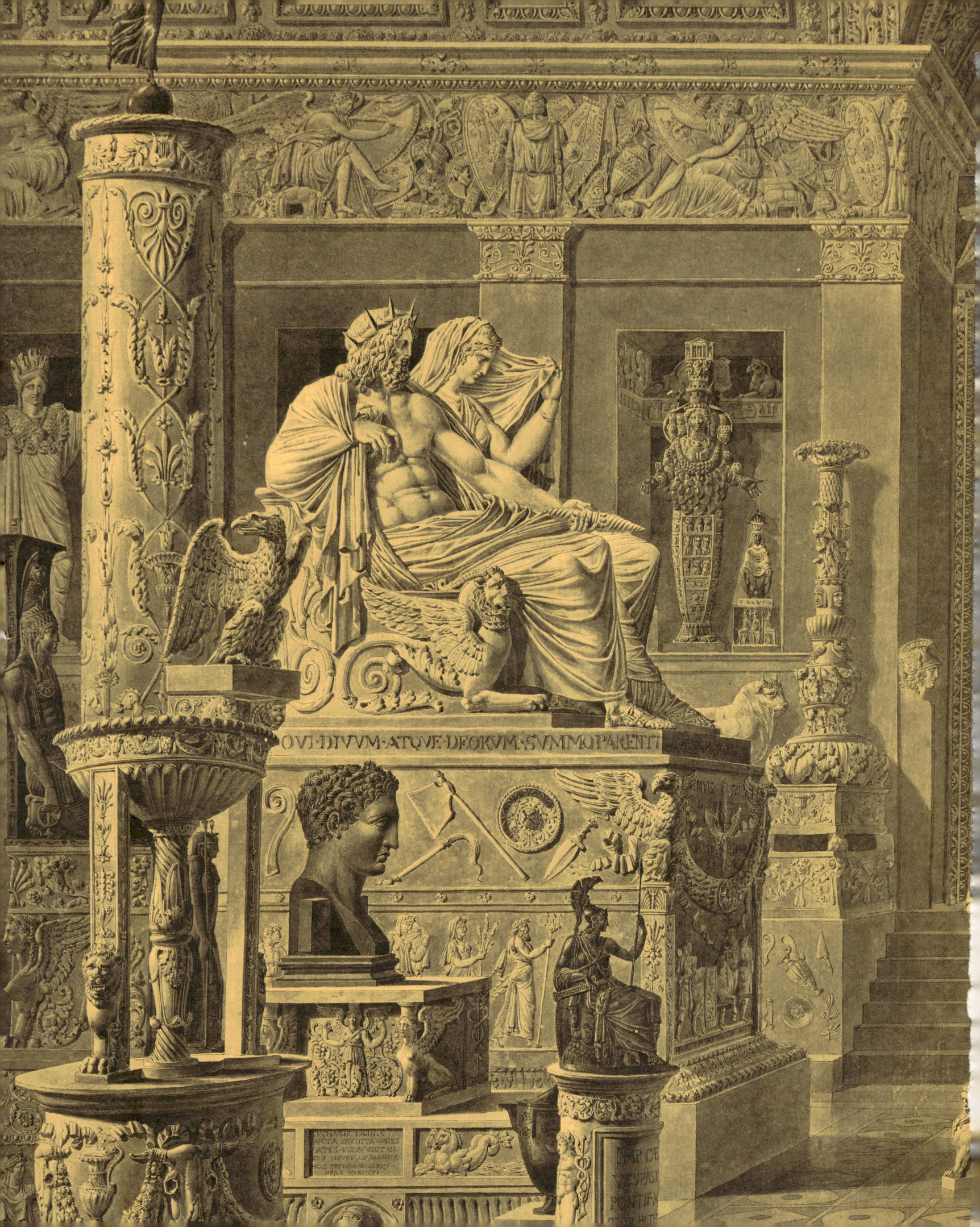

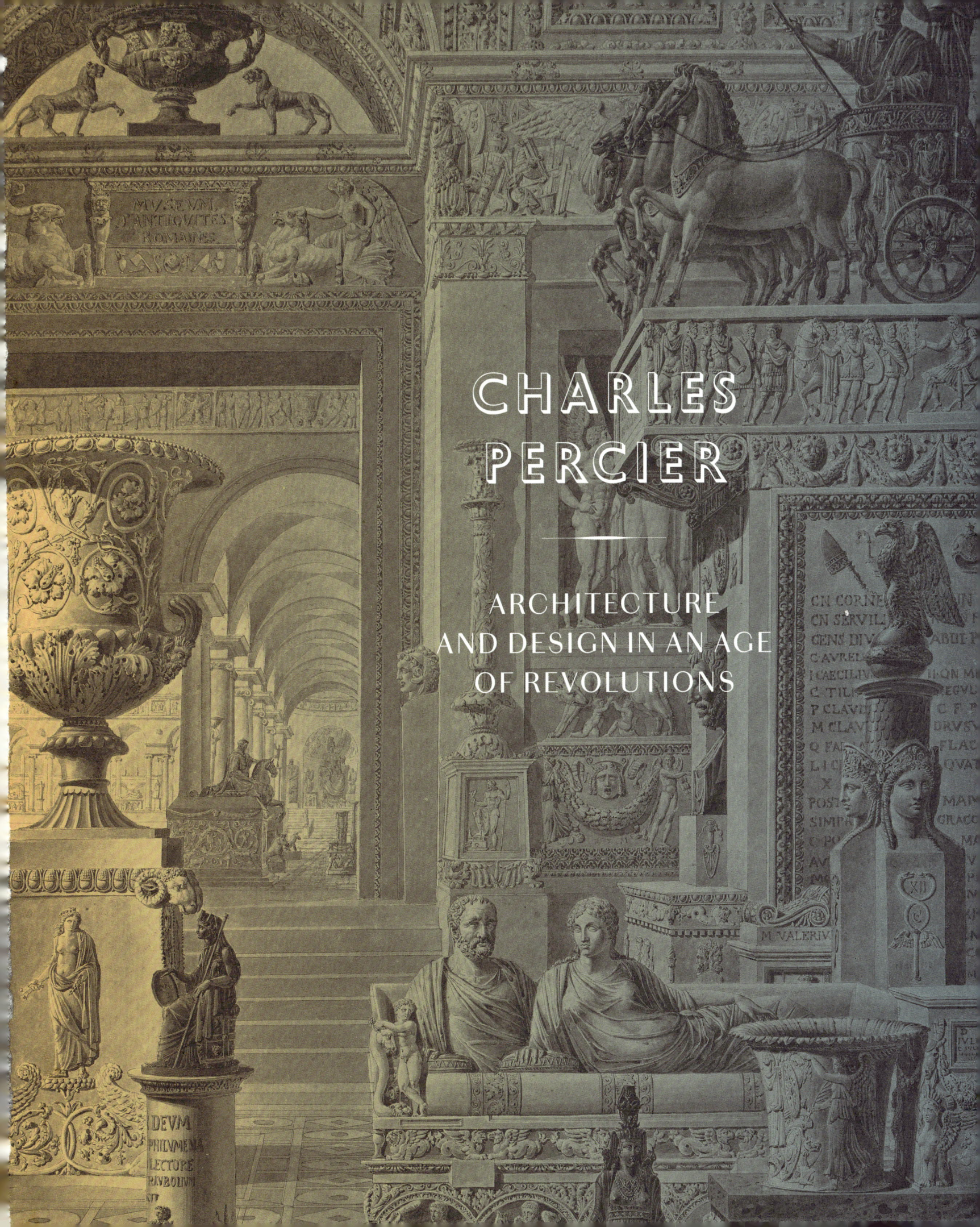

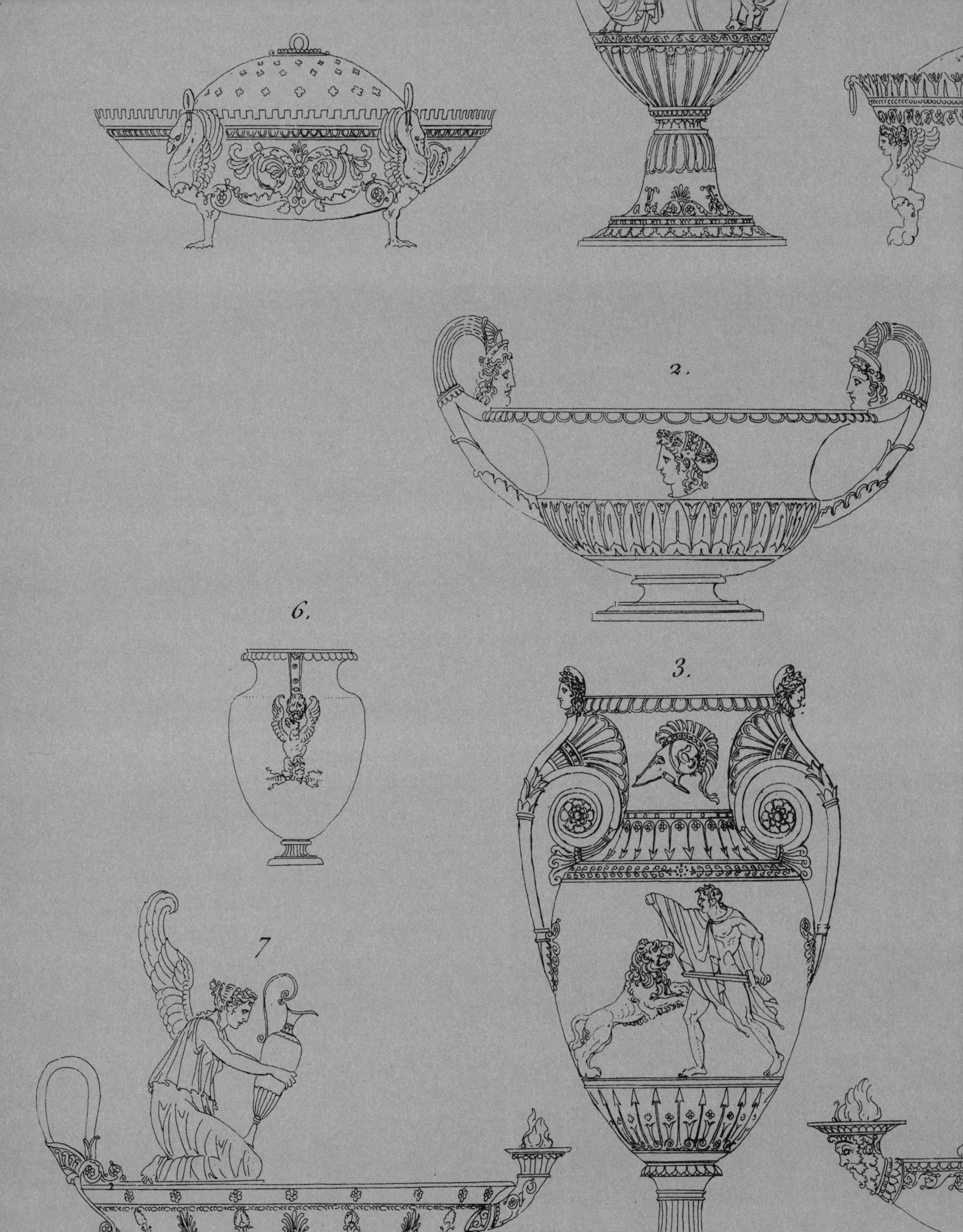

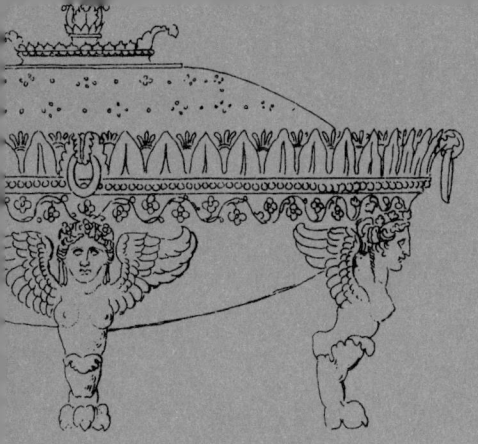
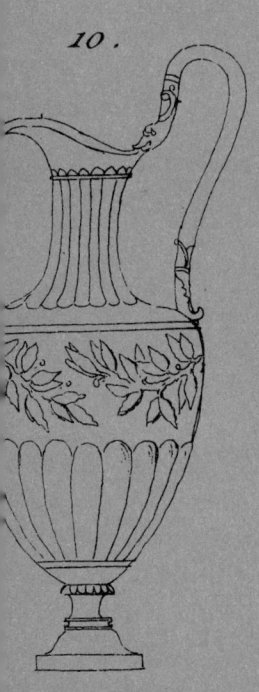

CHARLES PERCIER

ARCHITECTURE AND DESIGN IN AN AGE OF REVOLUTIONS

Jean-Philippe Garric, EDITOR

Jean-François Bédard, Jean-François Belhoste,
Christophe Beyeler, Vincent Cochet,
Anne Dion-Tenenbaum, Vincent Droguet, Jean-Philippe Garric,
Iris Moon, Thierry Sarmant, AND Letizia Tedeschi

WITH CONTRIBUTIONS BY Charlotte Duvette AND Saskia Wallig

PUBLISHED BY **Bard Graduate Center Gallery**, NEW YORK
Château de Fontainebleau, FONTAINEBLEAU
Réunion des musées nationaux–Grand Palais, PARIS
Yale University Press, NEW HAVEN AND LONDON

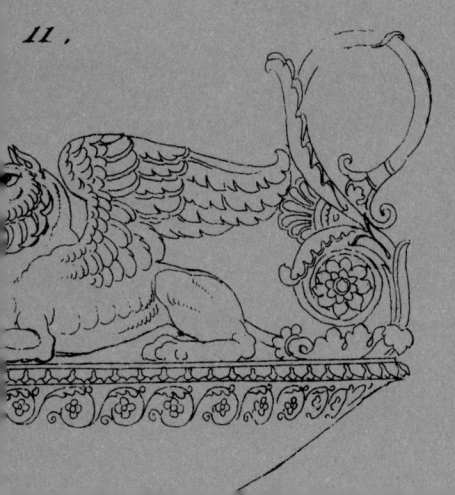

Support for *Charles Percier: Architecture and Design in an Age of Revolutions* has been generously provided by the Selz Foundation
with additional support from Max Blumberg and Eduardo Araújo, and other generous donors.

Published in conjunction with the exhibition *Charles Percier: Architecture and Design in an Age of Revolutions*, held at the Bard Graduate Center Gallery (November 18, 2016– February 5, 2017) and at the château de Fontainebleau, with the title *Charles Percier (1764–1838): Architecture et design* (March 18–June 19, 2017).

The exhibition and catalogue have been organized in association with the château de Fontainebleau and the Réunion des musées nationaux–Grand Palais, Paris.

Curator and Editor: Jean-Philippe Garric

Director, Bard Graduate Center Gallery and Gallery Publications: Nina Stritzler-Levine
Associate Director and Chief Curator: Marianne Lamonaca
Associate Curator and Project Coordinator: Cindy Kang
Manager of Rights and Reproductions: Alexis Mucha
Catalogue design: Barbara Glauber & Kellie Konapelsky/ Heavy Meta, New York
Copy editor: Barbara Burn
French-language translator: John Goodman
Catalogue production: Sally Salvesen, London
Printed and bound: Conti Tipocolor S.p.A., Italy

Copyright © 2016 Bard Graduate Center: Decorative Arts, Design History, Material Culture. Copyright for individual essays are held by the authors and Bard Graduate Center: Decorative Arts, Design History, Material Culture. All rights reserved. This book may not be reproduced in whole or in part, in any form (beyond that copying permitted in Sections 107 and 108 of the U.S. Copyright Law and except by reviewers for the public press), without written permission from the publisher.

LIBRARY OF CONGRESS CATALOGING-IN-PUBLICATION DATA

Names: Garric, Jean-Philippe, editor. | Percier, Charles, 1764–1838.
Title: Charles Percier : design in an age of revolutions / Jean-Philippe Garric, editor.
Description: New Haven : Yale University Press, 2016. | Includes bibliographical references and index.
Identifiers: LCCN 2016006831 | ISBN 9780300221589
Subjects: LCSH: Percier, Charles, 1764-1838—Exhibitions. | Neoclassicism (Architecture)—France—Exhibitions. | Decoration and ornament—France—Empire style—Exhibitions.
Classification: LCC NA1053.P5 A4 2016 | DDC 720.92—dc23
LC record available at https://lccn.loc.gov/2016006831

FRONT COVER: Charles Percier. Frontispiece for fascicle 8, Percier and Fontaine, *Palais, maisons et autres édifices modernes dessinés à Rome* (Paris: Authors, 1798), pl. 44. Watercolor over etching. Private collection, Paris; Charles Percier and Pierre Fontaine. Detail of the corbel of the arc du Carrousel, 1816–1810. Pen and wash, watercolor. Musée Carnavalet, Paris, CARD06681; Percier and Fontaine, *Recueil de décorations intérieures* (Paris: Authors and Pierre Didot l'aîné, 1801–12), pl. 64.

BACK COVER: Charles Percier and Pierre Fontaine. Bird's-eye view of the projected linking of the Louvre and Tuileries, from Charles Othon Frédéric Jean-Baptiste de Clarac, *Musée de sculpture antique et moderne*, (Paris: Texier, 1826–27), pl. 110bis.

ENDPAPERS: Percier and Fontaine. *Recueil de décorations intérieures* (Paris: Authors and Pierre Didot l'aîné, 1801–12), pl. 64.

HALF-TITLE: Charles Percier. View of a museum, n.d., Pencil, pen, and ink wash on paper. Musée Vivenel, Compiègne, Let.5703.

FRONTISPIECE: Percier and Fontaine, *Recueil de décorations intérieures* (Paris: Authors and Pierre Didot l'aîné, 1801–12), pl. 18.

➤ Charles Percier and Pierre Fontaine, *Recueil de décorations intérieures* (Paris; Authors and Pierre Didot l'aîné, 1801–12), pl. 19.

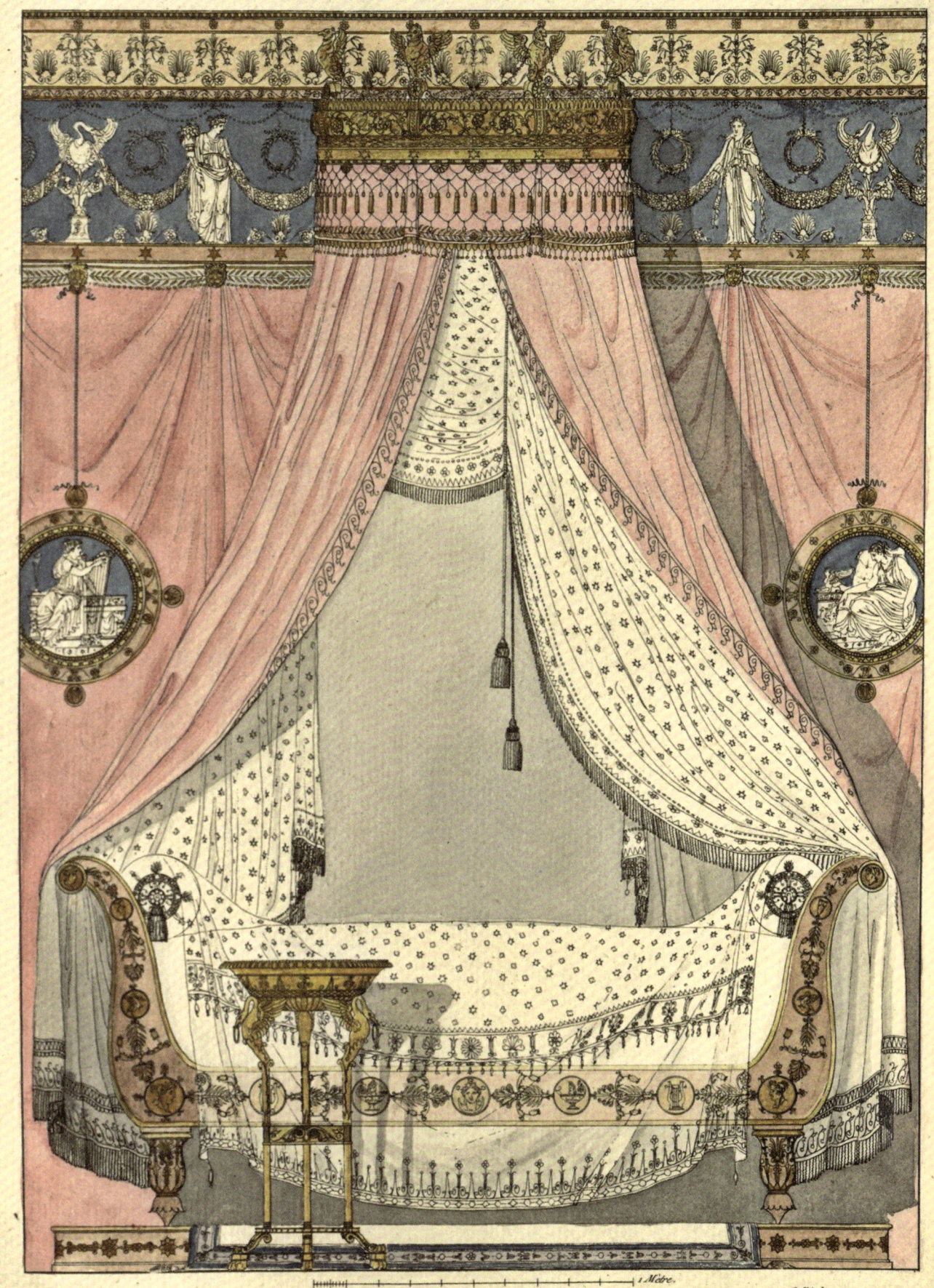

Pl. 19.

Lit exécuté à Paris pour Mme M.

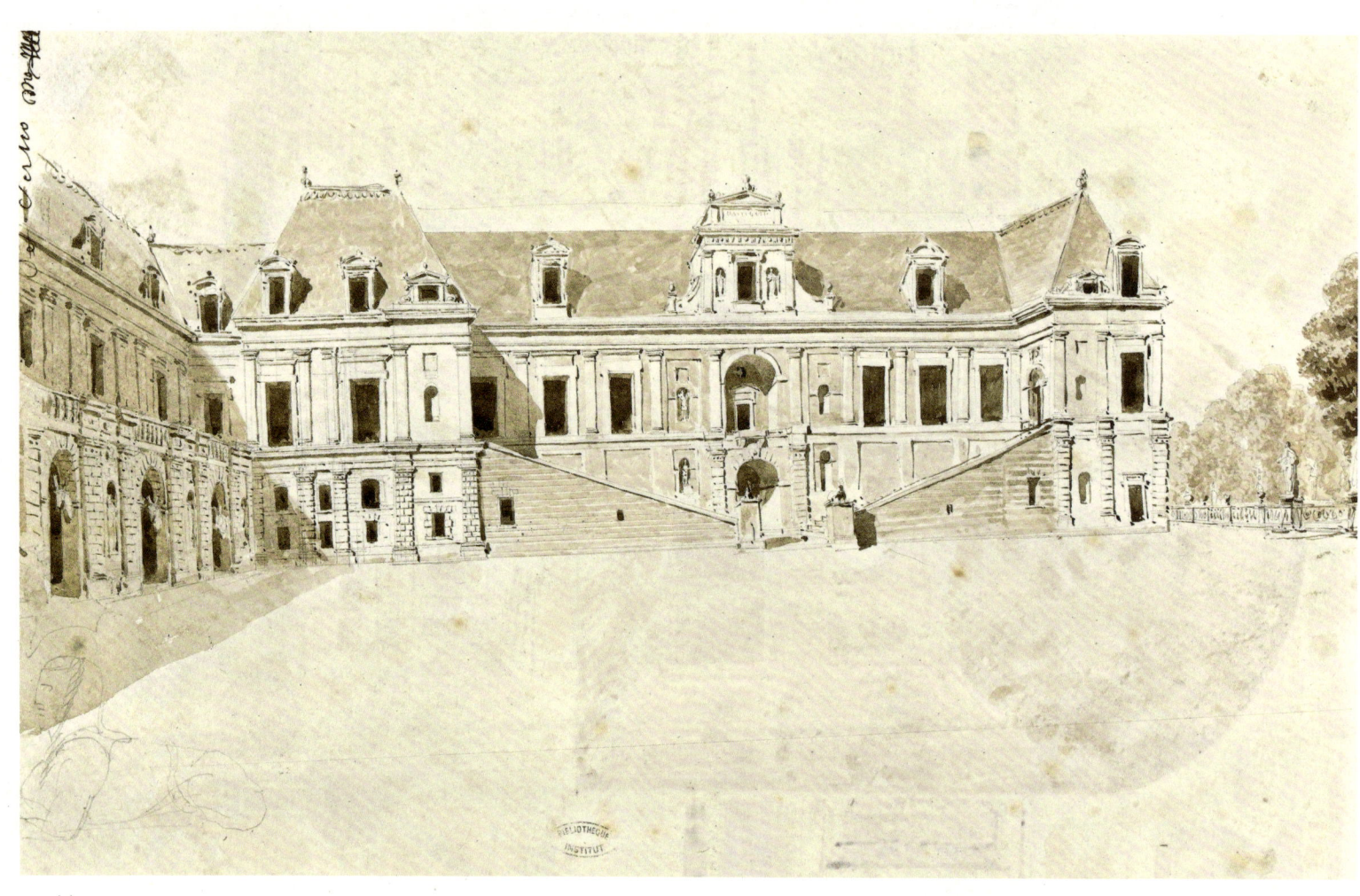

▲ Charles Percier. Wing of the Belle Cheminée, seen from the Cour de la Fontaine, château de Fontainebleau, and sketch of a sphinx, early 1790s. Pencil and sepia wash. Bibliothèque de l'Institut de France, Paris, Ms 1015, fol. 9, drawing 12.

EDITOR'S NOTE

This book is being published in two editions, one in English and one in French, and Bard Graduate Center's usual style has been adjusted to accommodate usage in both languages. For example, the use of hyphens between the components of French names was apparently established in the nineteenth century and continues today. In this volume, the editors chose to omit hyphens for all French individuals born before 1775. Another example is that French names for governmental and other institutions have been used throughout (with the English translation in parentheses at the first use), with the initial letter of the first word capitalized and subsequent words left lowercase. French place names, including museums and streets, are usually preceded by lowercase words followed by proper names in capital letters (musée du Louvre, rue de Rivoli, place de la Concorde, etc.).

    The checklist at the back of the book contains all of the objects that are on display in the exhibition that this publication accompanies; some will be exhibited in only one venue, as indicated on the checklist. The captions for all checklist items that are illustrated in the chapters include catalogue numbers that relate to the checklist numbers. In the dimensions given in the checklist entries, height precedes width and depth.

CONTENTS

FOREWORD
Susan Weber **11**

PREFACE
Jean-François Hebert **14**

BIOGRAPHY
Jean-Philippe Garric **16**

CHRONOLOGY
Saskia Wallig **19**

GOVERNMENT AND THE ARTS IN FRANCE, 1789–1848
Thierry Sarmant **24**

CHARLES PERCIER

1
PERCIER ALONE
Jean-Philippe Garric **36**

2
THE SCHOOLS OF PERCIER
Jean-Philippe Garric **50**

Percier's Ring
Jean-Philippe Garric **63**

The Atelier of Isabey
Vincent Cochet **66**

3
THE ROMAN SOJOURN
Letizia Tedeschi **71**

Letter to John Flaxman, November 1791
Charles Percier **76**

ARCHITECTURAL PATRIMONY

4
THE CHÂTEAU DE FONTAINEBLEAU
Vincent Droguet **82**

The Abbey of Saint-Denis, 1936
Georges Huard **99**

The Musée des Monuments Français
Jean-Philippe Garric **103**

ARCHITECT OF THE BOOK

5
GRAPHIC ART AS MATRIX
Jean-Philippe Garric **108**

Percier under the Loupe
Jean-Philippe Garric **118**

6
DOCUMENTING THE *RECUEIL DE DÉCORATIONS INTÉRIEURES*
Iris Moon **122**

The Italian Edition of the *Recueil*
Letizia Tedeschi **135**

7
THE *LIVRE DU SACRE*
Christophe Beyeler **140**

DECORATIVE ARTS

8
PERCIER AND FRANÇOIS HONORÉ GEORGES JACOB-DESMALTER
Jean-François Belhoste **154**

Two Commodes
Iris Moon **180**

A Scrapbook from Percier's Workshop
Jean-Philippe Garric **184**

9
DESIGNS FOR THE MANUFACTORIES AND THE GARDE-MEUBLE
Anne Dion-Tenenbaum **188**

Two Tureens and Their Variations
Anne Dion-Tenenbaum **201**

COURT ARCHITECT

10
THE SYNTHESIS OF ARCHITECTURE AND DECOR
Jean-François Bédard **206**

11
PERCIER AND THE IMPERIAL COUPLE
Vincent Cochet **213**

Josephine's Boudoir, Château de Saint-Cloud
Jean-François Belhoste **228**

12
THE LOUVRE AND THE TUILERIES
Jean-Philippe Garric **233**

The Arcades on the Rue de Rivoli
Charlotte Duvette **245**

13
A RHETORIC OF UNBUILT ARCHITECTURE
Jean-Philippe Garric **248**

14
PERCIER'S LEGACY
Jean-Philippe Garric **262**

CHECKLIST **268**
BIBLIOGRAPHY **286**
ABOUT THE AUTHORS **292**
INDEX **296**

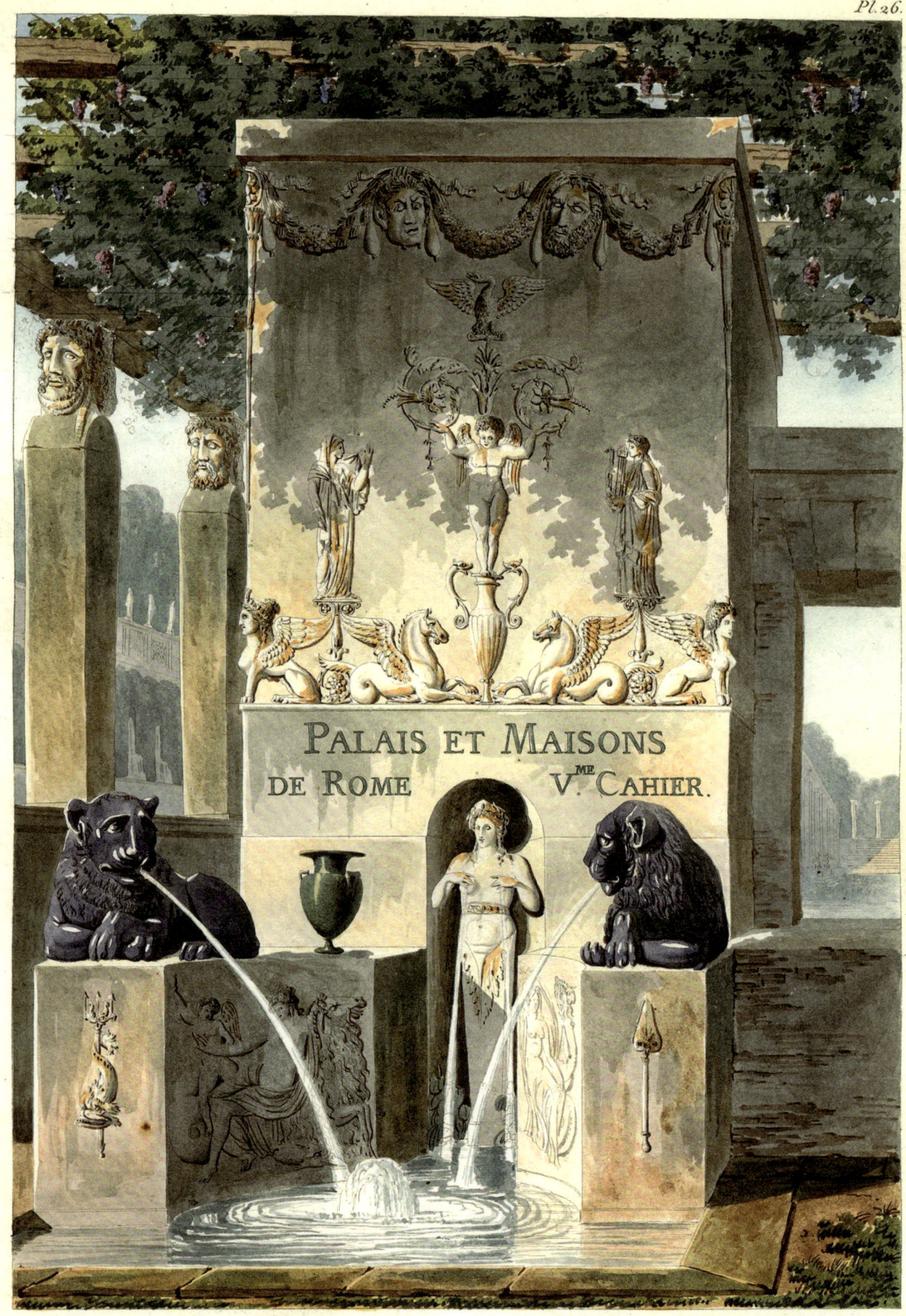

FOREWORD

FEW CHAPTERS IN WESTERN HISTORY have witnessed the kind of protracted political upheaval that characterized the years when Charles Percier emerged as a leading contributor to architecture and design in France. A man of exceptional creative gifts, he came from a modest background, which helped him avoid the fate that befell many of his contemporaries, whose lives were upended after the French Revolution in 1789 because of allegiances to the monarchy. Percier worked as an architect and as a designer from 1789 to 1838, the turbulent years that historian Eric Hobsbawm has called the age of revolution. Percier won the venerated Prix de Rome in 1786 and was in Rome when the Revolution broke out. After his prodigious sojourn in Italy, he made his way back to Paris and withstood all the regime changes that followed, including those that brought Napoleon Bonaparte to power as first consul and then as emperor. Despite these vicissitudes, Percier never stopped working; indeed, he was one of the most prolific architect-designers of the early nineteenth century in France.

Percier was a polymath whose accomplishments extended from major civic institutions, palaces, and churches to books, engravings, metalwork, horology, and furniture. He was as capable a draftsman as he was an urbanist who helped to create the rue de Rivoli and many of the monuments near the Louvre that are today identified with the city of Paris. Of these, the arc du Carrousel is among the best-known triumphal arches outside of France.

This volume calls into question conventional notions of who Percier was and what has become known as the Empire style. It is unprecedented in its assessment of Percier alone, as an individual creator and progenitor of that style separate from his closest collaborator, Pierre Fontaine. Largely because of their shared authorship of the *Recueil de décorations intérieures*, these two men have become so inextricably linked that many have questioned the viability of assessing Percier on his own. Yet as this book's editor, Jean-Philippe Garric, successfully argues, Percier demands to be recognized individually, as he was both the superior talent and a beloved and influential teacher. In addition to splitting the Percier-Fontaine pairing, *Charles Percier: Architecture and Design in an Age of Revolutions* introduces a more multifaceted and diverse interpretation of the so-called Empire style by showing how Percier's vision was more complex and varied in its sources than previously thought. As shown in the myriad themes on the contents page, he worked in a Pompeiian-inspired idiom, and he reworked and reinterpreted vocabularies from different moments in history, freely using Roman, medieval, and Gothic elements. Indeed, Percier can rightfully be considered one of the nineteenth century's pioneering eclectics.

◂ Charles Percier. Frontispiece for Percier and Fontaine, *Palais, maisons et autres édifices modernes dessinés à Rome* (Paris: Authors, 1798), pl. 26. Watercolor over etching. Private collection, Paris.

Jean-Philippe Garric originated the idea of examining Percier's independent career, and he has done the lion's share of the research on this subject. Bard Graduate Center is thrilled to have collaborated with the château de Fontainebleau and the Réunion des musées nationaux–Grand Palais (RMN–GP) on this important undertaking. At Fontainebleau, Jean-François Hebert, president, and Isabelle De Gourcuff, deputy director, offered their support of this project and of our collaboration from the outset, along with Sylvie Hubac, president; Valerie Vesque-Jeancard, deputy CEO; and Laurent Salomé, chief curator, at the RMN–GP. Professor Garric worked closely with Nina Stritzler-Levine, director of the Bard Graduate Center Gallery; Marion Mangon, head of the exhibition department at the RMN–GP; and Vincent Droguet, director of heritage and collections at the château de Fontainebleau, in establishing the partnership between our three institutions. Catherine Chagneau was the project coordinator in Paris and assisted with innumerable loan matters in conjunction with registrars Sarah Paronetto and Pauline Aronica. Considerable effort was required to realize the idea of a publication devoted solely to Charles Percier in both English and French. Clotilde La Batide-Alanore, head of the publications department at the RMN–GP, initially worked closely on this complicated task with Professor Garric, Mr. Droguet, Ms. Stritzler-Levine, Caroline Prual in the RMN–GP publications office, and Philippine de-Sartigas in the RMN–GP legal department. I want to thank Tim Ettenheim, chief operating officer at Bard Graduate Center, for working with Ms. Stritzler-Levine on the exhibition and publication agreements. Sally Salvesen, editor at Yale University Press, offered valuable advice and shared her expertise. Vincent Cochet, chief curator at the château de Fontainebleau, worked closely with Professor Garric in realizing the exhibition there.

I would like to thank the authors to this volume for their insights about Percier. Our understanding of his work in many practices has been enhanced by the contributions of Jean-François Bédard, Jean-François Belhoste, Christophe Beyeler, Vincent Cochet, Anne Dion-Tenenbaum, Vincent Droguet, Charlotte Duvette, Iris Moon, Thierry Sarmant, and Letizia Tedeschi.

A project of this complexity demanded extensive loan negotiations and the participation of the following institutions and their respective staffs. In France: Musées d'Angers: Isabelle Rotondaro; Bibliothèque Paul Marmottan, Boulogne-Billancourt; Musée national du palais de Compiègne: Emmanuel Starcky, Marc Desti; Musée Antoine Vivenel, Compiègne: Claire Iselin; Palais des Beaux-Arts, Lille: Bruno Girveau; Académie d'Architecture, Paris: Paul Quintrand; Banque de France: François de Coustin, Anne Brock; Bibliothèque de l'Institut de France: Gabriel de Broglie, Michèle Moulin; Bibliothèque de l'Institut national d'Histoire de l'art: Antoinette Le Normand-Romain, Eric de Chassey; Bibliothèque nationale de France: Bruno Racine, Sylvie Aubernas, Corinne Le Bitouzé; École nationale supérieure des Beaux-Arts: Emmanuelle Brugerolles, Anne-Marie Garcia; Les Arts décoratifs: Olivier Gabet; Mobilier national et Manufactures nationales des Gobelins, de Beauvais et de la Savonnerie: Hervé Barbaret, Christiane Naffah-Bayle; Musée Carnavalet: José de Los Llanos; Musée du Louvre: Jean-Luc Martinez, Sébastien Allard, Jannic Durand, Anne Dion-Tenenbaum, Xavier Salmon; Palais de l'Elysée: Jean-Paul Normand; Musée national des châteaux de Malmaison et Bois-Préau, Rueil-Malmaison: Amaury Lefébure, Isabelle Tamisier-Vétois; Cité de la céramique, Sèvres: Christine Germain-Donnat, Romane Sarfati; Musée national des châteaux de Versailles et de Trianon: Catherine Pégard, Jérémie Benoît, Frédéric

Lacaille, Béatrix Saule; Direction de la Mémoire, du Patrimoine et des Archives, Service historique de La Défense, Vincennes: Véronique de Touchet.

In the United States: Sterling and Francine Clark Art Institute: Francis Oakley, Jay Clarke; Cleveland Museum of Art: William M. Griswold, Heather Lemonedes, Gretchen Shie Miller; Cooper-Hewitt, Smithsonian Design Museum: Caroline Baumann, Matilda McQuaid, Lucy Commoner; The Metropolitan Museum of Art: Thomas P. Campbell, Nadine Orenstein, Femke Speelberg, Mary Zuber, Luke Syson, Daniëlle Kisluk-Grosheide, Emily Foss; Mount Holyoke College Art Museum: Ellen Alvord, Hannah Blunt; New-York Historical Society: Louise Mirrer, Margi Hofer, Roberta Olson; Smith College Museum of Art: Jessica Nichol, Aprile Gallant; Stanford University Libraries: Robert Trujillo, John Mustain, Malgorzata Schaefer; Wadsworth Atheneum: Thomas I. Loughman, Linda Roth.

This project benefited greatly as well from private collectors, including Duchess Oliva Salviati, Marguerite David-Roy, Benjamin Mouton, Odile Seyler and Jacques Lucan, Eric Plouvier, Philip Hewat-Jaboor, and several others who wish to remain anonymous.

Jean-Marc Chevalier, Marie-Laure Crosnier-Leconte, Anne Dary, Marie de la Chevardière, Emilie d'Orgeix, Paulette Hornby, Marc Langlois, Marc Le Cœur, Grégoire Massart, Serge Plantureux, Marc Rassiat, Hélène Servant, Carine Thuillier, Michelle Beiny, Sylvain Cordier, and Ulrich Leben generously shared information that enriched our knowledge of Percier.

At Bard Graduate Center, Marianne Lamonaca, chief curator; Cindy Kang, associate curator; Anne Tartsinis, former associate curator; and Eric Edler, registrar, provided considerable assistance with this project. Saskia Wallig was professor Garric's superb research assistant in Paris.

The catalogue production team at Bard Graduate Center involved the participation of many talented people. Foremost I want to acknowledge Barbara Glauber who created a magnificent design for this publication. Barbara Burn deserves a special note of thanks for her skillful and indefatigable copyediting. John Goodman was the primary translator of the French-language texts, bringing to the task considerable skill as well as knowledge of early nineteenth-century French architecture. Alexis Mucha managed the complex task of securing copyright and images for this volume.

Ian Sullivan created the thoughtful and beautiful exhibition design at Bard Graduate Center, and preparator Stephen Nguyen helped to coordinate the installation. Jesse Merandy, director of the Digital Media Lab, created engaging digital interactives. Art director Kate DeWitt designed a strong graphic program for the exhibition at the Bard Graduate Center Gallery.

Grace Johnstone and Hollis Barnhart skillfully coordinated the marketing and press campaign; Peter Miller and Melissa Gerstein developed the public education programs that accompany the exhibition; James Congregane, Chandler Small, and the staff of Bard Graduate Center facilities and security departments have ensured the smooth running of the gallery during the run of the exhibition.

Finally, I would like to acknowledge the generous support provided by Lisa and Bernard Selz for this exhibition and its accompanying publication.

I hope the reader will find this new and engaging interpretation of Charles Percier both enjoyable and a valuable contribution to their understanding of the work of a talent whose individual œuvre is finally receiving its long overdue recognition.

SUSAN WEBER
Founder and Director, Bard Graduate Center

PREFACE

THERE ARE FEW AREAS IN THE DOMAIN of the decorative arts in which Charles Percier did not exercise his creative gifts. From the design for the first currency bills issued by the Caisse d'escompte bank in 1800 and the delicate fan that the city of Paris presented to Josephine in 1798 to the vast urban projects for the rue de Rivoli in 1802 and the surroundings of the palace of the king of Rome ten years later, Percier worked in all scales and materials. Either alone or in collaboration with his faithful partner Pierre Fontaine, he was, in turn, set designer for the Paris Opera (1792–96), a fashionable interior designer in the era of the *Incroyables* and the *Merveilleuses* during the last years of the eighteenth century, designer of furniture for the assembly hall of the National Convention (1793) and, later on, for many residences remodeled and modernized by Napoleon, and, finally, architect of the arc du Carrousel and renovator of the Louvre. Percier was also the creator of refined and influential books, and—moving beyond his drawings and prints—his œuvre took form in stone and bronze and gold, in Sèvres porcelain and silk, and in a celebrated small room in Aranjuez, Spain. Not to be overlooked is his eminence as a teacher, one with nearly twenty winners of the Prix de Rome and seven members of the Institut de France to his credit.

Having risen from a modest background, Percier quickly distinguished himself as a student in the competitions of the Académie royale d'architecture and was the beneficiary of a royal grant to study in Rome. He returned to Paris when the Revolution was at its height and official architectural commissions were rare, but by reformulating ancient models to suit contemporary taste, Percier made signal contributions to the codification of a new style.

In spite of these accomplishments, it is surprising that this is the first exhibition devoted to Percier, the first to explore the full diversity and richness of his artistic production. If Waterloo put an end to his architectural hopes by radically reducing the number of actual buildings he left behind, collections both private and public, as well as the museums and palaces of the French Republic, abound in furniture and decorative art objects realized after his designs by the finest craftsmen of the era. His drawings, whose refinement spurred his contemporaries to admiration, number in the thousands and include student projects, studies of ornamental and architectural designs, several large albums bequeathed to the library of the Institut de France by his students, and drawings executed at the side of Alexandre Lenoir in the Musée des monuments français. The fact that Percier, whose importance is generally admitted, has not previously been presented to the public in a way befitting his stature is likely because of the very abundance and multiplicity of his production. Too much the architect for furniture historians, too much the ornamentalist for architectural historians, preeminently a designer and draftsman, and an inventor of the Empire style, as well as an enlightened and enthusiastic student of medieval and Renaissance decoration, he seems to constantly elude the usual frameworks and definitions.

This first Percier exhibition could not have a more fitting venue than the château de Fontainebleau. Received there by his revered teacher Antoine François Peyre, to whose care the monument had been entrusted, the young architect visited it on his way home from Rome in 1791 before returning to Paris. It was the final stop of his study trip, a place where he encountered, in its works by Rosso Fiorentino and Primaticcio, tokens of the Italy he had just left, above all the same intermingling of structure and decoration that had seduced him at Palazzo Te in Mantua. Percier returned in 1800 to document Fontainebleau in drawings before being asked, along with Fontaine, to remodel and furnish the building for the pope, who was coming from Rome to preside over Napoleon's coronation. From the many drawings Percier devoted to Fontainebleau, he fashioned the three albums, now in the Institut de France, that bear witness to his predilection for it.

The partnership that made this exhibition possible was the result of a proposal advanced by the Bard Graduate Center in New York. I would like to thank its founder and director, Susan Weber, as well as Nina Stritzler-Levine, director of its exhibition space and its publications, without whose steadfastness and commitment this enterprise would not have come to fruition.

JEAN-FRANÇOIS HEBERT
President, Château de Fontainebleau

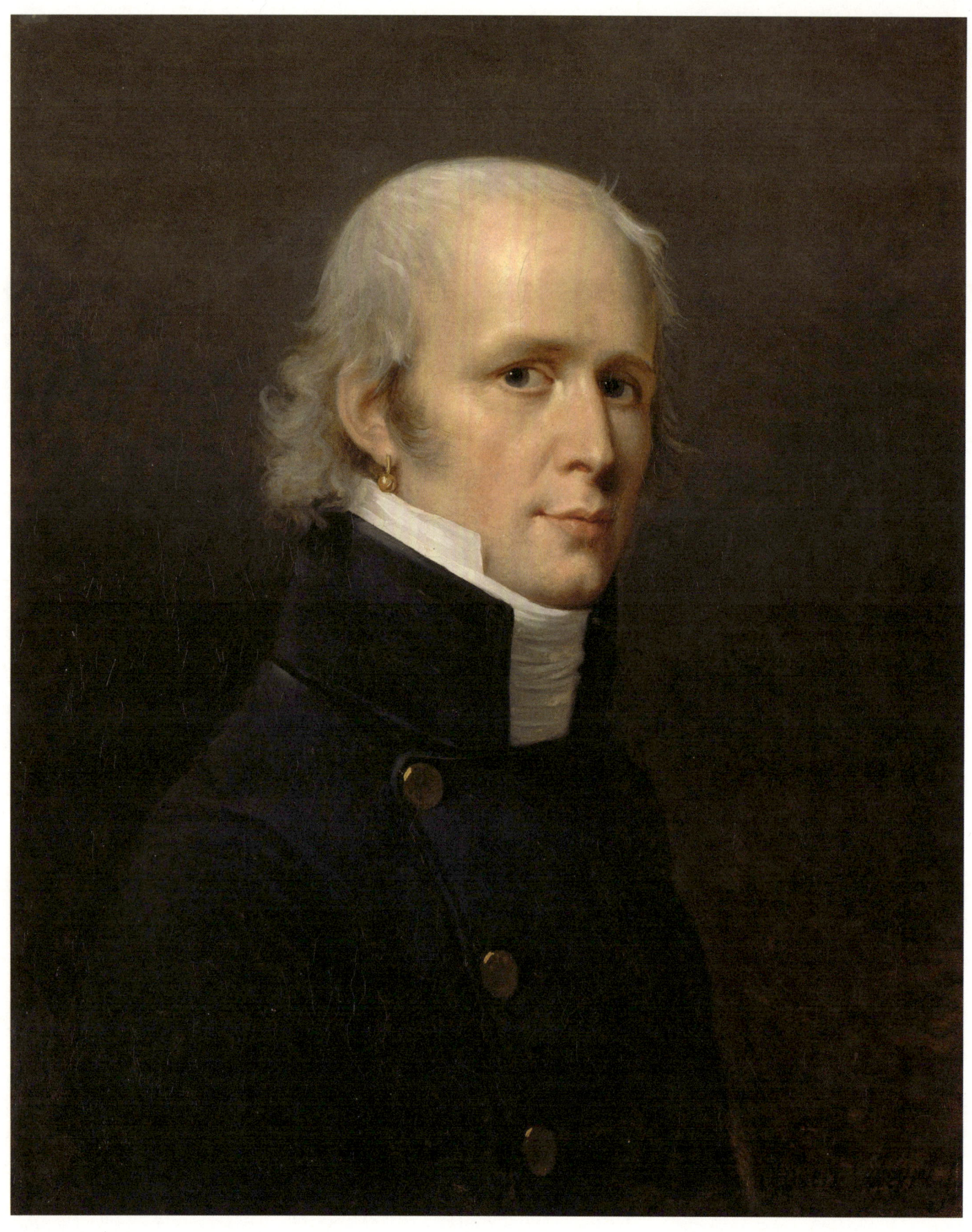

▲ **FIG i.1.** Robert Lefèvre. *Portrait of Charles Percier*, 1807. Oil on canvas. Château de Versailles et de Trianon, Versailles, MV 6313. Cat. 2.

BIOGRAPHY

JEAN-PHILIPPE GARRIC

CHARLES PERCIER WAS BORN IN PARIS on August 22, 1764, to parents of modest means. His father, a native of eastern France, was a porter in the Tuileries gardens; his mother, who came from Normandy, was a linen maid to Queen Marie-Antoinette. Charles was the eldest of their four offspring.

After a very rudimentary primary education—evidenced by the awkward handwriting and frequent misspellings in his letters—he learned to draw beginning at the age of twelve at the École gratuite de dessin (Free Drawing School), an institution established a few years earlier to expand access to artistic and artisanal training, especially among the disadvantaged. By 1779, at age fifteen, Percier was studying with Antoine François Peyre, one of the most important architecture professors of the period. It was in Peyre's atelier that he prepared entries for the competitions of the Académie royale d'architecture and where he met Pierre Fontaine. He attracted attention as a student and in 1786 won the Prix de Rome, thereby gaining access to a sojourn in Rome and a prestigious career. Throughout his life, Percier remained nostalgic for his five years in Italy, from whence he brought back three thousand drawings of monuments of all periods. When he returned to Paris in the summer of 1791, the capital was in the midst of the Revolution.

Percier immediately began to take on students, a practice then widespread. These were difficult times, but his reputation and modest origins won him powerful supporters, notably the painter Jacques Louis David. Toward the end of 1792, Percier was named architect of the Paris Opera, where his professional association with Pierre Fontaine began. The set designs they produced paid their bills and brought them attention. The following year they received their first important commission in furniture design, for the National Convention. Their increasing success made it possible for them to leave the Opera in 1796 to devote their energies to a fashionable private clientele and to prepare their first book, *Palais, maisons et autres édifices modernes dessinés à Rome* (1798).

In 1799, having come to the attention of Josephine and Napoleon, now first consul, Percier and Fontaine were commissioned to remodel Josephine's residence, the château de Malmaison, and were named co-architects to the government in charge of the Tuileries. Fontaine, the son of a contractor, was familiar with the world of construction. He was moderately well educated and knew how to comport himself among the elites of the ancien régime; accordingly, it was he who oversaw the construction sites and handled their professional relations, notably with the first consul. Percier, for his part, tirelessly imagined and drew the projects that were entrusted to them, as well as studies for the Musée des monuments français—a museum founded by Alexandre Lenoir for which he served as architect—and independent graphic productions. He invested considerable energy in the conception of the books he published with Fontaine and in the education of their students, whose successes in the Prix de Rome competitions soon multiplied.

In 1804, after Napoleon's coronation, the appointment of Fontaine as sole architect to the emperor reinforced the division of labor. Official commissions of various kinds, some of them never realized, succeeded one another at a rapid pace, from the design for the rue de Rivoli to festival decorations, from the restoration of venerable royal palaces to table services and furnishings, from renovations at the Louvre to construction of the arc du Carrousel and the project for a palace for the king of Rome. In 1811 Percier entered the Institut de France, the learned society that replaced the Académie royale in 1795; in 1812, the publication of the very influential *Recueil de décorations intérieures*, begun in 1801, reached completion.

In 1815 Percier decided to let Fontaine work for the new regime on his own, but they continued to collaborate, more episodically, on a few foreign projects. Thereafter, he increasingly turned his attention to teaching and graphic work, establishing order among his drawings and producing ornamental compositions for books as well as studies that he never published of Fontainebleau, the Palazzo Te in Mantua, and the basilica in Padua.

Percier died in Paris on September 5, 1838, leaving his drawing albums to his principal students and 100,000 francs to the École gratuite de dessin. He is buried in Père Lachaise Cemetery, together with his friends and business partners Pierre Fontaine and Claude Bernier, in a single tomb, in accordance with Fontaine's wishes. ●

CHRONOLOGY

SASKIA WALLIG

KEY
Life of Charles Percier
Art and culture in Europe
Politics of France

1764
- Birth of Charles Percier on August 22 in Paris
- First French translation of Johann Winckelmann, *History of the Art of Antiquity* (first German ed. 1763)

1775
- Construction of the Royal Salt Works at Arc-et-Senans after designs by Claude Nicolas Ledoux
- Coronation of Louis XVI

1778
- Deaths of Voltaire and Jean Jacques Rousseau

ca. 1780
- Percier enters the École gratuite de dessin, where he meets Louis Pierre Baltard and Charles Normand.

1783
- Percier places second in the Prix de Rome competition at age 19 with his design for a menagerie in the park of a royal château.

1784
- Percier meets Pierre Fontaine in the atelier of Antoine François Peyre.
- Project for *Newton's Cenotaph* by Étienne Louis Boullée
- Jean Germain Drouais paints *Christ and the Canaanite Woman* (Prix de Rome).

1785
- Fontaine places second in the Prix de Rome competition with his design for a sepulchral monument for the sovereigns of a great empire.
- Pierre Adrien Pâris named architect to the Paris Opera

1786
- Percier wins the Prix de Rome competition with his design for a building to house the academies and departs for Rome.

1788
- Percier makes meticulous drawings of Trajan's Column.
- Death of Drouais at age 25

1789
FRENCH REVOLUTION
- Jacques Louis David exhibits *Brutus* at the Paris Salon.
- Storming of the Bastille (July 14)
- Adoption of the Declaration of the Rights of Man (August 26)
- Nationalization of church property in France (November 2)

1790
- Edmund Burke publishes *Reflections on the Revolution in France*.
- Festival of the Federation in France (July 14)

1791

- Percier returns to Paris. He begins to teach and opens a free atelier.
- Percier visits the château de Fontainebleau and executes his first set of drawings there.
- Percier succeeds P.A. Pâris as director of set design at the Paris Opera.
- Mozart's opera *The Magic Flute* premieres in Vienna.
- First open salon in Paris
- Establishment of the Commune générale des arts
- Beginning of the Constitutional Monarchy in France
- Institution of patent laws in France

1792
FIRST REPUBLIC, NATIONAL CONVENTION

- Percier and Fontaine design five sets for *Lucrèce d'Arnault* at the Théâtre-Français.
- Percier and Fontaine named co-directors of set design at the Paris Opera (December)
- Fontaine, Jean Charles Bonnard, and Claude Bernier emigrate to England (September).
- Fontaine returns to France (December).
- Louis XVI and his family attempt to flee but are arrested at Varennes (June 20–21).
- Fall of the French monarchy and proclamation of the Revolutionary Paris Commune (June 20–August 10)
- Storming of the Tuileries and massacre of the Swiss Guards (August 10)

1793

- Percier collaborates with Georges Jacob for the first time, on furniture for the assembly hall of the National Convention in the Tuileries.
- Opening of the Muséum central des arts
- The National Convention abolishes the academies. Julien David Le Roy and Antoine Laurent Thomas Vaudoyer continue to teach architecture.
- Metric system adopted by the Constituent Assembly
- Publication of John Flaxman's illustrations of Homer's *Iliad*, engraved by Tomasso Piroli

- Execution of Louis XVI (January 21)
- Establishment of the Committee of Public Safety
- Assassination of Jean Paul Marat (July 13)
- Execution of Marie-Antoinette (October 16)
- Beginning of the Terror

1794

- Percier and Fontaine remodel the former church of Saint-Joseph to serve as the assembly hall of Section de Brutus in Paris.
- Percier and Fontaine submit *Design for a Monument to the Defenders of the Nation* (Competition of the Year II).
- Establishment of the École polytechnique and the École normale supérieure
- Robespierre initiates the Cult of the Supreme Being.
- Institution of the Law of Prairial, which marks the beginning of the Great Terror
- Thermidorian Reaction and execution of Robespierre

1795
DIRECTORY

- Percier executes plans and sketches of the Basilica of Saint-Denis.
- Establishment of the Conseil des bâtiments civils
- Opening of the Musée des monuments français, a project initiated by Alexandre Lenoir
- Establishment of the Institut, which restores the Prix de Rome competition
- Emmanuel Kant publishes *Perpetual Peace*.

1796

- Percier and Fontaine leave their posts at the Opera.
- Marriage of Napoleon and Josephine de Beauharnais

1797

- Percier and Georges Jacob collaborate on furniture for Benoît Gaudin at the Hôtel de Thur.
- Battle of Rivoli: Napoleon defeats the Austrian army.
- Treaty of Tolentino
- Napoleon's Egyptian Campaign

1798

- Percier and Fontaine design and execute interiors of the atelier of the artist Jean-Baptiste Isabey in the Louvre.
- Publication of *Palais, maisons et autres édifices modernes dessinés à Rome* by Percier and Fontaine
- Triumphal entry into Paris of "scientific and artistic objects gathered in Italy" on the occasion of the Festival of Liberty (July 28–29)
- Louis Léopold Boilly paints *Gathering of Artists in the Atelier of Isabey*.

1799
CONSULATE

- Publication of the edition of works by Horace illustrated by Percier
- Josephine Bonaparte engages Percier and Fontaine to remodel Malmaison.
- Percier and Fontaine are named co-architects of the Tuileries palace.
- Jacques Louis David paints *The Intervention of the Sabine Women*.
- Jean Nicolas Louis Durand publishes *Recueil et parallèle des édifices*.
- Augustin Grandjean de Montigny, a student of Percier, wins the Prix de Rome.
- 18 brumaire (November 9): coup d'état of Napoleon Bonaparte, who becomes first consul

1800

- Percier designs the Platinum Room in the Casa del Labrador in the gardens of the palace of Aranjuez, a residence of King Carlos IV of Spain.
- Percier is named architect of the Musée des monuments français and begins an official collaboration with Alexandre Lenoir.
- The *Annales du musée et de l'école moderne des beaux-arts* by Charles Paul Landon commences publication.

1801

- Percier and Fontaine are named co-architects to the government (January 1801).
- Renovation and redecoration of the Tuileries palace with Fontaine
- Publication of the first fascicle of *Recueil de décorations intérieures* (1801–12)
- First renovations at the château de Saint-Cloud, to serve as Napoleon's summer residence
- Consular authorization to begin construction of the rue de Rivoli in accordance with plans by Percier and Fontaine
- Publication of *Plans, coupes, élévations des plus belles maisons et hôtels construits à Paris et dans ses environs* by Jean Charles Krafft and Nicolas Ransonnette
- Construction of the Pont des Arts begins in Paris.
- Auguste Famin, a student of Percier, wins the Prix de Rome.
- Napoleon signs the Concordat with Pope Pius VII.

1802

- Publication of the fables of La Fontaine illustrated by Percier
- Decoration, in collaboration with Jacob, of General Moreau's townhouse on rue d'Anjou
- Publication of J.N.L. Durand's *Précis des leçons d'architecture*
- François René de Chateaubriand publishes *René*.

1803

- Designs for the restoration of the château de Fontainebleau for Napoleon
- Construction begins of the façade of the National Assembly, designed by Bernard Poyet.

1804
FIRST EMPIRE

- First redecoration of the Grande Galerie in the Louvre
- Percier and Fontaine design the decor for Napoleon's imperial coronation.
- Fontaine is named sole architect in charge of the Louvre and the Tuileries.
- Proclamation of the Empire and crowning of Bonaparte as Napoleon I (December 2)

1805
- Battle of Austerlitz: French forces victorious over those of Austria and Russia

1806
- Construction of the arc du Carrousel begins.
- Completion of renovation of the salle des Caryatides in the Louvre
- First projects by Percier and Fontaine to link the Louvre and the Tuileries
- Ingres paints *Napoleon on His Imperial Throne*.
- *Architecture toscane* by Grandjean de Montigny and Famin (1806–14) begins publication.
- Construction of the arc de Triomphe, designed by Jean François Chalgrin, begins.
- Battle of Jena: Napoleon victorious over Prussian forces (October 14)
- Berlin Decree initiates the continental blockade against Britain (November 21).

1807
- First designs for the château de Compiègne
- Competition for conversion of the church of the Madeleine into a "temple glorifying the grande armée"
- Thomas Hope publishes *Household furniture and interior decoration*.

1808
- Construction of the Paris Stock Exchange to a design by Alexandre Théodore Brongniart (1808–15)
- Achille Leclère, a student of Percier, wins the Prix de Rome.
- Antonio Canova completes *Venus Victrix* (Pauline Bonaparte).
- Napoleon installs his brother Joseph Bonaparte as King of Spain.

1809
- Percier and Fontaine publish *Choix des plus célèbres maisons de plaisance de Rome et de ses environs*.
- Construction of the north staircase in the Louvre colonnade block begins.

1810
- Prix décennal awarded to the arc du Carrousel.
- Initiation of the project to build a summer palace on the Chaillot Hill in Paris (future palace of the King of Rome)
- Jakob Ignaz Hittorff enters Percier's atelier.
- Construction of the Vendôme Column to commemorate the Battle of Austerlitz
- Napoleon divorces Josephine and marries Marie-Louise of Austria.

1811
- Percier becomes a member of the Institut, assuming the chair formerly occupied by Charles de Wailly and Chalgrin.
- Designs for an imperial residence in Terneuzen (present-day Netherlands)
- Birth of Napoleon II, dubbed the King of Rome

1812
- Publication of the complete edition of the *Recueil de décorations intérieures*

1813
- Augustin Caristie, a Percier student, wins the Prix de Rome.

1814
- Goya paints *The Third of May 1808*.
- Géricault paints *The Wounded Cuirassier*.
- First project for the Expiatory Chapel by Fontaine and Louis Hippolyte Lebas, a student of Percier
- Napoleon is dethroned and exiled to the island of Elba.

1815
RESTORATION
- Fontaine offers his services to the new regime.
- End of the Percier and Fontaine collaboration for government commissions
- Quatremère de Quincy publishes *Considérations morales sur la destination des ouvrages de l'art*.
- Louis XVIII accedes to the throne.
- The Hundred Days (March 20–July 8), Napoleon's attempt to return to power
- Battle of Waterloo (June 18)
- Napoleon exiled to the island of Saint Helena

1816
- Karl Friedrich Schinkel designs sets for Mozart's *The Magic Flute* for the Royal Opera House, Berlin.

1818
- Opening of the Musée du Luxembourg

1819
- Percier collaborates with François Gérard on a frontispiece for Voltaire's *La Henriade*.
- Project by Percier and Fontaine for the palace of the King of Wurtemberg, William I
- Project by Percier and Fontaine for the Potocki Palace in Krzeszowice, Poland
- Establishment of the École des beaux-arts

1820
- Horace Vernet paints *The Barrière de Clichy*.
- François Alexandre Villain, a Percier student, wins the Prix de Rome.
- Assassination of the duc de Berry, nephew of Louis XVIII and second in the line of succession to the French throne
- The Ultraroyalists return to power.

1821
- Death of Napoleon Bonaparte (May 5)

1823
- Construction of the church of Notre-Dame de Lorette after designs by Louis Hippolyte Lebas
- Death of Peyre

1824
- Henri Labrouste wins the Prix de Rome.
- Eugène Delacroix paints *The Massacre at Chios*.
- Death of Louis XVIII (September)
- Charles X mounts the throne.

1826
- Labrouste executes drawings of Trajan's Column.

1827
- Second edition of the *Recueil de décorations intérieures*
- Battle of Navarino: the coalition of France, the United Kingdom, and Russia is victorious over the Ottoman Empire (October 20).

1829
- Percier and Fontaine construct the Galerie d'Orléans at the Palais Royal (destroyed 1935).
- J.M.W. Turner paints *Ulysses Deriding Polyphemus*.

1830
- Les Trois Glorieuses (July 27, 28, 29); Charles X leaves France for England.

1830
JULY MONARCHY
- Louis-Philippe d'Orléans, "King of the French," assumes the throne.
- Delacroix paints *Liberty Leading the People*.
- Stendhal publishes *The Red and the Black*.

ca. 1830
- Percier organizes and completes his albums of drawings, notably one devoted entirely to Palazzo Te in Mantua.

1831
- Victor Hugo publishes *Notre-Dame de Paris*.

1833
- Percier and Fontaine publish *Résidences de souverains. Parallèle entre plusieurs résidences de souverains de France, d'Allemagne, de Suède, de Russie, d'Espagne et d'Italie*.

1836
- Construction of the Alexander Column in St. Petersburg to designs by Auguste Ricard de Montferrand, a Percier student

1838
- Death of Percier in Paris (September 5)

GOVERNMENT AND THE ARTS IN FRANCE
1789–1848

THIERRY SARMANT

THE "CENTURY OF REVOLUTIONS" designates the period of French history that commenced in 1789. For almost a hundred years, the country was periodically wracked by exceptional political instability as regimes succeeded one another at an accelerating pace: constitutional monarchy (1789–92), First Republic under the Convention (1792–95), Directory (1795–99), Consulate (1799–1804), First Empire (1804–14), First Bourbon Restoration (1814–15), a brief return to power of Napoleon I during the Hundred Days (1815), Second Restoration (1815–30), July Monarchy (1830–48), Second Republic (1848–52), Second Empire (1852–70), and, finally, the proclamation of the Third Republic (1870) and the tragic episode of the Paris Commune (1871).

This political volatility should not obscure the extent of the transformations that began in 1789 and foreclosed the possibility of a return to the ancien régime. The monarch was no longer the cornerstone of the political structure. In the final analysis, it was the nation that retained sovereignty, whatever the literal stipulations of the various constitutional acts. Even the authoritarian governments recognized the existence of public opinion and had to reckon with it. From the summit to the base of the various regimes, the number of assemblies, councils, and committees multiplied. Even when appointed and not elected, even when subject to those in power, these bodies instilled a habit of public deliberation.

These general conditions had an impact on public commissions. The official residences of the king or emperor were no longer the framework for important artistic and architectural projects. The personal taste of the head of state and that of his principal advisors played a less important role than they had in the years before 1789. No artist was permitted a monopoly. Although the old monarchy had built primarily in the Île-de-France and on the nation's borders, the new regimes built throughout the territory, in accordance with its division into a tight mesh of eighty-three *départements* in 1790. There was an unprecedented expansion of public architecture in these administrative regions, which was accompanied by economic development, growth of the state administrative apparatus, and the dissemination of public education.

THE ORIGINS OF THE MINISTRY OF CULTURE

New institutions sprang up to oversee these public commissions. Under successive monarchs, administrative entities heir to the former Direction générale des bâtiments du Roi (Office of the King's Buildings) were established, holdovers from the old courtly conception of government. But these entities shared their responsibilities with a new center of power, the Ministère de l'intérieur (Ministry of the Interior), also constituted in 1790.[1] The Ministry of the Interior's brief encompassed departmental and municipal governments, commerce, and public works, as well as "public instruction," a legislative brief born of the Revolution. Its Public Instruction division, established in 1791, oversaw "public education, the sciences and the arts, the academies, the theater, and everything pertaining to public instruction more generally."[2] Similarly, the Executive Commission of Public Instruction, which functioned under the Convention at the time the ancien-régime ministries were being eliminated, supervised "the conservation of national monuments, public libraries, museums, and natural history cabinets, and precious collections; the surveillance of schools and modes of instruction, of everything pertaining to inventions and scientific research, the fixing of weights and measures, the establishment of tables pertaining to population and political economy."[3]

In year IV (1795), the Ministry of the Interior established a Conseil des bâtiments civils (Council of Civic Buildings).[4] Its first members were the architects Jean Rondelet, Jean François Chalgrin, and Alexandre Théodore Brongniart. This bureaucratic entity had no ancien-régime equivalent and gave advice on countless building projects throughout France. The Bureau des bâtiments civils (Bureau of Civic Buildings), established in year VIII (1799), was subsequently elevated to the rank of a division, then of a managerial office—and from 1811 coexisted with the Direction des travaux de Paris (Office of Construction in Paris), dedicated solely to the capital.

It was also in year VIII that the bureau's organization chart first included a Bureau des beaux-arts (later renamed the Bureau des sciences et des beaux-arts, and later still the Bureau des sciences, belles-lettres, et beaux-arts), most often as a subdivision of the entity responsible for public education. This office supervised departmental museums, public monuments, historical sites, and artistic commissions. Becoming over the course of the nineteenth century a Bureau de direction (Bureau of Management), then an Under-Secretariat of State, it was the forerunner of the current French Ministry of Culture.

Despite the many changes of name and affiliation during the nineteenth century, these various bureaucratic entities employed many men whose work continued across regime changes, but none of whom held sufficient power to have a decisive effect on policy.[5] The same applies to members of the Conseil des bâtiments civils, as well as to those of the Académie des beaux-arts, for example Antoine Chrysostome Quatremère de Quincy, Louis Hippolyte Lebas, Antoine Laurent Thomas Vaudoyer, and Charles Percier and Pierre Fontaine, whose influence continued for decades. The members' work was by its nature collective, incremental, and prudent.

REVIVAL OF THE BÂTIMENTS DU ROI

In addition to these administrative offices of Revolutionary origin, we should note the periodic rebirth, until 1870, of administrative entities linked to court patronage. The ancien-régime Direction générale des bâtiments du Roi was reestablished, in more modest form, as l'Intendance des bâtiments de la maison de l'Empereur (the Intendancy of Buildings of the Emperor's Household) under the First Empire (1804–14), as the Ministry (1814–27), and then l'Intendance générale de la maison du Roi (General Intendancy of the King's Household; 1827–30) under the Restoration, and as the Intendance générale de la liste civile (General Intendancy of the Civil List) of King Louis-Philippe under the July Monarchy (1830–48), not to forget the Ministère de la maison de l'Empereur under Napoleon III (1852–70).

Under the First Empire, the Intendancy of Buildings of the Emperor's Household supervised the imperial buildings, the imperial museums, the mint, and the imperial manufactories.[6] Under the Restoration, the General Intendancy of the King's Household included an Intendancy of Buildings, Parks, and Gardens and a Department of Fine Arts, which oversaw court festivities, the royal museums, the mint, the royal manufactories, and the royal theaters. Under the July Monarchy, the General Intendancy of the Civil List included an Office of Buildings and an Office of Royal Museums, and also supervised the royal manufactories.

Under the three regimes, the heads of these institutions occupied an intermediary position between those responsible for setting government policy and the upper administrative echelons.[7]

To further complicate all of this, oversight of the great artistic, literary, and scientific establishments often passed from one bureau to another, from one ministry to another, even from the administrative bureaucracy to the court. Such was the case for the Bibliothèque nationale (dubbed, as political circumstances dictated, "du roi," "nationale," "impériale," or "royale"), the mint, the Musée du Louvre, the Conservatoire des arts et métiers, the École supérieure des beaux-arts, the Sèvres manufactory, the Gobelins manufactory, and so forth.[8]

PARIS AND THE DEPARTMENTS

This relationship between court and "civil" administrative structures was superimposed on, though it did not precisely coincide with, that between Paris and the *départements*. As under the ancien régime, the capital and its environs remained the heart of French political power, the center of the nation's artistic and literary life, and its international showcase. It was in Paris that the successive nineteenth-century regimes concentrated their most prestigious commissions in the realms of architecture, sculpture, and painting. "I began to dream," Napoleon observed on Saint Helena, "of making Paris the true capital of Europe. Sometimes I wanted it to become a city of two, three, four million inhabitants, something fabulous, colossal, hitherto unknown, and whose institutions would have been responsive to the people."[9] The accomplishments of the imperial regime in Paris are indeed impressive: not only monuments—the Vendôme Column, the arc du Carrousel, the arc de Triomphe, the Temple of Glory (subsequently the Madeleine), the "palace" for the Stock Exchange—but also public amenities, such as bridges, quays, fountains, markets, abattoirs, and cemeteries.[10]

From one government to the next, the centuries-long construction project at the Louvre and the Tuileries continued, encompassing the palace as well as the museum, the embellishment of the palaces of the legislative assemblies, the construction of new ministries, and the as-yet-unrealized plans to move or rebuild the national library. The Palais d'Orsay (on the site of the present Musée d'Orsay), intended under the Empire to house the Ministry of Foreign Relations, was not completed until the July Monarchy, when it became the seat of the Council of State and the Cour des comptes (Court of Auditors). The Temple of Glory-cum-Madeleine received its painted decor only under Louis-Philippe and was not consecrated until 1845.

➤ **FIG iii.1.** Jacques Louis David. *Self-Portrait*, 1794. Oil on canvas. Musée du Louvre, Paris, 3705.

The great building projects continued long after the regimes that had commissioned them.

In the provinces, public architecture flourished as never before; churches, town halls, prefectures, palaces of justice, museums, schools, hospitals, and prisons multiplied to house the new institutions generated by the tight mesh of departments, boroughs, cantons, and municipalities established during the Revolutionary years. Engineers improved the network of roads and canals and built many suspension bridges, the first industrial era's manifestos of metal architecture. Under the control of the Conseil des bâtiments civils, building types developed in Paris under the Convention were emulated from one end of the country to the other. The watchword was rational and economical architecture in which ornament was drastically reduced, even absent, in line with the teachings of Jean Nicolas Louis Durand at the École polytechnique and the publications of the engineer Louis Bruyère, director of public works in Paris.[11] As is well known, Jacobin centralization survived the fall of the Jacobins.

Although the museums at the Louvre and Versailles were affiliated with the monarch, sometimes to the point of taking his name ("Musée Napoléon" under the Empire, "Musée Charles X" under the Restoration), the provincial museums, which began to open under the Directory, were filled with government consignments initiated by the successive interior ministers François de Neufchâteau and Jean Antoine Chaptal.[12] This sums up the ambiguities of a century troubled by the opposition between, on the one hand, Paris, the "city of Enlightenment" and the "modern Babylon," and, on the other hand, the "provinces," perceived as backward, despite their having been transformed to a greater extent in the course of these few decades than over the entire preceding millennium.

OF TASTES AND REGIMES

In addition to these long-term developments, artistic ambitions differed from one regime to another. The period of the Convention (1792–95) was characterized by considerable originality but left no immediate legacy.[13] What has since come to be known as the French patrimony was henceforth considered the property of the French people. "All these precious objects that were kept far from the people or were shown only to engender awe and respect, all these riches belong to them."[14] Artists were called upon to serve the cause of the people. Royal commissions were replaced by "works of encouragement" (*travaux d'encouragement*), commissioned first by the Constituent Assembly and then by the Convention. It was recommended that artists imitate the ancient Greeks, in whose culture "all of the arts strove to support the actions of the government."[15] In 1791 responsibility for organizing the annual salon passed to the directorate of the department of Paris, "on the orders of the Ministry of the Interior" (decree of August 21, 1791). The Salon of September–October 1791 was the first open salon; all artists could exhibit there, regardless of whether or not they were members of the Académie de peinture et de sculpture. It was here that Jacques Louis David established himself as painter of the Revolution, with the preparatory drawing for his projected large canvas *The Tennis Court Oath*, intended to hang in the National Assembly [FIGS. iii.1, iii.2]. On August 8, 1793, the Convention decided to suppress the academies, the "last refuge of all the aristocracies" (David). The resulting void was filled for a time by the Commune générale des arts, established in 1791; presided over by Jean Bernard Restout and constituted "according to the model of deliberative assemblies," it was open to all artists. It organized the Salon of August–September 1793 before being replaced in turn by the Société républicaine des arts (October 1793).

The major figure of the period was David. He was famous before the Revolution, but his campaign for election to the Legislative Assembly ended in failure, although he succeeded in winning a seat in the Convention and sat on both the Committee of Public Instruction and the Committee of Public Safety. Pageant master of the Revolutionary

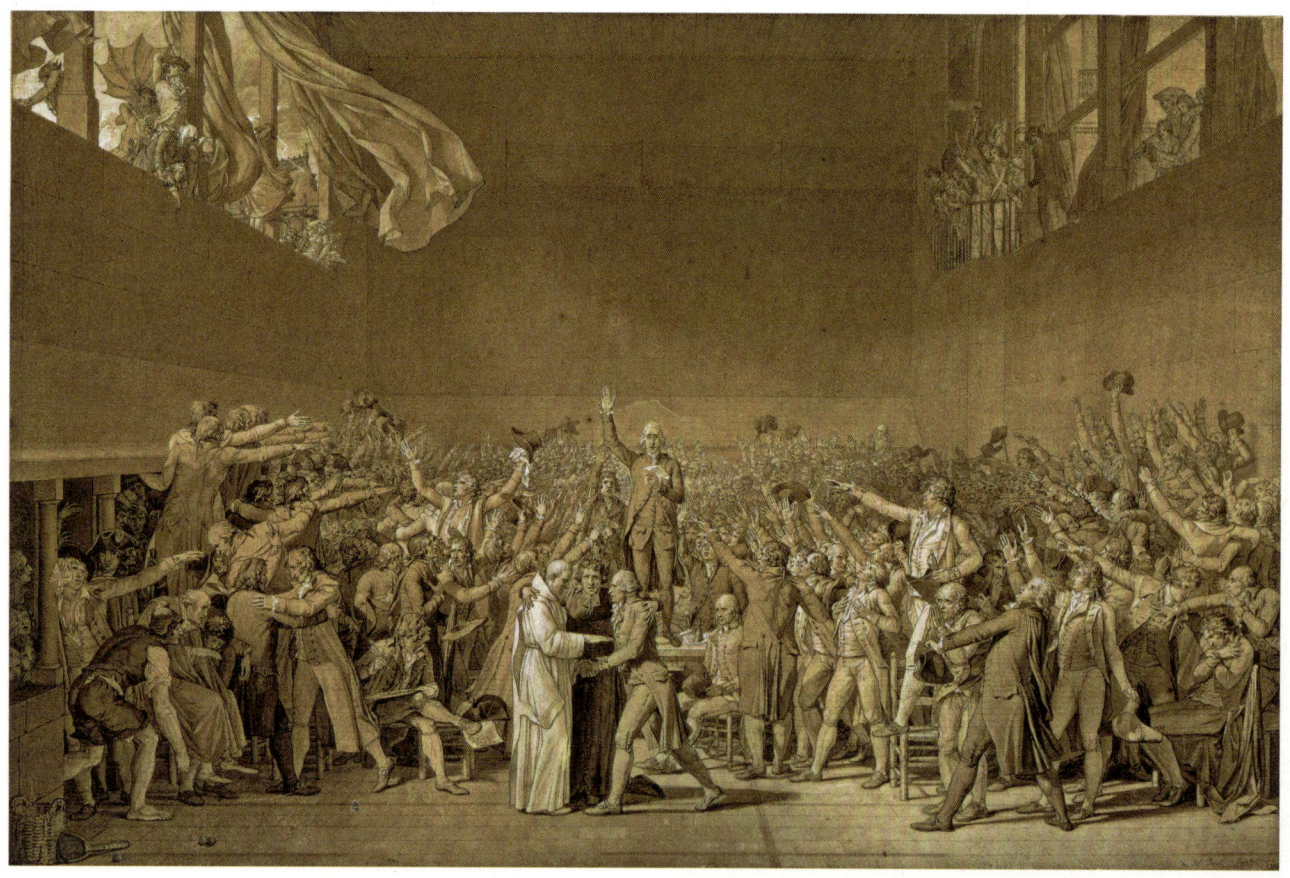

▲ **FIG iii.2.** Jacques Louis David. Sketch for *The Tennis Court Oath, 20 June 1789*, 1791. Pen and wash with brown ink, heightened with white on paper. Châteaux de Versailles et de Trianon, Versailles, MV8409; Dessins 736.

festivals, he painted portraits of Jean Paul Marat and Le Peletier de Saint-Fargeau for the assembly hall of the Convention. It was on the basis of a report written by him that a "jury of the arts" was named by the Assembly on 25 brumaire year II (November 15, 1793). David also promoted the establishment of the Muséum central des arts (now the Musée du Louvre), which was inaugurated on August 10, 1793, and opened to the public the following November 18. In a report of 27 nivôse year II (January 1794), he described the museum as an "imposing school": "May the genius of the arts, protector of the sublime works that we possess, be at the same time a creative genius and give birth to new masterpieces."[16] For David and his contemporaries, Republican art should be "masculine" and "severe" and find its inspiration in Greco-Roman antiquity.

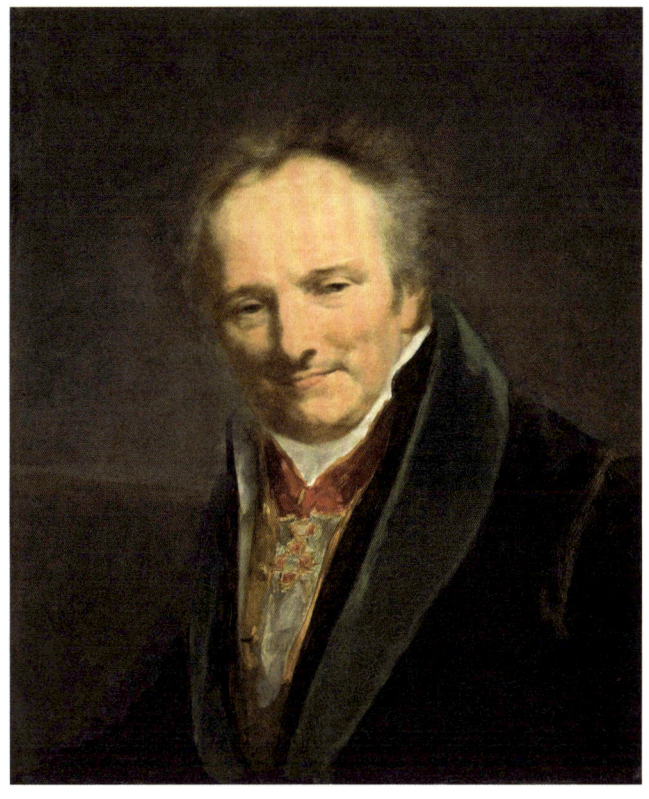

The epoch rejected the notion of art for pleasure (*arts d'agrément*) and denounced the preciosity (*mignardises*) fashionable under the ancien régime. The foreign wars and the civil war precluded the realization of large architectural, decorative, and pictorial projects. The government had to make do with the ephemeral decorations for Republican festivals and the recasting of the assembly halls, for which hemicycles in the antique style were considered de rigueur. Projects for monuments, often on a colossal scale, were stored away for better days.[17] For the time being, the Republican decorative lexicon—allegories, lictor's bundles, levels, liberty caps—proliferated in prints and on faience, coins, and medals.

From the Thermidorian Convention to the Directory, from the Directory and the Consulate to the Empire, there was a progressive "return to order." It was no longer a question of artistic democracy. David, implicated in the Terror, had to relinquish his political role. Still the most prestigious artist of the day, he was named "first painter" to Napoleon but never played a role analogous to that of Charles Le Brun under Jean-Baptiste Colbert during the reign of Louis XIV (r. 1643–1715), or to the one he himself had assumed at the height of the Revolution. The Ministry of the Interior, reestablished in 1795, reclaimed control of the Salon. The former academies were reborn as the Institut national des sciences et arts, established by the law of 3 brumaire year IV (October 25, 1795). The Musée des monuments français of Alexandre Lenoir, which opened September 1, 1795, showcased national sculpture saved from the "vandalism" denounced by the abbé Grégoire.[18] In year II, the minister François de Neufchâteau explained that the arts should be placed under "moral supervision" and become a "political institution." He maintained that history painting and sculpture "can flourish only if given special government protection" and that it was necessary to encourage the representation of battles, which "are today the most beautiful pages in the history of French glory."[19] Bonaparte was not far off.

The orchestrator of this politics of glorification under the Consulate and the Empire was

◀ **FIG iii.3.** Pierre Paul Prud'hon. *Baron Vivant Denon*, 1812. Oil on canvas. Musée du Louvre, Paris, MI723.

Dominique Vivant Denon, named general director of museums in 1802 [FIG. iii.3].[20] First attached to the Ministry of the Interior, he then simultaneously held posts there and in the Intendancy of the Emperor's Household—which did not prevent him from addressing himself directly to Napoleon whenever he deemed this necessary. A skilled courtier as well as a true connoisseur, this former gentleman to the bedchamber of Louis XV succeeded in holding his own against the upper echelon of administrators of the new regime, thanks as much to his extensive network of European contacts as to his technical expertise. Napoleon did not hesitate to employ Denon as his artistic advisor in ways that exceeded his formal responsibilities, which explains how the general director became involved, to Fontaine's considerable annoyance, in the planning of monuments such as the statue of General Desaix (whom he had befriended in Egypt), the arc du Carrousel, and the Austerlitz Column (now the Vendôme Column).

The reestablishment of internal stability reopened the way to public commissions. Much was built, sculpted, painted, and engraved.[21] It was a time for production on a massive scale; artists were more numerous, clients were in greater supply, artistic craftsmanship was being industrialized, and all genres were cultivated. The atelier of François Gérard became "a kind of factory."[22] A host of artists, the most remarkable among them being Antoine Jean Gros, set about realizing Neufchâteau's program by illustrating the military exploits of Napolean as first consul, then as the emperor [FIG. iii.4].[23]

If Napoleon and Denon believed in propaganda through the arts, they also had a more direct and utilitarian understanding of public commissions and maintained that they should improve the economy. Denon saw himself less as a promoter of official taste than as a paternalistic administrator of the arts, holding that it was necessary to distribute commissions in such a way that everyone thrived. This approach allowed little room for rigorous aesthetic distinctions. Support for the neoclassical ideal did not preclude the first intimations of eclecticism. Percier and Fontaine's design for the rue de Rivoli is more indebted to the Renaissance than to antiquity, and their work for Napoleon's coronation included a neo-Gothic portal in front of Notre-Dame. The salons under the Empire saw "troubadour" painting become ever more successful.[24]

The fall of the Empire and the advent of the constitutional monarchy did not result in any aesthetic rupture.[25] Funds were lacking and ambitions shrank. Louis XVIII settled into Napoleon's interiors in the Tuileries and while visiting Fontainebleau in 1816 remarked that the usurper had been "a good custodian." In official buildings, they made do with replacing initial "N"s and bees with "L"s and fleurs-de-lis. The regicide David went into exile, but other painters of the Empire, like its architects, eagerly placed themselves at the service of the Restoration [FIG. iii.5]. Fontaine designed the expiatory chapel and restored the Palais Royal for the duc d'Orléans. Gérard painted the coronation of Charles X. J.A.D. Ingres, who in 1806 had painted *Napoleon I on His Imperial Throne* [FIG. iii.6], executed the *Vœu de Louis XIII* (Vow of Louis XIII) for the cathedral of Montauban (1824).[26] The Madeleine, the Stock Exchange, and the arc de Triomphe were completed. Churches were built in an analogous neoclassical idiom derived from Chalgrin's Saint-Philippe-du-Roule. The château de Saint-Ouen, presented by Louis XVIII to his favorite, Madame du Cayla, was an Italian villa straight from the pages of the design compendia of Jean Charles Krafft. Taste for the

◀ **FIG iii.4.** Antoine Jean Gros. *Napoleon Distributing the Cross of the Legion of Honor to Artists During His Visit to the Salon on October 22, 1808*, n.d. Oil on canvas. Châteaux de Versailles et de Trianon, Versailles, MV6347.

▶ **FIG iii.5.** François Joseph Heim. *Charles X Distributing Prizes after the Salon of 1824 in the Louvre*, 1824. Oil on canvas. Musée du Louvre, Paris, 15-532301.

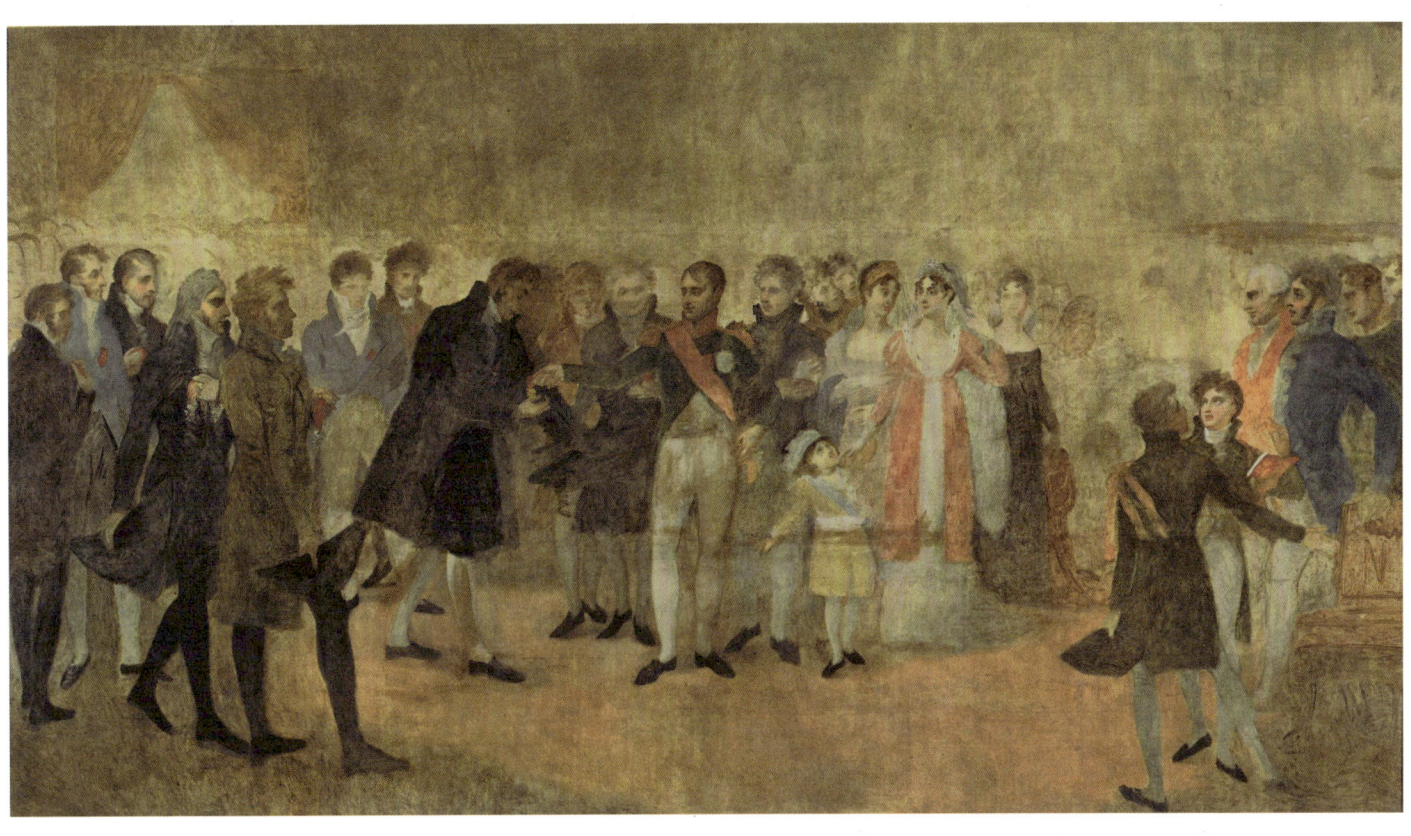

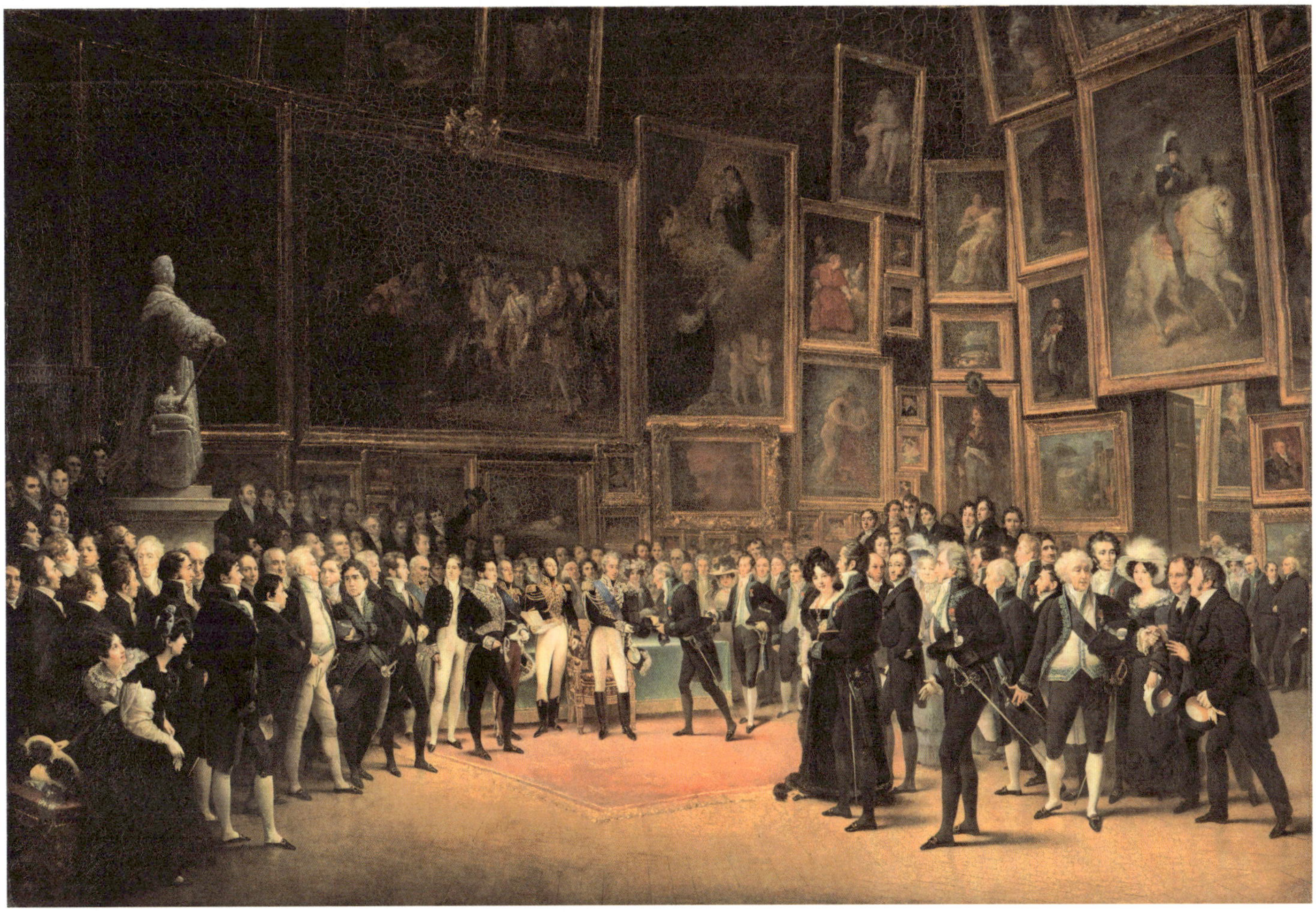

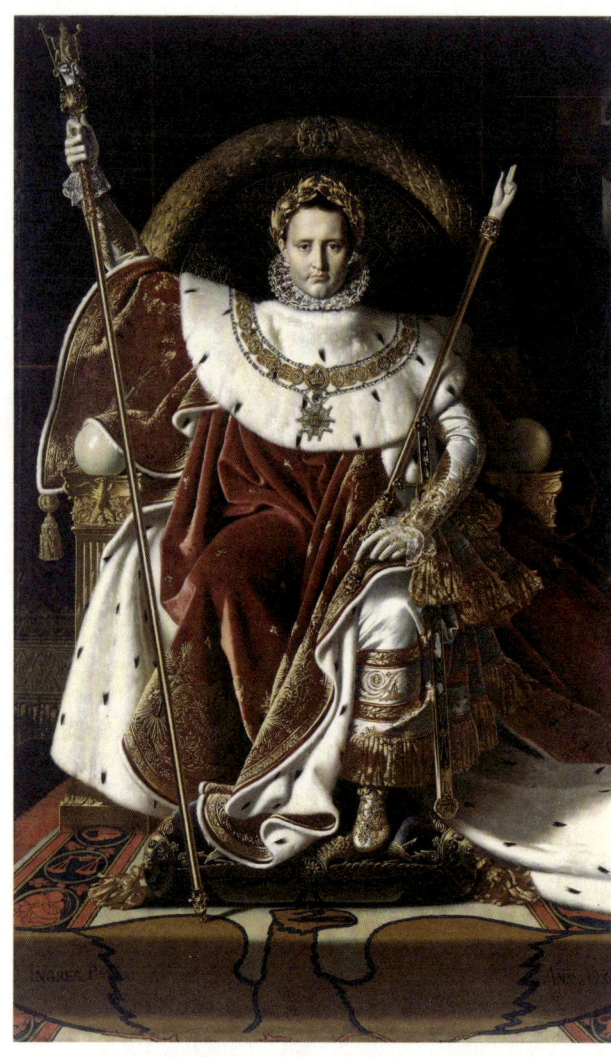

antique was rejuvenated by the audacious interior and exterior polychromy of Jakob Ignaz Hittorff, borrowed from Hellenistic Sicily.[27]

Under Louis-Philippe, a monarch virtually devoid of artistic sensibilities, eclecticism continued to spread [FIG. iii.7].[28] The king's personal taste ran to the meticulous touch of Horace Vernet, but his government also acquired *Liberty Leading the People* by the romantic Eugène Delacroix, who was appreciated by Adolphe Thiers and did not lack for prestigious commissions, such as the painted decorations in the Salon du Roi (1833) and the library (1838) of the Palais Bourbon and in the library of the palais du Luxembourg (1840). The July Monarchy, which instituted freedom of the press, was also a moment that saw the birth of an art of opposition in the caricatures of Charles Philippon and Honoré Daumier.

Neoclassicism evolved slowly, enriched itself with borrowings from the Italian and French Renaissance, and remained obligatory in official art. The regime's great Parisian building projects demonstrate this slippage from neoclassicism to eclecticism: the exterior of Saint-Vincent-de-Paul, by Hittorff, borrows from both antiquity and the Renaissance, while the interior looks toward Byzantium and cultivates all manner of technical innovations (enamel painting on lava, wax painting, decorative cast iron); the refurbishing of the palais du Luxembourg entailed the identical reconstruction of the garden façade designed early in the seventeenth century by Salomon de Brosse; and the monumental fountains that Louis Visconti designed for Paris are in a neo-baroque style. Henceforth, the pediments, porticos, and columns of public buildings in the provinces seemed out of sync with the innovations of private architecture. They projected the image of an official State style.

Neo-Gothic first found a niche in ephemeral architecture and interior decoration—and in the

▶ **FIG iii.6.** Jean Auguste Dominique Ingres, *Napoleon I on His Imperial Throne*, 1806. Oil on canvas. Musée de l'Armée, Paris, 4; Ea 89/1.

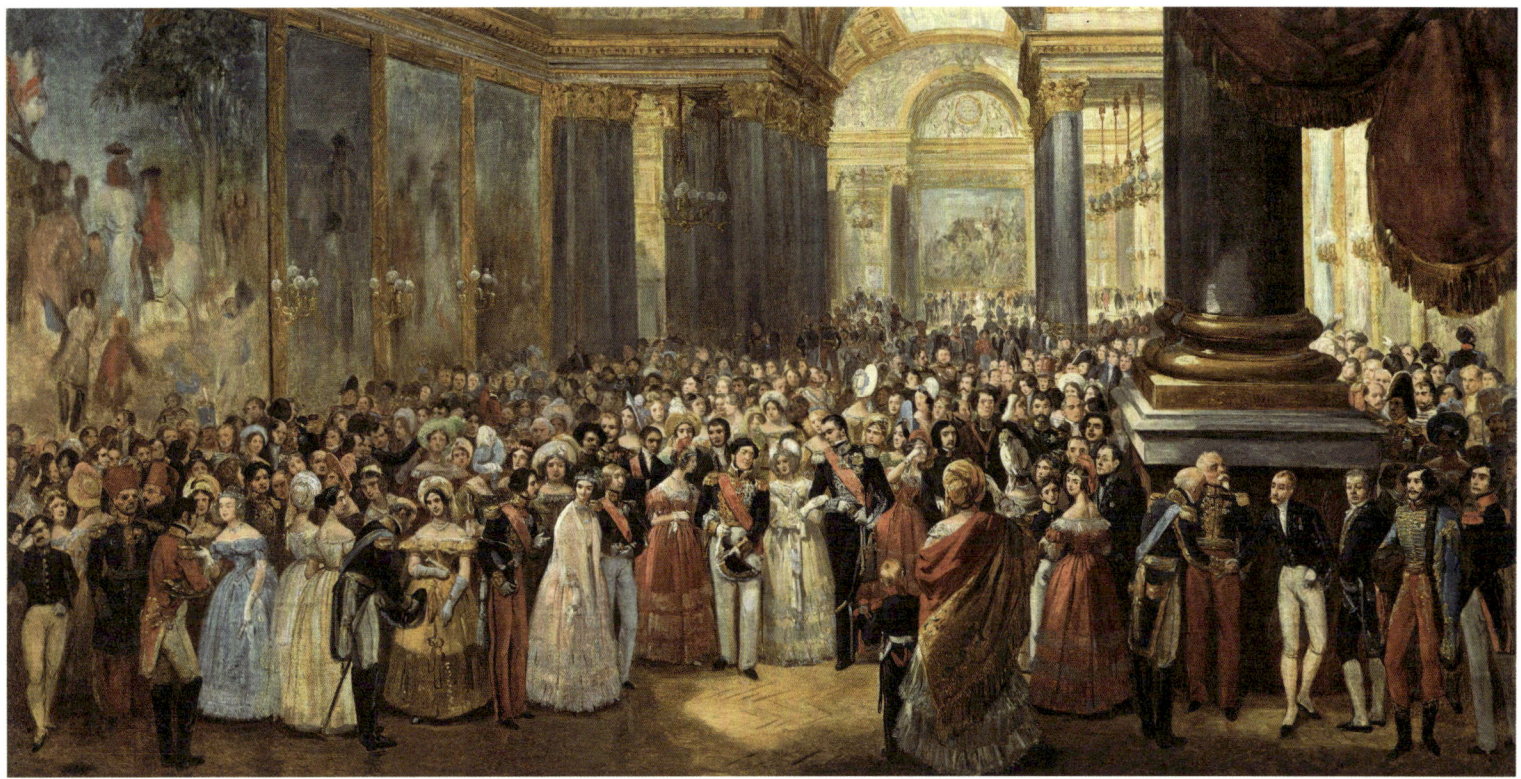

earliest restorations of Gothic buildings—before imposing itself as the new style of religious architecture. The grandest public commission in a neo-Gothic idiom, the Halls of the Crusades in the Musée de Versailles, was invisible from the exterior; all the other projects undertaken at Versailles by Louis-Philippe remained faithful to neoclassicism. Decorative programs inspired by the history of France, which under the Restoration concentrated on the tutelary figure of Henri IV, flourished and attained their apogee under a regime that presented itself as the culminating synthesis of the nation's history, devoted, like the Musée de Versailles, "to all the glories of France."

From the Directory to the July Monarchy, continuity prevailed over rupture. Percier and Fontaine, who traversed all of the regimes, from Louis XVI to Louis-Philippe, exemplified this art of survival that transcended revolutions. History remembers them primarily as Napoleon's architects, but they also served the Convention, the restored Bourbons, and the Orléans dynasty. The same could be said of most artists who worked in France between 1780 and 1840. During this period, the successive governments nourished the arts, directing them to a greater or lesser extent, but it cannot be said that they controlled their evolution. Which is to say that we should be prudent when proposing political readings of works produced during this period—readings that, if they are to remain pertinent, should never exclude other considerations. ◉

▲ **FIG iii.7.** Jean Auguste Bard. *Inauguration of the Galerie des Batailles, Versailles, on June 10, 1837* (exhibited at the Salon of 1850). Oil on canvas. Châteaux de Versailles et de Trianon, Versailles, MV7062.

The author would like to thank Philippe de Carbonnières for his assistance in the preparation of this text.

1 There is no synthetic history of this ministry, but see the thesis by Igor Moullier, "Le ministère de l'Intérieur sous le Consulat et l'Empire (1799–1814). Gouverner la France après le 18 brumaire," PhD thesis, Université de Lille III, 2004.

2 J. Guillaume, ed., *Procés-verbaux du Comité d'instruction publique de la convention nationale*, vol. 5. (Paris: Imprimerie nationale, 1904), 108.

3 Ibid., 112.

4 See the presentation by Léon Le Grand in sub-series F^{12} (Bâtiments civils) in the Archives nationales, accessible in the États sommaire des versements faits aux Archives nationales par les ministères, 1935, on the Archives nationales website, as well as the CONBAVIL database of INHA, which offers a systematic analysis of the proceedings of the meetings of the Conseil des bâtiments civils (1795–1840).

5 Pierre Louis Ginguené (1748–1816), Antoine Fourcroy (1755–1809), Amaury Duval (known as Charles Alexandre Amaury Pineux, 1760–1838), Toussaint Grille (1766–1850), John Pierre Barbier-Neuville (1754–1822), Pierre Paul Royer-Collard (1754–1822).

6 From 1808 to 1813, under the supervision of the Intendant of Crown Buildings, Baron Louis Costaz [1767–1842]. See Pierre Branda, *Napoléon et ses hommes: la Maison de l'Empereur 1804–1815* (Paris: Fayard, 2011).

7 The first Intendant of the Emperor's Household was Charles Pierre Claret de Fleurieu (served from year XII to 1805), formerly Minister of the Marine under Louis XVI; he was succeeded by Pierre Daru (served 1805–11), subsequently appointed Secretary of State and then Minister of War; Jean-Baptiste Nompère de Champagny took over this office from 1811 to 1814, having been "redeployed" there by Napoleon by way of consolation for having had to surrender the foreign relations dossier.
Under the Restoration, the post was occupied in succession by the comte de Blacas, Directeur Général du Ministère (served 1814–15), a favorite of Louis XVIII; the comte de Pradel (served 1815–20), the king's First Chamberlain; the marquis de Lauriston, Maréchal de France (served 1820–24); the duc de Doudeauville (served 1814–28), formerly postmaster general; and finally the comte de La Bouillerie (Intendant Général, 1828–30).
From 1824 to 1830, the vicomte de La Rouchefoucauld, aide-de-camp and familiar of Charles X, directed the Department of Fine Arts and worked directly with the king on related matters. Throughout the July Monarchy, Camille Bachasson, the comte de Montalivet, an intimate of Louis-Philippe, was Intendant of the Civil List, a post that he held concurrently with other ministerial positions (Interior, Public Education). Under the direction of the "king of the French," he created the Musée de Versailles and supervised the enlargement of the Louvre and the restoration of the châteaux of Fontainebleau and Pau. He was also the king's testamentary executor.

8 One of these institutions juggled between the courtly and administrative spheres is discussed in Thierry Sarmant, *Le Cabinet des médailles de la Bibliothèque nationale de 1661 à 1848* (Paris: École nationale des chartes, 1994).

9 "Il entrait dans mes rêves de faire de Paris la véritable capital de l'Europe. Parfois je voulais qu'il devînt une ville de deux, trois, quatre millions d'habitants, quelque chose de fabuleux, de colossal, d'inconnu jusqu'à nos jours, et dont les établissements eussent répondu à la population." *Le Mémorial de Sainte-Hélène*.

10 See Thierry Sarmant, Florian Meunier, Charlotte Duvette, and Philippe de Carbonnières, eds., *Napoléon et Paris: rêves d'une capitale*, exh. cat. (Paris: Paris Musées, 2015).

11 François Loyer, *Histoire de l'architecture française de la Révolution à nos jours* (Paris: Mengès-Éditions du Patrimoine, 1999), 24, 50–53.

12 Chantal Georgel, ed., *La jeunesse des musées: les musées de France au XIXe siècle*, exh. cat. (Paris: Réunion des musées nationaux, 1994).

13 For an overview, see Philippe de Carbonnières, "Les arts florissants," in Michel Biard, ed., *La Révolution française: une histoire toujours vivante* (Paris: CNRS-Biblis, 2014), 377–90; Pierre Arrizoli-Clémentel, Philippe Bordes, and Régis Michel, eds., *Aux armes et aux arts! Les arts de la Révolution française* (Paris: Adam Biro, 1988).

14 "Tous ces objets précieux qu'on tenait loin du peuple ou qu'on ne lui montrait que pour le frapper d'étonnement et de respect, toutes ces richesses lui appartiennent." La Commission temporaire des arts [Félix Vicq d'Azyr], *Instruction sur la manière d'inventorier et de conserver… tous les objets qui peuvent server aux arts, aux sciences et à l'enseignement* (Paris: Imprimerie nationale, an II [March 21, 1794]), 3.

15 "les arts s'empressaient tous pour seconder l'action du gouvernement." [François Antoine] Boissy d'Anglas, *Quelques idées sur les arts, sur la nécessité de les encourager et sur divers établissements nécessaires à l'enseignement public* (Paris: Imprimerie nationale, 25 pluviôse an II [February 13, 1794]).

16 "école imposante"; "Que le génie des arts, conservateur des ouvrages sublimes que nous possédons, soit en même temps un génie créateur et enfante de nouveau chefs-d'œuvre." Jacques Louis David, "…sur la nécessité de la suppression de la commission du Muséum, fait au nom des comités d'instruction publique et des finances, 1793," in Neil McWilliam, Catherine Méneux, and Julie Ramos, ed., *L'Art social de la Révolution à la Grande Guerre. Anthologie de textes sources*, INHA ("Sources"), 2014, published online July 7, 2014; http://inha.revues.org/6166.

17 Annie Jacques and Jean-Pierre Mouilleseaux, *Les architectes de la Liberté* (Paris: Gallimard, 1988).

18 Louis Courajod, *Alexandre Lenoir, son journal et le Musée des monuments français* (Paris: Honoré Champion, 1878–87); Dominique Poulot, *Musée, nation, patrimoine, 1789–1815* (Paris: Gallimard, 1997).

19 "direction morale"; "institution politique"; "ne peuvent fleurir que par la protection spéciale du gouvernement"; "sont aujourd'hui les plus belles pages de l'histoire de la gloire française." Instructions to the jury des arts, 30 pluviôse year VII (January 28, 1799).

20 Pierre Lelièvre, *Vivant Denon, homme des Lumières, ministre des arts de Napoléon* (Paris: Picard, 1993); Marie-Anne Dupuy, *Dominique-Vivant Denon l'œil de Napoléon*, exh. cat. (Paris: Réunion des musees nationaux, 1999).

21 Jean-Claude Bonnet, ed., *L'Empire des muses: Napoléon, les arts et les lettres* (Paris: Belin, 2004). On the industrialization of the decorative arts in this period, see also Jean-Philippe Garric, *Percier et Fontaine, les architectes de Napoléon* (Paris: Belin, 2012).

22 "une espèce de manufacture." The expression comes from Étienne Jean Délécluze, *Louis David, son école et son temps* (1855; Paris: Macula, 1983), 283–84.

23 David O'Brien, *After the Revolution: Antoine-Jean Gros, Painting and Propaganda under Napoleon* (University Park: Pennsylvania State University Press, 2006).

24 Udolfo van de Sandt, "Le Salon," in Bonnet, ed., *L'Empire des muses*, 59–78.

25 Jacques Robinet, *L'art et le goût sous la Restauration* (Paris: Payot, 1927).

26 Vincent Pomarède et al., eds., *Ingres (1780–1867)*, exh. cat. (Paris: Gallimard-Musée du Louvre Éditions, 2006), 142–45, 249–51.

27 Jakob Ignaz Hittorff, *Architecture antique de la Sicile*, 3 vols. (Paris: 1826–30; rev. ed. 1866–67).

28 Loyer, *Histoire de l'architecture française*, 66–131.

CHARLES
PERCIER

CHAPTER 1

PERCIER ALONE

JEAN-PHILIPPE GARRIC

*Percier, whose temperament and taste, indeed his gifts, were ill-suited to the trouble
and demands of business, left all practical matters to me. I handled
the correspondence as well as the accounts, and he focused almost exclusively
on study drawings and the composition of graphic productions.*
PIERRE FONTAINE, 1804[1]

THOUSANDS OF DRAWINGS IN PUBLIC AND PRIVATE COLLECTIONS, several architectural and urban interventions of prime importance in the heart of Paris, numerous furniture designs and interior decors for the most prestigious patrons, publications that left their mark on several generations of architects and decorators, sixteen Prix de Rome winners and seven members of the Institut de France among his students—the importance of Charles Percier was deemed self-evident by his contemporaries and subsequently acknowledged by historians of art and architecture. However, no exhibition or monograph has yet attempted an overview of his production as a whole.[2] This lacuna is not merely a form of injustice to him; given his central role in the arts at a time of transition between the ancien régime and the modern period and his proximity to those in power under Napoleon, it has compromised our understanding of the architecture and decorative arts produced during this period, not just in France but throughout Europe. How to explain this lack of recognition?

Three major difficulties have impeded the study of Percier's work. First, in order to grasp his specific contributions, one must distinguish him from his friend and associate Pierre Fontaine, with whom he has almost always been affiliated. Disengaging Percier from "Percier and Fontaine" is a complex but necessary operation, one that has often been dismissed. Second, Percier's many ventures in fields other than architecture, his nominal profession, raise questions about the real nature of his activity, a situation made all the more challenging by the tendency of some historians to honor traditional divisions, especially those hierarchies in which architecture is accorded a higher rank than the decorative arts. Finally, this hugely productive artistic life is poorly documented. Only a few letters survive, and there is no diary, much less a memoir. Most of the information available to us comes from Percier's contemporaries, first and foremost Pierre Fontaine. It follows that Percier's personality remains largely unknown.

▽ **FIG 1.1.** Julien Léopold Boilly. *Charles Percier and Pierre Fontaine.* From an album of 73 watercolor caricatures. Bibliothèque de l'Institut de France, Paris, ms 749, fol. 15, no. 12.

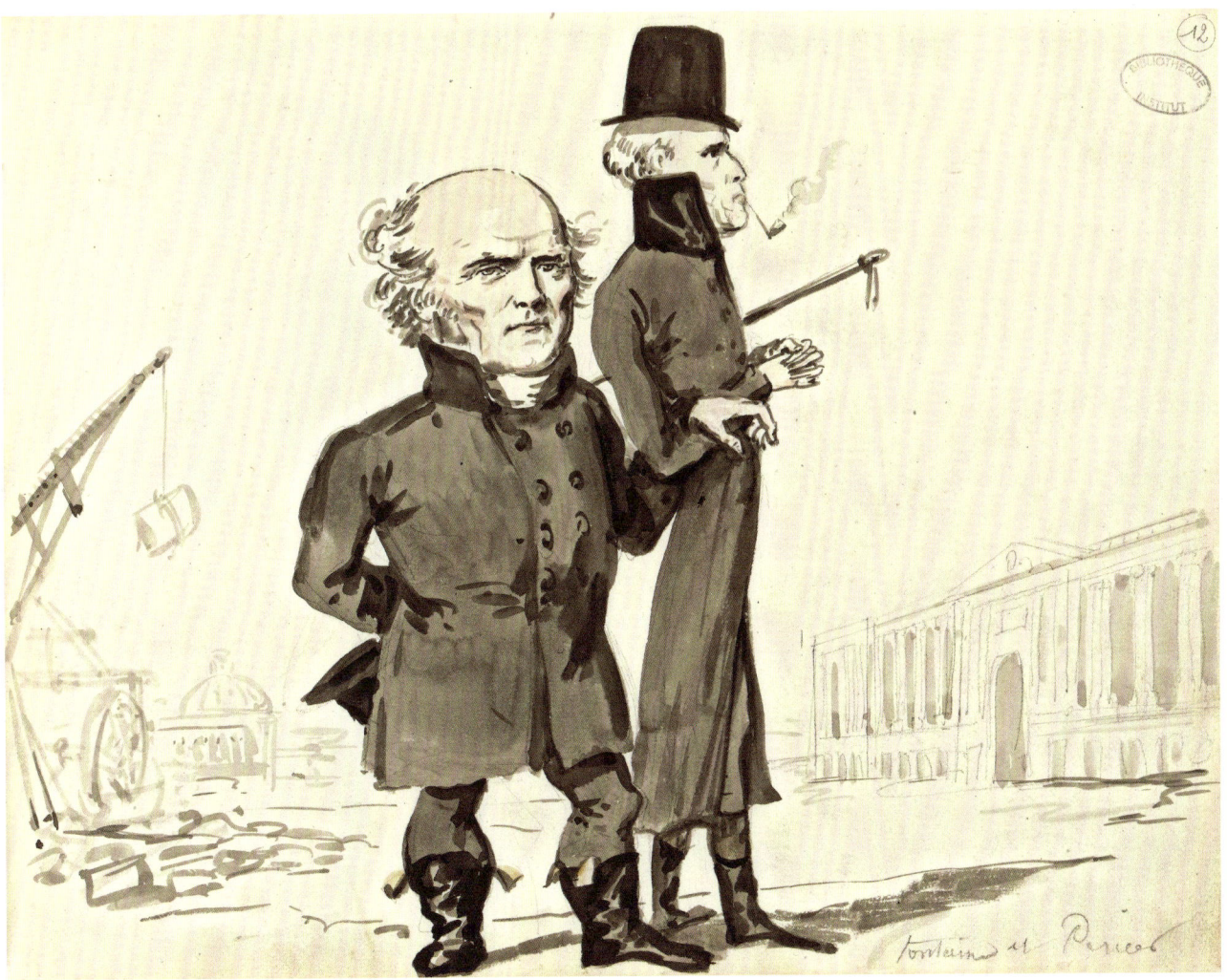

Although there are many surviving graphic documents and other works by Percier, there is no Percier archive. The principal sources—Fontaine's journal and memoirs,[3] the former written for posterity and the latter for his grandchildren—purport to be accurate but they omit or cover up entire aspects of reality. They fail to mention all of the projects undertaken by Percier alone and offer an idealized account of the association between the two men, one fashioned to appeal to "la France des notables"[4] under Louis-Philippe. Furthermore, Fontaine is by no means reliable about such sensitive matters as their political views during the Revolutionary years and the nature of their personal relationship.

Consequently, both the exhibition *Charles Percier: Architecture and Design in an Age of Revolutions* and this accompanying publication offer not a biographical synthesis but rather a thematic examination of Percier's career, with texts by various specialists focusing on specific projects, whether realized, published, or drawn. Although this approach may result in the juxtaposition of contradictory views, the ways in which it fosters acknowledgment of the full range of the architect's various creative endeavors justifies the risk. Likewise, we judged it necessary to admit that, despite recent advances in scholarship, several questions posed from the start of this undertaking are best left unanswered.

PERCIER WITHOUT FONTAINE

This exhibition breaks, then, with the tradition of considering Charles Percier and Pierre Fontaine together. This initial choice, shaped by the discovery of new documents relating to the production of the two partners, was dictated by a concern to free an individual career and a set of personal predilections from the double yoke securing Percier to Fontaine and then to the Empire style in order to grasp the contradictions and eclecticism of a complex period characterized by rapid change [FIG. 1.1].

The Platinum Room in the Casa del Labrador at Aranjuez in Spain offers an emblematic illustration of the shift in perspective afforded by recent research. This masterpiece has long been attributed to both Percier and Fontaine, solely on the basis of its inclusion in the *Recueil de décorations intérieures*. But according to Jean-François Bédard, documents relating to the commission recently published by Chantal Gastinel-Coural and, especially, Javier Jordán de Urríes[5] (notably, an extensive correspondence between the patron and the purveyor), as well as the discovery, during research for the exhibition, of unpublished original drawings from the Jacob workshops, now make it possible to attribute this major decorative ensemble to Percier alone.[6] The implications of this knowledge are significant: first, because the team assembled for the production of this luxurious little room prefigured the subsequent employment of a group of artists at Malmaison; and second, because it indicates that projects published in the *Recueil*, and thus effectively cosigned by Percier and Fontaine, might have been conceived by only one of them. Thus, it may make more sense to understand their conjoined signatures as something like a commercial brand, as opposed to an indication of shared artistic paternity.

A similar ambiguity comes into play in the realm of pedagogy. Although Victor Baltard published a brochure entitled "L'École de Percier,"[7] Louis Hautecœur, in his *Histoire de l'architecture classique en France*, opted for the phrase "the school of Percier and Fontaine," specifying further: "Fontaine, whose duties as official architect kept him very busy, left the direction of all these young people to Percier,"[8] a statement that aligns with Fontaine's own testimony in *Mia Vita*: "Percier had established a school of architectural students, the income from which he shared with me. He alone taught there. I have always thought that, in the matter of education, as in everything else requiring order and direction, the best system is to place one person in charge."[9] This use of the

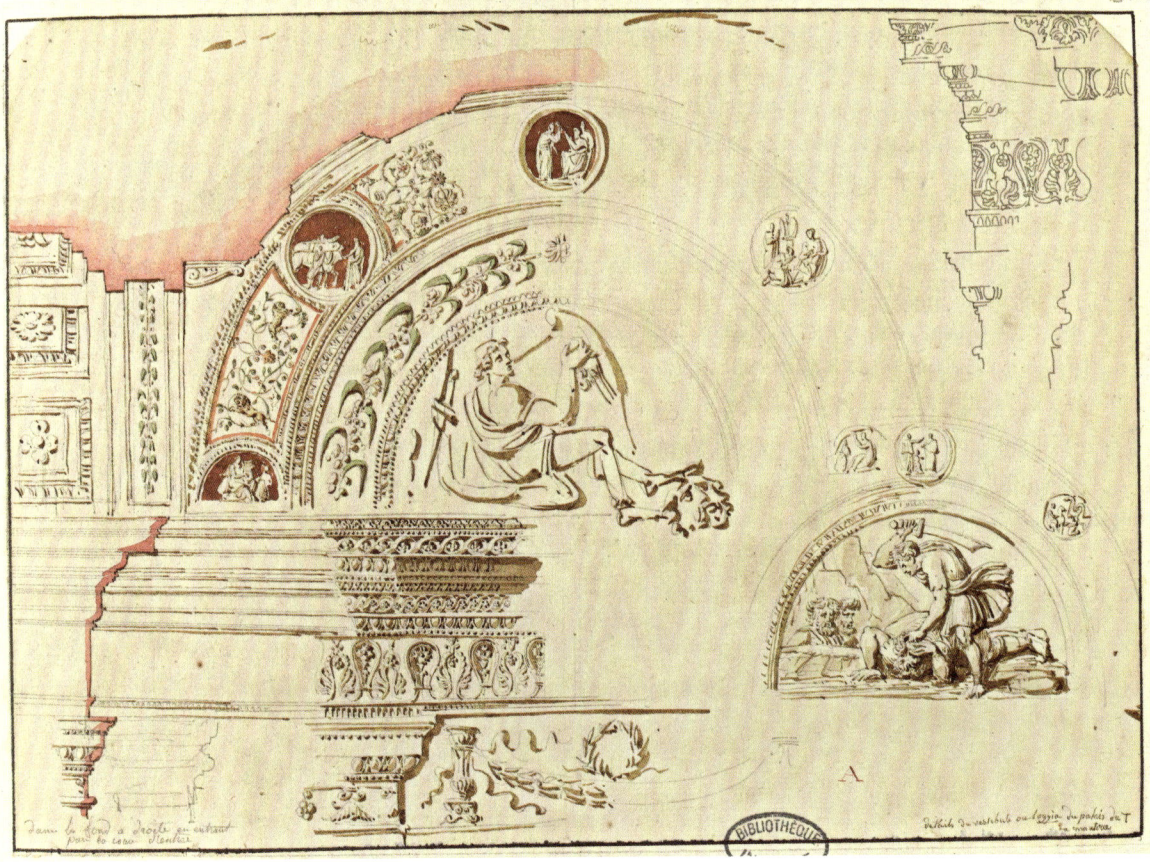

▶ **FIG 1.2.** Charles Percier. Details of the Loggia of Palazzo Te in Mantua, 1791. Ink, brown wash, and gouache on paper. Bibliothèque de l'Institut de France, Paris, ms 1010, fol. 219, no. 320.

designations "school of Percier" and "school of Percier and Fontaine" to designate one and the same thing aligns with the duality of the professorial role, which consisted on the one hand in educating students in their art, which was Percier's domain, and on the other hand in integrating them into a professional network and promoting their careers, a task assumed by Fontaine.

These examples shed light on the question of "Percier alone" versus "Percier and Fontaine," indicating that the two notions should not be placed on the same register. The former relates to the creative process and identifies authorship, while the latter pertains to professional structure, within which—despite the common signature and shared income—there was a clear division of roles.

Among the many works discussed in this book, for some the attribution is clear, whereas in other instances the question remains open. In the matter of drawings, whether study sketches or finished works, the extent of Percier's artistic autonomy is obvious. His sole authorship is verifiable in the case of drawings of buildings from the past, such as those in the albums devoted to Fontainebleau (discussed in this book by Vincent Droguet), to the Palazzo Te in Mantua [FIG. 1.2], and to the basilicas in Padua and Vicenza. This is also true in the case of the more creative ornamental compositions, from the large, highly finished drawings exhibited at the Salon to the composition for *La Henriade* consigned in 1819 with François Gérard [FIG. 1.3]. And in between there is the teeming overabundance of the frontispieces for the anthology of Roman palaces (1798), as well as the headpieces for the editions of Horace and La Fontaine published by Pierre Didot l'aîné and the decorative framing elements for the plates published in the volume commemorating Napoleon's coronation. This aspect of Percier's œuvre, which was especially dear to him and won the admiration of his contemporaries, was produced independently of Fontaine, who in their collaborative book projects was in charge of the perspective views,[10] a division of labor confirmed in the present volume in the chapter by Christophe Beyeler.

The division of labor in the realm of interior decoration is sometimes less clear than in the design of furniture and objets d'art, but most of the known drawings for them are from the

▽ **FIG 1.3.** François Gérard and Charles Percier. Frontispiece for Voltaire, *La Henriade*. Engraved by Henri Charles Müller (Paris: Firmin Didot, 1819–23) Chateaux de Versailles et du Trianon, Versailles, LP16.9.1. Cat 53a.

▷ **FIG 1.4.** Charles Percier. Design for a bedroom for Josephine Bonaparte, ca. 1802. Graphite, ink, wash, and watercolor on paper. Private collection, Paris. Cat. 63.

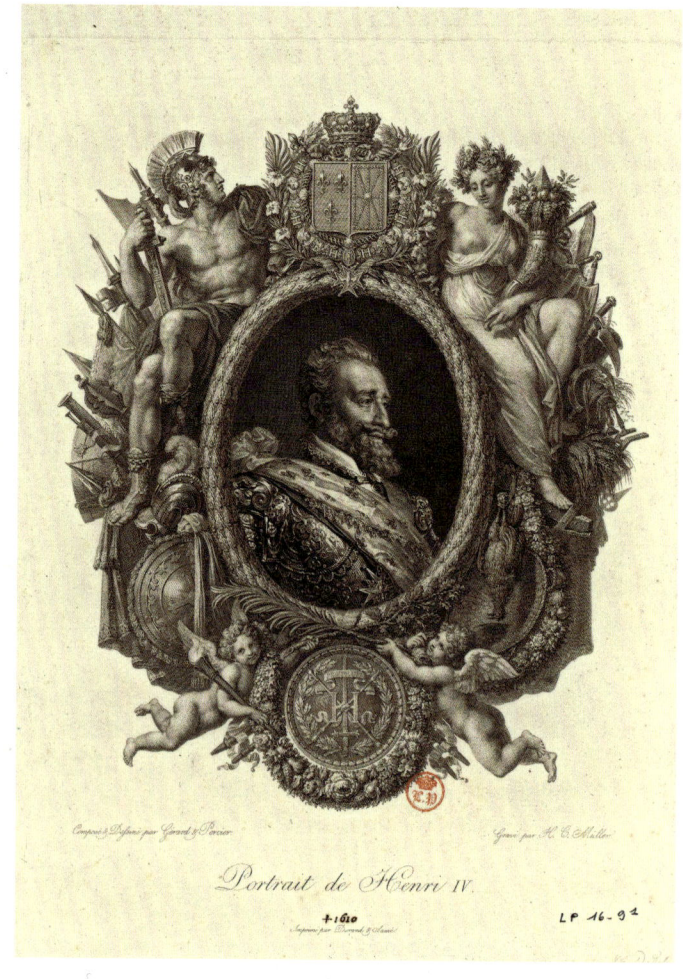

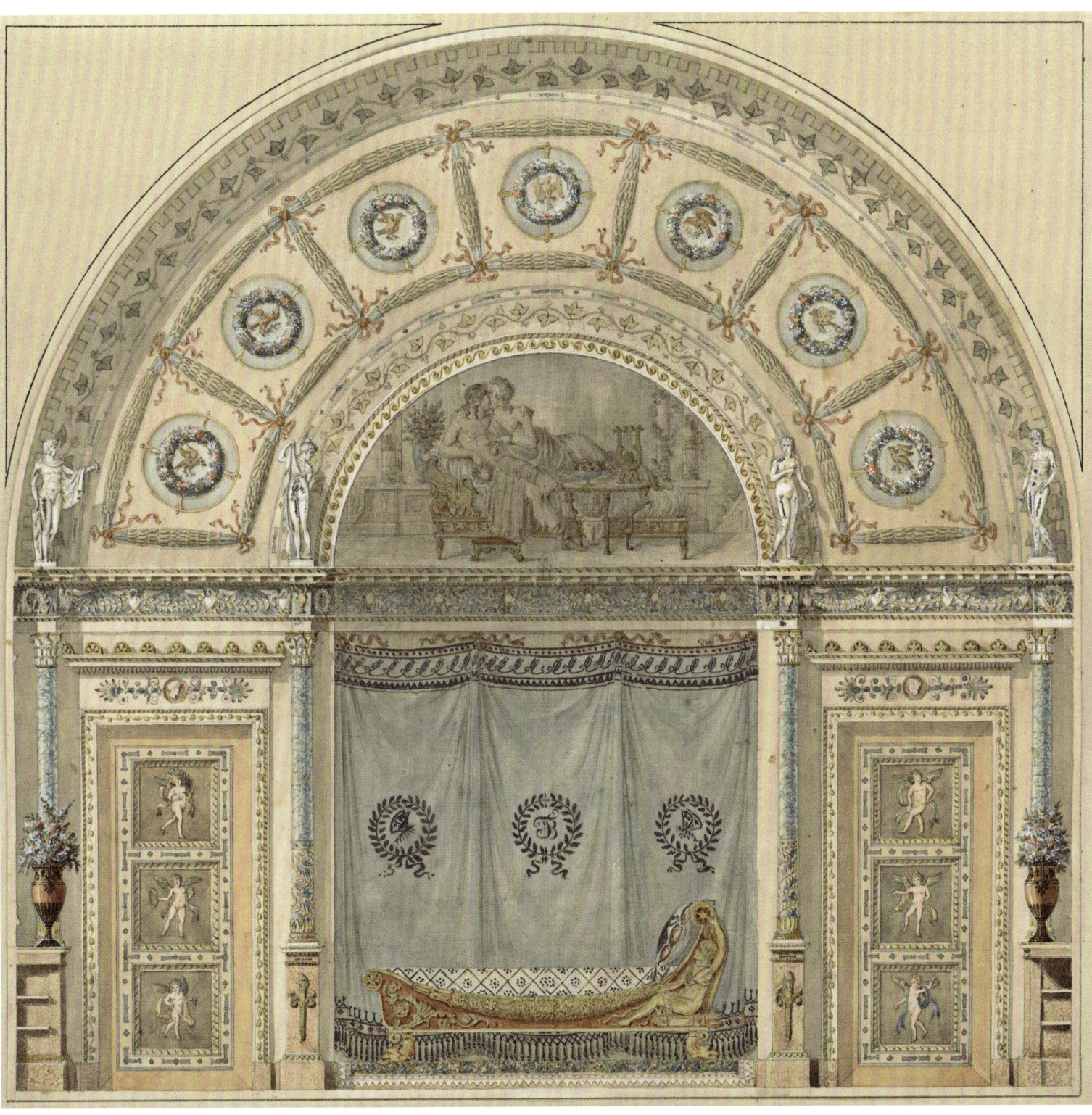

hand of Percier, who, often assisted by a student, regularly provided designs to fabricators, whether the Jacob and Biennais workshops or the Sèvres and the Gobelins manufactories, as Jean-François Belhoste and Anne Dion-Tenenbaum amply document in their respective chapters.[11] From the rapid sketches assembled in the Metropolitan Museum scrapbook, often annotated in Percier's hand, to meticulously finished compositions, such as the elevation drawing that may represent Josephine's first bedchamber in the Tuileries palace [FIG. 1.4], each characterized by extreme finesse, all of the available evidence confirms Fontaine's assertion in *Mia Vita* that the *Recueil de décorations intérieures* was largely the work of Percier.[12]

It is when we move into the realm of architecture per se that attribution generally becomes all but impossible, a situation wholly consistent with the collective nature of architectural design, which often results in drawings signed not by the actual draftsman but by the head of the firm. During the years when they were active as a team, the only architectural project clearly attributable to Percier alone is the one for the Musée des monuments français. Percier's close collaboration with Alexandre Lenoir around 1800, at a moment when Malmaison was being remodeled and the rue de Rivoli project was being developed, is completely ignored in Fontaine's diary, where Lenoir is not even mentioned. The collaboration was nonetheless quite real, occasioning many drawings, dozens of engravings, and an ambitious, original architectural project.

As for the rest, the fact that Percier was more oriented toward drawing and Fontaine more toward administration, notably when it came to linking the Louvre with the Tuileries or building the palace of the king of Rome, does not tell us much about the core dynamic of their creative collaboration, in which ideas were generated and important decisions were made. This part of their creative process definitely existed. It is central to their histories, both as partners and as individuals, and we should not be misled by the order in which their names appear on the title pages of their books, Percier having been listed first because he had won the Prix de Rome. Their published œuvre was a common enterprise, one equally indebted to each of them.

We must nonetheless draw attention to the originality in this regard of the architectural historian Sigfried Giedion, some of whose finest pages are devoted to Percier and Fontaine, pages that bear witness to the close attention he paid to them. Far from merging them together, this advocate of architectural modernism is among the few authors to consider them as individuals. Acknowledging what many scholars have refused to take into account, Giedion characterized Fontaine as a skillful builder and Percier as a talented draftsman,[13] descriptions that made it possible for him to assimilate their partnership to the architect-engineer relationship that Le Corbusier ardently advocated in the 1920s.[14]

THE ELUSIVE UNITY OF AN ŒUVRE

It is no easy task to select the proper framework within which to portray our subject: an imperfect architect, a painter without an easel, a stage director, even a historically precocious "designer," an Italophile curious about French Gothic art, and an antique revivalist partial to over-elaborate decorations. Doubtless the challenge has discouraged careful historians from taking it up. Moreover, in the context of French scholarship, Percier has the double disadvantage of straddling two chronological periods and several distinct areas of specialization, namely architectural history, furniture history, and the history of prints. Just as previous scholarship fails to transcend these categories, the various fields in which he was active—graphic arts, the design of furniture and objets d'art, interior decoration, architecture—correspond, despite their common reliance on a mastery of drawing, to different creative modes, some of which are by nature individual and autonomous, others more collective.

Louis Hautecœur, in his *Histoire de l'architecture classique en France*, had much to say about Percier and Fontaine. Some of his observations are scattered throughout the two volumes devoted to the period, whereas others are more focused, concentrated in a section entitled "Napoleon and Architecture" and in a discussion of their pedagogy and the work of their followers.[15] Hautecœur's assessment, comprehensive but insufficiently synthetic, emphasizes three things: their activity in service to Napoleon, their role in the establishment of the architecture department at the École des beaux-arts, and their contributions to the decorative arts, in which context they are mentioned many times. They are, however, considered not in terms of their specific achievement but rather as integral to the stylistic tendency of their era.[16]

Among more recent scholars to consider Percier apart from Fontaine, we should mention David Van Zanten,[17] whose work is largely concerned with Percier's pedagogy and the principles of composition at the heart of his teaching. Van Zanten's decision to examine projects developed by architecture students at the École des beaux-arts, from Charles Percier to Charles Garnier—a radical, almost provocative move[18]—led him to emphasize Percier's role as the initiator of a new school and to argue that he was a pivotal figure in the transition from the ancien régime to the nineteenth century. Van Zanten's approach left Percier the graphic artist and decorator entirely by the wayside, restricting his focus much as furniture historian and historians of the decorative arts do. Jean-Pierre Samoyault, who refused to sever Percier from Fontaine, accorded them major importance, notably in his book *Mobilier français Consulat et Empire*.[19] In this context, however, where the governing principle is classification by furniture type and the major concern is the attribution of individual pieces to specific craftsmen, it is difficult to separate Percier's own production from more or less meticulous reproductions of the models that he created, and from imitations still further removed from his originals.

POOR, REVOLUTIONARY, AND HOMOSEXUAL?
A FLAWED "GREAT MAN"

Percier came from a family of modest means but one with ties to royal power. His mother was a seamstress to Marie-Antoinette, his father a gatekeeper at the pivot bridge leading from the place Louis XV to the Tuileries gardens. Whatever the latter's political sympathies, he was an indirect victim of the Revolution; since his sole source of income was the rent paid for the restaurant of the Swiss Guards, he lost everything on August 10, 1792, when the siege of the Tuileries led to the sacking of the restaurant and the eradication of the guards.

What little we know about the architect's early education is consistent with such origins. A student at the École gratuite de dessin (Free Drawing School), an institution whose aims were in part philanthropic, he had a poor command of spelling, as can be seen in the letter addressed to John Flaxman recounting his return trip from Rome in 1791[20]; indeed, Percier was so prone to spelling errors that one wonders whether, without Fontaine's help, he would have been able to perform the administrative and social tasks that a prominent architectural career required.

Did these plebeian roots make him an advocate of the Revolution? Should we go so far as to assert, as Jean-François Bédard does in this volume, that he was a strong supporter of the Republican cause? In this same letter to John

Flaxman, Percier allows us to glimpse his disquietude. "I won't say anything about [political] affairs for fear of letter inspectors. But all goes well, thank god." This prudence, and the dissimulation it entailed, should prompt us to be circumspect when examining documents written during this period, given that they were likely influenced by concerns about self-preservation and the need to flatter those in power. Nonetheless, we can try to assess Percier's political positioning, if not his convictions, in light of what we know about their professional implications. Even here, however, the pertinent evidence emerges only when we read between the lines. In *Mia Vita*, Fontaine presents himself as a liberal and as someone close to Cardinal Loménie de Brienne, former minister of finance to Louis XVI. He emphasizes that he emigrated to London for several months and says that he was obliged to serve the Revolutionary government more or less under duress.[21] This account accords well with his connections during the Restoration and his friendship with Louis-Philippe, but is it consistent with his views in 1793? The commissions to design furniture for the assembly hall of the Convention and to remodel the offices of the Revolutionary *section de Brutus* (the only such project realized in France during the Terror), and his victorious submissions to the competition of the year II (1793) amount to a favorable list of credits, which points to some degree of official favor during these difficult years, especially when we add their appointment as architects to the Paris Opera between 1792 and 1796. All of this might owe something to the personal connections of Charles Percier, who then enjoyed the support of the painter Jacques Louis David, himself very committed to the Revolution. Percier's participation in the Commune des arts corroborates this hypothesis. In any case, it should be noted that his drawn architectural projects avoid the martial vocabulary and exaggerated rhetoric found in the more declamatory compositions of these years. Nor did his political views cause him trouble when the Empire fell, as did those of some of his more deeply implicated friends, including David and Joachim Lebreton, both of whom were exiled.

Finally, if we are to understand Percier's personality, we must explore the more intimate dimension of his sexual life, especially if we are to grasp the real nature of his very close and high-profile relationship with Pierre Fontaine. Unlike the latter, who cohabited until her death with Sophie Dupuis, the mother of his illegitimate daughter, and Claude Louis Bernier, their business partner, who was coupled with a woman and ultimately married, Percier, so far as we know, had no female liaisons. There was no open avowal of homosexuality on Percier's part, but Jeanne Duportal, made uneasy by the apparent lack of any heterosexual attachments, set out to discover one. Noting—with some emphasis—that the drawings by Percier in the Institut de France include five portraits of women, she paid special attention to one of them, the depiction of a "Roman lady" bearing a manuscript annotation in poor Italian, as was typical of Percier: "designato dalle Paolina Chatillon." Not realizing that this was probably an allusion to Pauline Chatillon, student and wife, in 1790, of the painter Louis Gauffier, she decided that the woman in question must have been a youthful love interest of Percier's: "If we remember," she writes, "that Percier remained single and that, in the last years of his life, he still dreamed of Italy to the extent of roaming the neighborhoods of Paris frequented by 'voiturins' [carters] so as to hear echoes of the speech from the banks of the Tiber, the image of this lovely woman with a fine Greek profile suggests a hypothesis. Until there is evidence to the contrary, would it be absurd to suppose that here we brush up against Percier's most intimate secret, that this small portrait is the last vestige of the youthful adventures of the most serious of architects?"[22] This hypothesis may seem amusing today, but it is significant. To construe the pleasure taken by the architect in frequenting voiturins and their spoken Italian, as evidence of a persistent nostalgia on his part for a youthful heterosexual affair betrays an eagerness on the author's part to clear her hero of what she, and others of like mind, apparently consider an embarrassing suspicion.

The fact that Percier, Fontaine, and Bernier are buried in the same tomb in Père Lachaise Cemetery has been construed as evidence in favor of the hypothesis that their relations exceeded the narrow bonds of close friendship. It is true that double and, especially, triple male tombs are very rare [FIG. 1.5].[23] But it is not clear that this octagonal stele decorated with masonic symbols, on which Fontaine stipulated that "Hi tres in unum sunt" (these three are one)—a startling allusion to the Holy Trinity—be engraved after his own burial, was intended as a public declaration of intimate union. A visit to the site reveals the monumental, almost official character of the tombs and grave markers in this part of the cemetery. The area brings to mind an open-air Pantheon, and in such a context the tomb in question comes

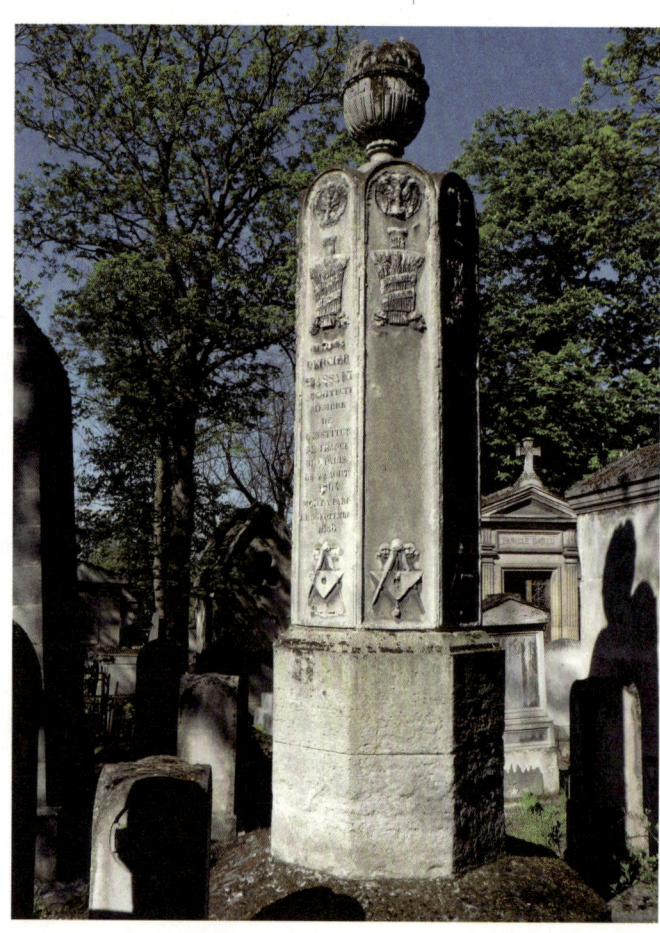

across more as a means of forever sealing an artistic union before History. And what are we to make of Bernier's role in this business? Denied a place on the title page of the book on Roman palaces,[24] was he included here solely to preclude the notion of a couple? Fontaine wrote in a letter six days after Percier's death: "I have lost half of myself; what now will be the days that are given to me?"[25] But isn't it anachronistic to interpret such a public avowal of friendship as an allusion to more intimate relations?

Ultimately, the only explicit elements available to us are perhaps a few of the illustrations for works by Horace and La Fontaine, which offered Percier's imagination fleeting opportunities to indulge in escapades outside the realm of architecture [SEE FIG. 5.7].

ARCHITECT OR DESIGNER?

Narrowing our focus from Percier and Fontaine to Percier alone also entails paying less attention to architecture and more to the graphic arts and the design of furniture and decorative arts. Should we, however, go so far as to claim that Percier was more a designer than an architect per se?

He did not, like Fontaine, come from the world of building, and his initial training at the École gratuite de dessin was structured around the graphic arts. Nonetheless, the discipline that enabled him to win the Prix de Rome, and later to become a member of the Institut de France and a celebrated professor, was that of architecture. He was indeed more inclined to perfect his drawings within the confines of his atelier and to deal with accomplished craftsmen than to engage with the coarser world of contracting and construction. But although he left all on-site work to Fontaine and preferred drawing to building, it does not follow that Percier completely abandoned the field of architecture; he just approached it more as a theoretician and pedagogue than as a practitioner. After all, when Percier and Fontaine took up garden design, when they prepared their book on Roman palaces and the *Recueil de décorations intérieures*, they did so in their capacity as architects.[26] What is most problematic about Percier's disciplinary orientation is not his remoteness from the practical side of architecture—a choice that might be likened to that of Étienne Louis Boullée—but the exceptional degree of his success in areas where architects' efforts tend to be less self-assured. Alexandre Lenoir effectively acknowledged this when he called Percier's headpieces for the Didot

◂ **FIG. 1.5.** Tomb of Charles Percier, Pierre Fontaine, and Claude Bernier. Père Lachaise Cemetery, Paris.

editions of Racine and La Fontaine "his most remarkable achievement, given that he's an architect."[27] Our intention here is not to diminish his architectural work but rather to emphasize the quality of his production in other realms.

That said, the importance of Percier's work in interior decoration, furniture, metalwork, and ceramics as well in the graphic arts—which the present book can by no means treat exhaustively—sets him very much apart from other architects of his generation, indeed from architects in general. Moreover, contrary to a pervasive tendency of his time, neither his preference for a stance that was more artistically oriented than building oriented, nor his friendship with painters, from Jean Germain Drouais to François Gérard, predisposed Percier toward the picturesque view of architecture favored by, among his intimates, Fontaine, Louis Pierre Baltard and especially Jean Thomas Thibault.

Neither an architect-builder nor an architect-painter, Percier eluded the dialectic that seems to have shaped the architectural profession in France in the years around 1800, opting instead for specialization in ornament, interior decoration, and set design. Thus he sidelined the pedagogical and professional priorities endorsed by the late eighteenth-century Académie royale d'architecture and the early nineteenth-century École des beaux-arts. But isn't it precisely Percier's capacity to stand apart, to cross boundaries and escape conventional categories in order to give free rein to his taste for detail and his preference for ornament, that constitutes his real masterpiece? ●

1 "Percier dont l'humeur et le goût, je puis dire les talents, s'accordaient mal avec les tracas et l'importunité des affaires, me laissait le soin de les diriger toutes en ce qui concernait l'exécution des choses. Je faisais la correspondance ainsi que la comptabilité, et il s'occupait presque exclusivement des études et de la composition des ouvrages de cabinet." This quote comes from page 118 (1804) of Pierre Fontaine's memoir, called *Mia Vita*, written from 1838 to 1844 for his grandchildren after Percier's death. It is a little-known source that documents the working relationship and ties between Percier and Fontaine. This text survives in a manuscript copy held by one of the architect's descendants and has been consulted by several historians; it will soon be published (*Mia Vita. Mémoires privés de Pierre François Léonard Fontaine (1762–1853). Architecte des princes à l'âge des révolutions*, forthcoming March 2017).

2 We must nonetheless mention Jeanne Duportal's publication of a selection of drawings, preceded by a substantial introduction, as well as the work by Hans Ottomeyer, which remains the most exhaustive yet devoted to Percier and interior decoration, despite its being limited to the period 1782–1800. Jeanne Duportal, "Charles Percier 1764–1838," in *Charles Percier. Reproduction de dessins conservés à la Bibliothèque de l'Institut* (Paris: Maurice Rousseau, 1931); Hans Ottomeyer, *Das frühe Œuvre Charles Percier (1782–1800)*.

Zu den Anfängen des Historismus in Frankreich (Munich: Ludwig-Maximilens-Universität, 1981).

3 Pierre François Léonard Fontaine, *Journal (1799–1853)*, ed. Marguerite David-Roy (Paris: École nationale supérieure des beaux-arts / Institut français d'architecture / Société de l'histoire de l'art français, 1987); Fontaine, *Mia Vita*.

4 André Jardin and André-Jean Tudesq, *La France des notables. Nouvelle histoire de la France contemporaine*, vols. 6 and 7 (Paris: Le Seuil, 1973).

5 See Chantal Gastinel-Coural, "Le cabinet de platine de la Casa del Labrador à Aranjuez. Documents inédits," *Bulletin de la société de l'histoire de l'art français* (1994): 181–205; Javier Jordán de Urríes y de la Colina, "Les décors d'Aranjuez: Les *Saisons* du cabinet de platine de la Real Casa del Labrador à Aranjuez," in *Girodet 1767–1824*, ed. Sylvain Bellenger (Paris: Gallimard–Musée du Louvre Editions, 2005), 261–65; Javier Jordán de Urríes y de la Colina, *La Real Casa del Labrador de Aranjuez* (Madrid: Patrimonio Nacional, 2009); Javier Jordán de Urríes y de la Colina and José Luis Sancho, "Sitel, Percier y el Gabinete de Platino," *Reales Sitios* 50, no. 195 (2013): 28–49; Javier Jordán de Urríes y de la Colina and José Luis Sancho, "El cabinete de platino de la Real Casa del Labrador en Aranjuez," in Sabine Frommel, Jean-Philippe Garric, and Elisabeth Kieven, *Charles Percier e Pierre Fontaine, dal soggiorno romano alla trasformazione di Parigi* (Rome: Silvana editoriale / Bibliotheca Hertziana, 2014).

6 Jordán and Sancho, "Sitel, Percier y el Gabinete de Platino."

7 Victor Baltard, "L'école de Percier (lu dans la séance publique annuelle de l'Académie des beaux-arts du 15 novembre 1873)" in *Journal officiel de la République française* (November 17, 1873), 7002–4.

8 Louis Hautecœur, *Histoire de l'Architecture classique en France*, vol. 6: *La Restauration et le gouvernement de juillet* (Paris: Picard, 1955), 166–89.

9 "Percier avait formé une école d'élèves en architecture, dont il me faisait partager les revenus. Il y enseignait seul. J'ai toujours pensé qu'en matière d'enseignement, comme en toute autre chose d'ordre ou de direction, le système d'un seul était le meilleur." Fontaine, *Mia Vita*, 84.

10 See the bibliography of works published by Percier and Fontaine and of books containing prints after drawings by Percier in this volume. Voltaire. *La Henriade* (Paris: Firmin Didot, 1819); Horace. *Quintus Horatius Flaccus* (Paris: Pierre Didot l'aîné, 1799); La Fontaine. *Fables de La Fontaine* (Paris: Pierre Didot l'aîné, 1802); Charles Percier, Pierre Fontaine, and Jean Charles Bonnard, *Choix des plus célèbres maisons de plaisance de Rome et de ses environs* (Paris: Pierre Didot, 1809–13).

11 The authorship of the rare drawings of interior decors found among Fontaine's papers remains unclear; in any case, there are too few of them to call Percier's predominance in this domain into question.

12 "…for while I was wholly occupied with architectural projects, he, virtually alone, drew and engraved, in addition to the frontispieces for the *Palais et maisons de Rome*, most of the plates that make up our anthology of furniture, decors, and other things"; "car, tandis que j'étais occupé tout entier aux travaux d'architecture, il a, presque seul, dessiné et gravé, outre les frontispices des *Palais et maisons de Rome*, la plus grande partie des planches qui composent notre recueil des meubles, des décorations et autres." Fontaine, *Mia Vita*, 119.

13 Sigfried Giedion, *Mechanization Takes Command* (New York: Oxford University Press, 1948), 289.

14 Le Corbusier, *Vers une architecture* (Paris: Crès, 1923).

15 Louis Hautecœur, *Histoire de l'Architecture classique en France*, vol. 5: *Révolution et Empire, 1792–1815* (Paris: Picard, 1953), 156–91; Louis Hautecœur, *Histoire de l'Architecture classique en France*, vol. 6: *La Restauration et le gouvernement de juillet* (Paris: Picard, 1955), 166–89.

16 Ibid., vol. 6, 332–92.

17 David Van Zanten, "Architectural composition at the École des Beaux-Arts, from Charles Percier to Charles Garnier," in *The Architecture of the École des Beaux-Arts*, ed. Arthur Drexler (New York: Museum of Modern Art, 1977), 111–324.

18 Jean-Philippe Garric, "L'Architecture Beaux-Arts: Objet d'expositions," *Les Cahiers du MNAM* 129 (Fall 2014): 38–49.

19 Jean-Pierre Samoyault, *Mobilier français Consulat et Empire* (Paris: Gourcuff-Granedigo, 2009).

20 See chapter 3a in the present volume.

21 Fontaine, *Mia Vita*.

22 Duportal, "Charles Percier 1764–1838," 22.

23 Alan Bray, *The Friend* (Chicago and London: University of Chicago Press, 2003).

24 Thanks to the buyback of his financial interest in the book in 1801.

25 Bibliothèque de l'Institut, manuscrit IX, 4484. See Marguerite David-Roy, "Introduction," in Pierre François Léonard Fontaine. *Journal (1799–1853)* (Paris: École nationale supérieure des beaux-arts / Institut français d'architecture / Société de l'histoire de l'art français, 1987), xii.

26 Charles Percier and Pierre Fontaine, *Le Recueil de décorations intérieures….* (Paris: Authors and Pierre Didot l'aîné, 1801–12); Percier, Fontaine, and Bonnard, *Choix des plus célèbres maisons de plaisance.*

27 "Ce que Percier a produit de plus remarquable pour un architecte." On this subject, see chapter 5, "Graphic Art as Matrix."

CHAPTER 2

THE SCHOOLS OF PERCIER

JEAN-PHILIPPE GARRIC

CHARLES PERCIER OWED A GREAT DEAL TO THE ACADEMIC WORLD, and he gave a great deal back to it. As noted in the introduction, this is one of the domains in which he distinguished himself from Fontaine, along with his success in the Prix de Rome competition and his role as professor. But this connection to teaching was not confined to his own training and the education of his students. It also led to the establishment of friendly ties and durable professional networks that constituted an informal but cohesive artistic community, one that managed to survive the period's political upheavals largely intact, thereby anticipating the autonomy of the École des beaux-arts from political power and its apolitical character.

After studying drawing at the École gratuite de dessin (Free Drawing School), an exemplary philanthropic institution of the last years of the ancien régime, Percier was a model student at the Académie royale d'architecture and then a very enthusiastic pensioner at the French Academy in Rome. He took students of his own in 1791—almost immediately after returning from Italy—and

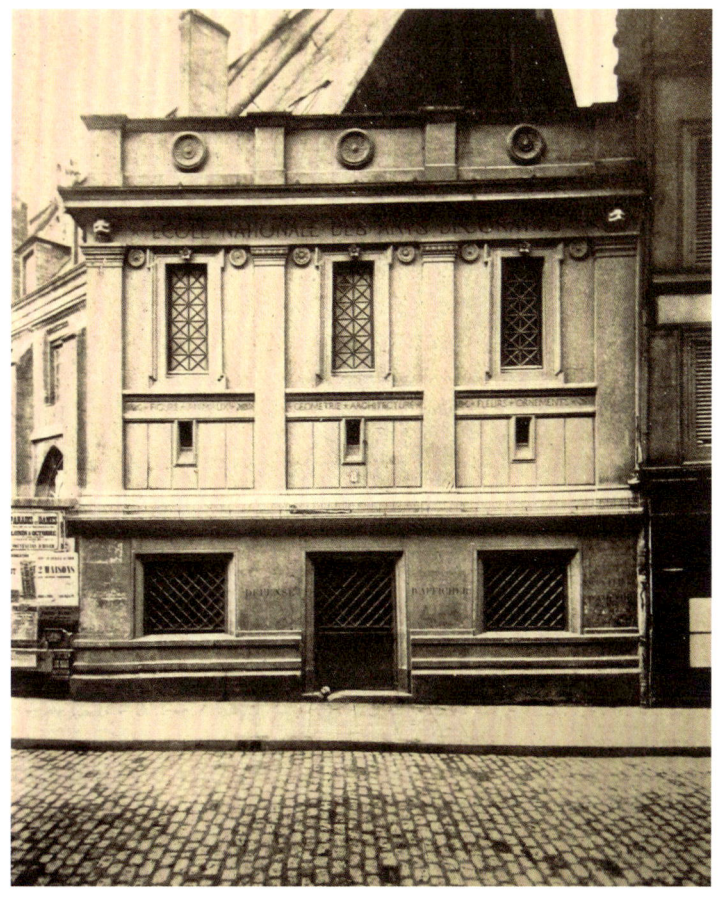

▲ FIG 2.1. Simon Claude Constant-Dufeux. Façade of the annex of the École gratuite de dessin, on the rue Racine, Paris. Photograph published in Maurice Testard, "L'École nationale des arts décoratifs de Paris," *L'Art décoratif, revue de l'art ancien et de la vie artistique moderne* (January 1911): 16.

◂ FIG 2.2. Attendance token for architecture class (recto and verso), École gratuite de dessin, Paris. Copper. Private collection Paris. Cat. 7.

gradually became one of the most important French architecture professors in the first third of the nineteenth century, entering the Institut de France in 1811. In his will, he bequeathed his drawings to several of his closest students, notably his nephew François Alexandre Villain, and he left a substantial sum to the school where he had begun his education, thereby enabling Simon Claude Constant-Dufeux to build a new wing and annex for it on the rue Racine [FIG. 2.1]. Despite his demanding career, Percier never completely abandoned the world of education. He lived alone but often worked with collaborators—Pierre Fontaine, the most important of these, was by no means the only one—and befriended many of his fellow Rome pensioners, as he would later do with several of his students, many of whom worked with him, either occasionally or on a more regular basis.

After moving into the former dissection amphitheater of the École de médicine in 1774, the École gratuite de dessin offered four two-hour classes every day of 125 students each. Students attended two classes per week and were given tokens to document their attendance [FIG. 2.2]. The instruction-through-copying practiced there was intended to prepare poor students to enter the elite cadre of French craftsmen. In addition to teaching Percier the rudiments of drawing, this method fostered not only his interest in decoration but also his preference for graphic perfection. It also gave rise to his first network of contacts.

Several of the young students he encountered at the school would likewise become architects, notably Louis Pierre Baltard, born the same year as Percier, and Charles Pierre Joseph Normand, one year their junior. Both would make significant contributions to contemporary publishing. Together with Percier, Normand can be considered the principal French advocate of neoclassical line engraving. The author of many prints, he also worked frequently

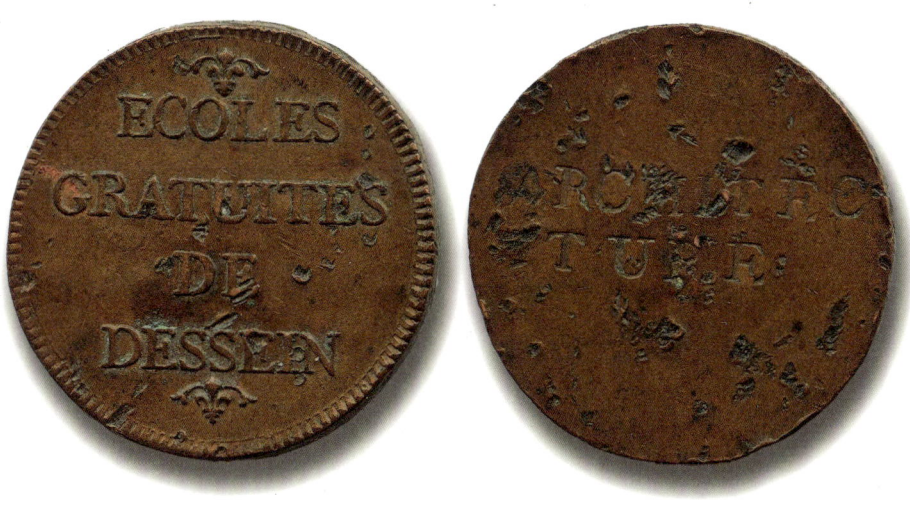

for others as an engraver, notably for the second part of Percier and Fontaine's *Recueil de décorations intérieures*.[1] Like that of Percier, Normand's œuvre extends well beyond architecture. He executed, for example, the plates of Charles Landon's *Annales du musée*, whose initial frontispiece was designed by Percier and engraved by Normand [FIG. 2.3].[2]

Percier's ties to Louis Baltard were even closer. Together with Claude Louis Bernier, Auguste Beudot, and Guillaume Guillon-Lethière, Baltard and Percier traveled from Paris to Rome in 1786.[3] Percier asked Baltard in 1792 to share the post of architect to the Paris Opera, but Baltard opted instead to rejoin the revolutionary armies as a combat engineer. The author of a collection of Roman views and of *Paris et ses monumens* (one of the period's most lavish architectural publications), he also engraved the plates for Alexandre de Laborde's *Voyage en Espagne*, including the frontispiece designed by Percier [FIG. 2.4], and—confining ourselves to projects in which both men were involved—made drawings of the arc du Carrousel that were published posthumously.[4]

It was probably also at the École gratuite de dessin that Percier first encountered the painter Anne Louis Girodet de Roussy-Trioson, with whom he later collaborated on the decoration of the Platinum Room in Aranjuez and at Malmaison. More generally, during this period he frequented circles analogous

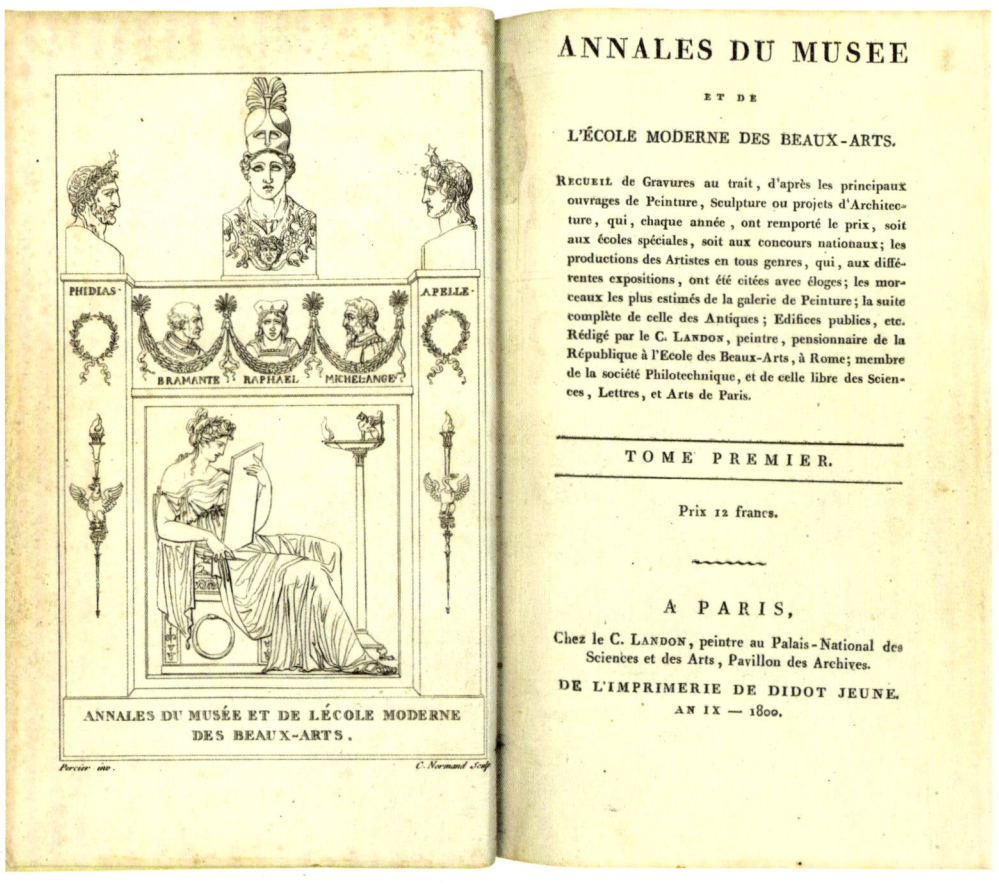

◄ **FIG 2.3.** Charles Normand, after Charles Percier. Frontispiece for Charles Landon, *Annales du musée et de l'école moderne des Beaux-Arts*. Etching (Paris: C. P. Landon, 1800), vol. 1.

► **FIG 2.4.** Charles Percier. Frontispiece for Alexandre de Laborde, *Voyage pittoresque et historique de l'Espagne*. Engraved by Georges Malbeste. (Paris: Pierre Didot l'aîné, 1806–20). Private collection, Paris. Cat. 51.

2 THE SCHOOLS OF PERCIER

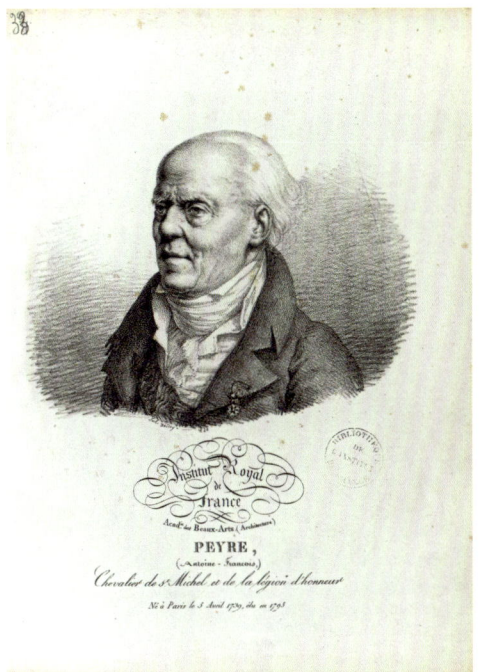

FIG 2.5. Louis Léopold Boilly. *Portrait of Antoine François Peyre*, 1820. Lithograph. Bibliothèque de l'Institut de France, 4°NS1039.

to the ones he would cultivate twenty years later, when his activity as a designer led him to become involved in interior decoration and furnishings.

Percier's second school—a more specialized one—was that of Antoine François Peyre, who led one of the principal ateliers then preparing architects for the Royal Academy competitions. Percier's new acquaintances there included Antoine Laurent Thomas Vaudoyer and Pierre Jules Delespine, with whom he would remain close. Baltard joined the atelier in 1784, and it was also there that Percier first met Pierre Fontaine. Throughout their lives, both men continued to revere this "master," to whom they devoted a passage in their last collaborative publication, on royal residences [FIG. 2.5].[5] The training imparted by Peyre also accorded a key role to drawing, but it was very different from that delivered at the École gratuite. Since the late 1770s, the academic architectural world had been dominated by grand monumental compositions featuring geometric and abstract forms, a rejection of the rococo affectations of the preceding period. The archi-

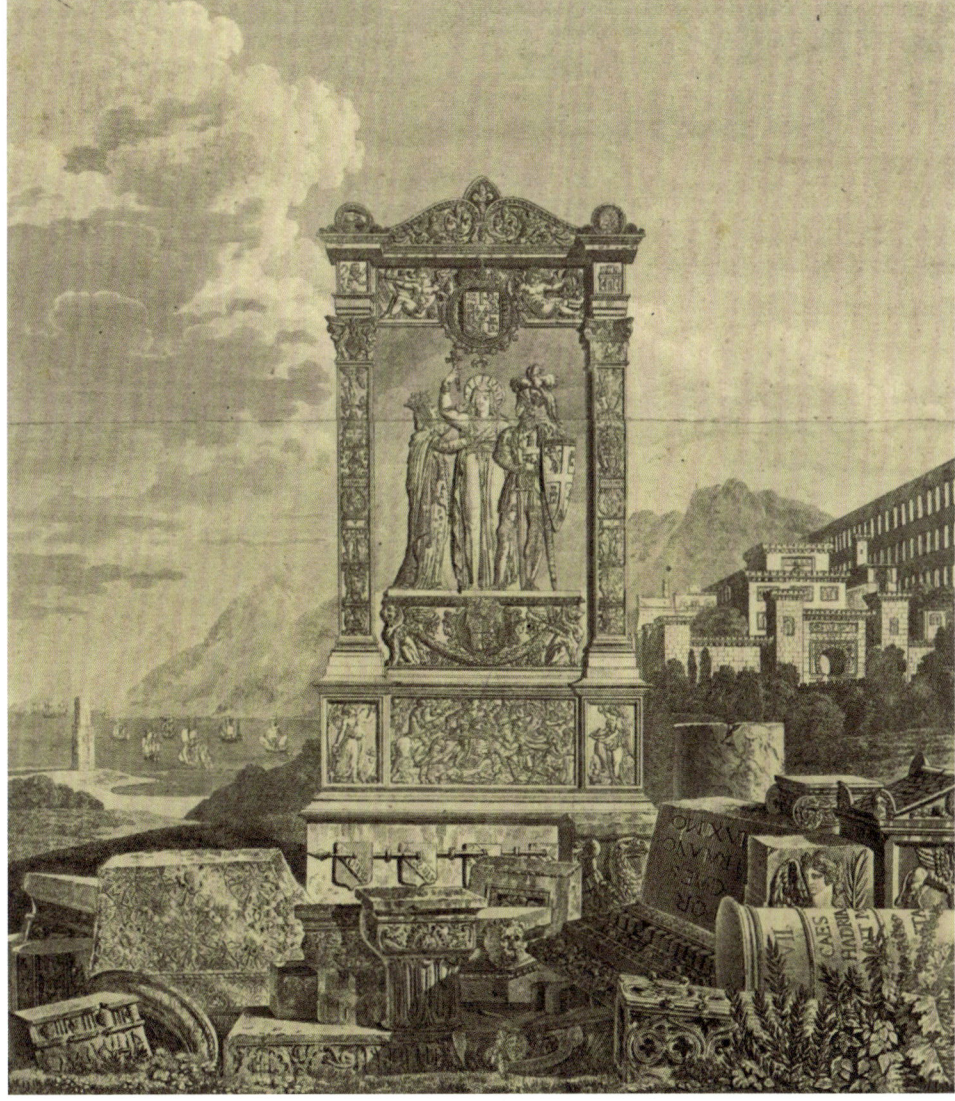

tectural conceptions and drawings of Étienne Louis Boullée had a huge influence on this development.

In 1783, when Percier first participated in the Prix de Rome competition, he won second place, a remarkable showing for a young man of nineteen. The assigned program, "a menagerie set within the park of a royal château," stipulated a square park 600 meters to a side and, as its set piece, "an open-air amphitheater and arena suitable for animal combats."[6] Like Vaudoyer, who won the competition that year, Percier drew a circular coliseum of extreme graphic simplicity [FIGS. 2.6, 2.7]. Nothing in this design betrays his taste for ornament nor his penchant for carved decoration and picturesque composition. In 1786 the submission with which he won first prize—on his second attempt—is even more severe and deferential to prevailing academic canons. For this "building to house the academies,"[7] he all but plagiarized the façade devised three years earlier by Boullée for his museum project, co-opting its linear horizontality, its drum obscuring a low-set dome, and even its flanking triumphal columns, which he transformed into obelisks [FIGS. 2.8, 2.9].

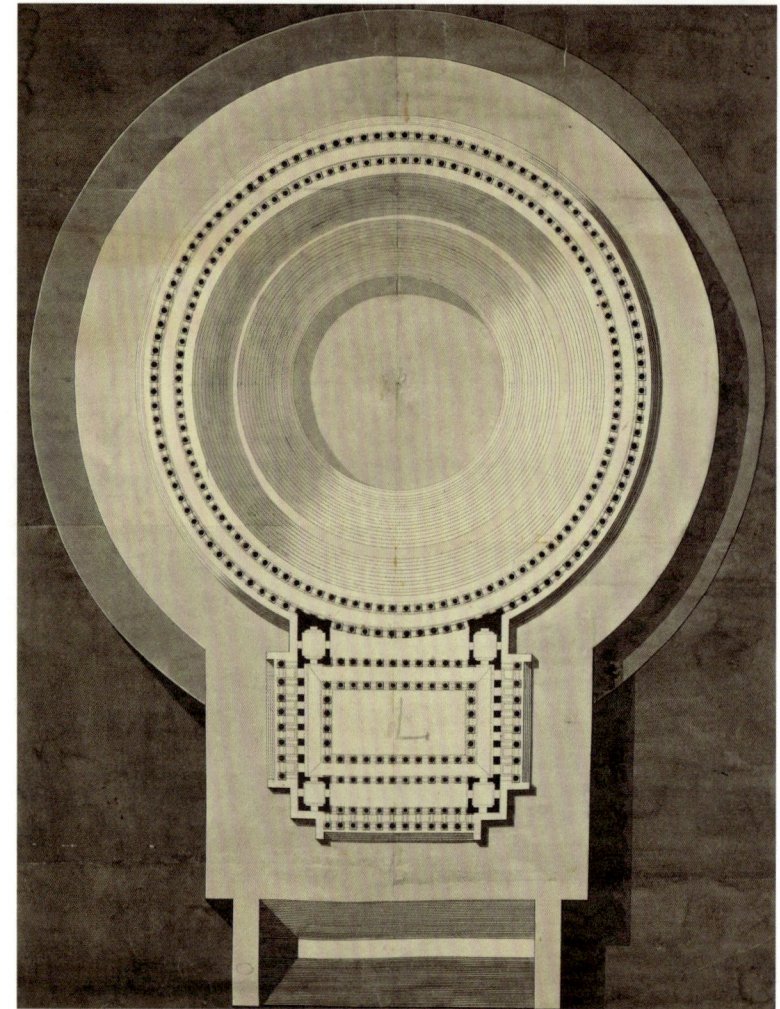

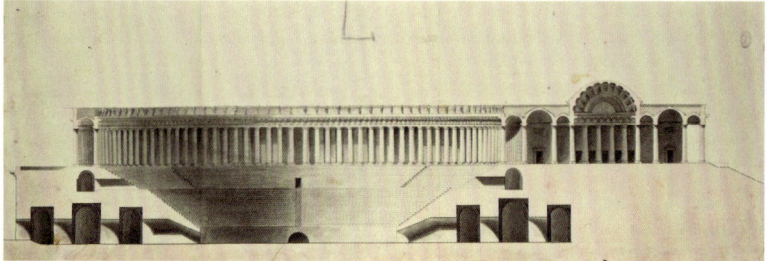

Percier's sojourn at the French Academy in Rome occasioned new friendships that he would maintain throughout his life. He was to divide his time between an assigned project, a study of Trajan's Column, and independent study. This monument was chosen for Percier by Pierre Adrien Pâris, architect of the Menus Plaisirs[8] under Louis XVI and a member of the architecture academy from whom Percier would later inherit the post of architect of the Paris Opera. Doubtless Pâris chose this monument, remarkable above all for its bas-reliefs, because of Percier's gifts as a draftsman and his penchant for sculpture; there had been several previous attempts to measure and draw it, beginning in the seventeenth century, but this one would have the novel aim of proposing a graphic restoration.[9] After ten

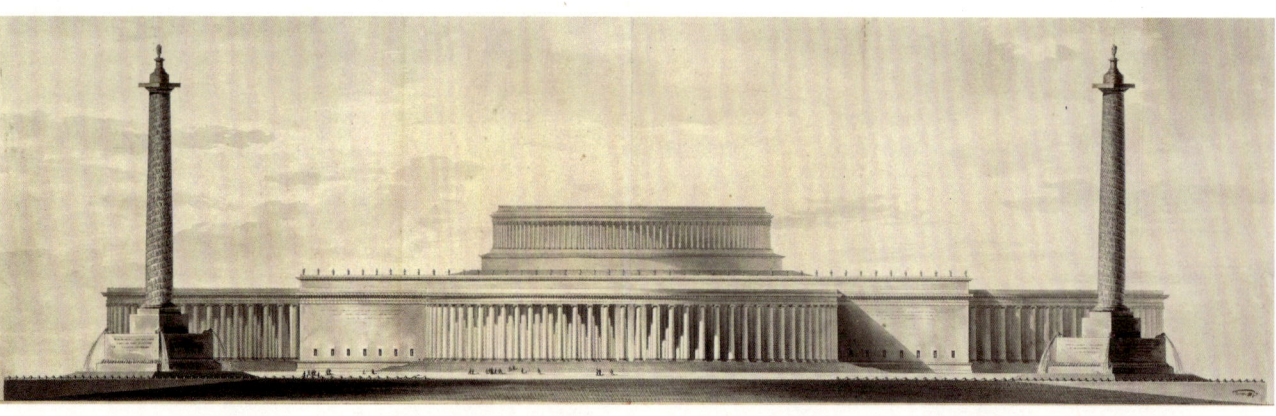

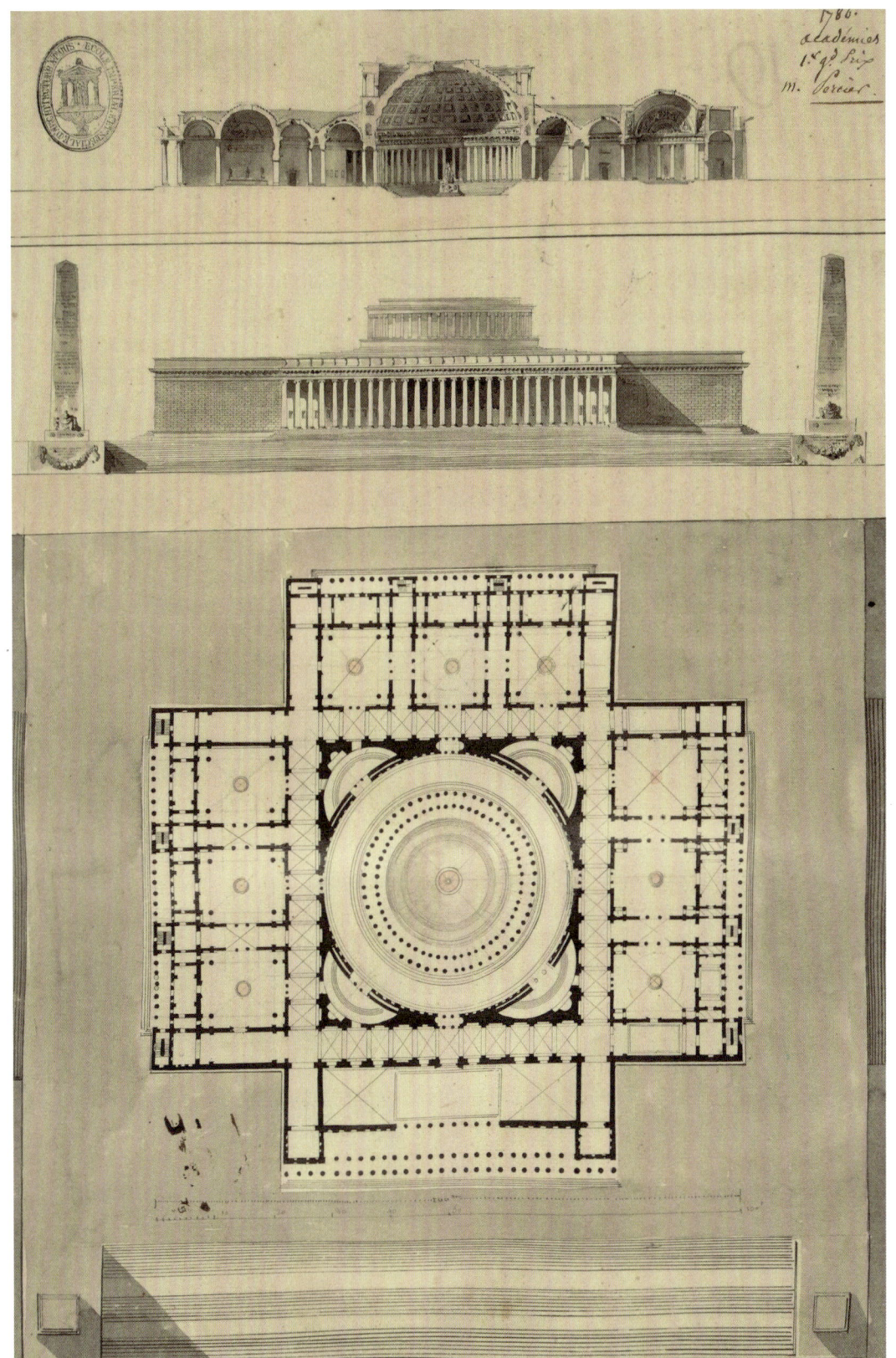

◁ **FIGS. 2.6 + 2.7.** Charles Percier. *Design of a Menagerie set within the Park of a Royal Château*, arena floor plan (top), arena cross section (bottom), 1783. Pencil, pen, and black ink, gray and pink wash on paper. École nationale supérieure des Beaux-Arts, Paris, PRA 104-10.

▷ **FIG 2.8.** Charles Percier. *Edifice to House the Academies*, longitudinal section, elevation, and plan, 1786. Pencil, pen, and black ink, gray and pink wash on paper. École nationale supérieure des Beaux-Arts, Paris, PRAE 1. Cat. 10.

▷ **FIG 2.9.** Étienne Louis Boullée. Elevation design for a museum, 1783. Pen and wash on paper. Bibliothèque nationale de France, Département des Estampes et de la Photographie, Paris, Est. Ha-56-Ft 7. Cat. 12.

months' work, four of which Percier carried out while suspended from the column's abacus in a basket, he managed to deliver a set of drawings of historic importance, effectively inaugurating the tradition of Roman *envois* sent to Paris by architect-pensioners at the Roman academy. (In 1826 this project was imitated, on a more modest scale, by Henri Labrouste, who devoted his second-year envoi to the same monument.) Percier's drawings were published in 1877, almost a century after their completion, at the beginning of a volume on the graphic restorations of ancient monuments by architect-pensioners of the French Academy in Rome [FIGS. 2.10, 2.11].[10]

Percier's independent studies in Rome are known through the two books that resulted from them, the volumes that he and Fontaine devoted to the palaces and villas of Rome,[11] as well as through hundreds of drawings now preserved in the Institut de France. These sketches and measured drawings executed on

▽ **FIG 2.10.** Charles Percier. Entry at the Base of Trajan's Column, 1788. India ink and wash on paper. École nationale supérieure des beaux-arts, Paris, Env 1-03. Cat. 13c.

▷ **FIG 2.11.** Attributed to Carlo Baldassare Simelli. Entry at the Base of Trajan's Column, ca. 1855. Albumen print from paper negative. Private collection, Paris. Cat. 16.

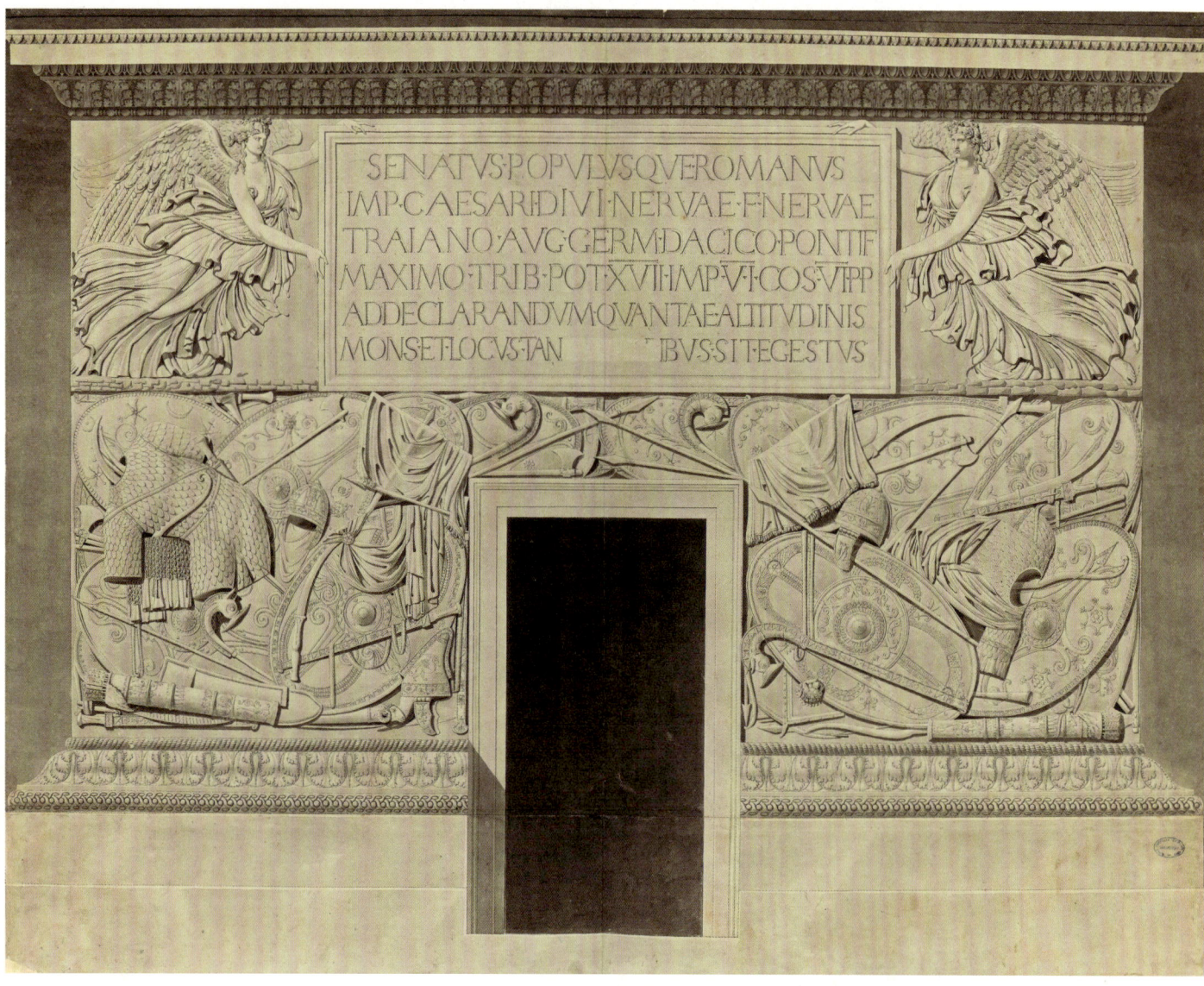

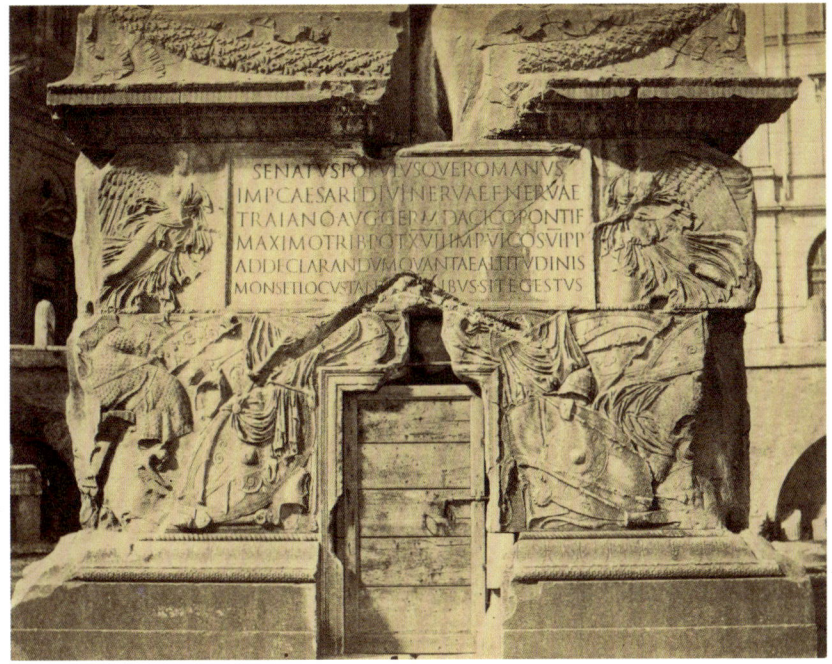

site and worked up in the evenings, after Percier returned to the atelier, encompass a much broader chronological and geographic range. In the papal city, Percier paid less attention to the great ancient monuments than to buildings of the Renaissance, the Middle Ages, and the eighteenth century. He was passionately interested in medieval churches and, above all, in statuary and ornamental sculpture, which figure prominently in his papers. He made his return trip a veritable study expedition, bringing back from the Marches, the Veneto, Emilia, Lombardy, and Piedmont hundreds of additional drawings. In addition to serving as the basis for Percier's publications, they were destined, on the one hand, to complete the young architect's education through close study of the masterpieces of the past, and, on the other hand, to constitute a collection of original documents, a kind of private graphic archive, that would prove useful to him in his own practice and design process as well as in his teaching.

Percier's first companion in these endeavors was not Fontaine, who later emphasized the originality of the corpus of buildings the two of them chose to investigate, but the painter Jean Germain Drouais, whose early death caused Percier great pain. Although brief, this friendship with one of David's favorite students made a profound impression on him. It strengthened his tendency to befriend contemporary painters, a pattern evidenced by his close personal and professional ties to Jean-Baptiste Isabey and, to an even greater extent, François Gérard. A drawing by Drouais of the exterior of the Sistine Chapel that closely resembles a view in one of Percier's albums in the Institut de France documents their shared drawing expeditions [FIGS. 2.12, 2.13]. The loss of Drouais sealed his association with Fontaine and Claude Bernier, the third friend and professional partner who, although more unassuming than the other two, remained close to

FIG 2.12. Charles Percier. View of the Sistine Chapel. Pencil, pen, and gray wash on paper. From *Vatican Sketchbook* (ca. 1787), fol. 11, drawing 23. Bibliothèque de l'Institut de France, Paris, Ms 1011.

FIG 2.13. Jean Germain Drouais. View of the Sistine Chapel, ca. 1787. Graphite, pen, and gray wash on paper. Musée Magnin, Dijon, 1938DF237.

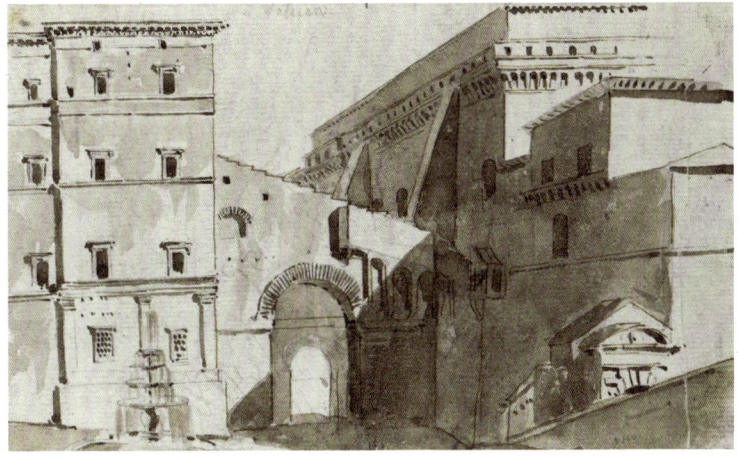
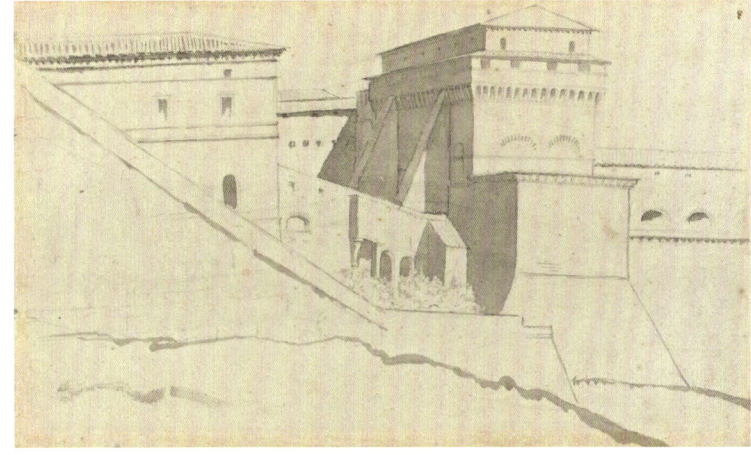

Percier. His apartment in the Louvre was close to Percier's, and he was buried with his two friends. Co-author of the book on Roman palaces (although not credited as such), Bernier became overseer of construction work at the Louvre.

Fontaine's role was, of course, exceptional. It is not without reason that most historians have treated him and Percier as a single entity and have merged their names. As emphasized in the introduction, it was Fontaine's social perspicacity and tact that enabled Percier's work to become so high-profile and influential. He was also an alter ego attached to Percier by deep affective ties. This is not to say that their partnership, of which Fontaine became the first and principal stage director and historian, was devoid of calculation and the occasional tension. Doubtless mutual self-interest played a part in it. But even after 1815, when the one chose to pursue his career by serving the new sovereign while the other opted to keep his distance, the two men continued to meet on a daily basis. Fontaine, although lacking his friend's strong commitment to education, nonetheless assisted him in this for a time by teaching classes on perspective.

In the last years of the eighteenth century, Percier's students began to climb into the front rank and sometimes to assist him. Under the challenging conditions that prevailed during the late Empire and the Restoration, as well as the more favorable ones fostered by the July Monarchy and the Second Empire, which saw the transformation of Paris, these disciples extended and greatly increased the influence of Percier's work and teachings, notably through the prominent roles they assumed in the realm of education.

This influence was not limited to France. The temporary expansion of the nation under Napoleon and the central role that Paris then assumed in European culture enabled the Belgian Tilman François Suys and the German Jacob Ignaz Hittorff to be French nationals for the duration of their studies in Percier's atelier, and in the case of the former during his sojourn at the Villa Medici. In 1818 Suys published, with Louis Pierre Haudebourt, a monograph on the Palazzo Massimi in Rome; he later served as architect to the king of Belgium and as professor and director of the architecture class at the Academy of Fine Arts in Amsterdam.

Other Percier students followed paths that took them still further from Paris. The most far-flung examples, both of whom emigrated in 1816, were Augustin Grandjean de Montigny, who worked in Rio de Janeiro, and Auguste de Montferrand, who worked in St. Petersburg. The former, who won the Prix de

FIG 2.14. Augustin Grandjean de Montigny and Auguste Famin. Frontispiece for *Architecture toscane* (Paris: Authors, 1806–15), book 10. Private collection, Paris. Cat. 29.

Rome in 1799, followed closely in the footsteps of his master, despite the fact that his effective exile to Brazil cut him off completely from Percier's circle. His book on Tuscan architecture, written with Auguste Famin, another Percier student (Prix de Rome 1801), was the first and most dutiful response to Percier's book on Roman palaces, whose interest in the early Renaissance it amplified. Grandjean de Montigny's gold medal at the Salon of 1808—for a composition of ancient fragments inspired by the frontispieces in the book on Roman palaces—further confirmed his artistic indebtedness to his professor [FIG. 2.14].[12]

Grandjean de Montigny wanted to work for a sovereign as Percier did, and his first opportunity—a dubious one, it turned out—was to serve Jérôme Bonaparte as architect of the short-lived and impoverished Kingdom of Westphalia (1807–13). After that, given the lack of prospects for him under the Restoration, Grandjean de Montigny left for Rio with the French artistic mission headed by Joachim Lebreton, in the reasonable but soon disappointed hope that he could play a prominent role in the transformation of the city into the new capital of the Portuguese empire.[13] In contrast with Lebreton and David, however, whose political engagement under the Revolutionary government and the Empire led to their exile, it seems safe to say—despite our ignorance of his political convictions—that Grandjean de Montigny's motives were above all professional. Although far from Paris and the atelier that had shaped him, he was a powerful echo of it outside Europe, becoming the first professor of architecture in Brazil, in the school of fine arts that he had helped to establish there and whose building he designed.

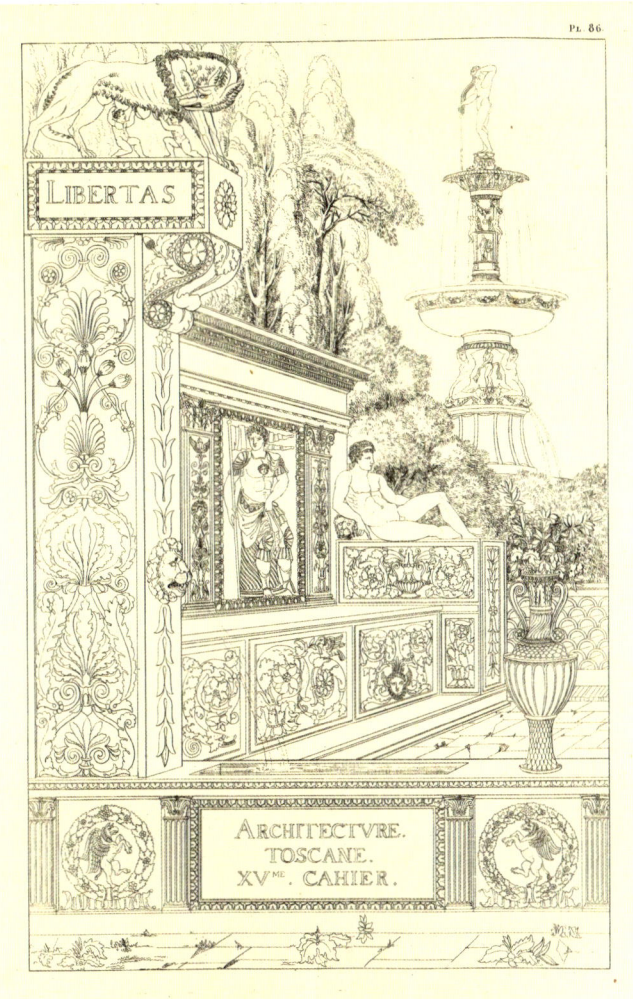

Auguste de Montferrand, whose destination was less exotic, had better luck. His emigration to Russia took him to St. Petersburg, where he realized buildings and monuments that were arguably more important than the school of fine arts in Rio, namely Saint Isaac's Cathedral, the Alexander Column, and the equestrian monument to Nicholas I. Before leaving his native land, Montferrand engraved illustrations for the architectural ornament catalogue of the Beunat manufactory that have been compared with those in the *Recueil de décorations intérieures*.[14]

As might be expected, the students who remained in Paris were more readily available for collaboration and discussion than were those who had tried their luck at the ends of the earth. Those closest to Percier—each of whom inherited a portion of his drawings—were François Debret, Louis Hippolyte Lebas, and Achille Leclère.[15] All three published collections of Italian models. Debret and Lebas collaborated on a monograph on Vignola that they never completed. Leclère edited a collection of lithographs meant to serve as a resource for students in his atelier, who assisted him in its realization.[16] Together with Grandjean, Famin, and a few others, they were among the followers of Percier and Fontaine who produced collections of Italian buildings after their example—and who prompted Viollet-le-Duc to denounce their sheeplike behavior: "they have made Roman houses rain down on us, to such an extent that we no longer see anything but terrace roofs, balconies with curved tiles, and porticos that are soon ruined by the Parisian fog. Moreover, thousands of works on the casinos and houses of Rome, Genoa, and Florence now clutter the print dealers."[17]

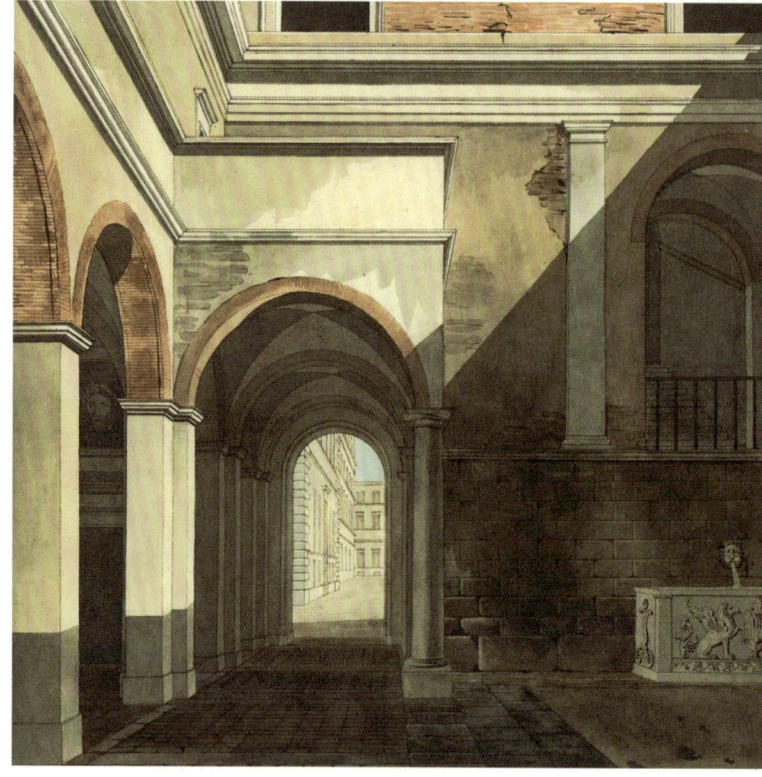

▲ **FIG 2.15.** Charles Percier and Pierre Fontaine. View of the courtyard of a Roman palace. Watercolor over engraving. From Percier and Fontaine, *Palais, maisons et autres édifices dessinés à Rome* (Paris: Authors, 1798), pl. 19. Private collection, Paris. Cat. 47.

▶ **FIG 2.16.** Saint-Ange Desmaisons, View of a Courtyard after Percier and Fontaine, n.d. Pen and watercolor on paper. Private collection, Paris.

Debret taught at the École des beaux-arts with his brother-in-law, Félix Duban, and his students there included Constant-Dufeux, whom we mentioned above as the builder of the new annex for the École gratuite de dessin. Leclère directed an atelier oriented more toward the training of beginners than preparation for the Prix de Rome competition, although his best students could pursue further study with Percier or Hippolyte Lebas. The latter, a devoted carrier of the flame, directed the most influential atelier of his time, first with Antoine Laurent Thomas Vaudoyer and then, after the latter's death in 1846, alone. Lebas, whose students included Henri Labrouste and Charles Garnier, was also, after 1840, professor of history at the École des beaux-arts.

As an architect, Debret took over one of the important projects on which Percier had been working before 1815, namely renovation of the monastery of the Petits-Augustins, which had been transformed into the Musée des monuments français (Museum of French Monuments) before becoming the École des beaux-arts. This is why he was chosen to inherit the album of drawings of this site, as well as another one devoted to France. Lebas collaborated closely with Percier. No mere assistant, he co-designed the vermeil tea urn, delivered in August 1810, for the tea service for Napoleon and Marie-Louise,[18] and after his professional affiliation with Percier and Fontaine had ceased, he helped the latter design the expiatory chapel before winning, over Achille Leclère, the competition for the design of the church of Notre-Dame de Lorette, which remains his masterpiece.

These were the principal figures, but other students in various domains also merit attention, such as Louis Saint-Ange Desmaisons, who on Percier's recommendation became an important carpet and tapestry designer.[19] One of his drawings paraphrases the view of a courtyard published in the volume on Roman palaces, thereby confirming his close connection with his master [FIGS. 2.15, 2.16].

Beyond Percier's "official" partnership with Pierre Fontaine and their more discreet friend Claude Bernier, there were other, overlapping circles of friendship, intellectual dialogue, and professional relations in his life. Not all of these ties began in the academic world (for example, he did not meet Alexandre Lenoir, founder of the Musée des monuments français, at the École), but his shared experience with his classmates and exchanges between master and student were the two principal foundations that made it possible for this solitary man to form several families for himself.

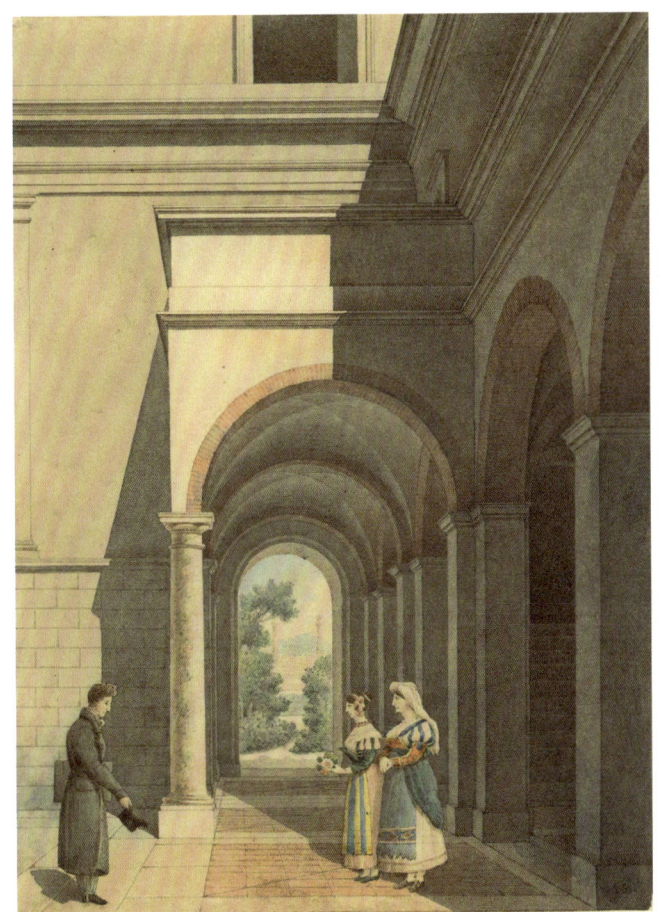

When Fontaine, who had built a house for Percier near his own on the rue de la Muette, near the Père Lachaise Cemetery, lamented his obstinate refusal to abandon his lodgings in the Louvre, he mentioned Percier's concern that such a move would result in "a reduction in the frequent visits of those who came to pay homage to his person and his gifts."[20] Doubtless there were many former students among the many admirers of the venerable architect. He could offer them advice and discuss his own ongoing research with them, for example, the collection of drawings of the château de Fontainebleau in which he proposed restorations of parts of it that had been destroyed, notably the Galerie de Diane and the Salle des Fêtes. He could also discuss works that he hoped to publish such as that devoted to the Palazzo Te in Mantua, which was almost ready to be engraved, or his graphic restoration of the palaces in Genoa, on which he had also begun work. •

1 See Jean-Philippe Garric, "Le *Recueil de décorations* de Charles Percier et Pierre Fontaine," in *Ornements XVe–XIXe siècles: Chefs-d'œuvre de la bibliothèque de l'INHA*, ed. Lucie Fréjou and Michaël Decrossas (Paris: INHA/Mare et Martin, 2014), 302–11. It is Normand's son who testified to his having been recruited by Percier and Fontaine; see Charles-Victor Normand, *Notice sur la vie et les ouvrages de C.P.J. Normand* (Paris, n.d.).

2 Charles Landon, *Annales du musée et de l'école moderne des beaux-arts*, vols. 1–6 (Paris: Landon, 1800–1808).

3 In Louis Pierre Baltard's book *Lettres ou voyage pittoresque dans les Alpes* (Paris: Author, 1806), the author describes Percier as impatient with the mountainous landscapes of the Alps and keen to arrive in Italy: "P[ercier] shared my joy at seeing the Alps; but after these peaks and mountainous curtains had passed before his eyes for a time without any interruption, impatience took hold of him" (p. 7: "P…a partagé ma joie en voyant les Alpes; mais depuis qu'il est au milieu de ces pics et de ces rideaux montueux, qui se déroulent devant ses yeux sans aucune interruption, l'impatience s'est emparée de lui").

4 Louis Pierre Baltard, *Paris et ses monumens, dessinés et gravés par Baltard, architecte, avec des Descriptions historiques par le cit[oyen] Amaury-Duval* (Paris: Author, 1803–5); Alexandre de Laborde, *Voyage pittoresque et historique de l'Espagne* (Paris: Pierre Didot, 1807–20); Louis Pierre Baltard, Charles Percier, and Pierre Fontaine, *Arc de triomphe du Carrousel édifié par Percier et Fontaine, architectes, gravé d'après leurs dessins par Louis Pierre Baltard* (Paris: Jules Claye, 1875).

5 Charles Percier and Pierre Fontaine, *Résidences de souverains. Parallèle entre plusieurs résidences de souverains de France, d'Allemagne, de Suède, de Russie, d'Espagne et d'Italie, à Paris chez les auteurs* (Paris: Authors, 1833), 160–61.

6 "une menagerie renfermée dans le parc du château d'un souverain"; "un amphithéâtre et arènes découvertes propres aux combats des animaux." See Jean-Marie Pérouse de Montclos, *"Les Prix de Rome": Concours de l'Académie royale d'architecture au XVIIIe siècle* (Paris: Berger-Levrault / École nationale supérieure des Beaux-Arts, 1984), 183.

7 "Édifice destiné à abriter les academies."

8 Menus Plaisirs du Roi (Lesser Pleasures of the King), Department de la maison du roi (Royal Household) responsible for the organization and design of royal ceremonies and festivities.

9 Philippe Morel, ed., *La Colonna Traiana e gli artisti francesi da Luigi XIV a Napoleone I* (Rome: Carte Segrete, 1988).

10 Charles Percier and Thomas Vaudoyer, *Restaurations des Monuments Antiques par les architectes pensionnaires de l'Académie de France à Rome…Colonne Trajane par Percier…Mémoire historique rédigé en 1839 par Thomas Vaudoyer* (Paris: Firmin Didot, 1877).

11 Charles Percier and Pierre Fontaine, *Palais, maisons et autres édifices modernes dessinés à Rome; publiés à Paris, l'an VI de la République française (1798, v. st.)* (Paris: Authors, 1798); Charles Percier and Pierre Fontaine [Jean Charles Bonnard], *Choix des plus célèbres maisons de plaisance de Rome et de ses environs* (Paris: Pierre Didot, 1809–13).

12 Augustin Grandjean de Montigny and Auguste Famin, *Architecture toscane* (Paris: Authors, 1806–15).

13 The emperor of Portugal's return to Lisbon, stipulated by the Congress of Vienna, precluded the construction of the new capital city that he had envisaged.

14 Valérie Nègre, "Les commencements de l'art industriel: Conception et usages des ornements d'architecture moulés au début de la période contemporaine," in *Le néoclassicisme dans les colonies européennes*, ed. Thierry Nicolas Tchakaloff (Saint-Denis de la Réunion: Musée des arts décoratifs de l'océan indien, 2013), 212–13.

15 See Annie Jacques, "I viaggi in Italia di Debret et Lebas (1804–1811)," in *Grand Tour: viaggi narrati e dipinti*, ed. Cesare De Seta (Naples: Electa, 2001), 60–73; Pierre Pinon, "Les Vaudoyer et les Lebas, dynasties d'architectes," in *Entre le théâtre et l'histoire: la famille Halévy, 1760–1960*, ed. Henri Loyrette, exh. cat. (Paris: Réunion des musées nationaux, 1996), 88–97; Adolphe Lance, *Notice sur la vie et les travaux de M. Achille Leclère, architecte, membre de l'Institut* (Paris: n.p., 1854).

16 François Debret and Louis Hippolyte Lebas, *Œuvres complète de Vignole* (Paris: Firmin Didot, [1815]); Achille Leclère, *Recueil d'architecture, lithographié en l'année 1826 par…élèves de Monsieur Achille Leclère* (Paris: Authors, 1826). On this last, see Jean-Philippe Garric, *Recueils d'Italie. Les modèles italiens dans les livres d'architecture français* (Liège: Mardaga, 2004), 97.

17 "ils nous ont fait pleuvoir les maisons romaines, si bien que nous n'avons plus vu partout que des toits en terrasse, des balcons en tuiles creuses et des portiques promptement délabrés par le brouillard de Paris. De plus, des milliers d'ouvrages sur les casins et maisons de Rome, de Gênes, de Florence, ont encombré les marchands d'estampes." Eugène Viollet-le-Duc, *Lettres d'Italie 1836–37* (Paris: Léonce Laget, 1971), 97.

18 Odile Nouvel-Kammerer, ed., *L'aigle et le papillon. Symboles des pouvoirs sous Napoléon* (Paris: Musée des Arts décoratifs, 2008), 300ff.

19 See chapter 9, "Designs for the Manufactories and the Garde-Meuble," in this volume.

20 "voir diminuer les visites habituelles de ceux qui viennent rendre homage à sa personne et à ses talents."

PERCIER'S RING

JEAN-PHILIPPE GARRIC

In December 1892, Léon Ginain addressed the annual assembly of architect-alumni of the École des beaux-arts, explaining that "one of his privileges in presiding over their reunion was that he was in possession of a ring, an engraved stone in a gold setting," which shone on his finger that night. This ring, he added, "belonged to Charles Percier, the uncontested head of the current school of architecture."[1] This story—a metaphor for the anxiety of transmission and for Percier's attachment to his friends, to whom he also left the drawing albums now in the Institut de France[2]—is likewise emblematic of the longevity of Percier's legacy and of the extent to which the French academic Beaux-Arts tradition, which survived until the student uprisings of May 1968, was rooted in the first years of the nineteenth century.

The origin of the practice of transmitting what has become known as "Percier's ring" from architect to architect dates to 1838.[3] Surviving letters of transmission document its journey and the sequence of its custodians; the object itself, a carnelian intaglio mounted on a gold ring [FIG. 2A.1]—described as ancient in the earliest of these letters [FIG. 2A.2], which was written by Achille Leclère ten days after the death of his master—is most probably a portrait of Marciana, the elder sister of Trajan, from the end of the first or beginning of the second century.[4] In fact, the first to transmit the ring was Julien David Le Roy, a member of the Académie royale d'architecture whose sponsorship had enabled Percier to compete for the Prix de Rome. Upon his death, Le Roy bequeathed the ring to Percier as a token of friendship, though his name was later eclipsed by that of his student.

Did Percier establish the protocol for the ring's transmission? On this point Leclère remained elusive, noting

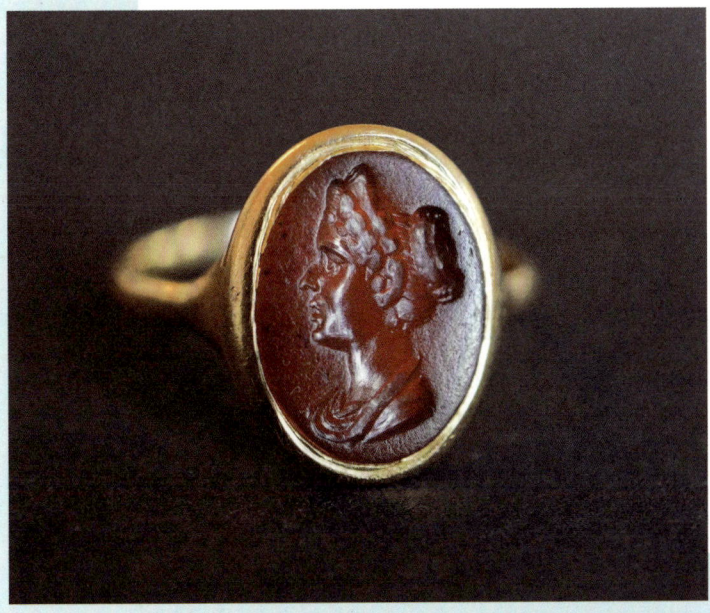

FIG. 2A.1. Percier's ring. Rome, Imperial period, late 1st century BCE–early 2nd century CE. Carnelian intaglio set in a gold ring. Private collection, Paris. Cat. 20.

only that the executors of Percier's estate delivered the precious talisman to him "with the most benevolent expressions," going on to explain: "I kept it; it cannot be sold. And after me [it goes] to Provost, with the stipulation that he is to transmit it to Lebas, member of the Institut, or failing him to the most skillful architect and also the finest man."[5] After this pronouncement, which established the rules governing transmission, Leclère inscribed: "Such is my will on this September 15, 1838."[6] But was it his will or Percier's?

The letter contains a correction. The name of Hippolyte Lebas, the initially designated successor, was crossed out and replaced with that of Jean Louis Provost, a friend of Leclère's since their youth, as evidenced by the double portrait of them drawn in Rome by J. A. D. Ingres [FIG. 2A.3]. Leclère and Lebas, both members of the Institut de France, were occasional rivals, as in the competition for the design of Notre-Dame de Lorette, which Lebas won in 1823. But Provost died before Leclère and Lebas indeed became the ring's second custodian, though he never chose a proper successor. On June 14, 1867, two days after Lebas's death, his daughter wrote to Charles Édouard Isabelle: "He bequeathed to you, sir, a ring that belonged, in succession, to his master Percier and his friend Achille Leclère. How should I convey to you this ring, which was for my dear father a veritable relic and which is now one for me? It never left his finger. I would very much like to give it to you myself."[7] Two days later, Esther Leclère, Achille's sister, wrote Isabelle in an informal tone, confirming her brother's desire that his student succeed Lebas: "I still remember how one day, when I spoke of this ring and its future, my father remarked: 'this ring,' he said, '...it will go to Isabelle!'"[8] Less well known than his predecessors, Isabelle, although not a student of Percier's, knew him well, and his major works, two books dedicated to circular buildings in which Italian examples predominate, belong to the tradition of published anthologies of Italian architectural models[9] [FIG. 2A.4].

Scarcely one month after receiving the ring, Isabelle chose as its future custodian Ginain, a product of Lebas' atelier and a professor at the École des beaux-arts. With him there began a second period: an extended one, for the ring would be held by his students until 1957. As demonstrated by the following passage from a letter written by the widow of Victor Blavette to Albert Louvet in September 1933, the principal criterion was affiliation with the atelier: "I am quite sure that I honor my husband's intentions by designating you, dear sir, his faithful friend and

◀ FIG. 2A.2. Letter from Achille Leclère establishing the terms of transmission and designating his successor as custodian of the ring, dated September 15, 1838. Pen on paper with wax seal of the ring. Private collection, Paris. Cat. 21.

▽ FIG. 2A.3. Jean Auguste Dominique Ingres. *The Architects Achille Leclère and Jean Louis Provost*, 1812. Graphite on paper. Smith College Museum of Art, Northampton, Massachusetts, purchased with the Drayton Hillyer Fund, 1937:5-1.

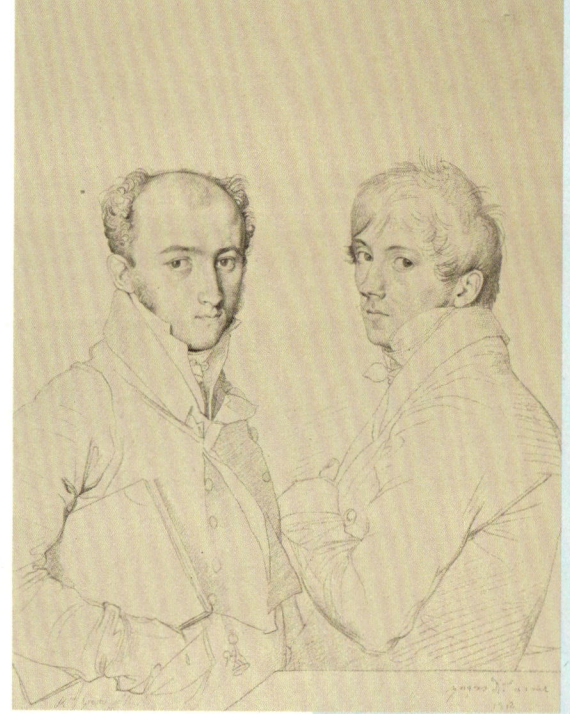

esteemed disciple, as the [next] possessor of this token, which should remain in the hands of an architect of talent and integrity, and preferably a student of Léon Ginain."10

However, Louis Varcolier, the penultimate Ginain student to be the ring's custodian, thought it useful to recall Percier's role in the story: "This ring, which belonged to my friend Louvet, was conveyed to me after his death by Madame Louvet, on July 13, 1936. Her husband had received it from Monsieur Blavette, to whom it had come after a series of analogous transmissions, beginning with its original owner, the architect Percier (First Empire). It will be transmitted under the same conditions after my death, either to a student of Ginain or, by default, to the Société Centrale."11 When there were no more Ginain students, the tradition was carried on through Paul Tournon, Yves-Marie Froidevaux, and now Yves Boiret, the ring's twelfth custodian. ●

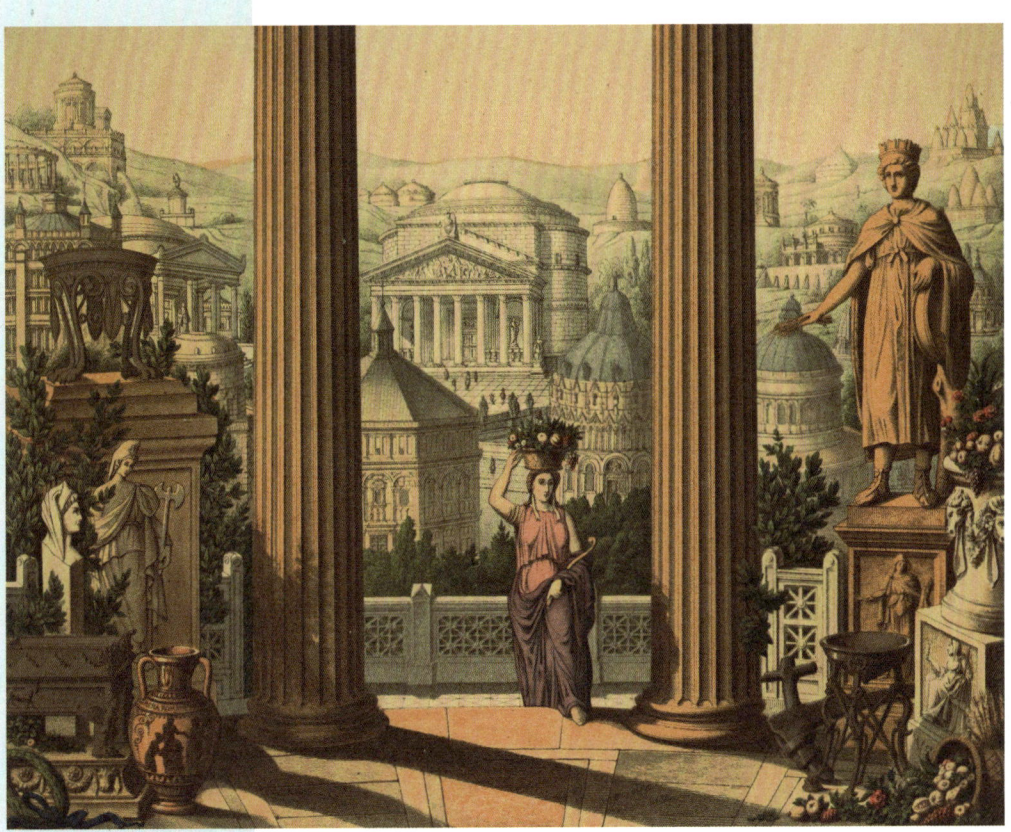

▲ **FIG. 2A.4.** Charles Édouard Isabelle. *Imaginary Composition of Circular Buildings in a Landscape* (detail). Chromolithograph. Frontispiece for *Parallèle des salles rondes de l'Italie*, 2nd ed. (Paris: Lévy, 1863).

1   "l'un des titres qu'il avait à présider leur reunion était d'être possesseur d'une bague, une pierre dure gravé, enchâssée dans l'or"; "a appartenu à Charles Percier, le chef incontesté de l'école d'architecture actuelle." "Les maîtres de l'architecture française—Léon Ginain," *La Construction moderne* (May 11, 1895): 373.
2   See Evelyne Saint-Paul, "Dons des dessins de Charles Percier par ses élèves," in Sabine Frommel, Jean-Philippe Garric, and Elisabeth Kieven, *Charles Percier e Pierre Fontaine dal soggiorno romano alla trasformazione di Parigi* (Milan: Silvana Editoriale, 2014), 159–65.
3   Jean-Pierre Epron, *Comprendre l'éclectisme* (Paris: Norma, 1997), 331.
4   A very similar ring belongs to the collections of the Museum of Fine Arts, Boston MFA 99-111. From the 18th century it was part of the collections of Lord Chesterfield, Lord Bessborough, and George 3rd Duke of Marlborough. The identification of Marciana is based on her very singular hairstyle.
5   "avec les expressions les plus bienveillantes"; "Je la garderai, elle ne peut être vendue. Et après moi à Provost [sic] et avec l'injonction de la transmettre à Lebas, membre de l'Institut, ou à son défaut au plus habile architecte et aussi au plus honnête homme."
6   "ceci est ma volonté ce 15 septembre 1838."
7   "Il vous lègue, Monsieur, une bague qui a appartenu successivement à son maître Percier et à son ami Achille Leclère. Comment dois-je vous faire parvenir cette bague qui était pour mon cher père une véritable relique et qui en est une aujourd'hui pour moi? Elle ne quittait jamais son doigt. Je désirerais vivement vous la remettre moi-même."
8   "un jour que je parlais de cette bague, de son avenir, cette parole de mon frère est toujours présente à mon souvenir: cette bague dit-il…ha…elle reviendra à Isabelle!"
9   Charles Edouard Isabelle, *Parallèle des salles rondes de l'Italie* (Paris: Firmin Didot, 1831); Charles Edouard Isabelle, *Les Édifices circulaires et les dômes, classés par ordre chronologique et considérés sous le rapport de leur disposition, de leur construction et de leur décoration* (Paris: Firmin Didot, 1835).
10 "Je suis bien certaine d'être l'interprète des intentions de mon mari en vous désignant, cher Monsieur, comme son ami de toujours et son très estimé considsciple pour posséder ce souvenir qui doit rester entre les mains d'un architecte de talent, intègre et de préférence élève de Léon Ginain."
11 "Cette bague appartenant à mon ami Louvet m'a été transmise après sa mort par Mme Louvet, le 13 juillet 1936. Son mari la tenait lui-même de Monsieur Blavette à qui elle était parvenue par une suite de transmissions analogues, depuis son propriétaire primitif, l'architecte Percier (1er empire). Elle sera à transmettre dans les mêmes conditions après ma mort, soit à un élève de Ginain, soit, à défaut, à la Société Centrale." The Société centrale des architectes français was established in 1840; in 1953 it was rechristened the Académie d'architecture, under which title it continues to function today.

THE ATELIER OF ISABEY

A Signboard for Percier and Fontaine

VINCENT COCHET

Although the existence of Jean-Baptiste Isabey's atelier as represented by Boilly remains uncertain,[1] the composition published at the beginning of the *Recueil de décorations intérieures* depicting the atelier remains one of Percier and Fontaine's most important works in the field of interior decoration. The public success of the painting at the Salon of 1798 undoubtedly contributed to the fame of the two architects.

On the occasion of the Salon of the year VI (July 19–October 7, 1798), one critic wrote: "There is nothing here by David, nothing by Regnault, there is but one history painting by Citizen Vincent.…The paintings by Citizen Boilly are, among all the productions exhibited at the Salon, the ones that have attracted the largest crowds. The familiar scenes can be judged by anyone, because no knowledge of history or mythology is required to appreciate them.…Doesn't the pleasure derived from recognizing the features of Gérard, Percier, Chaudet etc. largely explain the reception accorded Boilly's work?"[2]

The *Gathering of Artists in the Atelier of Isabey* is indeed a veritable portrait gallery [FIG. 2B.1]. At far left, the composer Etienne Nicolas Méhul converses with the critic François Benoît Hoffman. Proceeding across the canvas from left to right: beyond the easel, the painter Pierre Paul Prud'hon leans toward a group consisting of the sculptor Charles Louis Corbet, the painters Martin Drolling, Jean Louis Demarne, and Nicolas Antoine Tauney, while in the foreground Jean-Baptiste Isabey, the master of the place, wearing a red jacket and leaning on the keyboard of a pianoforte, examines one of his works with François Gérard, his friend and comrade from the David studio, shown seated. Behind them, the painters Guillaume Guillon-Lethière, and Carle Vernet, riding crop in hand, exchange glances; just beyond, the painter Jacques François Swebach, wearing a black hat, and the miniaturist Charles Guillaume Alexandre Bourgeois face the viewer. Behind Vernet, the engraver Jean Duplessis-Bertaux leans toward the actor Baptiste (seated, a drawing portfolio at his feet), who in turn looks toward Girodet (likewise seated and wearing a red vest, another portfolio at his feet) while—in the center of the composition and immediately below the bust of Minerva—Percier, in a bicorne hat, and Fontaine,

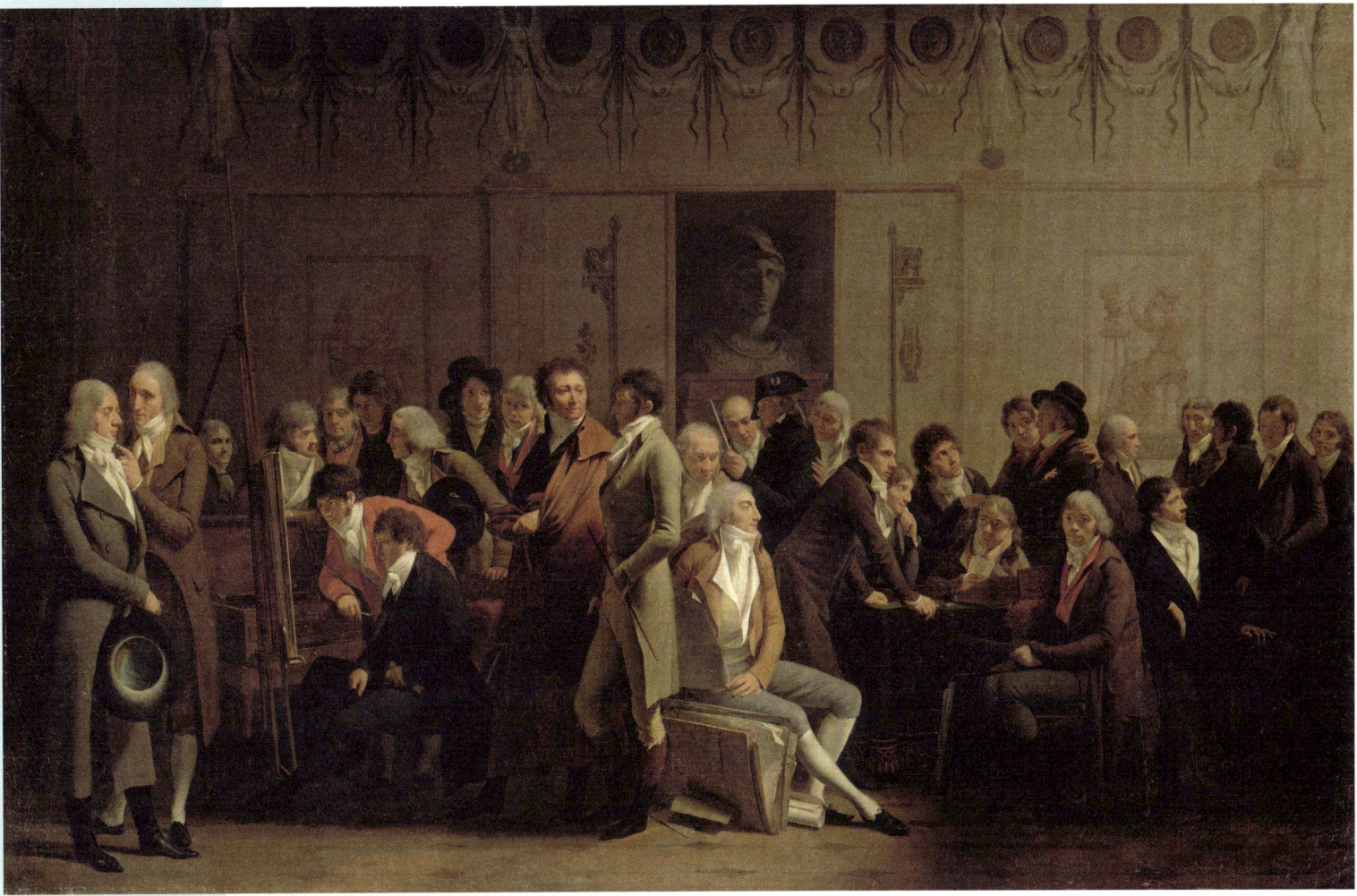

FIG. 2B.1. Louis Léopold Boilly. *Gathering of Artists in the Atelier of Jean-Baptiste Isabey*, 1798. Oil on canvas. Musée du Louvre, Paris, RF 1290bis. Cat. 4.

his bald pate exposed, admire an engraving or drawing. Directly behind Percier and looking over his shoulder is the architect Jean Thomas Thibaut. Around the table, the flower painters Jean François Van Daël (standing) and Pierre Joseph Redouté (leaning on one elbow), as well as the history painter Charles Meynier, admire a miniature. To their rear, the tragedian François Joseph Talma eyes the bass Simon Chenard, whose shoulder Boilly embraces. Behind them, the landscape painter Jean Joseph Xavier Bidauld converses with the engraver Maurice Blot and the sculptor François Frédéric Lemot. Seated in front of them, a guitar by his side, is the sculptor Antoine Denis Chaudet, who looks toward two standing figures, the painter Gioacchino Serangeli and the miniaturist Jean-Baptiste Jacques Augustin—like Isabey a native of Nancy.

This depiction of a cohort of young artists, practitioners of all genres and mediums, is both a group portrait and a genre scene. As pictured here, gathered around Isabey, they constitute something like a club of worldly sophisticates. Boilly emphasizes the characteristic postures and attitudes of each—from Isabey's concentration to Thibaut's curiosity, all rendered without descending into caricature but not without wit—as well as their respective roles within a remarkable social network of talent.

Boilly made many preparatory studies for the painting (Palais des Beaux-Arts, Lille; The Metropolitan

Museum of Art, New York), paying special attention to the various groups [FIG. 2B.2]. He then made oil sketches on cardboard of each artist to capture their features and expressions (SEE CAT. NOS. 3A–D) before integrating the results into the composition on canvas.³ Tension, reserve, smiles, and the play of glances imbue the final work with an atmosphere that is serious but congenial, redolent of the buzz of intellectual conversation.

The easel, the paint box, the chairs, even the portfolio of drawings, and the lining of a hat testify to the close attention Boilly paid to inanimate things. In addition to the paved floor, made of beige lias stone with darker inlay, he describes with considerable precision the rear wall, which is washed by light coming from the right. Subdivided by truncated pilasters, its central bay is pierced by a rectangular niche occupied by a large bust of Minerva.⁴ Presiding over the assembly, the bust is flanked by painted ensigns, one of which is decorated with a griffon and the other with an owl. The bays on either side are decorated with personifications of Painting and Sculpture executed in ochre monochrome. The wall is crowned by a high frieze punctuated by figures of Renown and upright torches, between which hang garlands of laurel secured with fluttering ribbons, above which are medallion profile portraits—painted to resemble patinated bronze—of great painters of the Italian school. At far left we see a portion of the end wall in sharp recession.

The painting's presence at the Salon of 1798 indicates that the depicted room was the atelier in Isabey's house at 27, rue Saint-Marc, and not his studio in the Louvre, which he began to occupy only in 1799, after the departure of the widow of the clockmaker Robin.⁵ The decoration, an example of a new neoclassical taste, was designed by Percier and Fontaine for their friend. Their introduction to Isabey, probably effected by David, dates back to the remodeling of the assembly hall of the

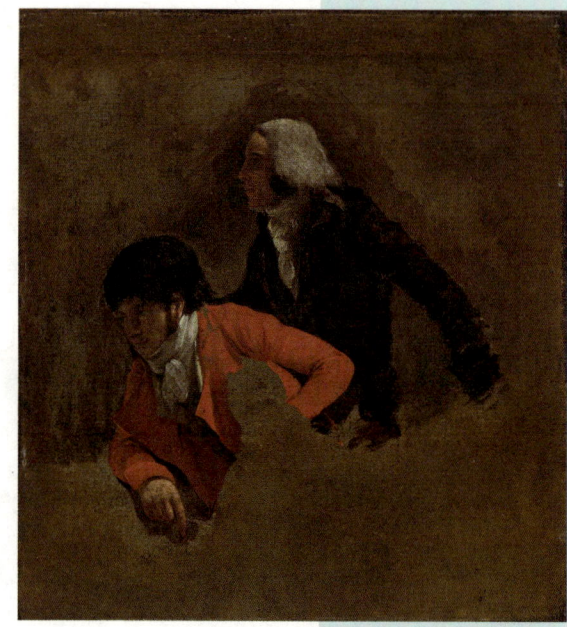

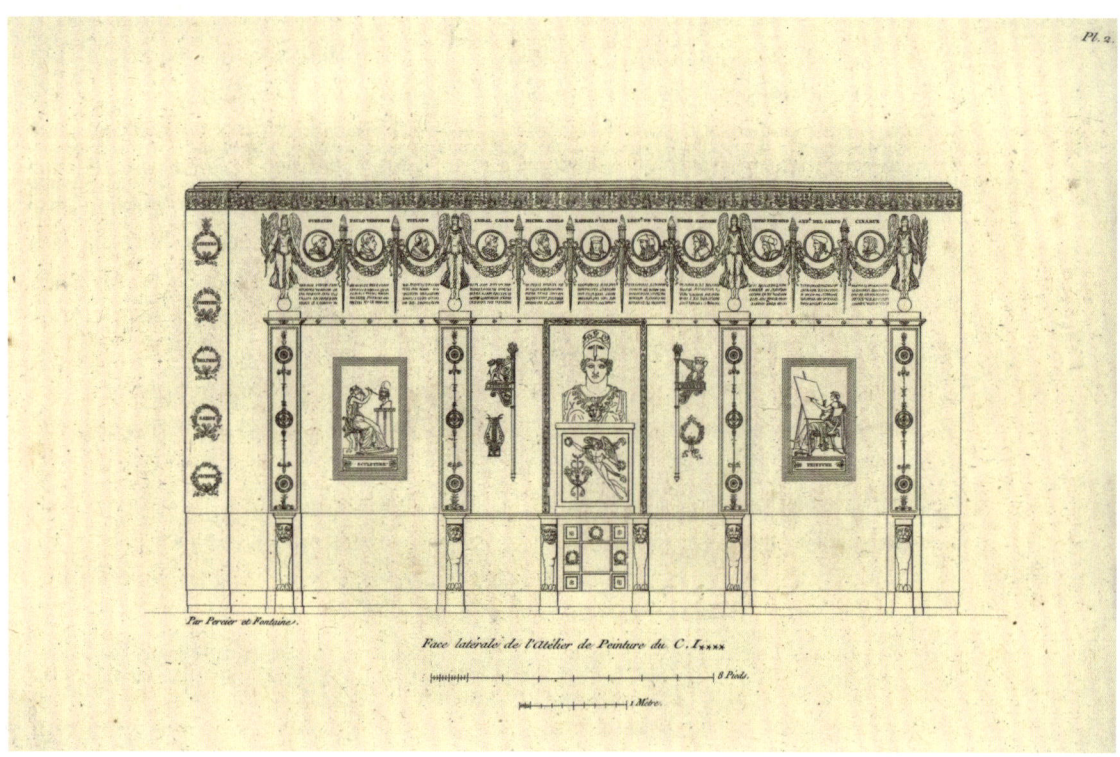

▲ **FIG. 2B.2.** Louis Léopold Boilly. Study for *Jean-Baptiste Isabey and Nicolas Antoine Taunay*, ca. 1798. Oil on canvas. Palais des Beaux-Arts, Lille, p. 375. Cat. 3d.

◀ **FIG. 2B.3.** Charles Percier and Pierre Fontaine. *Recueil de décorations intérieures* (Paris: Authors and Pierre Didot l'aîné, 1801–12), pl. 2.

▶ **FIG. 2B.4.** Charles Percier and Pierre Fontaine. *Recueil de décorations intérieures* (Paris: Authors and Pierre Didot l'aîné, 1801–12), pl. 3.

Convention, created in the Tuileries palace to designs by Gisors, for which Percier provided designs for the furniture—and where Isabey sketched the deputies at his leisure.[6] They would join creative forces in 1804, during the preparations for Napoleon's coronation at Notre-Dame, and all three contributed to the plates for the volume published to commemorate that occasion.[7]

Boilly's painting and the inclusion of five plates of Isabey's atelier in the first fascicle of the *Recueil de décorations intérieures*, published in 1801, testify to the precocity of the decor, and a similar frieze with profile artists' portraits would figure, in 1800–1812, in a room in the townhouse of General Moreau (SEE CATS. 66–69). The salon-atelier of Isabey can be considered one of the first private commissions of Percier and Fontaine.[8]

Far from being a space dedicated to labor, Isabey's atelier was a sanctuary of the muses, a kind of ancient lyceum over which Minerva kept watch. It was a large rectangular room with windows situated to the right, as indicated by the light source in Boilly's painting and by the "table explicative" in the *Recueil*. It "serve[d] simultaneously as a study and a bedchamber."[9] Plate I shows the bed on a platform situated slightly in front of the wall, which, below the stucco frieze, is hung with fabric in the ancient Roman style. The small bed is in the line of furniture that David designed for his own studio. The frieze continues along the wall opposite the one represented by Boilly; it also featured profile portraits of great artists, probably from the French and Northern schools, below which were personifications of Engraving and Architecture corresponding to those of Painting and Sculpture opposite (plate V). These must have flanked the door to the atelier, situated directly opposite the niche containing the heater that served as a base for the bust of Minerva [FIG. 2B.3]. On the ceiling, a central medallion containing the superimposed profiles of Apelles and Zeuxis was flanked, at either end, by painted lunettes—situated respectively above the windows and the bed—containing depictions of Day and Night, the latter shown in a chariot drawn by bulls [FIG. 2B.4; SEE ALSO FIG. 6.2]. Although Boilly's painting differs in many respects from what we see in the engraved plates, it still functioned as a gesture of friendship: as a high-profile demonstration of Percier's gifts as an interior decorator.

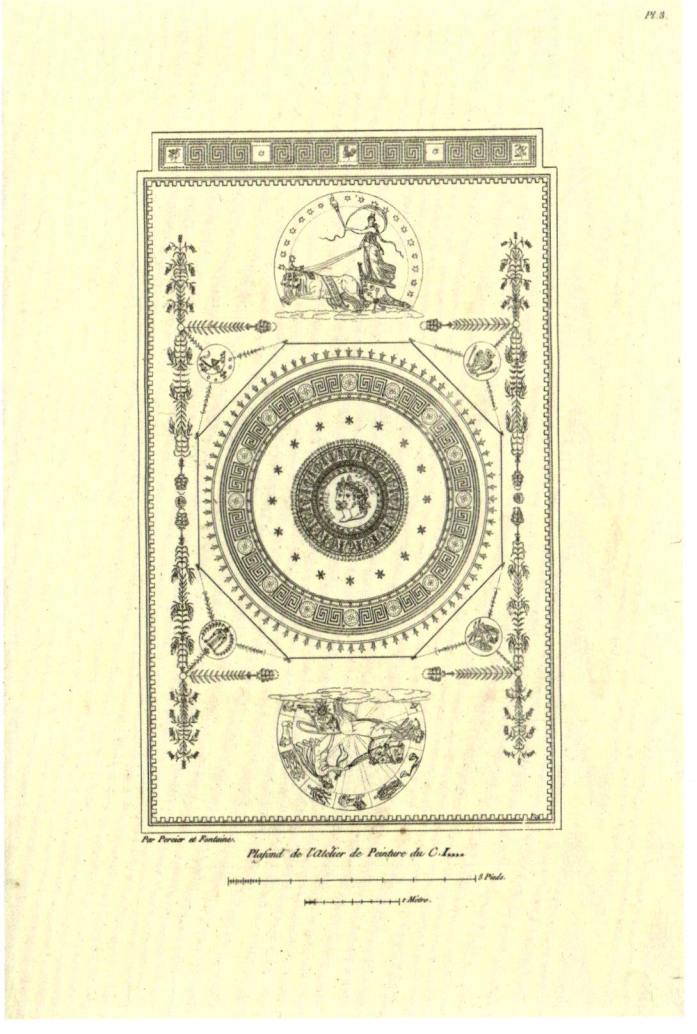

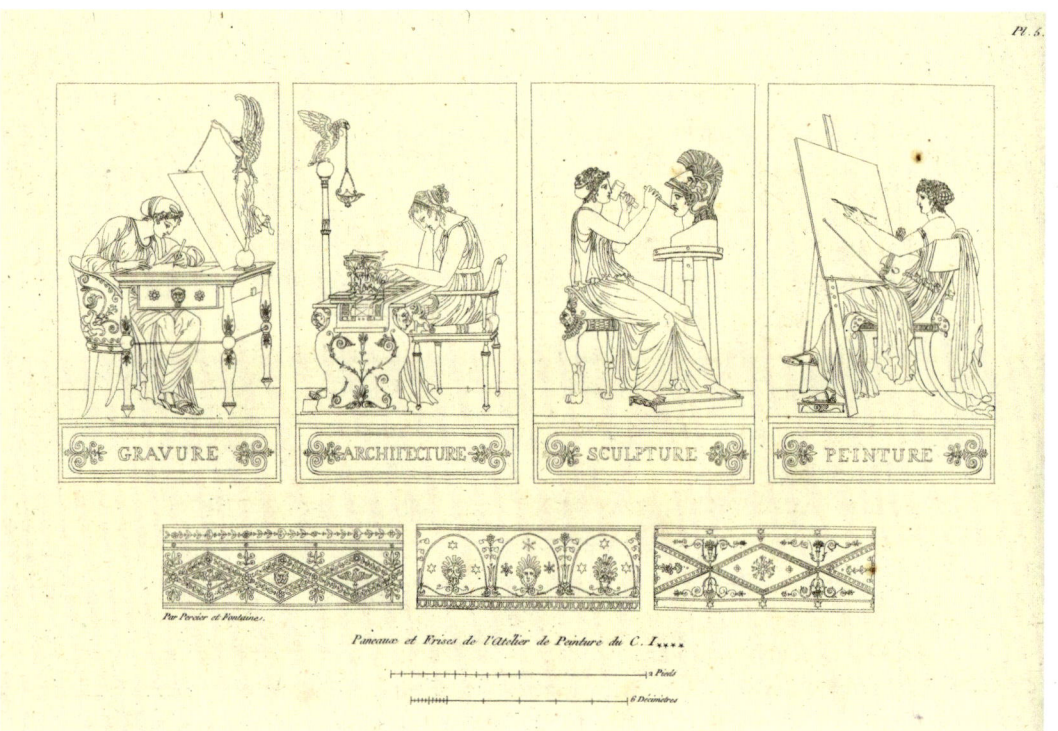

FIG. 2B.5. Charles Percier and Pierre Fontaine. *Recueil de décorations intérieures* (Paris: Authors and Pierre Didot l'aîné, 1801–12), pl. 5.

In addition to the plates representing the elevations and the ceiling, plates IV and V depict "détails et ajustements" (details and fittings), which is to say various decorative panels and one of the protome lion-head consoles that serve as bases for the pilasters, as well as a tripod, some vases, and a columnar candelabrum [FIG. 2B.5]. The juxtaposition on a single plate of architectural elements and furnishings brings to mind the presentation of plates in encyclopedias. Nonetheless, the oil lamp atop the *all'antica* candelabrum leaves no doubt about the contemporaneity of the depicted artifact. In his painting, Boilly staged a communion of contemporary artists and celebrated the new social world of the Directory for which Percier and Fontaine designed their interiors. ●

1   See Claire Bételu, "Réunion d'artistes dans l'atelier d'Isabey: processus créatifs de Louis-Léopold Boilly," 235-39. PhD thesis, Université Paris I–Panthéon-Sorbonne, 2015.
2   "On ne trouve ici rien de David, rien de Regnault, on ne voit qu'un seul tableau d'histoire du citoyen Vincent....Les tableaux du citoyen Boilly sont de toutes les productions exposées au Salon celles qui ont le plus attiré la foule. Les scènes familières ont tout le monde pour juge, parce qu'elles n'exigent pour être appréciées, aucune connaissance soit de l'histoire, soit de la mythologie....Le plaisir de reconnaître les traits de Gérard, de Percier, de Chaudet, etc. n'entre-t-il pas pour beaucoup dans l'accueil fait à l'œuvre de Boilly?" "Exposition des peintres vivants commencés le 19 juillet 1798," *Mercure de France*, BNF, ms., collection Deloynes, vol. 20, pp. 1, 45–47.
3   Bételu 2015, 75–100.
4   See the preparatory drawing in New York, The Metropolitan Museum of Art, acc. no. 2009.477. Cat. 54c.
5   See the dossier published by Sylvain Laveissière in *Boilly (1761-1845). Un grand peintre français de la Révolution à la Restauration*, exh. cat. (Lille: Musée des Beaux-Arts de Lille, 1989), 50–63.
6   See *Jean-Baptiste Isabey (1767-1855), portraitiste de l'Europe*, exh. cat. (Rueil-Malmaison: Musée national des châteaux de Malmaison et Bois-Préau / Paris: Réunion des musées nationaux, 2005), 19.
7   See Pierre François Léonard Fontaine, *Journal (1799-1853)*, ed. Marguerite David-Roy (Paris: École nationale supérieure des beaux-arts / Institut français d'architecture / Société de l'histoire de l'art français, 1987), 1:105.
8   See chapter 8 by Jean-François Belhoste in this volume.
9   "sert en même temps de cabinet de travail et de chambre à coucher."

CHAPTER 3

THE ROMAN SOJOURN

LETIZIA TEDESCHI

IN A LETTER THAT IS UNDATED BUT WAS CERTAINLY COMPOSED IN 1811, Charles Percier wrote in Italian to his friend Antonio Canova: "The little free time I have left I want to devote to the study of the fine arts that I love so much and [I] will tell myself by way of encouragement: 'work, you are almost Roman.'"[1] He recalled that he "brought back from Rome a number of drawings made after monuments and buildings there." And he added: "Every night before going to bed I spent two hours finishing them and in doing so forgot all my other tasks, thinking only of the sweet memories of my happy days."[2]

How are we to account for this profound attachment to Italy? Doubtless the principal reasons behind Percier's assertion that he was "almost Roman" are to be sought in the unforgettable experience of his study sojourn in the eternal city. Adding to that experience, after he had reached maturity in Paris and attained an exceptional degree of professional recognition there, he was made a member of the prestigious Accademia di San Luca in Rome, whose head at the time was Canova.

Several years later, this time posthumously, he received another mark of Italian recognition in the form of a publishing initiative, a subject to which I shall return in chapter 6a. Without pretending to deepen our knowledge of Percier's working methods, I will here attempt to cast light on his Italian years, when he was still a beginner, by examining the principal themes rooted in his experiences in Rome, where he spent his time studying both ancient models and models from other historical periods. This experience had a determinative effect on his subsequent projects, just as it proved crucial for the eventual Italian reception of the *Recueil de décorations intérieures*, one of the first books to treat the question of ornament in any depth.[3] That publication remained influential long after the end of the Napoleonic era, during which Percier and Fontaine strove to be emphatically of their time, thereby increasing their fame.

Let's try to imagine our young French architect diligently taking the measurements of various monuments in Rome and its environs, and then attempting to convey both the results and the attendant emotions in his drawings. He also ventured into excavation sites, collections, and museums, especially the Pio Clementino Museum in the Vatican [FIG. 3.1], an example of contemporary architecture that interested him greatly. He encountered different and various historical and stylistic horizons in succession, sometimes evidencing considerable originality in his chosen objects of study, such as productions of the early and high Middle Ages.

Percier was twenty-two in April 1786, when, having won the Prix de Rome, he presented himself at the door of the Palazzo Mancini, the seat of the French Academy in Rome.

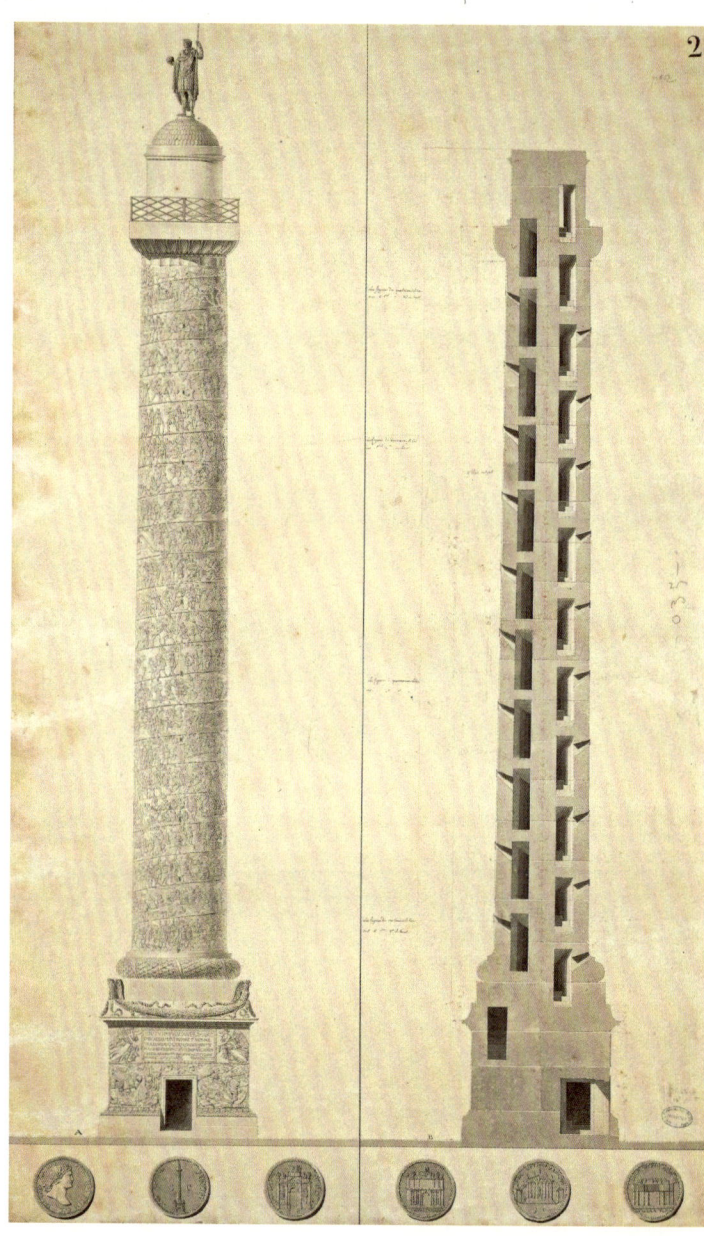

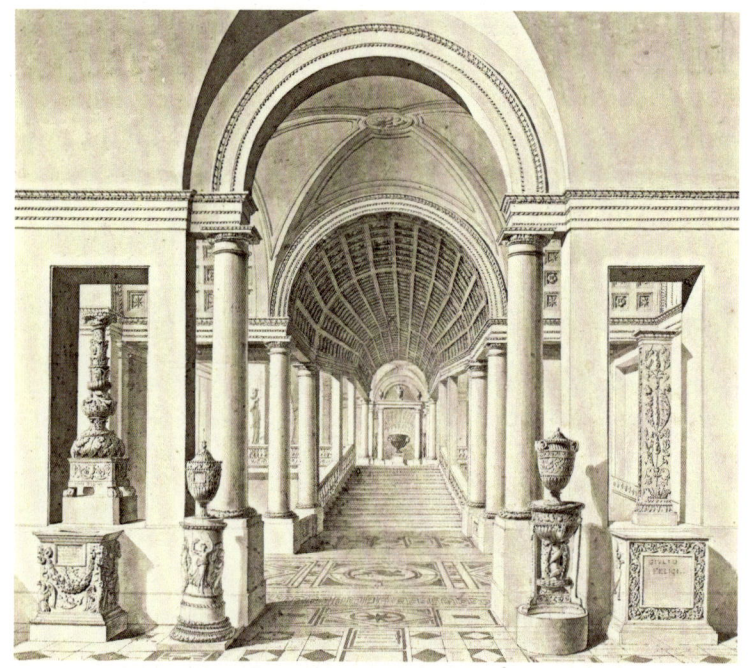

◂ **FIG. 3.1.** Charles Percier. The Simonetti Staircase Seen from the Gallery of the Candelabra, Pio Clementino Museum, Vatican, c.1789. Pencil, pen, and black wash on paper. Bibliothèque de l'Institut de France, Paris, ms 1011, fol. 53, drawing 100.

◄ FIG. 3.2. Charles Percier. Elevation and cross section of the Column of Trajan, 1788. Pen and ink, wash on paper mounted on canvas. École nationale supérieure des beaux-arts, Paris, Env. 1-02. Cat. 13a.

▽ FIG. 3.3. Charles Percier. Elevation of the left side of the Column of Trajan, 1788. Pen and ink, wash on paper mounted on canvas. École nationale supérieure des beaux-arts, Paris, Env. 1-06. Cat. 13b.

He would remain there until March 1791.[4] For his Roman assignment (his *envoi de Rome*), the academicians in Paris instructed him to produce both accurate drawings and an ideal graphic reconstruction of the Column of Trajan,[5] a project that he embraced with enthusiasm, thrilling to its bas-reliefs and the long dedicatory inscription on its base [FIGS. 3.2–3.4]. It is worth emphasizing Percier's determination to produce a scrupulous reconstruction, one whose meticulous precision sets it apart from the work of other scholarship students at the time, as well as from the version produced some ten years earlier by Piranesi. Having long been deeply interested in this monument, toward the end of his life Piranesi was able to study it closely from casts he had acquired from Charles Joseph Natoire's country house.[6]

The column was accorded considerable importance at the time, as is confirmed by the inclusion of two entries on it in Diderot's *Encyclopédie* ("Colonne Trajane"; "Trajane, colonne"); they are worth rereading in the context of Percier's reconstruction, for they enable us to better understand the concerns that guided him. But the column's perceived importance is also reflected, in another way, in the controversy that erupted over excavations in its immediate environs; this work had other implications, notably in the context of the birth of modern

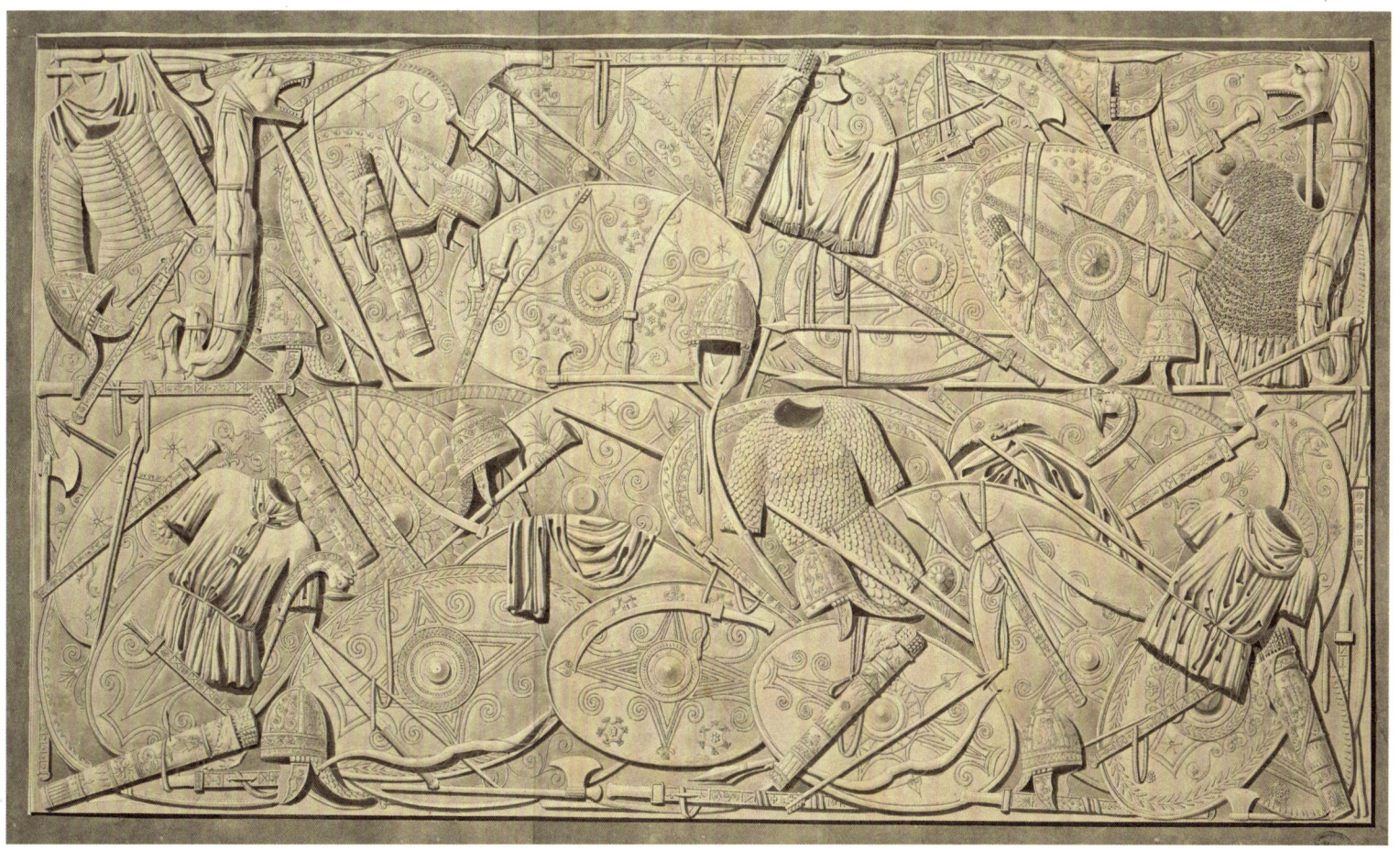

archaeology, which transformed the status of Roman ruins.[7] It can also be said, by way of synthesis, that Percier, benefitting from his Roman experience, managed to incorporate archaeological, typological, and morphological dimensions of rational analysis into his study project. In other of his undertakings, however, both contemporaneous and slightly later, he put into practice a conception of architecture as an assemblage of dissonant elements, one that, influenced by Rousseau, downplayed academic rules in favor of emotion, an approach consistent with the views of Étienne Louis Boullée [FIG. 3.5].[8] Moreover, it is worth recalling Percier's chronological proximity to the likes of Antoine Vaudoyer, a near contemporary who was in Rome just before him, between 1783 and 1786, as well as with such older architects as Pierre Adrien Pâris, who was there a few years earlier. Pâris visited the eternal city several times, and Pierre Pinon has amply demonstrated the relation between his "Études d'architecture" and the publications of Percier and Fontaine,[9] an affinity augmented by a concrete connection between the two men in December 1792, when, after returning to the French capital, Percier succeeded Pâris as architect-overseer of set design at the Paris Opera.

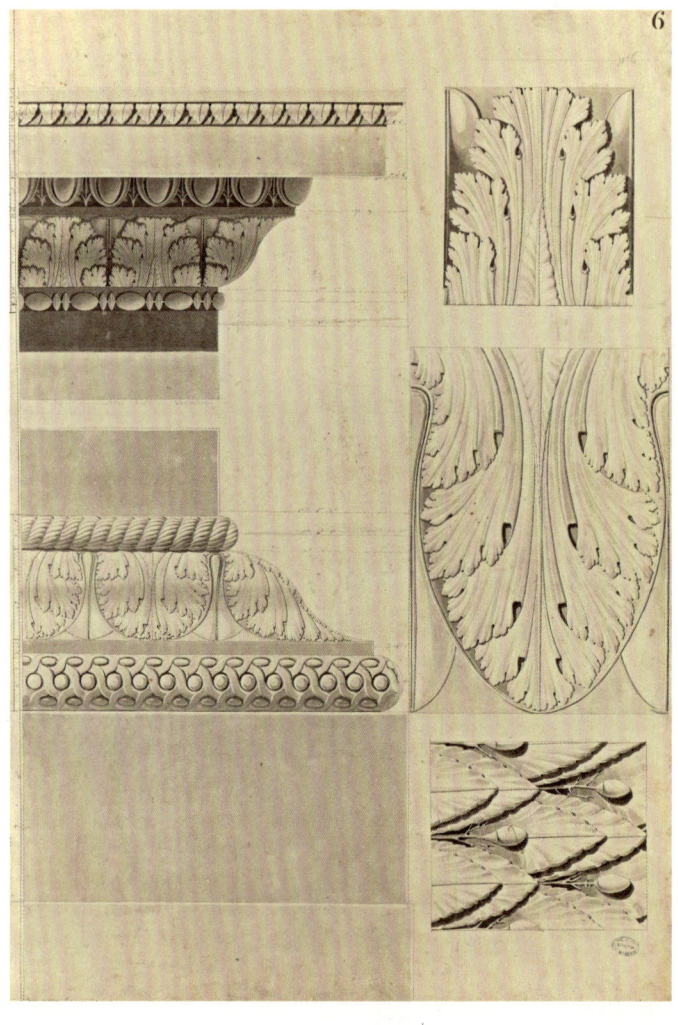

Some years later, in a development of the foundational Roman experience both surprising and predictable, the *Recueil de décorations intérieures*—a collaborative enterprise informed by many of the concerns evoked above—commenced publication, at a time when Percier and Fontaine were already quite famous, thanks in part to their first book, *Palais, maisons et autres édifices modernes dessinés à Rome* (1798). But their new opus manifested both a refinement and an extension of their method, aiming not only to provide resources for architecture and decoration but also to influence taste more generally, indeed the very way of life of a society then undergoing constant change: a society that, having irrevocably broken with the past, was entering the unaccustomed space of modernity.

Moreover, in these depictions of completed work, characterized by a diverse repertory of themes and subjects, we encounter, perhaps more directly than anywhere else in his publications, Percier's individual stylistic idiom, or, if you will, his

FIG. 3.4. Charles Percier. Details of the Column of Trajan, 1788. Ink, gray wash on paper mounted on canvas. École nationale supérieure des beaux-arts, Paris, 1-07.

FIG. 3.5. Charles Percier. Frontispiece for fascicle 15 of Percier and Fontaine, *Palais, maisons et autres édifices modernes dessinés à Rome*, (1798), pl. 86. Watercolor over etching. Institut National d'Histoire de l'Art, Paris, F° Est 688.

originality. This anthology of elegant forms, all richly ornamental, concentrated and unleashed (in the words of Jean-Philippe Garric) his "compulsive passion for details" and "unchecked penchant for drawing." We might say that Percier here honored the historical identity and material reality of his chosen models but sublimated these qualities by means of formal stylization, in the guise of geometric purification. This gave them a contemporary feel, introducing referential codes—including an ergonomic one—that bridged the gap between antiquity and modernity. In the process, he elaborated "a new kind of architectural design," one that was articulated in terms of historically specific ornamental forms and reflected the emergent historicist character of modern architecture. ●

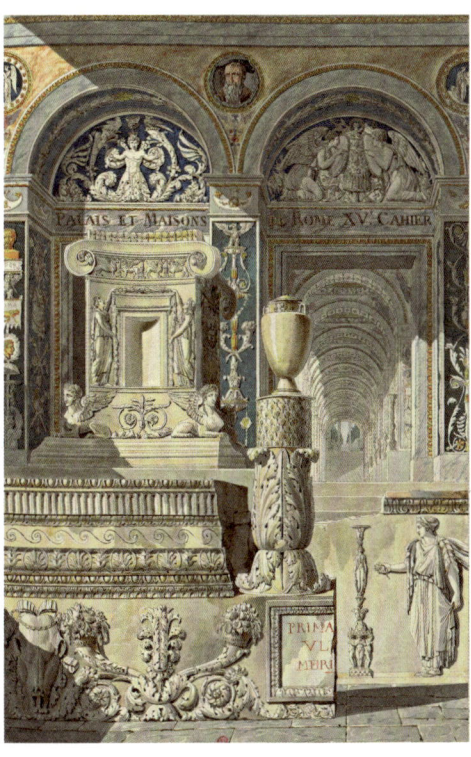

1 "Il poco tempo che mi resta di libertà lo voglio consacrare allo studio delle belle arti ch'io amo tanto e mi dirò per mio sostegno, lavora, to sei quasi romano." Letter published by Gian Paolo Consoli in "Un architetto 'quasi romano': Percier e I suoi rapporti con l'architettura e gli artisti italiani," in Sabine Frommel, Jean-Philippe Garric, and Elisabeth Kieven. *Charles Percier e Pierre Fontaine, dal soggiorno romano alla trasformazione di Parigi* (Rome: Silvana editoriale / Bibliotheca Hertziana, 2014), 63.

2 "Ho portato da Roma un numero di disegni fatti dappresso i monumenti e fabbriche di essa. Ogni sera prima di andare a letto me ci metto un paio d'ore per terminarli ed in tanto mi scordo di tutte le altre incombenze, non pensando ad altro che alla dolce remembranza dei giorni miei felici." Ibid.

3 Odile Nouvel-Kammerer, "La place du *Recueil de décorations intérieures* de Percier et Fontaine dans la question de l'ornement," in *Ornament, between art and design*. Proceedings of the international study day held on April 23, 2009, at the Istituto Svizzero di Roma, ed. A. Valera Braga (Basel: Schwabe, 2013), 32–43.

4 On Percier's Roman sojourn, see Desiré Raoul-Rochette, "Percier: Sa vie et ses ouvrages," in *Revue des deux mondes* 4, no. 24 (October 15, 1840): 246–68; Jeanne Duportal, "Charles Percier 1764–1838," in *Charles Percier: Reproduction de dessins conservés à la Bibliothèque de l'Institut* (Paris: Maurice Rousseau, 1931); M.-L. Morel d'Arleux, "Les voyages en Italie de Fontaine, Percier et Bernier, d'après leurs carnets de notes," *Bulletin de la Société de l'histoire de l'art français* 1 (1934), 88–103.

5 François Charles Uginet, *Roma Antiqua. Envoi des architectes français (1788–1924) Forum, Colisée, Palatin* (Rome: École française de Rome, Académie de France à Rome; Paris: École nationale supérieure des beaux-arts, 1985), 140–51.

6 Piranesi's version is the one that best exemplifies the anticomania of the time. See Giovanni Agostin and Vincenzo Farinella, "Il fregio della Colonna Traina e i Francesi," in *La Colonna Traiana e gli artisti francesi da Luigi XIV a Napoleone I*, ed. Giovanni Agosti, Vincenzo Farinella, and Giorgio Simoncini (Rome: Carta Segrete, 1988), 21–40.

7 Of the many publications on this subject, see especially Marcello Barbanera, ed., *Relitti riletti. Meta-morfosi delle rovine e identità culturale* (Turin: Bollati Boringhieri, 2009).

8 Jean-Philippe Garric, *Percier et Fontaine, les architectes de Napoléon* (Paris: Belin, 2012).

9 "it seems that the principal palaces and villas in the environs of Rome are present both in Pâris's Études and in the books of Percier and Fontaine. Pâris began to make his measured drawings in Rome in 1771, his successor in 1787." Pierre Pinon, "Rome antique et moderne vue par Pierre Adrien Pâris," in *Charles Percier e Pierre Fontaine dal soggiorno romano alla trasformazione di Parigi*, ed. Sabine Frommel, Jean-Philippe Garric, and Elisabeth Kieven, 25–39 (Milan: Silvana Editoriale, 2014), 31.

LETTER TO JOHN FLAXMAN

November 1791

CHARLES PERCIER

In the following letter,[1] which Percier sent to John Flaxman in November 1791, following his return to Paris, the architect, after alluding discreetly to fears prompted by the political situation there, lists the cities he had visited in the course of his return trip from Rome to France, which included what amounted to a study itinerary through northern Italy. From Rome he headed north to Rimini, the beginning of the via Emilia, and then he took a zigzag course through many urban centers, from Venice to Turin, from Bologna to Genoa. In the letter he mentions the notable monuments he saw at each stop, offering brief discussions of some of them. The lively but awkward style of the letter and the approximate spelling in the original manuscript reveal a passionate man, one understandably proud of having traveled more than 2,300 miles on foot but whose knowledge of classical culture was quite limited.

Sir,

Negligence is my only excuse. I am very aware that such a failing toward a man like yourself is almost unforgivable. However, I dare to hope that you will not have attributed a different one to me and [that] ingratitude cannot enter into the soul of a man so esteemed as yourself. Rest assured, sir, that not a day passed when I did not think about you, about your dear wife, about the advice you did me the honor of offering, and finally, if I may, about your friendship. Believe me, Mr. Flaxman, I think I am worthy of it. The idea of being loved and esteemed by a decent man, a gifted man, is the only thing capable of restraining me, even at the brink of danger.[2] I have been in Paris for two and a half months, a bit dazed in fact, often out of sorts, and constantly missing my beautiful, sublime Rome. No more monuments, no more beautiful skies, no more greenery; all anyone talks about is speculation and luxury. I won't say anything about [political] affairs for fear of letter inspectors. But all goes well, thank god. I've had a few small things to do in the way of drawings <u>ci vuol flemma</u>.[3] Now winter has arrived. I have retired to a small atelier, where I live in relative tranquility, perhaps too

▷ **FIG. 3A.1.** Map showing Percier's return route from Rome to France. The map, based on one published in 1790, the year before his journey, indicates contemporary political boundaries as well as the principal travel routes, which were the postal routes. This reconstruction of Percier's itinerary is based on the letter to Flaxman and the drawings executed during the trip, which are now in the Institut de France.

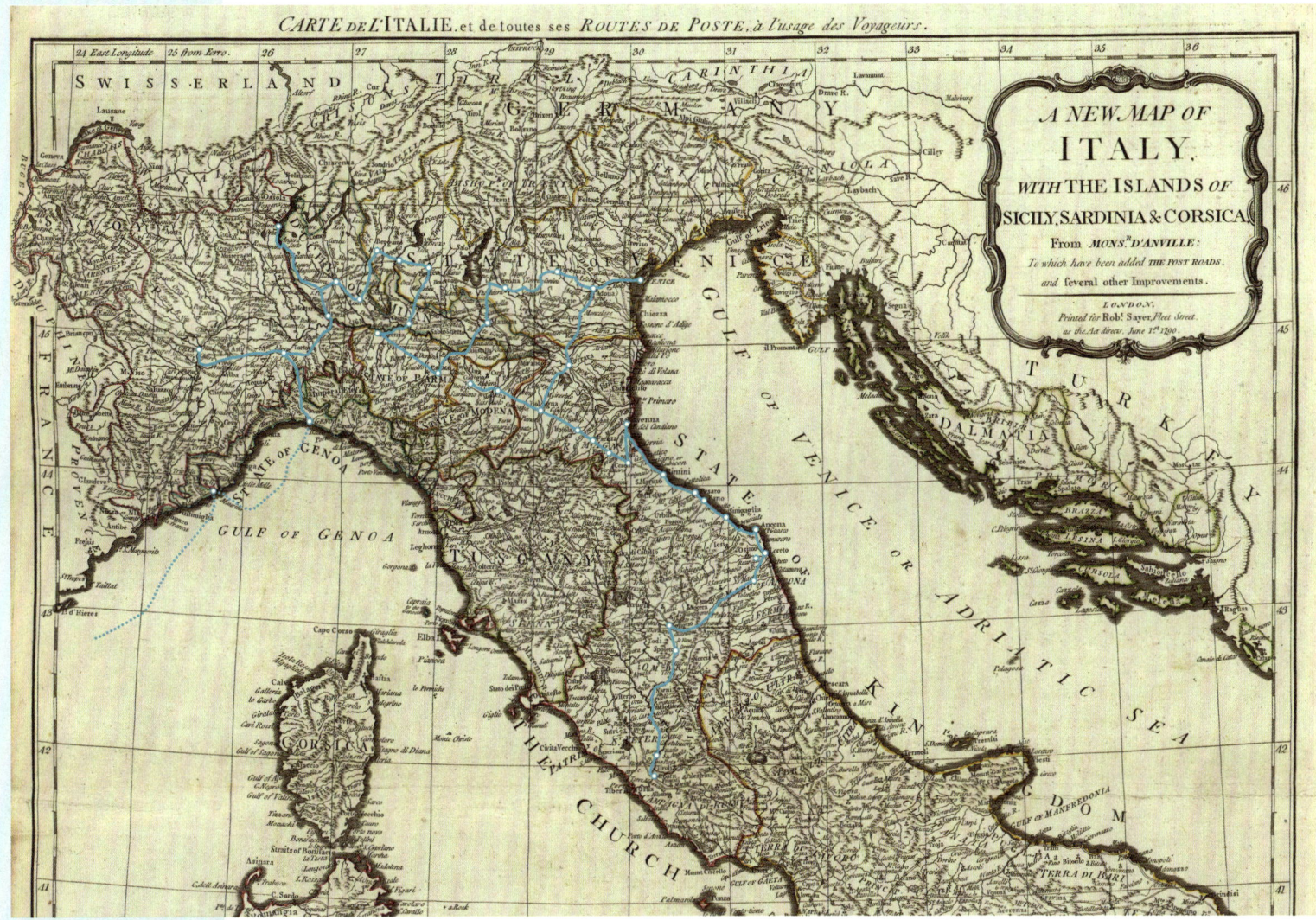

much for my own good. I will tell you about part of my trip, you know all of Tuscany. I'll begin with the Marche near Ancona. Foligno, a rather pretty small town; pretty buildings, beautiful paintings by Raphael. Tolentino, a [papal] consulate on the square [*un consul sur la place*]. Between these two cities the landscape is magnificent. Macerata, a beautifully conceived public square. Recanati, pretty buildings. Loretto, I wish you could see that place: seven bronze doors covered with bas-reliefs, baptismal fonts, apothecary vases after designs by Raphael. Ancona, the ancient arch on the port, superb palaces, a very beautiful slaughterhouse, a cathedral in a pretty gothic style. Senigallia, a regular city by the seaside. The porticos along the canal gave me much pleasure. Fano, a pretty small town, an ancient port. The good sense of the city officials prompted them to have engraved beside the gate, on part of the wall, its restored arch. In Pesaro, some palaces. There may be lots of paintings there; having little time, I limited myself to the architecture. The square there is beautiful, as in all the cities of the Marche, always one or two bronze statues of the pope, colossal and grandiose. On arriving in Rimini, an ancient arch, a first square with columns, a second one with porticos, a palace in the center, a statue of the pope opposite it.

From there to Ravenna, an ancient city. The churches resemble those in Trastevere, excepting that of San Vitale, where there are bas-reliefs, dedicated, I think, to Neptune. They show infants carrying shells and tridents. The same bas-relief can be seen in Venice, in the church of the Madonna dei Miracoli. Before arriving in that city, there is one of their very old churches, called Classe de fuori [*sic*].[4] From Ravenna to Cesena, from there to Forlì. Pretty square; I just passed through it. Faenza, beautiful square, beautiful palaces. Imola, here the Bolognese style begins: streets always lined with columns, a rather extraordinary theater, as in Modena. In Bologna, there's a lot to turn an architect's head. You know it. Reggio, Ferrara, a delicious city whose character is both solid and agreeable. I liked their idea of placing a seated figure of the pope atop a very thick column. The façade of the church seemed to me in a beautiful Gothic style. The palace of the duke, where the [papal] legate resides, is a beautiful structure. Venice completely disoriented me. It struck me as one of the most beautiful cities in Italy. The Grand Canal is a magnificent thing. San Marco, the square of the same [illegible], the surrounding islands, the marble, the water, the paintings, everything ravished me. However, in summer the small canals smell bad. That's the other side of the coin.

Padua. Il salone[5] is an immense thing, surrounded by columns; these same columns surrounded by shops and, finally, columns bring everything to a close. The church of Sant'Antonio is magnificent. Its chapel is covered with sculptures. They had the beautiful idea of placing all of their great men in a vast square. Vicenza is well known because of Palladio. The Casa Volpe outside the gates[6] is one of the prettiest of country houses. Verona, that's where I finally saw the idea of a Roman way. Two triumphal arches in succession on a grand, very wide street, a beautiful amphitheater, whose tiers are intact. The museum of the marquis of Maffei[7] is currently close and adjacent to the theater.[8] It contains some charming bas-reliefs, mostly tombs but like the ones in Volterra, not the ones in Rome. Mantua: the Palazzo Te is in my view worth the trip. The plan and the book that you gave me is [*sic*] completely accurate. I renew my thanks. The church of Sant'Andrea, the museum, the square, the streets are beautiful. Parma, the metropolitan church, the baptistery, but then you know it. Like Piacenza, Cremona is full of charming details, the cathedral in a beautiful Gothic style. Sixteenth-century paintings in the interior. Brescia, a delicious city, fountains like in Rome. The palace courtyards completely covered by vines, sometimes the streets as well. The square is very beautiful. The execution of the palace of the ragione is worthy of the antique. Bergamo, terraced buildings, as in Naples. Upper and lower parts of the city, the road is ancient. Loggias as in Rome. Bergamo is a beautiful region. Lodi, a beautiful hospital. Milan, the Palace of the Ragione, the hospital, the church of Sant'Ambrogio, the library, the merchants' loggia. Milan struck me as having a beautiful character, but greatly adulterated. I forgot an ancient temple at the church of San Lorenzo. I [went] to see the Borromean Islands and the statue on Lago Maggiore. The islands, largely untouched, struck me as worthy of Tasso. From there to Pavia; the famous Certosa, outside the town; in Pavia itself, the bridge, the Collegio Borromeo, another institute, the hospital, the square, a bronze

FIG. 3A.2. Letter from Percier to John Flaxman, November 13, 1791, describing his return trip from Rome to France. Fitzwilliam Museum, Cambridge, Flaxman Letterbook, 61.

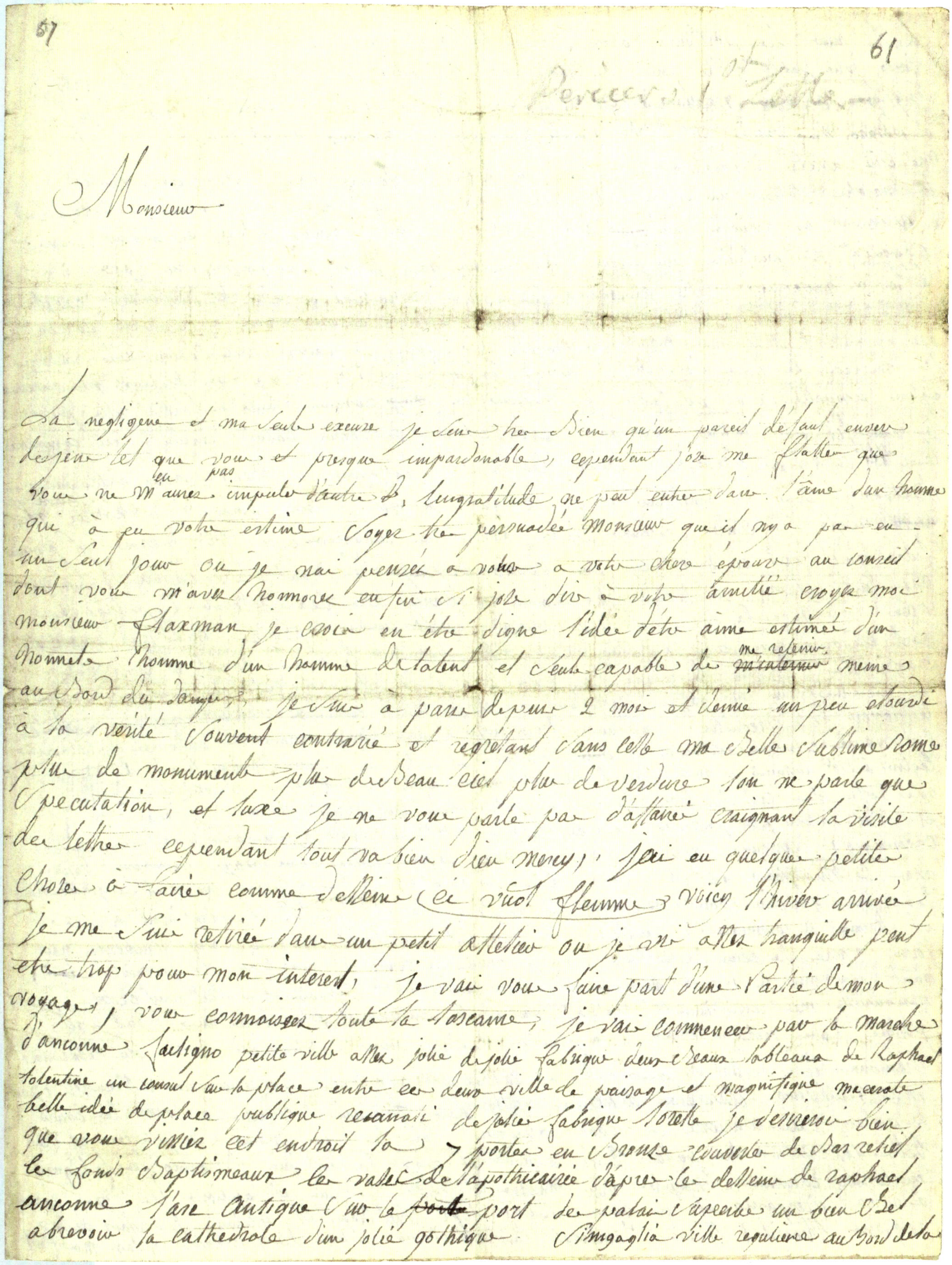

57   61

                                    Perçois 1.e Lettre

Monsieur

La negligence et ma seule excuse je sens bien Dieu qu'un pareil defaut envers
des gens tel que vous et presque impardonable, cependant j'ose me flatter que
vous ne m'aurez pas imputé d'autre B, l'ingratitude ne peut entrer dans l'ame d'un homme
qui a eu votre estime soyez très persuadée Monsieur qu'il n'y a pas eu
un seul jour ou je n'ai pensée à vous a votre cher époux au conseil
dont vous m'avez honorée enfin si j'ose dire à votre amitié croyez moi
Monsieur flaxman je crois en être digne l'idée d'être aimé estimé d'un
honnête homme d'un homme de talent et seule capable de me retenir même
au bord du danger. je suis à paris depuis 2 mois et j'ens un peu etourdi
à la verité souvent contrarié et regretant dans cette ma belle sublime rome
plus de monuments plus de beau ciel plus de verdure l'on ne parle que
specutation, et luxe je ne vous parle pas d'affaires craignant la visite
des lettres cependant tout va bien Dieu mercy, j'ai eu quelques petites
choses à faire comme d'Elena (ci vient flemme) voicy l'hiver arrivée
je me suis retirée dans un petit attelier ou je vis assez tranquille peut
être trop pour mon interest, je vais vous faire part d'une partie de mon
voyage, vous connoissez toute la toscanne, je vais commencer par la marche
d'ancone Jesigno petite ville assez jolie de jolie fabrique deux beaux tableaux de Raphael
tolentine un consul sur la place entre ces deux ville le paissage est magnifique macerate
belle idée de place publique recanati de jolie fabrique lorette je desirerois bien
que vous visiez cet endroit la portes en Bronse couverts de bas relief
les fonds Baptismeaux les vases de l'apothicairie d'apres le dessein de raphael
ancone l'arc antique sur le port de palais s'exerce un bien bel
abrevoir la cathedrale d'un jolie gothique. Sinigaglia ville reguliere au bord de la

equestrian figure. From there to Alexandria, Turin which you know, Susa also. Genoa, for architects, is an inexhaustible museum. The plans are really full of genius, the country houses superb. Farewell, Beautiful Italy, non te vedro mai più, queste parole sono teribile [sic] per me.[9]

France. Antibes, Toulon, Marseille. Beautiful on the Maggiore and at Saint-Victor. Ancient fragments in Aix, in the cathedral church, to the right as you enter. Remains from a baths, I think. In Saint-Remis a large well-preserved tomb. I know of nothing like it in Italy, remains from an ancient period. Arles, Mr. Flaxman, you might like to see the fragments of figures, ask Father Dumont, a former Minim and a very nice man, an amphitheater, the remains of a baths and a theater. At Nîmes, an amphitheater. A temple with a well-preserved exterior, of Diana, full of fragments. The public garden is curious. In Orange, an ancient arch, a large part of an immense theater. The façade is complete and 307 pieds high. Vienne in the Dauphiné, a temple, a tomb, some fragments, a church with a beautiful elevation, one of the most beautiful I've seen. Riom. Autun, two antique gates, one greatly superior to the other in workmanship. Cussy-la-Colonne, a column raised on an octagonal pedestal with eight niches where there are eight divinities. And from there to Paris, very few antiquities. My trip to my father's house was 981 leagues.[10] I made it, god be thanked, in peace and in health. The walk, far from discomfiting me, made me stronger.

My short relation, sir, less with the idea of giving you information than a kind of account of my trip. I dare to think that it might interest you somewhat. I told you above that I am living tranquilly among my drawings. Busying myself at the moment tidying up loose ends from my trip. I hope that my letter will be received with indulgence, and that in Paris you will come to see the few drawings that I will have made there. I also hope that you will not withdraw from me the role of cicerone that you promised me. You alone, sir, can obtain your wife's pardon for me. I ask that you not neglect, when you see Ms Canova, to convey my compliments. If Mr Read [?] remembers having seen me, [give him] my greetings, and you, sir, whom I consider my friend, rest assured that I am, despite occasional doubts [on your part], in gratitude, friendship, and esteem, your very humble servant.

Paris, November 13, 1791
Charles Percier

On the back of the letter:
Nov. 13 1791
Percier (architect Paris)
Account of his trip to Italy

Letter transcribed by Iris Moon and Jean-Philippe Garric

1 Fitzwilliam Museum, Cambridge, Flaxman Letterbook, 61.
2 Here and two sentences farther on, Percier discreetly evokes in this letter, dated November 1791, fears occasioned by the Revolution.
3 Roughly, "I must be patient."
4 The Basilica of Sant'Apollinare in Classe, near Ravenna.
5 The Palazzo della Ragione, or Palace of the Law.
6 Villa Volpe, also known as Villa Brusarosco, is in Vicenza just outside the Porta Lupia across the bridge of Campo Marzio.
7 Francesco Scipione, marquese di Maffei (1675–1755), author, art critic, and antiquarian. Upon his death he bequeathed his museum, built in 1745 to house his collection, to his native city. Now known as the Museo Lapidario Maffeiano, it remains in its original building.
8 The Teatro Filarmonico, Verona.
9 "I will never see you again, these words are terrible for me."
10 Here Percier calculates the total distance covered during his trip, which comes to approximately 2,360 miles.

ARCHITECTURAL PATRIMONY

THE CHÂTEAU DE FONTAINEBLEAU AND CHARLES PERCIER

ENCOUNTER WITH THE FRENCH RENAISSANCE OR NOSTALGIA FOR ITALY?

VINCENT DROGUET

I was still full of memories of Italy when, shortly after my return to France,[1] I visited the château de Fontainebleau.... [T]he bizarre overall effect of the château, compared with what I had just seen in Rome, Florence, Venice, in short, throughout Italy, did not satisfy me; but the various parts in which Serlio, Rosso, Primaticcio, Nicolò dell'Abbate had developed their talents reminded me for a moment of what I had just left behind.

CHARLES PERCIER[2]

THE LIBRARY OF THE INSTITUT DE FRANCE HAS IN ITS COLLECTION three albums of drawings by Charles Percier, all assembled and mounted under his direction and entirely devoted to the château de Fontainebleau.[3] Two of these albums are monographic in nature: Ms 1014 is dedicated to the Ballroom and its decoration, while Ms 1016 focuses exclusively on the Gallery of Diana. Only Ms 1015 brings together drawings of various buildings and decorative schemes at the château—the Oval Courtyard, the Porte Dorée, the Grotte des

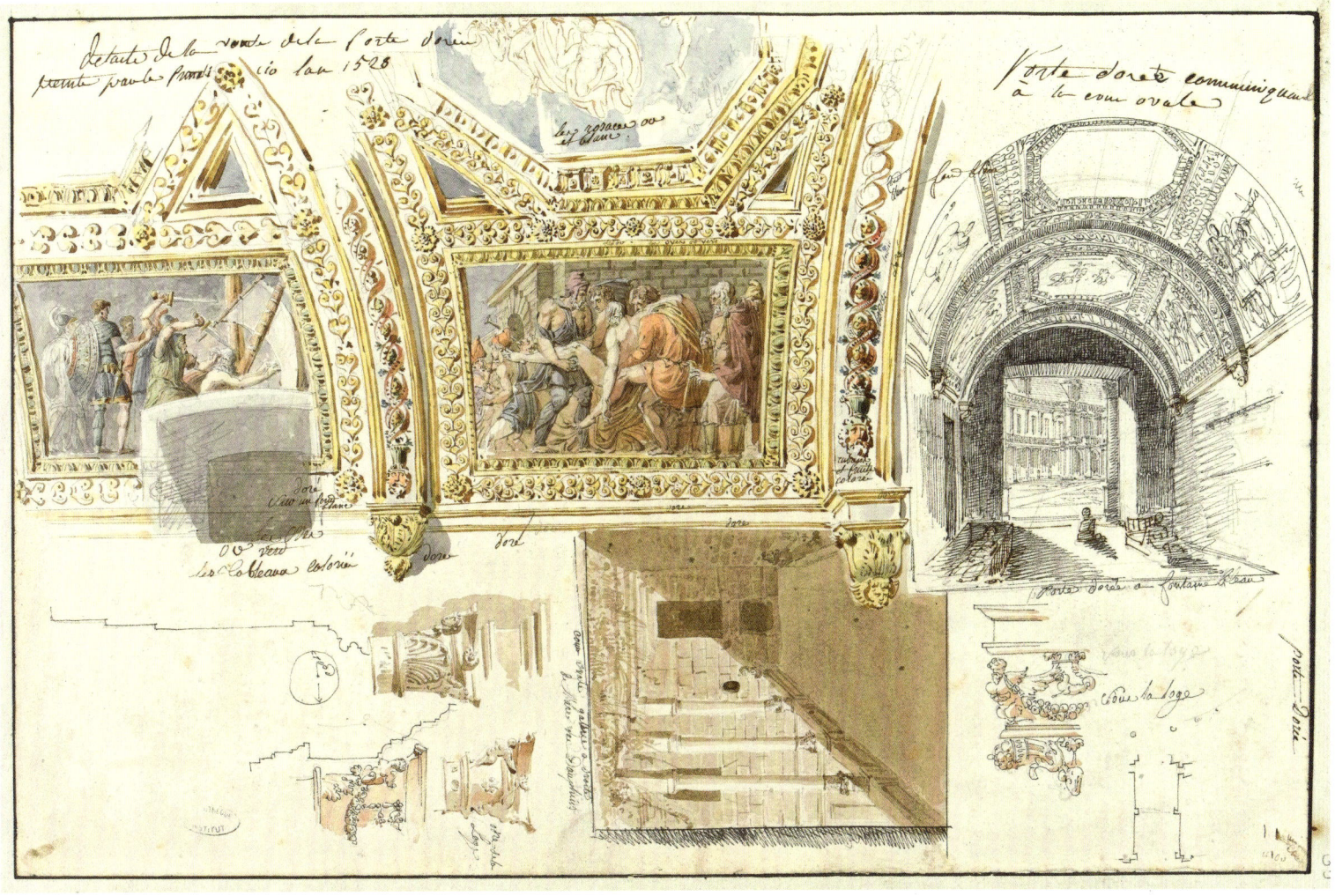

Pins, the Horseshoe Staircase, the Gallery of Francis I, and so forth—in a sort of compendium, one that does not extend beyond work completed during the reign of Louis XIII. There are almost a hundred pages in all, to most of which are affixed several drawings, many with multiple images and all attesting to Percier's intense interest in the château of Francis I and its grand decorative ensembles.[4] When these three albums were assembled, they constituted the most important collection of visual documentation of Fontainebleau yet compiled by a single

▲ FIG. 4.1. Charles Percier. Sketches of the vestibule vault over the Porte Dorée, the colonnade of the Oval Courtyard, and details of the loggia capitals from the Royal Apartments wing, château de Fontainebleau, ca. 1793–1800. Pencil, ink, and watercolor. Bibliothèque de l'Institut de France, Paris, Ms 1015, fol. 23, pl. 35.

artist.[5] This consideration alone amply justifies study of this corpus of drawings, but several related matters are also worth exploring: the specific context in which the drawings were made, the intentions that motivated their maker, and, finally, what they reveal about the role of Fontainebleau in the cultural mindset of an early nineteenth-century architect.

It will be best to begin with a basic question: When did Percier visit Fontainebleau? Two drawings in the albums offer a response that, although it might seem clear, is in fact incomplete; on two of his drawings—a rendering of the Ballroom (red chalk) and one of the left portion of the tympanum of the Porte Dorée (colored wash)[6]—Percier inscribed the same date: 6 brumaire year IX (October 28, 1800). There being no reason to doubt the authenticity of these annotations, it follows that the architect must have executed at least some of these Fontainebleau drawings toward the end of 1800, which is to say at a time when damage resulting from Revolutionary vandalism was visible on the buildings and their decor. However, in an autograph text in the album devoted to the Ballroom (see epigraph),[7] Percier states that when he visited Fontainebleau—for the first time?—he was "still full of memories of Italy," and that this was shortly after his return to France, which must have taken place in the summer of 1791. The same passage states that he was interested in the château because he saw it as an extension of the artistic legacy of the Italian Renaissance. If we can credit his assertion that his memories of Italy were still vivid during this drawing campaign, it seems reasonable to assume that his initial significant encounter with the château must have taken place shortly after 1791, not in 1800.

In this context, it is worth noting that some of the pages in the Fontainebleau albums have captions in Italian, which suggests that they date from shortly after the architect's sojourn on the peninsula.[8] It is true that, throughout his life, Percier retained a predilection for the Italian language, which he sometimes used when conversing with his former fellow pensioners. However, his use of Italian captions on drawings of decorative schemes at Fontainebleau executed by Italian artists indeed suggests that these sheets were executed shortly after his return to France, which is to say from the first half of the 1790s.[9]

Another piece of evidence should be considered in this connection, namely the observations made by Louis Pierre Baltard in *Paris et ses monumens, mesurés, dessinés et gravés par Baltard, architecte, avec des Descriptions historiques par le cit. Amaury Duval*, whose publication begun in year XI (1803). This book, whose title indicates that it will be concerned only with monuments in the capital, ultimately discussed several large buildings from the environs of Paris, notably the châteaux at Saint-Cloud, Saint-Germain, Meudon, and Fontainebleau. Several of the engraved illustrations for the chapter devoted to Fontainebleau are inscribed "C. Percier del.," which Amaury Duval, the author of the text, glossed in a note as follows: "A happy circumstance facilitated the work of M. Baltard, who wanted to bring together drawings of all the artistic productions that serve or have served in the decoration of Fontainebleau. Nine years ago one of our most distinguished architects, M. Percier, a passionate advocate of the taste that prevailed in the arts throughout the beautiful period of the reign of Francis I, was pleased to copy everything that was then most remarkable at the château....M. Percier kindly loaned all of these precious drawings to M. Baltard."[10] The first edition of Baltard's book bears the date 1803, but its publication was preceded by a subscription prospectus in 1802, by which time the texts must already have been written. It follows, then, in light of the precise indication in the above-cited note, that the drawings Percier loaned to his former fellow pensioner Baltard were executed about 1793, which is indeed shortly after his return to France.

The logical conclusion to be drawn from this web of information, and from examination of the drawings in the three albums, is that Percier must have visited Fontainebleau several times between his return from Italy and 1803, when the work undertaken by Bonaparte at the château commenced. During this long decade, Percier had ready access to an exceptional on-site interlocutor, one whose presence at the château must have had something to do with his successive visits to the palace and with his exceptional investment in it. This person was none other than Percier's former master, Antoine François Peyre, known as Peyre the younger.

Jean-Philippe Garric has rightly insisted on the crucial role played by Peyre in the education of Percier and Fontaine.[11] He was their supportive mentor, the master who cleared the way for them and made their brilliant double career possible. In their book *Résidences des souverains* (1833), they paid him glowing homage: "[T]he ties of affection and recognition that attach us to the memory of M. Peyre preclude for us, as regards this skilled man, all feelings other than those of the most sincere and respectful admiration."[12] Now, Antoine François Peyre, pensioner at the French Academy in Rome from 1763 to 1766, member of the Académie royale d'architecture from 1777, architect in the service of the Elector of Treves from 1780, was responsible for the buildings at Fontainebleau throughout the Revolutionary period. In this connection, he prepared a detailed plan of the château (dated December 1791), acted as guide to the members of the Commission temporaire des arts during their visit there (17 prairial year II [June 5, 1794]), and drafted plans for the transformation of the palace tennis court into a meeting hall for the Conseil des Anciens (September 1796).[13] Ultimately, Peyre's zealous defense of the château and its artistic treasures made him appear suspect, prompting his incarceration for a time in the palace itself.[14] In sum, prior to the appointment of the architect Alexandre Dufour in 1804, Peyre remained a key figure in matters pertaining to the maintenance and knowledge of the buildings at Fontainebleau.[15] Thus the close ties between Antoine François Peyre and Charles Percier cast a clarifying light on the latter's work at the château of Francis I.

Percier's engagement with Fontainebleau coincided with a singularly troubled moment in its history, one that saw the palace's continued existence called into question. This context makes it easier to understand the close attention that Percier paid to various decorative elements of the château, and it also explains some of the details in his drawings. For example, on a depiction of the right part of the tympanum of the Porte Dorée (Ms 1014, drawing 34), dated 6 brumaire year IX (October 28, 1800), Percier inscribed in the central medallion: "damaged scratched some remnants of color as if it had once been painted," an allusion to the disappearance of a royal coat of arms, elements that were systematically effaced during the Revolutionary years.[16] On another drawing [FIG. 4.1], he pointedly included, in a representation of the porch of the Porte Dorée, two statues in open crates as well as a bust left sitting on the ground,

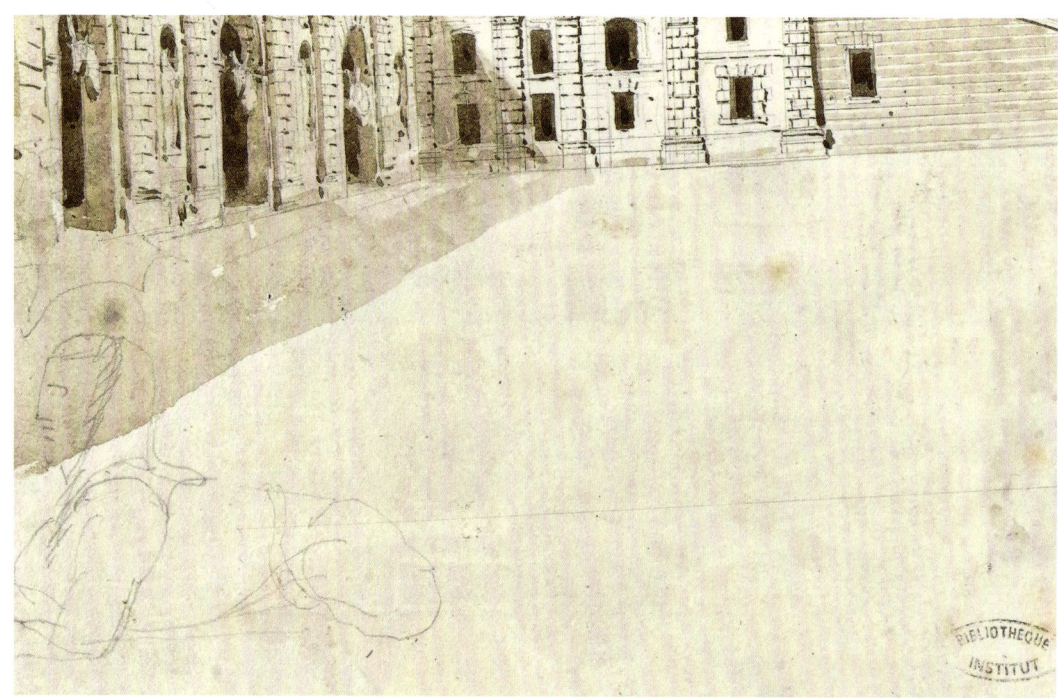

thereby bearing witness to current threats to the palace's sculpture collection and to the precariousness of its conservation.[17] Similarly, in the lower left corner of a drawing of the Fountain Courtyard [FIG. 4.2], he drew a faint pencil sketch of one of the bronze sphinxes cast under Francis I by Francesco Primaticcio, a sculpture that decorated the banister of the grand staircase in the wing of the Belle Cheminée. These two sphinxes, copies after antique models, were, like the satyrs integrated into the mantelpiece in the Ballroom, melted down by the Revolutionary government. Finally, although he was not much interested generally in the paintings on canvas incorporated into the decorative schemes, Percier indicated the six large compositions by Ambroise Dubois in the blind arcades of the upper chapel of Saint-Saturnin, whose religious subjects would have made them especially vulnerable to destruction in the near future [FIG. 4.3]. Clearly, Percier made a point of recording elements of the French patrimony that he knew to be seriously threatened.

He would have been all too aware of the reality of such threats, for since 1793 he had been an official participant in the work of the Commission des monuments. It was in this connection that he reestablished contact with Alexandre Lenoir, curator of the Musée des monuments français, and supervised the dismantling of the frontispiece of the château d'Anet and of the porticos of the château de Gaillon. His understanding of Fontainebleau, then, was shaped by a broader awakening to the interest of the great architectural achievements of the French Renaissance (Gaillon, Écouen, Anet), all of which were threatened with destruction—if not already undergoing demolition—during this period. Hans Ottomeyer has discerned, in Percier's drawings of Écouen, a greater sensitivity to ornament than is apparent in his drawings of Renaissance buildings in Rome. An "ornamentalist" at heart, Percier discovered in the decorative vocabulary of the French Renaissance a teeming world that appealed to his imagination.

However, Fontainebleau was a special case by comparison with the grand contemporary residences that Percier was exploring in these same years. Its painted decors were altogether exceptional; they had no equivalents at Gaillon or Anet, and it would seem that the famous painted mantelpieces at Écouen were not quite visible at this time.[18] Doubtless aware of their specific qualities as well as their vulnerability, Percier devoted most of his attention to these painted decors.

Nonetheless, it remains important to specify the choices that Percier made from the vast repertory available at the château. First, it is worth noting that his

◄ **FIG. 4.2.** Charles Percier. Wing of the Belle Cheminée, seen from the Cour de la Fontaine, château de Fontainebleau, and sketch of a sphinx (detail), ca. 1793–1800. Pencil and sepia wash. Bibliothèque de l'Institut de France, Paris, Ms 1015, fol. 9, drawing 12. The full image is reproduced on page 6.

ARCHITECTURAL PATRIMONY

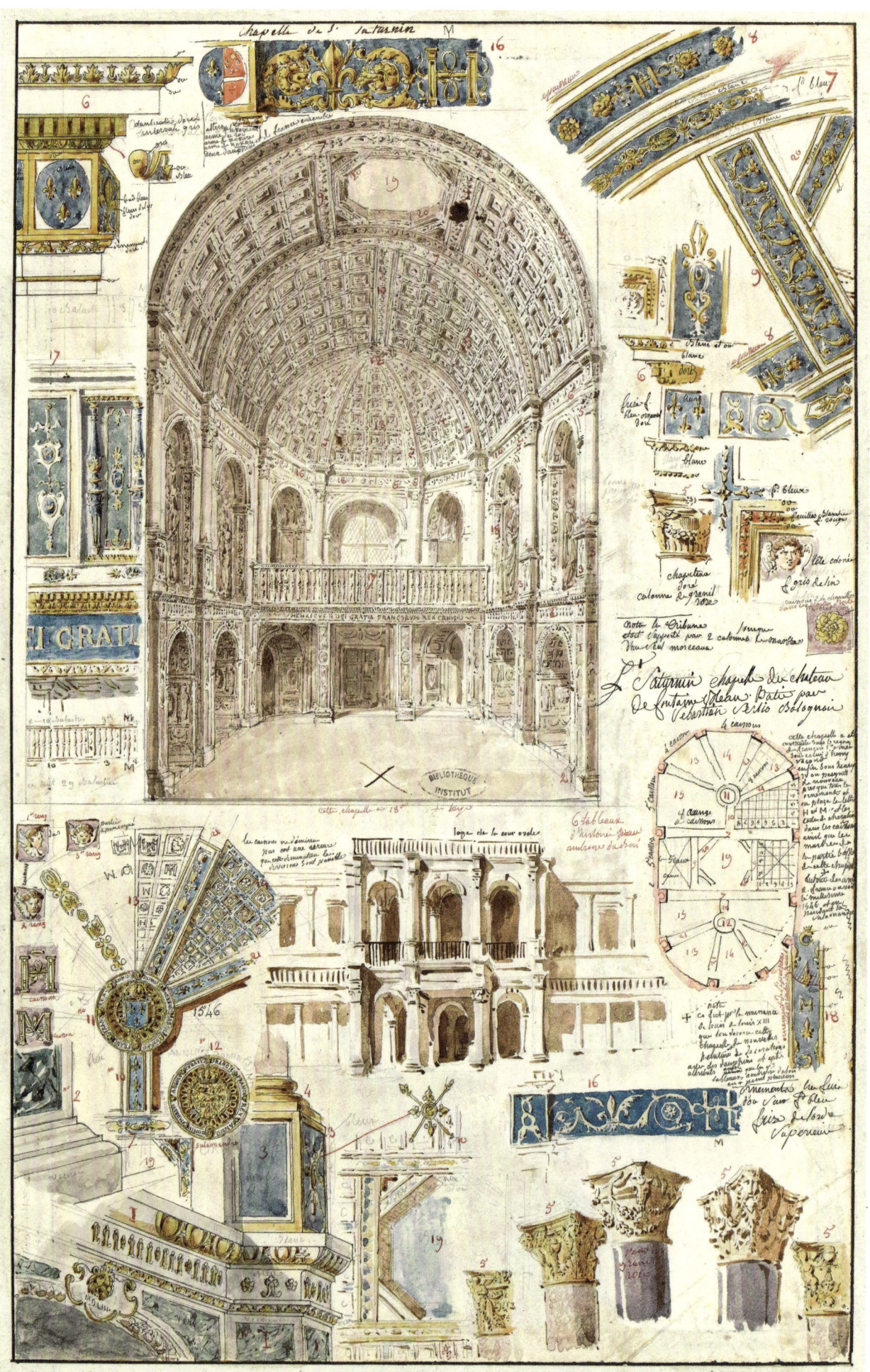

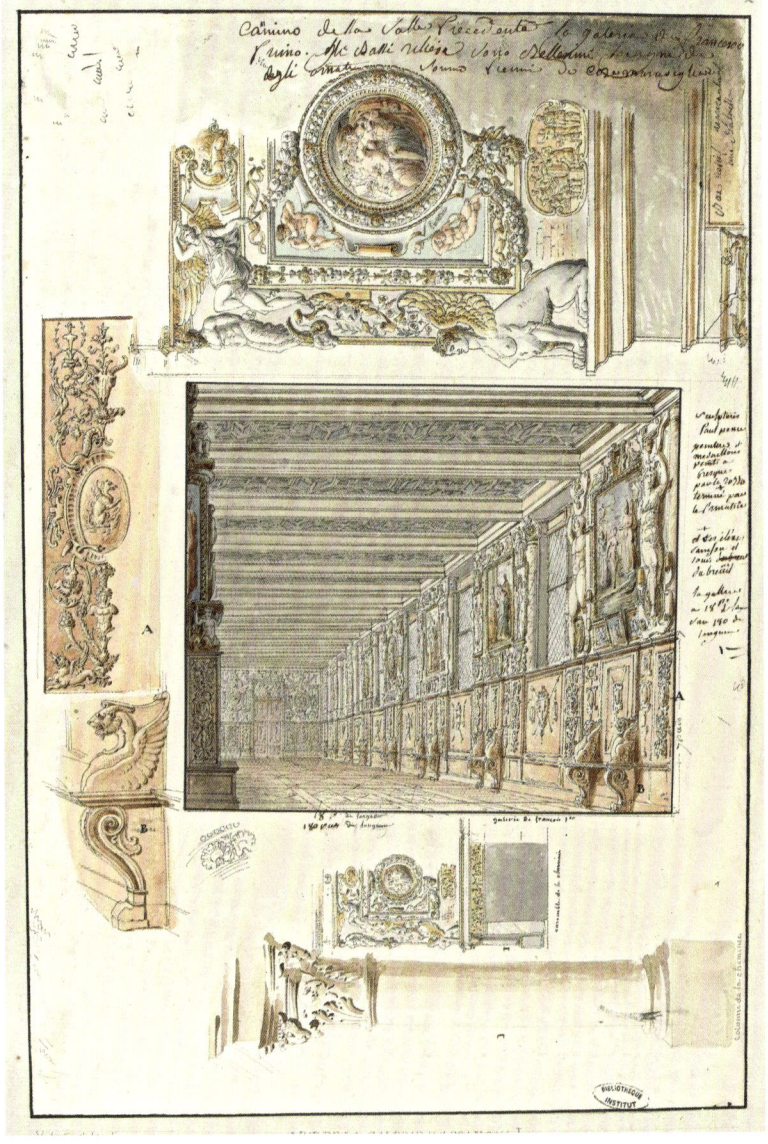

"coverage" of the Ballroom and the Gallery of Diana was exhaustive, and that no less than eight pages of Ms 1015 are devoted to the Porte Dorée,[19] whereas there are only three pages dedicated to the no less celebrated Gallery of Francis I. Also, regarding the Gallery of Francis I, Percier made do with a general perspective view and a few details of the stuccos and wood paneling, without delineating the frescos by Rosso Fiorentino.[20] Even more surprisingly, in the perspective view of the gallery [FIG. 4.4], only his rendering of the scene in the first compartment on the north wall—known as *Vénus frustrée* (Venus Frustrated)—is accurate, the sketch of the scene in the neighboring compartment—known as *L'Éducation d'Achille* (The Education of Achilles)—having nothing to do with Rosso's composition. This constitutes proof, if any be needed, that in this case Percier was interested only in the gallery's decorative system, admittedly, unique of its kind, and paid attention only to the stuccos and the paneling, thereby adhering to a pattern followed by all the commentators on the gallery since its completion.[21]

As already noted, Percier paid special attention to the ensemble of the Porte Dorée, including the frescoes on its porch and those in its vestibule as well as the sculpture on its tympanum. He recorded the flattened vault used there [FIG. 4.5], but being an architect thoroughly imbued with the classical aesthetic as well as an unstinting admirer of the achievements of the Italian Renaissance, he could not resist "rectifying" its shape in his overall views of the gate, making it a more canonical half-circle [FIG. 4.6]. Contrary to his apparent indifference—even disdain—for Rosso's paintings in the Gallery of Francis I, he drew almost all of the compositions by Primaticcio in the Porte Dorée, adding copious notations (either in the margins or within the drawings themselves) regarding their color schemes and indicating their exact placement on the vault by means of a numerical reference system [FIG. 4.7].[22] In

◀ FIG. 4.3. Charles Percier. Interior of Saint-Saturnin's Chapel, decorative details of the mural ornamentation and vaults, and loggia of the Royal Apartments wing overlooking the Oval Courtyard, ca. 1793–1800. Pencil, sepia wash, and watercolor. Bibliothèque de l'Institut de France, Paris, Ms 1015, fol. 9 verso, drawing 13.

▲ FIG. 4.4. Charles Percier. Gallery of Francis I, château de Fontainebleau, details of the benches and wood paneling, and decoration of the fireplace in the Salon of Francis I, ca. 1793–1800. Pencil, sepia wash, and watercolor. Bibliothèque de l'Institut de France, Paris, Ms 1015, fol. 2, drawing 2.

the case of the two scenes on the porch, the damaged state of which Percier meticulously recorded, he even sought out the sixteenth-century engraving after the original drawing and copied its composition into the album. In this instance, then, the prospect of eventual restitution was integral to his thinking from the start.

In the case of the Ballroom and its decor, he went much further: forty-five pages, with almost two hundred drawings, are devoted to this exceptional ensemble, which has its own album. In addition to general views of the room (including a very free one in red chalk dated 6 brumaire year IX [October 28, 1800]) and partial views of the fireplace wall, the wall with the musicians' tribune, and the painted spandrels, these sheets offer a multitude of details of the painted and sculpted decor and of the ornament on the paneling and benches. As with the Porte Dorée, Percier was interested in both the room's structure and its various decorative elements. He thought its unorthodox architectural disposition

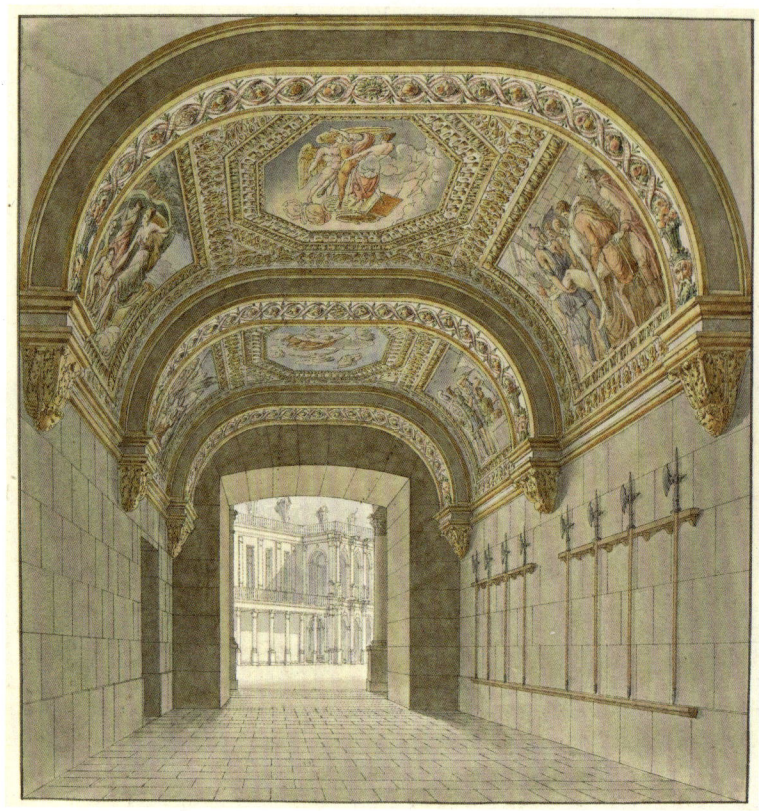

constituted evidence for an aborted ceiling design, which prompted him (he was attentive to what we would call the building's "archaeology") to propose a "restoration" of it with *arcs doubleaux*, or transverse arches [FIG. 4.8]. As for the painted decor, it was the object of many drawings, a mix of rapid sketches (their summary execution bringing to mind those of the Porte Dorée) annotated with comments on the frescoes' state of preservation and far more finished drawings, notably of the large compositions in the spandrels. The latter, if they don't suggest an actual

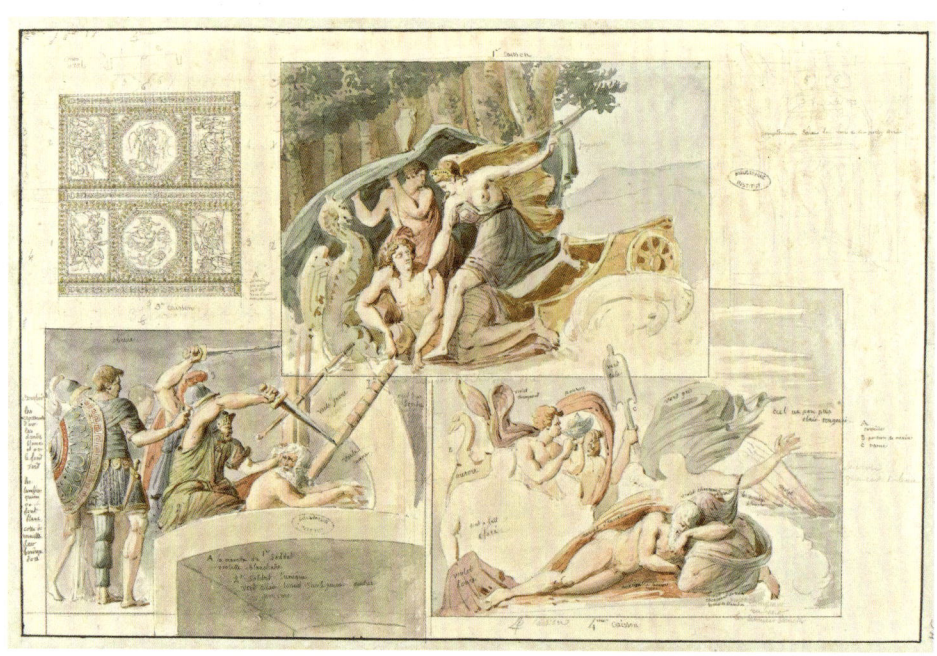

FIG. 4.5. Charles Percier. Decoration of the vestibule of the Porte Dorée, château de Fontainebleau, early 19th century. Pencil and watercolor on paper. Bibliothèque de l'Institut de France, Paris, Ms 1015, fol. 21, drawing 33.

FIG. 4.6. Charles Percier. Porte Dorée, château de Fontainebleau, details of the column capitals, early 19th century. Pencil, sepia wash, and watercolor on paper. Bibliothèque de l'Institut de France, Paris, Ms 1015, fol. 18, drawing 25.

FIG. 4.7. Charles Percier. Decoration of the vault of the Porte Dorée, château de Fontainebleau, ca. 1793–1800. Pencil, ink, and watercolor on paper. Bibliothèque de l'Institut de France, Paris, Ms 1015, fol. 22, drawing 34.

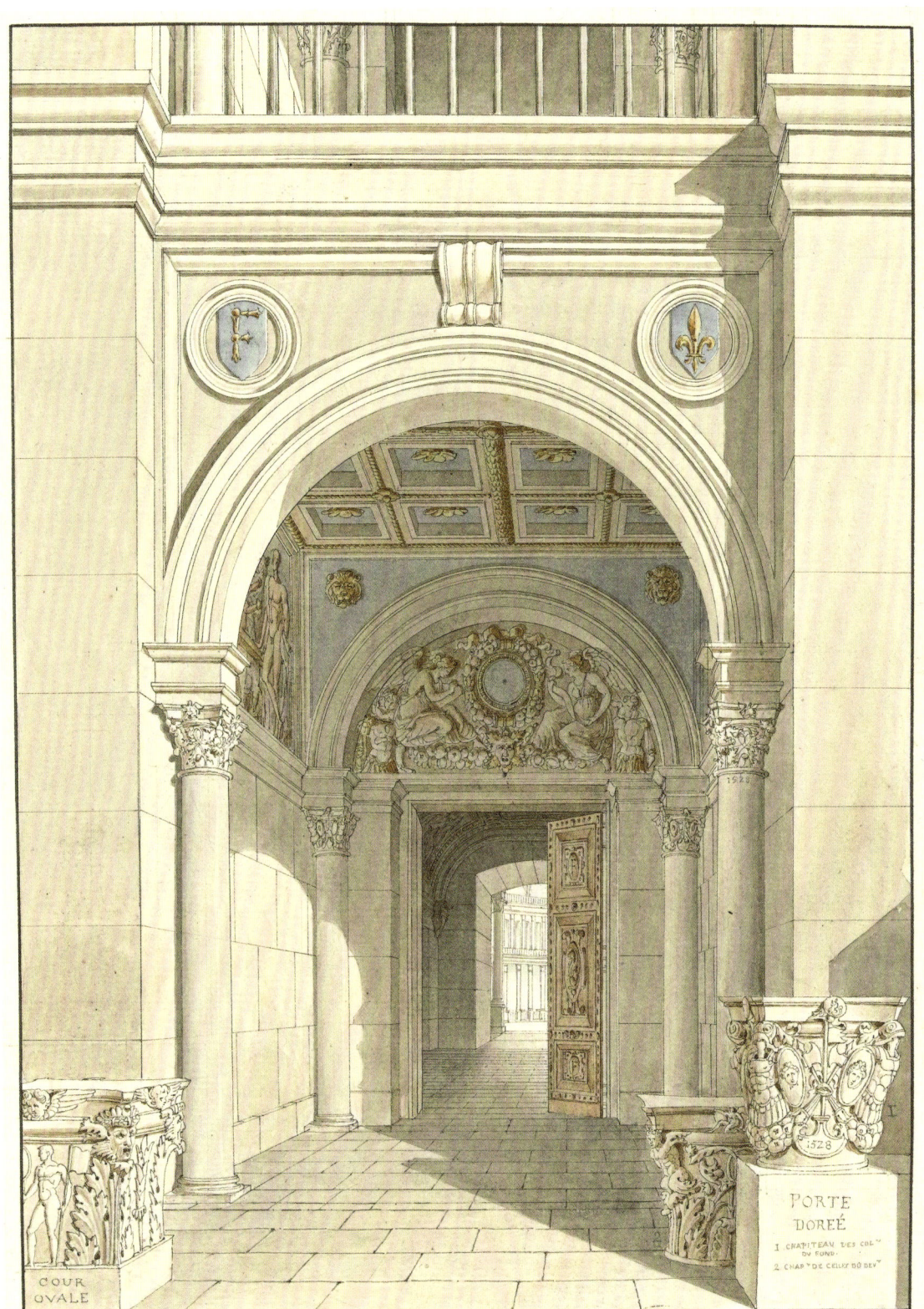

restoration project, effectively propose how such an enterprise might proceed, for they incorporate passages from engravings after the frescoes. At the bottom of one page with three tracings of prints by Alexandre Betou [FIG. 4.9], Percier made the following annotation: "having almost completed this album and having found some prints engraved after paintings in the ballroom [that are] now almost completely effaced I copied these to complete as well as possible the decoration of this room."[23]

The pages of this album, like those of the two other albums devoted to Fontainebleau, were prepared in view of a publication that never saw the light of day. A design for a title page—featuring the composition of one of the oval compartments in the decor of the former bedroom of the duchesse d'Étampes [FIG. 4.10]—was completed by Percier, who incorporated the following title: "Salle de Bal / décorée de peintures / executés / d'après les dessins / de Francesco Primaticcio / par Niccolo dell'Abate / Fontainebleau / Croquis et dessins."[24] The publication would have accorded pride of place to the room's painted decor, which Percier saw as exemplary in the perfection with which its painted elements harmonized with its architecture. In the text accompanying this album, he observes: "It is above all the Ballroom that makes the greatest impression on me and takes me back to Rome...and appears to me noble and rational, it is the necessary embellished...the surfaces of the walls were covered with paintings surrounded by stuccos serving to frame them and divide them, this decoration rested on paneling rising to a height appropriate for viewing....The architecture through the grandeur and skill of its dispositions created places for the painting and sculpture that would embellish it and never obscure it."[25]

But the Ballroom at Fontainebleau, because of its monumental volume, was meant, in this didactic context, to be compared with analogous large rooms in Italian and French palaces; a page of comparative drawings introduced into the album illustrates the Sala Reggia in the Vatican, the Salone del Cinquecento in the Palazzo Vecchio in Florence, the Grand Sala dei Collegio in the Palazzo Ducale in Venice, and, finally, the Grande Salle of the Hôtel de Ville in Paris [FIG. 4.11].

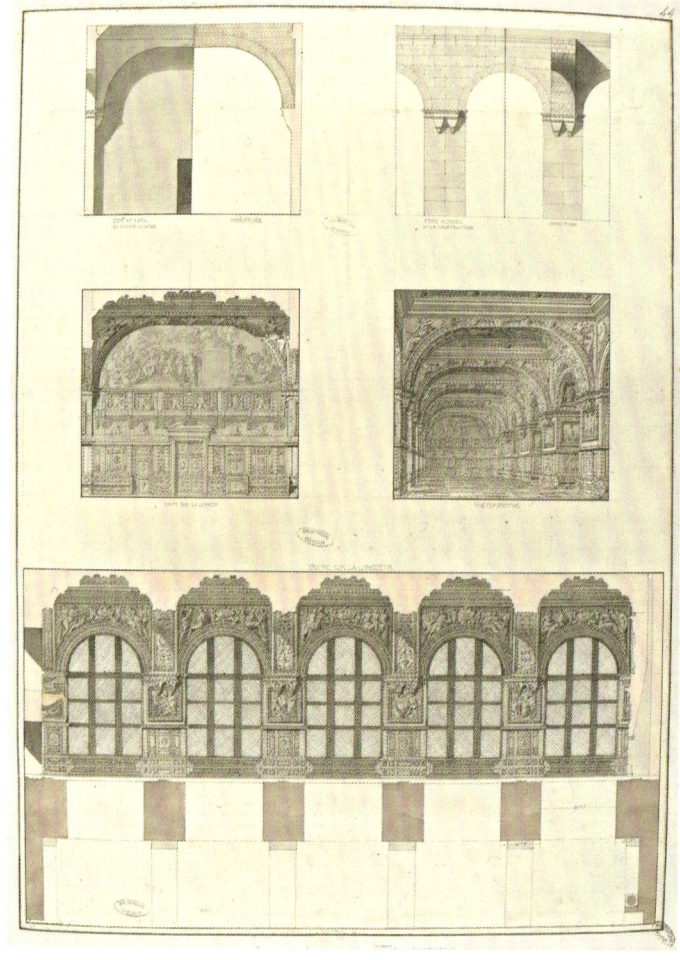

▲ **FIG. 4.8.** Charles Percier. Proposed restoration of the transverse arches in the Ballroom from the remaining consoles between the bays, château de Fontainebleau, early 19th century. Pencil, ink, and sepia wash on paper. Bibliothèque de l'Institut de France, Paris, Ms 1014, fol. 44, drawing 44.

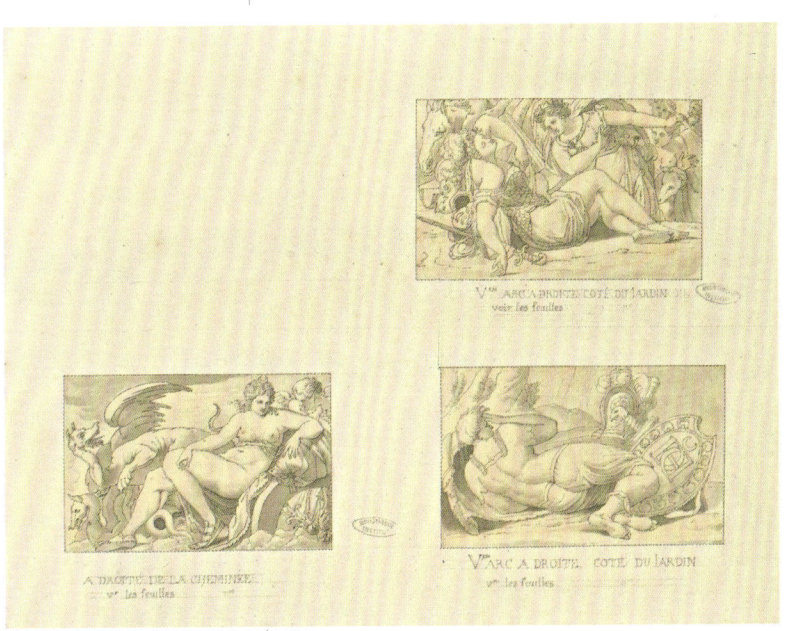
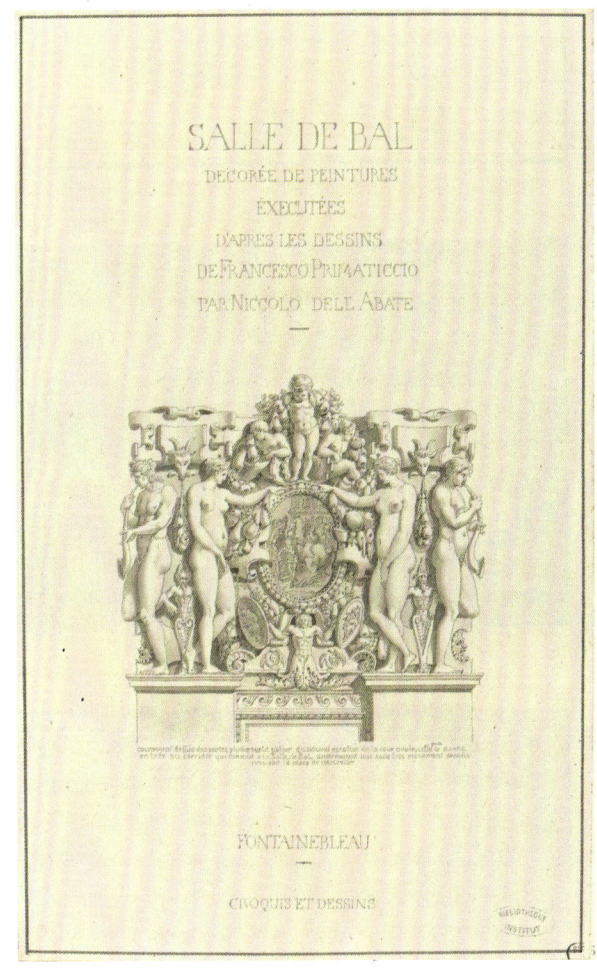

FIG. 4.9. Charles Percier. Figures from the fireplace wall and embrasures of the fifth arch on the garden side of the Ballroom, château de Fontainebleau, early 19th century. Pencil and black wash on paper. Bibliothèque de l'Institut de France, Paris, Ms 1014, fol. 35, drawing 35.

FIG. 4.10. Charles Percier. Title page, Fontainebleau Album, early 19th century. Pencil on paper. Bibliothèque de l'Institut de France, Paris, Ms 1014, fol. 4, drawing 2.

FIG. 4.11. Charles Percier. Four ballrooms: Sala Reggia, Vatican; Salone del Cinquecento, Palazzo Vecchio, Florence; Sala dei Collegio, Chamber, Palazzo Ducale, Venice; Grande Salle, Hôtel de Ville, Paris, early 19th century. Pencil, sepia wash, and watercolor on paper. Bibliothèque de l'Institut de France, Paris, Ms 1014, fol. 45, drawing 45.

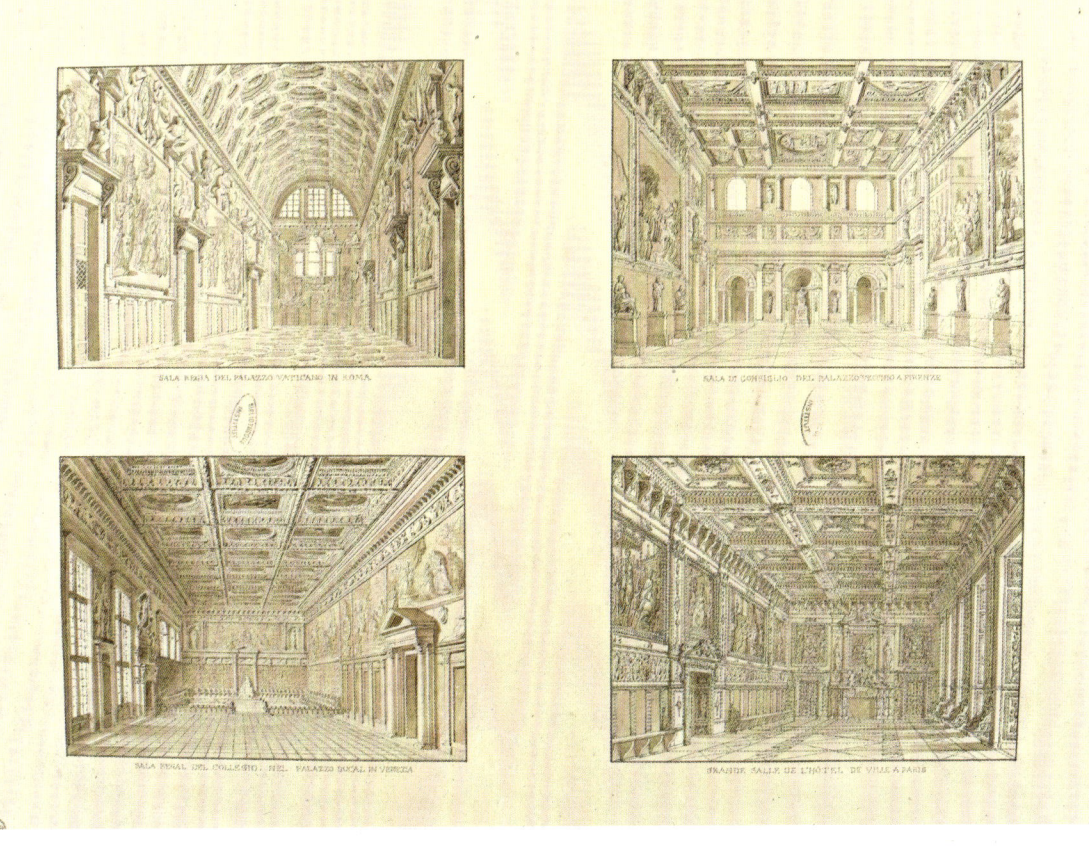

ARCHITECTURAL PATRIMONY

Beyond the exceptional interest of its painted decor, the Ballroom was pressed into service by Percier to advance a larger project: the identification of French Renaissance interiors that might withstand comparison with the great Italian examples that he so admired and would thus be valuable models when it came to creating the ideal residence of a sovereign, a notion that long haunted him.

More surprising, perhaps, is the close attention Percier paid to the decor of the Gallery of the Queen, also known as the Gallery of Diana, completed under the direction of Ambroise Dubois after 1600, most of whose painted decor would disappear under the First Empire. Percier was well aware of the relatively late date of the gallery (his title page for this album mentions it[26]), so it is clear that he did not see this as a problem; indeed, his inclusion of this ensemble among the most noteworthy in the château indicates how capacious his conception of the Renaissance was.

Here again, as with the Gallery of Francis I, it was the decorative system of this great nave-like space—262 feet long—that interested Percier. In the treatment of the walls, whose lower registers were decorated with compartmented and painted paneling and whose upper registers supported large mythological and martial compositions flanking portraits of the king and queen, he was interested only in the organizing principle and its underlying rhythms. For example, he recorded only the composition of one of the painted scenes [FIG. 4.12] and the portrait of the queen as Diana, which left it to the viewer to extrapolate the rest of the decor. However, Percier rendered the compartments and painted ornament of one section of the paneling very carefully, meticulously detailing the chromatic nuances of its camaïen decoration [FIG. 4.13].

But it was above all the vault, or rather the long ceiling subdivided into panels, that interested Percier, because of its teeming ornament. He drew half of it on a large folding sheet bound in the album, the better to convey the organizational scheme of this immense decor [FIG. 4.14]. The compositions within the compartments are indicated more or less summarily, for here again it was their inclusion within a larger decorative network that interested him. He delighted in

▸ **FIG. 4.12.** Charles Percier. Gallery of Diana, château de Fontainebleau, early 19th century. Pencil, pen, and watercolor on paper. Bibliothèque de l'Institut de France, Paris, Ms 1016, fol. 19, drawing 36.

▸ **FIG. 4.13.** Charles Percier. Dado of the Gallery of Diana, château de Fontainebleau, early 19th century. Pencil, pen, and watercolor on paper. Bibliothèque de l'Institut de France, Paris, Ms 1016, fol. 20, drawing 37.

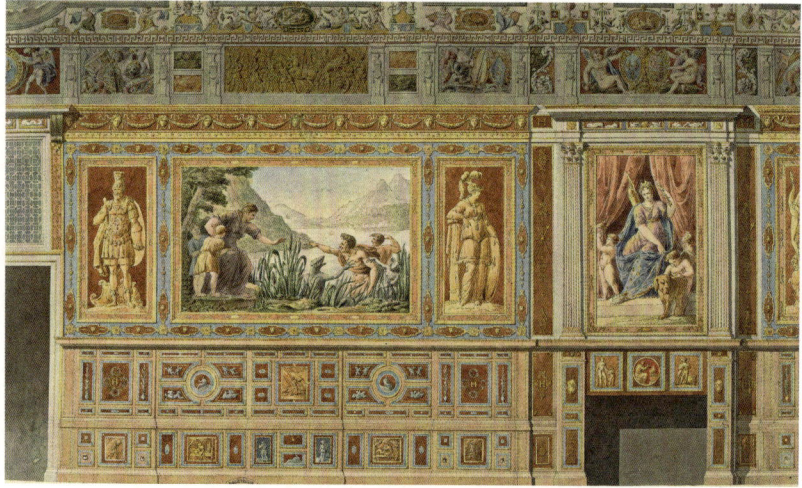

rendering the grotesque motifs within the framing elements, the compartments painted in grisaille, the medallions containing small landscapes, and above all the imbrication, the skillful integration of these various decorative figures, with their suggestion of a formidable number of different planes. He was just as attentive to—and doubtless just as enthusiastic about—the decoration of this ceiling as he had been, a few years earlier in his beloved Italy, to the decors of the loggia of the Villa Madama in Rome, the delightful Casino of Pius IV in the Vatican, the Palazzo Farnese in Caprarola, and the Palazzo Te in Mantua, a building whose formal coherence, masterminded by Giulio Romano, made a lasting impression on him.

For Charles Percier, Fontainebleau was of course not Italy, the lost paradise that he tried to keep alive in memory by conversing with his former fellow pensioners in its language. Nonetheless, as he himself said, the palace of the Valois, more than any other French monument, reminded him of a cherished moment in his recent past. When assessing Percier's interest in and attachment to Fontainebleau, which was given concrete form in this exceptional corpus of drawings, we must not neglect the role played by his nostalgia for Italy.

However, nostalgia alone does not suffice to explain the detail, attention, and acuity that characterize Percier's engagement with the architectural and decora-

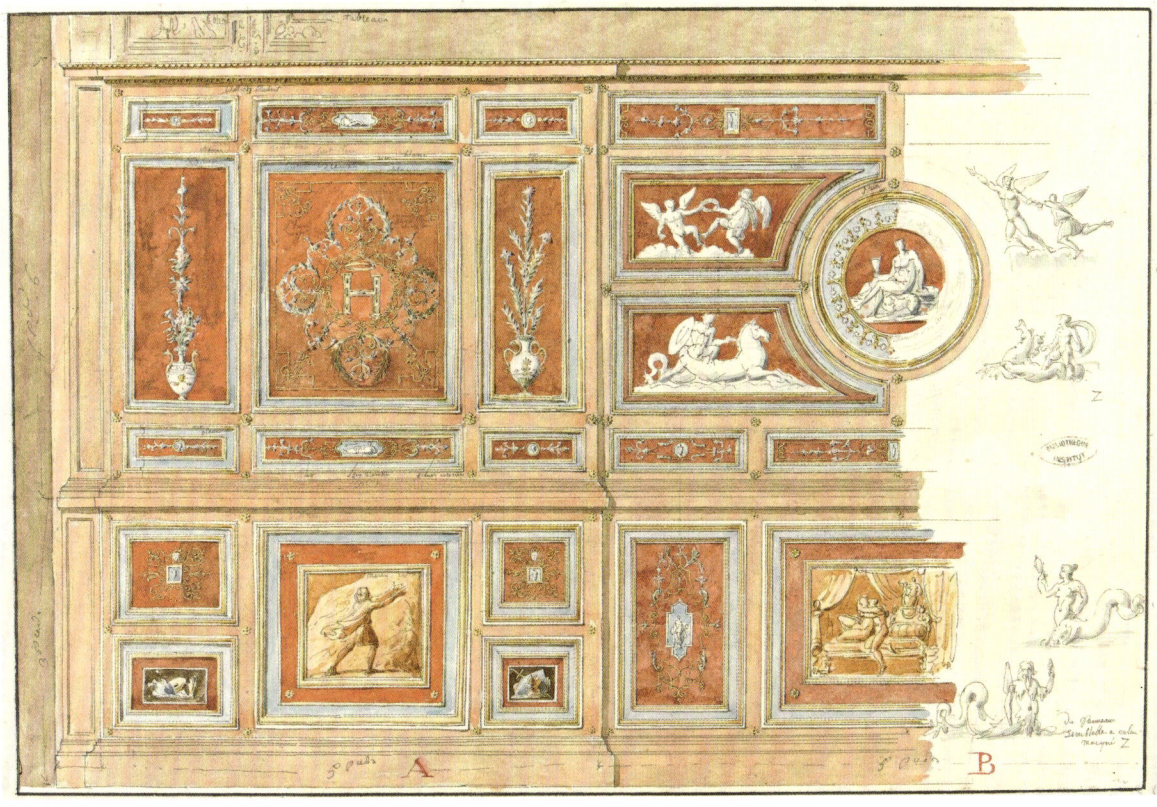

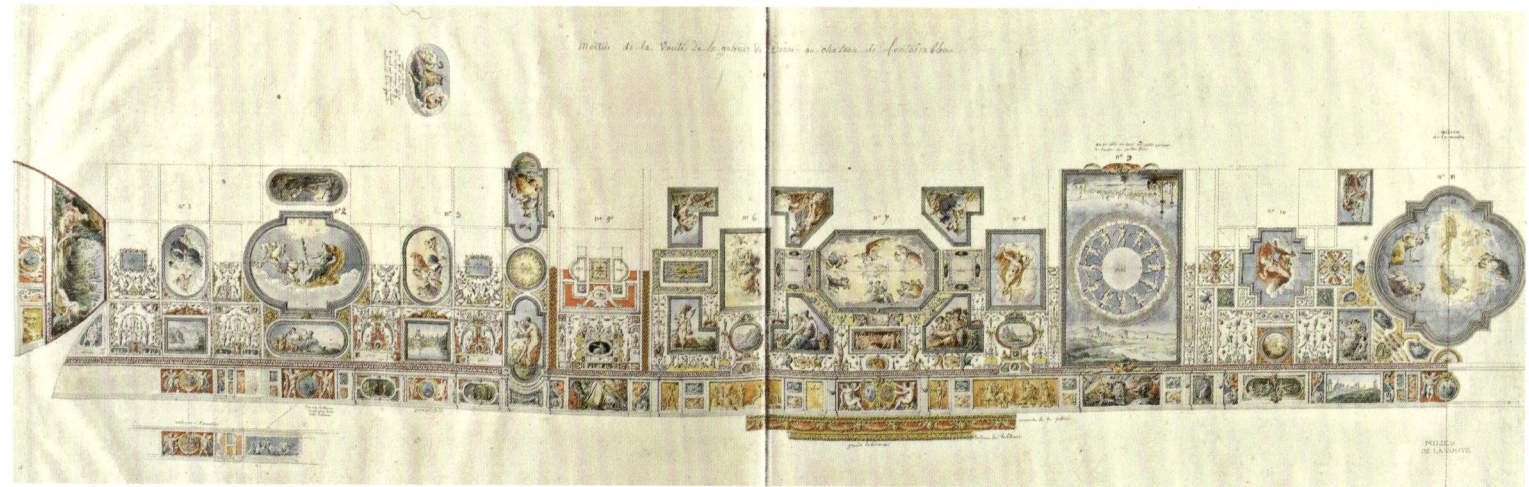

FIG. 4.14. Charles Percier. Half of the vaulted ceiling of the Gallery of Diana, château de Fontainebleau, early 19th century. Pencil, pen, and watercolor on paper. Bibliothèque de l'Institut de France, Paris, Ms 1014, fol. 5 verso, drawing 3.

tive elements of this great complex. Doubtless the château's precarious future at this time, the threats that then weighed so heavily on both its structural fabric and its grand decorative ensembles—threats that Antoine François Peyre was well placed to explicate—would have spurred Percier to heightened attention. Here he found superb examples of painted and sculpted decorations, unique of their kind and exceptionally large in scale, whose degree of integration with their architectural frameworks provided an architect smitten with ornament with much food for thought. At a time when the Revolutionary authorities were giving serious consideration to removing the frescoes from the Ballroom and the paintings from the "vault" of the Gallery of Diana, it was a matter of some urgency that they be drawn while they were still intact within their original architectural contexts, the only ones in which they made sense, and also, if possible, to argue for their preservation in situ. The many precise drawings executed by Percier, like his research into pertinent old engravings, must be understood within this very specific context.

Finally, we should also invoke the pedagogic aspect of this set of drawings. As we have already noted, Percier's Fontainebleau albums, as organized by him, were assembled in view of their eventual publication, in a form whose basic outlines are clearly indicated by their three title pages. The same intention is discernible in the album of drawings devoted to the Palazzo Te in Mantua, for which Percier also drew a title page, one that significantly accords equal importance to the patron, Federico I Gonzaga, and the artist and architect Giulio Romano. Percier, then, intended to devote an important publication to Fontainebleau and its decorative ensembles, a project that he may have abandoned when he entrusted a portion of his drawings to Baltard for his use in his own book, which appeared in 1803.

In his search for the most pertinent examples to serve as models for the ideal residence for a sovereign, at a moment when both ideals and dynasties were being renewed, it is readily comprehensible and, at base, natural that Percier should pay special attention to Fontainebleau, a palace that guaranteed the connection between the Italian ideal and the great French tradition. The publication that he had envisaged was never published, but the exceptional corpus of drawings contained in these three albums in the Institut still bears witness to Percier's ambition, and to the privileged place occupied by the "residence of kings" in the mind of one of the most influential architects of his era. ●

1 Percier returned to Paris in August 1791.
2 "C'étoit encore rempli des souvenirs de l'Italie que peu de tems après mon retour en France, je visitais le château de Fontainebleau....l'ensemble bizarre du château, comparé à ce que je venois de voir à Rome, à Florence, à Venise, enfin dans toute l'Italie, ne me satisfit pas; mais les divers parties où Serlio, le Rosso, Primaticcio, Nicolò dell'Abate avoient développé leurs talents me rappelèrent un moment ce que je venois de quitter." Manuscript at Bibliothèque de l'Institut, Ms 1014, fol. 49.
3 In his will, Percier left these three albums to his student Louis Hippolyte Lebas, who in turn left them to the library of the Institut.
4 The mounted sheets are of varying numbers and dimensions; in many cases they are complemented by drawings and inscriptions on the support page. It is clear that each page, composite or otherwise, was composed with a view to its eventual inclusion in a bound volume.
5 Louis Pierre Baltard used only a small part of the visual material assembled by Percier to illustrate the chapter devoted to Fontainebleau in his book *Paris et ses monuments mesurés*. Amaury Duval, the author of the text, had this to say about the matter: "We can state here with confidence, then, that nothing has ever been published on Fontainebleau, or perhaps on any modern building, more precise or complete than the engravings of it that we propose to offer." ("Nous pouvons donc assurer ici avec confiance, qu'il n'aura jamais été publié sur Fontainebleau, ni peut-être même sur aucun édifice moderne, rien de plus exact, rien de plus complet que les graveures que nous proposons d'en donner.") Louis Pierre Baltard, "Fontainebleau," in *Paris et ses monuments, dessinés et gravés par Baltard, architecte, avec des Descriptions historiques par le cit[oyen] Amaury-Duval* (Paris: Author, 1803–5), 2n.
6 Respectively, Ms 1014, drawing 46, and Ms 1015, drawing 30.
7 Ms 1014, folio 49.
8 On page 2 of Ms 1015, the drawing of the fireplace in the Salon of Francis I is captioned as follows: "camino della Salla Precedente la galleria di Francesco Primo—Gli bassi rilieve sono bellissimi...degli ornati sonno pieni de cose meravigliose" (fireplace in Preceding Room the gallery of Francis I—the low reliefs are very beautiful [illegible] of the ornaments are full of marvelous things). Page 17 of the same album, representing the so-called Stair of Francis I in the Oval Courtyard, bears this inscription: "Fabricate nel / tempo / di Francesco / Primo" (Made in the / period / of Francis / the First). There are many other Italian inscriptions on these drawings.

9 Certain pages in an album of drawings by Percier representing the château d'Écouen (Compiègne, Musée Vivenel) also have captions in Italian. According to Thierry Crépin-Leblond, the drawings in this album are securely dateable to 1793–94. Moreover, in October 1793 Percier wrote Maximilien Joseph Hurtault that he had just returned from Écouen, where he had seen details that "could withstand comparison with beautiful antiquities" ("pourraient figurer à côté des beaux antiques"). Cited by Hans Ottomeyer, "Das frühe Œuvre Charles Perciers (1782–1800). Zu den Anfängen des Historismus in Frankreich," PhD diss., Munich, 1981, 166.

10 "Une heureuse circonstance a facilité le travail de M. Baltard qui vouloit réunir les dessins de toutes les productions de l'art, qui servent ou ont servi à l'ornement de Fontainebleau. Il y a neuf ans, qu'un de nos architectes les plus distingués, M. Percier, partisan passionné du goût qui régnoit dans les arts pendant tout ce beau période du règne de François Ier, se plut à copier tout ce qu'il y avoit alors de plus remarquable dans le château…M. Percier a bien voulu offrir à M. Baltard tous ces précieux dessins." Baltard, "Fontainebleau," 2n.

11 Jean-Philippe Garric, *Percier et Fontaine, les architectes de Napoléon* (Paris: Belin, 2012), 20–24.

12 "les liens d'affection et de reconnaissance qui nous attachent à la mémoire de M. Peyre nous inderdisent à l'égard de cet homme habile, tous sentiments autres que ceux de la plus sincère et de la plus respectueuse admiration." Charles Percier and Pierre Fontaine, *Résidences de souverains. Parallèle entre plusieurs résidences de souverains de France, d'Allemagne, de Suède, de Russie, d'Espagne et d'Italie* (Paris: Authors, 1833), 164.

13 The plan of the château and the project to transform the tennis court into a meeting hall for the Conseil des Anciens were acquired in 2008 and 2009, respectively, by the Musée national du château de Fontainebleau.

14 Félix Herbet, "Fontainebleau révolutionnaire: Liste des personnes mises en arrestation au ci-devant château (1793–94)," *Annales de la Société historique et archéologique du Gâtinais* 25 (1907), 1–47, esp. 39–41.

15 Peyre's son-in-law, Antoine Laurent Castellan, turned the knowledge accumulated by his father-in-law to account in his book *Fontainebleau: Études pittoresques et historiques sur ce château* (Paris: Gaillot Libraire, 1840).

16 "usé graté [sic] quelques apparences de ton comme si il y avoit eu de la peinture." As a member of the Commune générale des arts, Percier was one of two architects "elected to work toward the destruction of the attributes of royalty" ("élus pour travailler à la destruction des attributs de la royauté"). See Garric, *Percier et Fontaine*, 70.

17 Half of the bronzes cast at Fontainebleau during the reign of Francis I (from molds brought back from Rome by Primaticcio) were melted down during the Revolutionary period. See Sylvia Pressouyre, "Les Fontes de Primatice à Fontainebleau," *Bulletin monumental* 127, no. 3 (1969): 223–39.

18 In any event, there are no drawings of these painted mantelpieces in the Percier album in the Musée Vivenel.

19 Two of the pages are, it is true, copies of prints by Léon Davent representing three of Primaticcio's compositions in their original state; when Percier saw them they were already seriously damaged.

20 He made do with the following notes in the margin of the perspective view of the gallery: "sculptures / Paul ponce / Paintings and medallions / painted in / fresco / by rosso / completed by Primaticcio" ("sculptures / Paul ponce / Peintures et médaillons / peints à / fresque / par le rosso / terminé par le Primatice").

21 On the critical "misfortune" of Rosso's paintings in the gallery, see Vincent Droguet, "Rosso Fiorentino à Fontainebleau: 'Personne n'a eu plus de génie et plus de feu que lui'," in *Le Roi et l'Artiste: François Ier et Rosso Fiorentino* (Paris: Réunion des musées nationaux, 2013), 90–97.

22 Page 35 bears the caption "détails de la voûte de la Porte dorée peinte par Primaticcio l'an 1528" ("details of the vault of the Porte dorée painted by Primaticcio in the year 1528"), a date Percier took from one of the capitals of the porch; in fact, the frescos must have been painted ca. 1540.

23 "étant prêt à terminer ce recueil et ayant trouvé quelques estampes gravées d'après les peintures de la salle de bal presque effacée aujourd'hui on a copié celles cy pour completer le mieux possible la décoration de cette salle." Ms 1014, drawing 35.

24 "Ballroom / decorated with paintings / executed / after drawings / by Francesco Primaticcio / by Niccolo dell'Abatte / Fontainebleau / Sketches and drawings"

25 "C'est surtout la Salle de Bal qui me fit le plus d'impression et me replaça encore une fois à Rome…et m'apparut noble et raisonnable, c'est le besoin embelli…les parois des murs étoient couverts de peinture entourées de stucs servant à les encadrer et les diviser, cette décoration reposoit sur un lambris élevé à une hauteur convenable pour voir.…L'architecture par la grandeur et la sagesse de ses dispositions préparait des places à la peinture et à la sculpture qui venoient l'embellir et jamais la voiler."

26 The title page for this album incorporates the following title: "Galerie de la reine dite de Diane par ordre d'Henry IV sur les dessins D [blank] peinte par Ambroise Dubois en MDC. Fontainebleau. Croquis" ("Gallery of the queen known as [gallery] of Diana built by order of Henry IV to designs D [blank] painted by Ambroise Dubois in MDC. Fontainebleau. Sketches).

THE ABBEY OF SAINT-DENIS[1]

(originally published as "L'Abbaye de Saint-Denis" in *Monuments historiques*, 1936)

GEORGES HUARD

M. Percier, whose predilection for the arts of antiquity is beyond dispute, was above all a man of taste, and, better yet, a man of feeling and sensitivity. Upon his return from Italy, he saw the church of Saint-Denis pillaged, devastated; he could not help but be moved upon seeing the scattered remains of so many artistic monuments accumulated over several centuries.... Occasionally we had the good fortune to hear M. Percier talk about this period in his artistic life; he was, perhaps without realizing it, the first who wanted to see and cultivate the appreciation of our old national art.

EUGÈNE VIOLLET-LE-DUC[2]

During his restoration of the abbey church of Saint-Denis, Eugène Viollet-le-Duc used various drawings of the building made during the Revolution by the architect Percier. He mentions the drawings several times in his *Dictionnaire raisonné* and thanks the architect Alexandre Villain, Percier's nephew, for having lent them to him....[3] The volume [containing these drawings], a large in-folio, is bound in green parchment and contains forty-seven leaves.[4] The first thirty are mounted with drawings of the château d'Ecouen and the tomb of Anne de Montmorency; the seventeen others pertain to the abbey church of Saint-Denis. This second part of the volume contains simple pencil sketches, lightly executed wash drawings, and highly finished renderings heightened with watercolor, representing various parts of the buildings, a few royal tombs, principally that of Dagobert, and stained-glass windows, floor pavings, and altars in apsidal chapels. None of these drawings, of which there are about forty, is dated. According to Viollet-le-Duc, they were executed in 1797.[5] However, we will see that the studies of the tomb of Dagobert must date from between brumaire and pluviôse of year II [between October 1794 and February 1795] and that those pertaining to the chapels might be slightly later than the date assigned them by Viollet-le-Duc, since the works depicted in them were not moved to the Musée des monuments français before fructidor year VII [August–September 1799].

One cannot insist too much on the interest aroused by these drawings, the work of an architect who, more than any other of his time, was to some extent capable of understanding and appreciating monuments of the Middle Ages. Was his interest in them stimulated by the teaching of his master Julien David Le Roy? What is certain is that the buildings of this period were already attracting his attention at the time of his departure for Rome in 1786.[6] Decidedly, his preferences always ran to ancient and Italian art and, among French buildings, to those of the Renaissance. It is nonetheless certain that he built a Gothic chapel for a Polish prince and that his decoration of Notre-Dame for the coronation in 1804 was strongly inspired by the same style.[7] In any case, no artist of his time knew better how to draw medieval monuments, as is demonstrated by his renderings of the cathedrals of Paris, Chartres, and Rouen. When, in thermidor year VIII (July–August 1800), Alexandre Lenoir protested to Chaptal against the demolition of the abbey church of Cluny, he implored him to at least have Percier execute a plan, sections, and elevations of the building, as he was the artist most capable of "bequeathing to posterity the memory of a monument as great as those of the Greeks, [but] which was built by the French."[8]

By that time, relations between [Percier and Lenoir] must have been well established. When the Musée des monuments français was still nothing but a simple depot, Percier was already drawing there.[9] He would continue to draw there until the Restoration, and it was one of his students, the architect Biet, who dedicated the collection to his master, who had executed the precious line engravings that enable us to have a clear idea of the rooms and Elysian Gardens of the Petits-Augustins.[10] In prairial year VII [May–June 1799], Lenoir called Percier his "comrade," his "special friend."[11] They visited Anet together[12]; at Gaillon, Percier had his inspector, Colliot, stand in for him.[13] To illustrate publications by Lenoir,[14] [Percier] drew and engraved a number of plates, many of them devoted to imagined arrangements.

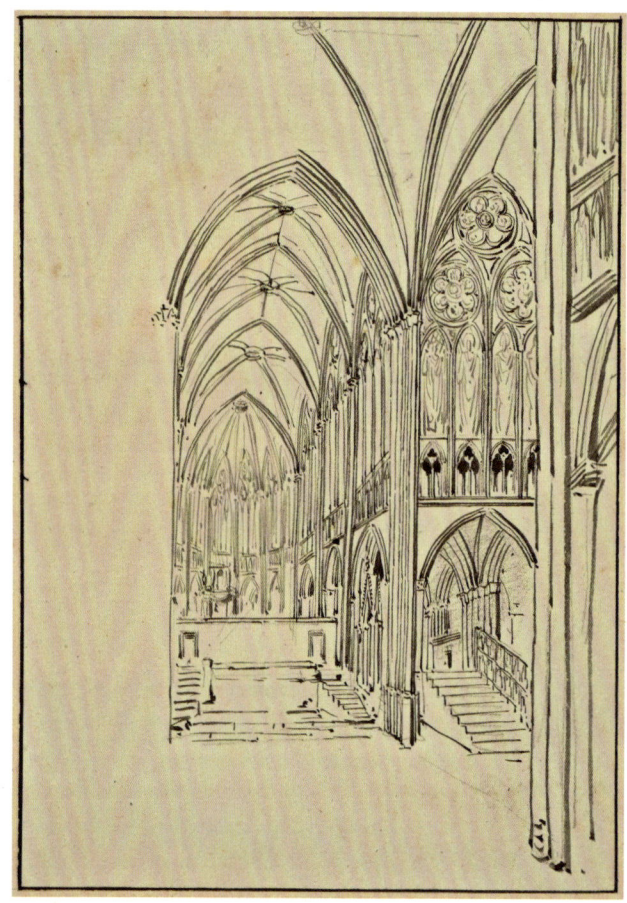

◁ FIG. 4A.1.
▷ FIG. 4A.2.

Although they depict a building that survives intact, some drawings, representing the interior architecture of the monument (the abbey church of Saint-Denis), are nonetheless extremely useful, for they show us elevations that reveal the disposition of its eastern part, hitherto known only through engraved plans dating from the early eighteenth century. Percier's plans and sketches help us to understand what were known as the core and chevet of Saint-Denis.... The most precious of these drawings (fol. 43 [FIG. 4A.1]), unfortunately made after the destruction of the high altar in ventôse or germinal of year II [February–March 1794], shows at the beginning of the chevet an enclosure pierced by two doors reached via two flights of stairs…; [the stairway] in the southern arm of the transept is also visible. Above the enclosure we see the so-called Altar of the Holy Martyrs or of Saint Denis, whose marble retable, erected under Louis XIII, occupies the full width of the central chevet arcade, rising as high as the clerestory windows. The royal tombs aligned in front of the high altar have disappeared in accordance with the decree of the Convention, with the exception of the monument to Dagobert, which was not dismantled until the beginning of the Consulate....

These dismantlements and transports, to which we must add Lenoir's application of a coat of oil paint, resulted in the removal from [Dagobert's] tomb of a very interesting

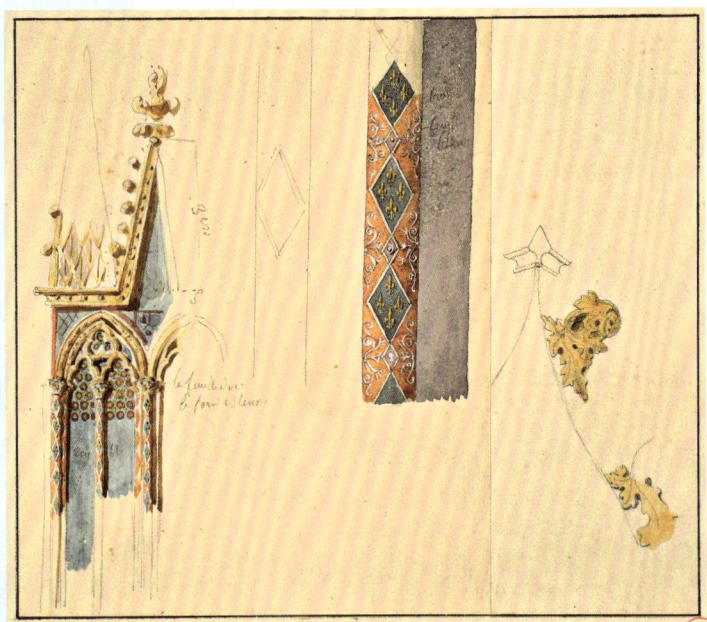

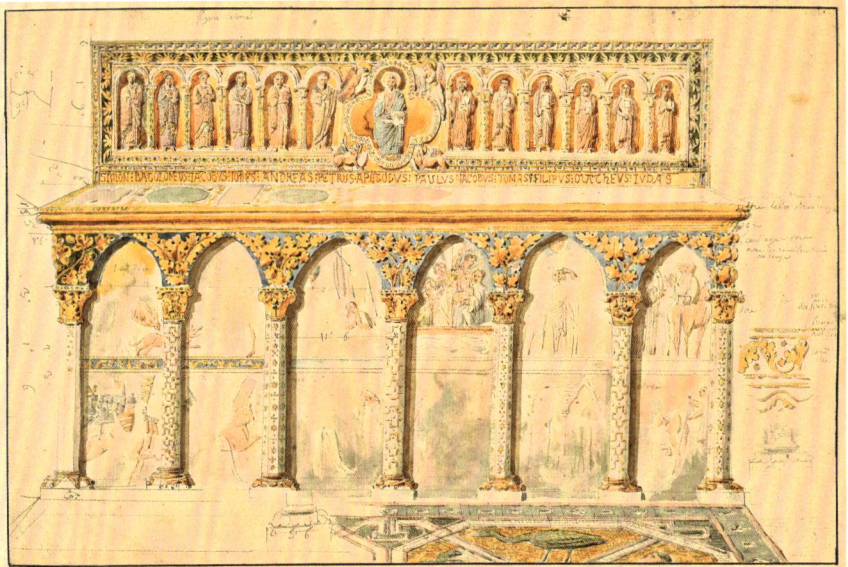

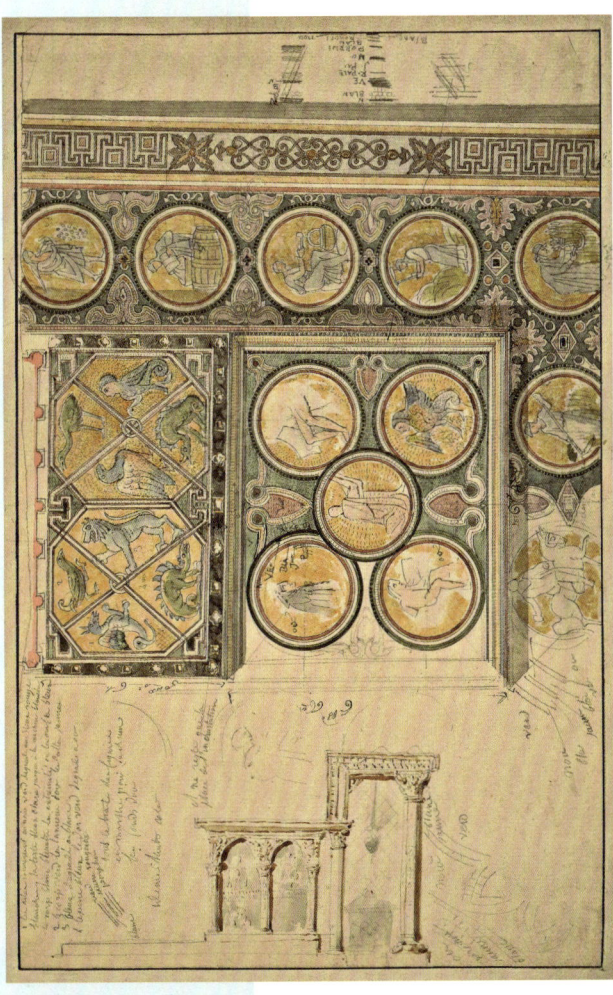

characteristic: its polychromy, a sufficient amount of which survived in year III to enable Percier to record important aspects of it. One watercolor, representing the upper portion of one its sides (fol. 37 [FIG. 4A.2]), shows us the blue ground speckled with red, the red colonettes with rhomboids containing fleur-de-lis, the arches and their tracery, the pinnacle turrets, the finials heightened with gold.

Also dating from the abbacy of Suger—or at least from the second half

▲ FIG. 4A.3.
◀ FIG. 4A.4.

of the twelfth century—is the mosaic paving of the chapel of Saint-Fermin, several parts of which, removed by Lenoir, are now in the Musée de Cluny.... Percier's drawing records both the overall design and the details of this flooring for posterity (fol. 38 [FIG. 4A.3]).

The second drawing, heightened with color, is a highly finished rendering of the altar of the chapel of Saint-Fermin (fol. 38; [FIG. 4A.4]), the principal fragments of which, mostly from the retable, are preserved at Saint-Denis. The anterior surface and the two sides of the block are decorated with polychrome arcatures whose colonettes are alternately cylindrical and octagonal, and whose spandrels are filled with foliage; the blind faces are decorated with two levels of half-effaced paintings that represent, according to Viollet-le-Duc, the siege of the château de Picquigny and Dagobert's conquest of the relics of Saint-Fermin.[15]

The details, they are the essential things. Consequently, why not use them in imagined arrangements? Why shouldn't Percier enshrine a statue within a tabernacle and install on the mosaic floor of the chapel of Saint-Fermin an altar sheltering gisant figures and surmounted by two superimposed retables (fol. 41v [FIG. 4A.5])? This is just an arrangement on paper, but Lenoir would act no differently at the Musée des monuments français... ●

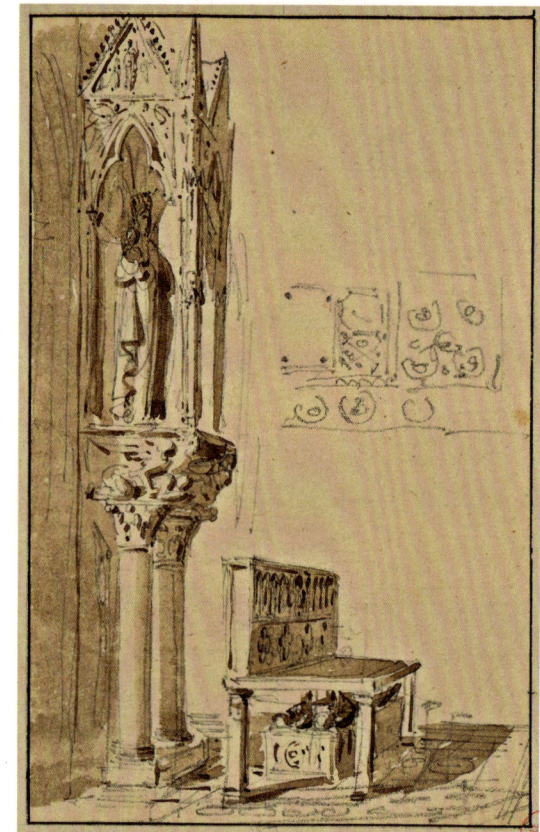

◁ FIG. 4A.5.

1 The texts and illustrations published here are taken from an article by Georges Huard published in the periodical *Monuments historiques* in 1936. See Georges Huard, "Percier et l'abbaye de Saint-Denis." *Les Monuments Historiques de la France* (1936): 5:134–44; 6: 173–82.
2 Eugène Viollet-le-Duc, *Dictionnaire raisonné de l'architecure française du XIe au XVIe siècle* (Paris: Bance, Morel, 1854–68), 2:40, no. 1.
3 From Alexandre Villain (d. 1884), the album passed to his nephew, Alexandre Sorel, president of the Tribunal Civile of Compiègne, who in 1901, near death, donated it to the library of that city. See Viollet-le-Duc, *Dictionnaire raisonné*, 2:40, 262–63; 5:14–16; 6:404; 9:32–35, 447–48.
4 The images in this album of Percier sketches date to the 1790s. The album is now in Compiègne, Musée Vivenel, inv. 6022.
5 Viollet-le-Duc, *Dictionnaire raisonné*, 2:40, 262; 6:404; 9:32.
6 Jeanne, Duportal, "Charles Percier 1764–1838," in *Charles Percier. Reproduction de dessins conservés à la Bibliothèque de l'Institut* (Paris: Maurice Rousseau, 1931), 12–13.
7 Desiré Raoul-Rochette, "Percier, Sa vie et ses ouvrages," in *Revue des deux mondes* 4, no. 24 (October 15, 1840): 261, 263.
8 "laisser à la posterité le souvenir d'un monument aussi grand que ceux des Grecs, qui fut bâti par les Français." *Archives du musée des monuments français. Inventaire général des richesses d'art de la France* (Paris: E. Plon, 1883–97), 1:180.
9 Ibid., 1:24.
10 Joseph Etienne Biet and Jean Pierre Brès, *Souvenirs du musée des monuments français. Collection de 40 dessins perspectifs gravés au trait...*
11 "camarade"; "ami particulier," 1:142, 157.
12 *Archives du musée des monuments français*, 1:142, 154.
13 Ibid., 1:154, 157. Editor's note: It was Colliot, not Percier, who made the plans and drawings needed to reconstruct the portal from Gaillon at the Musée des monuments français.
14 Principally for Alexandre Lenoir, *Musée des monumens français, ou Description historique et chronologique des statues en marbre et en bronze, bas-reliefs et tombeaux des hommes et des femmes célèbres, pour servir à l'histoire de France et à celle de l'art* (Paris: Author, 1800–1821).
15 Viollet-le-Duc, *Dictionnaire raisonné*, 2:43.

THE MUSÉE DES MONUMENTS FRANÇAIS

Composition and the Art of Context

JEAN-PHILIPPE GARRIC

It has long been known that Percier and Alexandre Lenoir were in contact with one another, but their interaction is sparsely documented and has been little studied, probably because it is inconsistent with the common view of Percier as inventor of the Empire style and exclusive collaborator with Fontaine. Jeanne Duportal dated the beginning of Percier's relationship with Lenoir to 1793, a view corroborated in part by Georges Huard.[1] More recently, Giovanna d'Amia, after completing a thorough study of the archives of the Musée des monuments français, was the first to demonstrate the importance of the collaboration between the two men.[2] Finally, the catalogue of the Alexandre Lenoir exhibition, organized in 2016 at the Louvre, presented an opportunity to propose a synthetic overview of the question.[3]

Although Percier produced many drawings for Lenoir and assisted him in his choices and construction projects at the museum, he was neither the first nor the only architect to work on renovations there. Toward the end of 1795, when the old convent of the Petits-Augustins officially became the Musée des monuments français, the architect Marie Joseph Peyre was put in charge of its maintenance and of a few structural modifications, notably the construction of two doors for the rooms devoted, respectively, to the sixteenth and seventeenth centuries and a semi-dome for the fifteenth-century room.[4] But in June 1800, Percier was officially named architect of the site, and he took on responsibility for drafting "plans, moldings, profiles, and in general everything pertaining to architectural stereotomy" in concert with the museum's director, Alexandre Lenoir [FIG. 4B.1]. Lenoir then informed the architects and contractors of the Petits-Augustins that the minister had appointed Percier in view of his "giving the architecture of the museum…the character appropriate to the physiognomy of the [various] centuries" that he wanted to "portray."[5] The two men had long been acquainted; they had both frequented Malmaison when work was under way there, and they had visited Anet together[6]; moreover, drawings made by Percier at the Abbey of Saint-Denis confirm that their first collaboration took place in 1795.[7]

Percier's interventions at the Petits-Augustins—which were few, in

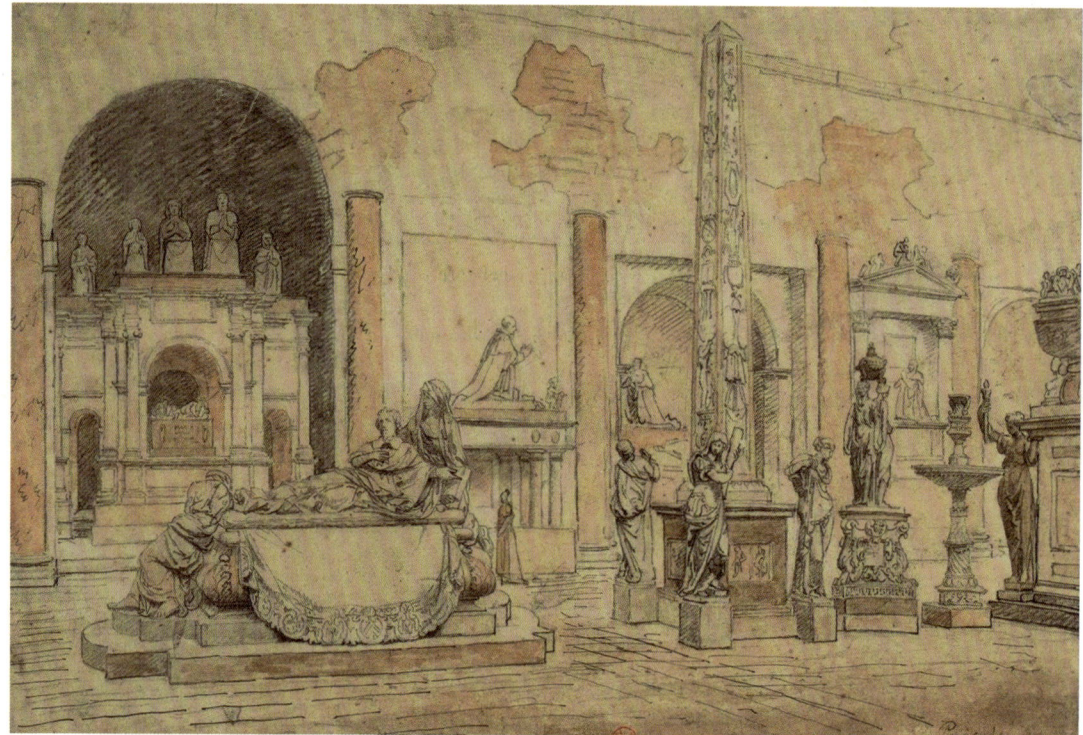

any case—are poorly documented, but we can safely attribute to him those parts that he himself engraved for the catalogue-cum-guide to the museum's collection:[8] the installation of fragments from the châteaux of Gaillon and Anet and, above all, the more ambitious and original project to create an ensemble of three courtyards adjacent to the extant complex [FIG. 4B.2]. The overall plan of this design was first engraved about 1802, "Dedicated to Citizen Chaptal, Minister of the Interior, by Alexandre Lenoir, administrator of this Museum."[9] The first state of the plate is unsigned, but a second state published in 1805—this time without a dedication to Chaptal, who opposed the proclamation of the Empire, had resigned in the interim—bears the unequivocal Latin indication "Percier del[ineavit] et sc[ulpsit]." This secures Percier's paternity of both the drawing of the plan and the engraving.[10] Four complementary plates offer more detailed renderings of the architecture of the first courtyard and the barrel-

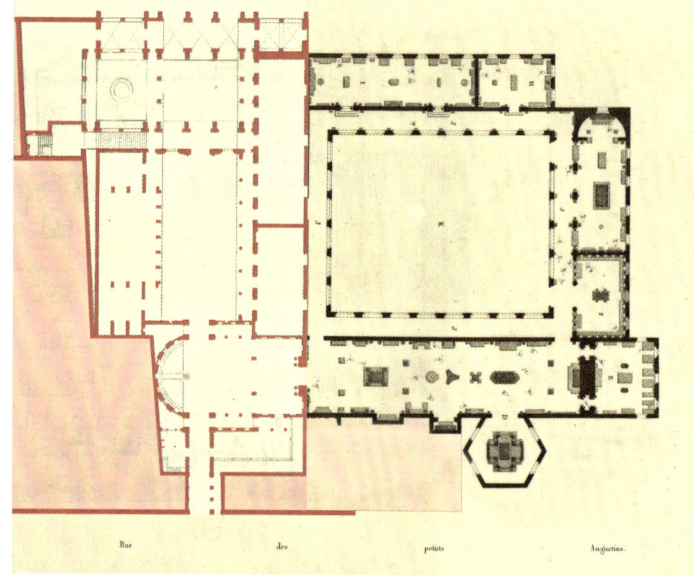

▷ FIG. 4B.1. Charles Percier. View of the 16th–17th-centuries gallery, Musée des monuments français, 1809. Pencil and watercolor on paper. Bibliothèque nationale de France, Département des Estampes et de la Photographie, Paris, VE-53 (C) 948. Cat. 36.

◁ FIG. 4B.2. Charles Percier. Project for an addition to the Musée des monuments français incorporating three courtyards, ca. 1802. This image combines the plan engraved ca. 1802 in rose with the plan of the museum published in Joseph Étienne Biet and Jean Pierre Brès, Souvenirs du musée des monuments français (Paris: Authors, 1821).

vaulted entry passage leading from the rue des Petits-Augustins,[11] notably a view from the street through the vestibule that could have come straight from Percier and Fontaine's book on Roman palaces [FIG. 4B.3].[12]

This project, hitherto ignored in the literature on the complex, was first

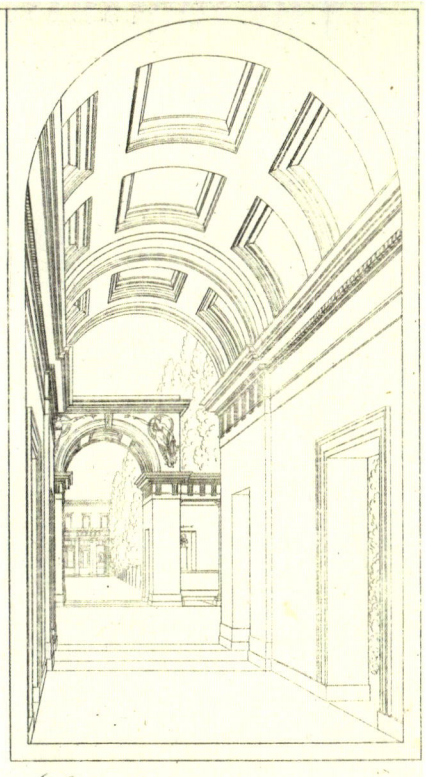

▷ **FIG. 4B.3.** Charles Percier. View of the entryway leading from the street to the first courtyard. From Alexandre Lenoir, *Description historique et chronologique des monumens de sculpture réunis au musée des monumens français* (Paris: Author, 1805), vol. 4, pl. 160. Cat. 37a.

of all a serious instance of disloyalty. At a moment when work was beginning on the rue de Rivoli and the two friends, joint architects to the government, were designing interiors for General Moreau, Percier alone drafted this significant project for a close friend, Alexandre Lenoir, for whom Fontaine had scarce affection and who goes completely unmentioned in his diary. That said, it is a remarkable architectural composition, in both its form and its program. The very idea of a series of museum courtyards organized by period and conceived for the presentation of elements taken from earlier buildings was without precedent. It anticipates the Cloisters (1934–39), the outpost of the Metropolitan Museum at the northern tip of Manhattan. But the didactic intention to illustrate the fourteenth, fifteenth, and sixteenth centuries is more directly linked to the educational aspirations of French museums in the wake of the Revolution. The first courtyard was organized around the façade at the sixteenth-century château d'Anet, the sole element of the plan to be erected (it remains in situ). The second was intended for the façades of the château de Gaillon[13] [FIG. 4B.4]. The third was conceived for the presentation of Gothic architecture—then called "arabic" architecture, in conformity with contemporary hypotheses about the eastern origins of Gothic—represented by elements seemingly unconnected to any known monument.[14]

The engraving is rudimentary, but it suffices to demonstrate the extreme sophistication of the overall plan. Instead of proposing three courtyards within which the historical architectural elements would be presented, the architect opted to incorporate these pre-existing components into their elevations. This approach dictated certain dimensions and dispositions, which generated binding constraints in addition to those already imposed by the irregular terrain and the extant convent buildings, which irrevocably established, for example, the point of entry into the old church.

It is interesting to consider this plan alongside that of Percier's 1786 Prix de Rome project (SEE FIG. 2.8). The comparison makes it possible to measure the difference between an autonomous academic composition—in this case, a building intended to house the royal academies—and one for which the architect had to exercise his skill to work within a pre-existing built context. Beyond this fundamental difference, however, it reveals many common features: the juxtaposition of symmetrical, independent parts arrayed along the grand axes of the composition and separated from one another by spaces for circulation; a doubling of the principal axis by galleries that constitute parallel axes; a dialectic between solid walls and isolated points of support; and finally, the importance accorded pilasters and the ends of walls perpendicular to the principal walls.

The difference between the two plans points to the realities that shaped monumental architecture in Paris during the first half of the nineteenth century. Designs oscillated between the grand abstract compositions of academic competitions and the need, in a design intended for the real world, of effecting ingenious negotiations with extant structures. Such a skill reached its culmination in the designs for the Bibliothèque nationale by Henri Labrouste, the Conservatoire des arts et métiers by Léon Vaudoyer, and the palais de Justice by Joseph Louis Duc and Étienne Théodore Dommey. ●

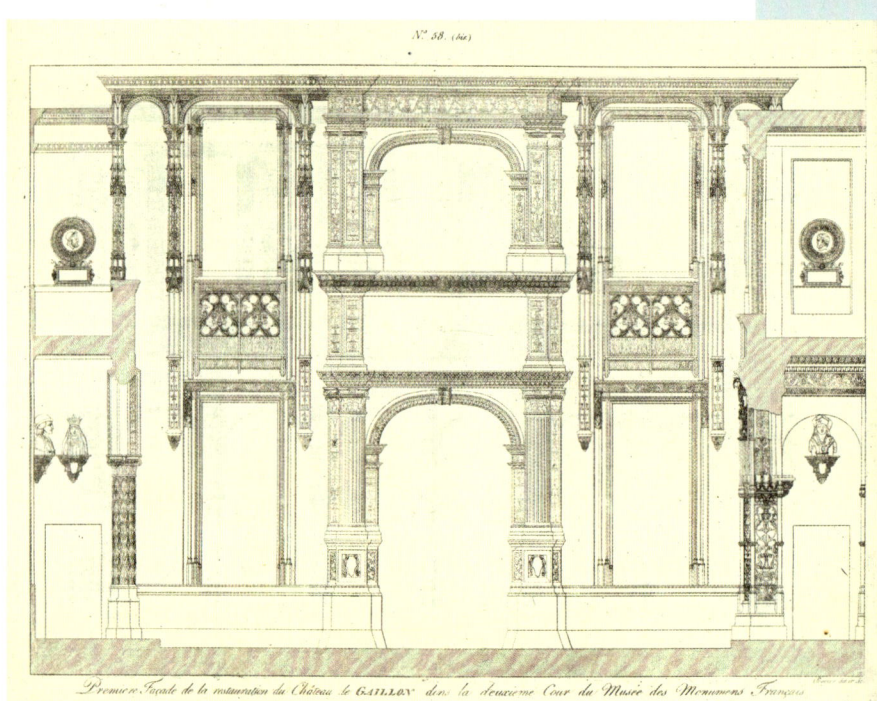

▼ FIG. 4B.4. Charles Percier. View of a façade from the château de Gaillon meant to be remounted in the second courtyard of the proposed addition to the Musée des monuments français. From Alexandre Lenoir, *Description historique et chronologique des monumens de sculpture réunis au musée des monumens français* (Paris: Author, 1805), vol. 4, pl. 163. Cat. 37b.

1 Jeanne Duportal, "Charles Percier 1764–1838," in *Charles Percier. Reproduction de dessins conservés à la Bibliothèque de l'Institut* (Paris: Maurice Rousseau, 1931), 39.
2 Giovanna D'Amia. "Memoria e rappresentazione della storia nel Museo dei Monumenti Francesi di Alexandre Lenoir," in *Memoria, identità, luogo. Il progetto della memoria*, ed. Davide Borsa (Milan: 2012), 523–48; *Archives du Musée des monuments français. Inventaire général des richesses d'art de la France* (Paris: E. Plon et Cie, 1883–97) [hereafter AMMF].
3 Geneviève Bresc and Béatrice de Chancel Bardelot, eds., *Alexandre Lenoir et le Musée des monuments français* (Paris: Musée du Louvre / Institut national d'histoire de l'art, 2016); Jean-Philippe Garric, "Le monument à La Pérouse: documenter la démarche d'Henri Labrouste," in *Le dessin d'architecture dans tous ses états II. Le dessin d'architecture, document ou monument?*, ed. Claude Mignot, 97–106 (Paris: Salon du dessin, 2016).
4 On the doors, see AMMF, 3:45, 5:4; on the apse, see Alexandre Lenoir, *Musée des monumens français ou description historique et chronologique des statues en marbre et en bronze, bas-reliefs et tombeaux des hommes et femmes célèbres, pour servir à l'histoire de France* (Paris: Author, 1800–1821), 7:207: ("Le cul de four qui termine cette salle de manière agréable, est de l'invention de M. Peyre le jeune, architecte" ["The apse that terminates this room so agreeably is an invention of M. Peyre le jeune, architect"]).
5 "plans, moulures, profils et en général tout ce qui tient à la stéréotomie de l'architecture"; "donner à l'architecture du musée…le caractère qui convient à la physionomie des siècles"; "peindre." ≠ 2 (June 16, 1800): 84; as cited in Georges Huard, "Percier et l'abbaye de Saint-Denis," *Les Monuments Historiques de la France* 1 (1936): 5: 134–44; 6: 173–82 (this quote on p. 136).
6 AMMF (May 23, 1799), 1: 85.
7 Huard, "Percier et l'abbaye de Saint-Denis," 135.
8 Lenoir, *Musée des monumens français*.
9 "Dédié au Cit. Chaptal Ministre de l'Intérieur, par Alexandre Lenoir, administrateur de ce Musée." BnF, Département des Cartes et Plans, GE D-1762; http://gallica.bnf.fr/ark:/12148/btv1b84406482.r=mus%C3%A9e+des+monuments+fran%C3%A7ais.langFR.
10 Lenoir, *Musée des monumens français*, 4:pl. 165.
11 Ibid., pls. 160, 160B, 161, 162.
12 Charles Percier and Pierre Fontaine, *Palais, maisons et autres édifices modernes dessinés à Rome; publiés à Paris, l'an VI de la République française (1798, v. st.)* (Paris: Authors, 1798).
13 Lenoir, *Musée des monumens français*, 4: pls. 163, 164.
14 Ibid., pl. 166.

ARCHITECT OF
THE BOOK

CHAPTER 5

GRAPHIC ART AS MATRIX

JEAN-PHILIPPE GARRIC

Percier's most remarkable achievements, given that he's an architect, are his drawings for the editions of Horace and the Fables *of La Fontaine published by Didot.*
ALEXANDRE LENOIR, 1805[1]

GIVEN THE EXTRAORDINARY RANGE OF HIS ACTIVITIES, FROM THE design of buildings, furnishings, and book ornaments to the staging of grand imperial festivities, how are we to make sense of the versatility of Charles Percier? Between the universal artist of the Renaissance and the brilliant contemporary jack-of-all-trades, what conception of the creative intelligence casts light on the singularity of a practice that far exceeded the bounds of architecture? Where should we look for the unifying thread in a production that is so large and various, as eclectic in its range of interests and points of reference as it is powerful in its capacity for synthesis?

As surprising as this might seem, the emphasis on Percier's graphic production in this chapter's epigraph was not unusual. Ten years earlier, a critic of the Salon of the year IV (1795) had already drawn attention, in four lines of verse, to Percier's singular penchant for graphic accumulation bordering on extravagance:

5 GRAPHIC ART AS MATRIX

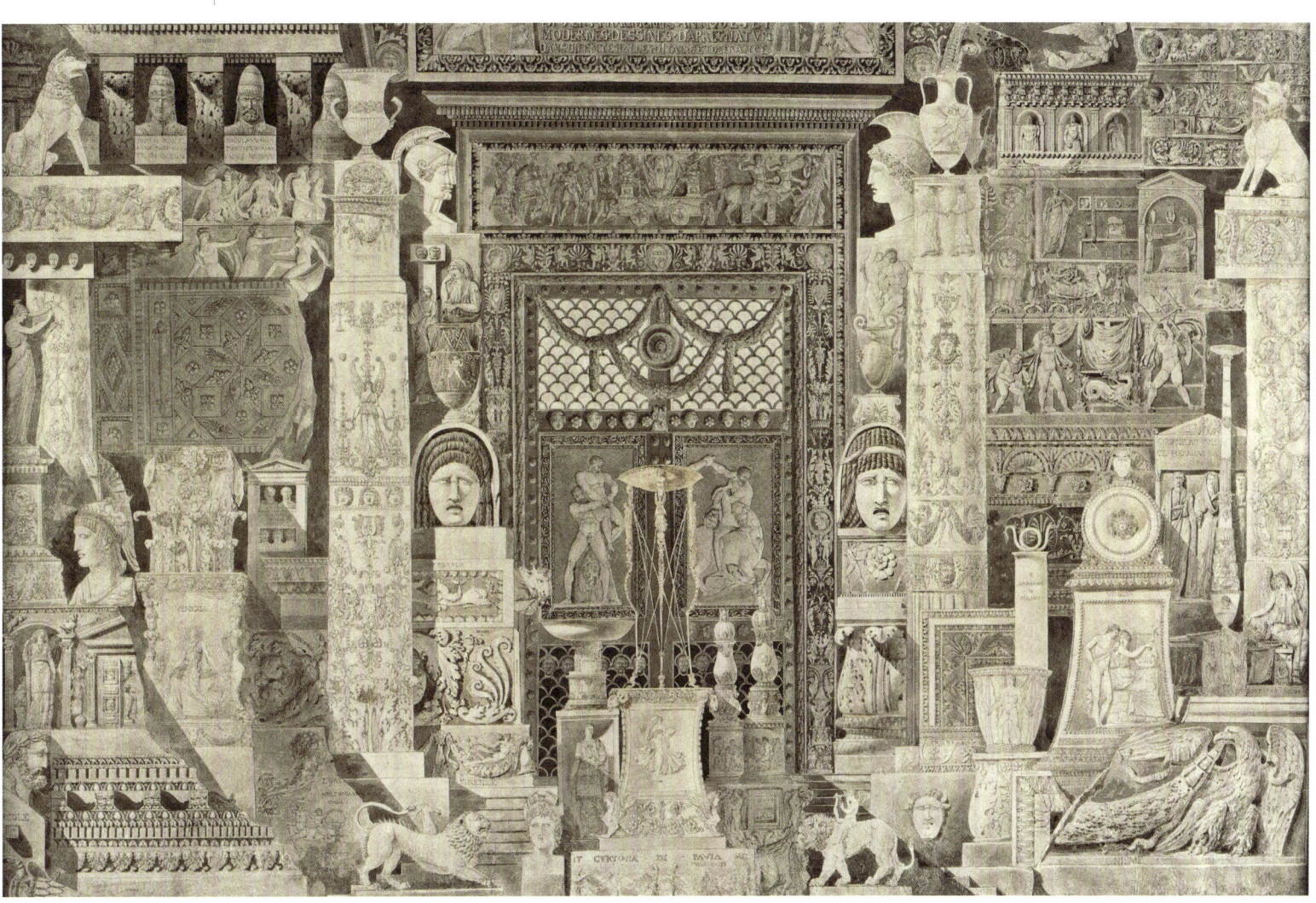

▲ FIG. 5.1. Charles Percier. *Various Modern and Antique Fragments from Different Cities in Italy and France Drawn from Nature*, 1791. Pen and brown ink, gray and ochre wash on paper. Musée du Louvre, Paris, RF TGF 52751. Cat. 39.

> *Percier*, in details multiplied with zest,
> Proves that he loves drawing best.
> He is—not to flatter—a bit confused.
> Knowing when to stop: a gift that him eludes.[2]

The anonymous author, whose irony is tinged with empathy, points to a compulsive passion for details and an unchecked penchant for drawing. We don't know what composition occasioned these lines, but we do know that it wasn't the work of a beginner. In September 1791, immediately after returning to France, Percier exhibited, at the first Revolutionary Salon that was open to all artists, a large wash drawing in ghostly shades of gray, effectively, the mental self-portrait of a newly repatriated Prix de Rome winner, his memory swamped with ancient fragments [FIG. 5.1].

In this sheet, an imposing door—shut to contain the superabundance of ornament—marks the central axis, flanked by symmetrically disposed piles and vertical groupings. But the implied spatial recession is contradicted by the contiguous distribution of forms across the foreground, as well as by the clear,

▽ **FIG. 5.2.** Charles Percier. *Archaeological composition: "8th year of the united and indivisible Republic,"* ca. 1799–1800. Pen and sepia wash on paper. École nationale supérieure des beaux-arts, Paris, PC31733.

◁ **FIG. 5.3.** Charles Percier. Frontispiece for fascicle 8, Percier and Fontaine, *Palais, maisons et autres édifices modernes dessinés à Rome* (Paris: Authors, 1798), pl. 44. Watercolor over etching. Private collection, Paris. Cat. 47.

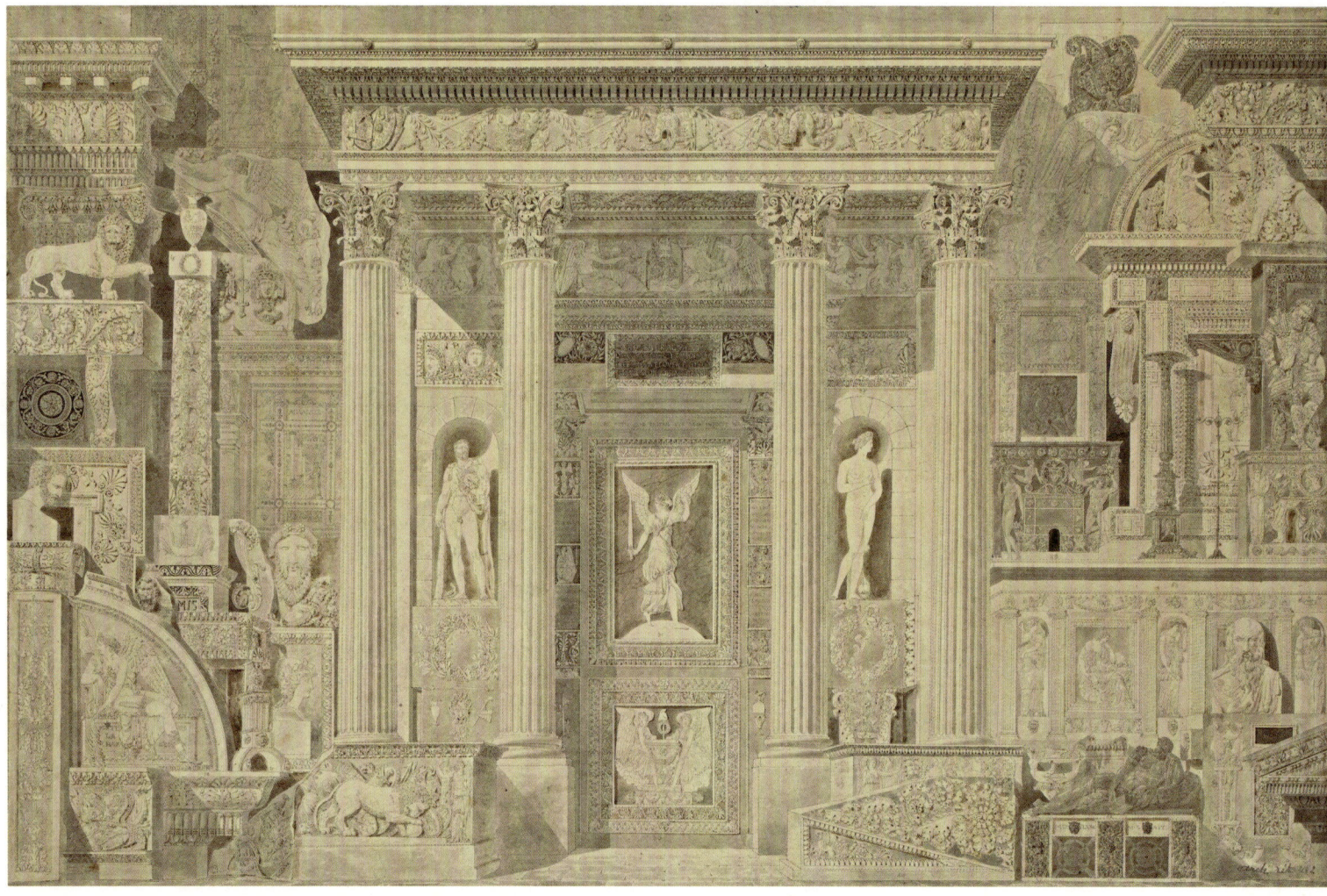

unvarying light. The composition as a whole oscillates between the evocation of depth—notably by means of cast shadows and gradations of value, from extremely bright to quite dark—and the flattening effect produced by the side-by-side juxtaposition of delicately rendered antiquarian motifs.

We find the same characteristics in another drawing, this one dating from about 1800: extreme linear precision, a profusion of ornament, symmetry—this time centered on a Corinthian portico—and a tension between perspectival construction and a mosaic of motifs that reasserts two-dimensionality [FIG. 5.2]. The handling of the central door epitomizes this contradiction; the interior of its bay, too pale to be a true opening, is blocked by a winged Victory atop a massive base.

These two examples illustrate ad nauseam a mania for drawing that, in its marked preference for ornamental linearity, is readily distinguishable from Renaissance *disegno*. Percier, in his many works, never attempted portraiture, and he rendered the human figure only in narrative headpieces and other decorative elements. This orientation was a direct consequence of his initial training at the École gratuite de dessin, where he took his first steps as a youth,

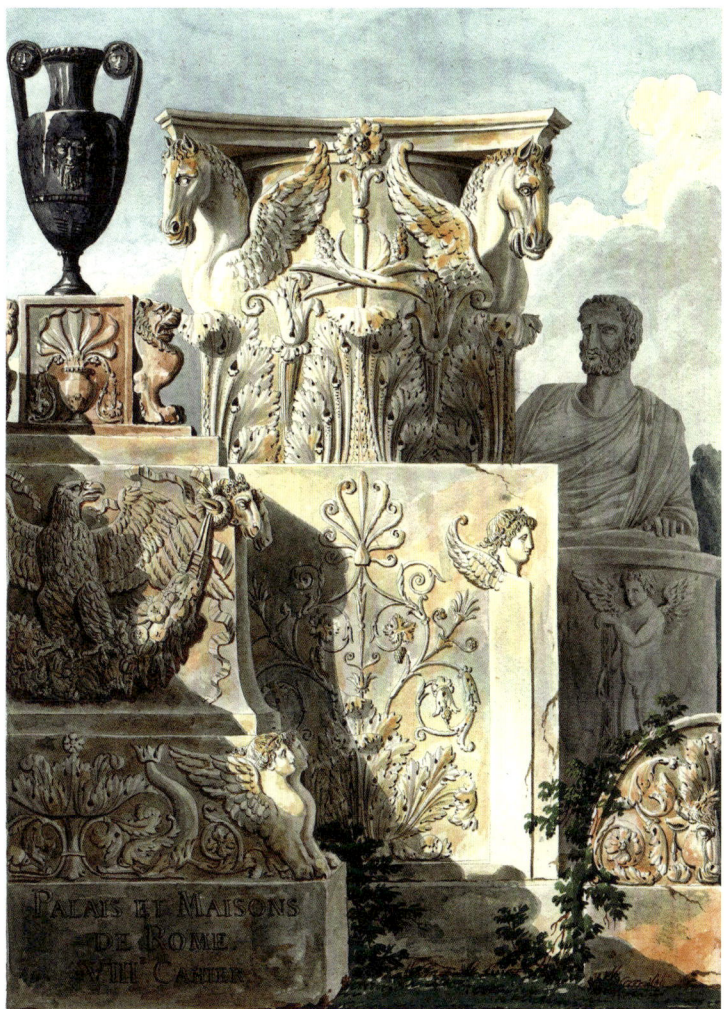

not drawing from the live model or making anatomical studies but diligently copying whatever prints the school provided to the students as two-dimensional models.

Just as the challenges he faced during this initial education-through-copying played a central role in his artistic awakening, the technique of engraving assumed a preeminent role in his production, beginning with two projects dating from the last years of the eighteenth century: the series of frontispieces for the book on Roman palaces (1798) and the headpiece illustrations for the edition of Horace, published the following year by Pierre Didot l'aîné.[3]

Regarding the first of these books, on which he collaborated with Pierre Fontaine and Claude Bernier, it is significant that Percier focused his contribution on the title pages, despite their having been marginal to the work's principal subject

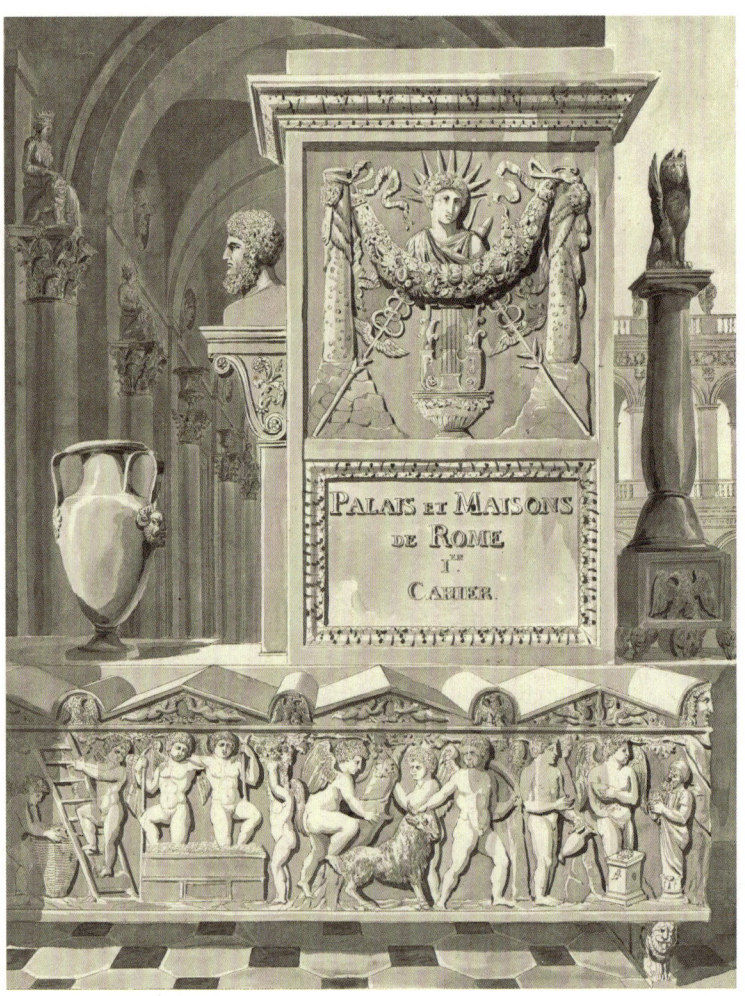 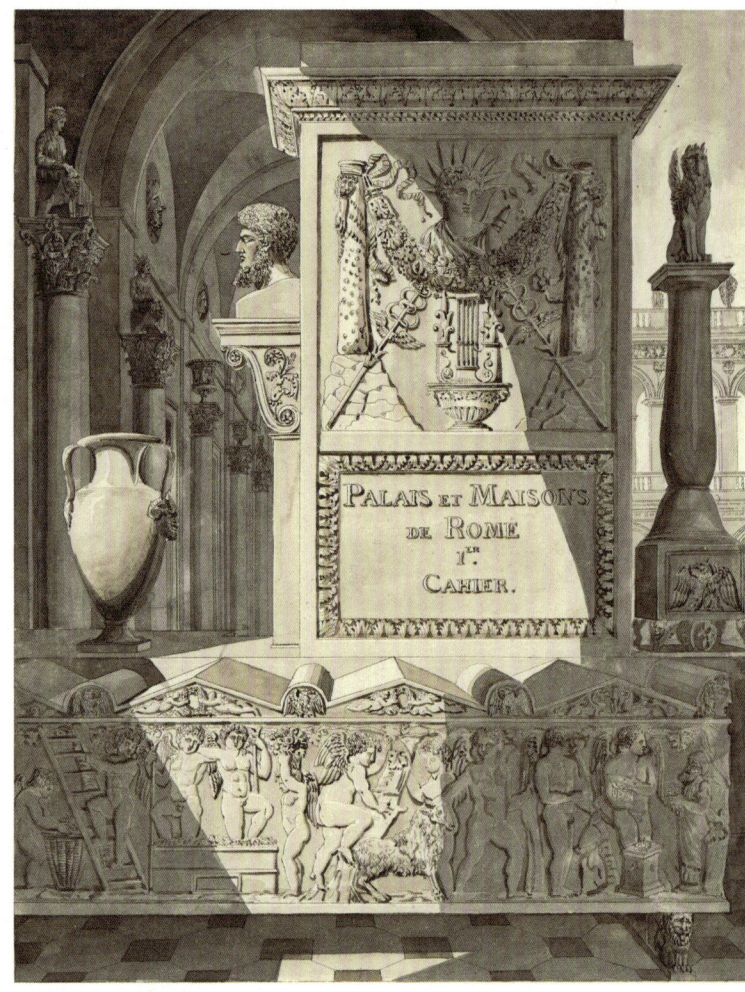

[FIG. 5.3]. The ambiguous choice of engraved renderings that were hand colored, but only in a few "prestige" copies, gives this ensemble a singular status. In their colored versions, these compositions resemble the larger works that Percier exhibited at the Salon, while the pristine linear versions, by far the majority, contributed to the fashion for neoclassical line engraving.

The exceptionally large number of these frontispieces—sixteen out of a total of a hundred plates, their inclusion linked to the initial sale of the book as sixteen

△ **FIG. 5.4.** Charles Percier. Two different versions of the frontispiece for fascicle 1, Percier and Fontaine, *Palais, maisons et autres édifices modernes dessinés à Rome* (Paris: Authors, 1798), pl. 1. Watercolor over etching. Private collection, Paris. Cat. 47.

▷ **FIG. 5.5.** Charles Percier. Frontispiece for Percier and Fontaine, *Choix des plus célèbres maisons de plaisance de Rome et de ses environs* (Paris: Pierre Didot l'aîné, 1808–15).

parts or fascicles[4]—allowed for variations. Some of the compositions are assemblages of sculpted elements and painted decorations, whereas others depict coherent architectural spaces; several play on a contrast between perspectival recession and planar decorative elements occupying much of the foreground. Such is the case with the first plate, which exists in several differently colored versions, some of which show the bas-reliefs on the sarcophagus and the pedestal in direct light, while others show these motifs partly obscured by cast shadows [FIG. 5.4].

The book on the villas of Rome did not repeat this division into fascicles, but its two frontispieces—devoted, respectively, to the Villa Borghese and the Villa Albani—made it possible for Percier to illustrate two opposing principles. The first is a perspective view of a series of sculptures in a garden landscape. The second, by contrast, eschews the picturesque in favor of a composition inspired by an ancient bas-relief in the Villa Albani collection that Percier had studied closely [FIG. 5.5].

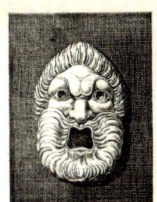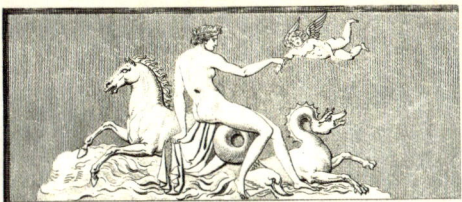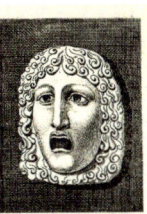

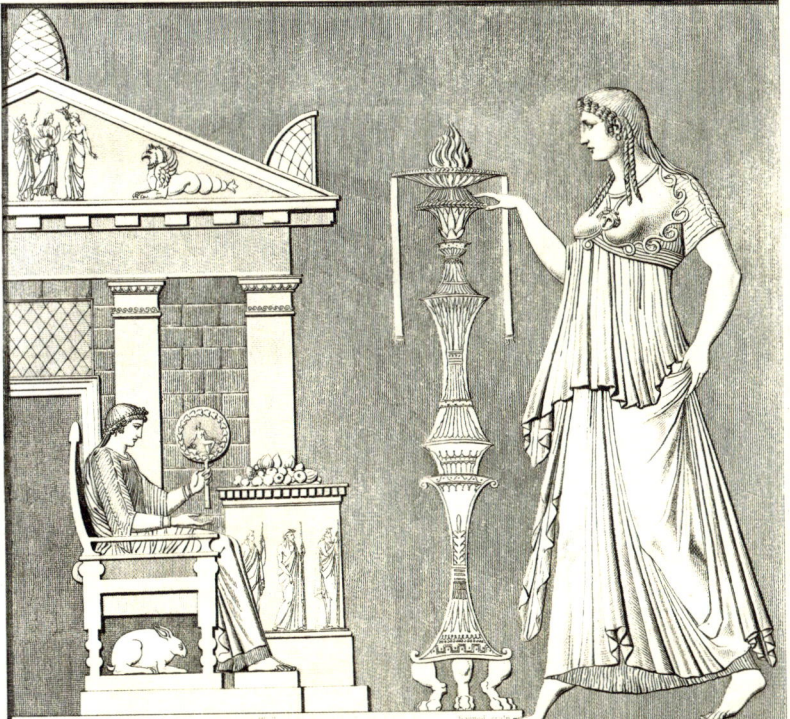

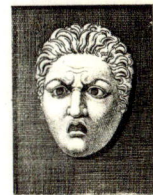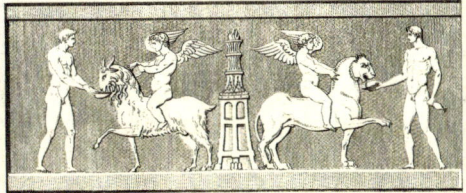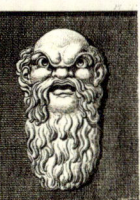

However, if the publications that Percier co-signed with Fontaine afforded him opportunities to use his gifts as a graphic designer, it was a commission from Pierre Didot l'aîné, which had nothing to do with architecture, that made his reputation as a true artist of the book. The result, a dozen decorative headpieces designed by Percier for the publisher's Horace edition, may seem insignificant, but these small engravings marked his entry into a field in which he would remain active into the 1820s. Admired by Thomas Hope for its erudition with regard to ancient Roman furnishings,[5] this set contains, in equal measure, perspectival compositions and planar ones imitating the appearance of bas-reliefs [FIGS. 5.6, 5.7].

The illustration at the head of the Epistles represents the dinner organized by the poet one summer night in honor of the wealthy lawyer

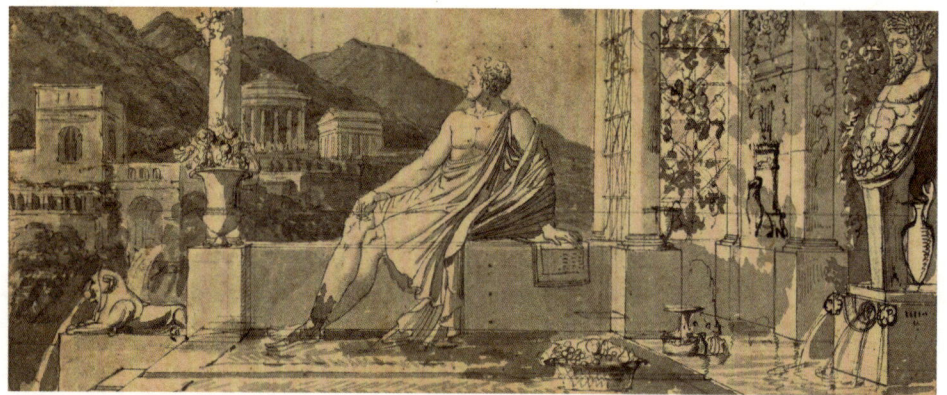

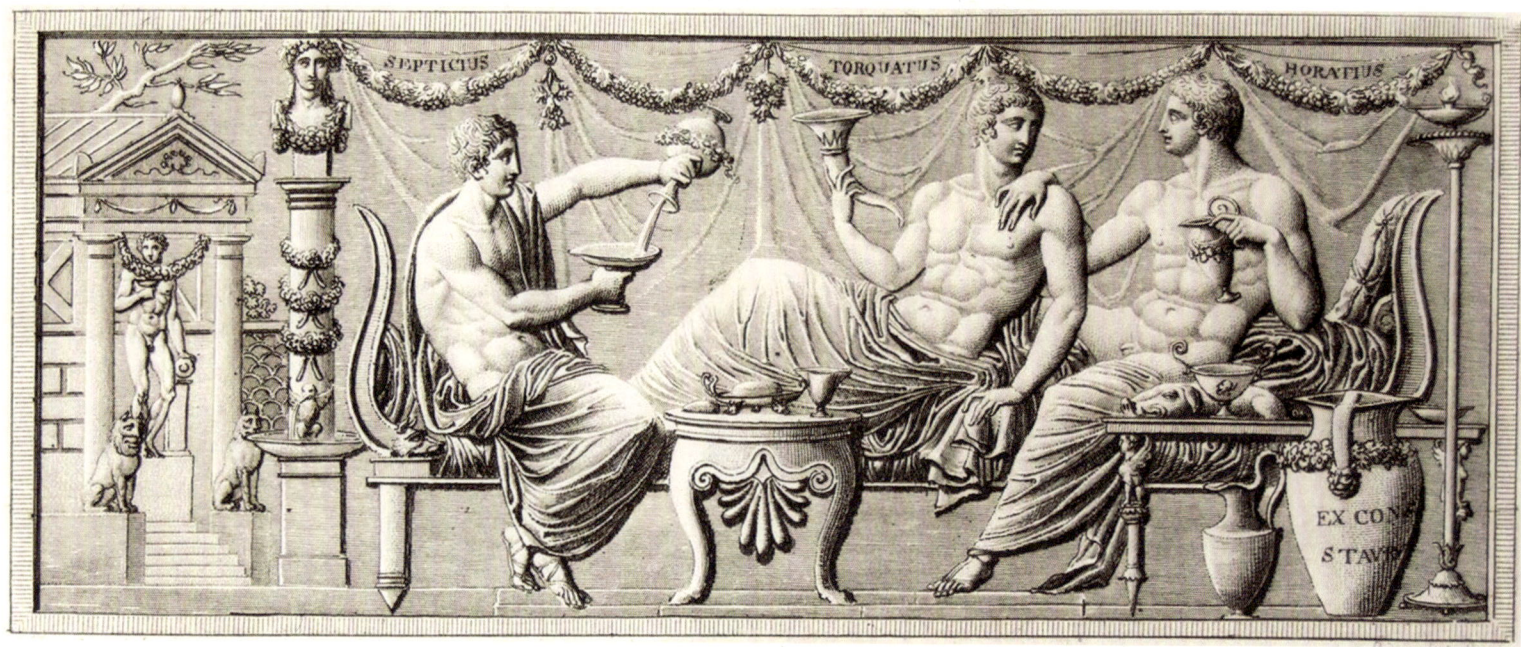

▼ **FIG. 5.6.** Charles Percier. Preparatory drawing for the headpiece of Horace's *First Book of Epistles* in *Quintus Horatius Flaccus* (Paris: Pierre Didot l'aîné, 1799). Pen, black ink, and brown wash on paper. Cliché musées d'Angers, MTC 120. Cat. 42.

▲ **FIG. 5.7.** Charles Percier. Headpiece for Horace's *Second Book of Epistles* from *Quintus Horatius Flaccus* (Paris: Pierre Didot l'aîné, 1799).

◄ **FIG. 5.8.** Charles Percier. Headpiece for Book 6 illustrating the poem "The Young Widow" from Jean de La Fontaine, *Fables* (Paris: Pierre Didot l'aîné, 1802).

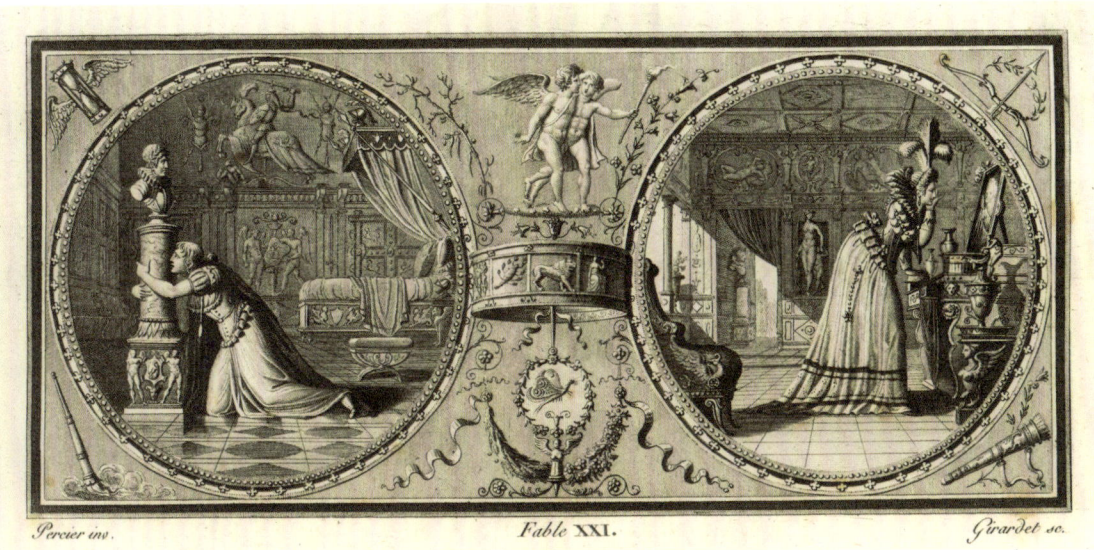

Fable XXI.

Torquatus. It is perhaps the most explicit expression of a homosexual imaginary in Percier's œuvre. The three semi-nude male guests converse while becoming intoxicated on a wine that Horace describes as rare and old. The couches on which they recline and the central table decorated with a large palmette anticipate the furniture in the *Recueil de décorations intérieures*. But the image is striking as well for the dark, complex rendering of the drapery folds, which contrasts sharply with the clarity and smoothness of the musculature.

The success of these designs prompted a second assignment from the publisher, this time more distant from antiquarian taste: a commission to provide illustrations for an edition of the fables of La Fontaine that would appear in 1802 in the same collection of very large-format books.[6] Percier's designs for these headpieces are more explicitly narrative in character, and thus consistent with the nature of La Fontaine's texts. Nonetheless, ornament is very prominent here. The engraving at the head of Book VI, for example, inspired by the poem "La jeune veuve" (The young widow), juxtaposes two views of elaborately decorated interiors, set within a frame that is rich in symbolic elements: at left, a winged hourglass and downturned torch; at right, Cupid's bow and quiver [FIG. 5.8]. First we see the young woman mourning her loss, and then, a few months later, she is a coquette studying her features in a mirror. Both times the figure is surrounded by designs in which Percier combined elements borrowed from the French seventeenth century and even the medieval period (see the jousting knight in armor, upper left) and furniture of his own devising, such as the chair at the right with armrests shaped like swans and the console table supported by a sphinx.

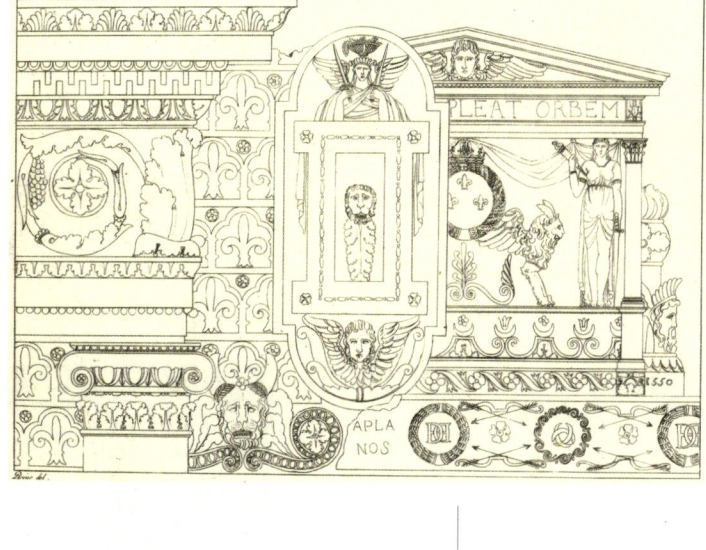

This exploration of the "classic" and medieval French decorative traditions, contemporaneous with his work as an architect-decorator in the service of Bonaparte, assumed greater amplitude during these same years in his collaboration with Alexandre Lenoir at the Musée des monuments français. In the words of Jeanne Duportal, there he designed "the rooms and the most important pieces of sculpture" and, "for his own pleasure, even sketched the tiniest bits of debris."[7] His contributions, as designer and/or engraver, to the illustrated catalogue of the museum published in 1800 were considerable.[8] In addition to executing preparatory drawings for many of the engraved illustrations of objects from various periods, he also engraved the most sophisticated architectural plates, as if he thought it necessary that he tackle these difficult challenges himself. One especially remarkable composition, captioned as depicting "lockplates and architectural detail[s] from the beautiful palace of Écouen" [FIG. 5.9], is conceived along the same lines

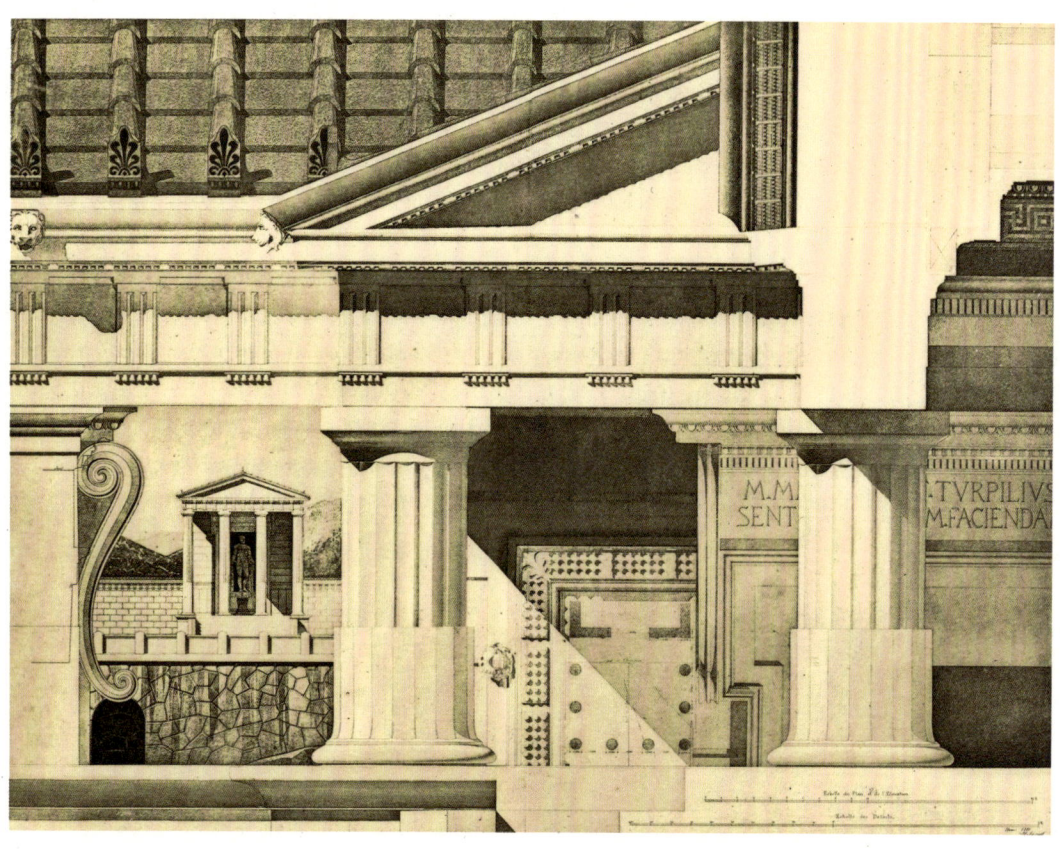

as the frontispieces in the book on Roman palaces. It shows an assemblage of fragments that juxtaposes decorative elements derived from ancient sources with a fleur-de-lis pattern dating from 1550. Here the architect, whose admiration for the art of Italy and the ancient world was well known, revealed his taste for the French Renaissance. But he also proposed an aggregation of characteristic elements from a single building, reproduced at different scales, intended as a synthetic portrait of it. This is a principle that, in 1867, was officially introduced into training exercises under the heading "éléments analytiques," a type of drawing and composition that was used until the mid-twentieth century to initiate architecture students at the École des beaux-arts [FIG. 5.10]. But it was above all a new form of architectural drawing, one whose objective—by contrast with plans, sections, elevations, and perspective views, which variously describe a structure's physical configuration—was to sum up a building's character. ●

1 "Ce que Percier a produit de plus remarquable pour un architecte, ce sont les dessins qu'il a fait pour un Horace et pour les contes de La Fontaine publiés par Didot." Alexandre Lenoir, *Musée des monumens français, ou Description historique et chronologique des statues en marbre et en bronze, bas-reliefs et tombeaux des hommes et des femmes célèbres, pour servir à l'histoire de France et à celle de l'art* (Paris: Author, 1805), 5:327.

2 "Percier, dans les détails abondant à l'extrême, / Prouve qu'en dessinant, il fait tout ce qu'il aime. / Il est un peu confus, soit dit sans le flatter. / Souvent c'est un talent de savoir s'arrêter."

3 Charles Percier and Pierre Fontaine, *Palais, maisons et autres édifices modernes dessinés à Rome; publiés à Paris, l'an VI de la République française (1798, v. st.)* (Paris: Authors, 1798); Horace, *Quintus Horatius Flaccus* (Paris: Pierre Didot l'aîné, 1799).

4 See my introduction to the facsimile edition of the copy in the collection of Jacques Doucet: Charles Percier and Pierre Fontaine, *Palais de Rome: Palais, maisons et autres édifices modernes dessinés à Rome*, ed. Jean-Philippe Garric (Wavre: Mardaga / Paris: Institut national d'histoire de l'art, 2008).

5 Thomas Hope, *Household Furniture and Interior Decoration, Executed from Designs by Thomas Hope* (London: Longman, Hurst, Rees, and Orme, 1807), 14, 53.

6 Jean de La Fontaine, *Fables de La Fontaine* (Paris: Pierre Didot l'aîné, 1802).

7 Jeanne Duportal, "Charles Percier 1764–1838," in *Charles Percier. Reproduction de dessins conservés à la Bibliothèque de l'Institut* (Paris: Maurice Rousseau, 1931), 39.

8 Lenoir, *Musée des monumens français*. See also the different publication containing only the plates of the preceding: A. Lenoir, *Recueil de gravures pour servir à l'histoire des arts en France* (Paris: Author, 1812). Not all of the engravings are signed, which makes it difficult to determine the precise extent of Percier's participation; of the total number of 164 plates, he signed 39 as designer, on 7 of which he is also identified as the engraver.

◂ **FIG. 5.9.** Charles Percier. *Composition of locks and architectural details from the Palais d'Écouen*. From Alexandre Lenoir, *Musée des monumens français* (1800–21), vol. 5, pl. 209.

▸ **FIG. 5.10.** Victor Auguste Blavette. *Composition of antique fragments after the Temple of Hercules in Cori* (Prix de Rome, 1879). From Hector d'Espouy, *Fragments d'architecture antique* (Paris, 1905), vol. 1, pl. 35.

PERCIER UNDER THE LOUPE

JEAN-PHILIPPE GARRIC

Charles Percier's contribution to neoclassical line engraving could not be more complicated. From his own books to his contributions to prestigious collaborative projects such as the folio editions of works by Horace and La Fontaine published by Pierre Didot l'aîné, the *Voyage en Espagne* by Alexandre de Laborde, and the *Voyages romantiques et pittoresques* by Justin Taylor and Charles Nodier,[1] everything suggests that his ambition constantly drove him to investigate forms of expression that were richer, more complex, and more sophisticated. He was on friendly terms with John Flaxman during his Roman sojourn,[2] but nothing in his own work indicates that he took the path opened by the publication, in 1793, of the radically simplified illustrations of the *Iliad* and the *Odyssey* of Homer designed by Flaxman and engraved by Tommaso Piroli.[3] However, two of the principal works that Percier co-authored with Pierre Fontaine, the book on Roman palaces and the *Recueil de décorations intérieures*, played an important role in the popularization of an architectural analogue of neoclassical outline engraving in France and throughout Europe.

The analogous architectural mode of engraving long predates the last years of the eighteenth century. In this context, in the years around 1650, it was already being used in France as a complement to carefully shaded images, figuring in works as important as the translation of *Palladio* by Pierre Le Muet and the *Parallèle* by Roland Fréart de Chambray.[4] After 1750 it was still being used by Jacques François Blondel in his *Cours d'architecture* and by Pierre Panseron, Fontaine's first teacher, in his *Cayers de profils* and his anthologies of ornament prints[5] [FIG. 5A.1]. This last case, in which rather freely etched lines are overlaid with shadows executed in wash, anticipates the technique used in *Palais, maisons et autres édifices modernes*. Here Percier both conceived and executed the frontispieces, the most artistic part of the whole, which are characterized by incised drawing of extreme sophistication and hand coloring of rare delicacy; they are also the least specifically architectural compositions in the book.

The plates meant to be hand colored in watercolor were printed on Holland paper in sepia ink, so as to avoid overly emphatic lines. Some of the more elaborate details executed by Percier are engraved with great finesse.

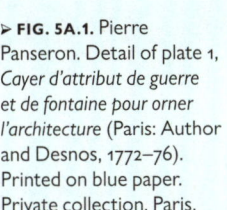 **FIG. 5A.1.** Pierre Panseron. Detail of plate 1, *Cayer d'attribut de guerre et de fontaine pour orner l'architecture* (Paris: Author and Desnos, 1772–76). Printed on blue paper. Private collection, Paris.

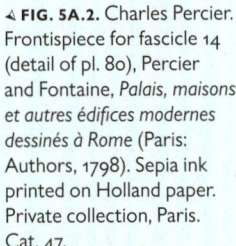 **FIG. 5A.2.** Charles Percier. Frontispiece for fascicle 14 (detail of pl. 80), Percier and Fontaine, *Palais, maisons et autres édifices modernes dessinés à Rome* (Paris: Authors, 1798). Sepia ink printed on Holland paper. Private collection, Paris. Cat. 47.

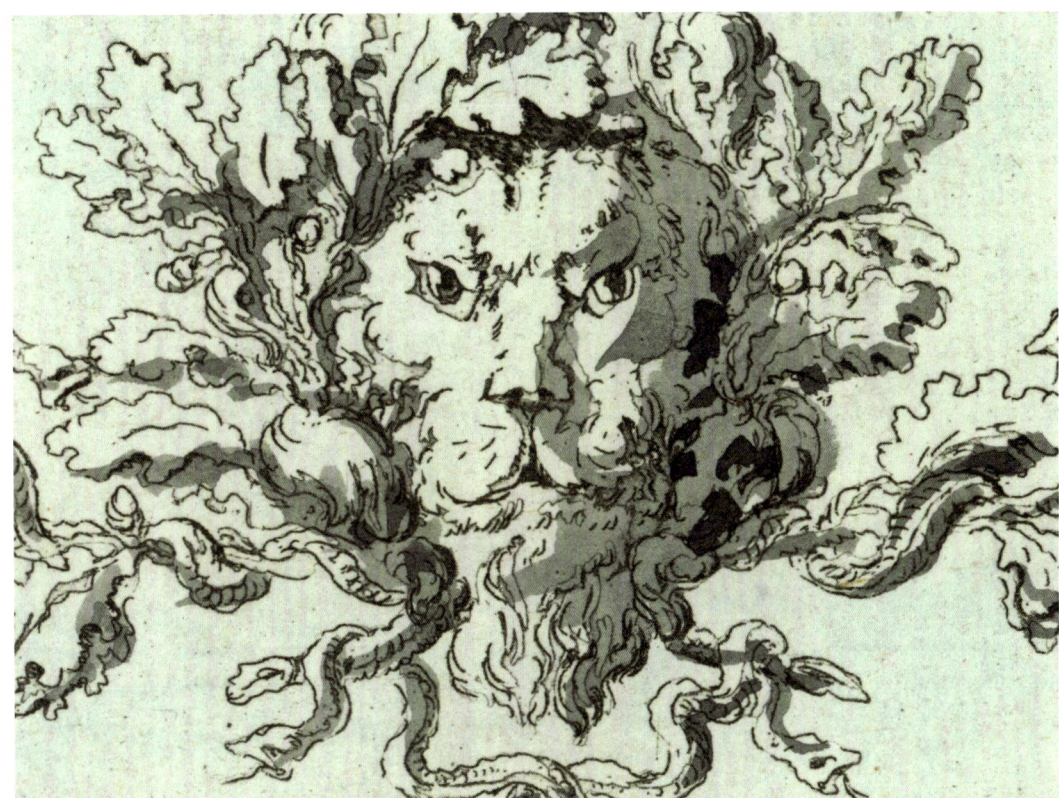

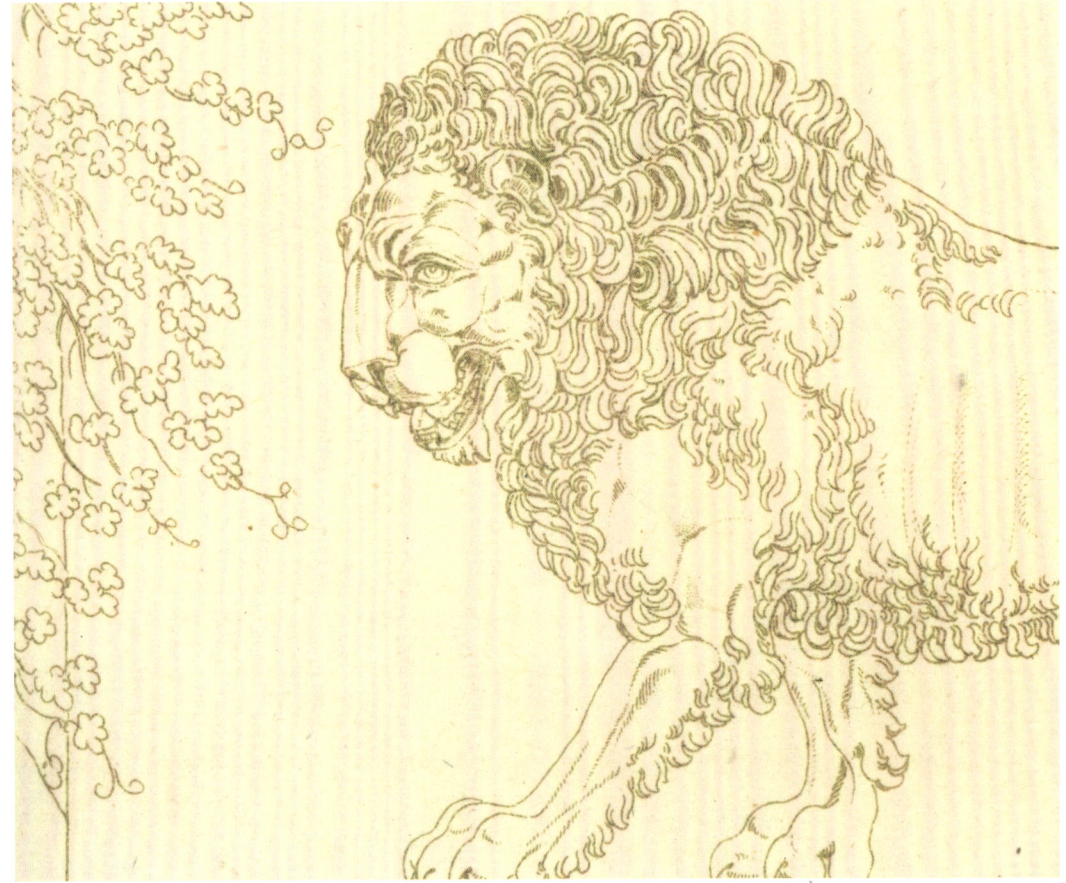

The lion that crowns the composition of the fourteenth frontispiece has a certain affinity with neoclassical line engraving, but there are also small areas of finely hatched shadow. Moreover, the lines here tend to intertwine, as opposed to remaining starkly independent; far from aspiring to a purist autonomy, they abound to the point of creating textures and shaping motifs [FIG. 5A.2].

The coloring, when present, adds another layer of complexity. The dark patches and touches of color toy with the grand lines of the composition, not always respecting their boundaries. The richness of tones, too, pays greater deference to graphic than to descriptive priorities; India ink nuanced with ultramarine, pale yellow with gamboge, a sienna tending toward orange, and a reddish burnt sienna function here less to differentiate various materials than to animate the surface of the paper by modulating the nuances of the fictive stone. Far from the dutiful application of technical drawing, here the brush is nimble as well as precise, leaving the upper corners of the blocks lighter in tone, thereby better articulating the successive planes and emphasizing the underlying geometry [FIG. 5A.3].

However, copies of the book colored with the brush were so expensive that very few of them found buyers, and contemporaries, like posterity, remembered it as a publication in black and white. The failure of the "deluxe" colored edition did not prevent Percier and Fontaine from embarking on the *Recueil de décorations intérieures*, the first fascicle of which was issued in 1801, but the outcome of this second undertaking was very different.

Completion of this volume, repeatedly delayed by the authors' many commissions and responsibilities, took more than a decade (an integral edition did not appear until 1812), and the hand-colored exemplars met with so little success that none has come down to us. In 1809 Percier and Fontaine changed their modus operandi for their third major publication, devoted to the villas of Rome, commissioning professional engravers to execute its plates; more discreetly, they acknowledged the success of the exclusively

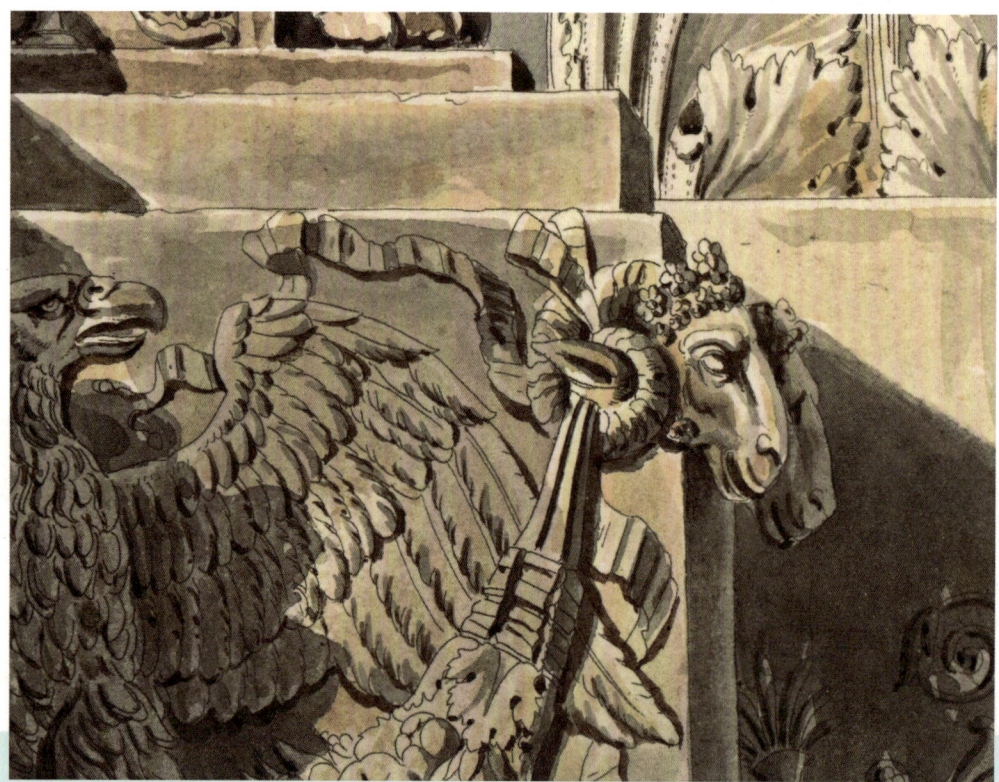

FIG. 5A.3. Charles Percier. Frontispiece for fascicle 8 (detail of pl. 44), Percier and Fontaine, *Palais, maisons et autres édifices modernes dessinés à Rome*. Watercolor over etching. Private collection, Paris.

FIG. 5A.4. Charles Percier. Allegory of Architecture (detail of pl. 5), interior decoration of Isabey's atelier. From Charles Percier and Pierre Fontaine, *Recueil de décorations intérieures* (Paris: Authors and Pierre Didot l'aîné, 1801–12).

FIG. 5A.5. Charles Normand. Fireplace from the Salle des Fleuves, Musée Napoléon (detail of pl. 72). From *Recueil de décorations intérieures* (Paris: Authors and Pierre Didot l'aîné, 1801–12).

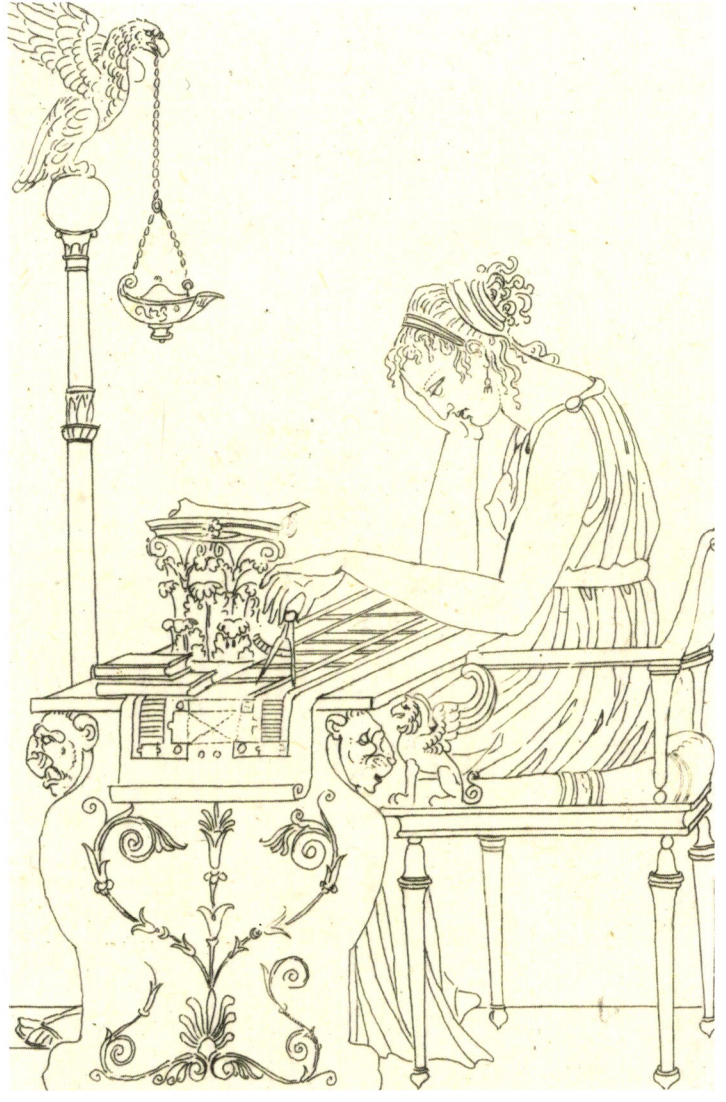

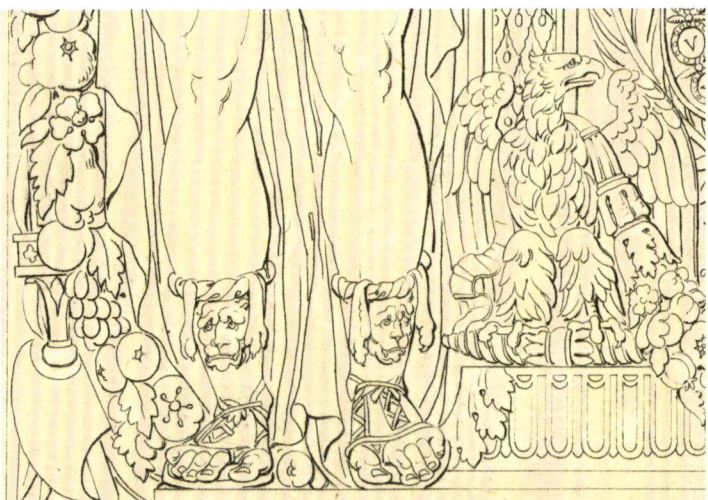

linear version of the earlier parts of the *Recueil de décorations intérieures* by abandoning coloring for its last plates and asking Charles Pierre Joseph Normand, a French specialist in engravings of this kind, to assist in their completion.[6] These last plates were clearly executed by a different hand, making it possible to contrast Percier's lissome but hesitant line in the earlier parts of the book with the powerful, plastically suggestive line of his former fellow student at the École gratuite de dessin, which is increasingly prevalent toward the end [FIGS. 5A.4, 5A.5]. Although Percier himself did not cultivate this style, he acceded to public taste on this point, thereby contributing—almost despite himself— to the popularization of a line-engraving aesthetic for which he had no particular predilection. ●

1 Horace, *Quintus Horatius Flaccus* (Paris: Pierre Didot l'aîné, 1799), drawings for 12 engraved headpiece illustrations; La Fontaine, *Fables de La Fontaine* (Paris: Pierre Didot l'aîné, 1802), drawings for 12 engraved headpiece illustrations; Alexandre de Laborde, *Voyage pittoresque et historique de l'Espagne* (Paris: Pierre Didot l'aîné, 1812), drawing for engraved frontispiece; Charles Taylor and Justin Taylor, *Voyages pittoresques et romantiques dans l'ancienne France, Franche Comté* (Paris: n.p., 1825), drawing for engraved headpiece on title page.
2 As evidenced by their correspondence; see the Flaxman letter book, Fitzwilliam Museum, Cambridge, accession ID f. 49; f.71-72; a translation of the letter is in chapter 3A in this volume.
3 The title pages of both series are dated 1793, the year in which Tommaso Piroli engraved the plates in Rome, but the latter were printed only later in London after Flaxman's return there, probably in 1795.
4 Andrea Palladio, *Traicté des cinq ordres d'architecture dont se sont servi les Anciens. Traduit du Palladio* (Paris: Langlois, 1645); Roland Fréart de Chambray, *Parallèle de l'architecture antique avec la moderne* (Paris: Edme Martin, 1650).
5 Jacques François Blondel, *Cours d'architecture ou Traité de la décoration, distribution et construction des bâtiments* (Paris: Desaint, 1771–77); Pierre Panseron, *Éléments d'architecture dédiés à Monsieur de Sartine*. 3 vols. (Paris: Author and Desnos, 1772–76).
6 The source for Percier and Fontaine's having solicited Charles Pierre Joseph Normand's assistance is Normand's own son. Although he alludes to this collaboration in connection with their books on Italian architecture, the only volume on which C.P.J. Normand can have participated is the *Recueil de décorations intérieures*. See Charles Normand, *Notice sur la vie et les ouvrages de C.P. J. Normand* (Paris: n.d.).

CHAPTER 6

DOCUMENTING THE *RECUEIL DE DÉCORATIONS INTÉRIEURES*

IRIS MOON

IN THE PRELIMINARY DISCOURSE TO THE *RECUEIL DE DÉCORATIONS intérieures*, Charles Percier and Pierre Fontaine write that the purpose of publishing their collection of furnishings and decorations is not to offer models for imitation but to contribute "to the dissemination and upholding of the principles of taste that we have derived from ancient art, and that we believe are linked, albeit by a less apparent chain, to those general laws of truth, simplicity, and beauty."[1] Comprising seventy-two plates of designs for interiors, furnishings, and objects issued in installments from 1801 to 1812, Percier and Fontaine's book exerted considerable influence on the development of the Empire style and the trajectory of nineteenth-century decorative arts.[2] Often grouped with contemporary pattern books and collections of ornament prints, the book is a complex document conceived by its authors as a pedagogical tool for educating students, artisans, and the public about what they termed the "industrial arts," and its role in cultivating the taste of a new era.[3] In a sense, Percier and Fontaine's book can be viewed as the precursor to nineteenth-century ornament manuals such as Peter Beuth and Karl Friedrich Schinkel's *Vorbilder für Fabrikanten und Handwerker* (1821–37), in which design was conceived as a means of social reform.[4] This essay will focus on the assembly, dissemination, and graphic language adopted by the *Recueil de décorations intérieures*, since much of its success depended upon these factors.

The *Recueil de décorations intérieures comprenant tout ce qui a rapport a l'ameublement comme vases, trépieds, candelabres, cassolettes, lustres, girandoles, lampes, chandeliers, cheminées, feux, poêles, pendules, tables, secrétaires, lits, canapés, fauteuils, chaises, tabourets, miroirs, écrans &, &, &,* formed the unexpected success of Percier and Fontaine's careers as published authors. In 1801, when an argument with Josephine Bonaparte over the design of the garden at Malmaison threatened to terminate the architects' budding relationship with their new client Napoleon, Fontaine comforted himself in knowing that his publications with Percier would provide them with financial security. Fontaine wrote in his journal that their book on the *Maisons de plaisance de Rome*, the "decoration book," and a less costly publication on the palaces and houses of Rome (*Palais, maisons et autres édifices modernes dessinés à Rome*) "appear to be resources [enough] for securing our existence and even our reputation."[5]

Much like their 1798 publication on Italian residences, the *Recueil de décorations intérieures* did not in fact begin its life as a bound book; it was disseminated instead through a series of installments over a twelve-year period. Percier and Fontaine's designs for furniture, decorative objects, and interiors were first printed in folio format, grouped in fascicles of six loose plates contained in blue paper wrappers [FIG. 6.1]. As the lengthy title page indicates, the book was available at paper sellers, bookstores, print shops, and *marchands de nouveautés*, the purveyors of luxury goods who had replaced the *marchands merciers* of the eighteenth century. Also sold on a subscription basis, the *Recueil* could thus be purchased in a variety of forms, including customizable types of paper. A set of plates printed

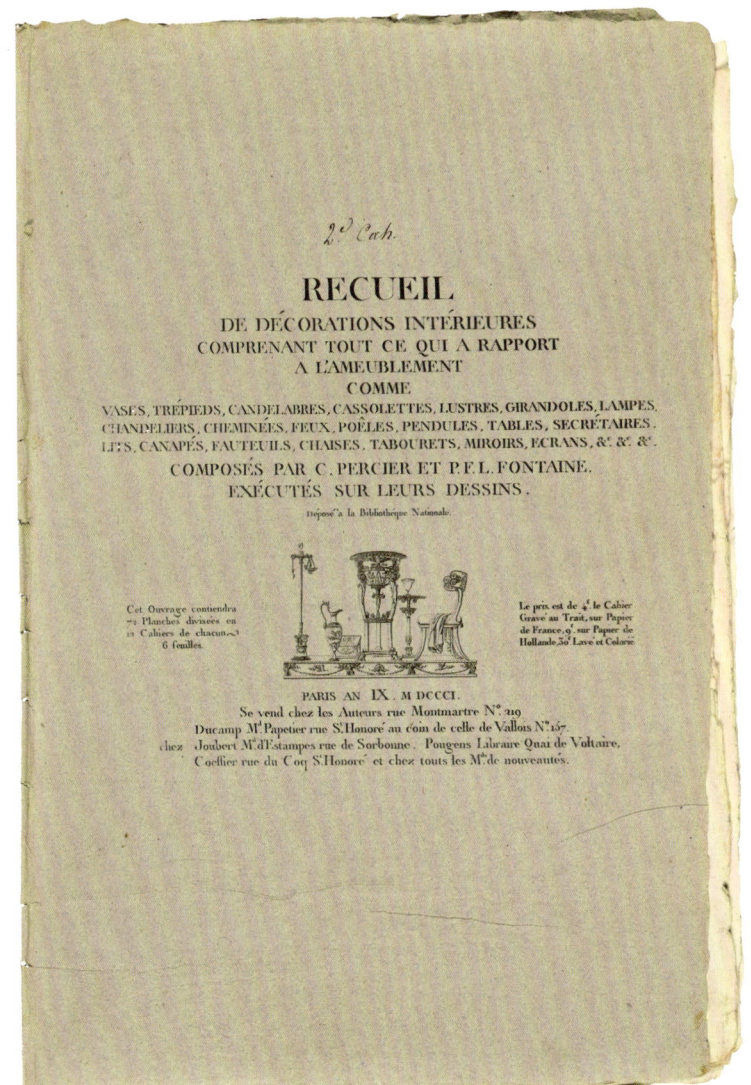

▼ **FIG 6.1.** Charles Percier and Pierre Fontaine. *Recueil de décorations intérieures* (Paris: Authors and Pierre Didot l'aîné, 1801–12), v. Title plate printed on blue wrapper. Getty Research Institute, Los Angeles.

on *papier de France* could be purchased for 4 francs, whereas a set printed on *papier d'Hollande* could be bought for 9 francs. For the costlier sum of 30 francs per fascicle, customers could purchase a set colored in wash and watercolor. Surprisingly few colored versions of the *Recueil de décorations intérieures* exist, suggesting that the original intention of issuing a complete colored set was abandoned by the architects, who were increasingly preoccupied with official building projects for Napoleon [FIG. 6.2].[6] It appears that rare hand-colored versions were gifted to exceptional clients.[7]

Percier and Fontaine took advantage of the trend of selling their books in installments, a practice adopted by an increasing number of early nineteenth-century architects who turned to self-publishing as a means of generating both income and publicity.[8] The fascicle format also reflected new consumer demand for fashion periodicals, with the *Journal des Dames et des Modes* promising to deliver of-the-moment fashions and decorating styles to its readers on a weekly basis.[9] Issuing the plates in such a manner was also more economical, since fascicles could be sold separately to subscribers and in shops and subsequently collated and bound more or less luxuriously, based on the tastes of the purchaser. Versions of Percier and Fontaine's book can today be found within other publications, in essence creating composite books.[10]

Contrary to earlier assumptions, there was no "original edition" published in 1801. Instead, the book appeared over a span of time, resulting in numerous printings of earlier plates alongside the printing of newer installments. The earliest publication announcement is found in 1801 in Charles Landon's *Nouvelle des arts*, which mentions that the first twelve plates had been issued.[11] More than half of the projects predate the beginning of the Empire period in 1804.[12] Although a copy was deposited at the Bibliothèque nationale on May 17, 1804, the final collection was not completed until 1812, the year Didot l'aîné issued the definitive bound edition that included all seventy-two plates, along with an explanatory table and preliminary discourse.[13]

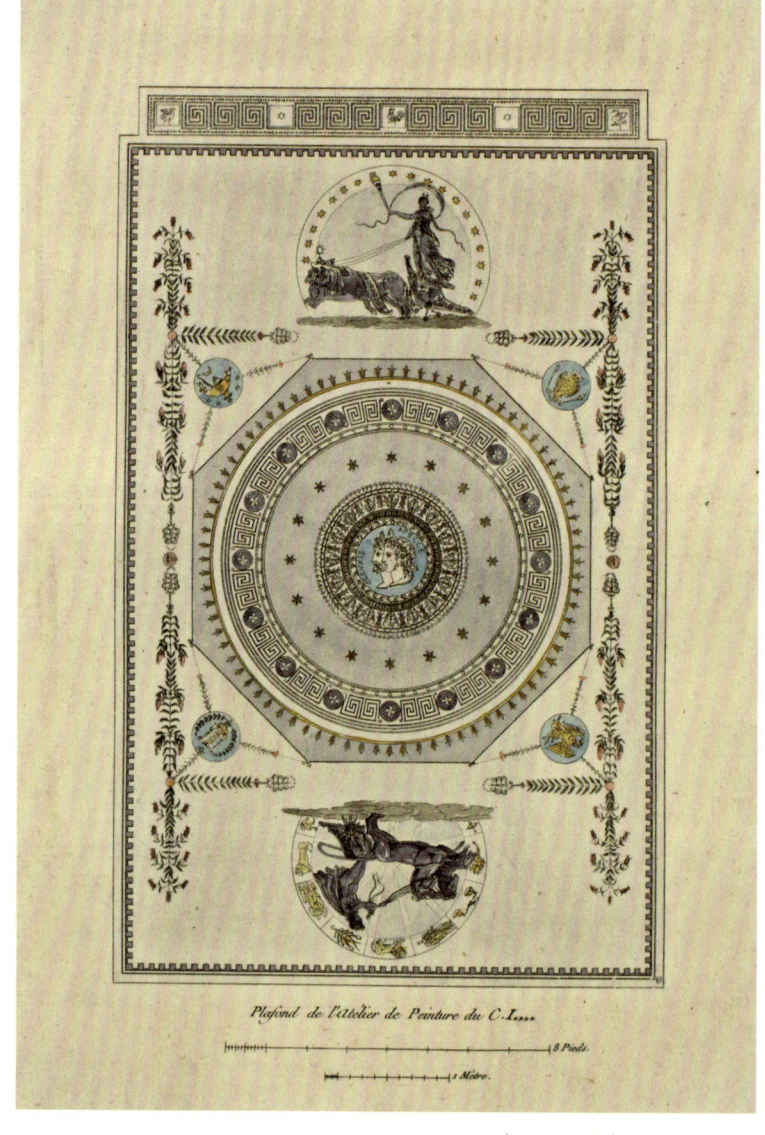

FIG 6.2. Charles Percier and Pierre Fontaine. *Recueil de décorations intérieures* (Paris: Authors and Pierre Didot l'aîné, 1801–12), pl. 3. Percier and Fontaine Collection, Ryerson and Burnham Archives, The Art Institute of Chicago, 747.240934 PR429r, supplementary volume.

FIG 6.3. Charles Percier and Pierre Fontaine. *Recueil de décorations intérieures* (Paris: Authors and Pierre Didot l'aîné, 1801–12). The notice is printed inside the blue wrapper. Getty Research Institute, Los Angeles, 83-B3068, copy 2.

Cet Ouvrage, dont le premier Volume in-folio est divisé en 12 Cahiers, de chacun 6 feuilles, sera composé en totalité de 72 Planches; il ne contiendra que des Meubles d'usage et des Décorations exécutés sur les Dessins de C. Percier et P. F. L. Fontaine. On y joindra les Plans et les détails nécessaires à l'intelligence des objets qui seront représentés, et on donnera, à la fin du 12.me Cahier, une Table explicative de chaque sujet, suivant son N°. Cette Table contiendra l'explication en abrégé des Meubles et des Décorations, avec l'indication des couleurs et des matières qui les composent. On rendra compte des moyens employés dans leur construction, pour en faciliter l'usage à ceux auxquels ils pourraient servir et répondre à la demande que la plupart des Souscripteurs en ont faite.

Se vend à Paris, chez les Auteurs, rue Montmartre, N.° 219;
Et chez tous les Marchands de Nouveautés.

On trouve chez les mêmes Auteurs, rue Montmartre, N.° 219, le Recueil des Palais, Maisons et autres Edifices modernes de Rome. Un volume in-folio, Prix 48 fr. gravé au trait, sur papier de France.

Et 384 fr. lavé et colorié sur papier de Hollande.

Although Percier and Fontaine were both highly invested in the editorial work of their publications, it appears that the *Recueil de décorations intérieures* was particularly meaningful to Percier. As is well documented, Percier studied object design from an early age at the École gratuite de dessin and, unlike Fontaine, believed that ornamental compositions constituted a central aspect of architectural knowledge.[14] His deep investment in publishing the book is expressed in a letter dated March 3, 1804, to his mentor and colleague, the architect-designer Pierre Adrien Pâris. Complaining that recent government commissions for Napoleon had delayed his work on the "l'ouvrage des meubles," Percier wrote, "I hope to soon apply myself to this work and to send it to you right away."[15] In addition to making preparatory drawings, Percier engraved a number of the images, although the later plates were executed by the talented architect-engraver Charles Pierre Joseph Normand, a cohort from the École gratuite.[16] Interestingly, the letter to Pâris suggests that even as Percier gained increasing fame with Fontaine as the architects of Napoleon, he viewed such publishing projects as quite independent from his official work, thus complicating the question as to what degree the decoration book was implicated in the propagation of imperial culture. In any case, the reproduced plates made publicly visible the importance Percier ascribed to the design of objects, a practice that he actively encouraged the students of his famous school, including Louis Hippolyte Lebas and François Debret, to pursue.[17]

Although we may never know exactly how the book was used within artisanal workshops, the importance Percier accorded to his work as a teacher makes it possible to conjecture that he and Fontaine originally intended the book as a kind of pedagogical tool for artisans and students.[18] The original notice for the *Recueil de décorations intérieures* indicates that it was directed toward specialists responsible for producing, rather than individuals consuming, interior decorations [FIG. 6.3]. The notice points out that plans "necessary to the intelligence of objects to be represented" and an

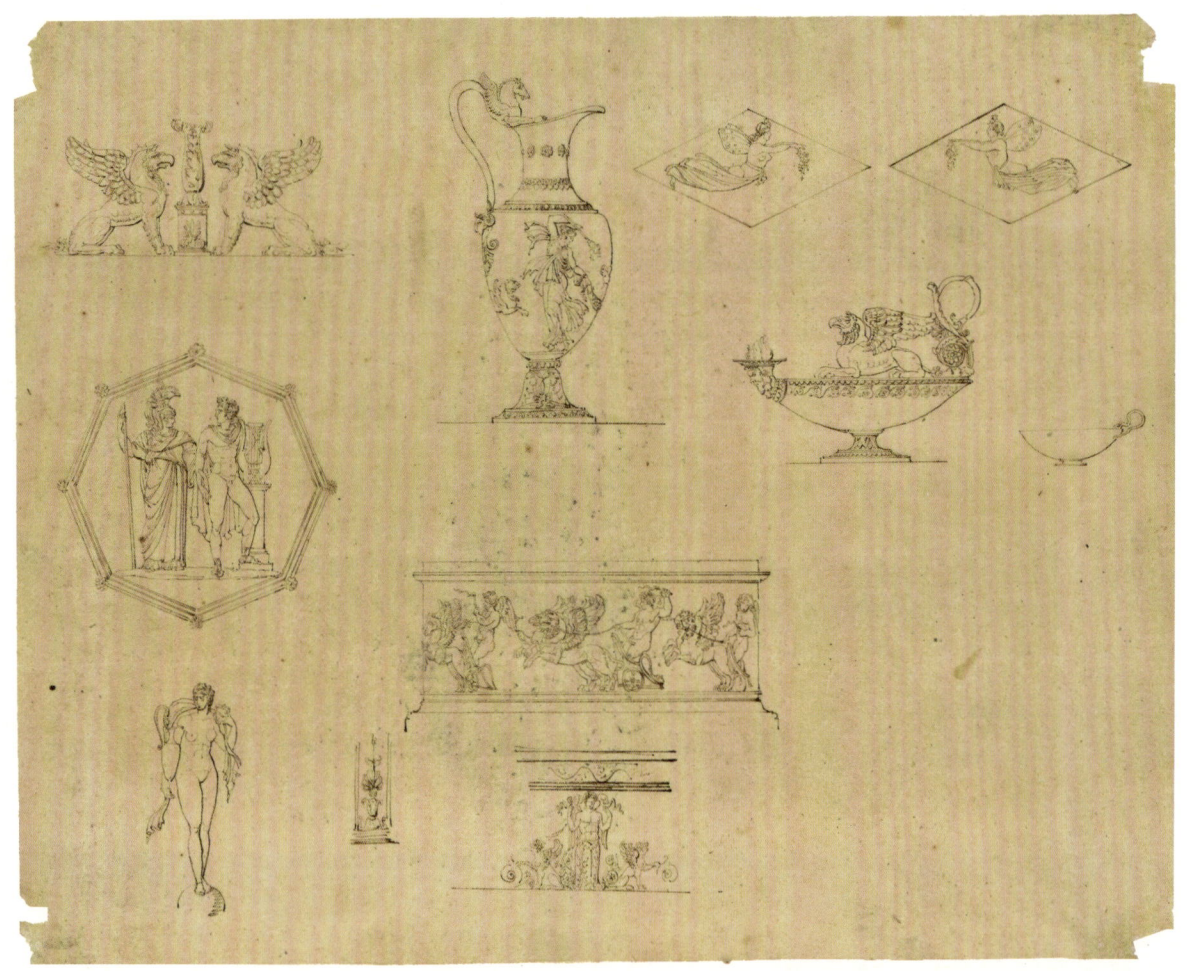
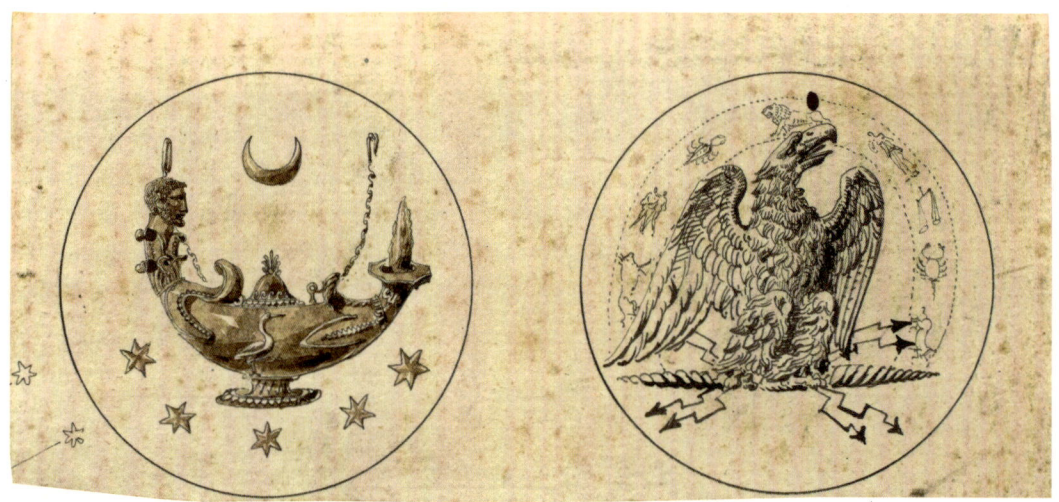

explanatory table would be included in future installments, yet there is no mention of the preliminary discourse.[19] This directed and limited readership is further indicated by Landon, who writes that "Not only artists and decorators, but also skilled workers in all areas related to interior decoration had desired the publication of such a collection."[20] Significantly, patrons are represented only with an initial, whereas a number of artisans and artists, such as the furniture firm of Jacob frères and the painters Anne Louis Girodet de Roussy-Trioson and Jean Joseph Xavier Bidauld, are collectively named, suggesting the loosening of the hierarchy of genres between the fine and decorative arts in the post-Revolutionary period.

What made Percier and Fontaine's book particularly accessible to the producers of decorative objects were the highly legible plates, reproduced in an outline engraving technique.[21] Several plates incorporate measurements in both pieds and the meter, the new system of universal measurement established by the Revolutionary government, thus allowing artisans to understand the dimensions of such furnishings. The sensitivity to the graphic intelligibility of the plates—from composition to line weight—was directly inherited from Percier's view of drawing as a form of communication.[22] Later in his career, Fontaine recalled being pleasantly surprised in 1814 when Alexander von Humboldt presented him, on behalf of Frederick William IV, with a porcelain cup based on the designs of their book that had been manufactured in Berlin.[23] Like the decision to publish in installments, the reliance on this radically reductive technique was initially economically driven. Less costly than the elaborate etching processes used in their book *Maisons de Plaisance* (1809), outline engraving was a relatively straightforward procedure that entailed using a single line to give shape to the contours of an object or a space.

The decoration book's use by students is evidenced by the numerous designs found in student notebooks of the period, clumsy copies that attest to the difficulty of mastering the draftsmanship techniques needed to design on the same level as Percier. Just as students studied ornament prints at the free drawing school Percier attended, his students rehearsed the designs found in the decoration book.[24] An example can be found in the album of his student Jules Frédéric Bouchet, where the architect has copied designs in brown ink from several different plates and arranged them on a single page [FIG. 6.4].[25] Another example in the Workshop of Percier album at the Art Institute of Chicago includes four medallions from the ceiling design of Jean-Baptiste Isabey's studio [FIG. 6.5].[26]

FIG 6.4. Jules Frédéric Bouchet. Album. Ink on paper. Getty Research Institute, Los Angeles. 2003.M.6.

FIG 6.5. Workshop of Percier. Sixty-three bound drawings. Percier and Fontaine Collection, Ryerson and Burnham Archives, The Art Institute of Chicago, OP 7, 2000.2.

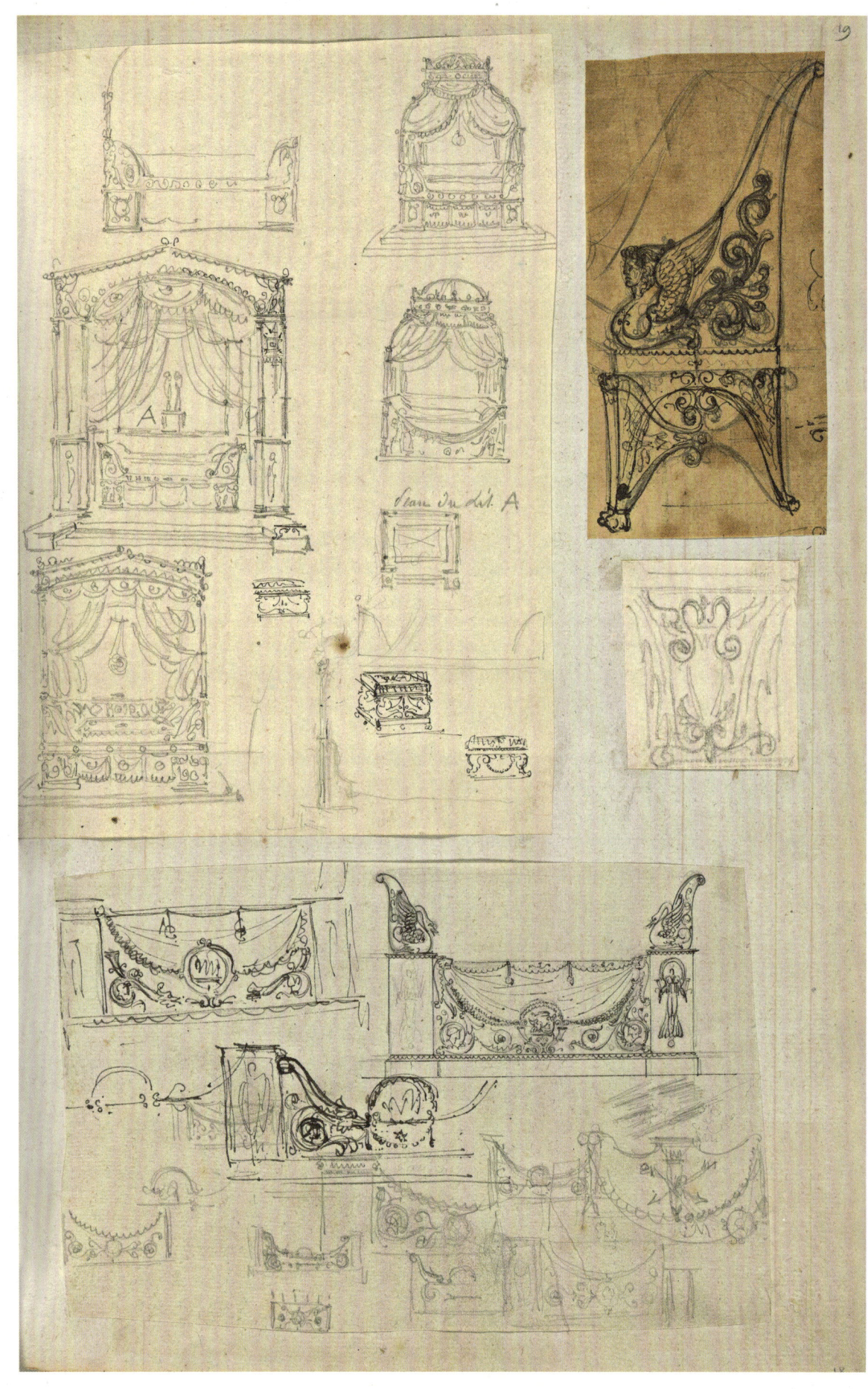

◀ **FIG 6.6.** Workshop of Percier. Scrapbook containing drawings and several prints of Architecture, Interiors, Furniture and Other Objects, fol. 19. n.d. Pen and black and gray ink, graphite, black chalk on paper. The Metropolitan Museum of Art, New York, The Elisha Whittelsey Collection, The Elisha Whittelsey Fund, 1963, 63.535. Cat. 59.

▽ **FIG 6.7.** Charles Percier and Pierre Fontaine. Plate 60 of *Recueil de décorations intérieures* (Paris: Authors and Pierre Didot l'aîné, 1801–12). Watercolor over etched plate. Musée Vivenel, Compiègne, L. 162. Cat. 58.

The medallions featured in plates 3 and 4 of the *Recueil* have been drawn in ink and watercolor and are shown in reverse. While hardly masterful, these copies demonstrate how the book would have allowed students to practice color schemes and hone their design techniques, skills that distinguished the Atelier de Percier from rival studios attended by students of the École des beaux-arts.

Nonetheless, this simple linear economy of the outline required an unforgiving degree of exactitude. This becomes apparent when one compares the plates of the *Recueil de décorations intérieures* with the informal series of compositions found in an album of designs attributed to the Percier and Fontaine workshop [FIG. 6.6]. One can observe the degree of difficulty entailed in editing down a multitude of possible furniture forms into a selection of designs, as well as the discipline entailed in reducing loosely drawn ink strokes into a single line. As Jean-Pierre Samoyault writes of the decoration book, "What is reproduced is not a catalogue of projects but a state of realized things (undoubtedly non-exhaustive), a veritable repertoire of forms and ornaments proposed as models."[27] Although a number of plates depict executed interiors, we can nonetheless capture glimpses of the design process, at a moment prior to the completion of a project. Samoyault notes that the plate depicting the boudoir of Madame Moreau proposes two alternative design choices for the legs of the extravagant *lit de repos*, along with the accompanying tassels grazing the floor [FIG. 6.7].[28]

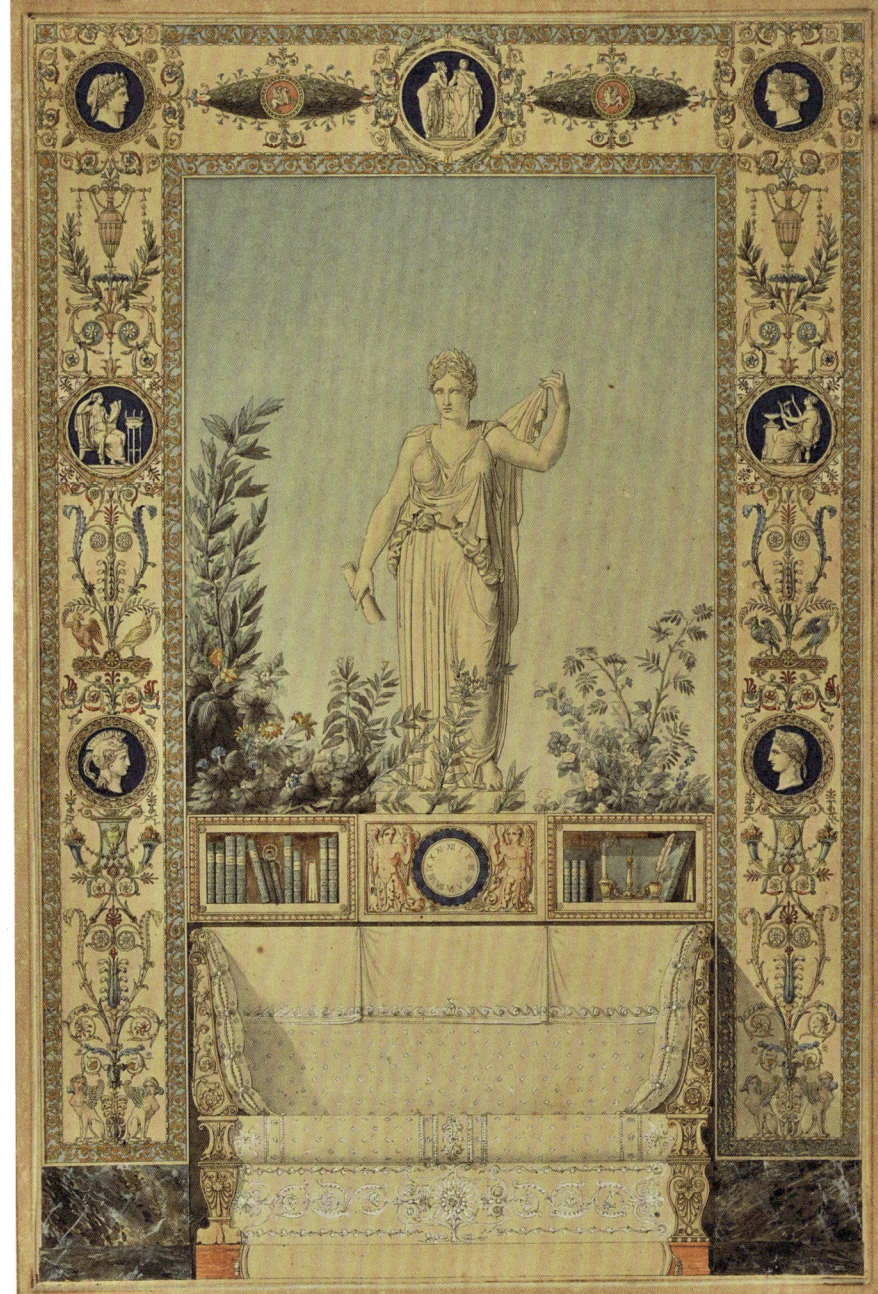

The simplicity of the outline engraving technique characteristic of countless other neoclassical publications is complicated by the alternative systems of representation found in the *Recueil de décorations intérieures*, namely the theatrical perspectival views that open a number of fascicles and establish the distinctive visual rhythm of the book. The technique of representing the interior by means of a perspectival view, more commonly utilized in depictions of outdoor *vedute*, can undoubtedly be tied to Percier and Fontaine's active work as scenographers at the Paris Opera from the end of 1792 to 1796.[29] The ways in which such perspectival views produce a sequential effect of moving through space can be observed in the first five plates, which feature the design for Isabey's atelier executed about 1798 in his home on 27, rue Saint-Marc and not, as is commonly believed, in his quarters at the Louvre.[30] The reader is invited into the atelier through a view that shows a bed dramatically placed on a dais and surrounded by portraits of famous artists, characteristic of the reductive aesthetics of the Directory period [FIG. 6.8]. The perspectival view is followed by an elevation of the right wall of the studio (SEE FIG. 2B.3), made famous as the backdrop to Louis Léopold Boilly's group portrait of artists (SEE FIG. 2B.1). A sketch by Boilly emphasizes the recession of the niche in which the bust of Minerva and the heating stove that served as its plinth were placed [FIG. 6.9]. Plate 3 [FIG. 6.2] shows the ceiling design, which includes profiles of Apelles and Zeuxis, a reflection of Isabey's profession as artist, whereas

▷ **FIG 6.8.** Charles Percier and Pierre Fontaine. Plate 1 of *Recueil de décorations intérieures* (Paris: Authors and Pierre Didot l'aîné, 1801–12). The Metropolitan Museum of Art, New York, Harris Brisbane Dick Fund, 1928, 28.40.1. Cat. 54c.

▷ **FIG 6.9.** Louis Léopold Boilly. Minerva (Study after a Sculpture). n.d. Conté crayon, stumping, heightened with white chalk on faded blue paper. The Metropolitan Museum of Art, New York, Gift of Louis de Bayser, 2009, 2009.477. Cat. 60.

◁ **FIG 6.10.** Charles Percier and Pierre Fontaine. Plate 25 of *Recueil de décorations intérieures* (Paris: Authors and Pierre Didot l'aîné, 1801–12). The Metropolitan Museum of Art, New York, Harris Brisbane Dick Fund, 1928, 28.40.1.

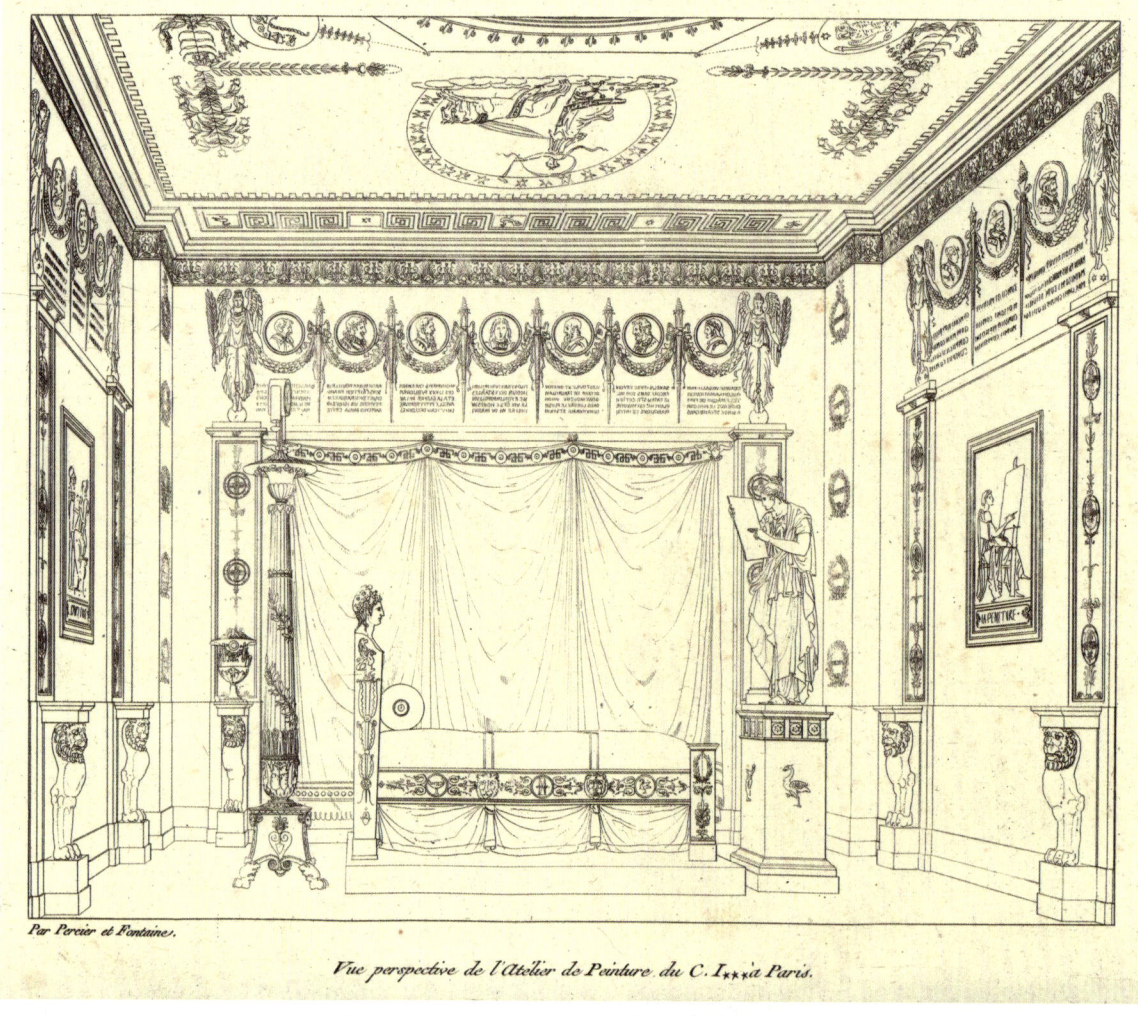

6 DOCUMENTING THE RECUEIL

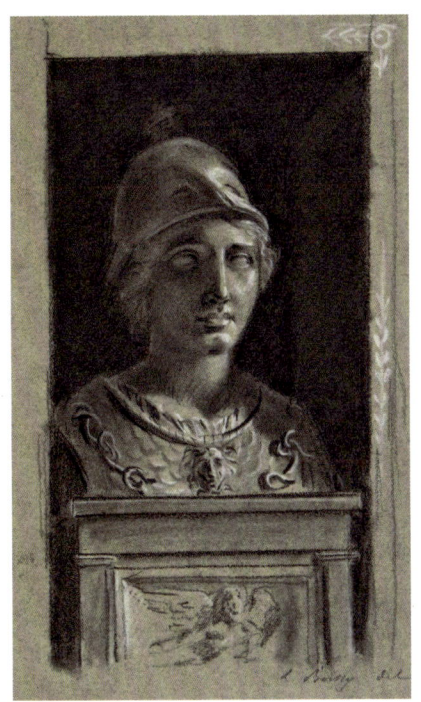

plates 4 and 5 (SEE FIG. 2B.5), respectively, show objects and ornaments decorating the space and walls of the atelier. By the time one arrives at the third fascicle, one is confronted by a dramatic perspectival view of a bedroom, an image that is upstaged in magnificence and complexity by the opening plates for the fourth and the fifth fascicles, a bedroom for Madame Moreau and a bedroom for Monsieur O. respectively (perhaps the financier Gabriel Julien Ouvrard) in the form of a Temple of Diana [FIG. 6.10].[31] From Isabey's studio to the final fascicle containing views of Percier and Fontaine's interventions at the Musée Napoléon, the images begin and end in the Louvre at very different aesthetic and political moments in time.

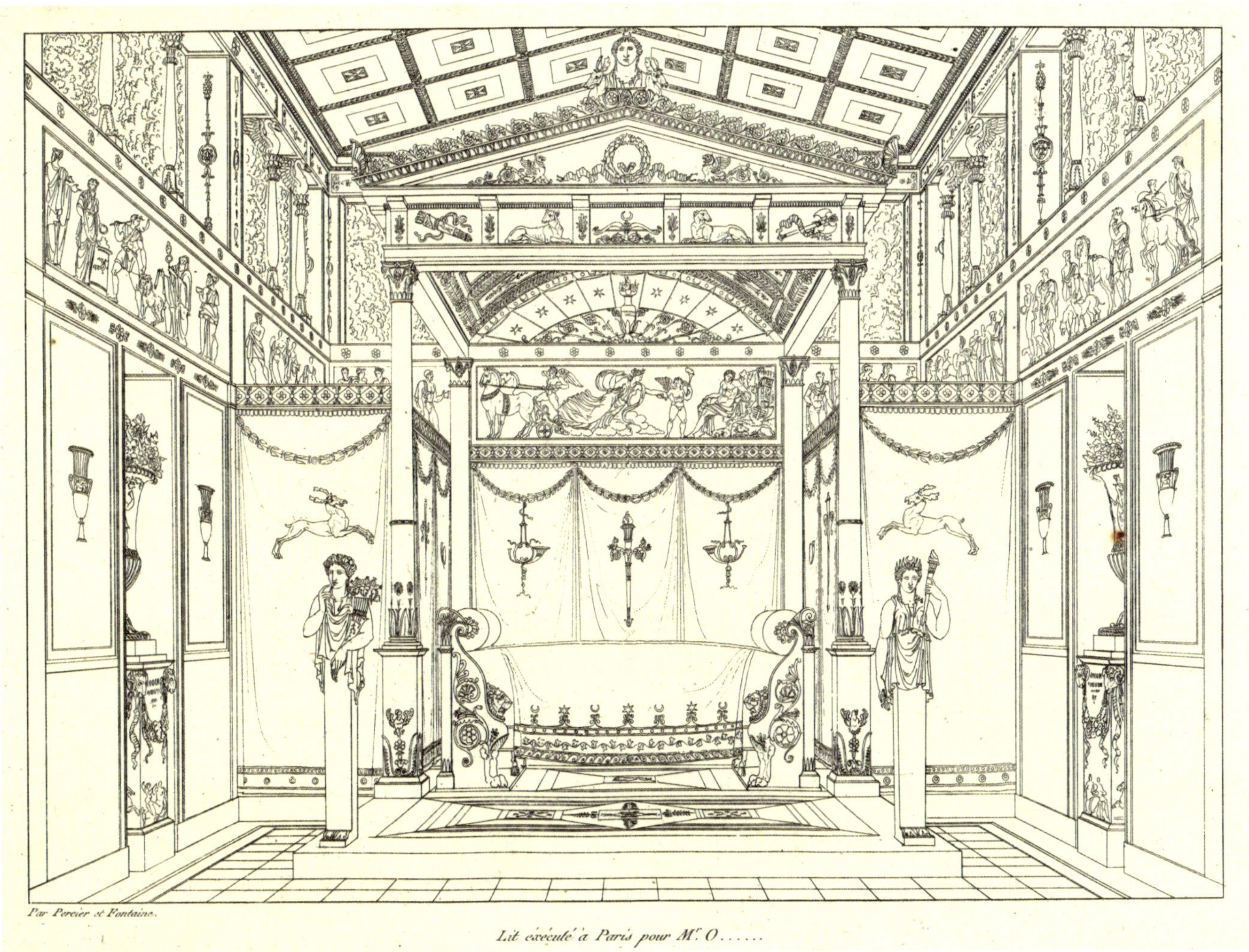

Coupled with the increasing presence of official commissions for Napoleon, the addition of the preliminary discourse in 1812 transformed the book into an idiosyncratic theory of interior decoration in which fixed Enlightenment ideals are coupled with a sense of historical change. This is the narrative thread that guides a text at once visionary and retroactive, penned at the end of the architects' careers as decorators when they were no longer in fashion. The architects speak to a readership well versed in the language of the *beau idéal*, as well as to those seeking to establish a legitimate place alongside architecture, painting, and sculpture for what they term "the industrial arts."[32] They argue against the fickle powers of fashion and describe the importance of "domestic utensils" for the fine arts and for understanding the spirit of an age. Echoing Winckelmann, they write that it was only at the end of the eighteenth century that the "simplicity of ancient taste" was restored. Antiquity, for the architects, is a moral imperative rather than a style to be copied.

Nowhere in the preliminary discourse does one find Napoleon mentioned, which raises the question of how Percier and Fontaine's celebrated interior decoration book became tied to the Empire, to the point where the twentieth-century edition was simply titled *The Empire Stylebook of Interior Decoration*. Whereas the association with Napoleon is evident in the commissions of the last plates, it must also be viewed in tandem with forms of collective memory, in which each subsequent edition of Percier and Fontaine's decoration book accumulated a stronger association with a polemical figure who haunted French political life throughout the nineteenth century. Although the 1827 edition of the *Recueil de décorations intérieures* 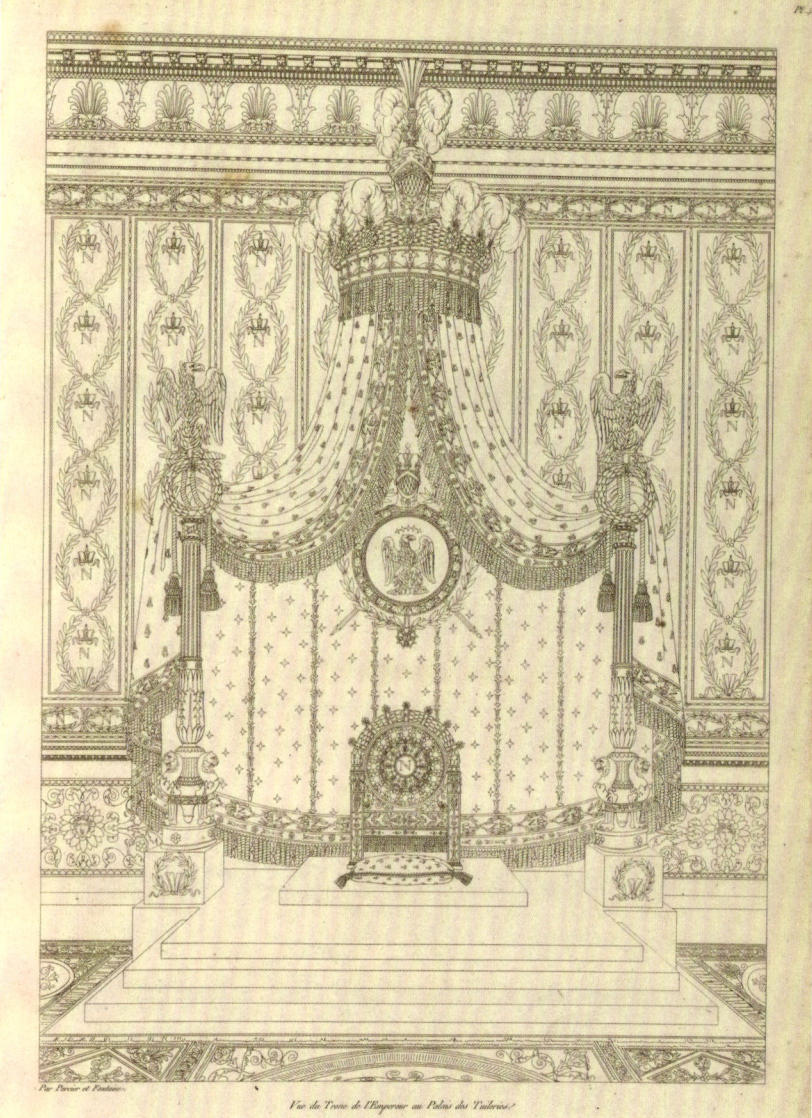 resembles the 1812 edition in format, the reactionary political climate of the Bourbon Restoration transformed the decoration book into an imperial souvenir, alongside the architects' decision the same year to publish their designs of the arc du Carrousel following Charles X's decision to remove Napoleon's statue from the triumphal arch and replace it with an allegorical figure of Restoration.[33] The political associations with Napoleon the book had acquired by the mid-nineteenth century were neutralized in the Italian decorator Giuseppe Borsato's highly revi-

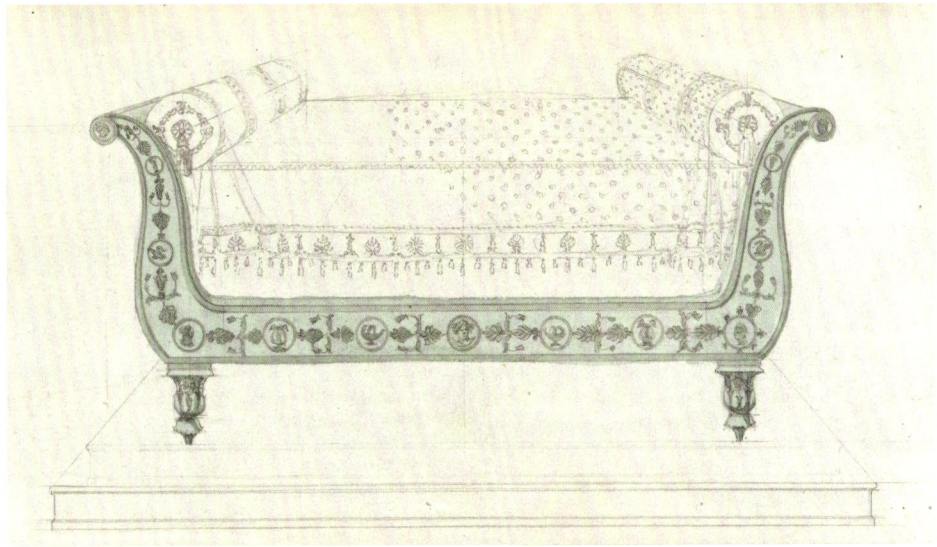

sionist edition of 1843, in which, in addition to appending his own designs and text, the Venetian removed Napoleon's initials from the Tuileries throne and published the book under the title *Raccolta di decorazioni interne* [FIG. 6.11; COMPARE FIG. 11.6].[34] Once more restored in the German edition from 1898, Napoleon's initials, along with Percier and Fontaine's designs, traveled to the United States in the twentieth century, at which point the decoration book had become a key reference for American designers seeking to bring a sense of French legitimacy into the homes of a class of wealthy patrons across the Atlantic [FIG. 6.12]. ●

▻ FIG 6.11. Giuseppe Borsato. *Charles Percier and Pierre Fontaine, Raccolta di decorazione interne che comprende quanto si riferisce all'addobabamento.* (Venice: G. Antonelli, 1843), pl. 48. Getty Research Institute, Los Angeles, 84-B8078.

◂ FIG 6.12. Ogden Codman. Design for a sleigh bed for Harold Brown Esq., 1893–94. Copied from Percier and Fontaine. Watercolor over graphite. The Metropolitan Museum of Art, New York, Gift of the Estate of Ogden Codman Jr., 1951, 51.644.76/78.

1 Charles Percier and Pierre Fontaine, "preliminary discourse," in Charles Percier and Pierre Fontaine. *Recueil de décorations intérieures* (Paris: Authors and Pierre Didot l'aîné, 1812), 1.

2 Jean-Philippe Garric, "Le *Recueil de décorations* de Charles Percier et Pierre Fontaine," in Lucie Fréjou and Michaël Decrossas, eds., *Ornements XVe–XIXe siècles. Chefs-d'œuvre de la bibliothèque de l'INHA (*Paris: INHA/Mare et Martin, 2014), 302–11.

3 The most comprehensive treatment of Percier's work in interior decoration remains Hans Ottomeyer, *Das frühe Œuvre Charles Percier (1782–1800). Zu den Anfängen des Historismus in Frankreich* (Munich: Ludwig-Maximilens-Universität, 1981). For an overview of Percier's work and his relationship with Fontaine, see Jean-Philippe Garric, *Percier et Fontaine, les architectes de Napoléon* (Paris: Belin, 2012).

4 See John E. Toews, "Building Historical and Cultural Identities in a Modernist Frame: Karl Friedrich Schinkel's Bauakademie in Context," in Mark Micale, Robert L. Dietle, and Peter Gay, eds., *Enlightenment, Passion, Modernity: Historical Essays in European Thought and Culture* (Stanford, CA: Stanford University Press, 2000), 167–206.

5 Pierre François Léonard Fontaine, *Journal (1799–1853)*, ed. Marguerite David-Roy. 2 vols. (Paris: École nationale supérieure des beaux-arts / Institut français

d'architecture / Société de l'histoire de l'art français, 1987), 1:32.

6 Garric, "Le *Recueil de décorations*," 259–60. The Art Institute of Chicago possesses a volume of 13 colored plates that have been interpreted as an "official" copy. See David Van Zanten, "Fontaine in the Burnham Library," *Art Institute of Chicago Museum Studies* 13, no. 2 (1988): 140.

7 Anne Dion-Tenenbaum, "Published Sources of Ornaments," in Odile Nouvel, *Symbols of Power: Napoleon and the Art of the Empire Style 1800–1815* (New York: Harry N. Abrams, for the American Federation of the Arts and Musée des Arts décoratifs, 2007), 68. The Soane Museum in London possesses a rare hand-colored edition of the *Palais, maisons et autres édifices* that was presented to Josephine shortly before Percier and Fontaine began work at Malmaison.

8 Ibid.

9 Annemarie Kleinert, *Le "Journal des Dames et des Modes" ou la conquête de l'Europe féminine (1797–1839)* (Stuttgart: Jan Thorbecke, 2001).

10 The Metropolitan Museum of Art has an example of plates from the *Recueil de décorations intérieures* bound with images from Dumont's *Parallèle de plans des plus Belles Salles de Spectacles d'Italie et de France* and a selection of plates from Amant Parfait Prieur's *Collection des prix. Salle de spectacles, plans et ameublement,* Department of Drawings and Prints, Rogers Fund, 52.519.157.

11 Landon lists successive issues: in 1802, the third fascicle was issued; in 1803, the fifth and sixth fascicles were issued; in 1804 the seventh. The last edition of Landon's book in 1805 mentions that the eighth and ninth fascicles had been issued. Ottomeyer, *Das frühe Œuvre Charles Percier*, 197.

12 Ibid., 195–200.

13 Ibid., 195–222. See also Nicolas Savage, British Architectural Library, and Royal Institute of British Architects et al., *Early Printed Books: 1478–1840: Catalogue of the British Architectural Library Early Imprints Collection* (London; New Jersey: Bowker-Saur, 1994–2003), 1424–45.

14 See Ulrich Leben, *Object Design in the Age of Enlightenment: The History of the Royal Free Drawing School in Paris* (Los Angeles: J. Paul Getty Museum, 2004). Fontaine's disdain for ornament is noted in his memoir, *Mia Vita*, in which he recalls having an argument with Percier over his decision to depict Trajan's column for his academic *envoi* in Rome. See Iris Moon, "Ornament after the Orders: Percier, Fontaine and the Rise of the Architectural Interior in Post-Revolutionary France," PhD diss., Massachusetts Institute of Technology, 2013, 78–83.

15 Paul Marmottan, "Percier à son collègue Pâris 1804," *Bulletin de la société de l'histoire de l'art* (1922): 329.

16 Garric, Le *Recueil*, 259.

17 See Charles Percier to Hippolyte Lebas, February 1, 1808, Hippolyte Lebas Correspondence, Los Angeles, Getty Research Institute (890012).

18 Dion-Tenenbaum, "Published Sources of Ornaments," 68.

19 Percier and Fontaine, *Recueil de décorations intérieures*, 83-B3068 Copy 1, Special Collections, Getty Research Institute, Los Angeles, CA.

20 Charles Landon, *Nouvelles des arts, peinture, sculpture, architecture et gravure* (Paris: Author, 1801).

21 On the publishing structure of Percier and Fontaine's books as a source of architectural design, see Jean-Philippe Garric, *Recueils d'Italie. Les modèles italiens dans les livres d'architecture français* (Liège: Mardaga, 2004), esp. 110.

22 Moon, "Ornament after the Orders," 123–26.

23 Fontaine, *Journal (1799–1853)*, 2:1105.

24 A copy of the *Recueil de décorations intérieures* was found in the library of Martin Guillaume Biennais. Dion-Tenenbaum, "Sources of Ornament," 69. On copying in the context of architectural education, see Marie-Laure Crosnier-Leconte, "Dessins d'école, bibliothèques d'ateliers: une affaire de copies," in *Bibliothèques d'atelier. Édition et enseignement de l'architecture, Paris 1785–1871*, ed. Jean-Philippe Garric (Paris: Institut national d'histoire de l'art, April 2011).

25 Frédéric Bouchet Album, acc. no. 1382-099 960040, Special Collections, Getty Research Institute. Bouchet was a Percier student who published prolifically and helped build Napoleon's tomb at Les Invalides. See Van Zanten, "Fontaine in the Burnham Library," 142.

26 Atelier de Percier, 63 bound drawings, OP 7, acc. no. 2000.2, Percier and Fontaine Collection, Ryerson and Burnham Archives, Ryerson and Burnham Libraries, The Art Institute of Chicago, IL.

27 Jean-Pierre Samoyault, *Mobilier français Consulat et Empire* (Paris: Editions Gourcuff-Gradenigo, 2009), 42.

28 Jean-Pierre Samoyault, *Le Mobilier du général Moreau, un ameublement à la mode en 1802* (Paris, Réunion des musées nationaux, 1992), 52–54.

29 Ottomeyer, *Das frühe Œuvre Charles Percier*, 152–59.

30 Vincent Cochet and Sylvain Levaissière, *Boilly, 1761–1845. Un grand peintre français de la Révolution à la Restauration* (Lille: Musée des beaux-arts, 1988), 52–53.

31 Ottomeyer, *Das frühe Œuvre Charles Percier*, 208–10.

32 Antoine Chrysostôme Quatremère de Quincy, *Essai sur la nature, le but et les moyens de l'imitation dans les beaux-arts* (Paris: Treuttel and Würtz, 1823).

33 Fontaine, *Journal (1799–1853)*, 2:736. A French version of the book was reissued in Naples in 1838, the year Percier died.

34 See chapter 6a, 'The Italian Edition of the *Recueil*,' in this volume.

THE ITALIAN EDITION OF THE *RECUEIL*

FIG 6A.1. Title page of Italian edition of *Recueil de décorations intérieures* (Naples: Fibreno, 1838).

LETIZIA TEDESCHI

As the international reputation of Percier and Fontaine grew, one might expect to see their work gaining a wider diffusion, especially in Italy during the period when it was largely under French control.[1] In the present state of scholarship, evidence of its impact there is less plentiful than might be expected, at least prior to a certain date, but much research remains to be done. It is surprising, for example, how little attention has been paid to the French-language edition issued in Naples in 1838, the year of Percier's death, by a "French" publishing enterprise, the Tipografia del Fibreno [FIG. 6A.1].[2] Its dimensions are identical to those of the original edition (1801–12) published by Pierre Didot l'aîné, and though it contains all seventy-two of the original plates, it lacks the preliminary discourse. At the time, the business was under the direction of Ernest Lefebvre, who had been affiliated with Firmin Didot in Paris for some time.[3] Doubtless future scholarship will shed light on both the circumstances surrounding this edition and the extent of its impact.

However, the most widely disseminated Italian edition of the *Recueil* is the one published in Venice in 1843. Entitled *Raccolta di decorazioni interne che comprende quanto si riferisce all'addobbamento composta da C. Percier e P.L.F. Fontaine* (Anthology of interior decoration that includes many designs by C. Percier and P.L.F. Fontaine), it featured (on facing pages) both the original French text and an Italian translation by the architect Francesco Lazzari [FIG. 6A.2]. This edition appeared about the same time as other Italian editions adapted from French books on architecture and decoration, a circumstance that increased the public's interest in it. Lazzari had previously executed the drawings for several plates in an anthology entitled *Fabbriche più cospicue di Venezia* (The most notable buildings in Venice; 1815–20), a publication in the series of Italian model books initiated by Percier and Fontaine's anthology of Roman palaces (1798), an augmented edition of which (1838–40) also included plates after drawings by Lazzari.[4] The *Raccolta* was published by Giuseppe Antonelli[5] and included additional notes by the artist Giuseppe Borsato, who had initiated the project.[6]

This new edition included a second part with forty-eight new plates and accompanying glosses illustrating work by Borsato, as well as a longer text by Francesco Zanotto entitled "Decorazione suppellettili ed altri oggetti d'ornamento del Prof. Giuseppe Borsato" (Decorations, furniture, and other decorative objects by Prof. Giuseppe Borsato). This supplement will orient my reflections, which will take into account the Venetian context that shaped his edition, which was strongly influenced by the Palladian heritage as well as by contemporary work like that of the architect Giannantonio Selva, whose radically abstract neoclassical idiom—for example, his design for the original theater of La Fenice (1790–92)—sparked controversy.[7]

When this expanded edition of the *Recueil* appeared, the Venetian architectural world had developed a new interest in the medieval buildings that would be published by Pietro Selvatico in *Sull'architettura e sulla scultura in Venezia. Dal Medio Evo sino ai giorni nostri* (On architecture and sculpture in Venice, from the Middle Ages to our own time; 1847).[8] This work was an outgrowth of Séroux d'Agincourt's six-volume history of European art and architecture from the fourth to the sixteenth century (1823),[9] whose parts on architecture were published in a one-volume Italian translation in 1826.[10] According to Guido Zucconi, the underlying strategy of Selvatico's book was one "that would become frequent in debates in the second half of the nineteenth century, [namely] pitting architectural relativism against the

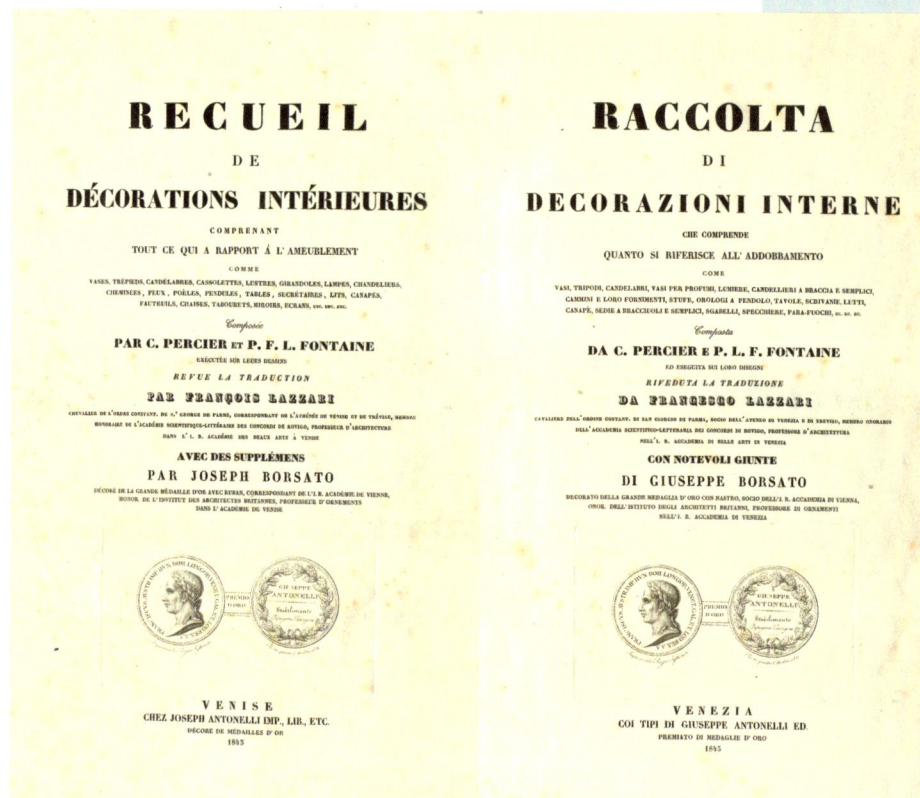

▲ FIG 6A.2. Title page of second Italian edition of the *Recueil de décorations: Raccolta di decorazioni interne che comprende quanto si riferisce all'addobbamento con notevoli aggiunte di Giuseppe Borsato* (Venice: Giuseppe Antonelli, 1845). Avery Architectural and Fine Arts Library, Columbia University.

uniformity of classical canons."¹¹ This approach was not far removed from the one that shaped the new Venetian edition of the *Recueil*.

This edition was only one of many works from preceding decades to be reissued during these years. The trend was spearheaded by the publisher Antonelli,¹² whose initiatives along these lines fostered the development of new theoretical formulations and a new lexicon consistent with the historicist movement that took hold after 1815. Surprisingly enough, this applies to Francesco Lazzari's *Compendio delle più interessanti regole di architettura tecnico-pratiche* (Manual of the most interesting techno-practical rules of architecture) of 1830, which was followed by *Principi dello stilo gotico* (Principles of Gothic style),¹³ a free adaptation of a book published by Friedrich Hoffstadt in 1853 that effectively reprised, in idealized form, some aspects of Percier's neo-Gothic designs.

Progressively, then, through the first half of the nineteenth century and after, there emerged a tendency to recast architecture, ornament, decoration, and sculpture into a single entity, one in which classical and romantic paradigms could coexist, sometimes uneasily, or even merge and mutually enrich one another to produce something new. In Venice, the transition from the preceding conceptual regime to the one we are attempting to describe found signal expression in the announcement, on February 20, 1847, of a competition to select a new professor of architecture at the academy. The announcement specified that the history of architecture was a field of study determined by "symbolic allegory, mythology, antiquarian knowledge, and art history among ancient peoples, especially the Greeks," and which emphasized "intermediate" periods. In a way consistent with the teachings of Selva, this was a flexible approach to canonical rules of composition, one that avoided giving privileged status to symmetry and other principles associated with the recent past and implicitly advocated an architectural design practice in which everything is more fluid and interconnected. All of the various elements are deemed to have equal value, including the decorative apparatus—conceived along lines consistent with the unity initially established by Percier and Fontaine—which functions, by way of drawing, as a guiding thread that connects the gestating forms that aggregate in architecture. It was not by chance that (as one scholar put it) Selvatico sought to approach architecture "on the one hand through a knowledge of its elementary constituents and on the other through a critical reading of the most significant examples offered by history." This was a procedure in which—note the parallels with Percier's practice—"drawing is the principal instrument of apprenticeship, before becoming the expression of the project."¹⁴

TRUTH AND FALSITY IN THE DISCOURSE ON ORNAMENT

What critical perspectives can we extrapolate from the above? By way of conclusion, I would like to examine, with an assist from Friedrich Nietzsche, the process whereby the ornamental and decorative system was redefined in a way that enriched the citational content of architecture. Thanks to the *Recueil de décorations intérieures* by Percier and Fontaine, as well as other publications, this movement was able to draw sustenance from both ancient and modern models in an unprecedented way. In question here—what we must strive to better understand—is nothing less than a redefinition of the entire architectural domain as something that oscillated, in terms of its formal vocabulary, between the historical and the contemporary, between literalism and invention, between materiality and immateriality.

This amounts to reflecting on how—during and after the rise of Napoleon, which contaminated everything by obliging it to revert to politics—the very being of architecture became false, in the sense that the truth of ornament, which completes a building and gives it emotional resonance, can be conceptualized only as "something that must be created and gives a name to a process,"[15] something incapable of determining, through its process, its own identity and form. For it is this very process that relativizes the certainties of materiality and historical truth: a creative process that, paradoxically, was mobilized within the very historical time that it negates. The history that it represents, through ornament, is a history of the past rather than of the present, an abstraction that is motionless and suspended as well as vital and fluid—and capable of tipping one way or the other. It is, moreover, a disassociated process, one that unfolds on an ideal plane and is constantly changing, like the forms and figures in which it traffics. It is a process parallel to reality but cut off from it, because it focuses solely on the representation of something that has no purpose of its own and remains alienated from the resulting whole, effectively petrifying ornament into an irrevocable sequence of forms and values.

From this perspective, the *Recueil* is a problematic point of reference. Unlike other contemporary publications, such as those of Jean Nicolas Louis Durand that advance, by means of an ideal system, a didactic and methodological agenda, the *Recueil* set out to recast the orders and paradigms inherited from the antique into a fictive hierarchical system and a new grammar. This knot, impossible to unravel, bound the values and dynamics of the new style both to a form-generating movement that had been active for decades and to an overcoming or sublation of classical architecture. This brought enrichments as well as limitations: irrefutable challenges that weakened the potential of classical historicism. This moment, then, gave birth to a truth both elusive and pointless, but inclined to manifest itself by isolating its own space of fantasy, the precise space that generated these ornaments, a confined realm situated between reality and unreality, since it possesses neither norms nor essence. It seems to be suspended between desire and imagination, insofar as it produces neither forms nor objects but rather—to borrow a conceit from philosophy—an "adventure," an imaginative process. Resorting to the geometric metaphor of an ellipse, we might say that its two foci were Descartes and Plato—evidence and pedagogy—or, alternatively, knowledge and non-knowledge, an opposition posited by Nietzsche when he declared: "The opposition is dawning between the world we revere and the world that we live."[16]

Finally, we arrive at a definition of classicizing ornament that presents itself in the terms summarily evoked above: an ornament whose identity is neither immediately classifiable nor fully anchored in the physical, mathematical, and morphological realities of architecture but which nonetheless refers to them, derives from them, and is justified by them. Such a new approach should open the way to a different reading of the "classical" architectural language in all its regional and individual inflections, envisioning its decorative elements as potential terms in a formula that would make it possible to surpass the limits of reality. It would enable us to envision other paradigms in keeping with a vision of the world as inhabited by men whom Joseph Rykwert called, in a now canonical text, the "first moderns"[17]: the inventors of a reality in which truth and fantasy coexist and mutually inform one another. This situation, which can be imagined as a "beginning,"[18] confirms the hypothesis of the initiatory role of Percier's Roman sojourn, and, finally, of the *Recueil de décorations intérieures*. ●

1 From 1797, when Napoleon established the Cisalpine Republic, until the fall of the empire in 1814.
2 The Tipografia del Fibreno was established in 1810 by Charles Antoine Béranger, a participant in the peaceful invasion of French writers, artists, and craftsmen attracted by the court of Joachim Murat, who already owned another printing enterprise. The new one was located in the former Carmelite convent of Santa Maria delle Forme in Tavernanova, near the island of Liri, premises granted free of charge by the French government. Both a character foundry and a printing establishment, it employed many French workers. See Vincenzo Trombetta, *L'editoria a Napoli nel decennio francese* (Milan: Franco Angeli, 2011), 57–58.
3 On the initiative of his father, Charles Lefebvre (1755–1858), who in 1822, on the death of Charles Béranger, became the sole proprietor of the Neapolitan firm, it became affiliated with the Parisian publisher Firman Didot in 1828. His son, Ernest Lefebvre, produced publications for the Royal Society of Naples as well as wallpaper. See Anna Dell'Orefice, "Ernesto Lefebvre," in *Dizionario Biografico degli Italiani* (Rome: Treccani, 2005).
4 Trained at the Accademia delle Belle Arti in Venice, Francesco Lazzari was the favorite student of the head of its architecture section, Gianantonio Selva. In 1819 he succeeded his teacher in that post, which he held until 1855. He also edited the Italian edition of Friedrich Hoffstadt's book on the Gothic style (*Principi dello stile gotico*, 1853). See Elena Bassi, "L'architetto Francesco Lazzari," *Rivista di Venezia* 13 (1934): 239–50; Massimiliano Savorra, "Francesco Lazzari," in *Dizionario Biografico degli Italiani* (Rome: Treccani, 2005), vol. 64; Giandomenico Romanelli, *Venezia Ottocento. L'architettura, l'urbanistica* (Venice: Officina Edizioni, 1988); and Guido Zucconi, *L'invenzione del passato: Camillo Boito e l'architettura neomedievale* (Venice: Marsilio, 1997), 60, 78, 80.
5 A publisher-printer based in Venice, his firm, which enjoyed an international reputation, employed artists and scholars as well as technicians. Recognized for the high quality of its lithographic work, his publishing house collaborated closely with the Accademia delle Belle Arti in Venice. See Paolo Tentori, "Antonelli Giuseppe," in *Dizionario Biografico degli Italiani* (Rome: Treccani, 1961), vol. 3.
6 Giuseppe Borsato (1779–1849) enrolled in the Venetian Accademia delle Belle Arti in 1791. In tandem with the entrepreneur Carlo Neumann Rizzi, he launched his professional career as a set designer, notably at the opera house La Fenice, where he was placed in charge of set design. He continued to work in that capacity until 1801, when he became an ornamentalist and a painter-decorator. In 1812 he was appointed to the chair of ornament at the Venetian academy, a post he retained until 1849. In 1806 he began to receive important commissions from the Napoleonic regime, designing festival decorations and ephemeral decors in addition to new interiors for rooms in the "royal palace" in Venice and in the apartments of Viceroy Eugène de Beauharnais in the villa at Stra. See Renato De Feo, "Une commande de Dominique-Vivant Denon à Giuseppe Borsato: les fêtes vénitiennes pour Napoléon I," *Revue du Louvre* 3 (2002), 66–75; Giuseppe Pavanello, ed., *La pittura nel Veneto: l'Ottocento* (Milan: Electa, 2003), 421–521; Ranieri Varese, "Giuseppe Borsato Accademico: l'orazione funebre per Antonio Canova," *Arte Documento*, no. 25 (2009): 213–19.
7 Romanelli, *Venezia Ottocento*, 68.
8 Pietro Selvatico, *Sull'architettura e sulla scultura in Venezia. Dal Medio Evo sino ai giorni nostri* (Venice: Paolo Ripamondi Carpano, 1847).
9 Jean-Baptiste Louis Georges Séroux d'Agincourt, *Histoire de l'Art par les Monumens, depuis sa décadence au IVe siècle jusqu'à son renouvellement au XVIe*, 6 vols. (Paris: Treutel et Würtz, 1823).
10 Jean-Baptiste Louis Georges Séroux d'Agincourt, *Storia dell'arte dimostrata coi monumenti dalla sua decadenza nel IV secolo fino al suo risorgimento nel XVI*, vol. 2 (Prato: Fratelli Giachetti, 1826). Another point of reference was *The Stones of Venice* by John Ruskin, who visited Venice in 1845 and again in 1849–50, when Selvatico was named secretary of the Venetian academy.
11 Guido Zucconi, *L'invenzione del passato: Camillo Boito e l'architettura neomedievale* (Venice: Marsilio, 1997), 62–63.
12 Antonelli specialized in lengthy reference works such as dictionaries and encyclopedias. In the years of interest to us here, his titles included Francesco Lazzari, *Compendio delle più interessanti regole di architettura tecnico-pratiche* (1830); *Le fabbriche e I monumenti cospicui di Venezia illustrati da Leopoldo Cicongnara, da Antonio Diedo e da Giannantonio Selva* (1831, 1838, 1840); *Le fabbriche civili ecclesiastiche e militari di Michele Sanmicheli* (1831); Melchior Missirini, *Del tempio eretto in Possagno da Antonio Canova* (1833); Jean Nicolas Louis Durand, *Raccoltà e parallelo delle fabbriche classiche di tutti i tempi* (1833); *Il palazzo ducale di Venezia, illustrato da Francesco Zanotto*, 4 vols. (1846–61); *Le fabbriche e i disegni di Antonio Diedo nobile veneto* (1846); and Léonce Reynaud, *Trattato di architettura contenente nozioni generali della costruzione e sulla storia dell'arte* (1853).
13 Francesco Lazzari, *I principi dello stile gotico cavati dai monumenti del medio-evo, ad uso degli artisti ed operai di Friedrich Hoffstadt tradotti dal francese* (Venice: Giovanni Brizeghel, 1853); Friedrich [Frédéric] Hoffstadt, *Principes du Style gothique exposés d'après des documents authentiques du Moyen Âge* (Paris and Liège: Noblet, 1854).
14 Zucconi, *L'invenzione del passato*, 79–80.
15 Friedrich Nietzsche, *The Will to Power*, ed. Walter Kaufmann (New York: Vintage Books, 1968), 298. In the continuation of this passage, Nietzsche goes on to say that Truth "has in itself no end," being "a *processus in infinitum*, an active determining."
16 Friedrich Nietzsche, *Nietzsche: Writings from the Late Notebooks*, trans. Kate Sturge, ed. Rüdiger Bittner (Cambridge: Cambridge University Press, 2003), 84.
17 Joseph Rykwert, *The First Moderns: The Architects of the Eighteenth Century* (Cambridge, MA: MIT Press, 1980).
18 In the sense elaborated by Husserl in "The Origin of Geometry," first published as an independent text in 1939 and later appended to *The Crisis of European Sciences*. Edmund Husserl, *L'origine de la géométrie* (Paris: Presses universitaires de France, 1962), app. 6, 353–78.

CHAPTER 7

THE *LIVRE DU SACRE*

AN ORNAMENTALIST AND HIS COLLABORATOR

CHRISTOPHE BEYELER

N AMED EMPEROR BY AN ACT OF THE SÉNAT CONSERVATEUR ON May 18, 1804, Napoleon I decided to mark the establishment of the empire with a ceremony combining the "coronation and *sacre* of His Majesty," which would take place not at Reims—now stripped of its prestigious ancien-régime status to the point that it was no longer even a bishopric—but in the metropolitan church of Notre-Dame de Paris. This revival of the monarchical rite entailed the publication of a commemorative *Livre du Sacre* conceived along the lines of those prepared for Louis XV and Louis XVI [FIG. 7.1]. This government project was quite distinct from the private initiative previously begun by Percier and Fontaine, a speculative enterprise published by Leblanc in 1807 and entitled *Description des cérémonies et des fêtes qui ont eu lieu pour le courronnement de Leurs Majestés Napoléon, empereur des Français et roi d'Italie, et Joséphine son*

▼ FIG 7.1. Jean-Baptiste Isabey, Pierre Fontaine, Charles Percier, and other collaborators, calligraphy by Baron, binding by Tessier. *Livre du sacre de S.M. l'empereur Napoléon dans l'Église métropolitaine de Paris le XI Frimaire an XIII* (Sunday, December 2, 1804) (Paris: Impr. impériale, 1804–15). Pen and brown wash drawings, engravings in black ink, and red morocco binding. Château de Fontainebleau, musée Napoléon Ier, Fontainebleau, GM Bibl. 3502.

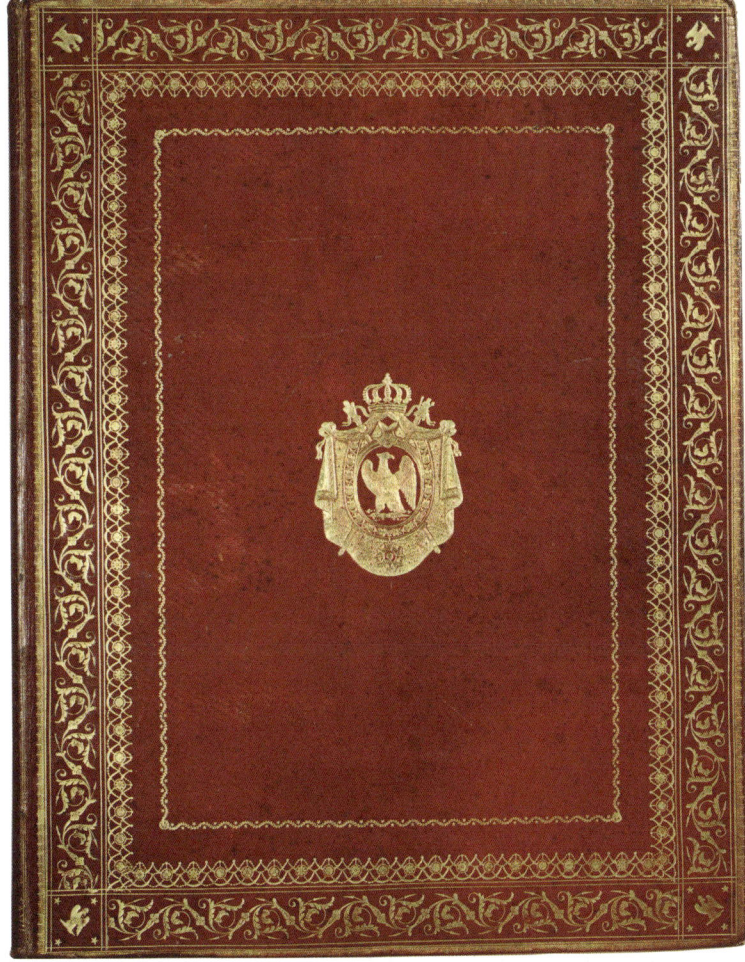

auguste épouse. Recueil de décorations exécutées dans l'église Notre-Dame de Paris et au Champ-de-Mars (SEE FIG. 13.8). This last had etched line engravings, but the *Livre du Sacre* would be illustrated with burin engravings, which meant that it would take much longer to prepare.

AN ENTERPRISE THAT CONTINUED THROUGHOUT THE REIGN

The project was announced in March 1805:

Work is now under way on the book of the *sacre* of their Imperial Majesties. The execution of this large book should be commensurate, in its magnificence, with the pomp of a ceremony that surpassed other solemn rites of this kind through its union of everything that is august and imposing. His excellency M. de Ségur, grand master of ceremonies, charged by His Majesty the Emperor with the general oversight of this beautiful enterprise, has determined its executants, as follows: the text will be prepared by M. Aignan, aide in charge of ceremonies, imperial secretary in charge of ambassadorial introductions; the illustrations will be prepared by M. Isabey, painter, designer of ceremonies and of the cabinet, and MM. Fontaine and Percier, architects to His Majesty. The former will execute the figures, the two others the architecture and ornament. The burin of the most celebrated engravers will be employed to consecrate these grand memories. The work will appear toward the end of next year.[1]

It soon became apparent that the stipulated time frame was not viable. The slow advance of the project can be followed in the account books of the grand master of ceremonies.[2] Eager for recognition, the artists—especially the engravers—wanted to exhibit their contributions at the Salon.[3] Motivated by other considerations, Fontaine, the operation's mainspring, tried to solicit the interest of the master of Europe, noting with annoyance on February 8, 1809: "I had assembled in the Gallery of Diana all the art objects that had some claim on his attention, like the drawings and engravings for the book of the sacre undertaken and overseen by MM. Isabey, Percier, and myself on the orders of the grand master of ceremonies [and] at the expense of the Crown Treasury.

A colored exemplar of the book that Percier and I had published on the same subject, some drawings by Monsieur Isabey, some models, and a large number of drawings of furniture of all kinds. This confusing array of different objects diverted the Emperor somewhat but interested him only slightly; he scarcely glanced at the furniture, he paid little attention to the drawings of the sacre."[4]

At the height of the Empire, the project was still unfinished. Fontaine made the following diary entry on May 7, 1810: "I have delivered to Monsieur de Ségur, grand master of ceremonies, twenty-six plates engraved at the expense of the Crown Treasury, against the funds for ceremonies, for the book of the sacre, for which MM. Isabey, Percier, and I made the drawings.[5] I still have 5,660 francs of the 100,000 francs given me on account to pay the engravers."[6] [FIG. 7.2]

When the Empire fell on April 6, 1814,[7] the day of Napoleon's unconditional abdication at Fontainebleau, Fontaine delivered the matrices of this official enterprise to a public institution: "I left at the engraving bureau, in the hands of M. Morel d'Arleux, its curator, the engraved plates of the sacre of the Emperor. This publication, undertaken by MM. Isabey, Percier, and myself under the direction of the grand master of ceremonies at the expense of the Crown Treasury, is completed. The related expenses have been paid, with the exception of those for drawings that are due to us, and against which we have received some advances. M. Morel did not give me a receipt for the forty-one engraved plates[8] that constitute the totality of the work, and which I left in his hands."[9]

Paradoxically, the work was finally printed only during the Hundred Days. In an entry dated December 13, 1815, Fontaine recounted bitterly: "We spent the three months of the Emperor's return finding some way to complete and publish the book of the sacre begun in February 1805....I think that I am finally rid for good of the annoyances of a publication that cost me so much care, that has lasted so long, the product of which has been so modest, and that circumstances condemn to obscurity. I readily sacrifice what remains due me so as never to hear it spoken of again."[10]

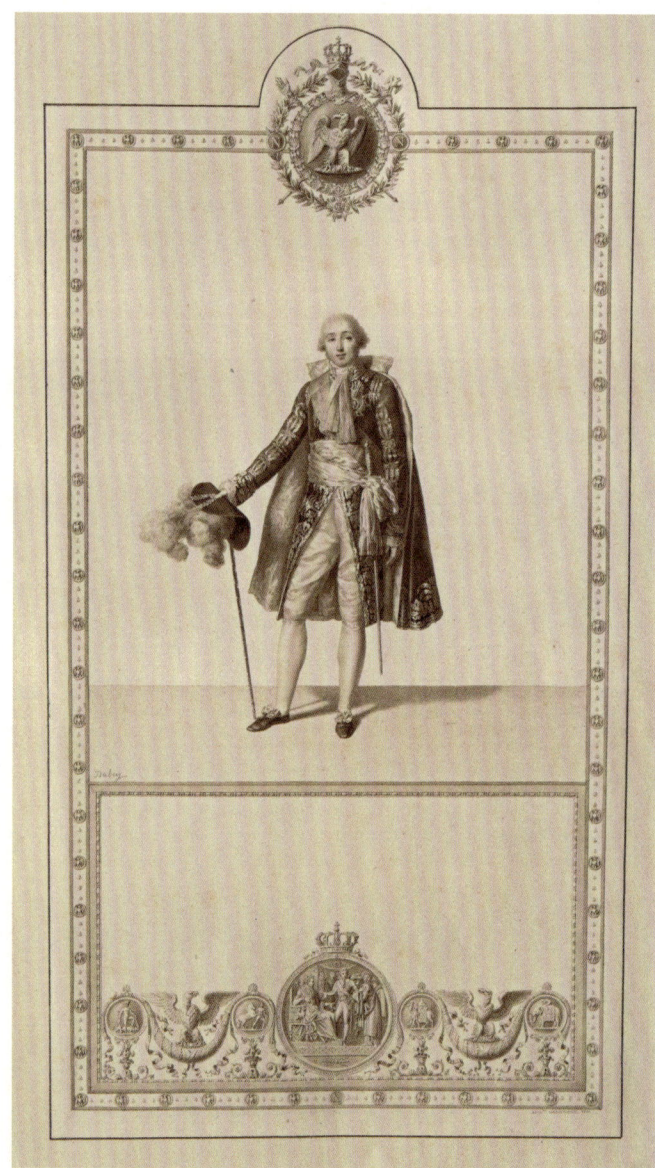

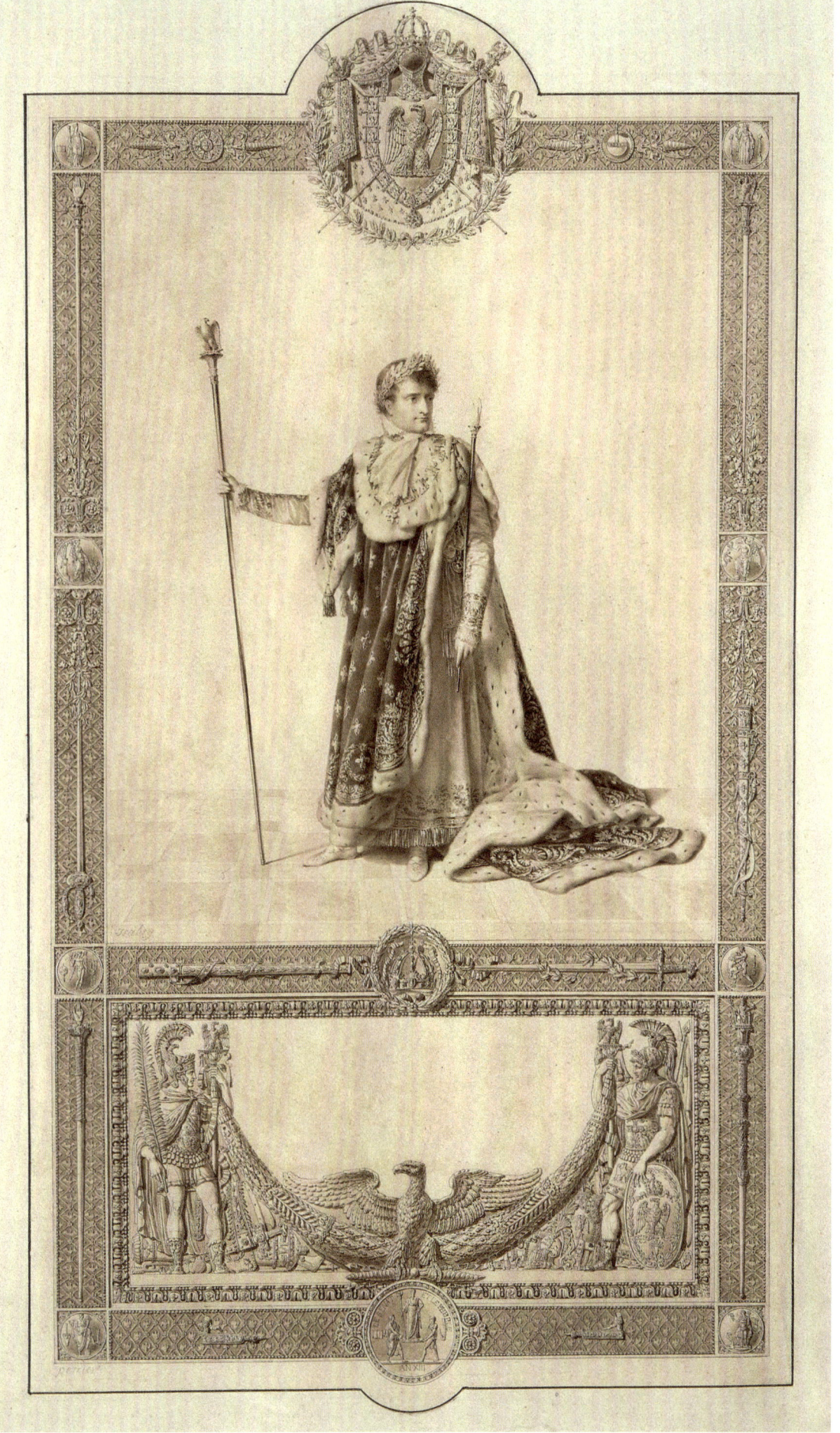

◁ **FIG 7.2.** Jean-Baptiste Isabey and Auguste Garneray. *Costume of a Grand Officer of the Crown*. Drawing for pl. xx of the *Livre du Sacre*, 1811. Pen and brown wash on paper. Château de Fontainebleau, musée Napoléon Ier, GM Bibl. 3502.

▷ **FIG 7.3.** Jean-Baptiste Isabey and Charles Percier. *The Emperor in Grand Ceremonial Dress*. Drawing for pl. ix of the *Livre du Sacre*. Pen and brown wash on paper. Château de Fontainebleau, musée Napoléon Ier, GM Bibl. 3502.

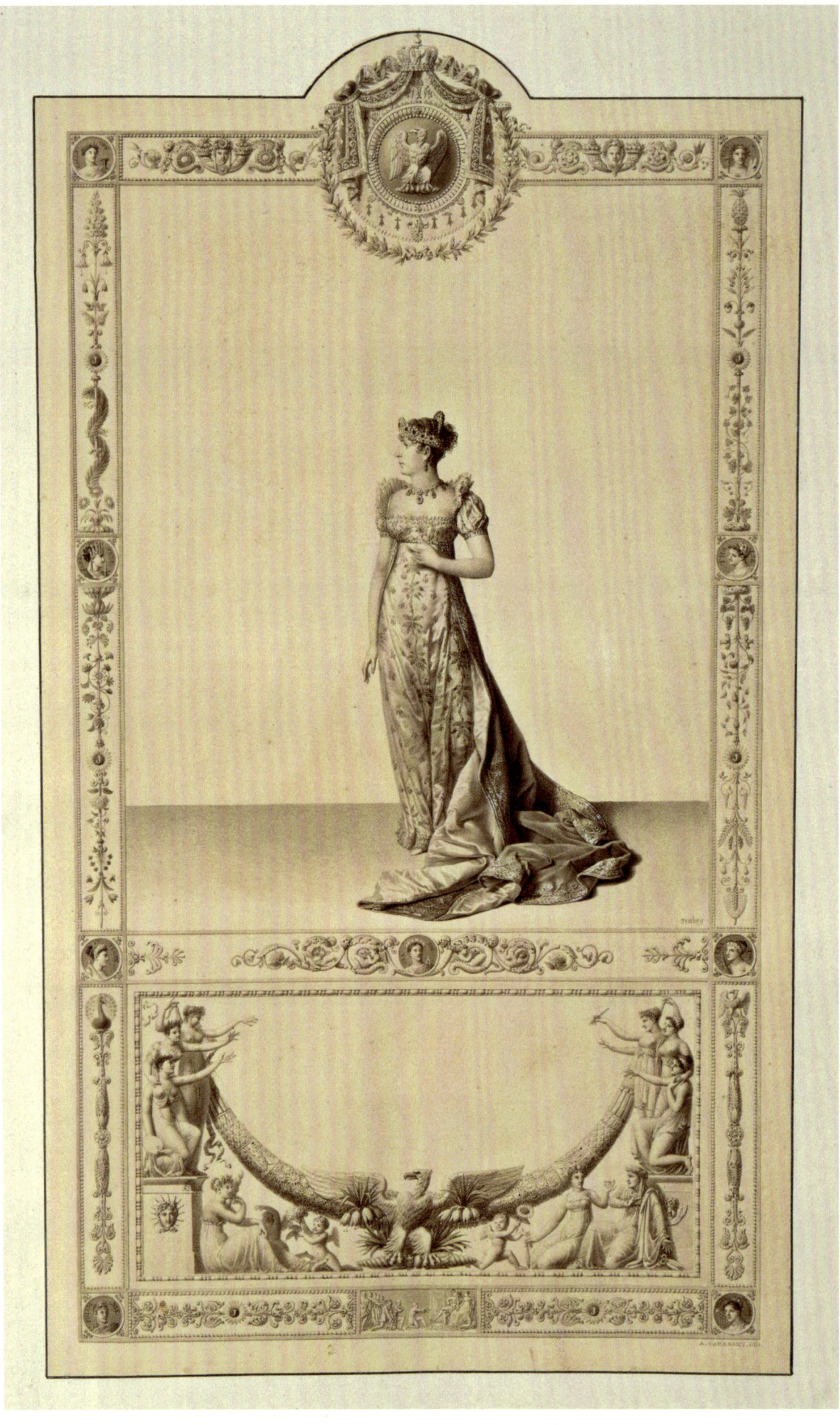

THE DISTRIBUTION OF TASKS: A FOURTH HAND FOR THE DRAWINGS?

A unique exemplar of the *Livre du Sacre*,[11] luxuriously bound by Tessier,[12] brings together a text of the ceremony executed in calligraphy by Baron, the original drawings that served as models for the engravings, and the engravings themselves, each mounted on a different sheet and bound with its model.

Is the distribution of roles in the execution of the drawings indicated on the engraved plates? The printed frontispiece indicates that Percier alone made the drawings ("Dessiné par Percier"). All seven of the "tableaux"—depictions of key moments of the ceremony with figures and extensive architectural backgrounds—carry the indication "Dessiné par Isabey et Fontaine," whereas the analogous phrase on almost all of the costume plates is "Dessiné par Isabey et Percier."

There are two exceptions to this signature associating Isabey and Percier. The first can be explained by the rank of the depicted figure, the first and most important one to appear in the "costumes" series; *L'Empereur en grand costume* (The Emperor in Grand Ceremonial Dress) [FIG. 7.3] reads the caption to this plate, on which the distribution of graphic tasks between draftsmen and engravers is explicitly indicated, for both the figure (double signature within the image: "Isabey Deline[avi]t" and "Alexandre Tardieu Sc[ulpsi]t"[13]) and the framing elements (another double signature: "Dessiné par Percier" and "Gravé par Malbeste et Dupréel"). The other exception is the *Grand officier de la Couronne*, whose features manifestly resemble those of Ségur [FIG. 7.2],[14] on which the indication reads "Dessiné par Isabey, Percier et Fontaine"; here again, the subject's status—in this case, both grand master of ceremonies and the official in charge of commissions relating to the book—made it important to identify all of the artists involved. If we can believe the engraved attributions, Isabey, Percier, and Fontaine provided all of the drawings.

However, careful examination[15] of the example of the *Livre du Sacre* at Fontainebleau, the only one that contains original drawings, reveals that six of these sheets bear the name of Auguste Simon Garneray[16]: the title page; depictions of two of the principals in the ceremony—Josephine[17] (*L'Impératrice en petit costume* [The Empress in Lesser Ceremonial Dress]) [FIG. 7.4], drawn in 1811, long after the divorce of December 1809), and Pius VII (*Le Pape*, which also bears the date 1811); *Le cardinal grand aumonier* (The Cardinal [and] Grand Chaplain; un-

◂ **FIG 7.4.** Jean-Baptiste Isabey and Auguste Garneray. *The Empress in Lesser Ceremonial Dress*, 1811. Drawing for pl. XII of the *Livre du Sacre*. Pen and brown wash on paper. Château de Fontainebleau, musée Napoléon Ier, GM Bibl. 3502. Cat. 49b.

dated), the features of which scarcely resemble those of Cardinal Fesch; a *Grand officier de la Couronne*, again dated 1811, clearly a portrait of Ségur; and, finally, the *Maître des cérémonies de l'Eglise* (Ecclesiastical Master of Ceremonies), also dated 1811.[18] Moreover, at least three additional sheets, although they are neither signed nor dated, can be attributed to Garneray on stylistic grounds: *Prince grand dignitaire*, *Colonel général des cuirassiers*, and *Colonel des dragons*.

BORDERS AND VIGNETTES: OUTLINES OF A COLLABORATION

The drawing for the title page [FIG. 7.5], in which a large space was left vacant to accommodate the printed title, is rectangular in shape. Here two hands are readily identifiable. The draftsmanship of one of them is soft, inclined to forms that are limp, even listless; this is Garneray, who signed the sheet at lower left: "AUGte GARNERAY." The other is taut, with drawing that is firm and resolute; this is Percier, who inscribed his signature at the bottom, in the center of the lower vignette: "C. PERCIER."

Garneray drew most of the framing elements for the title page. At the bottom of each side, a winged female Victory supports an attenuated staff bearing multiple attributes. The staff rising above the figure at left, who presents a metalwork crown and is accompanied by an eagle at her feet, is adorned with several attributes (bottom to top): shafts of wheat and the head of an ox surmounted by a plaque that reads "Agriculture"; attributes of the "Arts," so identified on a palette symbolizing Painting; a caduceus, the emblem of Commerce; a trophy of arms (helmet, crossed swords, shield) labeled "Guerre" (War); and, at the top, a culminating eagle, as on the emperor's scepter. The staff rising above the figure of Victory at right, who lifts a vegetal crown of victory and grasps a sword whose tip rests on the ground, also bears several attributes, in this case without identifying plaques (bottom to top): a laurel crown, scales of Justice, crossed swords, tables of the Law, a wreath

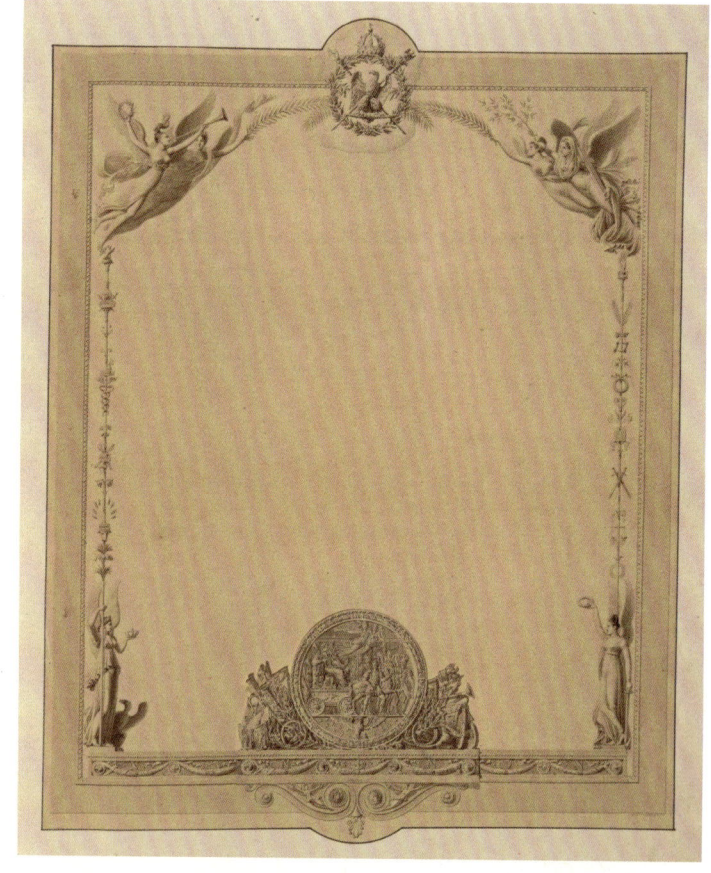

with fluttering ribbon attached, a bit alluding to the curbs of Temperance, and two palm fronds, the whole culminating in a block imprinted with an eye supporting a Hand of Justice, the organizing theme of this sequence.

At the top of the page, two pairs of winged female figures converge toward the center: a figure of Renown sounding her trumpet, two Victories carrying palm fronds, and Religion—the most fully dressed of these figures and the only one to be veiled—holding a cross and an olive branch, an allusion to the Concordat of 1801 and the gesture of religious pacification that returned Notre-Dame de Paris to the Catholic faith in 1802.

After Garneray drew the basic framing elements on this sheet, two vignettes were added. The first,[19] neatly cut from another sheet and then glued to the bottom of this one, includes a duplication, in darker brown ink and executed with more incisive draftsmanship, of the lower bar of the border, with its garlands and profile eagle heads. Above this, it incorporates the military attributes, standards, and musical instruments associated with a triumphal march, all flanking a large fictive medal. This medal shows the emperor and empress seated on a chariot drawn by four horses and accompanied by warriors, with figures of Renown and Religion hovering above. This scene, supported by an eagle—its wings spread wide—set against a starry ground, is circled by a laurel wreath into which are set the eight letters that spell NAPOLEON.

At the top center of the border another vignette, this one less carefully cut, was glued to the sheet. A combination of the *imperialia*, or emblems of the Empire, it shows an eagle grasping a thunderbolt and set against crossed eagle- and hand-of-Justice staffs, the whole set within a laurel wreath surmounted by a metalwork crown, effectively the keystone of the entire composition.

A similar collaboration[20] appears on the drawing for *Le Pape* [FIG. 7.6], where a vignette, carefully cut out, was glued to the sheet on which Isabey drew Pius VII and Garneray drew the surrounding border. As might be expected, given the subject depicted, this is the only sheet without the arms of the French Empire at the top; instead, it bears those of the papacy, in acknowledgment not only of the invitation issued to the Holy See in 1804 but also, more generally, of the agreement reached between the priesthood and the Empire, between the spiritual and temporal powers. At the top of the sheet, the framing border bears the pontifical arms, a combination of the heraldic emblems of the Chiaramonti family and the device "Pax" (Peace) chosen by the former Benedictine who was

◀ **FIG 7.5.** Jean-Baptiste Isabey, Charles Percier, and Auguste Garneray. Drawing for pl. I (frontispiece) of the *Livre du Sacre*. Pen and brown wash on paper. Château de Fontainebleau, musée Napoléon Ier, GM Bibl. 3502.

elected pope in March 1800. Additional motifs figure elsewhere within the border: on the sides, six medallions: at left, a chalice (captioned "Fides"), a sword ("Justicia"), and a bit ("Temperancia"); at right, a pelican giving its own blood to its offspring ("Caritas"), the decapitated head of a small devil set against crossed axes ("Fortitudo"), and a mirror ("Prudencia"); at the bottom, a putto set against a fictive semicircular hang of drapery; in the center of the transverse bar, a lamb reclining on a book with several hanging seals; in the upper border, shoots of grapevine circling a horizontal rod. Still more motifs figure within the lateral borders: at left (bottom to top), a cardinal's hat, a paten, and a patriarchal cross; at right, shafts of wheat, shoots of grapevine, and a crozier supported by an adoring angel, all supplemented by flowers and palmettes.

The center of the lower field is occupied by a fictive medal flanked by two flaming torches. Drawn by Percier, the medal shows Pius VII standing on a dais in front of the façade of a Gothic building, doubtless Notre-Dame de Paris, and surrounded by ecclesiastics, giving his benediction to four young people kneeling at his feet, their hands clasped.

THE CHOICES OF CHARLES PERCIER

We do not know what circumstances prompted Percier to solicit Garneray's assistance on this project; perhaps he was overwhelmed with work or had grown weary of an enterprise that seemed interminable. The collaboration, initiated at an unknown date,[21] was significant, definitely involving six sheets and very likely three more, which amounts to nine out of a total of thirty-one costume pages and a frontispiece, which inflected the ornamental borders for two figures of primary importance (the empress, duly represented even after her divorce, and the pope) and one who had played a key role in the very enterprise of the *Livre du Sacre* (the grand master of ceremonies), as well as the book's frontispiece. To be sure, Percier—a former pensioner of the king in Rome, a celebrated architect working for the government, and co-author with Fontaine of several reference works—never relinquished control, to the point of failing to acknowledge the role of his collaborator, whether or not by common accord we shall probably never know. It goes without saying that it was Percier, responsible for the "ornament," who defined the relative worth of the various plates of the *Livre du Sacre*. For the series devoted to costume, or ceremonial dress, the order of the figures

▷ **FIG 7.6.** Jean-Baptiste Isabey, Charles Percier, and Auguste Garneray. *The Pope*. Drawing for pl. XIII of the *Livre du Sacre*, 1811. Pen and brown wash on paper. Château de Fontainebleau, musée Napoléon I*er*, GM Bibl. 3502. Cat. 49a.

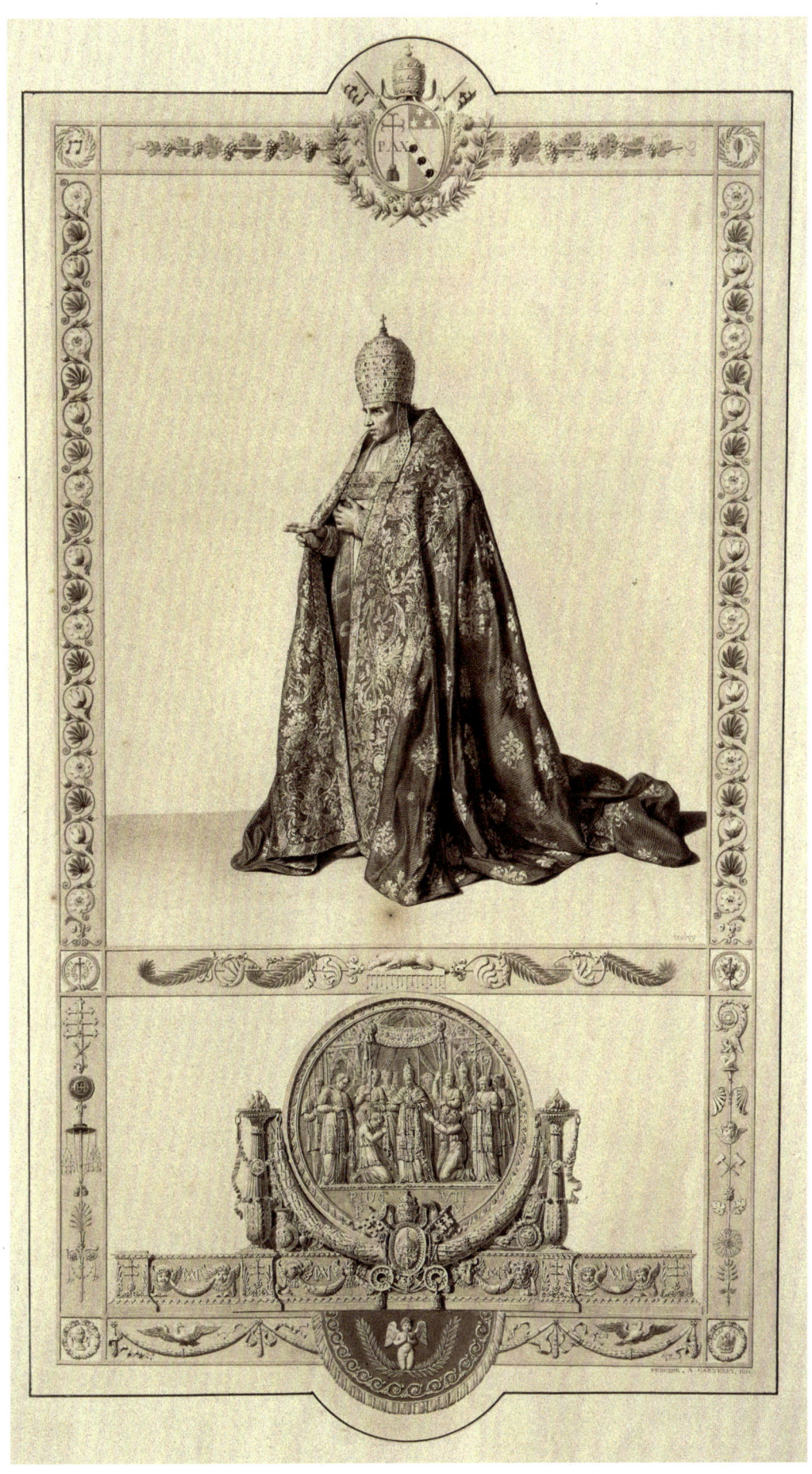

obviously corresponds to the importance of their role: first the emperor (twice), then the empress (twice), then the pope (once), a French prince (once), and so forth to the mayor of the city and the president of the canton [FIG. 7.7]. It was surely Percier who determined the various types of the imperial eagle in the upper borders of the costume pages. Likewise, he would have overseen the indication of the hierarchical status of the various figures by means of the relative elaboration of the attributes in the lower registers of these pages and adjusted the scale of their borders accordingly, making them larger and more elaborate for the first five pages, after which there is a decrescendo that parallels the decline in rank, with the final pages (Chef des hérauts d'armes [Chief Herald of Arms]) [FIG. 7.8], Huissier de la chambre (Keeper of the Bedchamber) being given only simple linear borders. Although assisted, partly in secret, by a lesser hand, Percier remained the controlling intelligence of the whole, on which he brought to bear his extraordinary gifts as a designer of ornament. ●

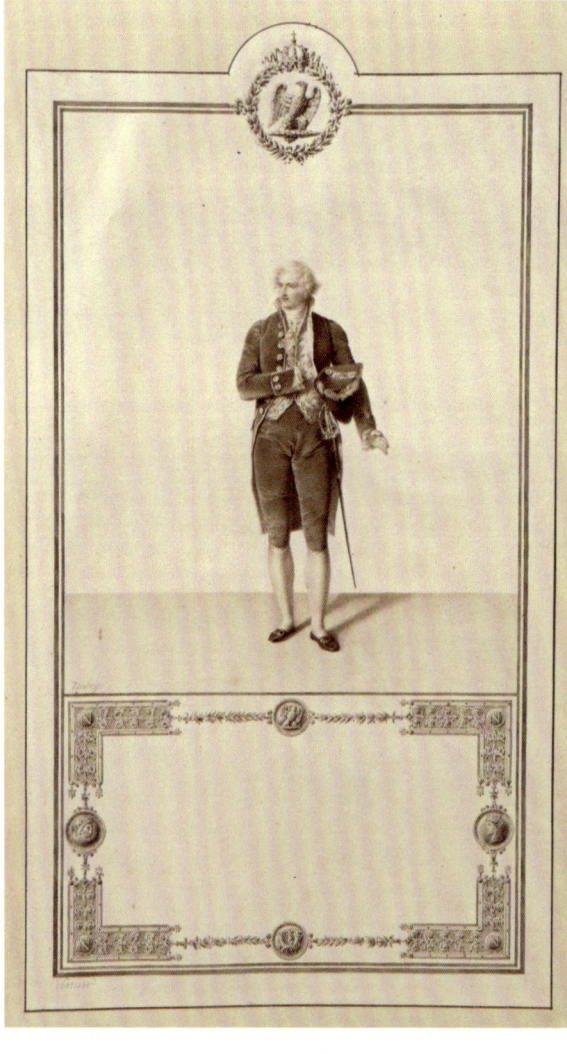
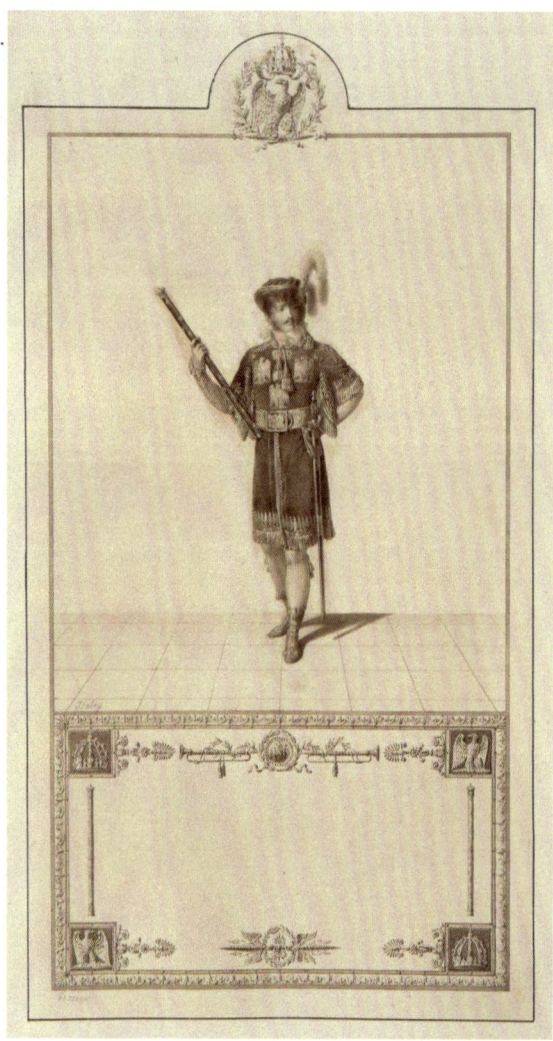

FIG 7.7. Jean-Baptiste Isabey and Charles Percier. *President of the Canton*. Drawing for pl. XXIX of the *Livre du Sacre*. Pen and brown wash on paper. Château de Fontainebleau, musée Napoléon Ier, GM Bibl. 3502.

FIG 7.8. Jean-Baptiste Isabey and Charles Percier. *Chief Herald of Arms*. Drawing for pl. XXXI of the *Livre du Sacre*. Pen and brown wash on paper. Château de Fontainebleau, musée Napoléon Ier, GM Bibl. 3502.

1 "On travaille actuellement au livre du sacre de Leurs Majestés Impériales. L'exécution de ce grand ouvrage doit répondre par sa magnificence à la pompe d'une cérémonie qui a surpassé les autres solennités de ce genre par la réunion de tout ce qui est auguste et imposant. Son Excellence M. de Ségur, grand maître des cérémonies, chargés par S. M. l'Empereur de la direction générale de cette belle entreprise, en a confié l'éxécution, savoir: pour la rédaction du livre, à M. Aignan, aide des cérémonies, secrétaire impérial à l'introduction des ambassadeurs; et pour le dessin, à M. Isabey, peintre, dessinateur des cérémonies et du cabinet, et à MM. Fontaine et Percier, architectes de S. M. Le premier est chargé des figures, les deux autres, de l'architecture et ornements. Le burin des plus célèbres graveurs sera employé pour consacrer ces grands souvenirs." "L'ouvrage paraîtra vers la fin de l'année prochaine." *Le Moniteur universel*, no. 181 (1 germinal year XIII [March 22, 1805]), 770.

2 A document dated April 22, 1806, indicates: "Execution of the Livre du Sacre. Nature of the expenditures: M. Isabey, as fee for 20 drawings made by him to be engraved: 10,000 francs; M. Percier, as fee for some vignettes and for borders for the above drawings: 5,000 francs" ("M. Isabey, pour prix de 20 dessins par lui faits pour être gravés: 10,000 fr.; M. Percier, pour prix des vignettes et bordures des dessins ci-dessus: 5,000 fr."). Apart from the stationer Coiffier, the printer Roussot, and the plate finishers Gallois and Tardieu, the only noteworthy collaborators named are four engravers: Urbain Massard fils, Remi Henri Delvaux, Jean Massard père, and Dupréel; there is also a collective mention of those "who undertook the execution of 10 plates that are not yet finished" ("qui ont entrepris l'exécution de 10 planches qui ne sont pas encore terminées"). (Archives nationales de France, O² 138, pièce 52, "Relevé des dépenses faites et des sommes payées à compte au 22 avril de l'an 1806"). In February 1807, 18 figures were engraved (ibid., pièce 56, 4e acompte); in April 1807, twenty-one (Ibid., pièce 58, 5e acompte).

3 At the salon des artistes vivants of 1808, Urbain Massard exhibited *Quatre costumes d'après Isabey, pour le sacre de l'Empereur* (no. 808 in the brochure), and Jean François Ribault some *Costumes de grands fonctionnaires* (no. 825). Similarly, Georges Malbeste presented at the Salon of 1812 *La Distribution des aigles au Champ de Mars par Sa Majesté l'Empereur et Roi* (no. 1249).

4 "J'avais rassemblé dans la galerie de Diane tous les objets d'art qui avaient quelques droits à son attention comme les dessins et les estampes gravées du livre du sacre entrepris et dirigé par MM. Isabey, Percier et moi, d'après les ordres de M. le grand maître des cérémonies aux frais du Trésor de la Couronne. Un exemplaire colorié du livre que Percier et moi nous avons publié sur le même sujet, quelques dessins de Monsieur Isabey, des modèles et un grand nombre de dessins de meubles de toute espèce. Cette confusion d'objets différents a distrait un peu mais a faiblement intéressé l'Empereur, à peine a-t-il voulu regarder les meubles, il a fait peu attention aux dessins du sacre." Pierre Fontaine, *Journal, 1799–1853*, ed. Marguérite David-Roy (Paris: École nationale supérieure des beaux-arts / Institut français d'architecture / Société de l'histoire de l'art français, 1987), 1:224.

5 An accounting document from October 1813 details the role played by each of the three draftsmen. Re Isabey: "7 grands dessins à 2,000 fr.: 14,000 fr., 31 costumes à 500 fr.: 15,500 fr." Re: Percier: "une vignette d'introduction: 500, 31 vignettes à 300 fr.: 9,300," which is to say for a total of 9,800 francs (7,310.40 of which had been paid and 2,489.60 of which remained due; ANF, O² 137, pièce 3, "Exécution du Livre du Sacre au 18 octobre 1813. État de proposition de la somme de douze mille deux cents francs, à payer par le Trésorier général de la Couronne, à MM. Isabey, Percier et Fontaine, peintres et dessinateurs, à compte des dépenses pour l'exécution du Livre du Sacre," October 18, 1813).

6 "J'ai remis à Monsieur de Ségur grand maître des cérémonies vingt-six planches aux frais du Trésor de la Couronne sur les fonds des cérémonies pour l'ouvrage du sacre dont MM. Isabey, Percier et moi avons fait les dessins. Il me reste encore 5,660 francs sur les 100,000 francs donnés à compte pour payer les graveurs." Fontaine, *Journal*, 1:261.

7 The project was still pending at the time of the fateful invasion of France (ANF, O² 137, pièce 10, "Dépenses extraordinaires. Livre du Sacre. Quittance de la somme de 2,400 francs à Mrs Isabey, Percier et Fontaine, pour neusvième [sic] à compte sur l'exécution du Livre du Sacre, pour avances faites pour écriture de lettres, etc. etc. pendant 1808," February 21, 1814).

8 The 39 plates numbered from I to XXXIX are supplemented by another plate entitled "Description des tableaux et explication des costumes" and incorporating a vignette by Percier. According to Fontaine, yet another plate was executed but was not used ("ne sert pas").

9 "J'ai déposé au cabinet de la chalcographie entre les mains de M. Morel d'Arleux, qui en est le conservateur, les planches gravées du sacre de l'Empereur. Cet ouvrage entrepris par MM. Isabey, Percier et moi sous la direction de M. le grand maître des cérémonies aux frais du trésor de la couronne est terminé. Les dépenses en sont acquittées à l'exception de celles des dessins qui nous sont dues [sic], et sur lesquelles nous avons touché quelques acomptes. M. Morel ne m'a pas donné reçu des quarante et une planches gravées qui composent la totalité de l'ouvrage et que j'ai laissées entre ses mains." Fontaine, *Journal*, 1:401.

10 "On s'était occupé pendant les trois mois du retour de l'Empereur des moyens de faire finir et de mettre au jour le livre du sacre commencé depuis le mois de février 1805....Je crois que me voilà débarrassé pour toujours des désagréments d'un ouvrage qui m'a coûté tant de soins, qui a duré tant de temps, dont le produit a été si modique et que les circonstances condamnent à l'obscurité. Je fais bien volontiers le sacrifice de ce qui me reste dû pour n'en plus entendre parler." Ibid., 481. The final payment was not made until much later, during the second Restoration: "They paid the outstanding debt, and contrary to my expectations, we have just received the amount still due us for execution of the book of the sacre of the Emperor." "On acquitte les créances arrierées, et contre mon attente, nous venons de toucher le solde de ce qui restait dû pour l'exécution du livre du sacre de l'Empereur." Ibid., October 20, 1817, 550.

11 The history of this exceptional copy is recounted by the series of stamps and labels that it bears: on the inside of the front cover, a small label printed with the monogram N surmounted by a crown and inscribed in ink with the copy number: "217"; on the printed frontispiece, an oval seal in red ink: a crowned eagle surrounded by the inscription "Cabinet de S. M. L'Empereur et Roi"; on the printed frontispiece, a round seal in red ink: "Bibliothèque du Roi / Louvre"; on the title page, an oval seal in red ink: "Bibliothèque du Louvre"; on the title page, a stamp in red ink: "Musée national de Malmaison." Presented to the Musée des souverains au Louvre during the Second Empire, this exemplar of the *Livre du Sacre* is now exhibited at the Musée Napoléon at the château de Fontainebleau, opened to a different page every three months.

12 On the back of the flyleaf, a printed label (6.9 × 9 cm) with a carefully executed border was glued; it reads: "Rue de la Harpe nº 45 / TESSIER / Relieur et Doreur de l'intendance de / la maison de l'empereur des ministre [sic] de / l'intérieur et du trésor publique [sic]...."

13 Doubtless this is the sheet exhibited by Alexandre Tardieu at the Salon of 1808 (no. 833 in the brochure): *Portrait en pied de S. M. l'Empereur et Roi*.

14 The designation of the printed caption is general ("grand officier de la Couronne"), but a manuscript list provides one that is more specific: "le grand maître des cérémonies" (ANF, O² 137, pièce 3).

15 Some of the questions raised by this "archaeological" approach to the *Livre du Sacre* cannot be answered now; too many primary documents are lacking, and we were unable to consult a mysterious "carnet du sacre" (a layout dummy?) now in a private collection.

16 Here the artist signs in capital letters "GARNERAY," preceded either by the initial "A." or by the abbreviated form "AUG^TE." Elsewhere, however, he sometimes opts, like his father François Jean, for the spelling "Garnerey," as in the brochure of the Salon of 1810, which indicates "Garnerey (Auguste), élève de son père et de M. Delanoix." Denon, in his review of "all the artists who might attract the eye [of His Majesty] when he deigns to visit the Salon," refers to him as "Garneret fils." The name of this family of artists is usually spelled "Garneray." Auguste Simon Garneray, the son of François Jean, was a student of Isabey and specialized in miniatures and watercolors. At the Salon of 1810 (no. 329), he exhibited a drawing entitled *Leurs Majestés l'Empereur et l'Impératrice entourés de la Famille impériale, sur le balcon élevé devant la façade du château des Tuileries, le jour de leur mariage* (château de Fontainebleau, cabinet des Arts graphiques, F 1980.1).

17 The features are clearly those of Josephine, and the monogram "J" appears six times in the border.

18 These four sheets are the only ones in the book that are dated.

19 This vignette was used again in the border of the "Description des tableaux et explication des costumes," where it bears the printed indications "Dessiné par Ch. Percier" and "Gravé par Ad^in Godefroy."

20 In the drawing, the figure is signed "Isabey" and the border is signed at lower right, in brown ink: "PERCIER, A. GARNEREY, 1811." By contrast, the indication on the print, which makes no reference to Garneray, reads simply: "Dessiné par Isabey et Percier."

21 Late in the day, if we rely on the indication "1811" inscribed on several sheets, what about the sheets that are undated? Moreover, an accounting document (ANF, O² 138, pièce 56) mentions an advance to Audouin "for the engraving...of the empress in lesser ceremonial dress" ("pour la gravure...de l'impératrice en petit costume") in February 1807, four years prior to the drawing of this subject by Garneray, which is dated "1811."

DECORATIVE ARTS

CHAPTER 8

PERCIER AND FRANÇOIS HONORÉ GEORGES JACOB-DESMALTER

THE ORIGINS OF MODERN FURNITURE DESIGN

JEAN-FRANÇOIS BELHOSTE

CHARLES PERCIER, WHETHER WORKING ALONE OR IN COLLABORAtion with Pierre Fontaine, was an exceptional furniture designer, one of the principal figures, perhaps the most important one, in what would become the Directory, Consulate, and Empire styles of interior decoration. More dominant in this domain than in that of built architecture, Percier left behind a considerable material legacy that, although unsigned and still largely unattributed, can gradually be restored to him through the careful scrutiny of objects, drawings, and written documents.

His body of work in furniture design was largely the result of a close collaboration—one that began quite early and continued into the 1830s—with the Maison Jacob, the principal furniture-making enterprise of the period, and above all with François Honoré Georges Jacob-Desmalter, who, with his elder

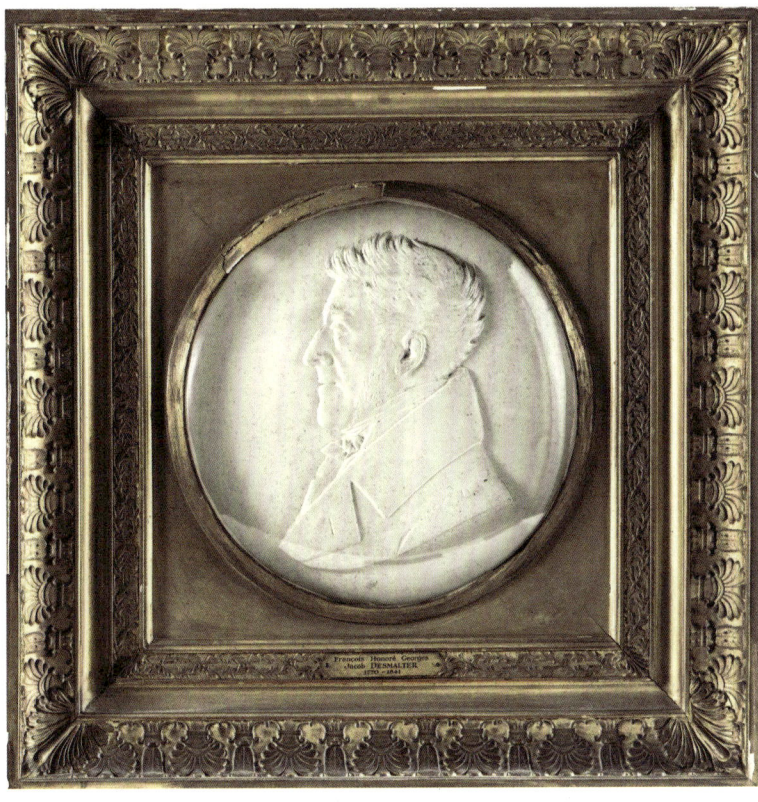

▲ **FIG 8.1.** Antoine Laurent Dantan, called Dantan l'aîné. *Portrait of François Honoré Georges Desmalter*, 1828. Relief medal in a wood and gilded stucco frame. Musée Carnavalet, Paris, S3489.

brother, Georges (who died prematurely in 1803[1]), succeeded his father as head of the firm in 1796 [FIG. 8.1].[2] This collaboration brought together a celebrated architect accustomed to working with very few people and the head of a business that, in about 1805, employed 300 to 350 workers. This was a novel situation and one that anticipated future arrangements in the realm of the decorative arts. First, it was unusual at this time for an architect to regard furniture as an integral part of interior decoration, most of them hitherto being concerned only with fixed decor. Second, expansion of the Jacob firm from the Directory onward transformed it into a veritable industrial enterprise, indeed one of the most important in First Empire Paris.[3]

This situation—new to the furniture-producing sector—was a consequence of both political revolution, which had freed it from the shackles of the ancien-régime guilds, and the industrial revolution, despite the still limited impact of mechanization. The success of Percier, who not only created design models but also set out to disseminate them widely and make them fashionable, was a result of his decision to work with large enterprises whose goal was the production of high-end furniture in small series. This is clearly stated in the preliminary discourse (first published in 1812) of the *Recueil de décorations intérieures*:

As regards execution, in many respects the industrial arts of the moderns have acquired, and should continue to acquire, the wherewithal to surpass those of the ancients. Everything dependent on experience can only improve over time, above all through applications bestowed on the arts by the physical sciences....France and especially its capital city possess, in the matter of materials needed for residential embellishment, infinite resources, and commerce guarantees the arrival there of every material—wood, stone, and so forth—that industry and taste might desire. The many manufactories of glassware, metalwork, and porcelain in and around Paris employ masses of skilled workers, but their talents need to be directed by good taste.[4]

Here, articulated with startling precocity, are the principles that—especially after the London Universal Exposition of 1851—would preside over the project to foster the application of the Fine Arts to Industry, the objective being, in the language of the day, to reconcile Beauty with Utility.

AN ENDURING FRIENDSHIP

It was apparently in late 1792/early 1793 that the dynasty's founding figure, the cabinetmaker Georges Jacob,[5] then fifty-three, took his first steps, spurred by the recommendation of the painter Jacques Louis David, whose atelier he had furnished in 1788 or 1789.[6] David paid a visit to the young Percier, then flush from the success of the sets he and Fontaine had designed for *Lucrèce*,[7] a politically charged play by Antoine Vincent Arnault, to seek his assistance in furnishing the new assembly hall for the National Convention in the Tuileries. David, who had been asked to make drawings for the furniture but agreed to take on only the armchair for the president, recommended the two young architects for the job.[8] The Convention held its first meeting in the new hall on May 10, 1793.

There ensued an intense and long-lasting collaboration that seems to have unfolded in an atmosphere of mutual esteem, a collaboration whose extent and nature we will attempt to assess here, despite the paucity of archival evidence. Several facts attest to this, beginning with the presence of Percier and Fontaine as witnesses at the marriage in March 1798 of François Honoré Georges Jacob-Desmalter and Adélaïde Anne Lignereux, daughter of the prominent furniture dealer Martin Eloy Lignereux [FIG. 8.2].[9]

It was doubtless this proximity to the two architects that prompted Georges Alphonse, the only son of the Jacob-Desmalter couple, to pursue their profession before he decided to become a cabinetmaker in turn. Admitted to Percier's atelier in June 1817,[10] he left the École des beaux-arts in May 1823, before completing his studies there, to assist his father before succeeding him as head of the firm by the end of 1824. Percier and Fontaine were witnesses to George Alphonse's marriage to Hortense Ballu, sister of the architect and future Prix de Rome winner Théodore Ballu.[11] But the most eloquent testimony to the closeness of their ties is found in their respective estate inventories. In his will, drafted in 1821, Percier used this suggestive turn of phrase: "I give to Madame Jacob-Desmalter, née Lignereux, as a token of my sincere attachment, the sum of 1,200 francs and that from my rings which will have greater value."[12] When François Honoré Georges Jacob-Desmalter died in 1841, several works by Percier and

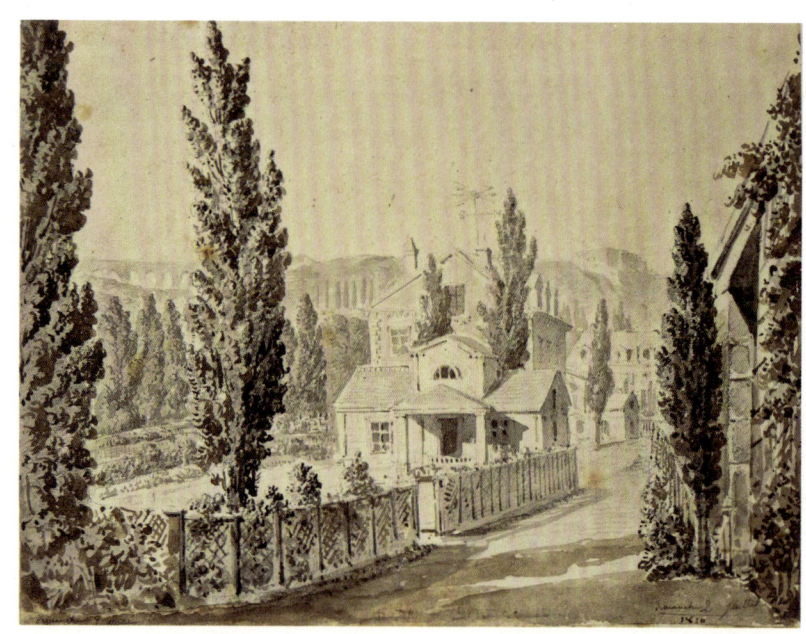

Fontaine were found among his many drawings, prints, and watercolors, notably four drawings of architectural fragments and two "large colored drawings representing diverse ornaments," all framed and bearing Percier's signature.[13] His library, which was rather large, included their three principal works: *Palais et Maisons de Rome*, *Résidences des souverains*, and, of course, the *Recueil de décorations intérieures*. In June 1847, Adélaïde Anne Jacob-Desmalter made a specific bequest to her son Georges Alphonse of ten drawings and copies of drawings by Percier and Fontaine.[14] It is perhaps some of these drawings (in fact watercolors) that Hector Lefuel, a descendant of Georges Alphonse, reproduced in his book, where he identified them as being in his personal collection[15] (specifically, designs for the jewel cabinets for Josephine and Marie-Louise, for malachite candelabra for the Tuileries, and for Napoleon's throne and bed, also for the Tuileries, all bearing Percier's signature).[16]

The relations between Percier and Jacob-Desmalter were nonetheless first and foremost professional, having been consolidated with the establishment of Maison Jacob frères in August 1796,[17] when Percier and Fontaine began to cultivate their interior-design practice. The Jacob enterprise expanded continuously until the last years of the Empire, and in 1807 it was considered "one of the finest furniture makers in France, and even in Europe. Ordinarily, it fabricat[ed] goods worth 700,000 francs [per annum], a third of which [was] for export."[18] Employing 300 to 350 workers, it was one of the largest enterprises in Paris. Its workshops were situated in the northern part of the city, on rue Meslay.[19]

The suppression of the guilds effected by the revolutionary government had, it is true, presented Jacob with an opportunity to diversify his production, and thus to expand the operation considerably. Such, at any rate, is the line taken by a description published in March 1803 in the *Moniteur Universel*, which reported that at the time the firm included "a workshop for architectural carpentry, two workshops for furniture carpentry, a workshop for figure sculpture and one for ornamental sculpture, one for lathe-turners, one for painting and gilding, one for cabinetmaking, one for inlay workers, one for chasers, one for founder-casters, one for molders, one for engravers, one for metal gilders, one for tapissiers, and one for locksmith-mechanics."[20] Maison Jacob frères was, therefore, equipped to handle almost anything, from woodwork to metalwork, from the realization of painting, gilding, and inlay work to upholstery and the hanging or application of fabric.

◂ **FIG 8.2.** Charles Percier. View of the country house of Mme Lignereux at Bougival. Sunday, May 9, 1810. Pencil and sepia wash on paper. Private collection.

The article also contains precious information about how the business was run. "The two Jacob brothers offer a confluence of talents that favors the prosperity of the establishment. The one [is] extremely well versed in the art of drawing, presiding over the details and daily operations of each workshop; the other, wholly dedicated to administrative matters, oversees everything pertaining to the accounts."[21] This distribution of responsibilities was foreseen from the time the business was established in 1796: "Citizen Jacob the elder will be responsible for record-keeping…for paying the workers and other expenses…Citizen Jacob the younger for the purchase of raw materials, for the direction and execution of works and tasks, for distributing tasks among the workers, for their surveillance, for the preparation of plans and drawings, and finally for everything pertaining to fabrication."[22] The "beauty of the designs" emphasized by the *Moniteur Universel* leaves little doubt about the artistic aptitude of François Honoré Georges.[23] His taste for art and architecture is evident from the size of the collection of drawings, prints, and paintings that was in his possession when he died in 1841.

INTERIOR DECORATION PROJECTS

Percier's interest in interior decoration, nourished by ancient models and facilitated by his experience as set designer for the Opera, blossomed under the Empire, with the renovation of the imperial palaces and more occasional projects such as the decorations for Napoleon's coronation. More or less consistently, when furniture was in question, he turned to Maison Jacob,[24] which had a large clientele, some of it international, and had already been entrusted with important public commissions. This situation established the contours of the collaboration with Percier. Unfortunately, the only known correspondence between them is a simple undated note from Percier, written on a red-chalk drawing of a capital and addressed to Jacob-Desmalter: "My dear comrade, I am leaving for Sceaux. I still haven't fin-

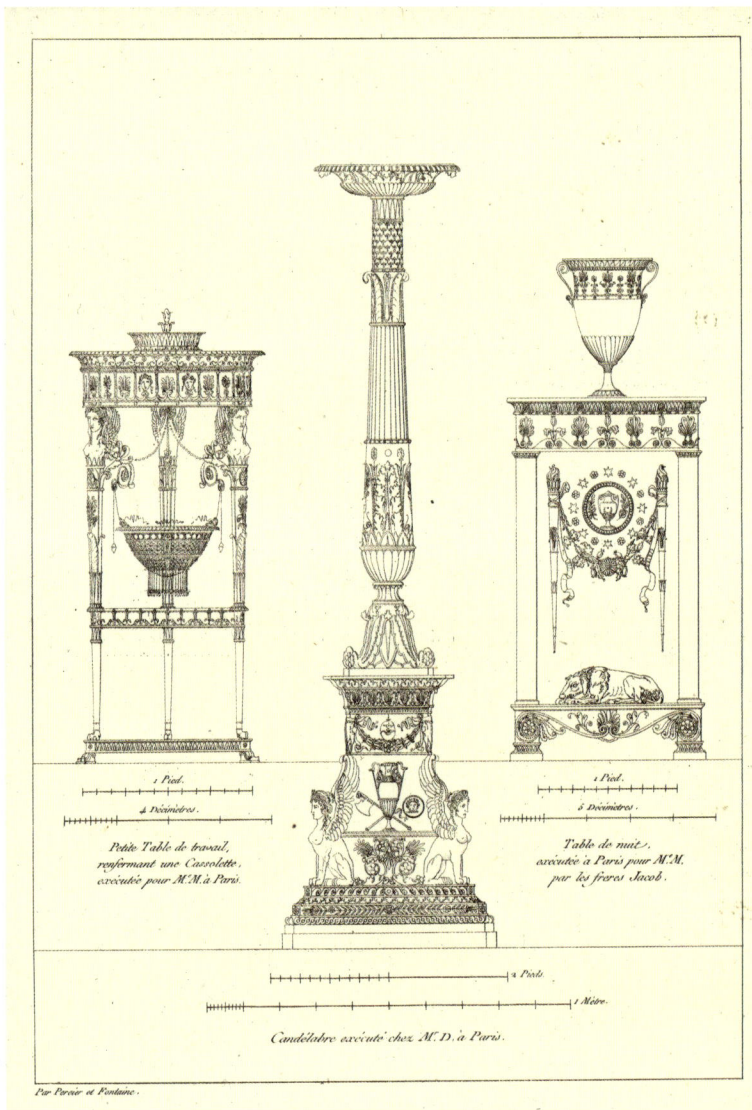

ished your candelabrum; it will be done soon. Yours truly, Charles Percier."[25]

It remains, then, to determine the nature of their collaboration before 1801, when Percier and Fontaine became "government architects." With regard to their previous activity, a note about the "ten best architects" of the time, prepared in late September 1800 by the painter and art dealer Jean-Baptiste Pierre Lebrun for the Minister of the Interior, Lucien Bonaparte, sheds some light. Percier and Fontaine, "architects united by friendship," are ranked eighth, and their names are glossed as follows: "Skilled in the finer points of their art, which they have drawn from antique sources; their productions are extremely polished; they are very successful in interior decoration and furniture design."[26] Percier, henceforth a specialist in interior decoration, had also become well known as an artist and, less predictably, enjoyed a degree of success as a furniture designer, which suggests that his collaboration with Jacob had already been tested. A primary document, the *Recueil de décorations intérieures* (1801–12), enables us to see things even more clearly. It contains both perspective views of rooms and designs for individual pieces of furniture, and the three earliest fascicles in the deluxe colored edition of the *Recueil* give us some idea of how important color was to Percier, both in the design of complete rooms and in that of independent pieces of furniture. Apart from one mention of the sculptor and furniture maker Alexandre Regnier,[27] the Jacob brothers are the only furniture makers identified in its pages, in texts (explanatory table, captions proper, and captions within the images) pertaining to five of the seventy-two plates in the *Recueil*, glossing tables, an armchair, and a roll-top desk [FIGS. 8.3, 8.4].[28] And this list is by no means exhaustive, as we know from the gloss on plate 32 in the explanatory table, which clearly states that "most" of the furniture in the preceding plates "was executed in the factory of MM. Jacob in Paris" (see note 28). This has been confirmed in several instances. Thus the "small work table or chiffonière" with an incense-burner illustrated in plate 23,[29] which unlike the night table in the same

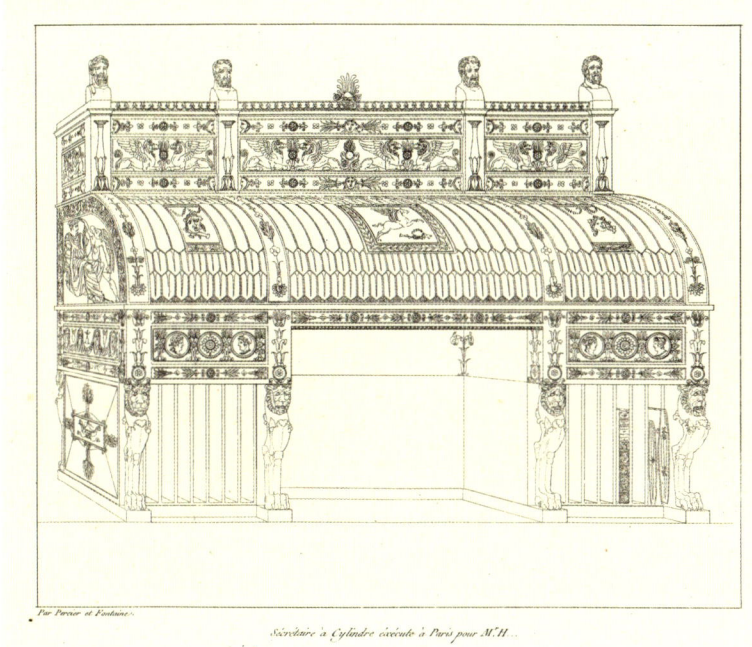

◂ **FIG 8.3.** Charles Percier and Pierre Fontaine. *Candelabra made by Mr. D*, Paris. From Percier and Fontaine, *Recueil de décorations intérieures* (Paris: Authors and Pierre Didot l'aîné, 1801–12), pl. 23.

▴ **FIG 8.4.** Charles Percier and Pierre Fontaine. *Cylinder secrétaire made in Paris for Mr. H*. From Percier and Fontaine, *Recueil de décorations intérieures* (Paris: Authors and Pierre Didot l'aîné, 1801–12), pl. 32.

plate is not attributed to Jacob, corresponds to a piece made for General Moreau and now at Fontainebleau that is stamped "Jacob frères, Rue Meslée [*sic*] (SEE CAT. 68)."[30] The bed made for the same patron, also now at Fontainebleau, and which appears in plate 19, bears the identical stamp [FIG. 8.23]. The same process of deduction applies to the guéridon in plate 39, a tea table "executed for Madame B"—in other words, for Josephine Bonaparte—which is now at Malmaison and is attributed to Jacob [FIG. 8.14],[31] and also to the "folding stool shaped like an X" that is illustrated in the same plate and described as having been "placed at Saint-Cloud" (SEE FIG. 11A.3).[32] Finally, although Anne Louis Girodet, Jean Joseph Xavier Bidauld, and Jean Thomas Thibault are identified as the painters of the Platinum Room for Aranjuez (plates 61–64; SEE FIGS. 10.2, 10.5, 10.6), there is no indication in the *Recueil* that the wood paneling was executed by the Jacob firm.

The plates in the *Recueil* that show rooms in perspective give us some idea of how Percier elaborated his decorative programs: how he dealt with the harmony of forms and the play of colors and determined the number and morphology of the furnishings, as well as their disposition in relation to one another and to the fixed decor. Such views,[33] to which we might add others of the same kind by Percier that survive,[34] make it possible to visualize these ensembles, in which furniture figured alongside bronzes, metalwork, tapestries and so forth. It is worth emphasizing the importance accorded mirrors—"placed between each subdivision, they repeat, in the dining room in the Tuileries, the infinite riches of the ceiling"[35]—as well as painted panels, which Percier usually entrusted to artists who were also his friends.[36] In any case, these interior views are strikingly reminiscent of opera sets. And it is interesting how Percier, in these compositions, did not limit himself to the fixed decors but also "staged" their furnishings. This theatricality is especially evident in the plates of the first fascicle, published in 1801, devoted to the decoration of the atelier of the painter Jean-Baptiste Isabey realized in 1798 (see chapter 2b). The sparse furnishings shown in these rooms were probably made by Jacob. Unfortunately, the "Citizen V." mentioned in the captions of the first plates has not been securely identified, but it seems likely that he was Ignace Joseph Vanlerberghe, the army provisioner who acquired the former Folie Baujon in October 1796. Seven plates are devoted to the designs for his residence, which makes it possible to envision the decoration of his bedchamber with some precision, especially given that colored exemplars of these prints survive. Here there can be no doubt about the collaboration

◂ **FIG 8.5.** Charles Percier and Pierre Fontaine. Plate 13 of *Recueil de décorations intérieures* (Paris: Authors and Pierre Didot l'aîné, 1801–12).

▸ **FIG 8.6.** Charles Percier and Pierre Fontaine. Plate 15 (detail) of *Recueil de décorations intérieures* (Paris: Authors and Pierre Didot l'aîné, 1801–12).

▸▸ **FIG 8.7.** Charles Percier and Pierre Fontaine. Plate 16 of *Recueil de décorations intérieures* (Paris: Authors and Pierre Didot l'aîné, 1801–12).

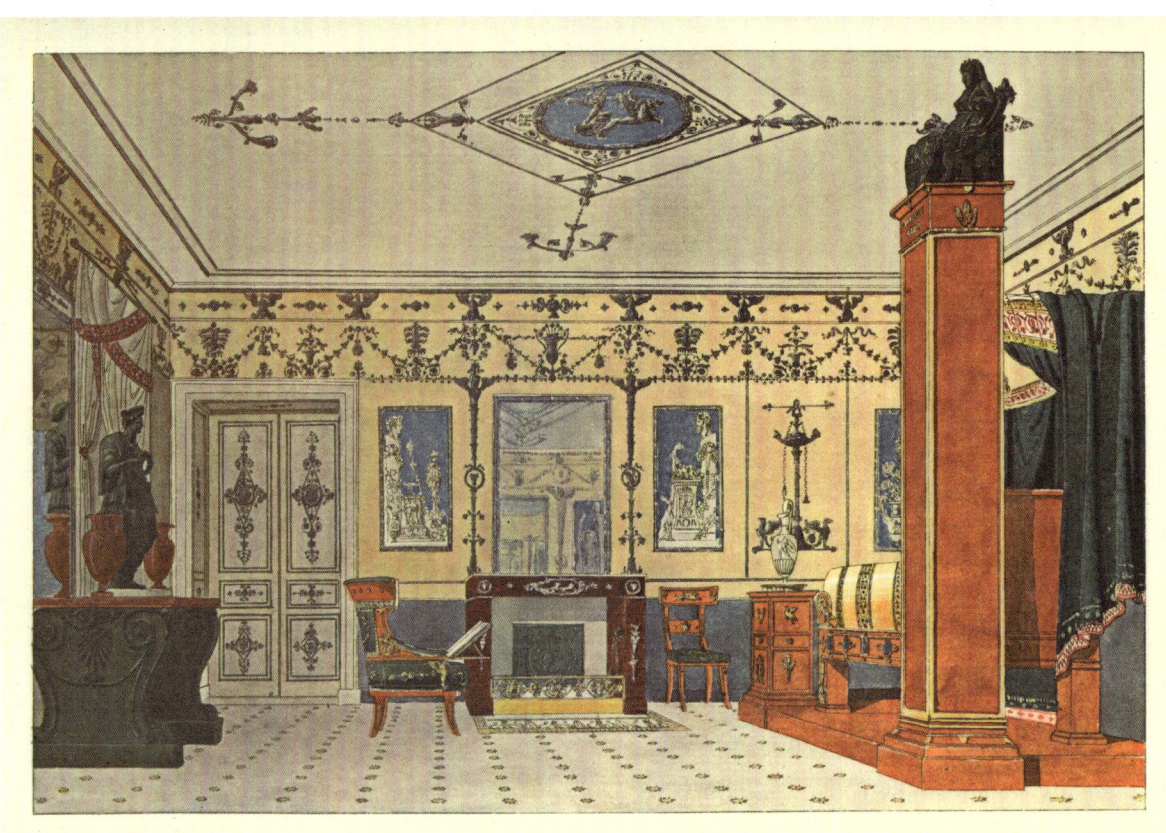

Vue perspective de la Chambre à coucher du Cit. V. à Paris.

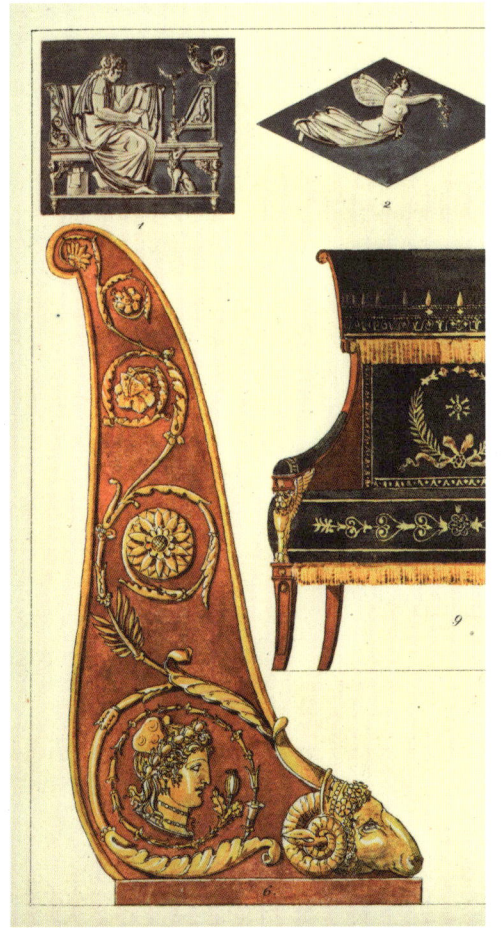

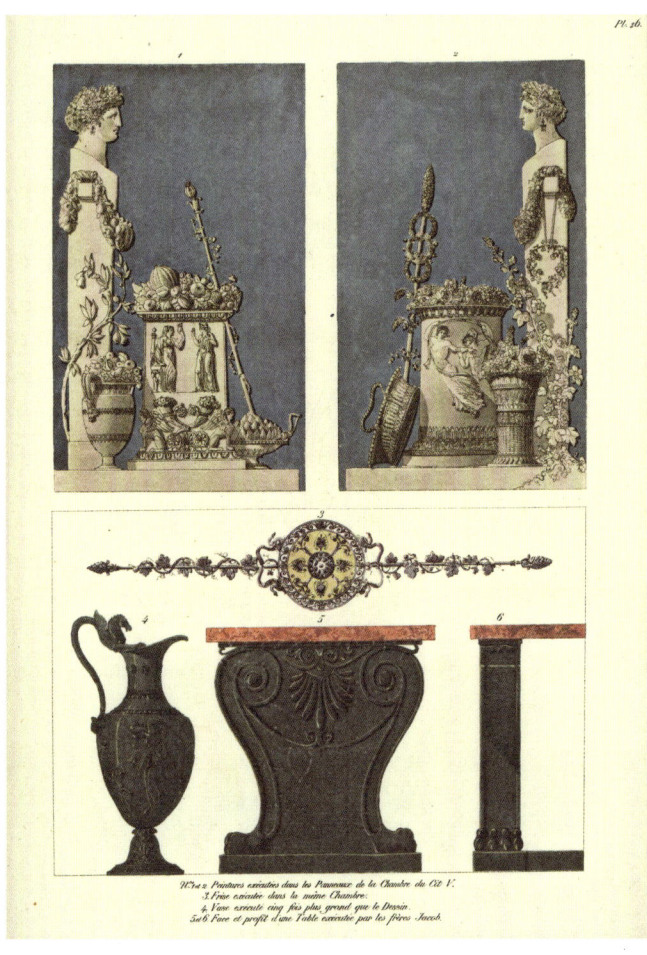

DECORATIVE ARTS

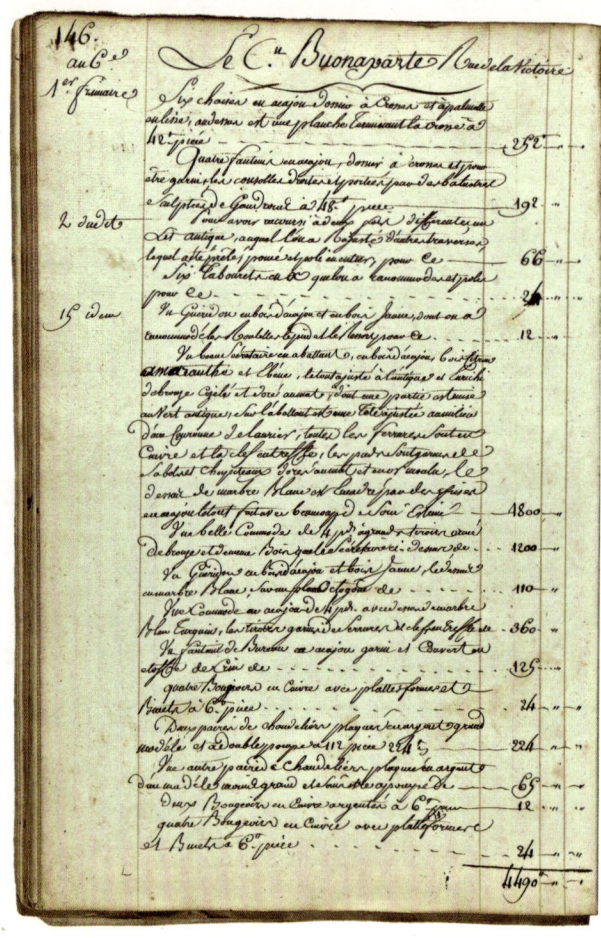

between Percier and the Jacob family, at least as regards an armchair and a table [FIGS. 8.5–8.7].[37]

In the *Recueil*, patrons are identified only with an initial: Citizens V., O., H., D., G., the comte de S., and so forth. Only a few of these figures have been securely identified, most notably General Jean Victor Marie Moreau and his wife ("M et Mᵉ M.") and Josephine Bonaparte ("Mᵉ B."). It is tempting to cross-reference these indications with an oft-cited comment made by Fontaine: "Bankers and provisioners dare to display the riches that they have acquired. Mssrs. Dumanoir, Gaudin, Ouvrard, Michel, and a few others asked us, then, to renovate and arrange their houses. I am not quite sure how, but we became fashionable."[38] "Citizen O." might be Gabriel Julien Ouvrard, a prominent financier and military provisioner. The Gaudin ("M. G") in question has long been thought to be Martin Michel Charles Gaudin, the future finance minister to Napoleon and the future duc de Gaëte, some of whose furniture, now in the Musée Carnavalet, is attributed to Jacob.[39] But it happens that another Gaudin, identified as residing on the rue du Faubourg Montmartre ("no. 1055"), figures among the principal clients of the Jacob brothers in the firm's sales ledger for November 1796–December 1797 [FIG. 8.8].[40] The furniture that he acquired between March and September 1797 consisted of pieces that would serve to furnish a salon, a dining room, a boudoir, and three bedchambers: one for the master of the house, another for his wife, and a "young ladies' bedchamber" containing two beds.[41] So the person in question cannot be the future minister, who did not marry until 1822.[42] The problem with identifying the Gaudin who was an important client of the Jacob brothers with the one mentioned in the above-cited passage by Fontaine is the fact that he did not reside in the Chaussée d'Antin quarter, the fashionable district that was home to most of Percier and Fontaine's interior decoration clients and precisely where Fontaine located his hôtel in *Mia Vita*.[43] A recent discovery resolves this quandary. On 17 messidor year IV (July 5, 1796), one Benoît Gaudin, a merchant residing on the rue du Faubourg Montmartre, acquired a small townhouse on the rue du Mont-Blanc[44] (as the rue de la Chausée d'Antin was known from 1793 to 1816): the hôtel de Thun, built around 1770 to designs by Étienne Louis Boullée.[45] Married at the time to Jeanne Sophie Moyroud, a native of Lyon, Gaudin was involved

▲ **FIG 8.8.** Sales ledger from the Maison Jacob, 1797. Detail of a page concerning Citizen Gaudin. Musée Carnavalet, Paris, ms A 6021.

◀ **FIG 8.9.** Anne Louis Girodet-Trioson. *Danaë Looking at Herself in a Mirror Held by Cupid*, 1798. Oil on canvas, Museum der bildenden Künste, Leipzig.

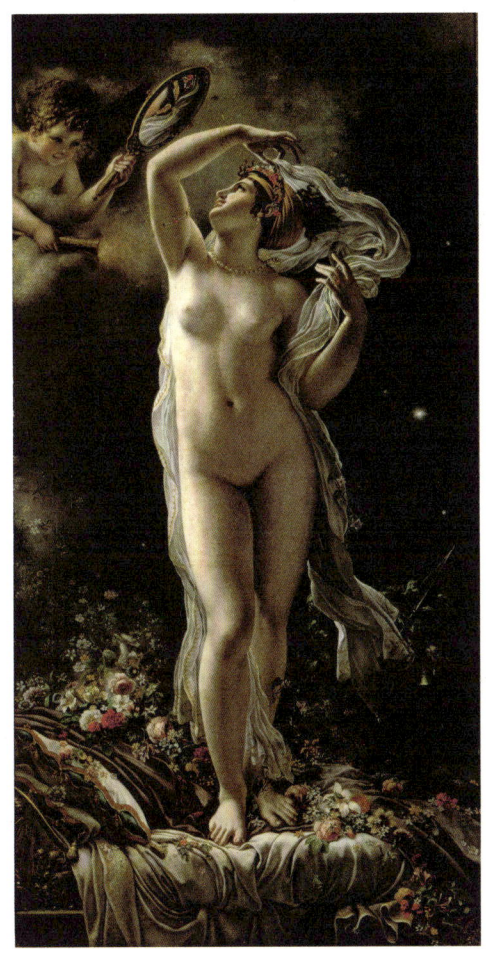

in military provisioning.⁴⁶ In December 1799 he sold the townhouse to Augustin Ouvrard,⁴⁷ the brother and business associate of Gabriel Julien Ouvrard, which suggests that he, like them, was close to Paul Barras, who served as president of the Directory from 1795 to 1799. The problem of identification is further clarified by the history of a celebrated painting by Girodet, his *Danaë* (1798; [FIG. 8.9]). According to Pierre Alexandre Coupin, the artist's first biographer, this canvas was "destined to decorate the salon of a small townhouse on rue du Mont-Blanc built by Mr. Percier for Mr. Gaudin."⁴⁸ Coupin already confused the patron of this work with the future duc de Gaëte, but recent scholarship has made it clear that the man in question was in fact Benoît Gaudin.⁴⁹

This point having been clarified, we can make more sense of the scant information available to us. The deed for the December 1799 sale of the townhouse contains precise descriptions (with valuations) of the furnishings, some of which tally with the purchases recorded in the Jacob sales ledger of 1797. Thus a "bed in antique form made of mahogany with ebony and pewter filets, and paintings of *petits sujets*," located in one of the bedchambers, corresponds to the bed "made of thick mahogany with a curved back of antique form…enriched with Etruscan ornament in ebony inlay" that was delivered for the bedchamber of Madame Gaudin.⁵⁰ Four chairs and four armchairs with scroll backs correspond with those listed in the ledger, where they are described as having scroll backs and arms with S-shaped grooves and, below, antique palmettes in ebony inlay."⁵¹ The most valuable piece was the desk—said to be in a "new form" and to incorporate a mirror and a clock—located in the man's bedchamber and described as having the upper part form an entablature "supported by four amaranth-wood columns and with a sprung mirror that can be pulled down in front of the columns."⁵² The 1799 inventory also details all of the textiles: violet taffeta curtains in the salon, a scarlet coverlet for the man's bed, and one made of poppy-colored taffeta with blue embroidery on that of his wife. These indications invite comparisons with the two corresponding plates in the *Recueil*. As described in the inventory, the man's bedchamber was sparsely appointed, its principal furniture consisting—in addition to the bed—of two bookcases, and its walls being hung with "pleated drapery over which valuable paintings are attached" [FIG. 8.10].[53] The wife's bedchamber, of which the *Recueil* depicts only a single wall elevation [FIG. 8.11], is said to have been notable for the "richness and abundance of [its] ornament," evidence, according to the inventory, that it "was made for a woman."[54] We also have three studies for this room executed in color by Percier, one of which depicts the bed in its original setting [FIG. 8.12].[55] It shows that the wall above was painted with a female figure in antique style, placed against a blue ground, that brings to mind Girodet's *Danaë* and *Flora Caressed by Zephyr* (1802; Musée de Grenoble) by François Gérard. We should add to this corpus of images plate 44 of the *Recueil*, which represents an astonishing mahogany and bronze tea table made "by MM. Jacob" for "M[onsieur] G." [FIG. 8.13],[56] as well as a drawing that bears the following annotation in Percier's hand: "console executed by Jacob for Gaudin."[57] The same sheet also has drawings of two chairs that, although not captioned, were likely for the same project. Thanks to the Jacob sale ledger, which indicates that the deliveries to Gaudin began in late March 1797, we can confidently assert that this is among the earliest, and possibly the first, of Percier's interior decoration commissions.

This chronological reference point enables us to position other, better-known projects more precisely as well, notably Josephine's commission for her townhouse on rue de la Victoire. On September 30, 1797, she wrote the architect-decorator Corneille Vautier from Italy that she wanted it furnished "with the utmost elegance."[58] There followed in November–December 1797, the very

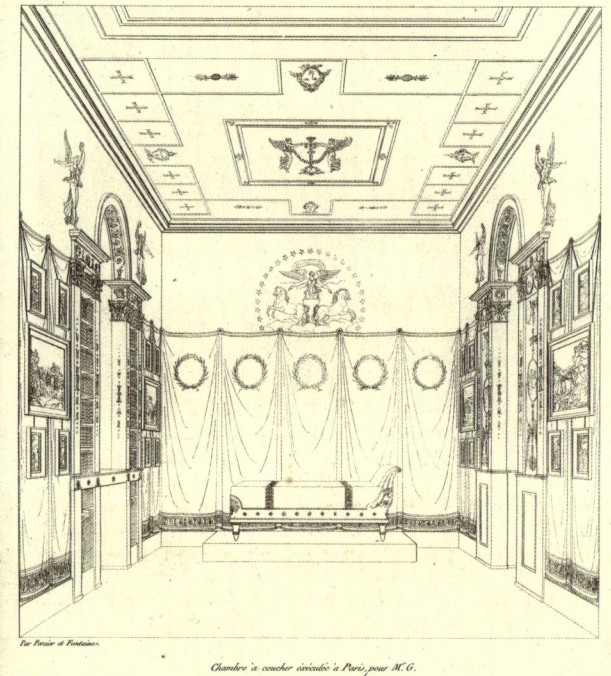

FIG 8.10. Charles Percier and Pierre Fontaine. Bedroom executed in Paris for Mr G., perspective view. From Percier and Fontaine, *Recueil de décorations intérieures* (Paris: Authors and Pierre Didot l'aîné, 1801–12), pl. 36.

FIG 8.11. Charles Percier and Pierre Fontaine. Façade for the bedroom of Mme G. From Percier and Fontaine, *Recueil de décorations intérieures* (Paris: Authors and Pierre Didot l'aîné, 1801–12), pl. 37.

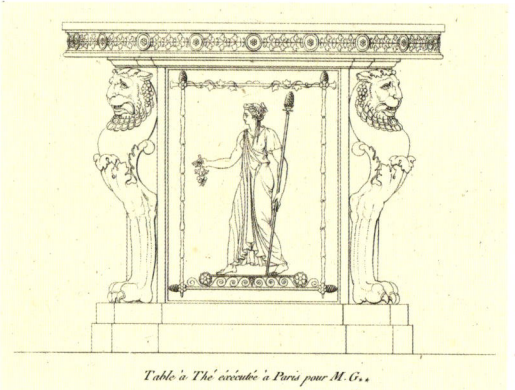

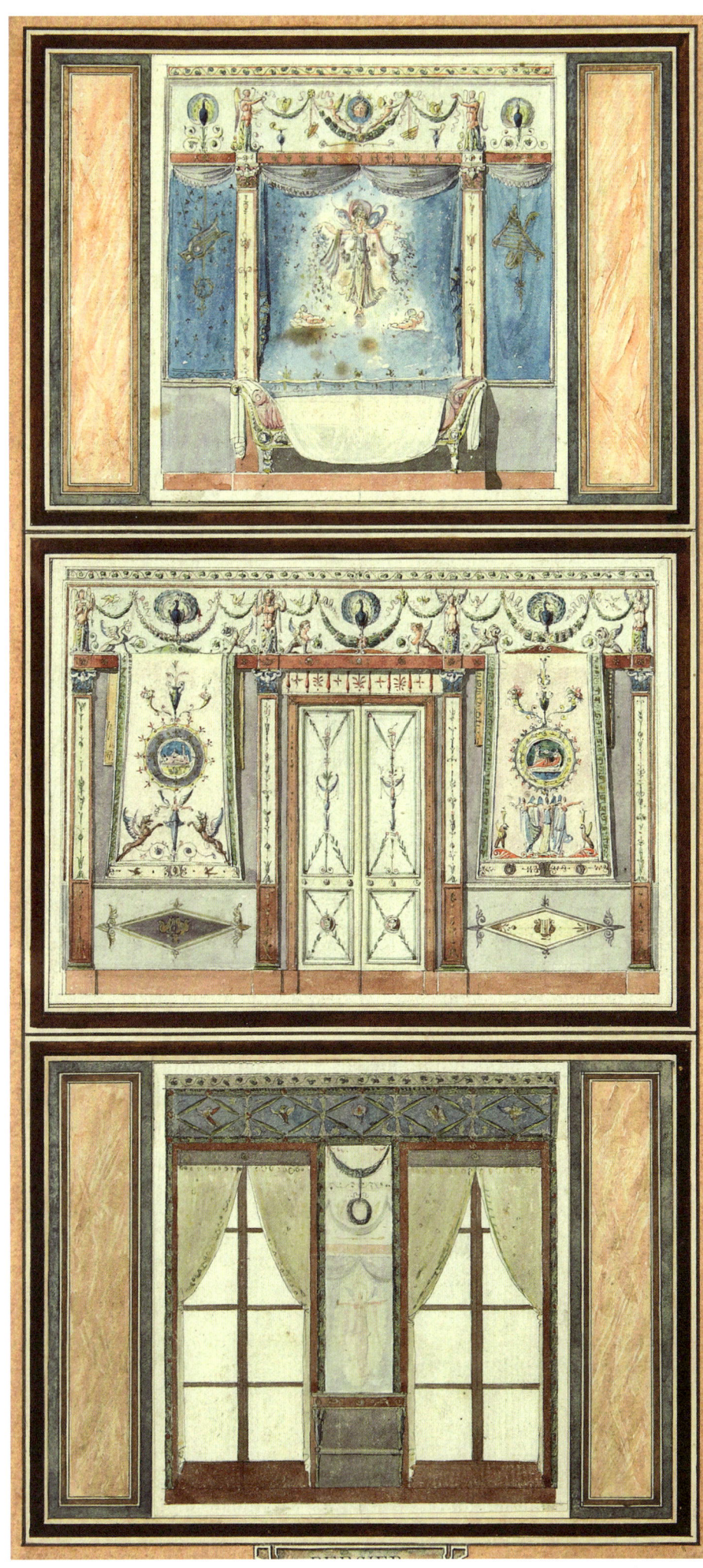

▷ **FIG 8.12.** Charles Percier. Three studies for the bedroom of Madame Gaudin, n.d. Pencil, pen, and watercolor on paper. Private collection, Paris.

◁ **FIG 8.13.** Charles Percier and Pierre Fontaine. Tea table executed in Paris for Mr G. From Percier and Fontaine, *Recueil de décorations intérieures* (Paris: Authors and Pierre Didot l'aîné, 1801–12), detail of pl. 44.

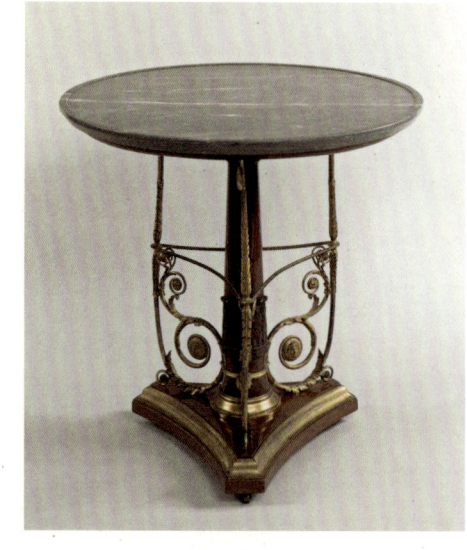

moment when the last deliveries were being made to Gaudin, a series of deliveries to the Bonaparte townhouse that are recorded in the Jacob sales ledger.[59] According to Fontaine, he and Percier encountered Josephine after she had seen their work at the residence of the former marquis de Chauvelin on rue de la Victoire, on which occasion she had asked them to assist Vautier.[60] Given the 1799 commission for Malmaison, likely a consequence of the one for Josephine's Parisian townhouse, it seems logical to situate this meeting in 1798 or 1799. However, in all likelihood the introduction was in fact arranged by the military provisioner Benoît Gaudin, doubtless less respectable than the former marquis de Chauvelin but whose townhouse was more original and would have attracted more attention, especially given the presence there of Girodet's celebrated *Danaë*. That would date the meeting to the summer or fall of 1797, when Josephine, short of cash, sought to profit from financial speculation related to provisioning the army through the intervention of Paul Barras. For obvious reasons, these transactions remained confidential.[61] In any event, if the timing implied by this information holds—if the commission for the Bonaparte townhouse indeed dates from late 1797, immediately after the one for the Gaudin townhouse—it means that the collaboration between Percier and the Jacob brothers commenced earlier, and on a more significant scale, than was previously thought. It should be noted here that, of the many pieces related to this commission and detailed in the Jacob sales ledger, a commode and a desk made of mahogany, lemonwood, amaranth wood, and ebony survive (Munich, Wittelsbacher Ausgleichsfonds).[62] The guéridon, or tea table with bronze legs, that corresponds to the one reproduced in plate 39 of the *Recueil* and now at Malmaison [FIG. 8.14] probably dates from somewhat later.

To date this collaboration more securely, we must look into other commissions suggested by Fontaine's list of clients, such as that for the hôtel de Montesson at 22, rue du Mont-Blanc, acquired in July 1798 by Gabriel Julien Ouvrard,[63] and that for 14, place Vendôme, acquired by Marc Antoine Grégoire Michel, known as Michel jeune.[64] The circumstances surrounding real-estate acquisitions made by such financiers tended to be much the same. Having rapidly grown wealthy through fiscal speculation, loans to the government, and provisioning of the armies, they suddenly found themselves in charge of significant holdings, properties previously owned by aristocrats and either sold by them out of necessity or seized by the government. These properties, frequently sumptuous but often ill-maintained and decorated in outdated styles, had to be

▲ **FIG 8.14.** Jacob frères, after Percier and Fontaine. Tea table from the Hôtel Bonaparte, rue de la Victoire, ca. 1798–1800. Mahogany, lemon tree wood, ebony, gilt bronze. marble. Château de Malmaison Rueil-Malmaison, M.M.D.30.3. Cat. 71.

▶ **FIG 8.15.** Louis Martin Berthault. Bedroom of Madame Récamier reconstructed at the Louvre. Châteaux de Versailles et de Trianon, on deposit at Musée du Louvre, Paris.

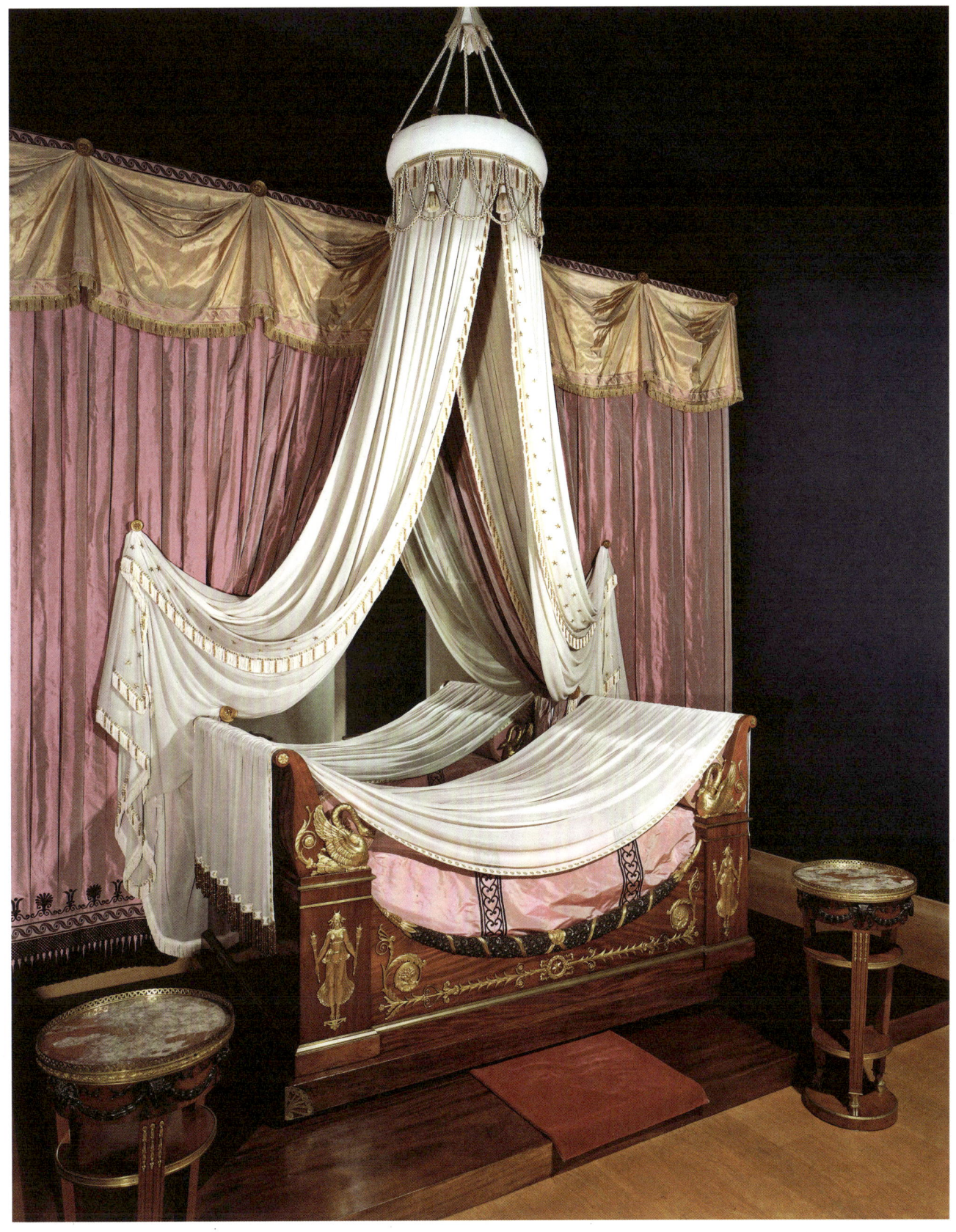

brought into line with current fashion, a task that Percier and Fontaine took up beginning early in 1797.

Unfortunately, most of the decors executed by them under the Directory and the Consulate have disappeared, and their constituent elements have been dispersed. A few, however, have survived or been reconstituted. The most emblematic example is perhaps the suite of interiors realized in late 1798 in Hôtel Récamier, two of which were recently reconstructed in the Musée du Louvre [FIG. 8.15].⁶⁵ Although Percier's involvement in the project is a matter of record, there is no trace of it in the *Recueil*, and the commission has not yet given up all its secrets. For one thing, the extent to which Percier and the Jacob brothers participated remains unclear. The architect officially in charge of the townhouse was Louis Martin Berthault, but the niece and adopted daughter of Juliette Récamier, Amélie Lenormant, later specified: "The restoration and furnishing of the townhouse on rue du Mont-Blanc was entrusted to the architect Berthault, who was given carte blanche for related expenses. He acquitted himself of this task with infinite taste and was assisted in this enterprise by M. Percier."⁶⁶ This account has gained in credibility with the recent discovery of five watercolors at the Bibliothèque nationale de France, four of which are proposed designs for various rooms in the house and the fifth, a design for Juliette's famous bed [FIGS. 8.16, 8.17],⁶⁷ for one of these watercolors bears the inscription "Percier f[eci]t." We

▽ **FIG 8.16.** Charles Percier. Dining room of Madame Récamier, ca. 1798. Pen and watercolor on paper. Bibliothèque nationale de France, Département estampes et de la photographie, Paris, VE-2160 (5)-BOITE FOL.

◁ **FIG 8.17.** Charles Percier. Salon and smoking room of Madame Récamier, ca. 1798. Pen and watercolor on paper. Bibliothèque nationale de France, Département estampes et de la photographie, Paris, VE-2160 (5)-BOITE FOL.

▷ **FIG 8.18.** Charles Percier. Study sketches for the bed of Madame Récamier, ca. 1798. Pen, black and gray ink, graphite, and Conté crayon on paper. Detail of fol. 19, The Metropolitan Museum of Art, New York, The Elisha Whittelsey Collection, The Elisha Whittelsey Fund, 1963, 63.535. Cat. 59.

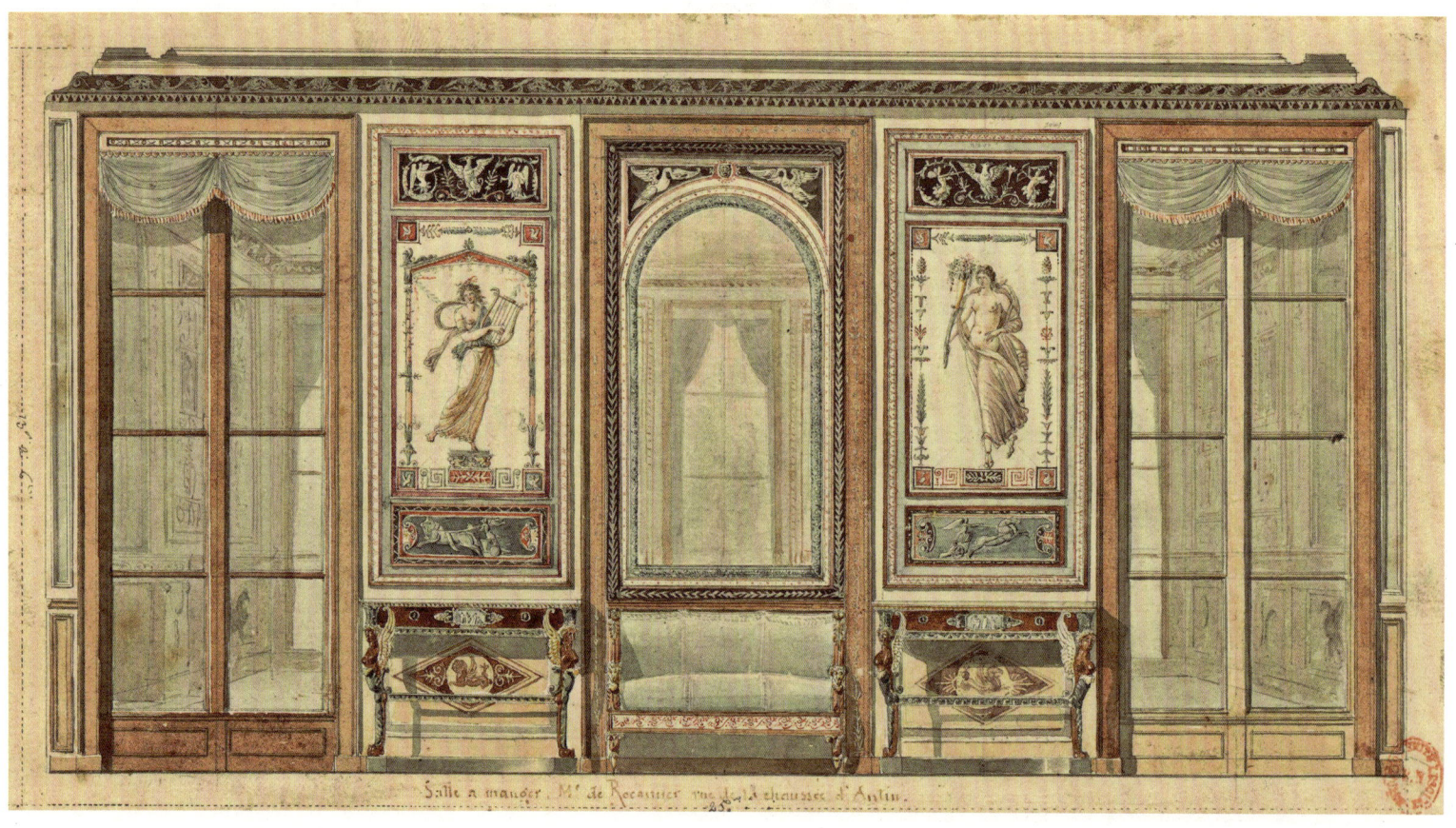

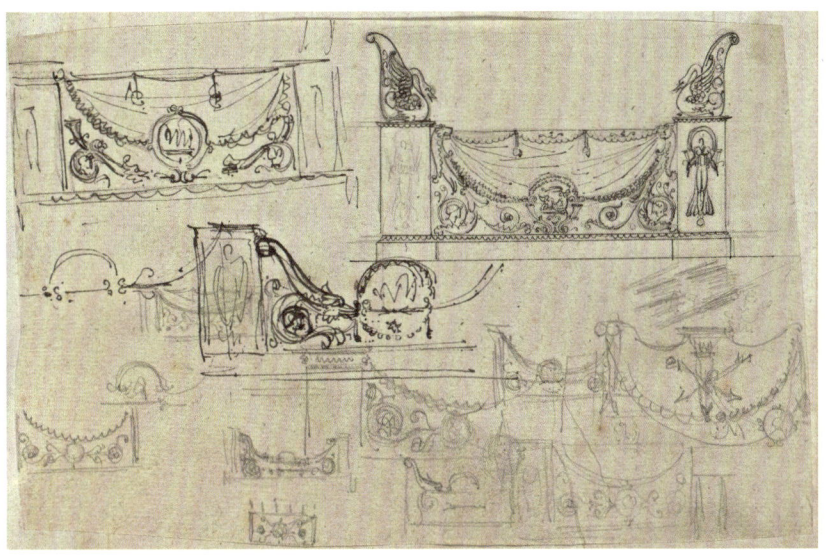

have long had evidence that Percier was responsible for the bed, in the form of a page of sketches in the workshop scrapbook in the Metropolitan Museum of Art [FIG. 8.18; SEE ALSO CHAPTER 8B], but this inscription tends to support his further participation in this decorative project. Similarly, no archival documents and maker's stamps attest to Jacob's having executed the surviving furniture for the bedroom and the salon now in the Louvre, with the exception of a guéridon with a marble top and a frieze with ebony and pewter inlay.[68] We do, however, have additional testimony from Amélie Lenormant, and it is unequivocal: "Every piece of furniture—bronzes, bookcases, candelabra, even the least important armchair—was designed and modeled to order. Jacob, a cabinetmaker of the first rank, executed the models provided him; this resulted in furnishings that bear the stamp of the era and will remain the best examples of the taste of that time."[69] Since one of the aforementioned watercolors bears the inscription "A. JACOB" (in ink) and the date "1827" (in graphite), there is reason to think that they once belonged to Georges Alphonse Jacob-Desmalter, and even that he inherited them from his father. So the better part of the furnishings for these celebrated rooms, which are known to us through various written accounts[70] and images,[71] and which prove a consummate mastery of the

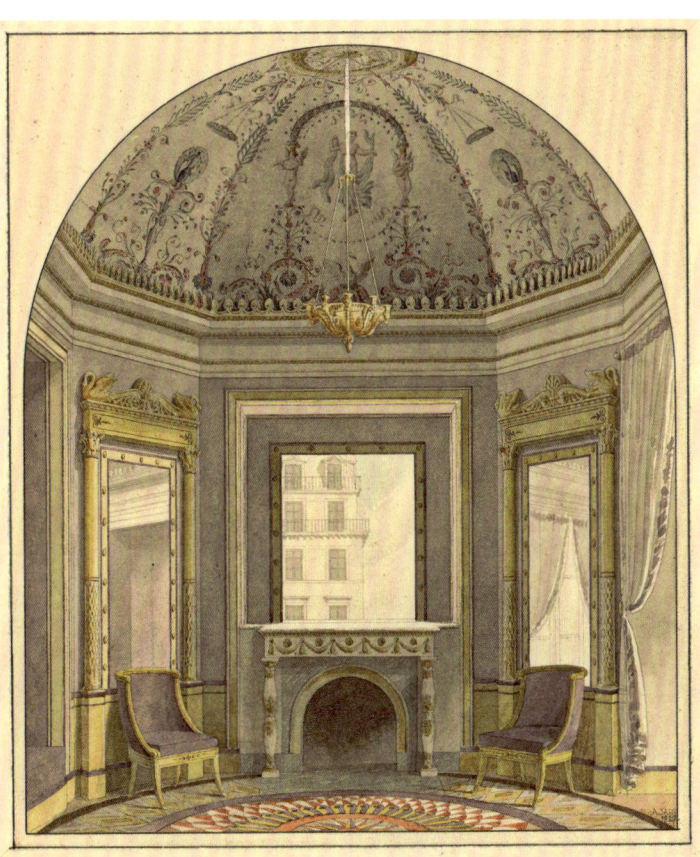

staging of interiors, almost certainly resulted from the collaboration between Percier and the Jacob brothers and should be regarded as belonging to a continuum that also includes the Gaudin and Bonaparte commissions.

The Platinum Room in the Casa del Labrador in the gardens of the royal palace at Aranjuez was one of last decorative projects undertaken by Percier before he became consumed, beginning in 1801, with remodeling the Tuileries and the château de Saint-Cloud. King Carlos IV of Spain issued the commission in February 1800, just after Percier and Fontaine were engaged to work on Malmaison.[72] Quite modest in scale (3.85 × 3.15 meters), this interior has the advantage of being largely intact and richly documented, which makes it possible to track its execution with some precision. The contractor-agent for the commission was Michel Léonard Sitel, a Parisian "fabricator of gold and silver appliqué work."[73] Once the contract was signed in Madrid in February 1800, he set about assembling a team by "engaging celebrated Parisian artists."[74] The overall conception was entrusted to Percier, who recruited as his principal collaborators "the best artists to be found in Paris."[75] Work on the project did not get under way until early 1801. The previous year Sitel had sent four drawings by Percier to Madrid (two line compositions and two in color), on the basis of which the king approved the design.[76] Executed in Paris, the various component elements were sent to Aranjuez, where they were assembled on site. The room was largely complete in 1804, but even then a few elements were lacking.

The participation of the Jacob firm, while long assumed,[77] has now been confirmed.[78] The room contained very little in the way of furniture: two chairs and two stools, as well as a richly decorated bronze table and two armchairs, all of which were fabricated not by the Jacob firm but by the Parisian cabinetmaker Xavier Hindermeyer.[79] The principal contribution of the Jacobs was the wood paneling, notably that of the remarkable barrel-vaulted ceiling [FIG. 8.19; SEE ALSO FIG. 10.2].[80] The various woods employed—mahogany, red palm, amaranth wood, lemonwood—

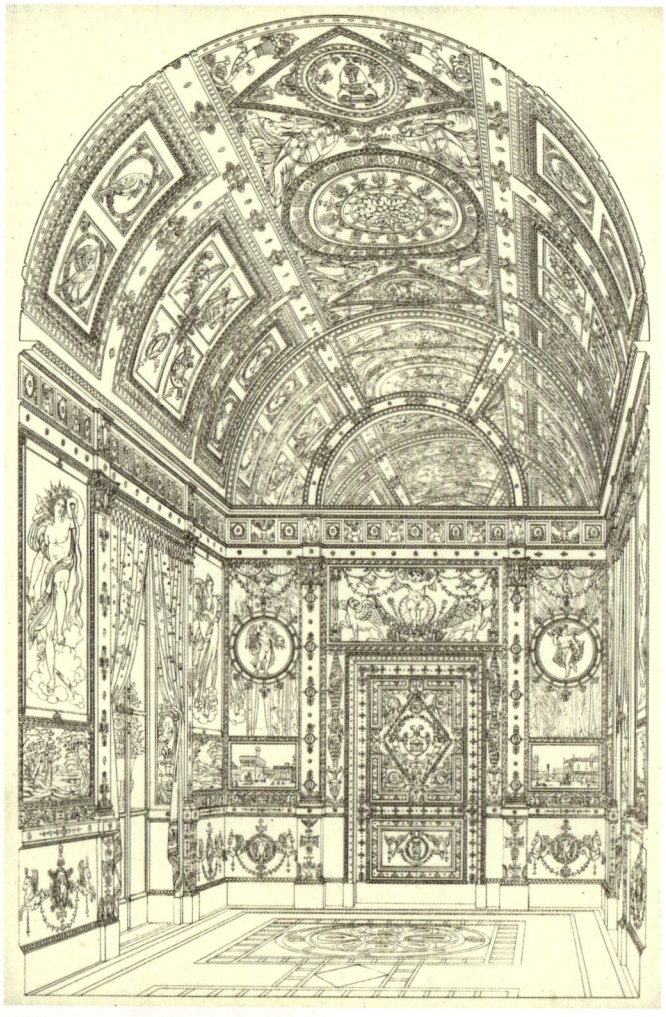

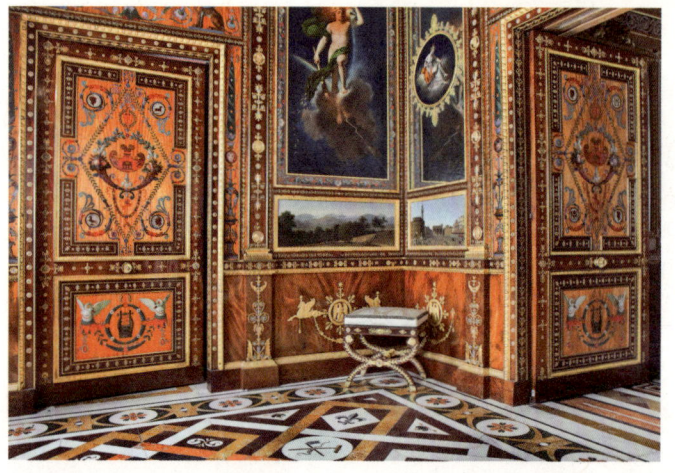

made it possible to obtain, in tandem with the gilt-bronze and platinum appliqués and the paintings by Jacques Barraband, a subtle play of colors [FIGS. 8.20]. The paneling was fabricated in 1801, shortly after Fontaine wrote with regard to the library at Malmaison, which doubtless served to some degree as a model: "M. Jacob, who was entrusted with the cabinetry and joinery work for the library, displayed in the execution of this project a rare intelligence."[81]

ARCHITECT VERSUS CABINETMAKER

The expression *de forme nouvelle* (in a new form) that is used in the texts, notably in the 1796–97 Jacob sales ledger, raises another question, that of the creation of furniture that was innovative in its form, purpose, materials, and stylistic references. If the Percier–Jacob collaboration is securely documented in the case of prestigious commissions, such as the celebrated jewelry cabinets made for Josephine and Marie-Louise and the armchairs with round backs intended for the throne rooms in the Tuileries and at Saint-Cloud, it is more difficult to prove in less exceptional instances. However, the scrupulous examination of texts, drawings, and surviving pieces makes it possible to draw certain conclusions. Although many of these new designs were occasioned by specific decorative commissions, others were perhaps conceived more independently, at the pleasure of their designer, who was free to propose them to Jacob for fabrication. This was certainly the case for small moveable pieces such as chairs and guéridons, a group of drawings for which was sold at auction in 2001.[82] Moreover, the extended caption for plate 52 of the *Recueil*, which describes "small everyday pieces" (*petits meubles usuels*), such as a washbasin, a lamp, and a toiletries cabinet, that were probably not fabricated by Jacob, qualifies them as "commercial pieces" (*meubles de commerce*) [FIG. 8.21]. The designs for which the firm was indebted to Percier were, by and large, those for beds and seating of various kinds, the firm's traditional specialties. New chair types proliferated, for example those with scrolled backs (*à crosse*) and curved backs (*cintrés*) whose legs and arm supports could be infinitely varied, incorporating lion

◀ FIG 8.19. Charles Percier and Pierre Fontaine. The Platinum Room at Aranjuez. From Percier and Fontaine, *Recueil de décorations intérieures* (Paris: Authors and Pierre Didot l'aîné, 1801–12), pl. 61. Cat. 54e.

▶ FIG 8.20. Entryway of the Platinum Room, Aranjuez. Photograph, n.d.

▼ FIG 8.21. Charles Percier and Pierre Fontaine. Plate 52 of *Recueil de décorations intérieures* (Paris: Authors and Pierre Didot l'aîné, 1801–12).

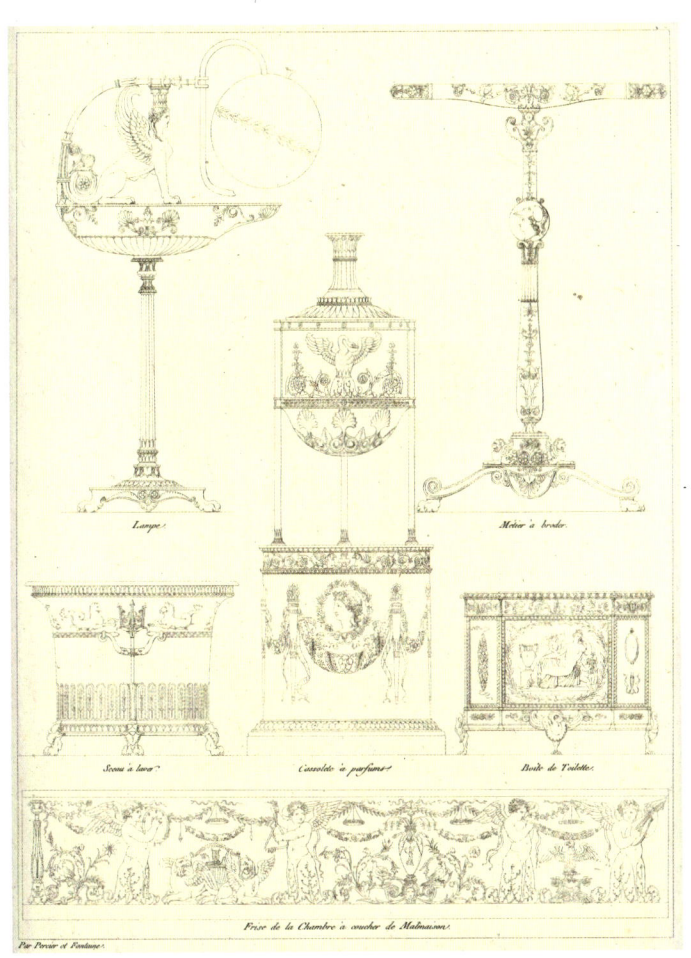

claws, winged sphinxes, swans, and so forth [FIG. 8.22]. New bed forms were also introduced, such as that for Madame Récamier with pilasters and two scrolled backs, and above all those shaped like a boat, in which, as the commentary on the one made for General Moreau's wife would have it, "all the contours...are rounded" so as to increase "comfort" [FIG. 8.23].[83] These seats and beds could be produced in readily transportable folding models suitable for the military campaigns of Napoleon and his entourage.[84] But Percier also made designs for more innovative pieces, notably in the case of consoles, desks, and commodes. With these pieces, his tendency was to increase the dimensions of their flat surfaces so that these offered larger fields for bronze decorative elements, as on the commode for Josephine's *petits appartements* at Saint-Cloud (see chapter 8a in this volume). In any case, it was thanks to the proliferation of these new models inspired by Percier that the Jacob firm was in a position, beginning with the Directory, to increase production and diversify their workshop activity.

We have not yet explored the process of transforming the design sketches into finished objects. The ways in which Percier and Jacob-Desmalter interacted must have been many and various. Percier may well have monitored the execution of his furniture designs in the workshops, but drawings must have been the crux of their collaborative process. Despite the abundance of surviving sheets from Percier's hand, just how these functioned has yet to be elucidated. Most of the pertinent drawings are highly finished, executed in graphite and ink, occasionally in watercolor as well. In some cases, they were meant to convince a patron, in others they were destined to be framed. The ones for the *Recueil* fall into the latter category. No intermediary technical drawings that would have facilitated the translation from design sketch to finished product survive.[85] This absence raises the question of the degree of latitude allowed the cabinetmaker. The available drawings are short on details, which suggests that the craftsmen were granted considerable liberty in the choice of woods, colors, and even dimensions, and that Percier did not get too involved in the more technical aspects of production. But his competence in the techniques of furniture construction must have been sufficient to preclude his submitting models that were unrealizable.

Most of the more detailed sketches that have come down to us lack indications regarding dimensions and other specifics. For this reason, the ones in the workshop scrapbook at the Metropolitan Museum

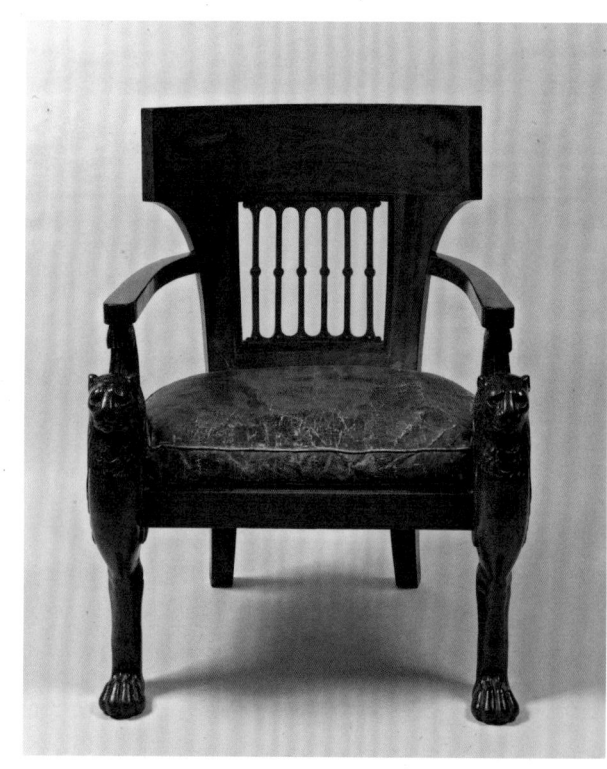

FIG 8.22. Charles Percier. Desk chair of Corvisart, 1793. Made by Georges Jacob. Mahogany, copper inlay, and green leather seat cushion. Châteaux de Malmaison et Bois-Préau, Rueil-Malmaison, MM61. Cat. 77.

FIG 8.23. Jacob frères, after Percier. Bed for the townhouse of General Moreau, 1802. Mahogany, gilded and enameled bronze. Château de Fontainebleau PFH 1992-0024-A. Illustrated in Percier and Fontaine, *Recueil de decorations intérieurs* (Paris: Authors and Pierre Didot l'aîné, 1801–12), pl. 19 (see p. 5). Cat. 67.

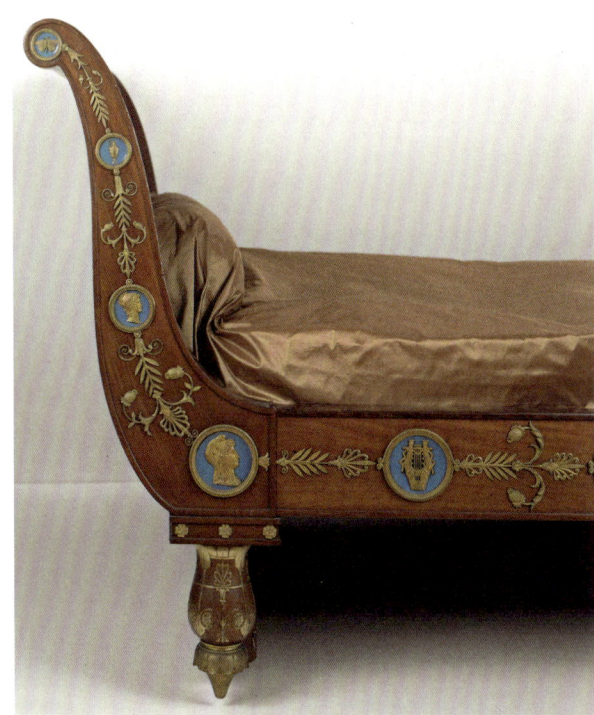

are especially precious, notably a remarkable page of drawings pertaining to the furniture for Josephine's bedchamber at Saint-Cloud, which has several such indications about its "gondola" armchairs (see chapter 11a).[86] This suggests that most of the more technical drawings were retained by the firm. The material that Jacob-Desmalter ceded to his wife in 1813 included, in addition to the commercial property of the firm and its equipment, "all the models whether in bronze or made of plaster and wood and all the plans and drawings pertaining to them."[87] This makes it clear that the working drawings and models were considered integral parts of the enterprise. The existence of templates made of wood and plaster suggests that models were fabricated, doubtless at less than full scale.[88] It is worth recalling here the wording employed by Amélie Lenormant in her comment about the furniture for Hôtel Récamier: "Every piece…was designed and modeled to order."[89] Not all of the drawings retained by the firm were from Percier's own hand; most were probably made by competent in-house professionals, notably F. H. G. Jacob-Desmalter, about whom Lefuel remarked that he could "execute designs for furniture in the current taste and make impeccable copies of watercolors" composed for this purpose by Charles Percier.[90] Doubtless it was Jacob-Desmalter who was responsible for bridging the gap between a sketch and the design for a viable piece of furniture, by making sure that the materials employed were mutually compatible, specifying how the components should be assembled, and anticipating the effect produced by the various colors. It would also have fallen to him to verify that the finished piece was consistent with Percier's original design, especially when it had been conceived as part of a decorative ensemble. Given the size of the Jacob firm, it must have employed several draftsmen whose identities are unfortunately lost to us.

We have yet to raise the question of intellectual property, or what would now be termed copyright. There is no trace of payments made to Percier by the Jacob firm that might correspond to the acquisition of such rights. Percier was, of course, remunerated by his patrons, and the firm was free to make use of his designs to devise variants, usually simplified ones, for its own commercial market and that of Martin Eloy Lignereux, who was, until he retired in late 1804, the most important furniture merchant in Paris. Such, at any rate, is suggested by the *Collection de meubles et objets de goûts* published by Pierre La Mésangère beginning in 1802.[91] Many of Percier's designs are recognizable here: the X-shaped stool in plate 39 of the *Recueil* (La Mésangère, *Collection de meubles et objets de goût*, vol. 1, plate 13), the gondola armchairs with white swans for Josephine's bedchamber at Saint-Cloud (vol. 2, plate 87), the bed for General Moreau (vol. 3, plate 120), the roll-top desk in plate 32 of the *Recueil* (vol. 4, plate 191) [FIGS. 8.24, 8.25]; (SEE ALSO FIGS. 11A.3, 11A.5, AND PAGE 5).

Without underestimating the importance of financial considerations, it seems clear that Percier was less preoccupied with defending such rights than he was with assuring the diffusion of his designs on the largest possible scale. That was one important purpose of his decorative ensembles for the fashionable Parisian townhouses of wealthy clients, which effectively functioned for him as showrooms. Potential patrons could also assess some of his innovative designs when they were displayed in the Cour Carrée of the Louvre in 1801 and 1802, during the first exhibitions of the products of French industry. Publication of the *Recueil* (1801–12) advanced the process of dissemination still further.

By way of closure, let us consider some reflections from the preliminary discourse of the *Recueil* that strike an especially modern note. "Decoration and furnishing are becoming for houses what clothes are for people: things of this kind also become outmoded."[92] What then is the role of the artist in relation to the manufacturer? "Among the many ways of fashioning a chair, for example, some are dictated by the shape of our bodies, by considerations of necessity and comfort which are so delicate that instinct alone enables us to find them. Such is [the role of] nature in productions of this kind. What remains for art? To purify the forms dictated by decorum, to combine them with the simplest contours and make of these natural givens a rationale for ornament that fits the essential form without ever disguising its type or denaturing the principle that gave birth to them."[93]

The following commentary on the proper role of the architect sounds very much like a defense of Percier and his collaboration with Jacob-Desmalter: "We think that, given the close

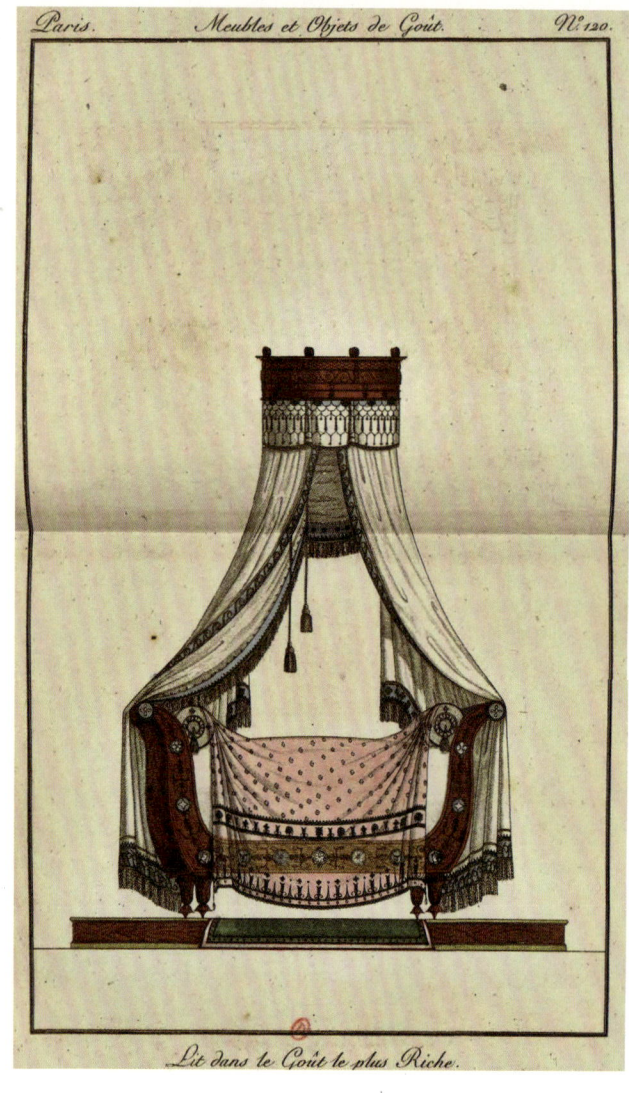

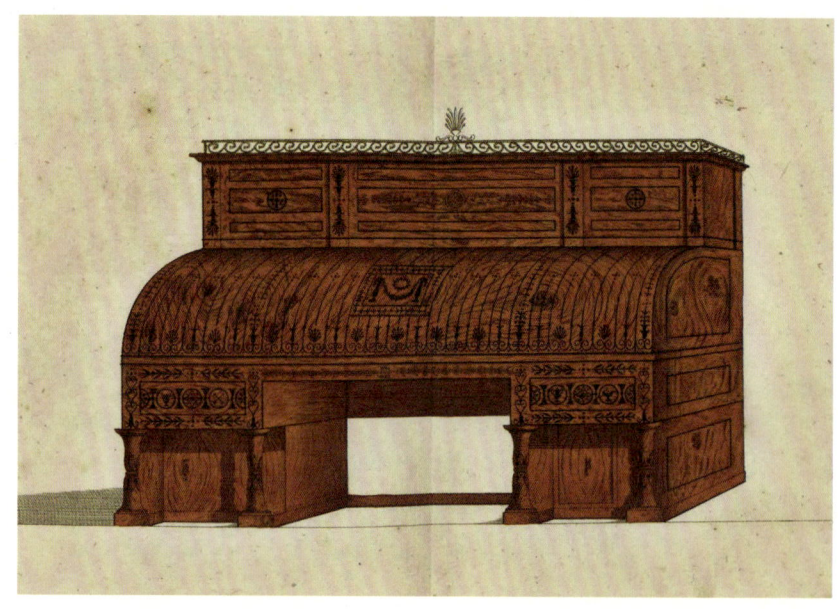

relationship that holds between architecture and furniture, architects should not only avoid ceding control of it to workers' routine, but that, out of an interest in art and in their own honor, they cannot exercise too much care over a part of it whose good or bad implementation affects the very future of architecture. Furniture is too closely connected to interior decoration for the architect to remain indifferent to it."[94] ●

FIG 8.24. Pierre La Mésangère. The bed of General Moreau. Hand-colored plate. From Pierre La Mésangère, *Collection de Meubles et objets de goût* (Paris: Author, 1802–15), vol. 3, pl. 120.

FIG 8.25. Pierre La Mésangère. Cylinder secrétaire. Hand-colored plate. From Pierre La Mésangère, *Collection de Meubles et objets de goût*. (Paris: Author, 1802–15), vol. 4, pl. 191.

1 Estate inventory of Georges Jacob fils, 11 brumaire year XXII (November 3, 1803), Archives nationales de France, Minutier Central (hereafter ANF-MC), Étude LXX, 723.

2 Société des Citoyens Jacob fils, 16 thermidor year IV (April 3, 1796), ANF-MC, Étude XXII, 134.

3 Louis Bergeron, *Banquiers, négociants et manufacturiers parisiens du Directoire à l'Empire* (Paris: Éditions de l'École des Hautes Études en Sciences Sociales, 1978), 41.

4 "En fait d'exécution, sur beaucoup de points les arts industriels des modernes ont acquis, et doivent encore acquérir de quoi surpasser ceux des anciens. Tout ce qui dépend de l'expérience ne peut que se perfectionner par le tems, et surtout par les applications que les arts reçoivent des sciences physiques....La France, et surtout sa ville capitale, possèdent en matières propres à embellir les habitations, des resources infinies, et le commerce y fait arriver en bois, en pierres, etc., tous les matériaux que l'industrie et le goût peuvent désirer. Les nombreuses manufactures de verreries, de métaux, de porcelaines que Paris possède, ou dont cette ville est entourée, y entretiennent une foule d'ouvriers habiles; mais leur talent a besoin d'être dirigé par le bon goût." Charles Percier and Pierre Fontaine, Preliminary discourse to *Recueil de décorations intérieures* (Paris: Authors and Pierre Didot l'aîné, 1801-12), 16–17.

5 On the elder Jacob, see Hector Lefuel, *Georges Jacob, Ébeniste du XVIIIe siècle* (Paris: Morancé, 1923). The same author later published a book on F. H. G Jacob-Desmalter, cited in note 15 below.

6 Étienne Jean Delécluze, *Louis David, son école et son temps* (Paris: Didier, 1855), 20.

7 The play, which dealt with ancient Rome's fraught transition from a monarchy to a republic, was first performed May 4, 1792; the sets by Percier and Fontaine were presumably designed shortly before. The set for Act III, which is set in Lucretia's rooms, included furniture after antique models.

8 Lefuel, *Georges Jacob*, 145–46. Percier and Fontaine provided drawings and models for a presidential bureau, a speaker's tribune, two secretarial bureaus, oil-burning floor lamps, and stalls for the 760 deputies. It is worth citing another source regarding this commission: "When it came time to furnish the hall for the Convention, G[eorge] Jacob was the obvious choice for this important project....Although a skillful designer, as evidenced by his previous compositions, he did not want to take on the heavy responsibility of designing this furniture; moreover, he feared he was not yet sufficiently well informed about the new taste. Spurred by a happy inspiration, he solicited drawings from Percier and Fontaine, who lived miserably in a poor room in a hovel in the rough Saint-Martin quarter." ("Quand il fut question de meubler la salle de la Convention, G. Jacob se trouva naturellement désigné pour cet important travail....Quoique adroit dessinateur, comme le témoignent ses compositions antérieures, il ne voulut point assumer une responsabilité aussi lourde que celle de dessiner ce mobilier; d'ailleurs il craignait de ne point être encore au fait du goût nouveau. Poussé par une heureuse inspiration, il alla demander aux architectes Percier et Fontaine, qui vivaient misérablement dans une pauvre chambre d'une triste masure de ce populacier quartier Saint-Martin de faire ces dessins.") Paul Lafond, *Une famille d'ébénistes français: Les Jacob: Le mobilier de Louis XV à Louis-Philippe* (Paris: E. Plon, 1894), 12.

9 Marriage contract dated 26 ventôse year VI (March 14, 1798), ANF-MC, Étude XXIV, 1070. On this document, see Jean-Pierre Samoyault, "The Jacob-Lignereux alliance (14 March 1798)." *Furniture History* 43 (2007): 20–28. On Jacob's side, their friend and collaborator Claude Louis Bernier also took part as a witness. It is also worth noting here Fontaine's intervention with Napoleon on the elder Jacob's behalf in November 1813, when they encountered Napoleon and Fontaine emerging from the construction site of the palace of the King of Rome. See Lefuel, *Georges Jacob*, 106.

10 Marie-Laure Crosnier-Leconte, *Dictionnaire des élèves architectes de l'École des Beaux-Arts (1800–1968)*, published online: http://agorha.inha.fr/inhaprod/jsp/

reference.jsp?reference=INHA_METADONNEES_7

11   Marriage contract dated May 8, 1832, ANF-MC, Étude LXXV, 1110.

12   "Je donne comme un gage de mon attachement sincère à Madame Jacob-Desmalter née Lignereux une somme de 1200 francs et celle de mes bagues qui aura plus de valeur." Posthumous inventory of Charles Percier, September 11, 1838, ANF-MC, Étude XLVI, 905.

13   "grands dessins coloriés représentant divers ornements." Will dated February 15, 1821, and recorded September 8, 1838, ANF-MC, Étude XLVI, 905.

14   Will dated June 30, 1847, and posthumous inventory dated October 11, 1847, ANF-MC, Étude XXIV, 1337.

15   Hector Lefuel, *François-Honoré-Georges Jacob-Desmalter, ébéniste de Napoléon Ier et de Louis XVIII* (Paris: Morancé, 1925).

16   Other legatees of the widow Jacob-Desmalter included Achille Leclère and the wife of the architect Louis Visconti, who frequented Percier's atelier during the same period as Georges Alphonse. The latter received, among other things, "a small, four-legged bedside table that came from the Empress Josephine" ("une petite table de lit à quatre pieds venant de l'impératrice Joséphine").

17   Articles of incorporation dated 16 thermidor year IV (August 3, 1796), ANF-MC, Étude XXII, 134.

18   "l'une des plus belles fabriques de meubles que possède la France et même l'Europe. Il s'y fabrique, en temps ordinaire, pour la valeur de 700,000 francs, dont un tiers à l'exportation." ANF, AF IV, 1060. This description comes from a dossier on a government loan granted in 1807, when the French economy was in the midst of a general slowdown. "At present," the text reads, "it employs only 100 [workers]. It is suffering from the decline in exports and foreign sales" ("En ce moment elle n'en occupe que 100. Elle souffre du défaut d'exportation et de vente à l'extérieur").

19   The physical expansion of the workshops provides a useful index of this development, for in 1801 and 1809 the Jacob family purchased two buildings adjacent to their initial property. Sale by Michel Desprez, April 18, 1801, ANF-MC, Étude LXX, 692; sale by Jean Vallée, November 16, 1809, ANF-MC, Étude LXX, 796.

20   "un atelier de menuiserie en bâtiments, deux ateliers de menuiseries en meubles, un atelier de sculpture en figures et un de sculpture en ornements, un de tourneurs, un de peinture et dorure, un d'ébénisterie, un d'incrusteurs, un de polisseurs, un de fondeurs-mouleurs, un de mouleurs, un de ciseleurs, un de doreurs en métaux, un de tapissiers et un de serruriers-mécaniciens.") *Moniteur Universel*, March 26, 1803, in an article occasioned by a visit to the facilities by Interior Minister Chaptal; as cited by Lefuel, *François-Honoré-Georges Jacob-Desmalter*, 61.

21   "Les deux frères Jacob présentent une réunion des talents qui concourt avantageusement à la prospérité de l'établissement. L'un très versé dans l'art du dessin, préside aux détails et à la manutention habituelle de chaque atelier; l'autre, tout entier à l'administration, dirige tout ce qui appartient à la comptabilité." Ibid.

22   "Le citoyen Jacob aîné sera chargé de la tenue des écritures…du payement des ouvriers et autres dépenses…le citoyen Jacob jeune de l'achat de matières premières, de la direction et exécution des ouvrages et travaux, de la distribution du travail aux ouvriers, de leur surveillance, du dressé des plans et dessins, et enfin de tout ce qui a rapport à la confection des travaux." Articles of incorporation, 16 thermidor year IV (August 3, 1796), ANF-MC, Étude XXII, 134.

23   After retiring, he sojourned in Rome and Naples, where he made many drawings and watercolors, including an album of ninety sepia drawings representing ancient marbles in the Vatican Museum as well as several landscapes. See Lefuel, *François-Honoré-Georges Jacob-Desmalter*, 12–13.

24   Regarding work executed for the coronation—specifically, woodwork for the ceremonial platform—see the invoice for carpentry (*menuiserie*) dated December 1804, ANF, O2 558.

25   "Mon cher camarade, je pars pour Sceaux. Je n'ai pu encore terminer votre candélabre: il le sera sous peu. Tout à vous, Charles Percier." Lefuel, *François-Honoré-Georges Jacob-Desmalter*, 28.

26   "architectes que l'amitié a réunie"; "Habiles dans les détails de leur art qu'ils ont puisé dans l'Antiquité; leurs productions sont extrêmement soignées; ils ont beaucoup de succès dans la décoration des intérieurs et dans les dessins des meubles." Memorandum written by the prominent art dealer in his capacity as "commissaire expert" at the Musée central des arts, and doubtless drafted under the influence of the architect Jean Arnaud Raymond; as quoted in Anatole de Montaiglon, "Artistes français en 1800," *Nouvelles Archives de l'Art français* (Paris: 1872), 1:431.

27   Percier and Fontaine, *Recueil de décorations intérieures*, pl. 14, caption proper: "Bed of Citizen V. executed by Alexandre Regnier" ("Lit du citoyen V. exécuté par Alexandre Regnier").

28   Ibid., pl. 15, caption proper: "Fauteuil exécuté…par les frères Jacob"; pl. 16, caption proper: "une table exécutée par les frères Jacob"; pl. 23, caption on plate: "Table de nuit exécutée par les frères Jacob"; pl. 32, explanatory table (p. 30): "Secrétaire à cylindre. Ce meuble, ainsi que le plus grand nombre de ceux que l'on vient de voir, a été exécuté dans la fabrique de MM Jacob à Paris." ("Rolltop desk. This piece, like most of those previously illustrated, was executed in the factory of MM. Jacob in Paris"); pl. 44, explanatory

28 table (pp. 34–35): "Ces deux meubles sont exécutées en acajou et en bronze. On peut reconnaître au fini et à la perfection du travail qu'ils sont de la fabrique de MM Jacob" ("These two pieces of furniture [i.e., a tea table and a jardinière] were executed in mahogany and bronze. The finish and perfection of the workmanship identify them as having come from the factory of MM. Jacob").

29 Ibid., pl. 23, caption proper: "petite table de travail ou chiffonière"; caption on plate: "Petite table de travail, renfermant une cassolette."

30 Jean-Pierre Samoyault and Colombe Samoyault-Verlet, eds., *Le mobilier de Général Moreau: un ameublement à la mode en 1802* (Paris: Réunion des musées nationaux, 1992), 81.

31 Jean-Pierre Samoyault, *Mobilier français, Consulat et Empire* (Paris: Gourcuff-Gradenigo, 2009), 117, fig. 198.

32 Percier and Fontaine, *Recueil de décorations intérieures*, pl. 39, caption proper: "tabouret pliant dans la forme d'un X"; list of plates: "placé à St. C."

33 E.g., ibid., pl. 1 ("Vue perspective de l'atelier du citoyen I. à Paris"); pl. 13 ("Vue perspective de la chambre à coucher du citoyen V. à Paris"); pl. 25 (perspective view of a bedchamber executed in Paris for "M. O"); pl. 36 (perspective view of a "Chambre à coucher exécutée à Paris pour M. G").

34 "Projets pour la chambre et le salon de l'hôtel Moreau," rue d'Anjou (see Samoyault, *Le mobilier de Général Moreau*, 17); "Trois études pour la chambre à coucher de Mme G." See Elisabeth Caude and Christophe Pincemaille, eds., *Joséphine et Napoléon. L'hôtel de la rue de la Victoire* (Paris: Réunion des musées nationaux, 2013), 59.

35 "placées entre chaque subdivision, elles répètent, pour la salle à manger des Tuileries, à l'infini les richesses du plafond." Percier and Fontaine, *Recueil de décorations intérieures*, "Table explicative," gloss on pl. 43.

36 See Anne Lafont, "A la recherché d'une iconographie Incroyable et Merveilleuse: les panneaux décoratifs sous le Directoire," *Annales historiques de la Révolution française* 2 (2005): 5.

37 Percier and Fontaine, *Recueil de décorations intérieures*, pls. 13–17: table, bed, armchair, pedestal-armoire, tripod washstand; pl. 20: roll-top desk; pl. 22: "miroir mobile" (cheval mirror) and jardinière.

38 "Des banquiers, des fournisseurs se hazardèrent à montrer les richesses qu'ils avaient acquises. Messieurs Dumanoir, Gaudin, Ouvrard, Michel, et quelques autres encore nous chargèrent alors du rétablissement et de l'arrangement de leurs maisons. Nous devînmes, je ne sais trop comment, hommes de vogue." Passage from Fontaine's manuscript *Mia Vita*, as cited by Hans Ottomeyer, *Das frühe Œuvre Charles Percier (1782–1800). Zu den Anfängen des Historismus in Frankreich* (Munich: Ludwig-Maximilens-Universität, 1981), 203. Fontaine continues (ibid.): "Various projects more profitable to us than the income from our books necessitated a slight delay in the timely publication of the installments of our *Édifices et palais de Rome*" ("Divers travaux plus lucratifs pour nous que les revenus de nos ouvrages nous obligèrent à suspendre un peu et à ne pas publier avec la même exactitude des livraisons des édifices et palais de Rome").

39 Anne Foray-Carlier, *Le mobilier du Musée Carnavalet* (Paris: Faton, 2000), 242.

40 Musée Carnavalet, ms A 6021.

41 "chambre des demoiselles." Ibid., fol. 91. Between 9 germinal year V (March 28, 1797) and 28 frimaire year VI (December 18, 1797), Gaudin made furniture purchases from the Jacob firm amounting to 9,382 livres.

42 April 2, 1822, ANF-MC, Étude XLII, 789.

43 "Chez Messieurs Chauvelin et Gaudin, près…de la rue Chantereine (aujourd'hui rue de la Victoire), les appartements que nous avions récemment décorés," from Pierre François Léonard Fontaine, *Journal (1799–1853)*, ed. Marguerite David-Roy (Paris: École nationale supérieure des beaux-arts / Institut français d'architecture / Société de l'histoire de l'art français, 1987), 2:1333.

44 17 messidor year IV, ANF-MC, Étude CXV, 1032.

45 Jean-Marie Pérouse de Montclos, *Etienne-Louis Boullée (1728–1799)* (Paris: Flammarion, 1994), 225–27 (purchase history of hôtel de Thun, p. 226).

46 A Gaudin corporation was mentioned during a session of the Council of Five Hundred in 1799. See the *Journal des débats et lois du Corps législatifs*, séance des Cinq Cents du 14 vendémaire year VIII (October 6, 1799).

47 1 nivôse year VIII (December 22, 1799), ANF-MC, Étude CXV, 1044.

48 "destiné à décorer le salon d'un petit hôtel rue du Mont-blanc construit par Mr Percier pour Mr Gaudin." Pierre Alexandre Coupin, ed., *Œuvres posthumes de Girodet-Trioson…précédé d'une notice historique* (Paris: J. Renouard, 1829), 1:xiv.

49 See Sylvain Bellenger, *Girodet 1767–1824* (Paris: Gallimard–Musée du Louvre Editions, 2005), 256–59.

50 "lit de forme antique en bois d'acajou avec filets d'ébène et étain, et petits sujets peints." ANF-MC, Étude CXV, 1044; ["en acajou massif… à un dossier renversé d'une forme antique…enrichi d'ornement étrusque en ébène incrusté."] Musée Carnavalet, ms A 6021, fol 91.

51 "dossiers à crosse." ANF-MC, Étude CXV, 1044; "dossiers à crosse…, les accotoirs en S cannelés," "avec au dessus des palmettes antiques en ébène incrusté." Musée Carnavalet, ms A 6021, fol. 91.

52 "forme nouvelle"; "le haut formant chapiteau est

52 porté par quatre colonnes en amarante et renferme un miroir se tirant à ressort et s'abattant sur la devanture des colonnes." Musée Carnavalet, ms A 6021, fol. 98. Sold for 1,000 livres in 1797, this desk is ascribed a value of 1,500 livres in the 1799 inventory.

53 "draperies plissées sur lesquelles sont attachés des tableaux de prix." ANF-MC, Étude CXV, 1044.

54 "la richesse et l'abondance des ornements"; "a été fait pour une femme." Ibid.

55 Private collection; reproduced in Caude and Pincemaille, *Joséphine et Napoléon,* 59.

56 Percier and Fontaine, *Recueil de décorations intérieures,* pl. 4: "table à thé exécutée à Paris pour M. G"; list of plates; "en acajou et en bronze"; "sont de la fabrique de MM. Jacob"; caption proper.

57 "console exécutée par Jacob chez M. Gaudin." Paris, Drouot, Binoche and Godeau sale (March 22, 1991), cat. lot 31 (reproduction). The console represented on this sheet seems to be different from the one for Madame Gaudin's bedchamber, described as follows in the 1800 sale catalogue: "made of mahogany [and] supported by four legs with winged female heads in gilt bronze" ("en bois d'acajou supportée par quatre pieds à tête de femmes ailées bronzées et dorées").

58 "Je désire que ma maison soit meublée dans la première élégance." As cited by Elisabeth Caude in Caude and Pincemaille, *Joséphine et Napoléon,* 42.

59 Musée Carnavalet, ms A 1060, fol. 146; published in Lefuel, *François-Honoré-Georges Jacob-Desmalter,* 46–49. The aggregate price of the delivered goods was 7,381 livres.

60 Fontaine, *Journal,* 1:72, 5 pluviôse year XII (entry dated January 26, 1804): "C'est au voisinage de cette petite maison (de la rue de la Victoire) avec celle de M. Chauvelin, ex-ambassadeur en Angleterre, dans laquelle nous avions fait travailler, que nous sommes redevables de la bienveillance de Madame Bonaparte qui nous a mis dans la situation où nous nous trouvons. C'est qu'en y voyant ce que nous avons fait qu'elle a bien voulu augurer favorablement de nos talents et qu'elle nous a fait appeler près d'elle...." ("It is to the proximity of this small house [on rue de la Victoire] to that of M. Chauvelin, the former ambassador to England, in which we had done some work, that we are indebted for the benevolence of Madame Bonaparte, who placed us in the situation in which we now find ourselves. It was upon seeing what we had done there that she decided we were promising and summoned us to her side" etc.).

61 We do not know the extent of Bonaparte's complicity in these transactions; he did not return to Paris until December 1797, after the deliveries from Jacob had begun.

62 See Caude and Pincemaille, *Joséphine et Napoléon,* 104.

63 9 thermidor year VI (July 27, 1798), ANF-MC, Étude LXLX, 852. Ouvrard sold the house to Narcisse Dorothée Michel, known as Michel l'aîné, on 12 pluviôse year XI (February 1, 1803). Cf. the subsequent sale: March 29, 1822, ANF-MC, Étude XV, 1674. In his diary, Fontaine says that he and Percier were still working for Ouvrard in September 1801. He also mentions work under way for General Marmont, who had married the daughter of the banker Perregaux in April 1798. The work in question was probably in their townhouse at 9, rue de la Chaussée d'Antin, which was next to that of the Récamiers (Fontaine, *Journal,* 1:34, entry dated September 23, 1801),

64 Michel jeune sold the furniture in the house to his wife on December 11, 1814 (ANF-MC, Étude XCII, 3151). Appended to the deed of sale is a detailed list of the furniture, some of which is now at the château d'Azay-le-Féron (Indre), which was also owned by Michel jeune at the time.

65 Anne Dion-Tenenbaum, "Le mobilier Récamier," in Stéphane Paccoud and Léna Widerkher, *Juliette Récamier: muse et mécène* (Paris: Hazan, 2009), 173–201.

66 "L'hôtel de la rue du Mont-Blanc fut confié à l'architecte Berthault pour être restauré et meublé, et on lui donna carte blanche pour la dépense. Il s'acquitta de sa tâche avec un goût infini et se fit aider dans son entreprise par M. Percier." Amélie Lenormant, *Souvenirs et correspondances tirés des pàpiers de Madame Récamier* (Paris: Michel Lévy frères, 1859), 1:25.

67 Maria-Teresa Caracciolo, "Juliette Récamier et Charles Percier: nouveaux dessins pour l'hôtel de la rue du Mont-Blanc," *Les Cahiers d'Histoire de l'Art* 12 (2014): 61.

68 This guéridon is stamped "Jacob frères / rue Meslée." See Dion-Tenenbaum, "Le mobilier Récamier," 199.

70 "Chacune des pièces de l'ameublement, bronzes, bibliothèques, candélabres, jusqu'au moindre fauteuil, fut dessiné et modelé tout exprès. Jacob ébèniste du premier ordre, exécuta les modèles fournis; il en résulta un ameublement qui porte l'empreinte de l'époque, mais qui restera le meilleur échantillon du goût de ce temps" Lenormant, *Souvenirs et correspondances,* 25.

70 E.g.:"To each arrival, Madame Récamier said: 'Would you like to see my bedchamber?'...Whereupon a cortege of cavaliers rushed toward the sanctuary" ("A chaque arrivant, Mme Récamier disait: Voulez-vous voir ma chambre?...Un cortège de cavaliers se pressaient sur leur pas vers le sanctuaire.") Johann Friedrich Reichardt, *Un hiver à Paris sous le Consulat (1802–1803)* (Paris: Tallandier, 2003), 133.

71 For example, a watercolor by Robert Smirke ("Chambre de Madame Récamier," 1802). London, Royal Institute of British Architects, SD84/2 (1).

72 Chantal Gastinel-Coural, "Le Cabinet de platine de

la Casa del Labrador à Aranjuez: Documents inédits," *Bulletin de la Société de l'histoire de l'Art français* (1993): 181.

73 "fabricant parisien de placqué et doublé d'or et d'argent," *Almanach du commerce* (Paris, 1807).

74 "des engagements avec de célèbres artistes de Paris." Sitel to Pedro Cevallos, June 12, 1801 (Madrid, Archivo Histórico Nacional, Estado, vol. 3924), as cited by Javier Jordán de Urríes y de la Colina and José Luis Sancho, unpublished first version of "El gabineto de la Real Casa del Labrador en Aranjuez," in Frommel, Garric, and Kieven, *Charles Percier et Pierre Fontaine*, 133–43.

75 "artistes les meilleurs qui se trouvent à Paris." Martinez de Hervas to Pedro Cevallos, September 23, 1801 (Madrid, Archivo Histórico Nacional, Estado, vol. 3924, as cited in ibid.).

76 Letter from Ignacio Muzquiz to Pedro Cevallos, January 20, 1801 (Madrid, Archivo Histórico Nacional, Estado, vol. 3924, as cited in ibid.).

77 "The execution of the cabinet of the King of Spain, Carlos IV, after designs by Percier won Mr [Jacob-] Desmalter ample and honorable praise" ("L'exécution du cabinet du roi d'Espagne Charles IV sur les dessins de Percier valut à Mr Desmalter de nombreux et honorables suffrages.") Edouard Foucaud, *Les artisans illustres* (Paris: Béthune et Plon, 1841), 489.

78 In an accounting of expenditures prepared in July 1806, the aggregate cost of their contributions amounted to 31,209 francs, out of a total of 456,996. Memoir by Sitel to S.M.C., cited by Jordán de Urríes y de la Colina and Sancho, "El gabineto de la Real Casa," 142 n.27.

79 Gastinel-Coural, "Le Cabinet de platine," 190.

80 The central panel of the ceiling features a large rosette flanked by two lozenges containing roundels decorated with "Etruscan" vases; the panels immediately above the walls are decorated with trophies and exotic birds.

81 Fontaine, *Journal*, 1:13, 1st Complementary (September 18, 1800).

82 Group of drawings by Charles Percier from the archives of the Jeanselme family, which purchased the holdings of Maison Jacob in 1847; catalogue of the Rieuner and Bailly-Pommery sale, Drouot, January 15, 2001, lots 27–29.

83 "La commodité a été le but principal...tout est arrondi dans les contours des dossiers, des traverses et des pieds." Percier and Fontaine, *Recueil de décorations intérieures*, pl. 19, caption proper.

84 Jehanne Lazaj, ed., *Le bivouac de Napoléon: luxe et ingéniosité en campagne* (Milan: Silvana Editoriale, 2014); Christiane Naffah-Bayle and Jehanne Lazaj, eds., *L'esprit et la main*, exh. cat. (Paris: Gourcuff-Gradenigo, 2015).

85 However, there exist a few sketches or study drawings that once belonged to Pierre Fontaine, for example a group of forty such sold at auction in 1991, notably a watercolor annotated in ink: "chaise courante exécuté par M. Jacob" ("standard chair executed by M. Jacob"); and another sheet, mentioned previously (note 56), that is inscribed "console exécuté par Jacob chez m. Gaudin." Paris, Drouot, Binoche and Godeau sale (March 22, 1991), lots 33 and 31 (reproductions).

86 On this commission, see chapter 8b in this volume.

87 "tous les modèles tant en bronzes qu'en plâtre et bois et tous les plans et dessins y relatifs." Deed of assignment transcribed into an agreement recorded on May 14, 1824, ANF-MC, Étude XXIV, 1216.

88 There is reason to believe that the preparation of reduced-scale models had long been standard workshop practice, at least in the Jacob firm. See Lefuel, *Georges Jacob*, pl. II (a wooden model of a chair that Lefuel thinks was Jacob's *chef-d'œuvre*, or certification piece qualifying him for entry in the guild) and pl. X, Lefuel's caption to which reads: "Desk chair, wax maquette from the Louis XV period and attributed to Georges Jacob."

89 "Chacune des pièces...fut dessinée et modelée exprès." For the full French quote, see note 69.

90 Lefuel, *François-Honoré-Georges Jacob-Desmalter*, 12.

91 Pierre La Mésangère, *Collection de meubles et objets de goût*, 8 vols. (Paris: Author, 1802–15). These volumes contain a total of 421 colored plates.

92 "La décoration et l'ameublement deviennent aux maisons ce que les habits sont aux personnes: tout en ce genre vieillit aussi." Percier and Fontaine, "Discours Préliminaire," *Recueil de décorations intérieures*, 9.

93 "Entre toutes les façons d'un siège, par exemple, il en est qui sont dictées par la forme de notre corps, par des rapports de nécessité et de commodité, tellement sensibles que l'instinct seul nous les ferait trouver. Voilà la nature en ce genre. Que reste-t-il à l'art? D'épurer les formes dictées par les convenances, de les combiner avec les contours les plus simples, et de faire de ces données naturelles les motifs d'ornement qui s'adapteront à la forme essentielle sans jamais déguiser son type, ni dénaturer le principe qui leur donna naissance?" Ibid., 13–14.

94 "Nous pensons que sous ce rapport de correspondance qui existe entre l'architecture et l'ameublement, non seulement l'architecte doit se garder d'en abandonner la direction à la routine des ouvriers, mais que, par intérêt pour l'art et pour son propre honneur, il ne saurait trop soigner une partie dont le bon ou le mauvais emploi réagit sur le sort même de l'architecture. L'ameublement se lie de trop près à la décoration des intérieurs pour que l'architecte puisse y être indifférent." Ibid., 15.

DECORATIVE ARTS

TWO COMMODES

IRIS MOON

The *Recueil de décorations intérieures* played a decisive role in establishing a new taste in the realm of furnishing and luxury objects at the beginning of the nineteenth century in Europe. While primarily serving to publicize the architects' designs, its wide dissemination also helped revive a fragile luxury industry in Paris, which was still recovering from the adverse political and economic effects of the French Revolution. Famous clients, notably Napoleon Bonaparte and his wife Josephine, influenced the direction of the architects' designs. However, the publication was propelled by Percier and Fontaine's extensive studies of antiquities, museum collections, and Renaissance buildings, which they had undertaken as students in Rome. Foremost, the book marks the authors' awareness that the design of furnishings and decorative objects was crucial to securing their reputation as practicing architects. This is particularly evident in the preliminary discourse, where they signaled that furnishings were too important for architects to ignore, since their "good or bad employment affects the very fate of architecture."[1]

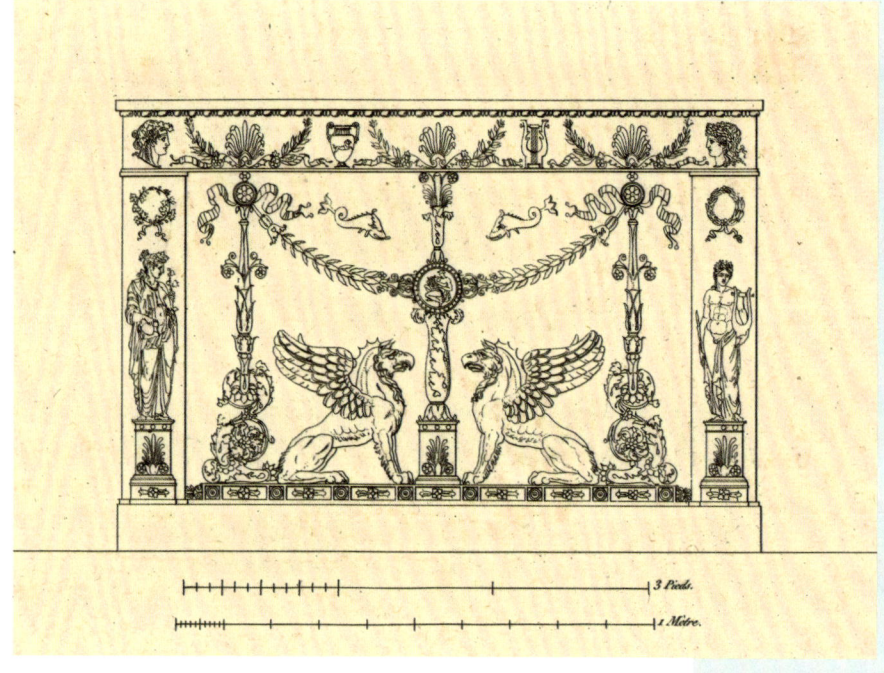

Early in their careers, Percier and Fontaine catered to the tastes of the urban elite centered in Paris and created some of the most notable interior decorations of the Directory period (1795–98). The members of this new wealthy class included bankers and financial speculators, military contractors and generals, and, importantly, women of the minor nobility who had managed to survive the Terror and came to dominate the heady, fashionable world of *Merveilleuse* society.[2] Marie Joseph Rose de Tascher de La Pagerie, who became Josephine Bonaparte upon marrying the Corsican general Bonaparte in 1796, would eventually come to dominate post-Revolutionary Parisian society. The newly designed beds, curtains, and chairs found in the refurbished residences of women such as Josephine and

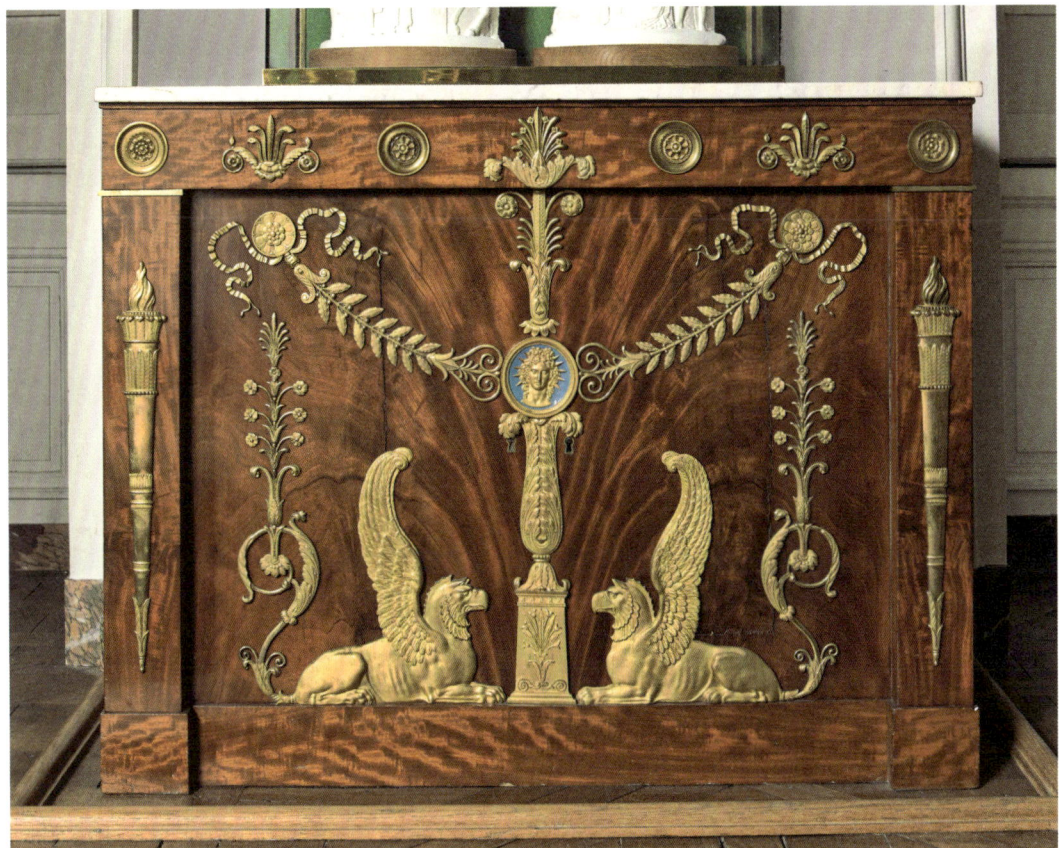

▷ **FIG 8A.1.** Jacob frères after Charles Percier. Commode from the bedroom of Josephine's apartments, château de Saint-Cloud, 1802–3. Mahogany, gilt bronze, white marble, enamel. Château de Fontainebleau, F3927. Cat. 86.

◁ **FIG 8A.2.** Charles Percier and Pierre Fontaine. Plate 26 of *Recueil de décorations intérieures* (Paris: Authors and Pierre Didot l'aîné, 1801–12).

◁ **FIG. 8A.3.** Georges Jacob and François Honoré Georges Jacob-Desmalter. Writing Cabinet, 1810–13. Mahogany, oak, marble, gilded bronze mounts. Philadelphia Museum of Art, Gallery 299, European Art 1500–1850, Philadelphia, The Henry P. McIlhenny Collection, in memory of Frances P. McIlhenny, 1986-26-86.

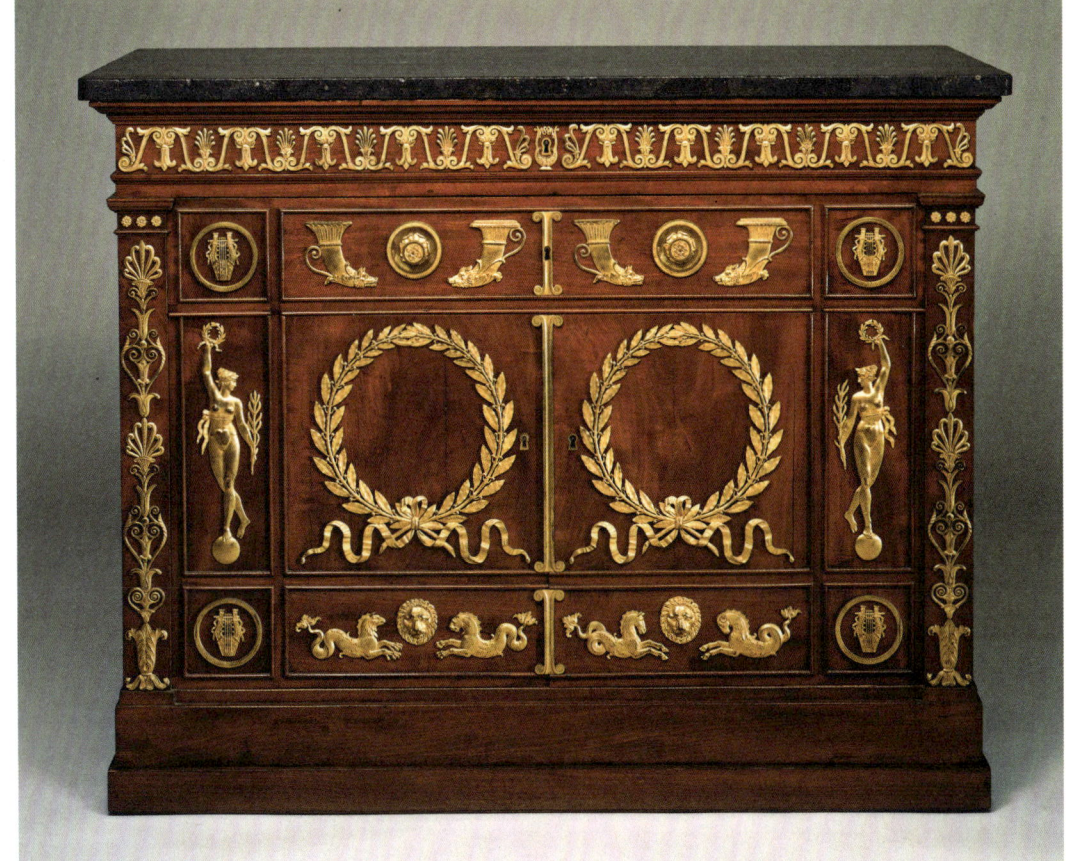

her rival, Juliette Récamier, attracted as much attention as the diaphanous and risqué fashions they wore. Both fashion and furnishing were crucial to the continual process of self-fashioning that was vital to establishing and securing one's socioeconomic status in the volatile and highly competitive realm of post-Revolutionary Paris. Of course, Percier and Fontaine's decoration book was not the only source for furniture design. Although architectural ornament and decoration books could be found at Parisian print sellers and luxury goods shops throughout the eighteenth century, post-Revolutionary fashion publications such as Pierre de la Mésangère's *Journal des Dames et Modes*, issued from 1797 to 1839, and its supplementary catalogue, *Meubles et objets de goût,* did much to market a taste for new furniture. Such journals were marketed toward a more geographically and socioeconomically diverse readership, namely rural female consumers who sought news of the latest fashions in Paris.[3]

However brief, the Consulate period (1799–1804) saw subtle if significant transformations emerge in the realm of domestic furnishings, as evidenced by a commode designed in 1802–3 for the private apartments of Josephine at Saint-Cloud and attributed to Jacob frères, today located at the château de Fontainebleau [FIG. 8A.1]. Whereas earlier Louis XVI designs by cabinetmakers such as Guillaume Benneman combined marquetry with neoclassical motifs that incorporated intricate foliate decorations, the Jacob *commode à vantaux*, or chest of drawers with panels, is distinguished by its severe cubic form. The architectonic effect is heightened through the recession of the central panel and the protruding horizontal elements of the upper drawer and the thick pedestal at the base. A flat, planar effect is achieved by obscuring the opening of the two central panels behind a vertically positioned gilded bronze candelabrum pierced by a curving garland. The central medallion of Apollo, set against a blue enamel ground and positioned slightly above the two keyholes, is similar to the ornaments found on the bed designed by Percier and Fontaine for General Moreau (cat. 67, also located at Fontainebleau), and evokes Wedgwood blue jasperware cameos.[4] Flanking the central candelabrum are seated griffons, torches, and a garland with ribbons, gilded bronze ornaments organized along a central axis. On plate 26 of the *Recueil*, Percier and Fontaine offer an alternative, more ornate model to the commode at Fontainebleau [SEE FIG. 8A.2]. In the plate, the winged griffons are shown in a half-seated position and are flanked by two candelabra emerging from foliate rinceaux. In addition to wreaths, statues, and dolphins, the design features a central medallion of a seated Apollo holding his lyre.[5]

Gilded-bronze ornaments played a visible role in the furniture designs of the Consulate and Empire periods. The case furniture produced by the Jacob firm during the period typically featured flat surfaces, rather than the combination of marquetry, highly carved segments of joined woodwork, and gilded-bronze ornaments favored by ancien-régime cabinetmakers. As Jean-Pierre Samoyault notes, despite the prominent role of bronze *fondeurs* and *ciseleurs* in the furnishings of the period, few are known by name. Two notable exceptions are Philippe Thomire and Lucien François Feuchère, collaborators of Jacob frères, as well as Percier and Fontaine, who, in addition to supplying bronze ornaments for furniture makers, separately created chandeliers, lamps, candelabrum, and clock cases.[6] Significant too is the fact that the Jacob firm had space for a bronze foundry within their large factory on rue Meslay in Paris.[7] The remarkable rhythmic effects that could be achieved by the application of bronze ornaments can be seen in a *commode secrétaire*, or writing cabinet, by the Jacob firm at the Philadelphia Museum of Art [FIG. 8A.3]. Attributed to the period 1810–13, the two panels in the front are divided into two sections, emphasized by the repeating ornaments of wreaths, nude figures of victory, and pairs of lyres set within rings found on either side of the three Ionic colonettes in the central axis. Terminated at either end by narrow pilasters and a thicker pedestal at the base, the commode's entablature features an alternating motif of Greek palmettes and floral design. A drawer of the commode opens up to reveal small storage compartments and a writing surface, created by folding down the hinged drawer.

Heavier and more simplified forms of furniture featuring larger amounts of gilded-bronze ornaments characterized the furniture of the Empire period (1804–15), which was for the most part dominated by official commissions for the imperial court of Napoleon. The year 1805 marked a turning point in the consolidation of taste, as Napoleon reinstated court etiquette that year and set about refurnishing the royal residences he had taken over, including Saint-Cloud, Fontainebleau, and Compiègne. Like Percier and Fontaine, Parisian luxury producers were increasingly occupied with fulfilling imperial commissions, even as the declaration of the Continental Blockade of November 21, 1806, which sought to block all English commerce from the European continent, severely curtailed access to foreign materials and export markets.[8] Although Percier and Fontaine established a new vocabulary of splendor for the Napoleonic regime, the architects' designs were nonetheless accompanied by the continual threat of bankruptcy, material scarcity, and the instabilities of war. ●

1 Charles Percier and Pierre Fontaine, *Recueil de décorations intérieures…* (Paris: Authors and Pierre Didot l'aîne, 1801–12), "preliminary discourse," 14.
2 On notable women of the Directory period, see Thierry Lemoine, ed., *Au temps des merveilleuses: la société parisienne sous le Directoire et le Consulat*, exh. cat. (Paris: Paris Musées, 2005), esp. 75–110.
3 For the readership of the fashion journal, see Anne-Marie Kleinert, *Le journal des Dames et des Modes: ou la conquête de l'Europe féminin* (Stuttgart: J. Thorbecke, 2001).
4 On the decoration and furnishings of General Moreau's house, see Jean-Pierre Samoyault and Colombe Samoyault-Verlet, eds., *Un ameublement à la mode en 1802: le mobilier de Général Moreau* (Paris: Réunion des musées nationaux, 1992).
5 Jean-Pierre Samoyault, *Mobilier Français Consulat et Empire* (Paris: Gourcuff-Gradenigo, 2009), 87.
6 Ibid., 45.
7 Hector Lefuel, *François-Honoré-Georges Jacob-Desmalter* (Paris: A. Morancée, 1925), 61. For the Jacob firm's role in transformations in furniture making in early 19th-century Paris, see chapter 8 in this volume.
8 Samoyault, *Mobilier Français*, 149–52.

DECORATIVE ARTS

A SCRAPBOOK FROM PERCIER'S WORKSHOP

Understanding the Genesis of Forms

JEAN-PHILIPPE GARRIC

The Metropolitan Museum of Art in New York has in its collection an unusual album (cat. 59).¹ Containing more than 450 drawings, the album casts a unique light on the creative process of Charles Percier, but its nature, like its origins, remains somewhat enigmatic. The contents are heterogeneous, ranging from summary sketches to relatively finished renderings. Executed on supports of varying character and dimensions, these drawings were at some point assembled and fixed into a volume bound in repurposed parchment,² an account book (39 × 25 cm) that still bears the label of the stationer's shop where it was purchased and which reads: "A L'Empereur, rue de la lanterne, au coin de celle des Marmouzets, au bas du pont Notre-Dame."³ This label, with its reference to the "emperor," dates the volume to somewhere between 1804 and 1814.

Containing a total of 128 pages, the album has suffered somewhat; a few of its drawings have been cut out and others pulled out. Its central pages are blank, all of the drawings having been laid onto its first pages and its last,

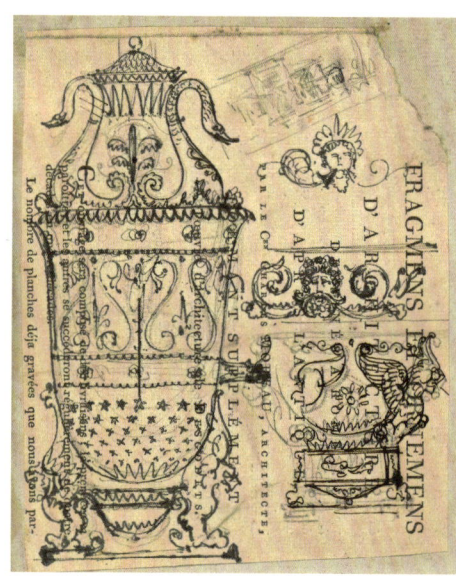

meant to be viewed respectively from the front cover or, after the album had been flipped, the back cover. All of those in the front section relate to ornament, furnishings, and decoration, all of those in the back to architecture [FIG. 8B.1]. All of the drawings are fixed to the album's pages, none having been executed directly in it, with only the rectos (relative to the two alternative viewing orientations) being used for this purpose, and each page supports anywhere from one to twelve pieces of paper. The latter fall into four different categories: thin white vellum paper, oiled serpentine paper (used for tracing before the invention of tracing

▷ **FIG 8B.1.** Workshop of Percier. Folio 10 of scrapbook containing drawings and several prints of architecture, interiors, furniture, and other objects, 1804–14. Pen and black and gray ink, graphite, black chalk on paper. The Metropolitan Museum of Art, New York, The Elisha Whittelsey Collection, The Elisha Whittelsey Fund, 1963, 63.535.1–.128 (hereafter MMA Scrapbook)

◁ **FIG 8B.2.** Workshop of Percier. Study sketches for a tea urn drawn over a prospectus for an ornament album by Charles Moreau. Detail of fol. 7, MMA Scrapbook.

▽ **FIG 8B.3.** Workshop of Percier. Cover of the MMA Scrapbook, with traces of an old business card with the name of Chatillon. MMA Scrapbook.

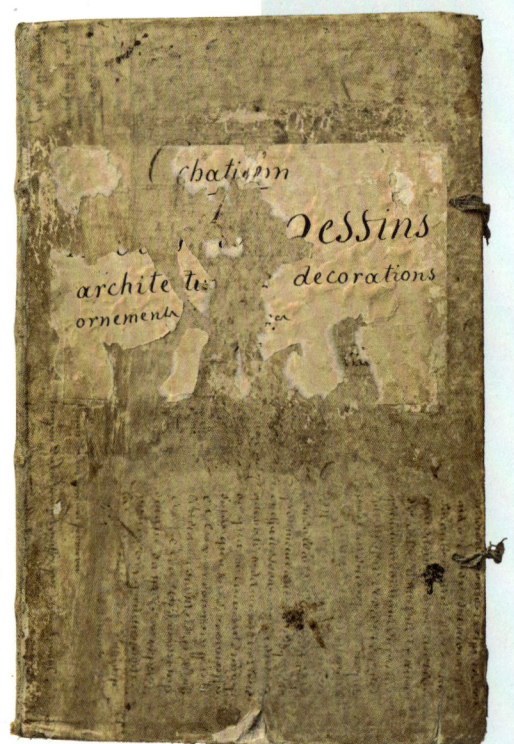

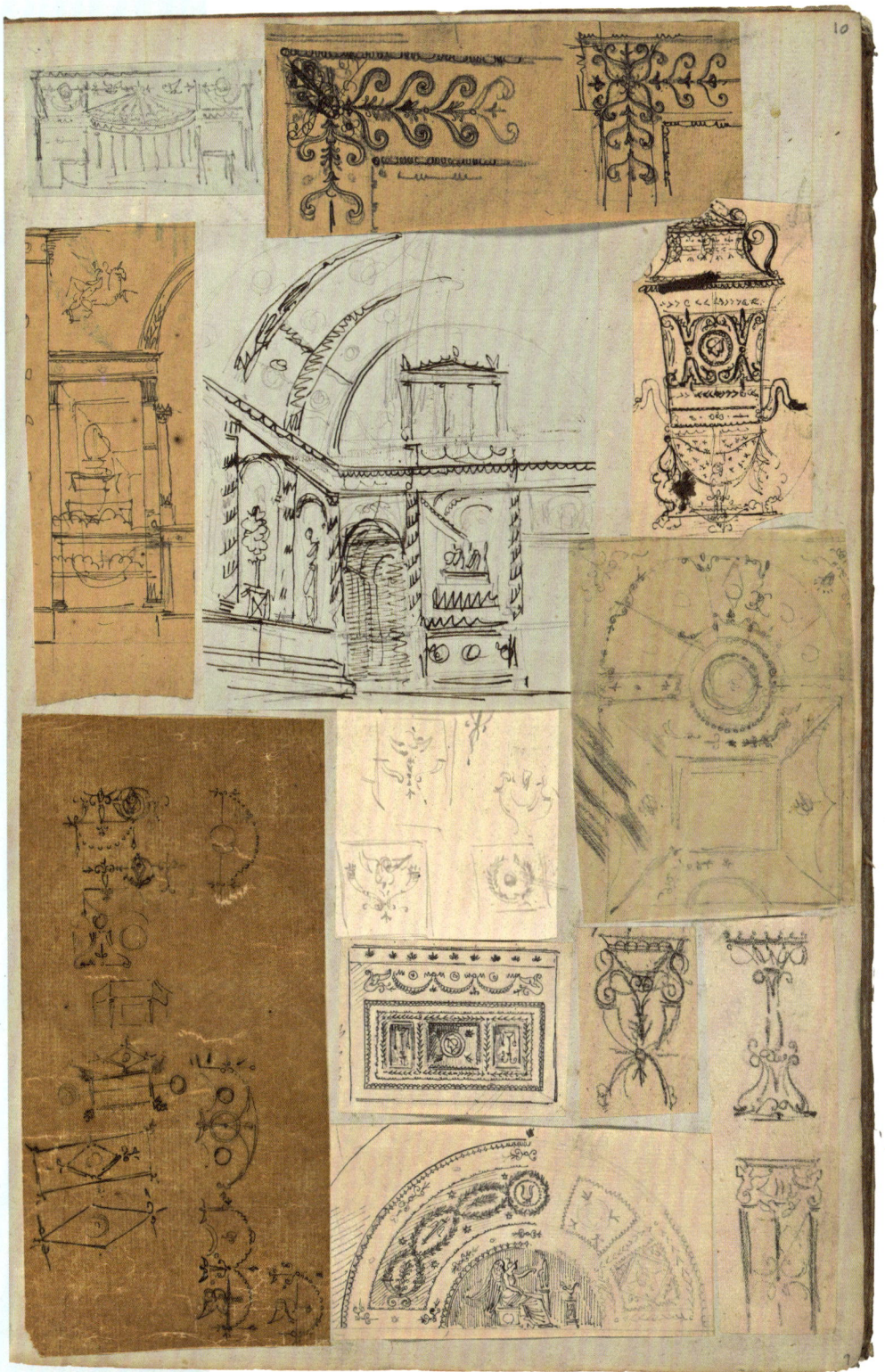

paper), modern tracing paper (which became available shortly before 1810), and paper salvaged from publications, notably pieces of the delivery wrappers for the book on Roman palaces by Percier and Fontaine and parts of the prospectus for Charles Moreau's *Fragmens et ornemens d'architecture* [FIG. 8B.2].[4]

Although the hands of several draftsmen are in evidence, there can be little doubt about Percier's authorship of a large number of these drawings, especially those that pertain to known projects by him and bear inscriptions in his handwriting. Nonetheless, he did not compile the volume himself; this was done by an assistant who was also one of his architecture students. Percier, then at the peak of his celebrity, would not have used so crude a support, nor would he have incorporated two copies of an engraving cut from the delivery wrappers of his book on Roman palaces[5]; finally, he would not have included, in the architecture section, a copy of an academic project by Jean Thomas Thibault.[6]

The cover of the volume bears the remnants of a label, parts of which have been torn away, that puts us on the track of a student who was preparing Prix de Rome projects during the pertinent time frame, and one whose proximity to Percier would have made it possible for him to gather up sketches otherwise fated to disappear. Still legible on the label, above the inscribed words "dessins, architecture, décorations, ornements," is a last name that might correspond to André Marie Chatillon, who competed for the Prix de Rome from 1803 to 1809 [FIG. 8A.3]. The dates coincide perfectly, and an examination of the drawings lends credibility to this attribution.[7]

The album contains drawings of several different types, corresponding

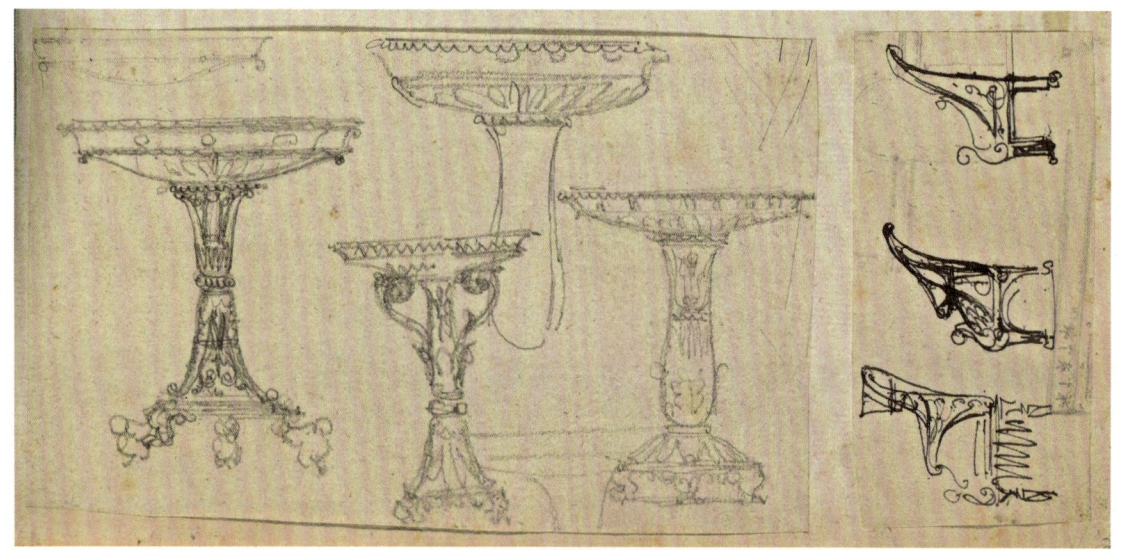

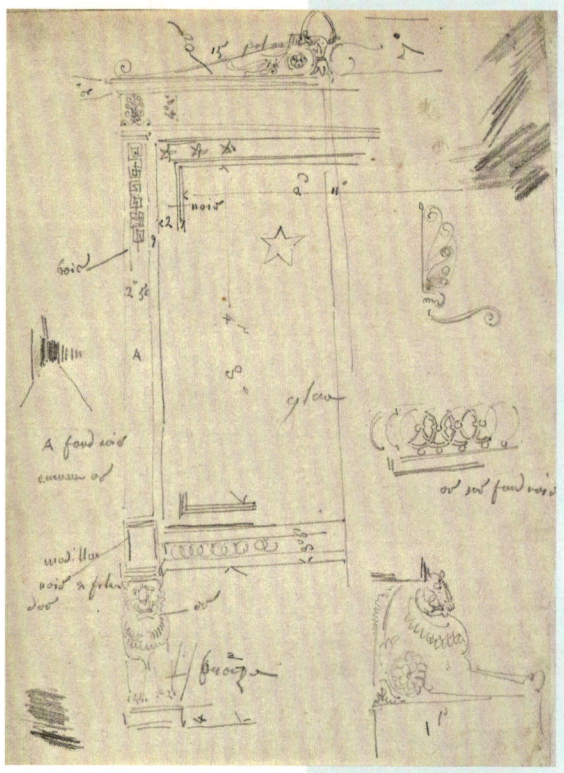

FIG 8B.4. Workshop of Percier. Study sketches for a tea table and an armchair. Detail of fol. 24, MMA Scrapbook.

FIG 8B.5. Workshop of Percier. Study for a mirror. Detail of fol. 21, MMA Scrapbook.

FIG 8B.6. Workshop of Percier. Study sketches for lanterns on the entrance gate to the Tuileries Palace, beginning of 1805. Detail of fol. 35, MMA Scrapbook.

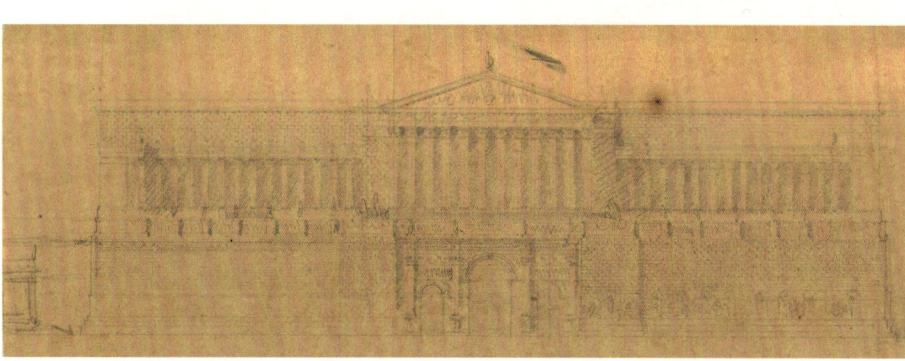

to successive steps in the design and realization of various works. The largest group consists of free study sketches—often rapidly executed, rendering the object with varying degrees of precision—that document the emergence of a formal solution [FIG. 8B.4]. A smaller group documents the various stages of fine-tuning. Drawn with a ruler or T-square, these drawings made it possible to determine the dimensions. By contrast, other drawings were apparently intended to transmit the final design. They bear annotations that specify colors, materials, and dimensions, which suggests that they were destined either for an assistant charged with executing a more finished drawing or for a craftsman capable of producing working drawings. One notable example is a sheet devoted to the boudoir at Saint-Cloud (SEE FIG. 11A.1). Finally, a few tracings that do not belong in the previous three groups were probably made to serve as records of a completed design.

Although the summary sketches illustrate the movements of an individual creative mind, the annotated drawings bear witness to a collective process. Like the sheet related to the boudoir at Saint-Cloud, another pertaining to the project for a mirror contains information of various kinds [FIG. 8B.5].[8] But it does not offer a depiction of the object's overall appearance: it is neither a means for the designer to assess the quality of his conception nor a presentation drawing, summary or otherwise, intended for the client. It is rather a visual memorandum sent to a partner capable of deciphering the data that it contains. And these

FIG 8B.7. Workshop of Percier. Sketch of the elevation of the arc du Carrousel and a new façade of the Tuileries Palace, 1806. Detail of Fol. 43A, MMA Scrapbook.

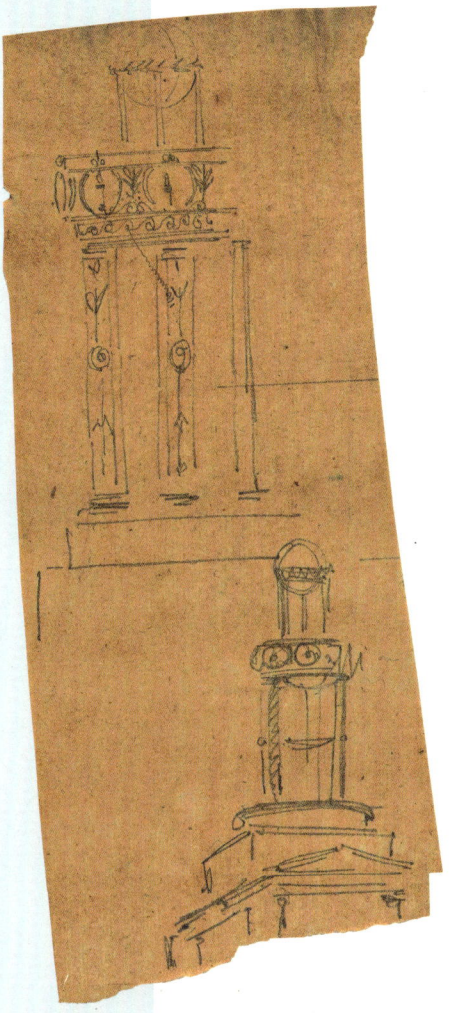

data are plentiful: the principal dimensions, in ancien-régime measurements; specifications as to color and materials (black, bronze, gold, mirror); a detail of the bronze lion feet, shown in profile; a detail of the gilded frieze below the mirror; and a detail of the palmette above the side posts. The summary and informal character of the whole indicates that it was a message exchanged between persons sharing a common culture and vision.

Finally, the presence of several drawings relating to the arc du Carrousel corroborates the other indices confirming the album's date. Two sketches, one more developed than the other, merit special attention. The more summary one is a study that predates the decision to build a triumphal arch, from a moment when Napoleon's intention, stated early in 1805, was to build two monumental lanterns above the gate of the place du Carrousel to illuminate it [FIG. 8B.6].[9] But military victories prompted a shift to more grandiose ideas, and the lanterns atop the guardhouses gave way the following year to the project for a triumphal arch, of which the album contains both a rather detailed compositional drawing and studies of its ornamental details [FIG. 8B.7].[10] Percier and Fontaine even went so far—doubtless on their own initiative—as to imagine a complete redesign of the palace façade in an antique style more in keeping with that of their new monumental gateway.[11] Both the decorative details of the arch, in the part dedicated to furniture and ornament, and the overall compositional studies for it, in the architecture part, are situated toward the end of their respective sections, which suggests that the compilation of the drawings in the album, which began around 1804, came to an end rather quickly, about 1808–9, when the sculpted ornament on the arch was still being designed. ●

1 Workshop of Charles Percier, *Scrapbook containing Drawings and Several Prints of Architecture, Interiors, Furniture and Other Objects*, New York, The Metropolitan Museum of Art, The Elisha Whittlesley Collection, The Elisha Whittlesley Fund, 1963, 63.535.1–158.
2 After the French Revolution, which occasioned the suppression of religious houses and the sale of property belonging to emigrés, many archives and old documents on parchment were dismantled and their pages reused for ordinary, utilitarian bindings.
3 "At the Empereur, on rue de la lanterne at the corner of rue des Marmouzets, at the foot of the pont Notre-Dame." This address was located on the Île de la Cité.
4 Charles Moreau, *Fragmens et ornemens d'architecture dessinés à Rome, d'après l'antique* (Paris: Vilquin, 1800). On February 19, 1800 (30 pluviôse year VIII; no. 42, p. 5), the *Journal des arts, des sciences et de la littérature* announced: "citizen Moreau, architect, designer, and painter combined, won the first prize in architecture in 1785; after his return from Italy, the second prize in painting in 1792; few artists have a double talent and this particularity [deserves] mention. The decorations in the hall of the Théâtre de la République, as they currently exist, are due to Citizen Moreau." ("le citoyen Moreau, Architecte, Dessinateur, et Peintre tout ensemble, a remporté en 1785 le 1er Prix d'Architecture; à son retour d'Italie, le second Prix de Peinture en 1792: Peu d'artistes offrent un double talent, et cette particularité digne de remarque. La décoration de la salle du Théâtre de la République, telle qu'elle existe, est due au citoyen Moreau."
5 Fols. 28 and 34.
6 Fol. 31A. This project, not previously identified, might be an entry in the competition for the prix d'émulation held in January 1782, the assigned subject for which was a hippodrome (racecourse). See Jean-Marie Pérouse de Montclos, *Etienne-Louis Boullée (1728–1799)* (Paris: Flammarion, 1994), 169.
7 Two sketches for plans on fol. 59 seem to correspond to Chatillon's prize-winning project. This is discussed in detail in David Van Zanten, "Architectural composition at the Ecole des Beaux-Arts, from Charles Percier to Charles Garnier," in *The Architecture of the Ecole des Beaux-Arts*, ed. Arthur Drexler (New York: Museum of Modern Art, 1977), 130ff.
8 Fol. 21.
9 Pierre François Léonard Fontaine, *Journal (1799–1853)*, ed. Marguerite David-Roy (Paris: École nationale supérieure des beaux-arts / Institut français d'architecture / Société de l'histoire de l'art français, 1987), 1:102 (January 15, 1805). Fol. 35.
10 For the elevation and section of the arch: fol. 58A; for the bas-reliefs of Victories: fols. 43 and 44.
11 A presentation drawing of the arc du Carrousel with, in the background, a new monumental façade for the Tuileries, was included in the recent exhibition *Napoléon et Paris* (Paris: Musée Carnavalet, 2015). See Sarmant et al., eds., *Napoléon et Paris: rêves d'une capitale* (Paris: Paris Musées, 2015), no. 205.

CHAPTER 9

DESIGNS FOR THE MANUFACTORIES AND THE GARDE-MEUBLE

A MODEL FOR THE INDUSTRIAL ARTS

ANNE DION-TENENBAUM

IN 1805 THE *JOURNAL DU COMMERCE* PUBLISHED THIS DELIGHTFUL description of Percier's influence on the industrial art products then known as *objets de goût*, or objects of taste: "Jewelers, goldsmiths, engravers, cabinetmakers, and wallpaper manufacturers draw upon the work of Percier, such that it is not unusual to find in a single apartment a tapestry, a clock, a table service, and a women's parure with the same design elements."[1]

According to Raoul-Rochette, it was the collaboration of Percier and Fontaine with Georges Jacob on furniture for the Convention that brought the pair other commissions of the same kind. "From that moment forward, the pen and pencil of M. Percier and his friend had no other occupation than the design of

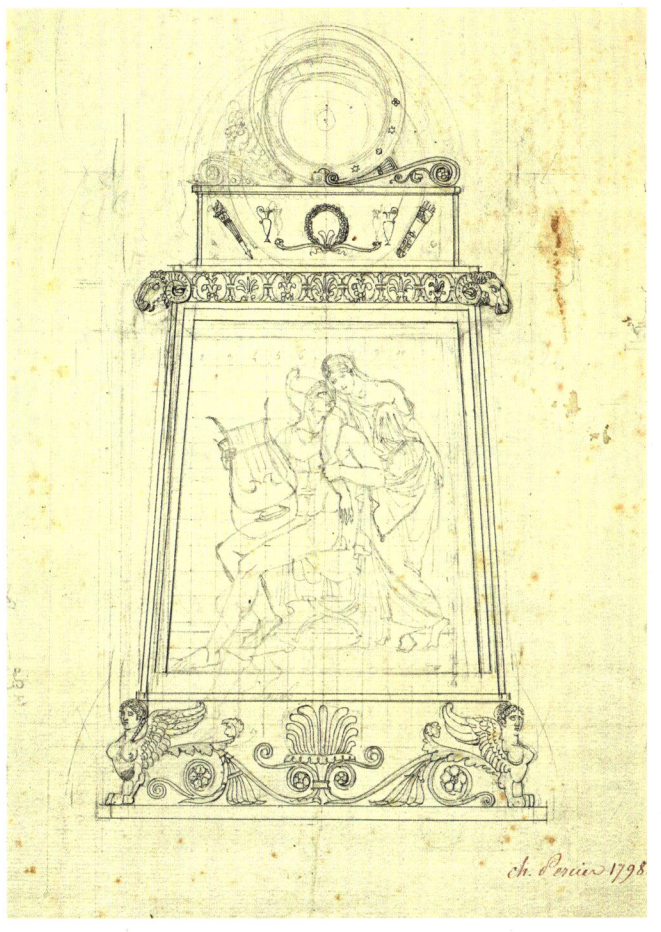

fabrics and the sketching of furniture; they worked for the carpet and wallpaper manufactories; they designed theatrical decors; they made models for bronzes, crystal, and goldsmith work."[2] Percier's earliest designs in the service of the decorative arts are poorly documented. Sometimes they were occasioned by ties of amity. Such was the case for a series of designs for bronze furnishings (clocks, candelabra, and so forth), dated 1798,[3] intended for Pierre Maximilien Delafontaine,[4] a student of Jacques Louis David who quickly abandoned painting to devote himself to his family's bronze atelier. Two clock designs from this group feature the central motif of David's *Les Amours de Paris et Hélène* (The Loves of Paris and Helen) of 1787 [FIGS. 9.1, 9.2].[5] Another clock design, in the form of a cippus flanked by torches and enriched with an ivy garland, celebrates the friendship between the two men.[6]

Percier's work for the state manufactories, notably Sèvres, is easier to grasp. He functioned there as an inventor of forms and ornament, as a decorator, and simply as a source of ideas. When Alexandre Brongniart was named administrator of the Sèvres porcelain manufactory in 1800, his first concern was to renew the forms it had inherited from the ancien régime. He sought Percier's help, although to a lesser extent than that of his father, the architect Alexandre Théodore Brongniart. In May 1801, the younger

▷ **FIG 9.1.** Jacques Louis David. *The Love of Paris and Helen*, 1788. Oil on canvas. Musée du Louvre, Paris, 3696.

▲ **FIG 9.2.** Charles Percier. Design of a clock for Delafontaine after David, 1798. Black ink and graphite on paper. Musée des beaux-arts, Rennes, 74.73.375.

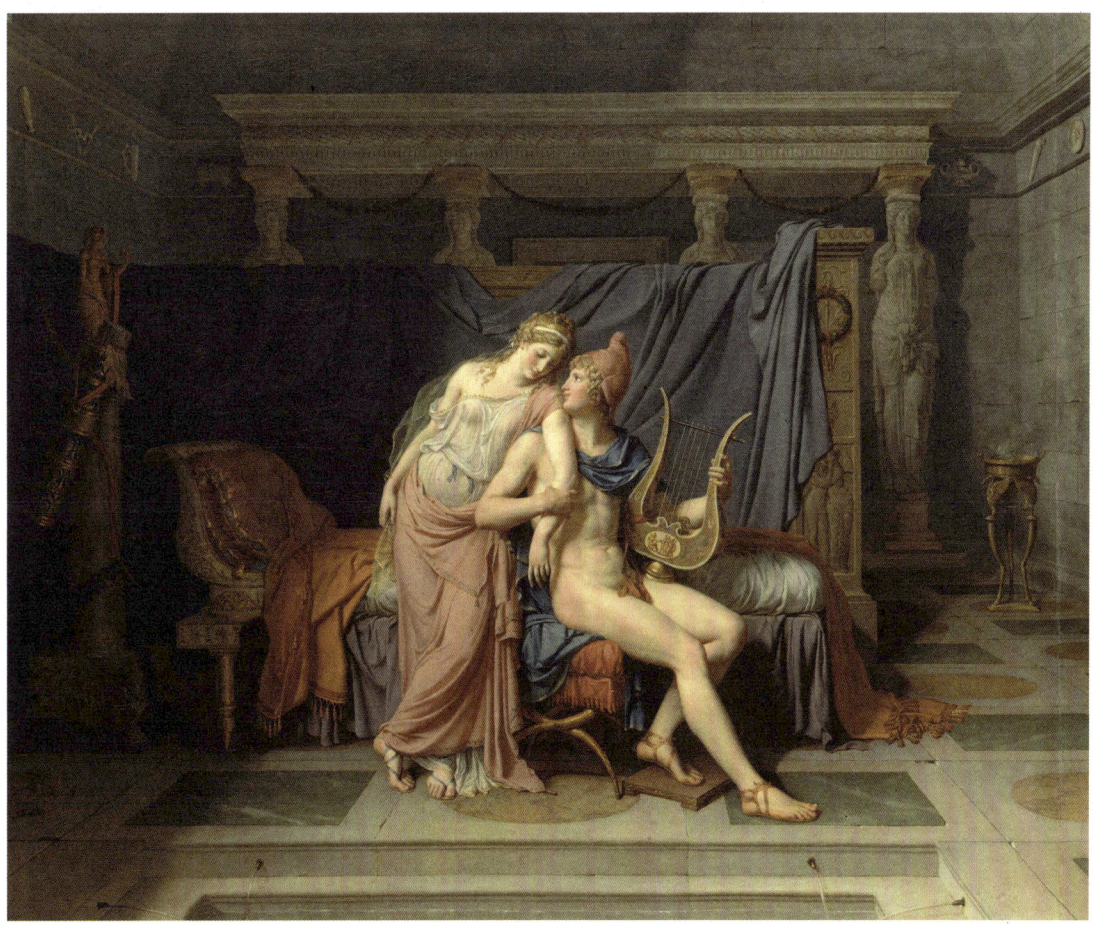

Brongniart congratulated himself on having seen his efforts crowned with success: "most of the forms have been changed or corrected...distinguished artists have provided drawings and models."[7] At about this time, Percier was earning 48 francs for each of his drawings.[8] The new forms were named after their inventor and are readily identifiable: in year X, a Percier dinner plate made its appearance; in year XII, Percier cups, carafes, and ewers; in year XIII, "Jasmine" vases in a Percier form, as well as "Etruscan" vases with rolled handles similar to one illustrated in the *Recueil de décorations intérieures* (plate XVIII, figure 1). This last form was adopted for the monumental vase decorated with a frieze showing "the entry into Paris of the principal monuments that constitute the Musée Napoléon" (1813),[9] as well as for the so-called Londonderry Vase, now in Chicago [FIG. 9.3].

In their capacity as decorators, Percier and Fontaine selected vases from the manufactory's inventory to adorn the apartments redecorated by them at Saint-Cloud and the Tuileries. Occasionally they issued new commissions, as for the medallions after their designs for the library of the first consul at Saint-Cloud. (This interior was short-lived; in 1804 the room was transformed into the emperor's *grand cabinet*, or study.) They called for the installation of ninety-six such medallions bearing profile depictions of celebrated authors and other great men, all suggesting either Wedgwood (white against a blue ground) or cameos, high along the walls of the bays of the library.[10] Eighty-four were delivered in Messidor year XI (June–July 1803),[11] at the same time as an oval plaque representing the Battle of Marengo, and there was a supplementary delivery in May 1804.[12]

Percier also influenced the artists at Sèvres indirectly, through his publications. Thus, his engraved headpieces for the Didot edition of Horace (1799) were adapted by the painter Jean Georget for a "Litron" cup in 1805,[13] and by the painter Jean Alexis Girard for two "Medicis" vases in 1806.[14] Also in 1806, the Queen of Württemberg received a gold ground cabaret (coffee or tea service) with subjects painted in grisaille after Percier's illustrations for the Didot edition of the fables of La Fontaine (1802).[15] More predictably, the *Recueil de déco-*

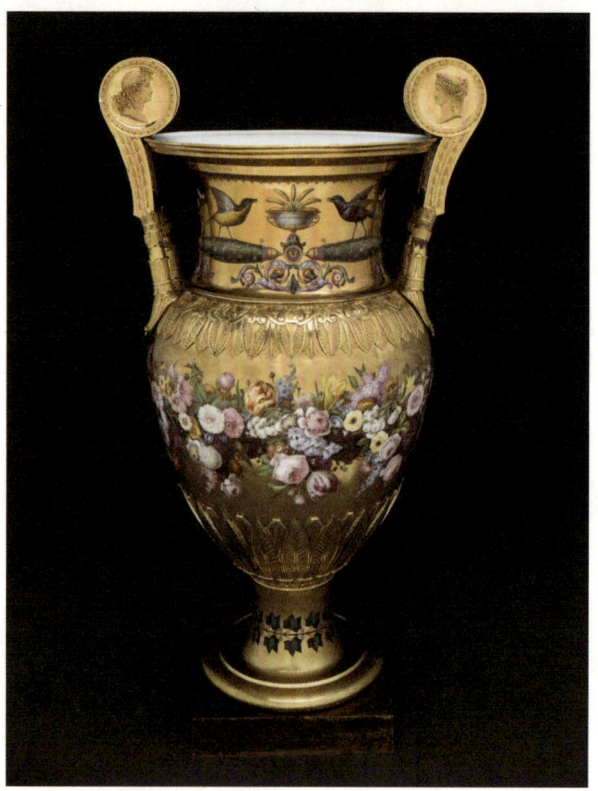

▲ FIG 9.3. Charles Percier. Londonderry vase, 1813. Made by Sèvres Porcelain Manufactory; decoration designed by Alexandre Brogniart; painted by Gilbert Drouet and Christophe Ferdinand Caron. Hard-paste porcelain, poly-chrome enamels, gilding, and gilt bronze mounts. The Art Institute of Chicago, Gift of the Harry and Maribel G. Blum Fund and the Harold L. Stuart Endowment, 1987.1.

rations intérieures was exploited. At the beginning of 1813, Brongniart anticipated the confection of a "rich pedestal in biscuit representing the four seasons and analogous ornaments surmounted by a cup and enclosing a clock, after Percier."[16] The engraving had been published in 1803 (plate XXXVIII, figure 4); moreover, the form recalls one of the designs Percier made for Delafontaine in 1798. Above the clock face, Apollo drives his chariot; below, four female figures symbolizing the seasons dance around a two-faced herm representing time [FIG. 9.4]. The following year, Brongniart called for the execution of four new clocks.[17]

In a few exceptional cases at Sèvres, Brongniart, who enjoyed relative autonomy in the choice of independent collaborators, called on Percier. There is no trace in the manufactory's archives of the platter decorated with Paris and Helen that, according to the *Recueil de décorations intérieures* (plate XXXV, sixth fascicle, 1803), was executed by the manufactory for one "Mme B," so as "to provide an example of its most perfect production methods."[18]

In 1806, when Napoleon commissioned a table showing him surrounded by his generals, Percier provided drawings for a round tabletop with a radial compo-

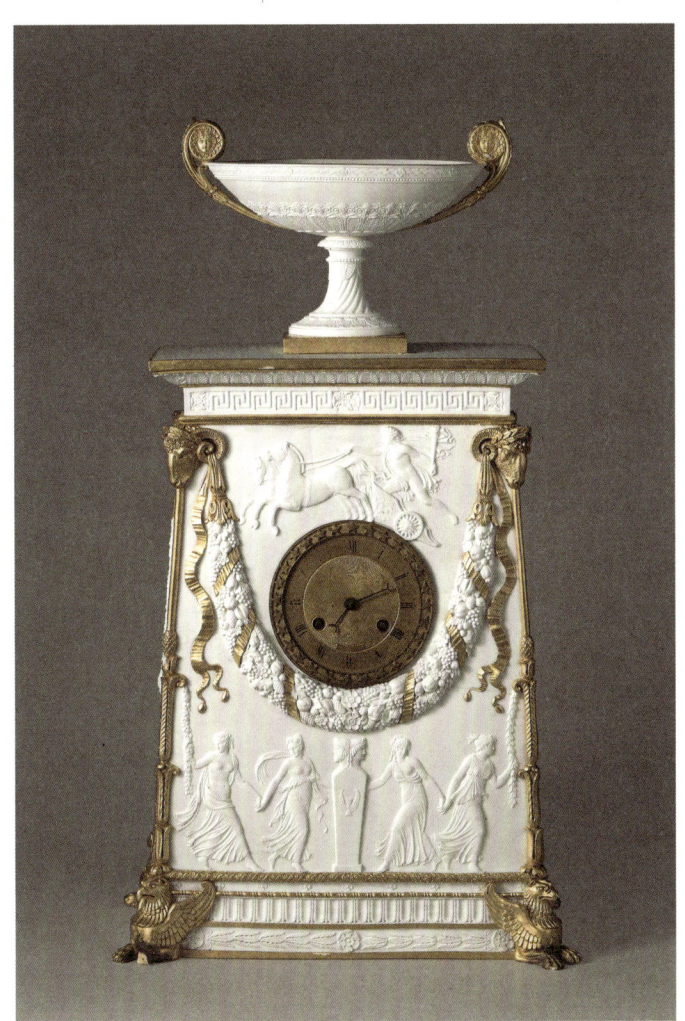

▽ **FIG 9.4.** Charles Percier. Clock in the shape of an antique altar dedicated to the sun with representations of the four seasons on the pedestal, 1813. Made by Sèvres Porcelain Manufactory. Bisque porcelain, gold highlights. Cité de la Céramique. Sèvres, MNC 13022. Cat. 104.

◁ **FIG 9.5.** Charles Percier. Design for the Marshall's table (Austerlitz table), 1806. Pen and ink, gouache on paper. Cité de la Céramique, Sèvres, 2012.1.1660.

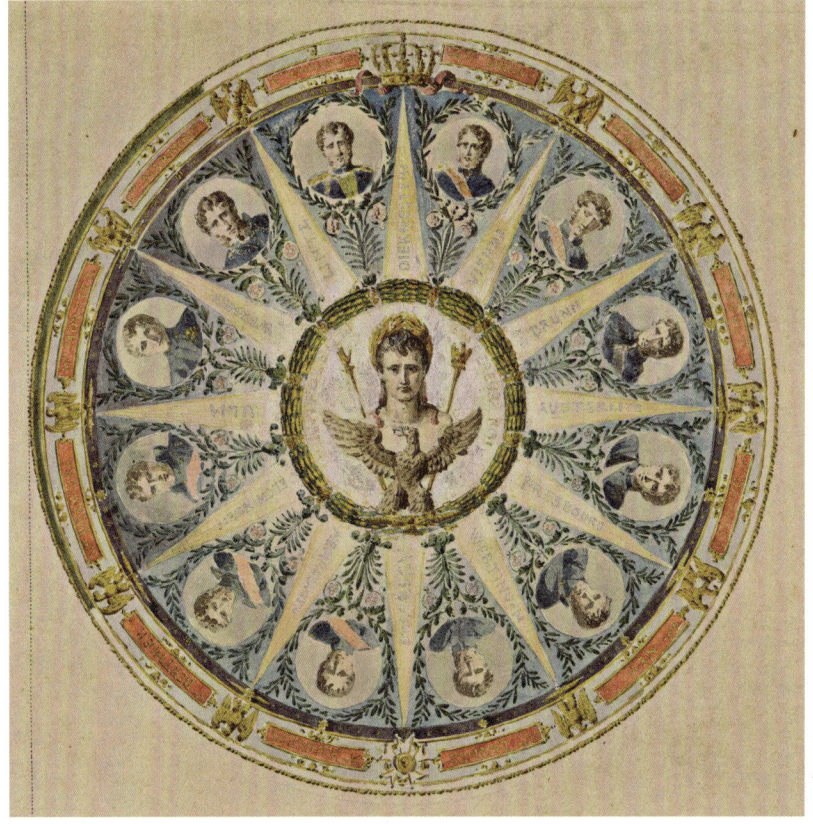

sition featuring a central portrait roundel of the emperor circled by analogous roundels of the generals [FIG. 9.5] and for a columnar pedestal support decorated with personifications of martial virtues.[19] He was paid 240 francs for these designs. That same year, a *biscuit surtout* representing the château des Tuileries and the arc du Carrousel was contemplated but quickly abandoned.[20]

In 1817, under the Restoration, Brongniart asked Percier to design a round table illustrating several rooms of the Musée royal and their new installations,[21] necessitated by the restitution of artworks to the victors of 1815. Supported by a pedestal shaped like a palm tree, its top featured a central medallion showing Minerva presenting France with the museum restored by the king. Around this, in octagonal cartels, are depictions of four rooms in the sequence then called the Musée des antiques—the salles de Diane, des Romains, de Melpomène, and des Cariatides [FIG. 9.6]—and four hexagonal compositions incorporating celebrated antiquities, notably the Piranesi candelabrum and statues from the Borghese collection [FIG. 9.7]. Percier received 400 francs for a watercolor showing one third of the overall design, the ornamental elements, and the four cartels.[22] This guéridon, which was displayed at the exposition of products of the manufactory in 1820, was gifted to Leopold of Saxe-Coburg in 1824.[23]

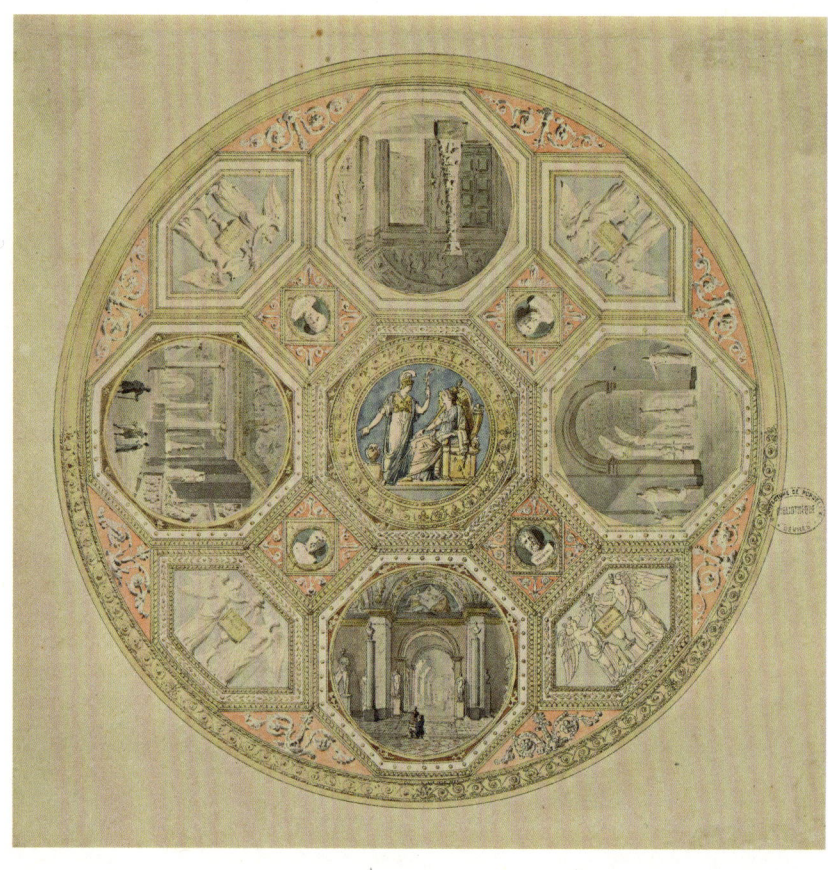

In March 1820, at Brongniart's request, Percier proposed a design for a mantelpiece in the château de Fontainebleau, but it remained unrealized.[24] The design featured four figures symbolizing winter on the vertical framing elements and three allegorical paintings on the band across the top, all separated by six signs of the zodiac [FIG. 9.8].

At the beginning of the Consulate, in an initiative analogous to that of Brongniart, Nicolas Cyprien Duvivier, director of the Savonnerie manufactory, sought a painter suitable to undertake a renewal of its outdated models. To

▲ **FIG 9.6.** Charles Percier. Design for the Royal Museums table, 1817. Graphite, India ink, gouache, wash on paper. Cité de la Céramique, Sèvres archives, 2012.1.227. Cat. 107b.

◁ **FIG 9.7.** Charles Percier. Design of a cartel for the Royal Museum's table (antiquities from the museum with candelabra by Piranesi), 1819. Graphite, India ink, gouache, wash. Cité de la Céramique, Sèvres, 2012.1.228. Cat. 107d.

▷ **FIG 9.8.** Charles Percier. Design for a fireplace in marble and bronze, inlaid with porcelain, March 1820. Pen and ink, graphite, gouache. Cité de la Céramique, Sèvres, 2012.1.1631.

9 MANUFACTORIES AND THE GARDE-MEUBLE

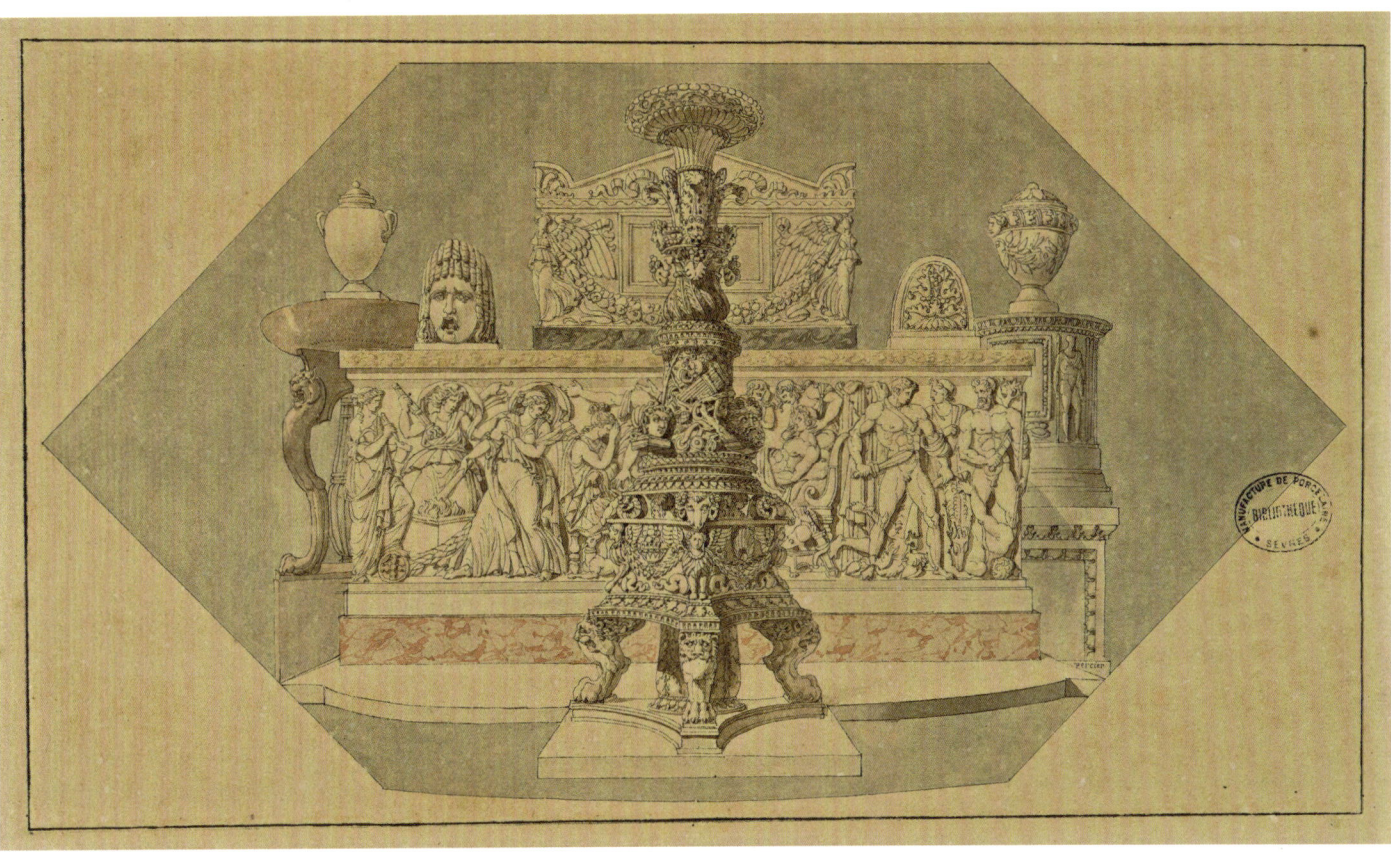

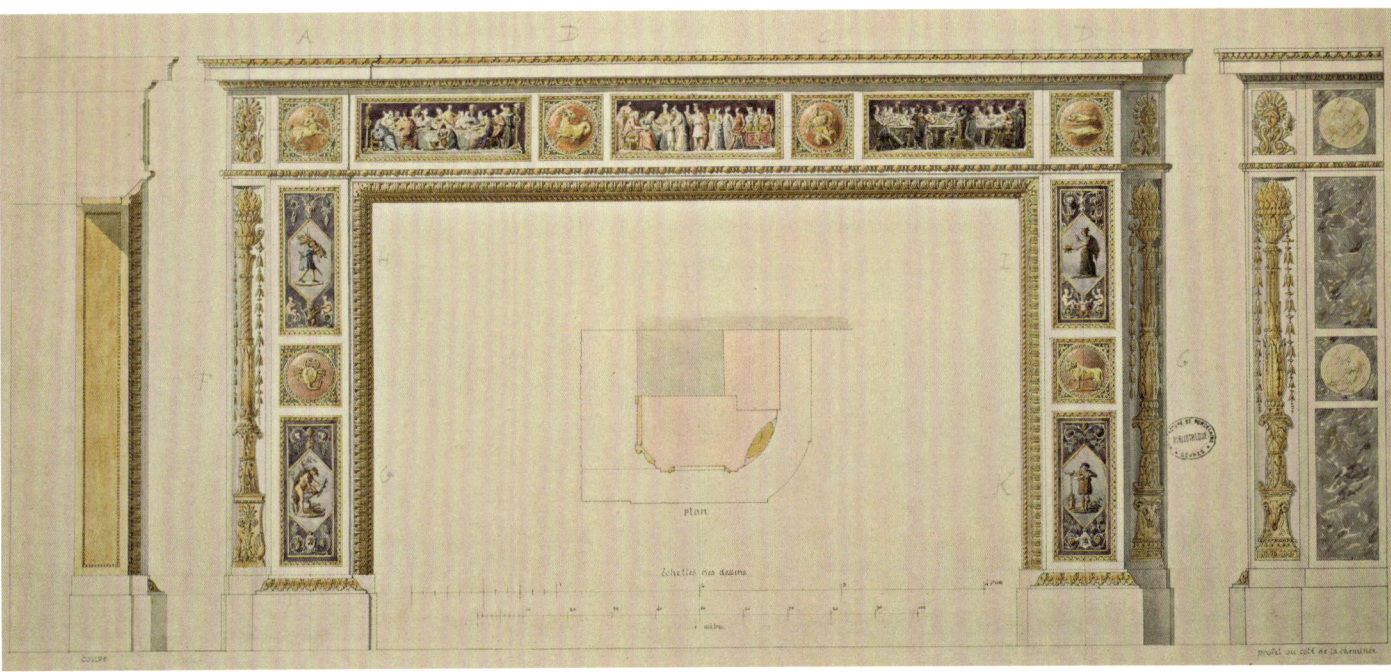

this end, he consulted both Percier and the painter Jean Jacques Lagrenée.[25] Initially Lagrenée assumed the task, sometimes working after Percier's sketches. Carpet designs were usually commissioned in tandem with an overall interior design project, making such assignments consistent with the architect's customary brief. In 1801 Duvivier wrote that he had "received from Citizens Percier and Fontaine the proposed designs for carpets to be made for the first rooms to be occupied in the apartments of the palace of the Consuls at Saint-Cloud"; they were to be executed "in the genre and taste that the architects have established for their decoration as a whole."[26] The full sum of 1,800 francs allotted by the minister for these cartoons was absorbed by the one for the carpet for the First Consul's bedroom. An arabesque design against a brown ground with a decorative border, this carpet was delivered December 1, 1803.[27]

In 1806 N. C. Duvivier requested that new models be provided for the imperial palaces with "nobler and more majestic composition[s]," [28] but Percier lacked the necessary time. The example of the carpet destined for the room of the Conseil d'État (Counsel of State) is symptomatic. Related correspondence indicates that a design by Percier was awaited with impatience.[29] Finally, one of Percier's students, the architect François Debret, "made the small colored drawing that Percier was unable to make,"[30] probably working from a sketch provided by his master [FIG. 9.9/CP-338X].[31] (Debret had previously assisted Percier in the design of a large vase of varnished sheet metal, in the Egyptian style, commissioned in 1804 from the varnished metal manufactory on the rue Martel.[32]) The carpet, now dismembered and transformed, consisted of two lateral strips bearing an "N" with bolts of lightning and a larger rectangular composition featuring the attributes of War, Justice, Navigation, and the Arts disposed around the grand imperial arms (Musée du Louvre) and complemented by eagles in the corners; it was finally installed in the throne room in 1810. In 1808 Percier, still unavailable, recommended that another of his students, Jacques Louis de La Hamayde de Saint-Ange be enlisted to design the carpet for the Grand Cabinet in the Tuileries. Duvivier explained to Pierre Daru—Intendant Général and

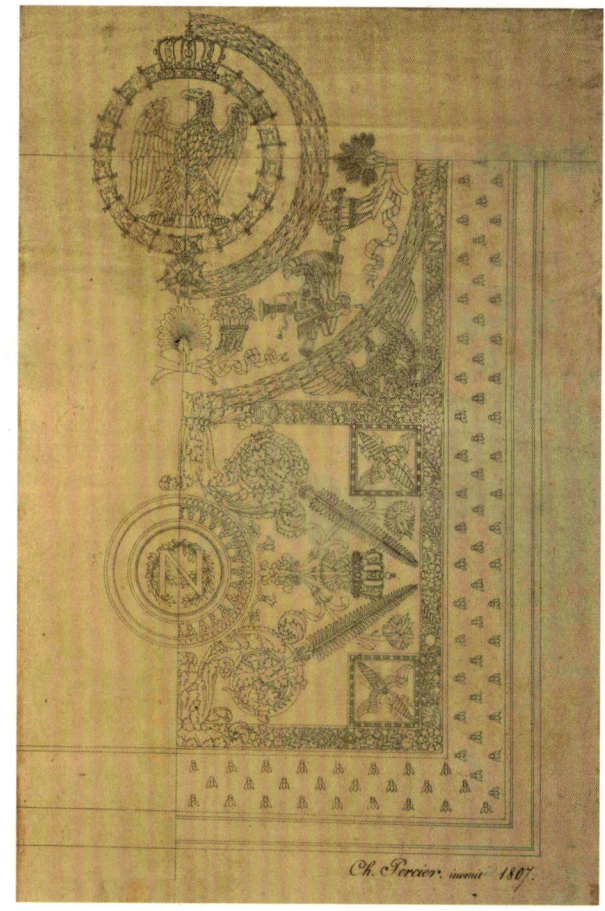

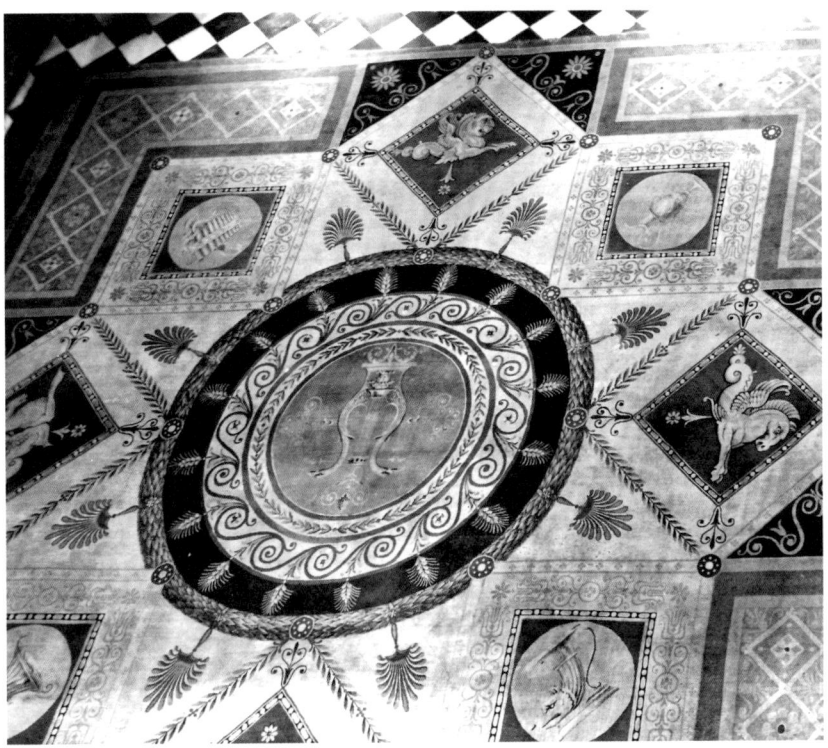

thus his superior—how, by way of assuring "that this design accords with the dignity of the place, by conforming with the overall taste of its furnishings," he had contacted Percier, who, too busy, had recommended one of his former students, Saint-Ange, "known favorably through [his] pleasing compositions."[33] Here again, we might suppose that it was under Percier's oversight that Saint-Ange conceived this carpet, whose design features the attributes of the sixteen "cohorts" of the Legion of Honor arrayed around the Legion's star (Musée du château national de Compiègne). In the case of the portière tapestries for this same Grand Cabinet in the Tuileries, to be woven at the Gobelins manufactory, the process was similar. In 1808 Percier enlisted his student Gilles Barthélémy Blanchon to design the first two, which were to represent Victory and Renown. For the four remaining portière designs he turned to Saint-Ange, who charged lower fees than his colleague.[34]

It seems likely that, in 1809, Percier was consulted regarding the design by Saint-Ange of a carpet for the emperor's bedroom in the Tuileries, since he had designed the room's ceiling; like the ceiling, the carpet is organized around a central octagon.

Perhaps owing to the cost of cartoons and to weaving delays at the Savonnerie, the Garde-Meuble sometimes turned to private manufactories, notably that of Piat Lefebvre in Tournai, which on several occasions worked from designs by Percier. A carpet in the Savonnerie manner for the music room at Saint-Cloud, delivered by their representative Bellanger on October 30, 1804, was woven after a design by Percier.[35] Chantal Gastinel-Coural has identified this carpet in the collection of the château de Malmaison; it features a central lyre surrounded by eight medallions, four of which contain attributes of music and the other four the heads of seahorses [FIG. 9.10].[36] The same scholar has attributed to Percier the design of another carpet delivered by Bellanger on the same day, this one destined for the Salon des Consuls at Saint-Cloud.[37] Its central rosette is decorated with arabesques incorporating vases and putti, motifs that bring to mind the analogous one in Percier's

◂ FIG 9.9. Jacques Louis de La Hamayde de Saint-Ange. Copy of Percier's design of a carpet for the room of the Conseil d'État made by the Savonnerie Manufactory, 1807. Pencil on tracing paper mounted on paper. Collection du Mobilier national, Paris.

▴ FIG 9.10. Charles Percier. Carpet for the music room, château de Saint-Cloud, 1804. Made by Piat Lefebvre Manufactory. Musée national du château de Malmaison et Bois-Préau, dépôt du Mobilier national, Rueil-Malmaison, GMT 2091.

frontispiece for the fifth fascicle of *Palais, maisons et autres édifices modernes dessinés à Rome* (1798). These two carpet designs might have figured among those for Saint-Cloud that Percier initially entrusted to N. C. Duvivier in 1801.

In November 1804, a fitted carpet for the throne room in the Tuileries was delivered by the same Bellanger, consisting "of a large compartment of gilded ornaments, containing various arms and initials of His Imperial Majesty. An analogous border for the rest of the carpet, the whole executed after the designs of Messrs. Percier and Fontaine, architects of the imperial palace."[38] An identical model was provided for Saint-Cloud. In 1805 Percier and Fontaine decorated a large music room, with hemicycles at either end, in Josephine's apartments in the Tuileries. In 1806 Bellanger delivered a carpet of the Savonnerie type with a "design of arabesque ornaments, with medallions containing the attributes of music and war, [and] a large rosette against a blue ground" in the center, after Percier and Fontaine.[39] The blue ground harmonized with the blue stucco decoration in the hemicycles. In April of 1806, Bellanger provided, again after Percier, a very large fitted carpet with bronze-colored compartments and framing elements with the arms and monogram of Napoleon.[40] This carpet was used in the Salon des Grands Officiers when concerts were held there.

The relationship between Percier and the Piat Lefebvre manufactory, then, was not a direct one but was mediated by the Maison de l'Empereur. The same could be said of all the ateliers who worked for the crown, for example Jacob-Desmalter, Thomire, and Biennais. As with carpets, the Garde-Meuble, now the Mobilier impérial, turned to Percier to design furniture and bronze pieces out of a concern for the overall harmony of a room's decoration. As an example, we might cite a clock made of griotte marble, delivered by Thomire in 1809 for the emperor's bedroom at the Tuileries, for which Percier had also designed the bed, which was executed by Jacob-Desmalter. The clock, originally surmounted by an eagle, is decorated with a gilt-bronze appliqué representing a seated personification of France contemplating a trophy of arms [FIG. 9.11].[41]

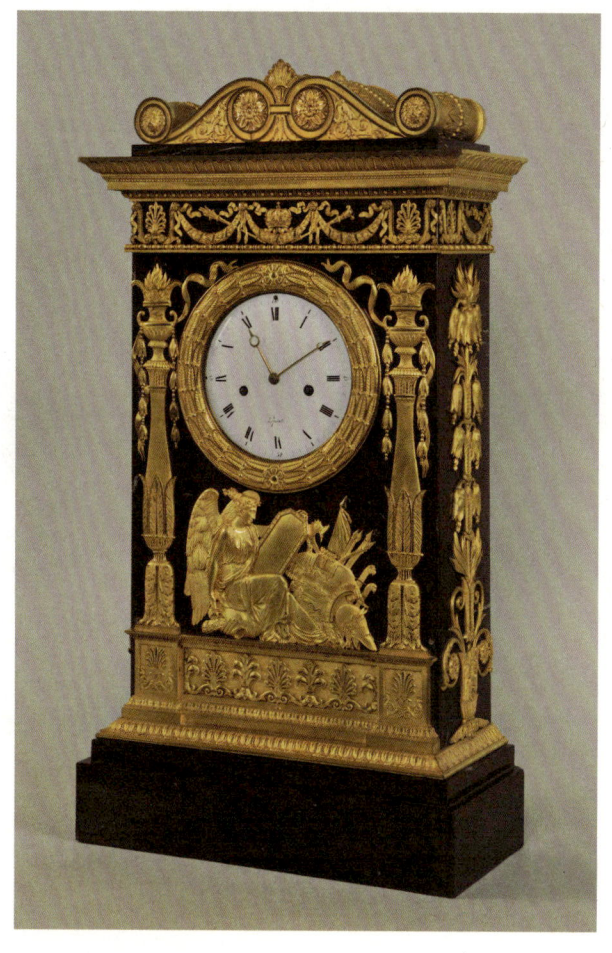

▲ **FIG 9.11.** Charles Percier. Clock from the Emperor's Grand Cabinet at the Tuileries Palace, 1809. Made by Pierre Philippe Thomire. Mobilier national, Paris, GML 2891. Cat. 105.

▷ **FIG 9.12.** Charles Percier. Tea service commissioned by Napoleon for Josephine de Beauharnais, Empress Josephine. Made by Martin Guillaume Biennais with maker's mark of Marie Joseph Gabriel Genu. Gilt silver. Private Collection.

Martin Guillaume Biennais became interested in the publications of Percier and Fontaine in 1798, for he was among the subscribers to *Palais, maisons et autres édifices modernes dessinés à Rome* and then acquired the various installments of the *Recueil de décorations intérieures* before purchasing a complete copy.[42] Nonetheless, his first documented contact with the two architects dates from 1801, when Biennais was commissioned to make a vermeil tea service for the first consul [FIG. 9.12]. It seems likely that it was at Josephine's instigation that the designs, published in part in the *Recueil de décorations intérieures*, were solicited from Percier.[43] Henceforth Percier would provide many designs for the Crown goldsmiths. The ragout tureen on plate XXXIV (sixth fascicle, 1803) might be the one made for the Crown silver service, decorated with a "frieze of half-length winged

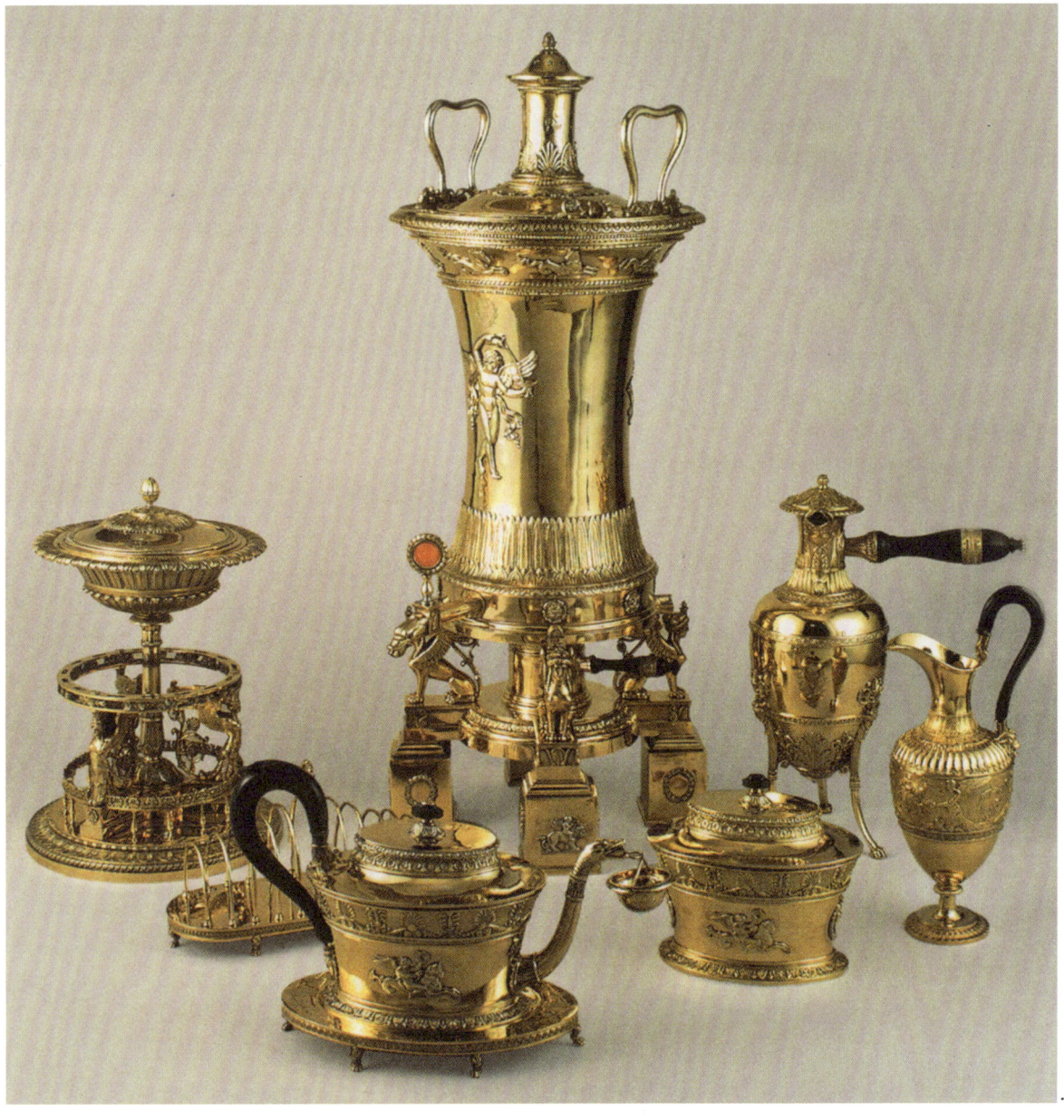

figures with bull's heads,"[44] now lost. The ragout tureen for Empress Josephine (pl. XLVI) won Biennais a gold medal at the Exposition of 1806. Nonetheless, scholars may have been overgenerous in their attributions to Percier among the drawings from the Biennais atelier (Paris, Musée des Arts décoratifs). These drawings, which were acquired by the Union central des Arts décoratifs from the print dealer A. Rapilly in 1885, came from the estate sale of Biennais' widow (December 24, 1859). The title page of the sale catalogue specifies drawings executed by Percier for Biennais, goldsmith to Napoleon I, but the pertinent language in the estate inventory is rather different, referring to "four large portfolios and a lot [consisting] of drawings by Percier and Fontaine and others for the goldsmith atelier and the jewelry atelier."[45] Very few sheets in this collection actually bear Percier's signature[46]: a coin cabinet in the Egyptian style [FIG. 9.13],[47] commissioned by Napoleon in 1814, and a large candelabrum with Apollo driving two winged horses [FIG. 9.14],[48] published in the *Recueil de décorations intérieures* (plate LIX). The 1859 sale catalogue mentions a drawing (current location unknown) "signed by Charles Percier and Fontaine" for Josephine's ragout tureen.[49] A few other drawings related to crown commissions can also be attributed to Percier. Still more are variations after original designs by Percier executed by anonymous draftsmen in the workshop. It must be acknowledged: the entirety of Biennais' production bore the imprint of the "Percier style." Particular attributions can always be uncertain, for example—despite their being inscribed "Charles PERCIER"—those of two designs for religious metalwork (a ciborium and a chalice commissioned in 1814 by Czar Alexander) recently acquired by the Metropolitan Museum of Art.[50]

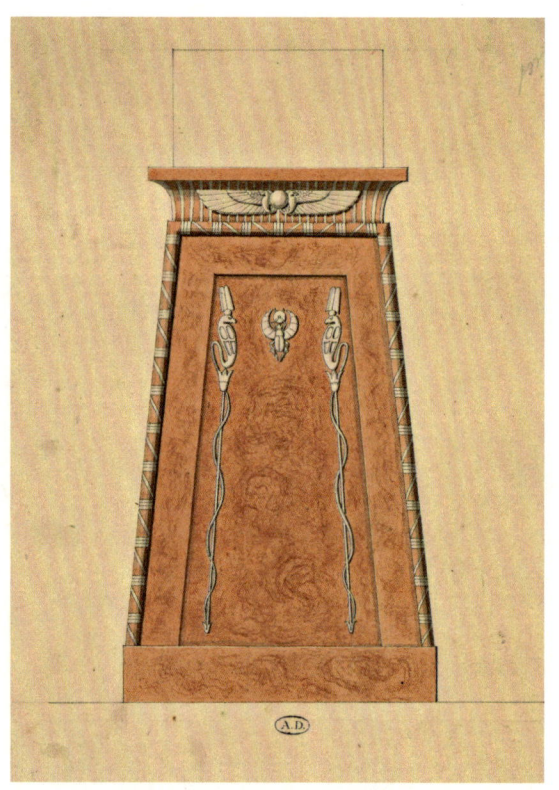

It is not clear that, after the Revolution period had passed, Percier provided models directly to the craft ateliers. He received government commissions from the agencies administered by the Maison de l'Empereur, which was responsible for selecting executants as well as designers. Even so, nothing prevented both the private and state manufactories from making use of the models that Percier had originally provided under official aegis, and from making infinite variations on them. The official style set the period tone. Moreover, the *Recueil de décorations intérieures* made available to craftsmen models for furniture and objects,

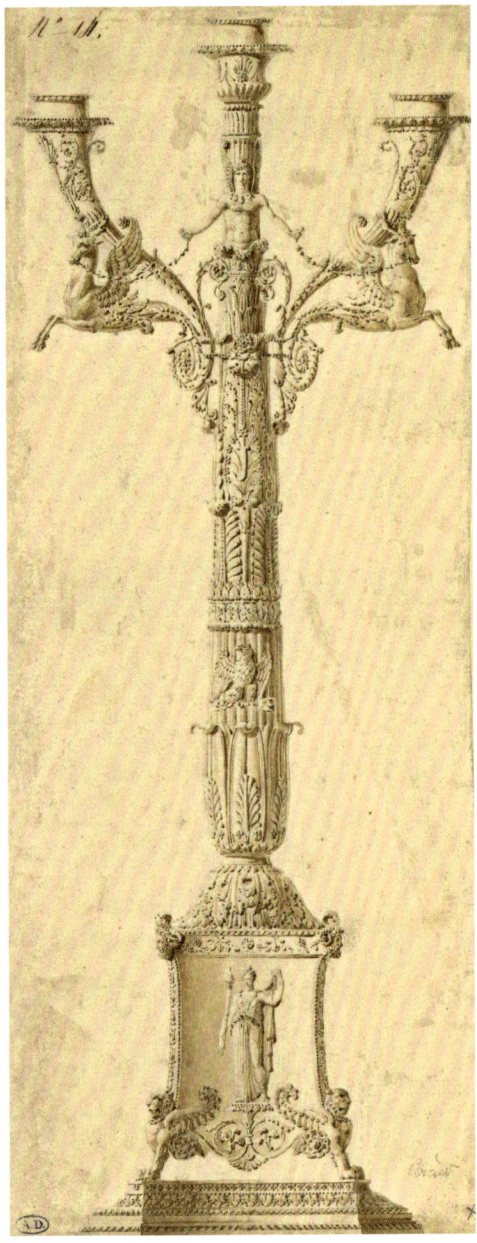

some of which, the text specifies, "have been repeated several times, sometimes with variations, by the fabricators of Paris."[51] The book disclaimed any pretense "to offer artists models for imitation,"[52] but there is no denying its influence on contemporary taste. ●

1 "Joailliers, orfèvres, ciseleurs, ébénistes, fabricants de papier, puisent dans l'œuvre de Percier, en sorte qu'il n'est pas rare que dans le même appartement, la tapisserie, la pendule, le service de table et la parure des dames offrent les mêmes dessins." *Journal du commerce*, 16 vendémaire year XIV (October 7, 1805).
2 "Dès ce moment, la plume et le crayon de M. Percier et de son ami ne furent plus employés qu'à dessiner des étoffes, qu'à esquisser des meubles; ils travaillent pour les manufactures de tapis et de papiers peints; ils produisent des compositions pour les décorations de théâtres; ils font des modèles pour les bronzes, les cristaux, l'orfèvrerie." Raoul-Rochette, "Percier, Sa vie et ses ouvrages," in *Revue des deux mondes*, ser. 4, 24 (October 15, 1840): 257.
3 Drawing album by Drouais acquired by the Musée des Beaux-Arts, Rennes, from Mme Rosset in 1974.
4 Fontaine describes him as a friend in a journal entry dated January 13, 1837. Pierre François Léonard Fontaine, *Journal (1799–1853)*, ed. Marguerite David-Roy (Paris: École nationale supérieure des beaux-arts / Institut français d'architecture / Société de l'histoire de l'art français, 1987), 2:880.
5 Rennes, Musée des Beaux-Arts, inv. 74.73.375 recto and verso. See Hans Ottomeyer and Peter Pröschel, *Vergoldete Bronzen die Bronzearbeiten des Spätbarock und Klassizismus* (Munich: Klinkhardt & Bermann, 1986–87), 2:no. 5.5.3, 344.
6 Rennes, Musée des Beaux-Arts, inv. 74.73.376; see Ottomeyer and Pröschel, *Vergoldete Bronzen*, 318. Translation of inscription on this sheet: "Sweet friendship, under your empire / Time has fixed happiness. / You are the heart's reason; / Love is but delirium."
7 "la plupart des formes sont changées ou corrigées…des artistes distinguées ont donné des dessins et des modèles." Report to the minister, 6 germinal year IX (March 27, 1801), Archives de la Cité de la Céramique (hereafter ACC), Vc 2, fol. 84.
8 9 germinal year IX (March 30, 1801); see ACC, Vf 51 bis, fol. 37.
9 "l'entrée dans Paris des principaux monuments qui composent le musée Napoléon." Sèvres, Cité de la Céramique, MNC 1823. See Odile Nouvel-Kammerer, "Le vase étrusque à rouleaux représentant l'entrée dans Paris des principaux monuments qui composent le musée Napoléon," in *Les vases de Sèvres XVIII*e*–XXI*e *siècles. Éloge de la virtuosité*, ed. Antoinette Faÿ-Hallé (Dijon: Éditions Faton, 2014), 128–39.
10 Correspondence of Brongniart with Percier and Fontaine, 27 vendémiaire year X (October 19, 1801) (ACC, Vc 2, fols. 104 and 106); 8 brumaire year X (October 30, 1801) (T 1 L 3).
11 ACC, U 21, liasse 1.
12 Letter from Brongniart to Percier and Fontaine, 12 floréal year XII (October 19, 1801)(Vc 2).
13 Sale of 16 floréal year XIII (May 6, 1805) (ACC, Pb 1, 194/216).
14 Work carried out during the second semester of 1806 (ACC, Pb 1 L 1).
15 List of gifts to the queen and the princesses of Württemberg, July 10, 1806 (Pb 1 L 1 and Vy 17 fol. 26); sale, Fontainebleau, Me Osenat, December 11, 2005, no. 438.
16 "riche piédestal en biscuit représentant les quatre saisons et ornements analogues surmonté d'une coupe et renfermant une pendule d'après Percier." Marcelle Brunet, "Eine Dokumentation zu einer Uhr aus Sèvres-Biskuitporzellan nach dem Entwurf von Charles Percier," *Weltkunst* 3 (1979): 162–64. Percier received no payment for this clock.
17 Two of these clocks have been located, one in the Musée de Céramique, Sèvres (inv. MNC 13022; see Odile Nouvel-Kammerer, ed., *L'aigle et le papillon. Symboles des pouvoirs sous Napoléon*, exh. cat. [Paris: Musée des Arts décoratifs, 2008], no. 125); the other in the Hessisches Landesmuseum, Kassel [inv. 1997/42; see Ekkerhardt Schmidberger, *Schatzkunst 800 bis 1800*, exh. cat. (Neu-Isenburg: Edition Minerva, 2001).
18 "donner un exemple de ses moyens de fabrication les plus parfaits."
19 Tamara Préaud, ed., *The Sèvres Porcelain Manufactory: Alexandre Brongniart and the Triumph of Art and Industry, 1800–1847*, exh. cat. (New York: Bard Graduate Center, 1997–98), 182, no. 16.
20 Letter from Brongniart to Fontaine requesting elevations of the arc du Carrousel, April 30, 1806 (ACC, Vc 3 fol. 64 and Vb 1 fol. 27).
21 Préaud, *The Sèvres Porcelain Manufactory*, 224–25, no. 45. See also ACC, Pb 4, Vv 1.
22 ACC, Y 21, fol. 65.
23 ACC, Vbb 6. The current location of this guéridon is unknown.

◄ **FIG 9.13.** Attributed to Charles Percier. Design for a medal cabinet, ca. 1814. Pen, black ink, watercolor on paper. Les Arts décoratifs, Paris, CD 3240. Cat. 91.

▲ **FIG 9.14.** Charles Percier. Design for a candelabra. Pen and brown wash on paper. Les Arts Décoratifs, Paris, CD 3248.

24 Bernard Chevallier, *Les Sèvres de Fontainebleau: porcelaines, terres vernissées, émaux, vitraux (pièces entrées de 1804 à 1904)* (Paris, Réunion des musées nationaux, 1996), 207, and Préaud, *The Sèvres Porcelain Manufactory*, 235, no. 53.

25 N.C. Duvivier to Chaptal, 11 nivôse year IX (January 1, 1801)(Arch. nat., O² 908).

26 "reçu des citoyens Percier et Fontaine les projets de dessins pour tapis à exécuter pour les premières pièces à occuper dans les appartements du palais des consuls à Saint Cloud"; "dans le genre et le goût que les architectes ont fixés pour l'ensemble de leurs décorations." Duvivier to Chaptal, 21 frimaire year X (December 12, 1801). (Arch. nat., O² 908).

27 Receipt of the concierge of the palace of Saint-Cloud, 9 frimaire year XII (December 1, 1803) (Arch. nat., O² 908); for details and schedule of execution, see the fonds Duvivier AnF (497 AP); the cost came to 12,216.50 francs (Arch. nat., 497 AP 4); 1807 Saint-Cloud inventory, no. 163 (Arch. nat., AJ¹⁹ 292).

28 "composition plus noble et plus pompeuse." Report of N.C. Duvivier, May 1, 1806 (Arch. nat., O² 909).

29 N.C. Duvivier to Daru, May 1, 1806 (Arch. nat., 494 AP4).

30 "fait le petit dessin coloré que n'a pu faire l'architecte Percier." See Jean-Pierre Samoyault, "L'Ameublement des salles du Trône dans les palais impériaux sous Napoléon 1ᵉʳ," *Bulletin de la Société de l'histoire de l'art français* (1985): 196–97, 204 n. 34.

31 A tracing made by Saint-Ange in 1827 of a drawing signed "Ch. Percier invenit 1807" is now in the Mobilier national (published by E. Dumonthier, pl. 3).

32 Samoyault, "L'Ameublement des salles du Trône,"

33 "que ce dessin fut convenable à la dignité du lieu, en s'assortissant au goût général de l'ameublement"; "connu avantageusement par d'heureuses compositions." Duvivier to Daru, June 10, 1808 (Arch. nat. O² 909).

34 Guy René and Christian Ledoux-Lebard, "La décoration et l'ameublement du Grand cabinet de Napoléon aux Tuileries," *Bulletin de la Société de l'Histoire de l'Art français 1941–1947* (1947): 185–258, and Chantal Gastinel-Coural, ed., *La manufacture des Gobelins au XIXᵉ siècle, tapisseries, cartons, maquettes* (Paris: Mobilier national, 1996), nos. 1–6.

35 For the price of 7,300 francs, see the report by Bellanger dated 3 nivôse year XIII (December 24, 1804) (Arch. nat. O² 558).

36 Dépôt du Mobilier national, GMT 2091; see Chantal Gastinel-Coural, "Tapis à histoires: Des Savonneries qui n'en sont pas. Quelques identifications de tapis impériaux et royaux," *Bulletin de la Société de l'Histoire de l'Art français, 2006*, (2007): 262, fig. 1, n. 15.

37 Mobilier national, GMT 8059; see ibid., pp. 268–70.

38 "d'un grand compartiment d'ornemens doré, renfermant les divers attributs des armes et chiffres de Sa Majesté impériale. Une bordure analogue au reste du tapis, le tout exécuté d'après les dessins de Messieurs Percier et Fontaine, architectes du palais impérial." Report of 8 pluviôse year XIII (January 28, 1805) (Arch. nat. O² 558).

39 "dessin d'ornements arabesques, avec médaillons contenant des attributs de musique et de guerre, une grande rosette sur un fond bleu." Ledger of accounting documents, year XIV, fol. 138 (Arch. nat. O² 1189); cf. Gastinel-Coural, "Tapis à histoires," n. 192.

40 Ibid., fol. 143.

41 Marie-France Dupuy-Baylet. *Pendules du Mobilier national 1800–1870,* (Paris: Éditions Faton, 2006), 127–29, no. 59.

42 See the estate inventory of Biennais' wife, November 16, 1859, Arch. nat. MC, II/1108.

43 Tea urn and creamer, pl. XXXIV; incense burner (location unknown), pl. LII. See Anne Dion-Tenenbaum, *L'orfèvre de Napoléon, Martin-Guillaume Biennais*, exh. cat. (Paris: Réunion des musées nationaux, 2003), 38, 39, 46.

44 "frise avec figures ailées, à demi-corps et têtes de bœufs." Biennais added the imperial arms to this ragout tureen in 1806 (Arch. nat., O² 17).

45 "quatre grands portefeuilles et un lot des dessins par Percier et Fontaine et autres pour l'orfèvrerie et la bijouterie."

46 Pierre Arizzoli-Clémentel, "The Percier and Biennais Album in the Musée des Arts décoratifs, Paris," *Burlington Magazine* (March 1998): 195–201.

47 Paris, Musée des Arts décoratifs, inv. CD 3240. Two medal cabinets of this design are known: one (formerly coll. Vivant Denon) is now in the Metropolitan Museum of Art, New York (cat. 90); the other was recently acquired by the Victoria and Albert Museum, London.

48 Paris, Musée des Arts décoratifs, inv. CD 3248.

49 1859 sale, lot 29, under the erroneous title *sucrier* [sugar dish]. When Mantz published it in 1863 (p. 246, ill. p. 245), it was in the Bérard collection.

50 The Metropolitan Museum of Art, ACC. no. 2013.544.1 and 2013.544.2 (cats. 98, 99). These sheets probably correspond to lots 8 and 9 in the 1859 sale. The Met dates these drawings to 1804 for the coronation of Napoleon I.

51 "ont été répétés plusieurs fois, et même avec quelques variantes, par les fabricants de Paris." (Charles Percier and Pierre Fontaine, "Table explicative," in *Recueil de décorations intérieures* (Paris: Authors and Pierre Didot l'aîné, 1801–12), 38, pl. 52.

52 "nous sommes fort éloignés de prétendre offrir aux artistes des modèles à imiter." Percier and Fontaine, *Recueil de décorations intérieures*, "Preliminary Discourse," 1.

TWO TUREENS AND THEIR VARIATIONS

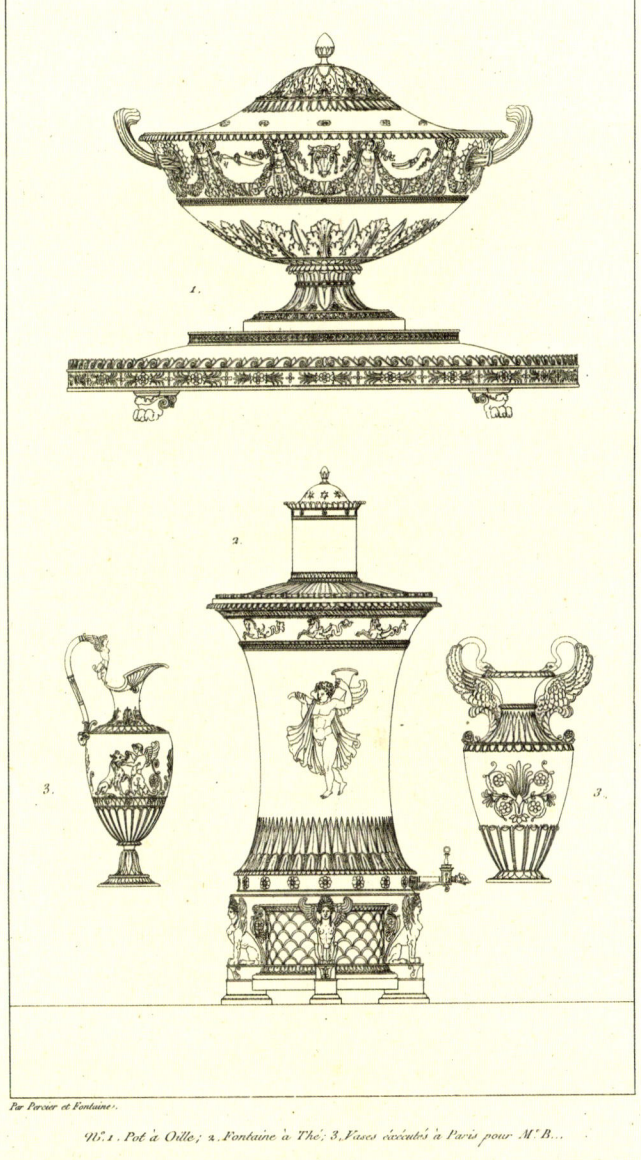

FIG 9A.1. Charles Percier and Pierre Fontaine. *Tureen, Tea urn, and Vases made in Paris for Mr. B...* From Percier and Fontaine, *Recueil de décorations intérieures* (Paris: Authors and Pierre Didot l'aîné, 1801–12), pl. 34.

ANNE DION-TENENBAUM

The *Recueil de décorations intérieures* includes two designs for tureens, both of which were fabricated by the goldsmith Martin Guillaume Biennais. The first one (plate 34; sixth fascicle, 1803) [FIG. 9A.1], corresponds to descriptions of the tureens in the first silver service of the first consul household; when Biennais added the imperial arms in 1806, these pieces had friezes of "winged half-length figures and ox heads."[1] Biennais had probably delivered these silver tureens (in their original form) to the first consul in June 1802, shortly after the silver-gilt tea service, designs for which were also included in the *Recueil*. At this early date, Percier seems to have been in constant demand for the design of works for the first consul.

The second design is identified in the *Recueil* (plate 46; eighth fascicle, 1804) [FIG. 9A.2] as a "[t]ureen executed in silver for the service of Empress Josephine," and the commentary, written in 1812, informs us that it "attracted attention at one of the expositions of the products of French industry."[2] The exposition in question was clearly the one held in 1806, where

Biennais exhibited for the first time and was awarded a gold medal. (A variant of this tureen is recognizable on the professional card that Biennais had printed after the exposition to exploit this award [FIG. 9A.3]). In this design, the stand, supported by hooved feet, is decorated with garland swags suspended between vases and ox heads; the base and support (in the form of a Corinthian capital) are enriched with acanthus leaves, and the lower body of the vessel is decorated with a scale pattern. A bas-relief composition on the upper body shows two women, kneeling on one knee, flanking a monogram "J" surmounted by a crown and framed by two cornucopias. Each of the two handles is supported by two winged female nudes emerging from vegetation. Finally, the finial on the cover represents a seated woman holding a vase overflowing with fruit and flanked by two infants holding fruit, one standing and one sitting. The sale of drawings from Biennais' workshop,[3] organized after his widow's death in 1859, included a design (present location unknown), signed by Percier and Fontaine, for this very tureen for Josephine, which does not survive.[4]

Biennais worked several variations on this design by Percier. The most literal reprise is a silver soup tureen (*soupière;* FIG. 9A.4); exhibited at the Centennial Exposition of 1900, when its owner was identified as the "baron de Bethman," it is currently in the collection of the Banque de France.[5] Here we again find acanthus leaves on the base and support, the fish-scale ornament, the kneeling-women-with-cornucopias motif, and the handles supported by pairs of winged female nudes. By contrast, the finial on the cover represents Bacchus and Ariadne, and the stand is decorated with a relief inspired by the Aldobrandini Wedding,[6] a

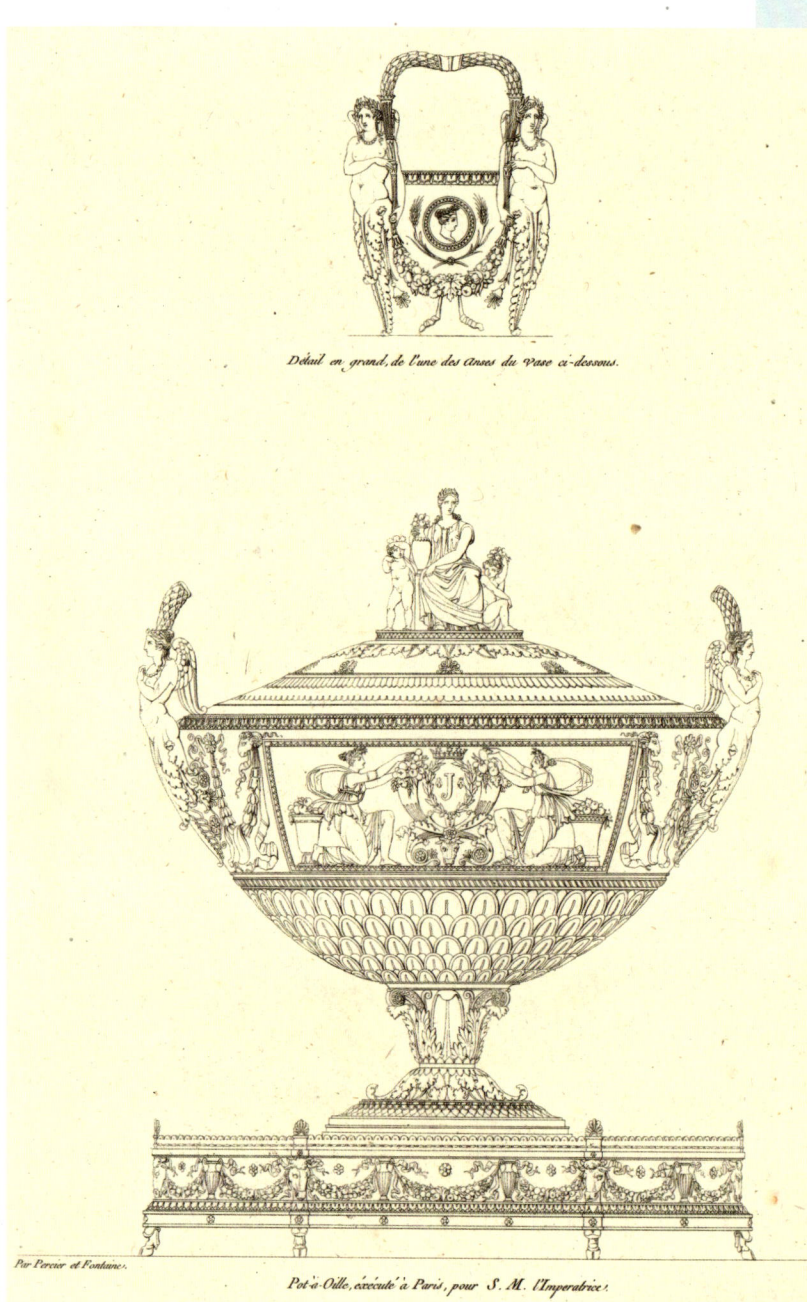

▼ FIG 9A.2. Charles Percier and Pierre Fontaine. *Tureen made in Paris for HM the Empress.* From Percier and Fontaine, *Recueil de décorations intérieures* (Paris: Authors and Pierre Didot l'aîné, 1801–12), pl. 46.

◀ FIG 9A.3. Professional card of Martin Guillaume Biennais after the 1806 Paris Industrial Exposition.

▶ FIG 9A.4. Charles Percier. Tureen, n.d. Manufactured by Martin Guillaume Biennais. Silver. Collection Banque de France, Paris, 15667. Cat. 96.

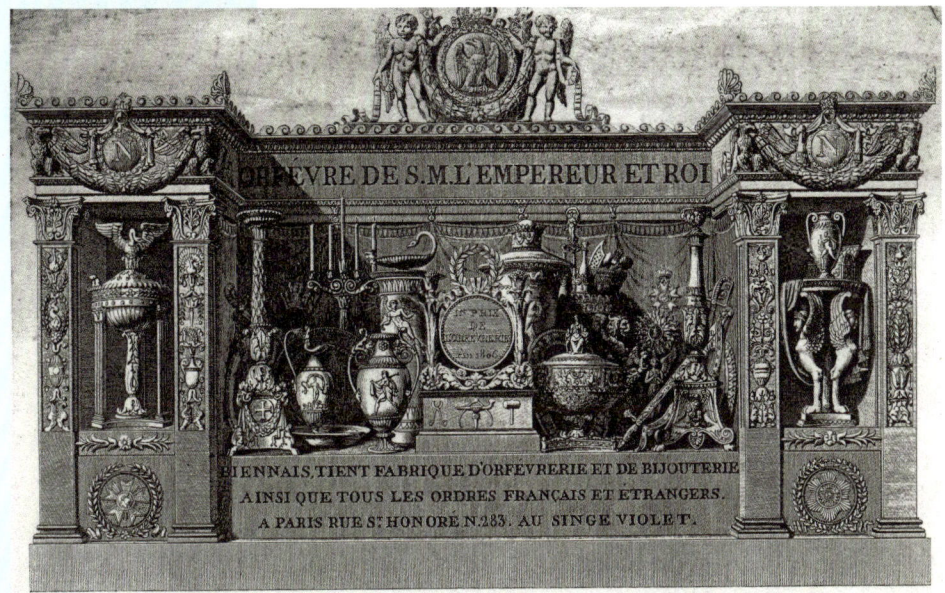

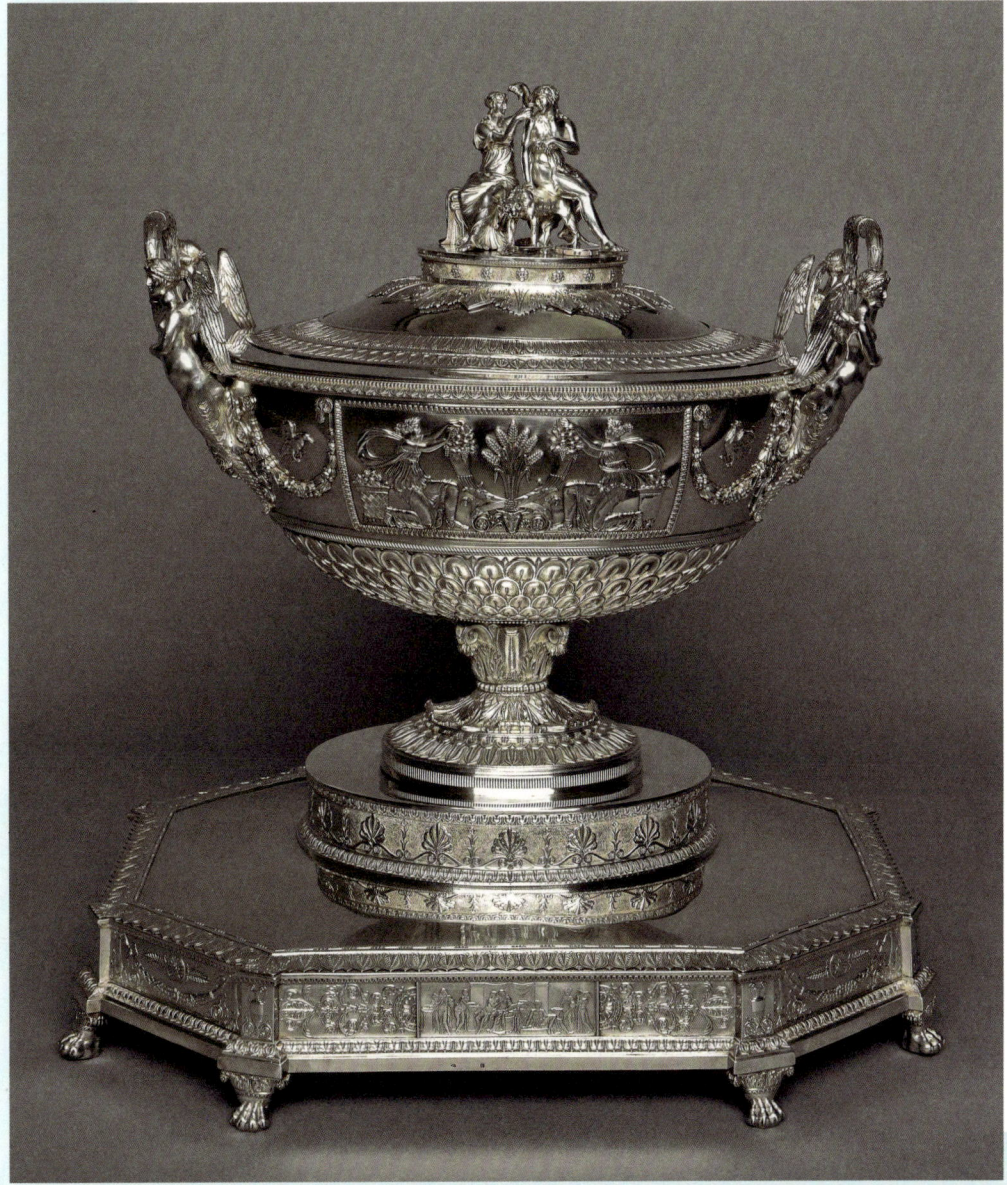

composition that Biennais used repeatedly in his work beginning in 1810. This piece corresponds precisely to a drawing whose provenance from the Biennais workshop is certain (SEE CAT. 93), but the recipient of the initial realization of this design is unknown.

There are many iterations of the culminating group of the 1804 design (a woman accompanied by two infants). In 1808, Biennais was commissioned to make a silver-gilt service as well as a silver service for Napoleon's sister Elisa, the grand duchess of Tuscany. The silver-gilt tureens are now lost, but they were described in some detail when Biennais delivered them in 1809.[7] Their stands were supported by claw feet (*griffes*), the friezes on their upper bodies were decorated with winged human figures emerging from scrolled rinceaux and, above, ravens, roosters, and antique ox heads; the handles were shaped like winged figures, and groups of Ceres or Cybele with infants dominated the covers. The latter figural template, apparently close to the one on Josephine's tureen (the 1809 description specifies the iconography of the seated women), was often used by Biennais. These lost tureens of the grand duchess of Tuscany were probably very similar to a pair delivered by Biennais at roughly the same date to the viceroy of Italy in Milan. These were joined by two more tureens in 1811, when the Milanese goldsmith Eugenio Brusa

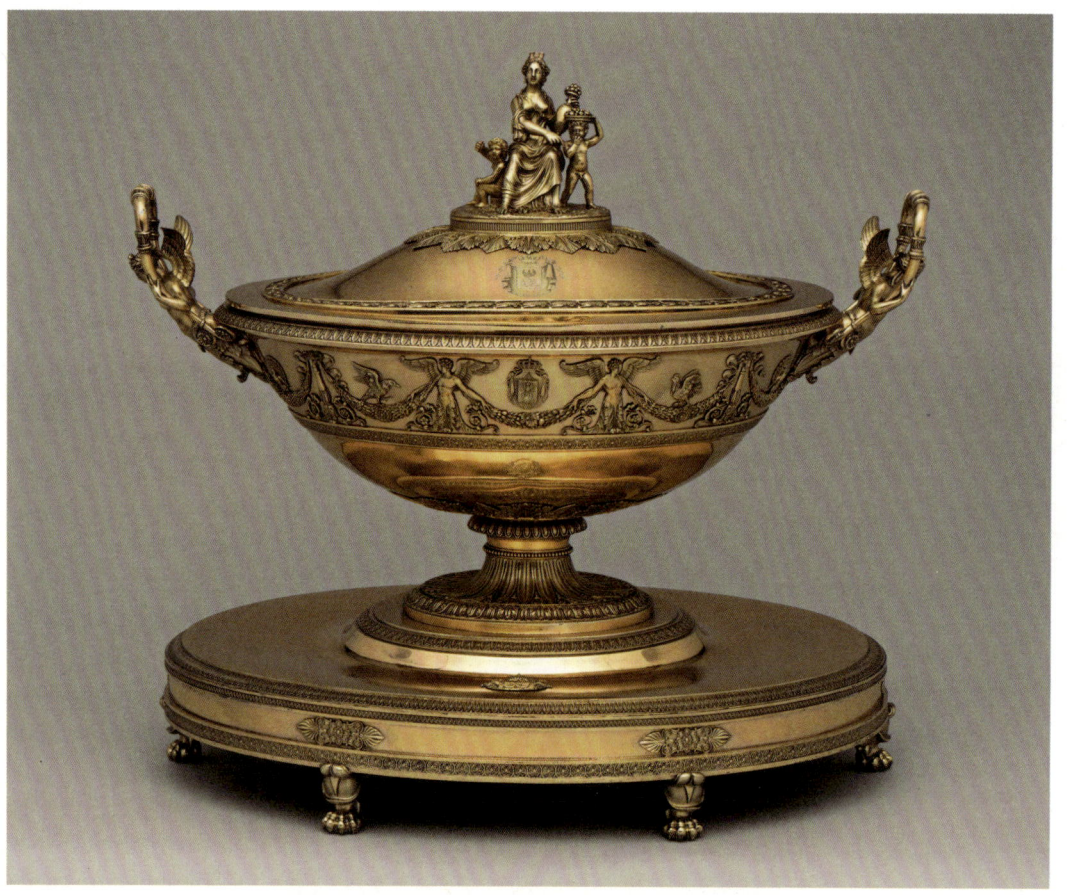

FIG 9A.5. After Charles Percier. Tureen, 1794–1814. Made by Martin Guillaume Biennais. Silver gilt. The Metropolitan Museum of Art, New York, Purchase, Joseph Pulitzer Bequest, 34.17.1a-c. Cat. 95.

fabricated an additional pair to create a set of four illustrating the four seasons; the tureen with Ceres became a representation of summer, the one with Cybele of autumn. The resulting quartet of tureens, brought to Vienna in 1816 by Francis I of Austria, survives (Vienna, Bundesmobilienverwaltung-Silberkammer). The important service commissioned by Prince Camillo Borghese, sometime between 1809 and 1814, included very similar tureens, as is demonstrated by one that survives, in the Metropolitan Museum of Art [FIG. 9A.5]. As in the Milanese pieces, the seated woman wears a mural crown, a substitution for the laurel crown in Percier's original drawing.

These variations on two designs by Percier demonstrate how different motifs borrowed from the architect were reworked and recombined in the studio. In this way, Percier's style came, more or less directly, to permeate the entire production of the Biennais workshop. ●

1 "figures ailées à demi corps et têtes de bœuf." Biennais invoice dated June 1806 (Paris, Archives Nationales, O² 17).
2 "Pot à l'oille exécuté en orfèvrerie pour la vaisselle de l'impératrice Joséphine"; "Il a été remarqué dans l'une des expositions publiques des produits de l'industrie française."
3 Sale of December 24, 1859, no. 29. See Anne Dion-Tenenbaum, *L'orfèvre de Napoléon, Martin-Guillaume Biennais*, exh. cat. (Paris: Réunion des musées nationaux, 2003), 16 n.28.
4 This drawing was published in Paul Mantz, "Recherches sur l'histoire de l'orfèvrerie française," *Gazette des Beaux-Arts* 1 (1863): 245, where it is mistakenly identified as a sugar dish (*sucrier*).
5 Henri Bouilhet, *L'orfèvrerie française aux XVIIIᵉ et XIXᵉ siècles: 1700–1900* (Paris: H. Laurens, 1863), 2:94.
6 A celebrated ancient fresco discovered in Rome ca. 1600; now in the collection of the Vatican Museums.
7 Arch. Nat., O² 23. Pieces from this service are now in the Palazzo Pitti.

COURT
ARCHITECT

CHAPTER 10

THE SYNTHESIS OF ARCHITECTURE AND DECOR

JEAN-FRANÇOIS BÉDARD

DESPITE CHARLES PERCIER'S STAUNCH SUPPORT OF THE REPUBlican cause—as a preeminent designer during the French Revolution, Percier served on the committee mandated to replace the royal insignia in 1793—his approach remained remarkably similar to that of royal architects. His teacher Antoine François Peyre and his mentor Pierre Adrien Pâris, both of whom were trained and employed by the monarchy, provided a model and shaped the young Percier's outlook.[1] Spanning a wide range of scales from diminutive ornamental designs to large urban planning schemes, his work combined Pâris's dexterity as an ornament designer with Peyre's skills in architectural composition. Percier's production, like theirs, fulfilled the multifarious demands placed on architects by a court culture that the Revolution failed to obliterate.

Courts had always relied on the arts to buttress their authority. The Regency of Philippe II d'Orléans, for instance, saw a conscious revival of seventeenth-century forms, appropriating the grandeur of the Sun King's reign to stress political continuity at a time of fragility for the monarchy.[2] Gilles Marie Oppenord was the principal orchestrator of the Regency's visual culture. His career is strikingly similar to Percier's. Like Percier, he completed his architectural training at the French Academy in Rome. Like Percier, he produced an extensive array of designs: book illustrations, ornamentation for domestic objects and furniture, interior decoration, sets for festivities, architectural projects, and garden and urban schemes. Like Percier, he was a consummate draftsman and an inventive ornament designer. Like Percier, he used prints to disseminate his work and, thus, the image desired by the political elite who employed him. And like Percier, he made a lucrative commerce of his drawings. Despite the formal differences that set Percier's cool neoclassicism apart from Oppenord's rich baroque, the two artists share a remarkable coherence of purpose: Percier is far closer to his noble forerunner than to his contemporaries in the employ of bourgeois industrialists.

Trained in the tradition of courtly "artistic directors," Percier was ideally suited to serve Napoleon's reinstatement of a court in France after 1804.[3] The Empire paid closer attention to architectural and decorative forms as heralds of political power than previous regimes had done. Percier's first project in a court context, however, was for a well-established monarchy. In 1800, King Carlos IV of Spain ordered the decoration of a cabinet for the Casa Real del Labrador in Aranjuez, the so-called Platinum Room.[4] To supervise the project, the king employed Michel Léonard Sitel, a French metalsmith who had recently settled in Madrid. Sitel, in turn, called upon Percier to design the room and its furnishings. He also delegated to the architect the selection of the artisans needed to carry out the work. One of the few projects conceived by Percier without the participation of his lifelong partner Pierre Fontaine, the Platinum Room is Percier's most accomplished decorative scheme.[5]

Located at the end of an enfilade in the east wing of the Casa Real, the Platinum Room is a richly decorated rectangular room covered by a barrel vault

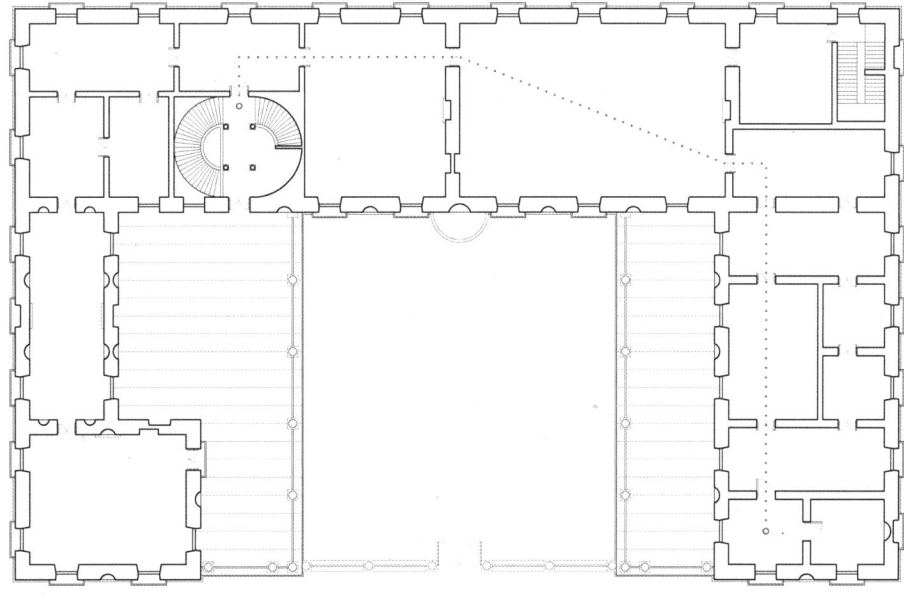

▷ **FIG 10.1.** Plan of the second floor of the Casa Real del Labrador, Aranjuez, showing the location of the Platinum Room.

[FIG. 10.1]. A thin pilastered order, on pedestals and surmounted by gilded bronze capitals, subdivides the walls. On the north and south walls, these pilasters frame pairs of rectangular canvases by Anne Louis Girodet representing the seasons; below them are landscapes by Jean Joseph Xavier Bidauld. Mirrors take the place of Girodet's paintings on the east and west walls, and views of famous urban sites by Jean Thomas Thibauldt that of Bidauld's canvases. Mirrors also fill the lunettes over the east and west walls. This arrangement creates the illusion of an infinite vaulted gallery, an effect Percier emphasized in the perspective published in the second edition of Percier and Fontaine's *Recueil de décorations intérieures* [FIG. 10.2; SEE ALSO FIG. 8.19].[6] Gilded bronze ornaments cast and chased by Pierre Auguste Forestier cover the entablature, pilaster shafts, pedestals, and wainscoting. Some are enhanced with platinum plate, giving the room its name. Painted grotesques, birds, flowers, emblems, and other figures decorate doors, overdoors, and the compartmented ceiling. The seats—two armchairs, two chairs, and two stools executed by the Parisian cabinetmaker Xavier Hindermeyer after designs by Percier—are richly appointed with gilded bronze ornaments in harmony with the room.

The perfection of the cabinet's unified decor is a tribute to Sitel's exacting supervision and Percier's inventiveness with ornament, furniture, and architecture.[7] During the ancien régime, these domains were often the purview of specialists from different departments of the royal administration. Broadly speaking, the Bâtiments du Roi specialized in permanent buildings and supervised royal manufactures. The Administration de l'argenterie, menus plaisirs, et affaires de la chambre du roi (known as the Menus Plaisirs) took care of temporary decors for spectacles, fireworks, balls, and other special occasions.[8]

Percier's mentor, Pierre Adrien Pâris, was the preeminent designer at the Menus Plaisirs at the century's end. As Dessinateur de la Chambre et du Cabinet du Roi between 1778 and 1792, he conceived and supervised the decors of the monarchy's final years. With Pâris's support, Percier became the set designer at the Paris

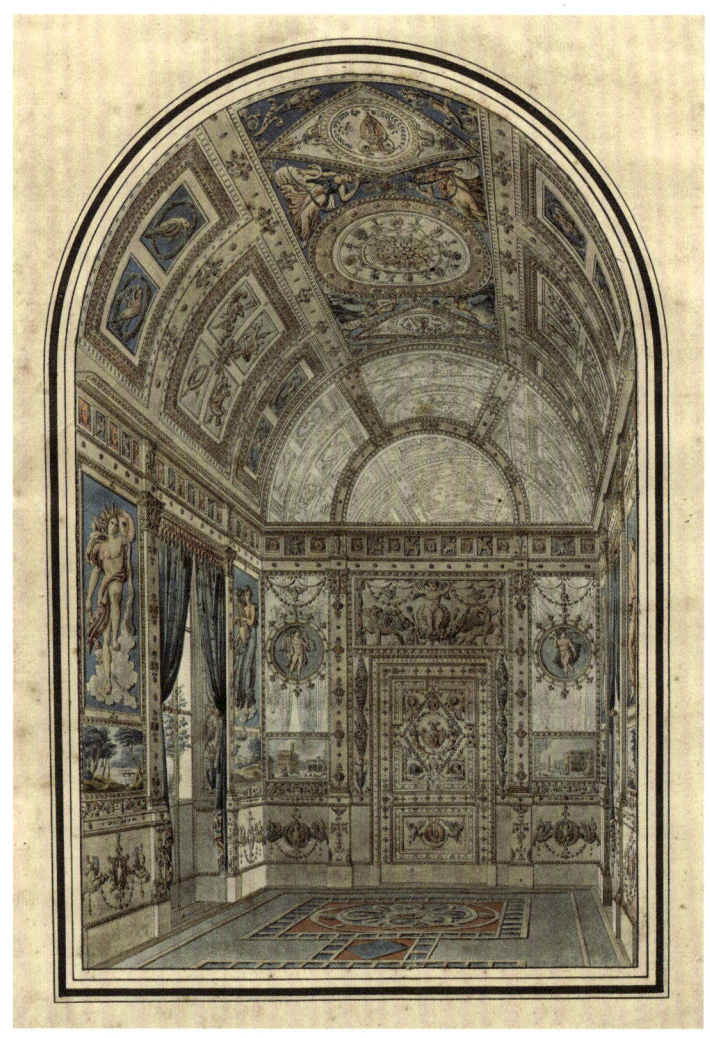

▲ FIG 10.2. Unknown watercolorist and Charles Percier, designer and printmaker. Perspective of the Platinum Room, Casa Real del Labrador, Aranjuez, Spain (1800–1806). Watercolor over pl. 61. From Percier and Fontaine, *Recueil de décorations intérieures* (Paris: Authors and Pierre Didot l'aîné, 1801–12). Bibliothèque Paul-Marmottan, Ville de Boulogne-Billancourt, Académie des Beaux Arts, France, 70–424.

▶ FIG 10.3. Pierre Chenu, printmaker, after Juste Aurèle Meissonnier, architect and draftsman. "Cabinet of Count Bielinski, Grand Marshal of the Polish Crown, executed in 1734," from *Œuvre de Juste-Aurèle Meissonnier* (Paris, 1738–1751), pl. 87.

Opera during the Revolution. This experience left its mark on his Spanish project of 1800. At Aranjuez, the spatial dematerialization that results from the use of opposing mirrors, the shine of precious wood veneers, and the glittering ornaments—all no doubt heightened when illuminated by candlelight—conjure up the magic of a stage set. The theatricality of the Platinum Room echoes that of other decors realized by Percier and Fontaine around the same time, such as the salle du Conseil at Malmaison, which was designed as a military tent with martial attributes.

Theatrical influences pervaded the architectural work of artists at the Menus Plaisirs. Between 1734 and 1736, one of Pâris's predecessors, Juste Aurèle Meissonnier, Dessinateur de la chambre et du cabinet du Roi from 1726 to 1750, designed a room for the Polish count Franciszek Bielinski.[9] As Percier would sixty-five years later for the Platinum Room, Meissonnier orchestrated mirrors, paintings, and furniture into a cohesive environment. He similarly disposed mirrors face to face and crafted lavish ornamentation that recalled the fantasy world of the theater [FIG. 10.3]. Even the manner of construction of both rooms suggests set design: they were prefabricated and exhibited in Paris before being shipped to their patrons in crates. Though far different in appearance, the Platinum and the Bielinski rooms nonetheless share the formal extravagance of spectacle in meeting the demands of a court elite that relished enchanting interiors.

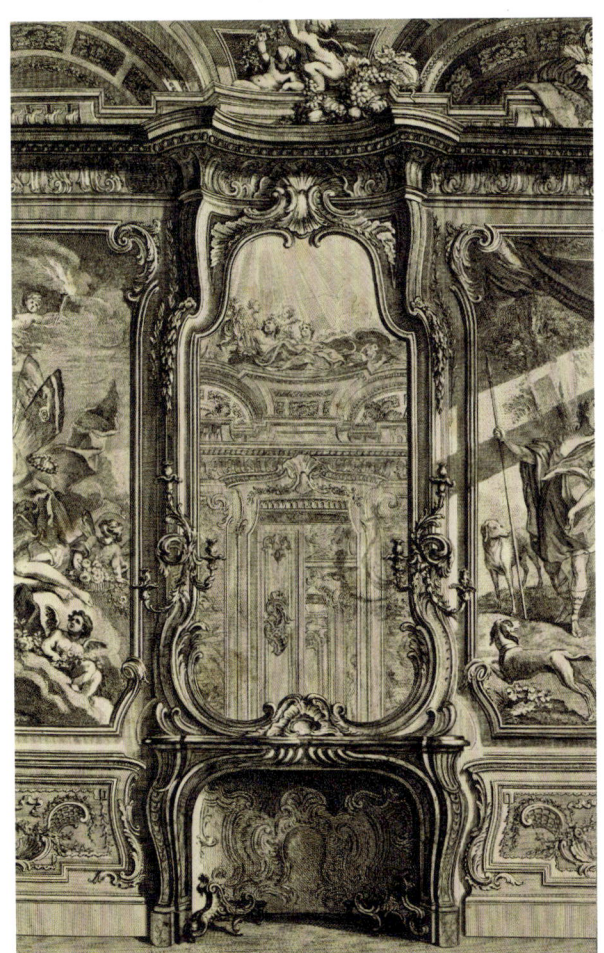

As Dessinateurs of the Menus Plaisirs, Meissonnier and Pâris were accomplished inventors of ornament. Percier, too, placed ornament design at the center of his practice [FIG. 10.4].[10] Unlike Meissonnier's plastic and curvilinear decor for Bielinski, however, Percier's decoration at the Platinum Room preserved the simple geometry of the space. He encrusted every surface with an overall field of planar ornaments. The engraved view of the room intensifies this visual saturation (SEE FIG. 10.2). Percier's two-dimensional ornamentation points to the tradition of grotesque decoration. Pâris nurtured Percier's interest in that formal style, which had influenced architects and decorative artists since the rediscovery of ancient Roman models in the fifteenth century.[11] Following Pâris's lead, Percier learned from celebrated grotesque compositions such as Raphael's and Giovanni di Udine's Vatican loggie.[12] Inspired by the grotesque, Percier maintained an "epidermic" ornamental strategy throughout his career.

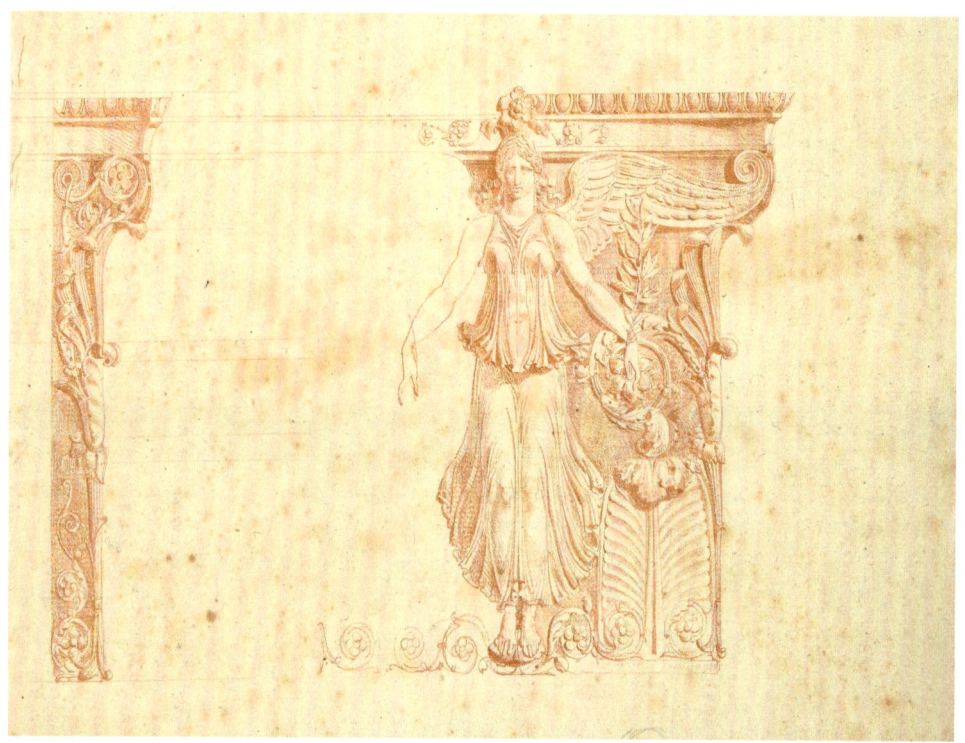

Percier's mastery of the grotesque also influenced his design method. The combinatory arrangement at different scales of geometric, plant, and animal components characteristic of this decorative style may be sensed in the illustrations of the Platinum Room in the *Recueil de décorations intérieures*.[13] Plates 62 and 63, devoted respectively to the upper parts of the room's order and to the pedestals, wainscoting, and furniture set against an enlarged portion of the door panels' frames [FIGS. 10.5, 10.6], record the decor in abbreviated fragments, at different scales, superimposed on each other much as in a grotesque composition. The *Recueil*'s engravings are meant not so much to document a final architectural design as to depict a stage in the compositional process that could be pursued by other designers.

Schooled in the tradition of ancien-régime architects and designers, Percier mastered the planning of the total environments that distinguished court architecture. Ornament held a central place in these settings. It reflected social hierarchies as it proclaimed political prestige—both crucial concerns for aristocratic regimes. Percier's dexterity in decorative invention helped him tackle the different scales at play in these theatrical settings. The Platinum Room at Aranjuez exemplifies his approach. There, he implemented a decorative

▷ **FIG 10.4.** Charles Percier. Study of a capital for the Platinum Room, Casa Real del Labrador, Aranjuez (detail), 1800. Graphite and red chalk on paper. Private collection, Paris. Cat. 61.

◁ **FIG 10.5.** Charles Percier and Pierre Fontaine. Entablature, capital, and details from the Platinum Room, Casa Real del Labrador, Aranjuez. From the *Recueil de décorations intérieures*, pl. 62. Cat. 54D.

▷ **FIG 10.6.** Charles Percier and Pierre Fontaine. Wainscoting, armchair, tripod, vases, and other accessories executed for the Platinum Room, Casa Real del Labrador, Aranjuez. From *Recueil de décorations intérieures* (Paris: Authors and Pierre Didot l'aîné, 1801–12), pl. 63.

10 ARCHITECTURE AND DECOR

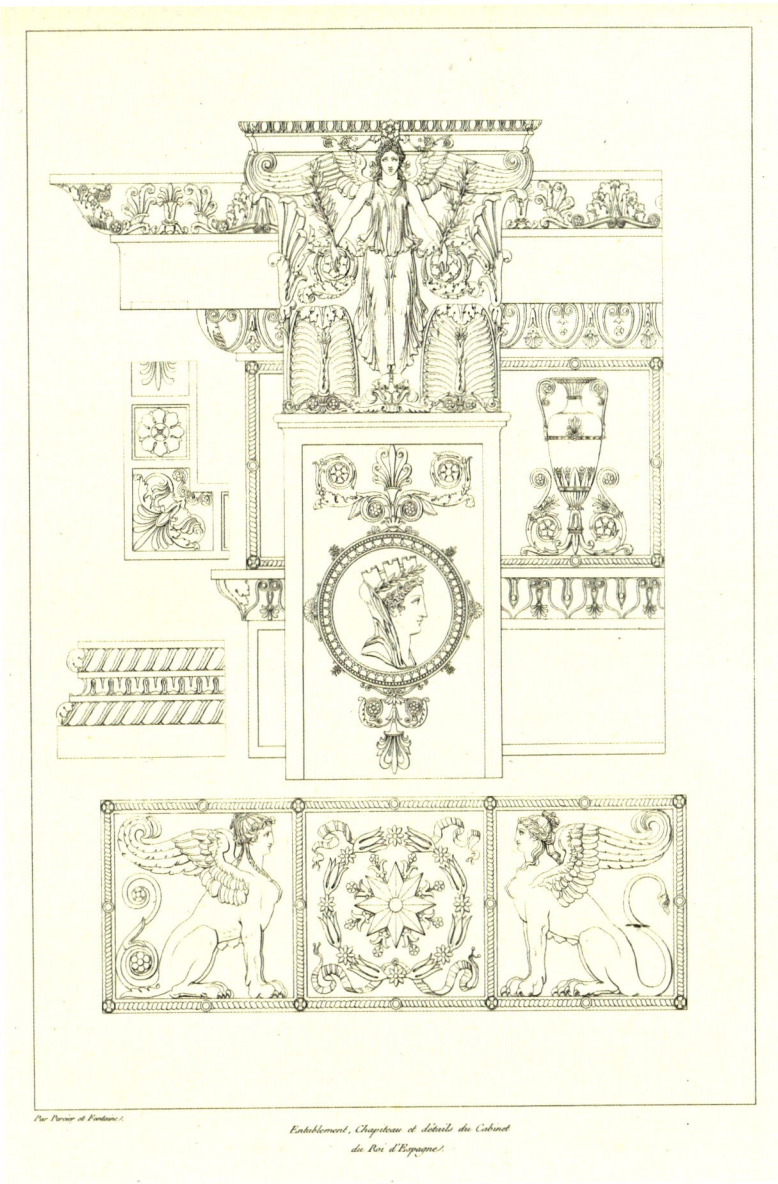

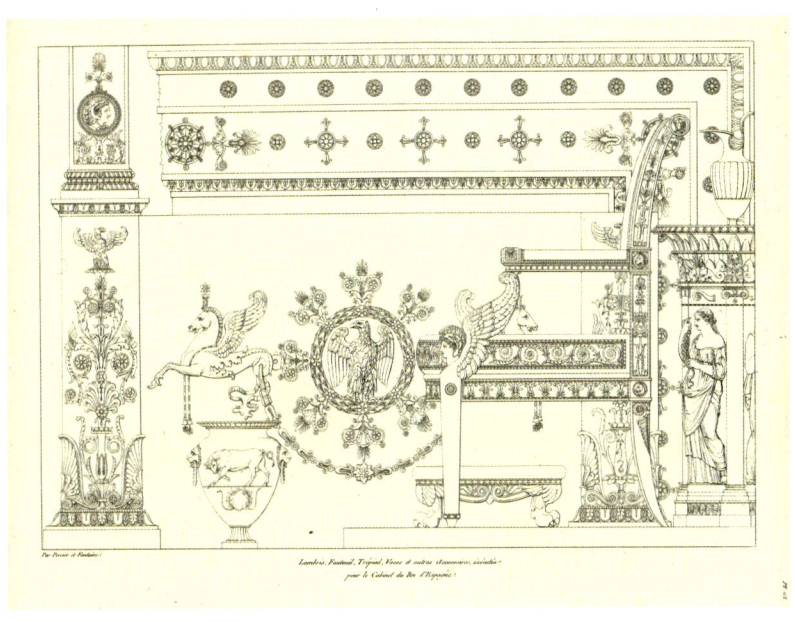

211

method in the grotesque tradition. Not only the metallic ornaments disposed on the room's surfaces but also the painted decoration of the wood veneers and the barrel vault are in this formal mode. Even the way the room is illustrated in the *Recueil de décorations intérieures* heightens the fragmentation of geometric, figurative, and architectural elements as in grotesque designs. With the accession of Napoleon Bonaparte to the rank of Emperor of the French, Percier fully deployed his ornamental strategy in the service of the upstart imperial court and fulfilled his ambitions as court architect. ●

1 On Antoine François Peyre's importance as a teacher, see Jean-Philippe Garric, "L'Académie royale d'architecture aux origines de l'art de la composition (1779–1799)," in *L'atelier et l'amphithéâtre: les écoles de l'architecture, entre théorie et pratique*, ed. Guy Lambert and Estelle Thibault (Wavre: Mardaga, 2011), 23–50.
2 Jean-François Bédard, "Political Renewal and Architectural Revival during the French Regency: Oppenord's Palais-Royal," *Journal of the Society of Architectural Historians* 68, no. 1 (March 2009): 30–51.
3 Following Martin Warnke's expression. Martin Warnke, *The Court Artist: On the Ancestry of the Modern Artist* (Cambridge: Cambridge University Press, 1993), 176.
4 On the Platinum Room, see Chantal Gastinel-Coural, "Le cabinet de platine de la Casa del Labrador à Aranjuez: Documents inédits," *Bulletin de la Société de l'histoire de l'art français* (1994), 181–205; Javier Jordán de Urríes y de la Colina, "Les décors d'Aranjuez: Les *Saisons* du cabinet de platine de la Real Casa del Labrador à Aranjuez," in *Girodet, 1767–1824* (Paris: Gallimard and Musée du Louvre Éditions, 2005), 261–65; Javier Jordán de Urríes y de la Colina, *La Real Casa del Labrador de Aranjuez* (Madrid: Patrimonio Nacional, 2009), esp. 176–84; Javier Jordán de Urríes y de la Colina and José Luis Sancho, "Sitel, Percier y el Gabinete de Platino," *Reales Sitios* 50, no. 195 (2013): 28–49.
5 Percier's sole authorship is noted by Jordán de Urríes and Sancho, "Sitel, Percier," 28.
6 Charles Percier and Pierre Fontaine, *Recueil de décorations intérieures, comprenant tout ce qui a rapport à l'ameublement, comme vases, trépieds, candélabres, cassolettes, lustres, girandoles, lampes, chandeliers, cheminées, feux, poêles, pendules, tables, secrétaires, lits, canapés, fauteuils, chaises, tabourets, miroirs, écrans, etc. etc. etc. composé par C. Percier et P. F. L. Fontaine, exécuté sur leurs dessins* (Paris: Authors and Pierre Didot l'aîné, 1812).
7 Jordán de Urríes argues for Sitel's important role in the design of the cabinet; Jordán de Urríes and Sancho, "Sitel, Percier."
8 For a more nuanced account of the relationship between the Bâtiments and the Menus Plasirs, see Jérôme de La Gorce, "Quand les Menus Plaisirs et les Bâtiments du roi s'associent pour servir la monarchie," *Les Menus Plaisirs du roi (XVIIe–XVIIIe siècles)*, ed. Pierre Jugie and Jérôme de La Gorce (Paris: Presses de l'Université Paris-Sorbonne, 2013), 101–15. On the Menus Plaisirs, see also Jérôme de La Gorce and Pierre Jugie, *Dans l'atelier des Menus Plaisirs du roi: spectacles, fêtes et cérémonies aux XVIIe et XVIIIe siècle* (Versailles: Éditions Artlys, 2010).
9 On the Bielinski cabinet, see Peter Fuhring, *Juste-Aurèle Meissonnier: un génie del rococo 1695–1750*, 2 vols. (Turin: Umberto Allemandi & C., 1999), 2:213–14. <which volume?>
10 Noted by Jean-Philippe Garric, "Présentation," in Charles Percier and Pierre Fontaine, *Palais de Rome: Palais, maisons et autres édifices modernes dessinés à Rome*, ed. Jean-Philippe Garric (Wavre: Éditions Mardaga, Institut national d'histoire de l'art, 2008), 16.
11 On Pâris's study of grotesques, see Marc-Henri Jordan, "L'étude de l'ornement et l'art du décor," in *Le cabinet de Pierre-Adrien Pâris, architecte, dessinateur des Menus-Plaisirs* (Besançon: Musée des Beaux-Arts et d'Archéologie de Besançon, 2008), 40–57.
12 Eighteen engravings of Raphael's *loggie*, colored and in gilded frames, hung in Percier's Louvre apartment at the time of his death. His library also contained a volume documenting this decorative ensemble. See the probate inventory of Charles Percier, Archives nationales de France, Minutier central, étude XLVI, no. 905, September 11, 1838, respectively fol. 6r, no. 30, and fol. 7v, no. 54. Two original drawings for arabesques, most likely by the architect, are also mentioned on fol. 5v, no. 25.
13 Jean-Philippe Garric points to a similar combinatory strategy at play in Percier's decorative frontispieces; Garric, "Présentation," 25.

CHAPTER 11

PERCIER AND THE IMPERIAL COUPLE

VINCENT COCHET

Percier resided at the Louvre; he lived like a philosopher, in extreme simplicity; the walls of his cabinet were of neutral gray plaster, completely covered with precious old master drawings and painted sketches by his friends, who were then the likes of David, Gérard, Girodet, etc. Percier always wore a long gray frock coat, buttoned all the way up; his health was delicate and he almost never went out; it was Fontaine who took care of external business.... He was a good man and had exquisite manners but was very sparing with his time; he dreaded the distraction of visitors.

THÉOPHILE VAUCHELET, 1808[1]

AS PIERRE FONTAINE'S BUSINESS PARTNER, CHARLES PERCIER seemed content to remain in the shadows of his office, from which there emerged, at a rapid clip, projects intended to satisfy Bonaparte, now Emperor Napoleon, and his wife Josephine. Fontaine forced himself to write and was forthcoming about what he felt in the face of events, but Percier expressed himself only through his drawings and the publications that he supervised. In the second-person plural, Fontaine left an account of the two friends' extraordinary double career, from the Consulate to the fall of the Empire, in the form of diary entries. How did this partnership go about securing commissions? What was the nature of Percier's relations with his patrons?

CHARLES PERCIER: A SHORT OFFICIAL CAREER

When the last fires of the Empire had been snuffed out, Fontaine declared: "We have enjoyed for more than thirty years the perfect harmony of a sweet friendship that has never been troubled and will end only when we do....Reputation, profits, exhaustion, we have shared everything, and if circumstances have dictated...that I alone take official credit for some projects, neither of us has ever ceased sharing equally in their execution."[2] The binomial "Percier and Fontaine" originated in Italy, where the pair, both students of Antoine François Peyre, found themselves in 1786. A shared admiration for antiquity and for the study of Renaissance architecture sealed their friendship, which ended only with Percier's death in 1838.

One year after returning to Paris in 1791, Percier embraced an official career, succeeding Pierre Adrien Pâris as supervisor of scenery at the Paris Opera at the end of 1792. After emigrating to England, Fontaine returned to Paris to design trompe-l'œil architectural sets with his friend. Percier traversed the Revolutionary turbulence by way of a seemingly endless series of administrative initiatives; a member of the Commission générale des arts, he contributed to the refurbishment of the assembly hall of the Convention overseen by Guy de Gisors in the Tuileries Palace, providing, on Jacques Louis David's recommendation, models for its furniture, which was executed by Georges Jacob [FIG. 11.1].

In this new society erected over the ruins of the old, museums such as the Musée des monuments français collected the wreckage of vandalism, while those with newly minted fortunes sacrificed to the gods of fashion.[3] Under the Directory, Percier was a prominent designer who, from theatrical scenery to bedchamber by way of furniture, bronzes, and goldsmith work, exceeded the bounds of architecture per se to create interiors whose archaeological cast accorded with the aspirations of a society steeped in antiquity, frivolous as well as heroic. Accordingly, he worked for real estate speculators and provisioners to the armed forces, in-

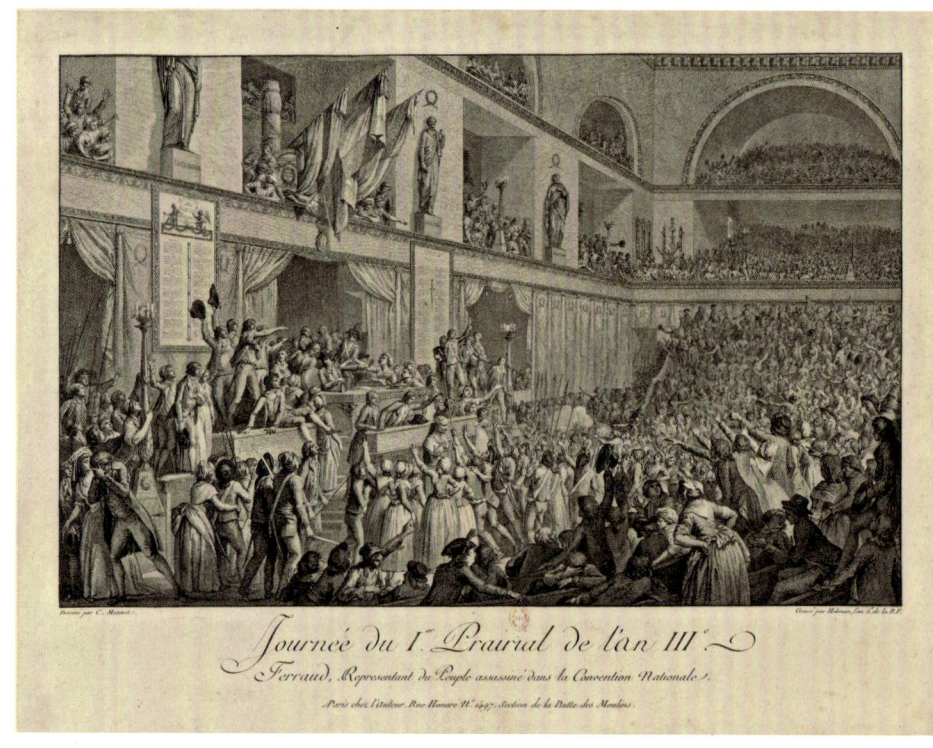

FIG 11.1. Isidore Stanislas Helman after Jean Duplessis-Bertaux. *View of the Hall of the National Convention at the Tuileries during the assassination of Deputy Jean Bertrand Féraud, 1 prairial year III* [May 20, 1795], 1796. Etching. Bibliothèque nationale de France, Paris, Département des Estampes et de la Photographie, De Vinck, 6574.

cluding Benoît Gaudin, the Ouvrard brothers, and François Bernard Chauvelin (see chapter 8), who had settled into the townhouses of the former aristocracy or erected pretty houses of their own in the new quarters of the city. It was these private commissions that brought Percier close to the seat of power.

In tandem with recommendations provided by the painters Jean-Baptiste Isabey and David, Percier's interiors functioned like visiting cards for the wife of General Bonaparte. The acquisition of Malmaison in April 1799 prompted her to undertake work there. "She wants to make this property into a place of delights.…We are going to propose new construction projects," Fontaine noted after a visit to the property with Percier and David shortly after the coup d'état of 18 brumaire.[4] It was Josephine who introduced the architects to the first consul, who was more interested in plans for the embellishment of Paris than in improvements to his own residence. Percier was self-effacing before the man in power, but Fontaine asserted himself as both a man of the arts and an audacious courtier. Before long the two architects were crossing the Seine in Bonaparte's carriage, together with David and Joachim Murat, on their way to the Louvre to examine the antiquities that had been brought back from Italy, which the consul wanted to exhibit under the dome of the Invalides. Percier and Fontaine's plans for this monument were approved in January 1800, whereupon work commenced immediately.[5] Regarding Malmaison, Josephine accepted the ambitious project proposed by the two men, who were appointed architects of the residence, but she preferred to begin with some "small changes necessary for the occupancy of the first consul, who seems predisposed to come here to take the air every ten days."[6] With this enterprise, Percier initiated his practice of retiring to his study to prepare the designs while Fontaine supervised the work. This division of responsibilities placed Fontaine on the front lines, which fostered his contact with Bonaparte.

The day after the attempted assassination of the first consul on rue Saint-Nicaise, Étienne Chérubin Lecomte, the architect responsible for the Tuileries, was discharged, and on 28 nivôse year IX (January 18, 1801), Fontaine was appointed architect to the government. His advocacy for Percier and the intervention of Josephine resulted in a joint appointment of the two partners and the provision of lodgings for them in the Louvre.[7] They then began restoring the apartments in the château de Saint-Cloud, in addition to their Parisian projects. This activity prompted Percier and Fontaine to devote themselves exclusively to government commissions and "to get rid of all our other projects as they are completed,"[8] among them the townhouse of General Moreau on rue d'Anjou[9] and the incredible Platinum Room of the Casa Real del Labrador at Aranjuez for King Carlos IV of Spain.[10] At the same time, Louis Martin Berthault asked Percier to decorate the Parisian townhouse of the banker Jacques Rose Récamier, but apparently he did nothing but provide the designs, leaving supervision of the work to others.[11]

However, in December 1804, responsibility for organizing the services of the emperor's household was assigned to one man; Fontaine alone was named "architect of the Tuileries Palace, the Louvre and its dependencies, the imperial manufactories for tapestries at the Gobelins and for carpets at the Savonnerie, the marble storehouses, and all Crown buildings situated within the walls of the city of Paris."[12] Percier was sidelined for reasons of administrative propriety, but despite the prospect of individual glory, Fontaine did not abandon his partner: "I alone will be visible, but we will continue to share the pains and profits as in the past."[13]

Percier's official career ended shortly after Napoleon's coronation. Designing its ephemeral decorations had excited his imagination, and the results were surprising, notably the painted portal in front of the cathedral, with its medieval allusions, and the immense tribune pavilion facing the Champ-de-Mars, unfortunately damaged by wet snow [FIG. 11.2; SEE ALSO FIG. 13.7]. The architect, whose fame both in France and abroad was growing apace, effectively hid from the emperor behind Fontaine. Percier's close ties to Fontaine led him to devote himself exclusively—apart from his publications and his teaching responsibilities—to official projects, as evidenced by a shift in focus in the later parts of the *Recueil de décorations intérieures*.[14] However, his name appeared one last time in the papers of Louis-Philippe, comte de Ségur, Grand Master of Ceremonies, in connection with the *Description des cérémonies et des fêtes*, the lavish volume commemorating Napoleon's coronation (February 1805).[15] In 1811 his peers acknowledged his work by making him a member of the Institut, shortly before awarding the same honor to Fontaine.

MALMAISON: THE APPLE OF DISCORD

Percier and Fontaine elaborated an ambitious project to transform the small château de Malmaison, whose greatest asset, in their eyes, was the extent of

FIG 11.2. Charles Percier and Pierre Fontaine. *Sketch for the tribune built for the distribution of the eagle standards on the occasion of Napoleon's Coronation,* 1804. Pencil, pen, and watercolor on paper. Private collection, Paris. Cat. 136.

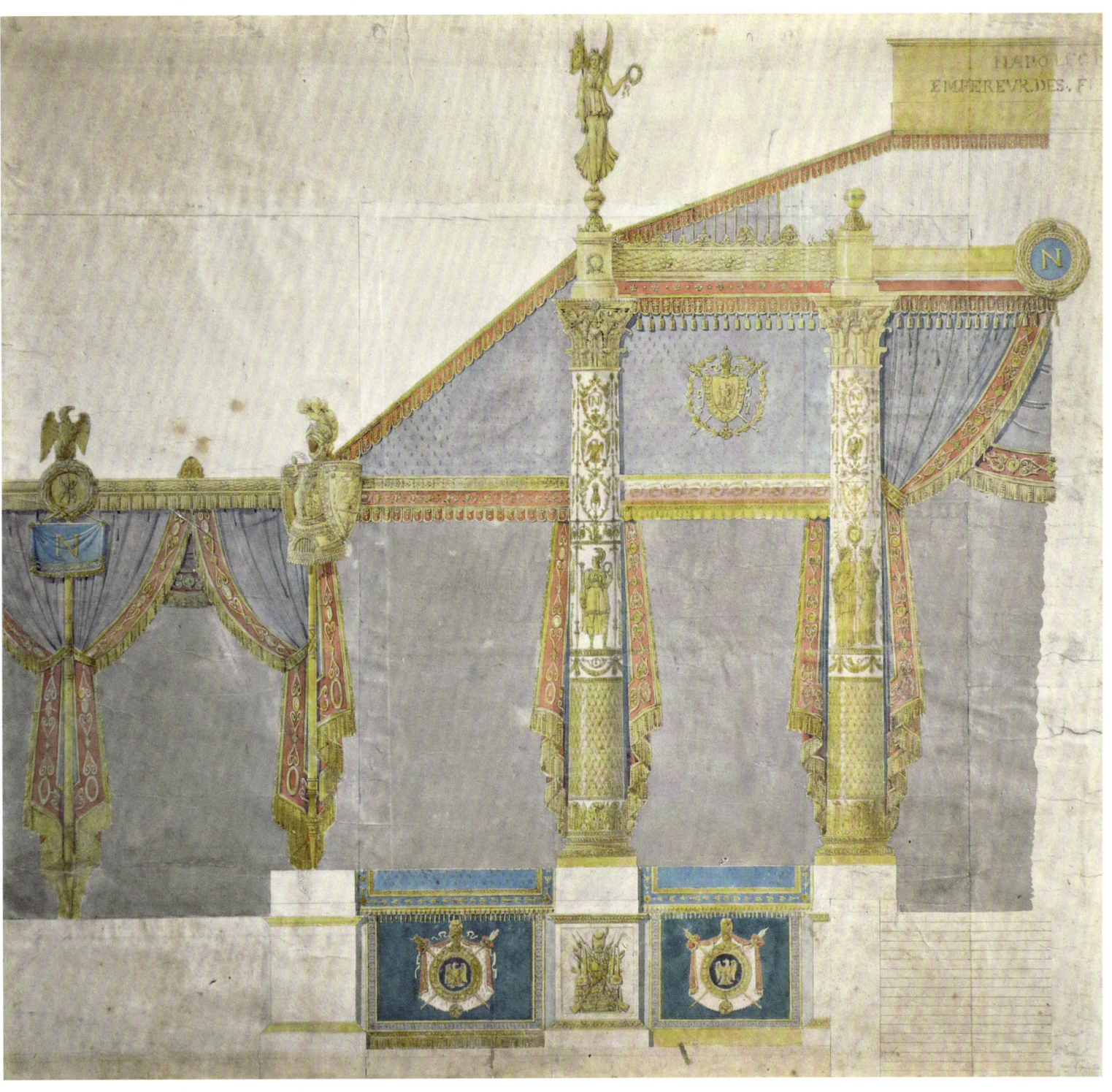

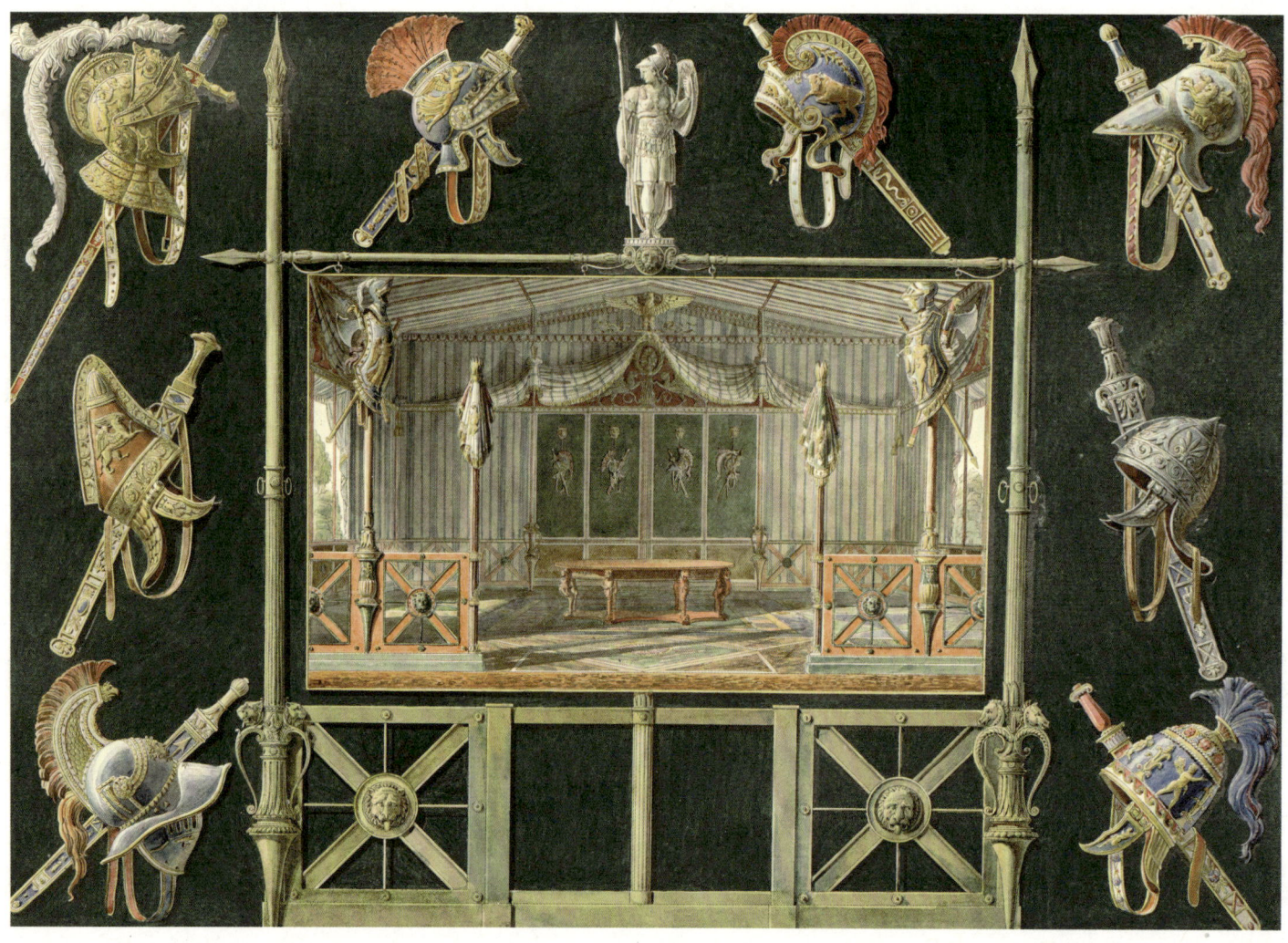

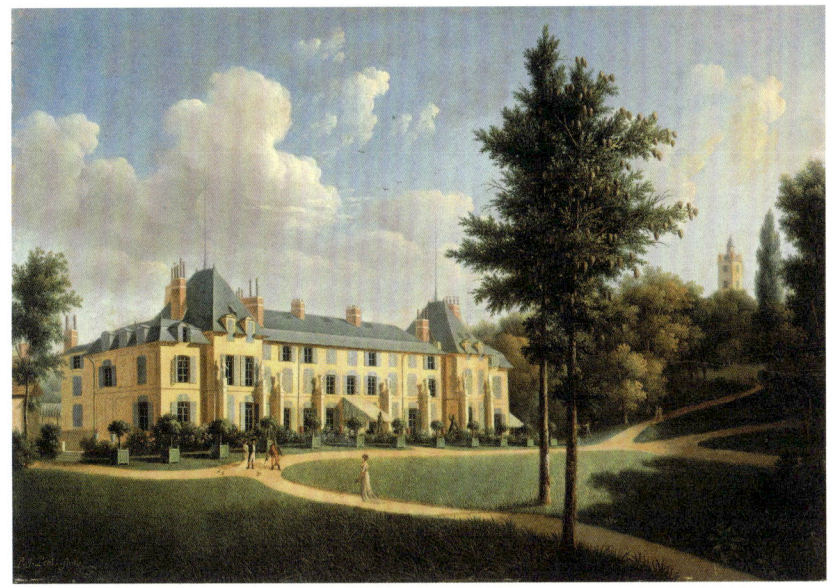

▲ **FIG 11.3.** Pierre Joseph Petit. *View of Château de Malmaison* (façade facing the park), ca. 1802–7. Oil on wood. Châteaux de Malmaison et Bois-Préau, MM.40.47.591.

▼ **FIG 11.4.** Charles Percier and Pierre Fontaine. *View of the Council Room at Malmaison*. Watercolor by Benjamin Gotthold comte de Schlick. From Percier and Fontaine, *Recueil de décorations intérieures* (Paris: Authors and Pierre Didot l'aîné, ca. 1825), pl. 42. Les Arts Décoratifs, Paris, 33761.36.

its park on the banks of the Seine. They envisioned reshaping its building, which they deemed "frightful,"[16] into a residence fitted out with porticos for the reception of family and friends, connected, like its modern pendant for the ministers, to the main house by galleries.

The idea seduced Josephine, who asserted herself as the real project manager. But the Bonaparte couple's country house became a rural annex of the Consular government, which made a thorough restoration of the old residence obligatory [FIG. 11.3]. Work progressed rapidly between the first consul's visits every ten days, that is, at the end of each *decade*.[17] Structural reinforcements offered occasions to recast the interiors in the latest style. The central vestibule was transformed into an atrium with stucco columns; then the northern wing was reworked into a music room opening onto a gallery with mahogany paneling executed by Jacob frères and decorative paintings by Simon Frédéric Mœnch. When Bonaparte visited, he made his reactions known; he disliked the wooden structures for the porter and the guard house as well as the stucco columns, and he found that "the vestibule shaped like a tent" resembled an "animal house at a fair."[18] As for the gallery, "the first consul, who, it is said, is not easy to please, seemed satisfied."[19] At this same moment, refurbishment of the billiards room and the dining room was nearing completion. Later Bonaparte "ordered that we decorate the salon, that we make a Council Room in the place of the ground-floor bedroom and a library."[20] According to Fontaine, the salon, completed in ten days, did not produce the desired effect, but the Council Room, finished just as quickly, resembled—thanks to the skill of the *tapissier*—set designs by Percier and Fontaine [FIG. 11.4]. The library, produced by combining three rooms, exemplifies the ease with which the architects managed to exploit the constraints of the existing building [FIG. 11.5]; they concealed the chimney flue rising from the basement kitchens with a projecting pavilion lined with mirrors, supported by mahogany columns at the corners. Multiplied (there are four), these projections support the two transverse arches of the flattened vault, which was decorated in ten days after designs by Percier; Minerva and Apollo dominate the

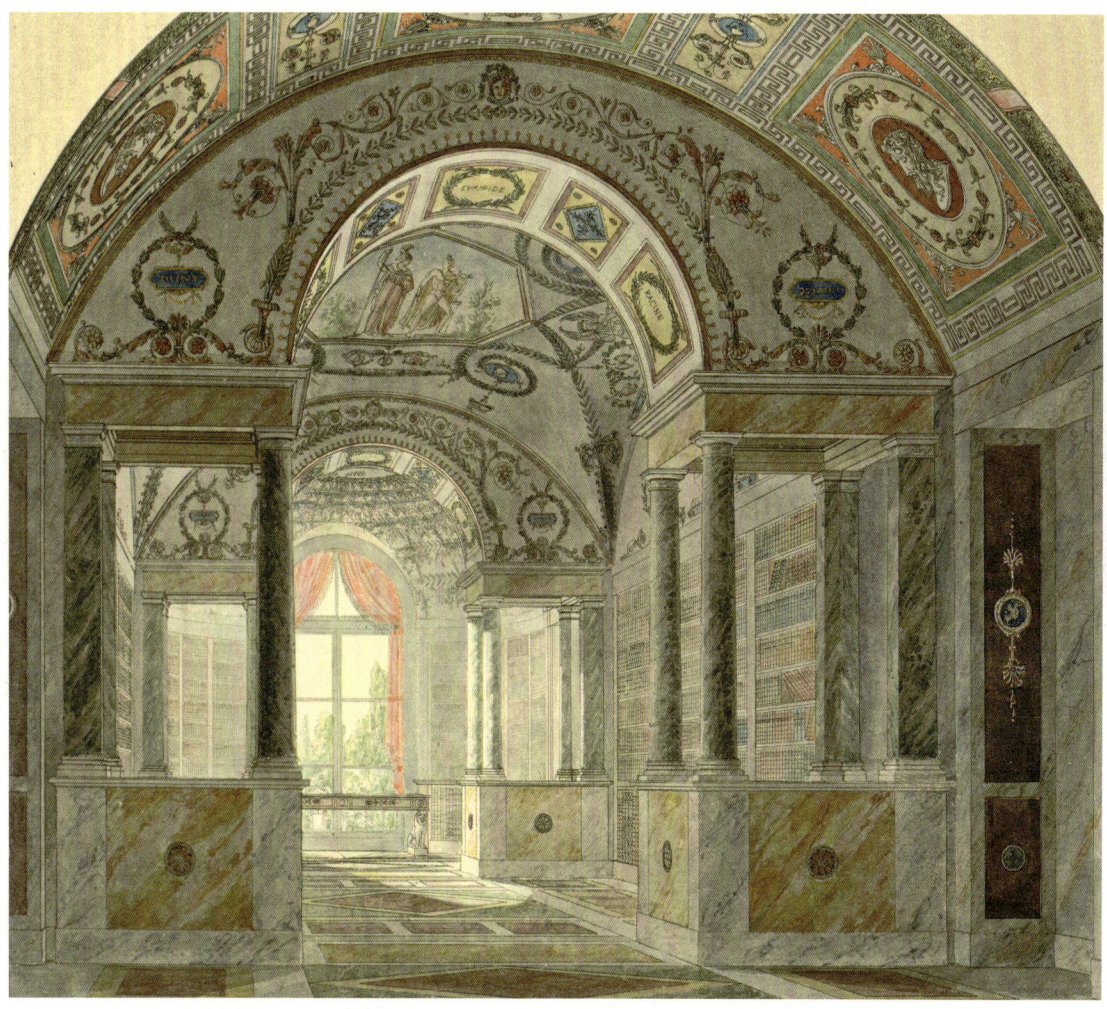

iconography, while portraits of ancient and modern authors adorn the scrolling rinceaux inspired by Raphael's Loggia in the Vatican, the whole being complemented by trompe-l'œil bowers at either end. This interior transformation appealed to Napoleon, who "continues to give orders for the refurbishment of this residence. We are spending lots of money without honor and almost without results."[21]

In his diary, Fontaine recorded only his exchanges with the first consul. What, then, was the part played by Josephine, who initiated these "small changes"? It seems likely that her recommendations greatly influenced the final results, but the extreme rapidity of the work left no room for dithering. If Bonaparte wanted stables, Josephine seized upon this as an occasion to introduce changes in the landscaping; "she wants us to turn our attention to the gardens, to waterworks, to hothouses, finally to everything that might help to make this residence, which she regards as her particular property, more agreeable. Her projects are always changing. She is forever desirous of something and whenever we convince her to adopt a plan, a steady advance toward the goal, she becomes inclined to wait."[22] Misunderstandings between the patron and her architects were exacerbated by their plan to create allées in the park, for T-square and compass had no place in this realm. Like many eighteenth-century women, Josephine had succumbed to Anglomania and was smitten with botany; accordingly, she never for a moment entertained the possibility of subjecting the park at Malmaison to the laws of symmetry. What she required was the picturesque: "To speak of order and regularity in the matter of gardens was to commit blasphemy."[23]

To satisfy her desires, Jean Marie Morel was engaged. This landscape gardener, author of *Théorie des jardins* (1776), condemned Percier and Fontaine's work: "Nothing that had been done seemed tolerable to him.... Everywhere he saw insults against nature and war against art."[24] The two partners experienced this judgment as a direct affront. It occasioned the irrevocable abandonment of their grand project for Malmaison and their fall from grace in the eyes of Josephine. So much effort expended to achieve what was, after eight years, merely an "old château in new clothing, composed of riches piled up in disorderly fashion and surrounded by all the idiocies of gardening in the English manner."[25]

This offense, coupled with Bonaparte's inability to understand how so much money could have been spent, prompted Percier and Fontaine to submit their resignation. They received no response but were liberated from the torments of Malmaison, or more precisely from the caprices of Josephine, whose "desires are orders that one cannot refuse, and whose outcome even the subtlest would be unable to foresee."[26] They were immediately replaced by the architect Jean-Baptiste Lepère.

This episode left indelible traces on the relations between Josephine and the two partners. At Saint-Cloud, the task of renovating the château fell to Percier and Fontaine, thanks to the protection of Charles Victoire Emmanuel, General Leclerc, the husband of Pauline Bonaparte. The remodeling of Josephine's apartments was in line with her taste and exceptionally refined, incorporating furniture that Percier designed for the project in 1802 (SEE FIG. 8A.1).[27] Upon becoming empress, Josephine asked that her apartments in the Tuileries also be trans-

▸ **FIG 11.5.** Benjamin Gotthold, comte de Schlick, after Charles Percier and Pierre Fontaine. *View of the Library at Malmaison*, ca. 1825. Watercolor over pl. 42 from Percier and Fontaine, *Recueil de décorations intérieures* (Paris: Authors and Pierre Didot l'aîné, 1801–12). Les Arts Décoratifs, Paris, 33761.42. Cat. 56.

formed,[28] and in March 1808 Fontaine found himself wrestling with her demands. The funds allocated by Napoleon were meant to pay for "magnificence, gold, Gobelins tapestries, large paintings....The empress, who attended the presentation of our work, who now had less confidence in our taste than in the past, and who regarded us as outmoded, insisted, entreated us, wanted everything in her rooms to be gray and gold with pretty arabesques and ancient stuccos."[29] But these requests, which were repeated constantly, "in whatever manner we executed them increased the total expenditure still further."[30] The equation was insoluble, and the results could not satisfy the expectations of the empress, who, on viewing them, found nothing to like.[31] Imbuing his account of this episode with resignation and disappointment, Fontaine focused not on the empress's whims but rather on the specific ideas that Percier and Fontaine were unable to execute because of insufficient funds. They were prisoners of an imperial couple whose female sovereign, contrary to ancien-régime custom, had no architect attached to her household.

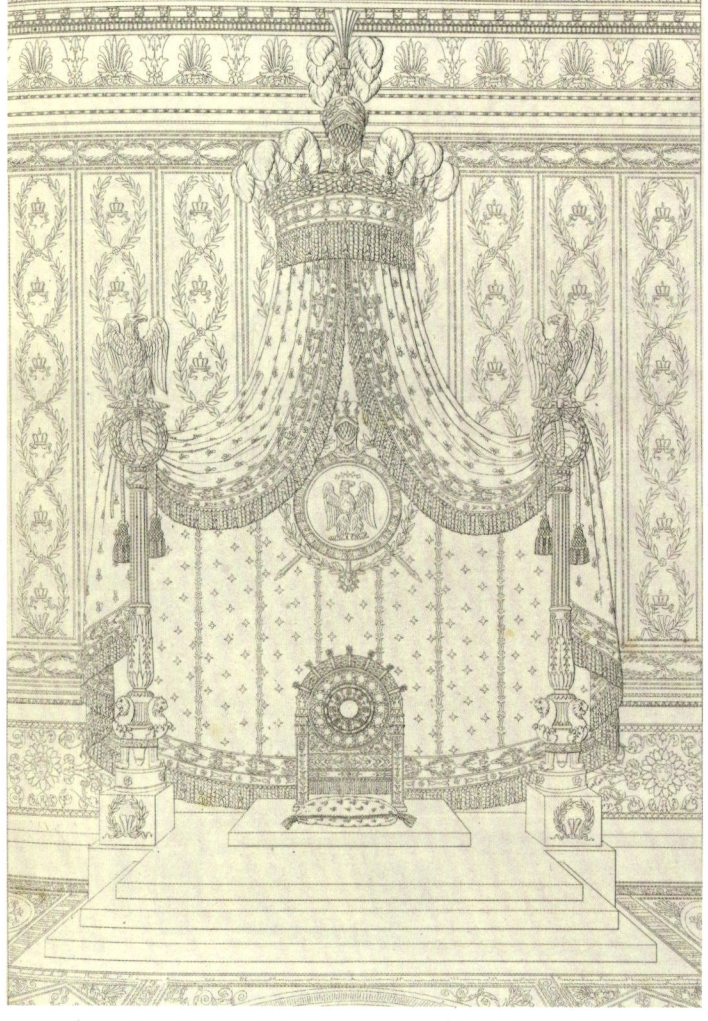

CHARLES PERCIER: WORKING IN THE SHADOWS

After the proclamation of the French Empire in May 1804, the ephemeral constructions for the coronation at Notre-Dame de Paris and for the Distribution of the Eagle Standards on the Champ-de-Mars were the last official realizations of Percier, who, together with Fontaine, had become designer of the nascent imperial pageantry and crafted the models of Napoleonic splendor. With extreme attention to detail, Percier designed the throne to be used at Notre-Dame, although "nothing precise had been provided us in this regard. The emperor, uncertain about what should be done, had not communicated his thoughts. The coats of arms...had not been definitively decided upon; finally, the grand master of ceremonies, even the Council of State, consulted about the matter, offered nothing more than vague indications."[32] Executed under the control

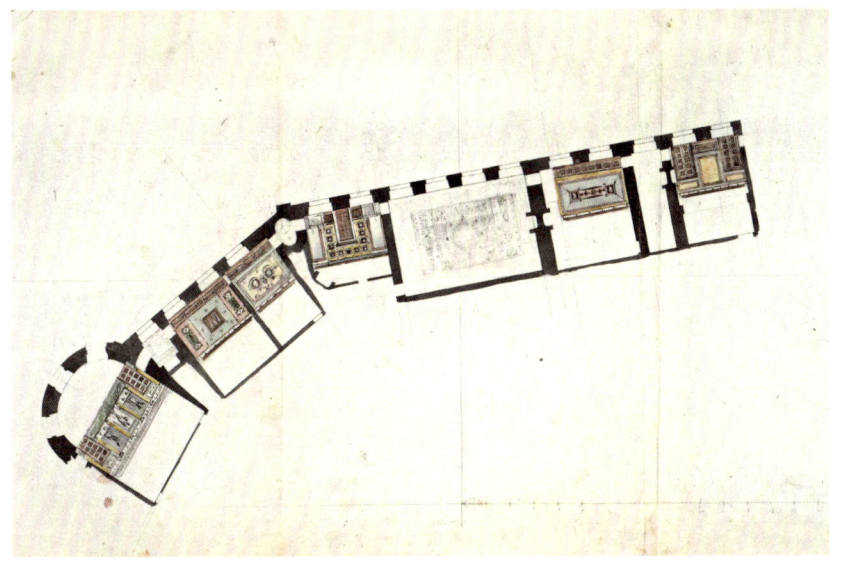

▼ **FIG 11.6.** Charles Percier and Pierre Fontaine. The Throne at the Palais des Tuileries. From Percier and Fontaine, *Recueil de décorations intérieures* (Paris: Authors and Pierre Didot l'aîné, 1801–12), pl. 48.

▲ **FIG 11.7.** Charles Percier. Project for redecorating the "Petits Appartements" of the empress at Fontainebleau, ca. 1807. Pen and watercolor on paper. Château de Fontainebleau, archives.

of the Mobilier impérial, the armchair and dais in Figure 11.6 became the archetype for the throne rooms in the palaces of Saint-Cloud and the Tuileries.

However, Percier's dismissal upon the establishment of the Emperor's Household did not mean that he no longer worked on the projects henceforth officially entrusted solely to Fontaine, who became "First Architect to His Majesty the Emperor and King" on April 25, 1813. His bureau, which consisted of an inspector, a verifier, a draftsman, two administrators, and an office boy, could not have done without Percier. Fontaine was now granted access to the palace interiors and was afforded proximity to the sovereign, whose "marks [of recognition] indicated confidence… [and] obliged me to remain almost continuously at his service [and] close to his person."[33] These direct relations entailed a correspondingly significant recommitment, in the way of endurance and the occasional audacity, in order to satisfy an emperor who was impatient but also indecisive and torn between dreams of grandeur and his commitment to thrift. Thus the project for a summer villa for Napoleon in the gardens of Monceau, the former extravagance of Louis-Philippe d'Orléans, duc de Chartres, was dismissed from consideration almost as soon as it had been initiated.[34] In addition to work on buildings in Paris, Fontaine was also given special briefs, such as furnishing the palace of Fontainebleau "as if by enchantment" prior to the arrival of Pope Pius VII in November 1804, or overseeing work undertaken at the various imperial residences, from Rambouillet to Compiègne by way of Fontainebleau, Versailles, and Trianon.

Such oversight responsibilities, which Fontaine found unappealing but which were consistent with his friendly ties to his colleagues, reveal how the bureau operated. Refurbishment of the small apartments at Fontainebleau for the empress began as early as 1805, but no real progress was made until 1807, when the plan of Napoleon's interior apartment was changed.[35] The architect Antoine Leroy, then charged with implementing work "ordered in accordance with designs made by me," wrote Fontaine, was in fact working from designs by Percier, who had proposed painted decorations, ultimately unrealized, along the lines of the designs inspired by antique models at Malmaison [FIG. 11.7].[36] Moreover, Percier continued to produce designs for furnishings for the imperial palaces, notably the furniture executed in 1809 by Jacob-Desmalter for the malachite artifacts presented by Czar Nicholas I and the beds for Napoleon and Josephine in the Tuileries [FIG. 11.8].[37]

But Percier's most important activity concerned the embellishment of Paris, from connecting the palace of the Louvre with the Tuileries to projects for the Chaillot hill. The installation of the first consul in the Tuileries in 1800 and the further expansion of the museum into the Louvre brought increased attention to the problem of unifying this gigantic urban ensemble, which was completely enclosed to the south, along the Seine, by the Grand Gallery. Its central expanse, however, was occupied by disordered buildings, without a delimiting structure to the east or the alignment that the laws of perspective rendered indispensable. Napoleon regarded this linkage as a challenge for his reign. Orders to address the challenge were given to Fontaine as early as January 1805, and successive projects were assessed until 1814, either in private meetings or by specially established commissions—and even by the public, for models were exhibited, which prompted the formulation of competing proposals by architects such as François Joseph Bélanger. The lack of a fully articulated program did not preclude the allocation of funds in budgets prepared by the Bâtiments. Fontaine tirelessly prepared new design solutions with Percier, but Napoleon was unable to commit to any of them. The architects had a taste of victory, however, with construction of the arc du Carrousel between 1806 and 1810. This small, exceptionally elegant monument was a first step toward achieving the desired relationship between the two palaces. The new wing between the pavillon de Marsan and the pavillon de Rohan, along the rue de Rivoli, was a second step.

Similar indecision prevented advances on the project that Fontaine succeeded in convincing the emperor to adopt. The construction of a palace in the Perrache district of Lyon was abandoned in favor of a new building, just as ambitious, on the Chaillot Hill opposite the École militaire.[38] This palace of the "king of Rome," envisioned (like the project for Malmaison) as a combination of architecture and gardens, would serve to anchor the imperial dynasty in the capital. Despite the commencement of terracing work and the preparation of a considerable number of designs, in which Fontaine as well as Percier worked out many stylistic variations on the palace, Napoleon backed away from the extent of his own ambition and, in

FIG 11.8. Charles Percier and Pierre Fontaine. Bookcase with a malachite tabletop presented by Czar Alexander I, 1809. Made by François Honoré Georges Jacob-Desmalter. Ebony, gilt bronze, two-way mirror, Siberian malachite. Grand Trianon, châteaux de Versailles et de Trianon, T 176 C.

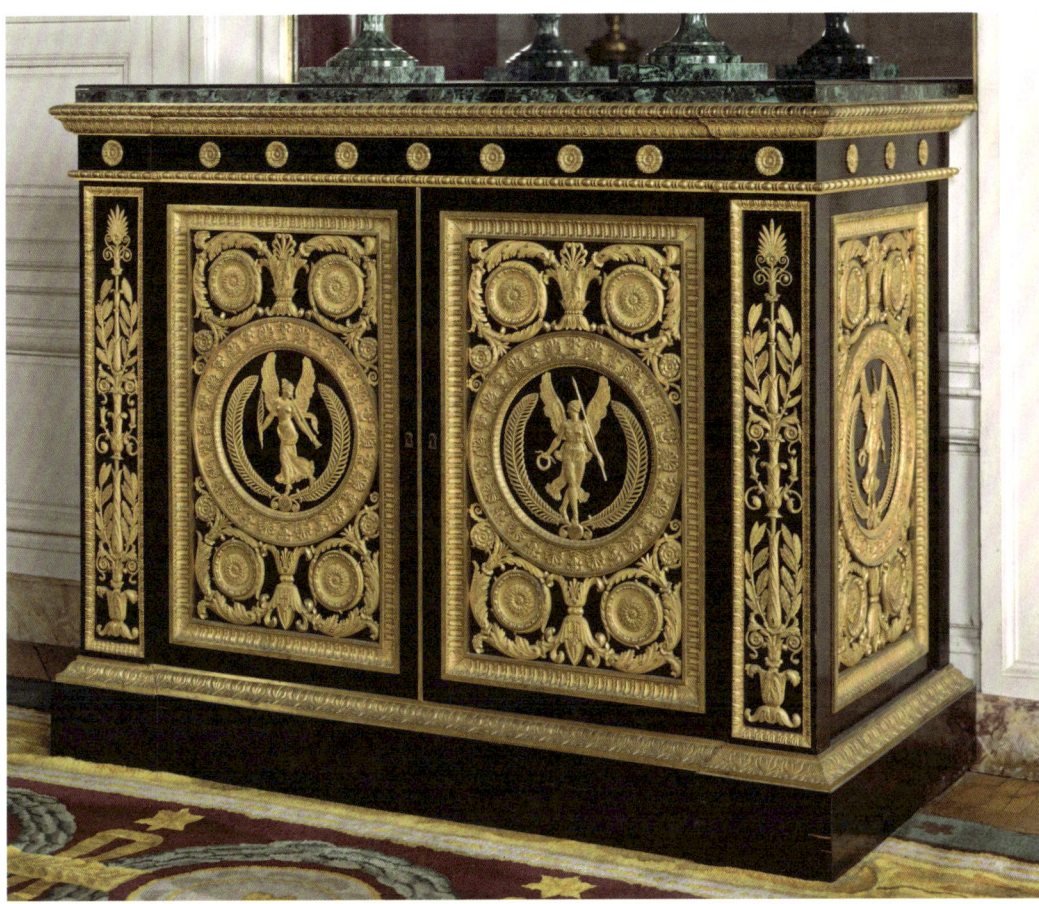

the face of military reversals, abandoned the gigantism of this dream palace in favor of a "small retreat, a Sans-Souci, a villa like those of Italy."[39] Although working in Fontaine's shadow, Percier continued to feed Napoleon's fantasies.

The troubled period in the course of which Percier began his architectural career offered him few occasions to translate his thoughts into stone. Instead of masonry it was plaster, stucco, wood, and even canvas that became his materials of predilection in the service of interior decoration and the decorative arts. The encounter with Josephine proved decisive, but the promise of the grand design for Malmaison remained unfulfilled. Apart from the arc du Carrousel, his grandest realizations were ephemeral. His partnership with Fontaine provided him with a welcome bulwark from which to confront the circles of power. His displacement to the sidelines in 1804—more formal than real—afforded him a distance that he found congenial. He experienced the advances and postponements of imperial projects through Fontaine. Enthusiasm and successes, like disappointments and chicanery, were shared in secret within the office. Josephine, oddly faithful to the Pompeian grace of the Directory, abandoned Percier and tolerated Fontaine. If "the antique succeeded in becoming the most fecund source for the genius of fashion."[40] Percier was apparently insensitive to the inflection introduced into the art of the court around 1806, despite his having been instrumental in its elaboration. On the other hand, the emperor, timorous and indecisive when it came to architecture, deferred fully to "his" architect—who had a double in the person of Percier—when it came to giving his reign and his dynasty the stuff of grandeur. These fifteen dazzling years, dominated by paper pipedreams, left Percier without sufficient strength to confront the Restoration. ●

1 "Percier demeurait au Louvre, il vivait en philosophe, dans une grande simplicité; les murs de son cabinet étaient de plâtre gris, bien unis, sans aucune tenture, ils étaient recouverts entièrement de précieux dessins d'anciens maîtres et d'esquisses peintes de ses amis, qui étaient alors, les David, les Gérard, les Giraudet [sic], etc. Percier avait toujours une longue redingote grise, boutonnée jusqu'en haut, il était d'une santé délicate et ne sortait presque jamais; c'était Fontaine qui faisait les affaires du dehors….Il était bon et d'une politesse exquise, mais très avare de son temps, il redoutait beaucoup qu'on vienne le distraire." Théophile Vauchelet, "Mémoires de Théophile Vauchelet (1802–1873)," 58, manuscript held by the painter's descendants. This memoir, which continues into the July Monarchy, includes accounts of events predating the Revolution based on the memories of various family members. The cited passage is one such secondhand account.

2 Pierre François Léonard Fontaine, *Journal (1799–1853)*, ed. Marguerite David-Roy (Paris: École nationale supérieure des beaux-arts / Institut français d'architecture / Société de l'histoire de l'art français, 1987), 1:525 (entry dated May 1816).

3 Madame de Genlis, entering these fashionable interiors, exclaimed: "To show that the new ideas precluded neither *grace* nor *gallantry*, men and women tied back the curtains of their beds with the attributes of love and transformed their night tables into *altars*. We saw conspirators who had been drenched in blood sleep on sumptuous beds decorated with cameos representing Venus and the Graces! And we saw suspended above their heads not the sword of Damocles but a little arrow and wreaths of roses!" ("Pour montrer que les nouvelles idées n'excluaient ni la *grâce* ni la *galanterie*, les hommes et les femmes rattachaient les rideaux de leurs lits avec les attributs de l'amour, et transformaient en *autels* leurs tables de nuit. On vit des conspirateurs qui s'étaient baignés dans le sang, se coucher sur des lits somptueux, ornés de camées représentant Vénus et les Grâces! et l'on voyait suspendue sur leurs têtes, non l'épée de Damoclés, mais une flèche légère ou des couronnes de roses!" Félicité de Genlis, *Mémoires inédits sur le dix-huitième siècle et la Révolution française, depuis 1756 jusqu'à nos jours* (Paris: L'advocat, 1825–28), 5:105–6.

4 Fontaine, *Journal*, 1:7 (entry dated 9 frimaire year VIII).

5 Ibid., 1:7–8.

6 "petites dispositions nécessaires à l'habitation du Premier Consul qui paraît disposé à venir y prendre l'air tous les dix jours." Ibid., 1:10.

7 Ibid., 1:17, and Ferdinand Boyer, "L'installation du premier Consul aux Tuileries et la disgrâce de l'architecte Lecomte (1800–1801)," *Bulletin de la Société de l'histoire de l'art français* (1941–44): 142–84 (on the double appointment and the allocation of lodgings, see 179–80).

8 "nous défaire de tous nos autres travaux à mesure qu'ils se termineront." Fontaine, *Journal*, 1:51 (June 15, 1802).

9 *Le Mobilier du général Moreau, un ameublement à la mode en 1802*, exh. cat. (Paris: Réunion des musées nationaux, 1992).

10 Chantal Gastinel-Coural, "Le cabinet de platine de la Casa del Labrador à Aranjuez. Documents inédits," *Bulletin de la société de l'histoire de l'art français* (1994): 181–205.

11 Maria-Teresa Carraciolo, "Juliette Récamier et Charles Percier: nouveaux dessins pour l'hôtel de la rue du Mont-Blanc," *Les Cahiers d'histoire de l'art*,

no. 12 (2014): 61–70.

12 "architecte du palais des Tuileries, du Louvre et dépendances, des manufactures impériales des tapisseries des Gobelins et des tapis de la Savonnerie, des magasins des marbres et de tous les bâtiments de la Couronne situés dans l'enceinte de la ville de Paris."

13 "Je paraîtrai donc seul mais nous continuerons à exercer en communauté de peines et de profits comme par le passé." Fontaine, *Journal*, 1:99 (December 29, 1804).

14 Jean-Philippe Garric, "Le *Recueil de décorations* de Charles Percier et Pierre Fontaine," in *Ornements XVe–XIXe siècles: Chefs-d'œuvre de la bibliothèque de l'INHA*, ed. Lucie Fréjou and Michaël Decrossas (Paris: INHA/Mare et Martin, 2014), 302–11.

15 Fontaine, *Journal*, 1:105 (February 29, 1805).

16 "affreuse." Ibid., 1:9 (9 frimaire year VIII).

17 A *decade* was the period of ten days that replaced the week of seven days during the Revolution.

18 "le vestibule en forme de tente"; "une loge d'animaux à montrer à la foire." Ibid., 1:31 (20 fructidor year IX).

19 "le Premier Consul, qui, dit-on, n'est pas facile à contenter, en a paru satisfait." Ibid., 1:11 (1 germinal year VIII).

20 "ordonne que l'on décore le salon, que l'on fasse une salle de Conseil en place de la chamber à coucher au rez-de-chaussée et une bibliothèque." Ibid., 1:13 (20 messidor year VIII).

21 "continue à donner des ordres pour la mise en état de cette habitation. Nous dépensons beaucoup d'argent sans honneur et presque sans fruit." Ibid., 1:13 (1 fructidor year VIII).

22 "elle veut qu'on s'occupe des jardins, des eaux, des serres chaudes, enfin de ce qui peut contribuer à rendre plus agréable cette habitation qu'elle regarde comme sa propriété particulière. Ses projets varient sans cesse. Elle désire toujours et nous ne pouvons parvenir à lui faire adopter un plan, une marche réglée pour arriver au but qu'elle se propose d'atteindre." Ibid., 1:14 (5 vendémiaire year IX).

23 "Parler d'ordonnance, de régularité en fait de jardins c'était blasphémer." Ibid., 1:31 (20 fructidor year IX).

24 "Rien de ce qui était fait ne lui avait paru supportable….Partout il avait vu injure à la nature et guerre à l'art." Ibid., 1:20 (25 pluviôse year IX), 31 (20 fructidor year IX); *Joséphine: la passion des fleurs et des oiseaux*, exh. cat. (Paris: Artlys, 2014), 19.

25 "vieux château rhabillé de neuf, composé de richesses entassées sans ordre, et entouré de toutes les niaiseries du jardinage à l'anglaise." Fontaine, *Journal*, 1:231 (March 19, 1809). Fontaine wrote in a similar vein about Fontainebleau: "Hurtault undertook wild expenditures in English-style gardening at Fontainebleau" ("Hurtault a entrepris à Fontainebleau des dépenses folles en jardinages à l'anglaise"). Fontaine, *Journal*, 1:373 (October 1, 1813).

26 "les désirs sont des ordres auxquels on ne peut résister, et dont le plus habile ne saurait prévoir le terme." Ibid., 1:52 (July 1, 1802).

27 Jean-Pierre Samoyault, "Furniture and Objects Designed by Percier for the Palace of Saint-Cloud," *Burlington Magazine* 868 (July 1975): 457–65.

28 Fontaine, *Journal*, 1:149 (March 6, 1807).

29 "de la magnificence, de l'or, des tapisseries des Gobelins, et de grands tableaux…. L'impératrice qui assiste à la présentation de notre travail, qui n'a plus dans notre goût la confiance qu'elle avait autrefois, et qui nous regarde comme des gens passés de mode, insiste, nous recommande, veut que chez elle tout soit gris et or avec de jolies arabesques et des stucs antiques." Ibid., 1:204 (March 23, 1808).

30 "de quelque manière que nous les exécutions augmentent encore la somme des dépenses." Ibid., 1:212 (July 19, 1808).

31 Ibid., 1:214 (August 16, 1808), 218 (December 4, 1808).

32 "rien de précis ne nous avait été ordonné à cet égard. L'empereur, incertain sur ce qui devait être fait n'avait pas communiqué sa pensée. Les armoiries…n'étaient pas une chose définitivement arrêtée, enfin le grand maître des cérémonies, le Conseil d'État même, consultés sur ce sujet, n'avaient donné que des instructions assez vagues." Ibid., 1:87 (October 12, 1804).

33 "les marques signalées de confiance…m'obligent à résider comme étant presque continuellement de service auprès de sa personne." Ibid., 1:175 (November 1, 1807).

34 Ibid., 1:194–98 (February 28, 1808).

35 Ibid., 1:175–76 (November 1, 1807); Vincent Cochet, "Les petits appartements de l'empereur et de l'impératrice," in *Fontainebleau, 'La vraie demeure des rois,'* ed. Vincent Droguet et al. (Paris: Swan, 2015), 268–345.

36 Ibid., 1:187, and Vincent Cochet, "Le salon jaune de Joséphine. La sauvegarde d'un décor déraciné," *Revue du Louvre et des musées de France*, no. 5 (2014): 66–77.

37 Pierre Arizzoli-Clémentel and Jean-Pierre Samoyault, *Le Mobilier de Versailles. Chefs-d'œuvre du XIXe siècle* (Dijon: Faton, 2009), 58–67, 70–77, 174–80.

38 Fontaine, *Journal*, 1:262 (June 17, 1810).

39 "petite maison de convalescent, un Sans-Souci, une villa comme celles d'Italie," Ibid., 1:353 (March 3, 1813).

40 "l'antique parvint à être la source la plus féconde pour le génie de la mode." Charles Percier and Pierre Fontaine, *Recueil de décorations intérieures* (Paris: Authors and Pierre Didot l'aîné, 1801–12), 7.

JOSEPHINE'S BOUDOIR, CHÂTEAU DE SAINT-CLOUD

JEAN-FRANÇOIS BELHOSTE

Shortly after the coup d'état of 18 brumaire (November 9, 1799), Napoleon Bonaparte launched an ambitious program to renovate some of the former royal residences, with an eye to both habitation and the exercise of power. It was in this context that, in January 1801, Percier and Fontaine were named architects to the government, appointments that effectively obliged them to bring their work on private projects to an end. One of the most important of these, their commission for the townhouse of General Moreau, was completed in June 1802 (SEE CATS. 66–69). The first project to which they turned their attention in their new capacity was at the Tuileries, where renovations had been under way since 1800.[1] Then, in September 1801, work began on the château de Saint-Cloud, which, to the detriment of Malmaison, was to become the principal summer residence of the consular couple. "The renovations at the château de Saint-Cloud are complete. The apartments are furnished. We oversaw the selection, fabrication, and placement of every piece," wrote Fontaine on August 12, 1802.

At Saint-Cloud, as at the Tuileries, some of the new furnishings came from the Garde-Meuble and the palaces of the Republic. But a few pieces, notably those for Josephine's apartments, were newly commissioned, which meant that Percier could continue the work he had begun for private clients in the fashionable townhouses of the Chaussée d'Antin. Located in the left wing of the château, Josephine's Saint-Cloud apartment consisted of (in sequence) a dining room, two salons, a music room, a bedchamber, a bathroom, and a boudoir, all of which disappeared in the fire at the château in 1870. Situated at the corner of the wing, the boudoir had two windows overlooking the *cour d'honneur* (forecourt), as well as a fireplace and four large mirrors. Here Percier created a decor in the most fashionable taste; such, at any rate, is suggested by two inventories dating from 1805 and 1807, the particulars of which seem to correspond in large part to the 1802 redecoration campaign.[2] The room had white taffeta curtains and cerise draperies, and the whole featured gold motifs and was dominated by a red, white, and gold color scheme that was echoed in the upholstery. The boudoir contained several precious objects: two large

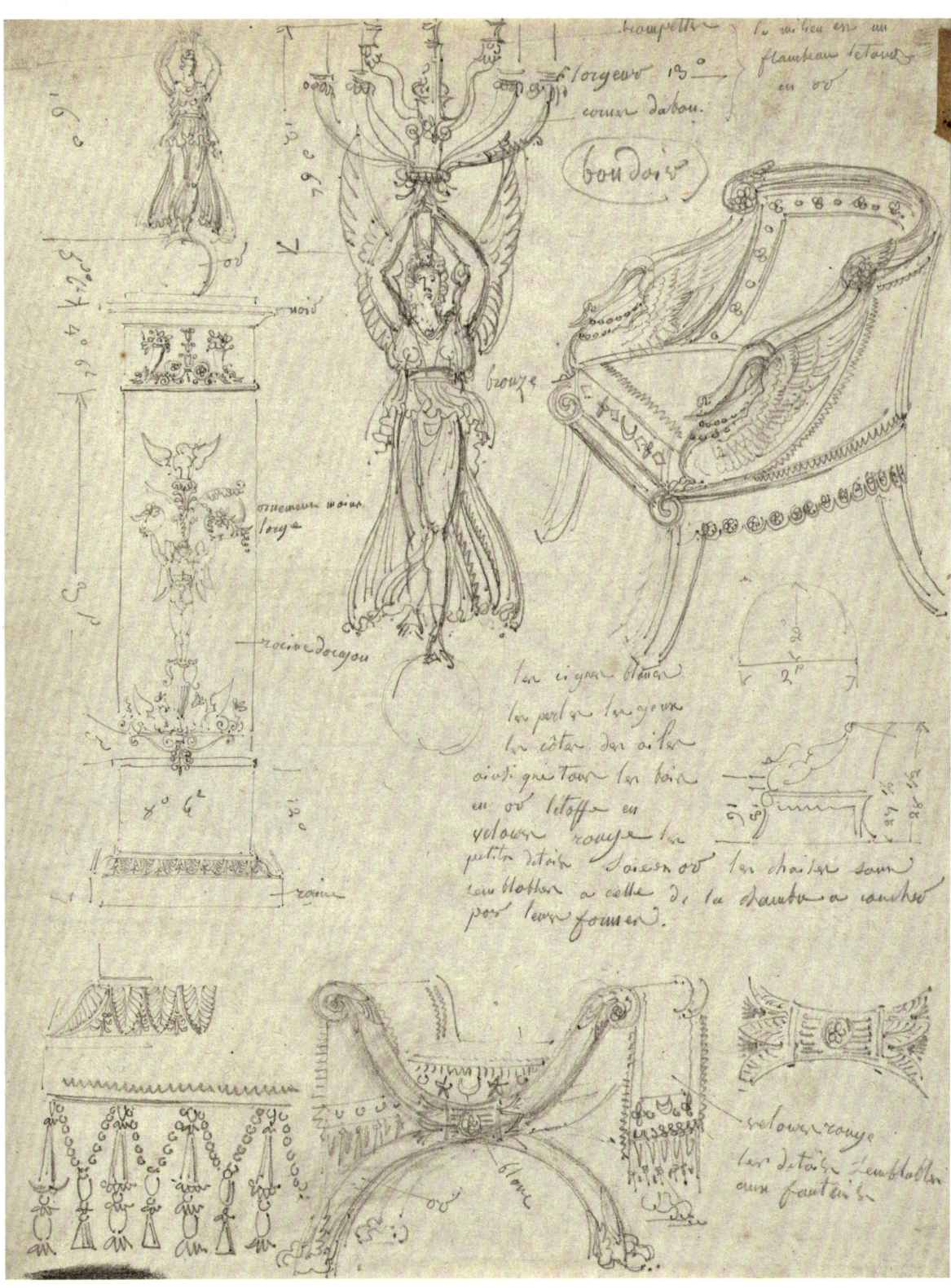

▶ **FIG 11A.1.** Workshop of Charles Percier. Study sketches. Detail of fol. 20. Graphite on paper. The Metropolitan Museum of Art, New York, The Elisha Whittelsey Collection, The Elisha Whittelsey Fund, 1963, 63.535, 1–128. Cat. 59.

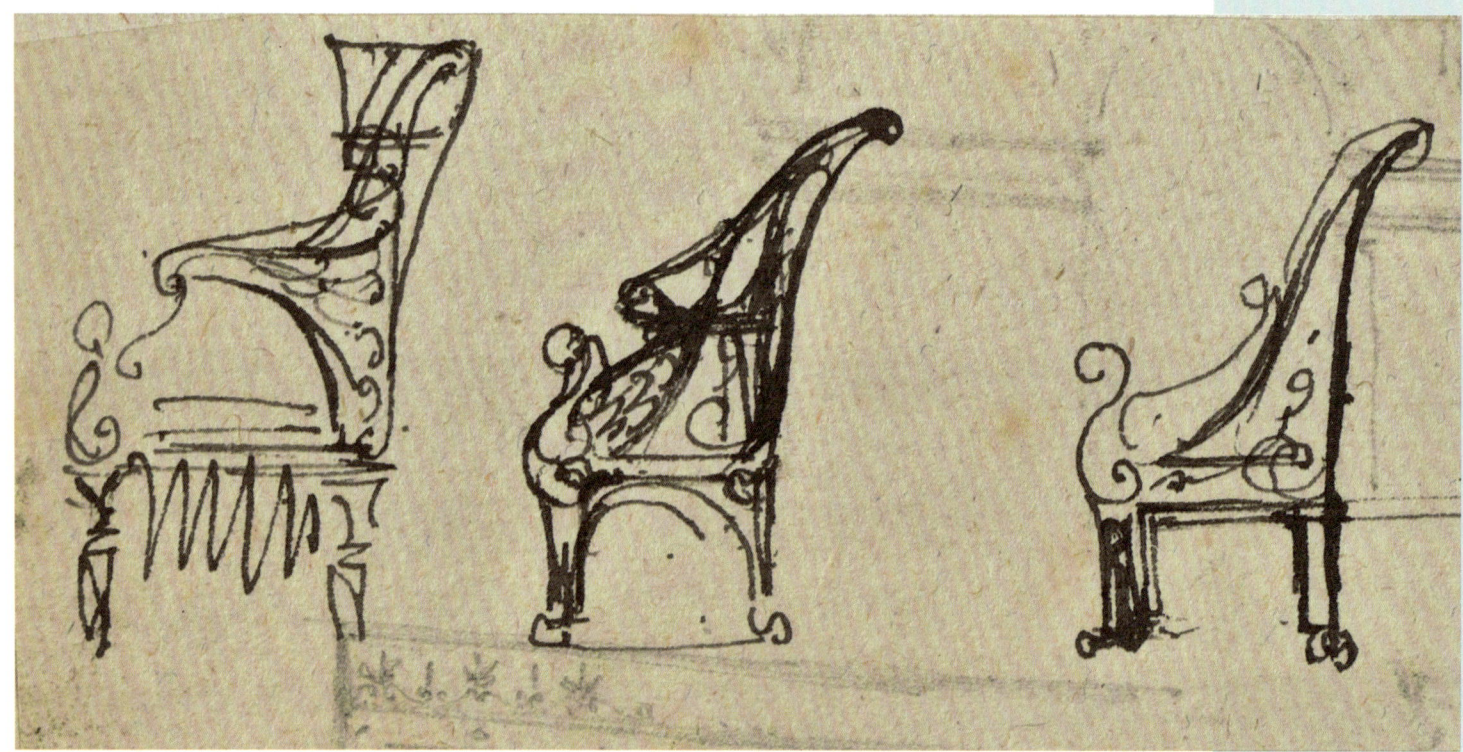

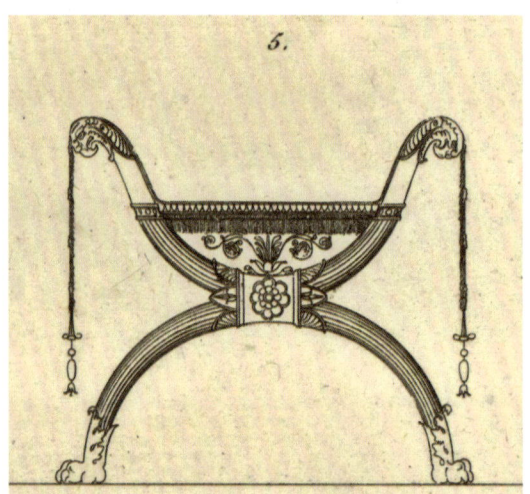

porcelain Sèvres Medici vases, some goblets made of "oriental agate," a Lepaute clock supported by two chimeras, and even two stuffed fish. The furniture included a hexagonal tea table made of yew wood with legs incorporating winged female figures made of gilt-bronze, as well as two console tables, now at Fontainebleau, made of the same wood with mirrored tops and Egyptian figures. These tables were probably acquired from the merchant Martin Eloy Lignereux,

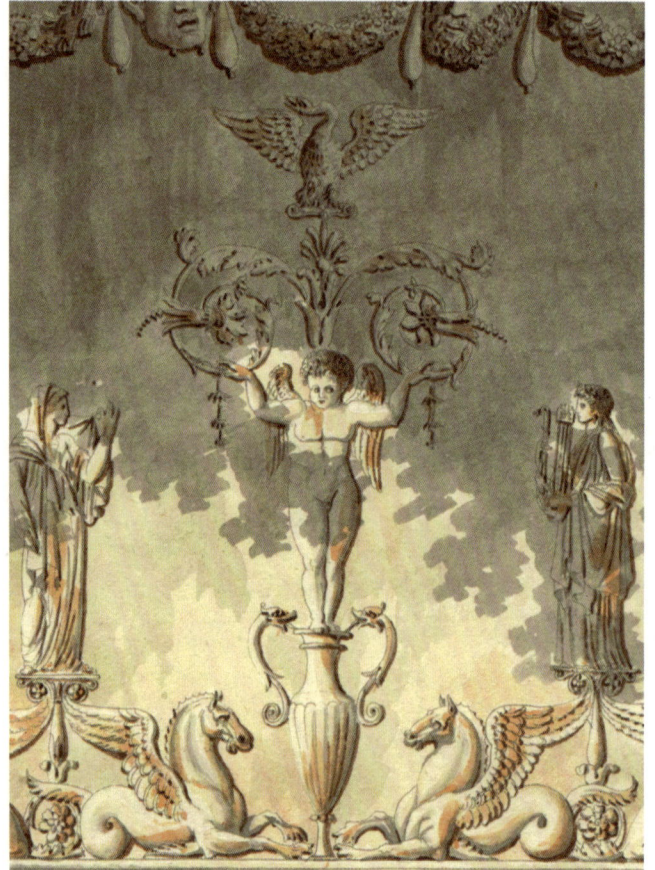

> **FIG 11A.2.** Workshop of Percier. Three ink studies of an armchair. Detail of fol. 24, MMA Scrapbook.

◂◂ **FIG 11A.3.** Charles Percier. X-frame stool. Detail of pl. 39 from Percier and Fontaine, *Recueil de décorations intérieures* (Paris: Authors and Pierre Didot l'aîné, 1801–12), pl. 39.

◂ **FIG 11A.4.** Charles Percier. Detail of frontispiece for Book 5 of Percier and Fontaine, *Palais, maisons et autres édifices modernes dessinés à Rome* (Paris: Authors, 1798), pl. 26.

▸ **FIG 11A.5.** Jacob-Desmalter, after Charles Percier. Gondola chair from the Salon d'Argent of the Elysée Palace, 1805. Carved and silver-gilt wood. Collection du Mobilier national, GME 18590. Cat. 82.

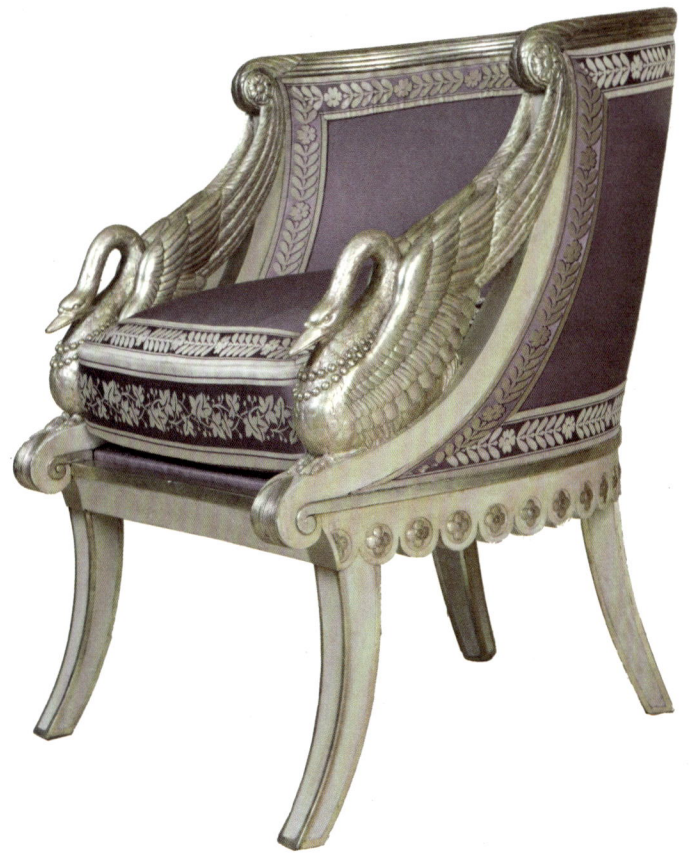

Jacob-Desmalter's father-in-law.[3] The design of the seating was quite innovative. The ensemble consisted of a canapé, four armchairs, four chairs, and four X-shaped stools, or *curule tabourets*, all made of gilded beech wood and upholstered in cerise silk velvet. Apart from the *curule tabourets*, all of these pieces had armrests that incorporated striking carved swans that were painted white.

The new "gondola" form of the armchairs, with deep convex backs derived from the ancient klismos chair, would subsequently enjoy a degree of success in boudoirs and petits salons. The workshop scrapbook in the Metropolitan Museum of Art includes an interesting sketch for it from Percier's hand [FIG. 11A.1]. It is annotated with precious instructions as to textiles, colors, and shapes: "The white swans, the beading, the eyes, the sides of the wings as well as all of the wood in gold; the fabric in red velvet, the small details [in] silk and gold. The chairs are like those in the bedchamber as regards their form."[4] A few dimensions are indicated on the sketch situated immediately below in the scrapbook, notably the total height: 28½ *pouces*, or roughly 29½ inches. Three drawings on another page explore design possibilities for the swan armrests [FIG. 11A.2]. The gondola armchairs now at Malmaison are not stamped, but their attribution to the Jacob firm is relatively secure, for a sheet with a drawing of one such chair—as well as frontal and profile views of the canapé—was once among the firm's holdings.[5] The scrapbook sheet with the gondola armchair design also has, at the bottom, small drawings of the *curule tabourets* for this boudoir (SEE FIG. 11A.1).

Equally novel for the period, inspired by ancient and Renaissance curule chairs but incorporating armrests and lion-claw feet, this design is illustrated in plate 39 of the *Recueil de décorations intérieures* [FIG. 11A.3]. The drawings in the Metropolitan Museum focus on the red silk fabric with (according to the 1807 inventory) "crescents, stars, fringes, crests, and fringe pendants of white silk, cerise, and gold."[6] The same page also has drawings for a third design for the boudoir, a lighting unit consisting of a winged Victory supporting a seven-branch candelabrum and resting on a tall pedestal made of yew wood (SEE FIG. 11A.1).[7] Variants of this Victory figure—clearly of ancient inspiration—appear elsewhere in the *Recueil*, notably in engravings of the atelier of Isabey. The pedestal dimensions inscribed on this sheet correspond roughly to those recorded in the inventories; the gilded appliqués of swans and chimeras,[8] which were derived from one of the frontispieces in *Palais et Maisons de Rome* [FIG. 11A.4], are likewise consistent with the 1807 description, and the indication "noir" (black) beside the drawing also matches the color of the marble indicated in the inventory.[9] The gondola armchair design seems to have made quite an impression. It was repeated around 1805 for the boudoir of Princess Murat (Caroline Bonaparte) in the Elysée Palace, where four exemplars remain in the Silver Salon [FIG. 11A.5]. It was also reproduced, in simplified form, about 1803 in the *Collection de meubles et objets de goût*,[10] where it was called a desk chair (*fauteuil de bureau*), a designation then customarily applied to armchairs with convex backs.

The inventories of 1805 and 1807 also describe the furniture in Josephine's bedchamber. Beside the bed, described as "en chaire à prêcher" (in the form of a pulpit)—a designation that indicates the presence of a headboard, a footboard, and an elaborate canopy—was a mahogany "somno" (night table) in a new form, the base of which was, per the 1805 inventory, decorated with a sleeping dog, a feature that brings to mind the night table—pictured in plate 23 of the *Recueil* (SEE FIG. 8.4) and now at Fontainebleau—delivered to General Moreau by the Jacob firm at roughly the same time [FIG. 11A.6]. The workshop scrapbook contains a design for a similar night table corresponding to one that, according to the 1805 inventory, was then in the emperor's bedchamber (cat. 85),[11] but which may previously have been in that of Josephine. The same folio features on an adjacent sheet a drawing for a mahogany cheval mirror with an ebony frame resting on two lion heads, alongside which are notations regarding materials, colors, and dimensions (SEE FIG. 8B.5). Here again, correspondence with descriptions in the inventories makes it clear that this piece was intended for Josephine's bedchamber.

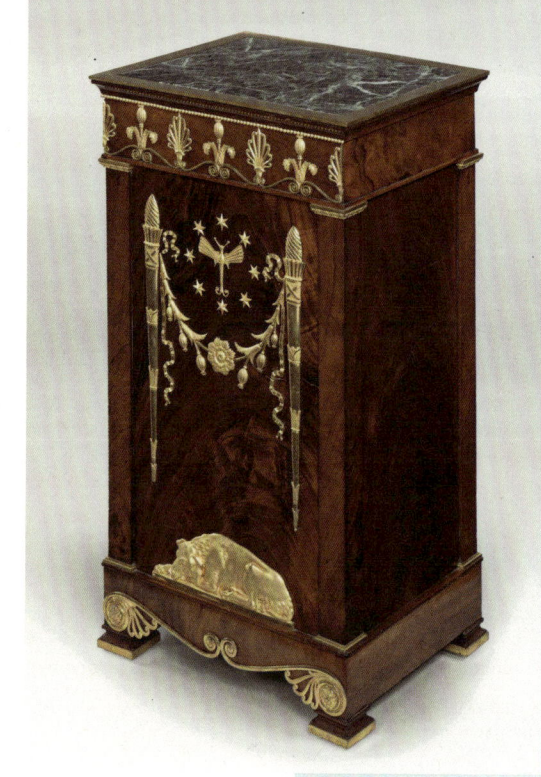

▲ **FIG 11A.6.** Jacob-Desmalter. Night table from the *petits appartements* of the empress at Fontainebleau, 1804. Mahogany, gilt bronze, green marble. Musée national du château de Fontainebleau, F.4070; GME6879. Cat. 84.

1 Jean-Pierre Samoyault. "L'Appartement de la générale Bonaparte, puis l'impératrice Joséphine aux Tuileries (1800–1807)," *Bulletin de la Société de l'Histoire de l'art français* (2000): 215–43.
2 ANF, O² 730. See Jean-Pierre Samoyault, "Furniture and Objects Designed by Percier for the Palace of Saint-Cloud," *Burlington Magazine*, no. 868 (July 1975): 457–65.
3 Jean-Pierre Samoyault, *Mobilier français Consulat et Empire* (Paris: Gourcuff-Gradenigo, 2009), 110.
4 "Les cygnes blancs, les perles, les yeux, les côtés des ailes ainsi que tous les bois en or; étoffe en velours rouge, les petits détails soie et or. Les chaises sont semblables à celles de la chambre à coucher par leur forme." Cf. the description in the inventory of 1807: "The armrests represent swans painted white, with a double circle of gilded beads...decorated and covered with cerise-colored silk, decorated with crescents, lozenges, small crests in white and gold silk" ("Les accotoirs représentent des cynges peints en blanc, avec un double tour de perles dorées...garni et couvert de soie couleur cerise, orné de croissants, losanges, petites crêtes en soie blanche et or").
5 Hector Lefuel, *François-Honoré-George Jacob-Desmalter, ébéniste de Napoléon Ier et de Louis XVIII* (Paris: Morancé, 1925), pl. VIII, the caption of which specifies "exécuté pour Saint-Cloud."
6 "avec croissants, étoiles, franges, crêtes et mollets"
7 Description in the 1805 inventory: "Two girandoles [with a] winged female figure in burnished bronze, holding in their hands a group of seven lights in mat gilt bronze, resting on a mat gilt-bronze globe and on [yew] wood pedestals 42 pouces high" ("Deux girandoles figure de femme ailée en bronze couleur antique, tenant en leurs mains un groupe de sept lumières en bronze doré or mat, posées sur un globe de bronze doré or mat et sur des piédestaux de 42 pouces de haut en bois de racine").
8 "Decorated with chimeras, swans, and palmettes of gilded copper" ("Orné de chimères, cygnes et palmettes en cuivre doré or moulu").
9 Additional exemplars of this pedestal design were also produced. One is now in the Mobilier National; it was *mis en consignation* by the Maison Thomire in 1807, when the latter firm succeeded that of Lignereux.
10 Pierre de La Mésangère, *Collection de meubles et objets de goût*, vol. 2. (Paris: Author, 1806–18), pl. 87.
11 Fol. 21 reproduced in Samoyault, "L'Appartement de la générale Bonaparte," 458.

CHAPTER 12

THE LOUVRE AND THE TUILERIES

A PALACE, A QUARTER, A MUSEUM

JEAN-PHILIPPE GARRIC

AT THE END OF THE 1820S, THE COMTE DE CLARAC, THEN CURATOR of antiquities at the Musée du Louvre, published several documents based on drawings by Percier and Fontaine that pertained to the restoration, completion, and linking of the Louvre and the Tuileries, notably a plan of the entire projected complex and two bird's-eye views [FIGS. 12.1, 12.2].[1] Formulated shortly before the fall of the Bourbons and the coronation of Louis-Philippe, who chose to reside at the Palais Royal, this design may be considered the final version of a project that had been studied countless times.[2] It is also among the most elaborate in terms of its program, incorporating an opera house (in the lower center) and a palatine chapel (left of the opera house, at the corner of the Louvre). In the plan, portions "extant in July 1828" are shown in black and those not yet built are shown in gray. After twenty-five years of reflection and many changes, as well as the completion of several constituent elements, the project remained largely unfinished. Almost as much remained unbuilt as had been erected since the Renaissance. Construction—begun during the Empire—of a wing connecting the Louvre and the Tuileries on the side facing the city, one that would be a symmetrical counterpart to the wing along the Seine dating from early in the seventeenth century, was only half complete.

Before we can grasp what was at stake in this exceptional undertaking, we must differentiate its three principal ambitions. The first and oldest one was to connect the Louvre with the Tuileries, thereby creating a palace of unmatched magnitude. As heir to the Enlightenment and the Revolution, Napoleon could not reside at Versailles, and he wanted to complete a project that a century of royal rule had been unable to bring to fruition. The Tuileries became the principal consular and then imperial residence, with all the practical and symbolic consequences that this entailed. The second ambition was to transform the surrounding city. Given their dimensions and location, connecting the Louvre with the Tuileries meant recasting the heart of Paris. From this perspective, the operation constitutes a link between the great urban embellishment projects of the eighteenth century and those of the Second Empire. Finally, the third ambition, doubtless the most contemporary one, was cultural in nature: to complete and restore buildings considered jewels of French architectural patrimony as well as to create, within the Louvre, the world's largest museum.

All of these intentions predated Bonaparte's earliest projects. Antoine François Peyre, Percier and Fontaine's teacher, had proposed an analogous synthetic undertaking on July 17, 1796, in a lecture at the Institut national, in which he made a case for completing the Louvre, linking it with the Tuileries, and establishing an expanded national museum and a dedicated school of the arts within the complex.[3] His plan combined patrimonial conservation with a political project for the arts, all within a framework of consolidating the young nation state:

The old Louvre, built to designs by Pierre Lescot and decorated with superb sculptures by Jean Goujon, is a magnificent masterpiece without example in Antiquity. The architecture of the Tuileries palace and of the gallery of the Museum, although less regular, nonetheless contains passages of rare beauty. This architecture, some of which was built during the shift from the Gothic genre to the taste for Greek architecture, has a special meaning for our nation. It falls to this nascent Republic, with its achievements in the sciences and the arts, to complete this superb edifice.[4]

12 LOUVRE AND TUILERIES

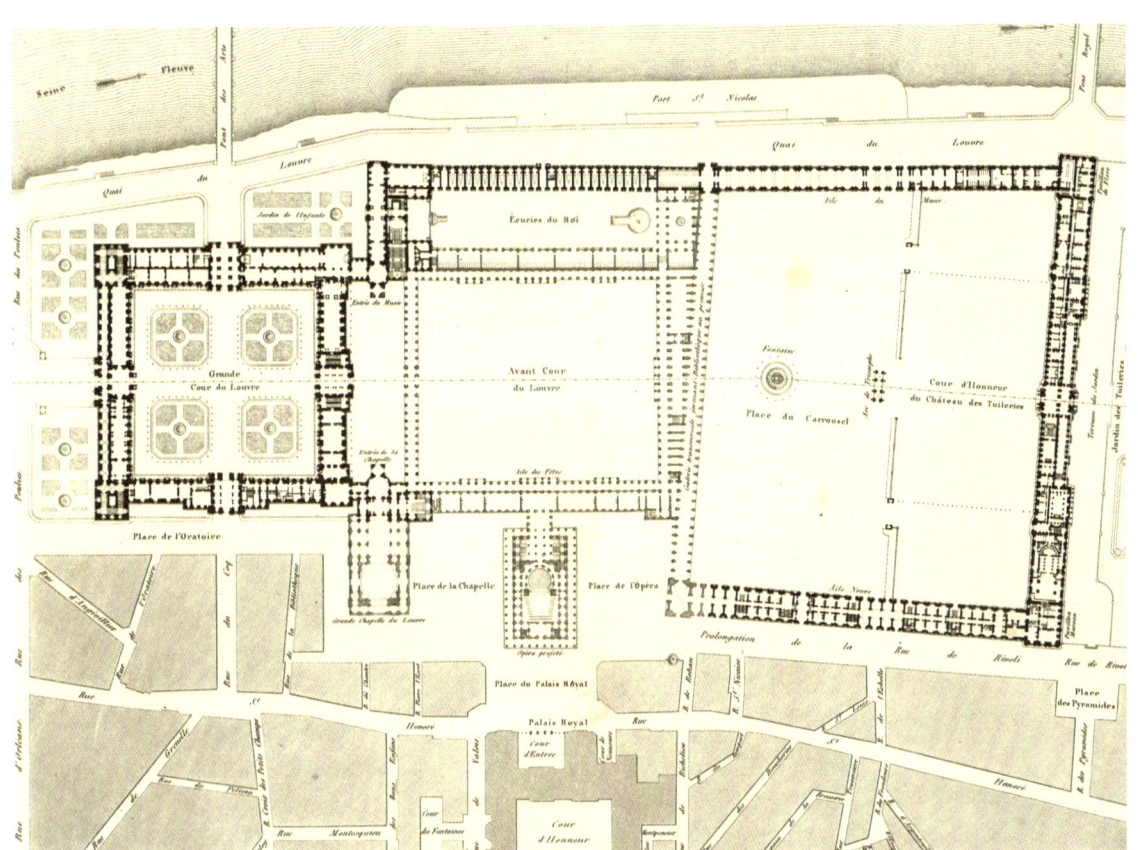

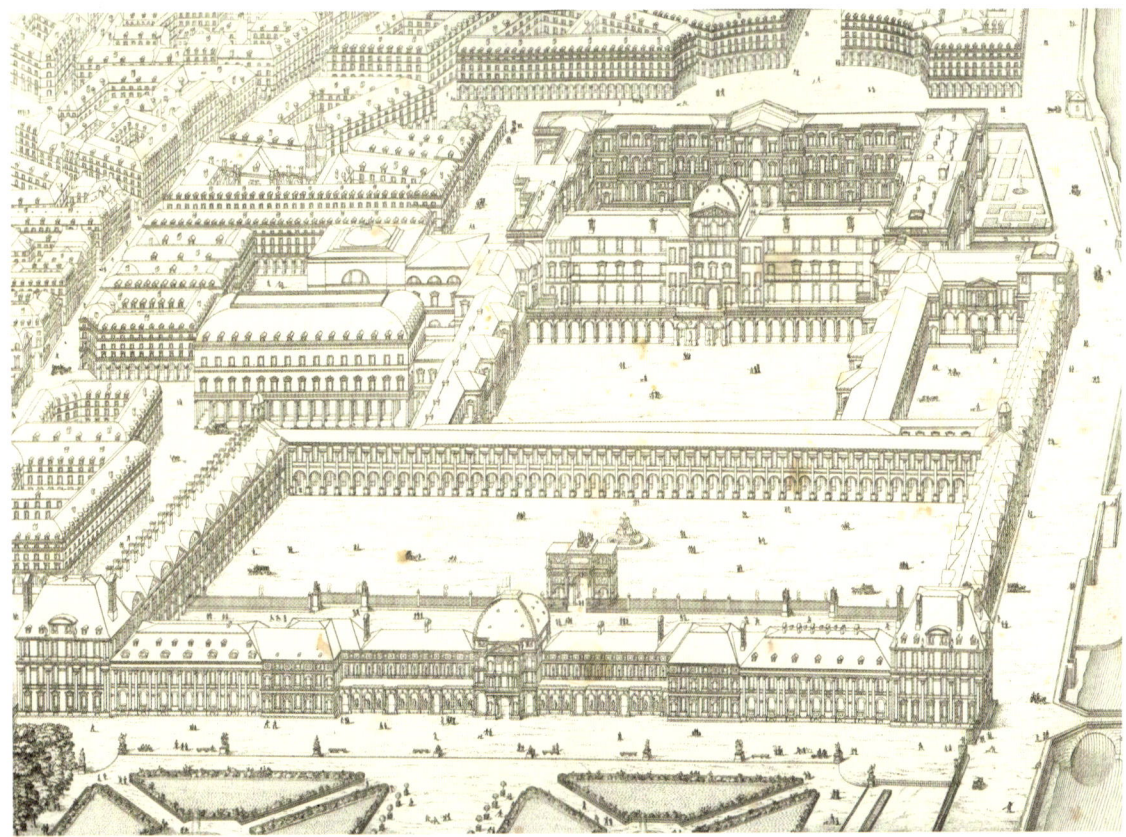

◀ **FIG 12.1.** Charles Percier and Pierre Fontaine. Plan for the projected linking of the Louvre and Tuileries in 1828. From Charles Othon Frédéric Jean-Baptiste de Clarac, *Musée de sculpture antique et moderne* (Paris: Texier, 1826–55), pl. 110.

▶ **FIG 12.2.** Charles Percier and Pierre Fontaine. Bird's-eye view of the projected linking of the Louvre and Tuileries in 1828. From Charles Othon Frédéric Jean-Baptiste de Clarac, *Musée de sculpture antique et moderne* (Paris: Texier, 1826–55), pl. 110bis. Cat. 115.

235

Thus Napoleon and his architects cast themselves as heirs to the Enlightenment, whose project they set out to realize, despite the fact that this was a program for an imperial palace, and thus a significant departure from the republican aims of Peyre.

MAGNIFYING THE HEART OF PARIS[5]

The "Turgot" map of Paris, which dates from the late 1730s, shows the Louvre and the Tuileries enmeshed in the urban fabric [FIG. 12.3]. Later structures encroached upon the Louvre Colonnade, and other buildings occupied even the Cour Carrée. Moreover, the aerial view leaves no doubt about the palace's incomplete state, clearly showing that the blocks on two sides of the courtyard were unroofed, their upper floors exposed to the elements. An entire neighborhood, with its own streets and two squares, filled the space between the Louvre and the Tuileries. As for the Tuileries gardens, they were bordered by the very irregular rear façades of the buildings fronting the rue Saint-Honoré. As late as 1800, this state of affairs remained largely unchanged.

The creation of the rue de Rivoli, extending from the place de la Concorde to the place du Palais royal, made it possible to separate the city from the palace and to give it a more majestic urban environment. The project approved on 1 floréal, year X (April 21, 1802), drew on earlier schemes. A street following the same route, from the place de la Concorde to the present rue du Louvre, had figured in the "plan des artistes" of 1793, which was a synthesis of earlier projects.

A more complete project, recently rediscovered and published here for the first time, immediately preceded that of Percier and Fontaine. This anonymous

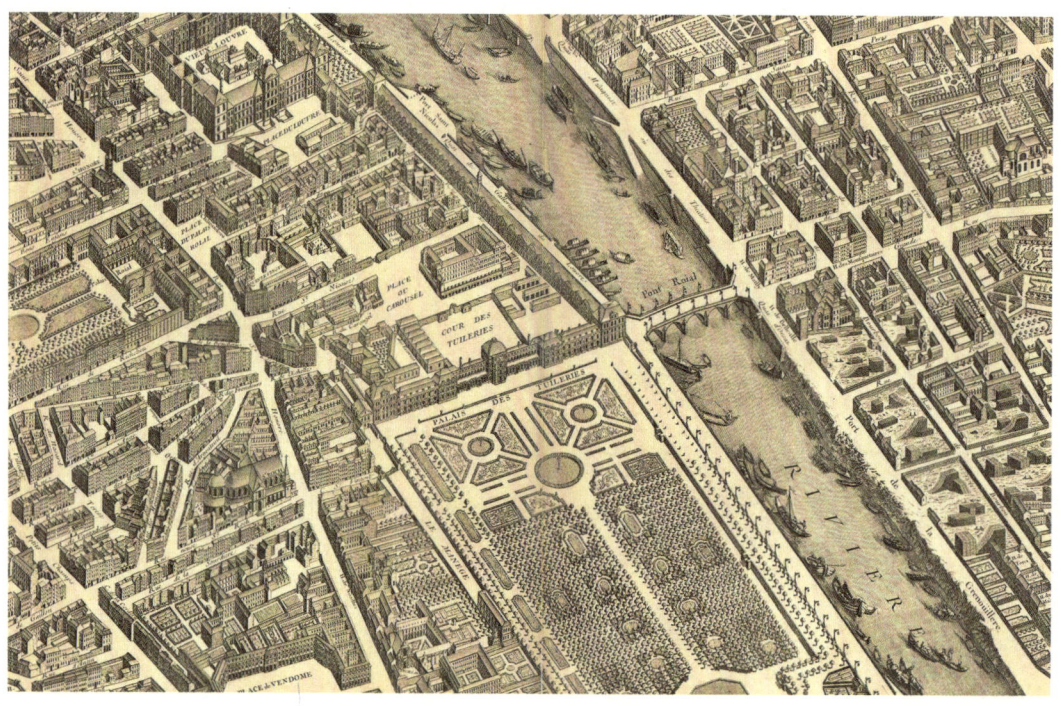

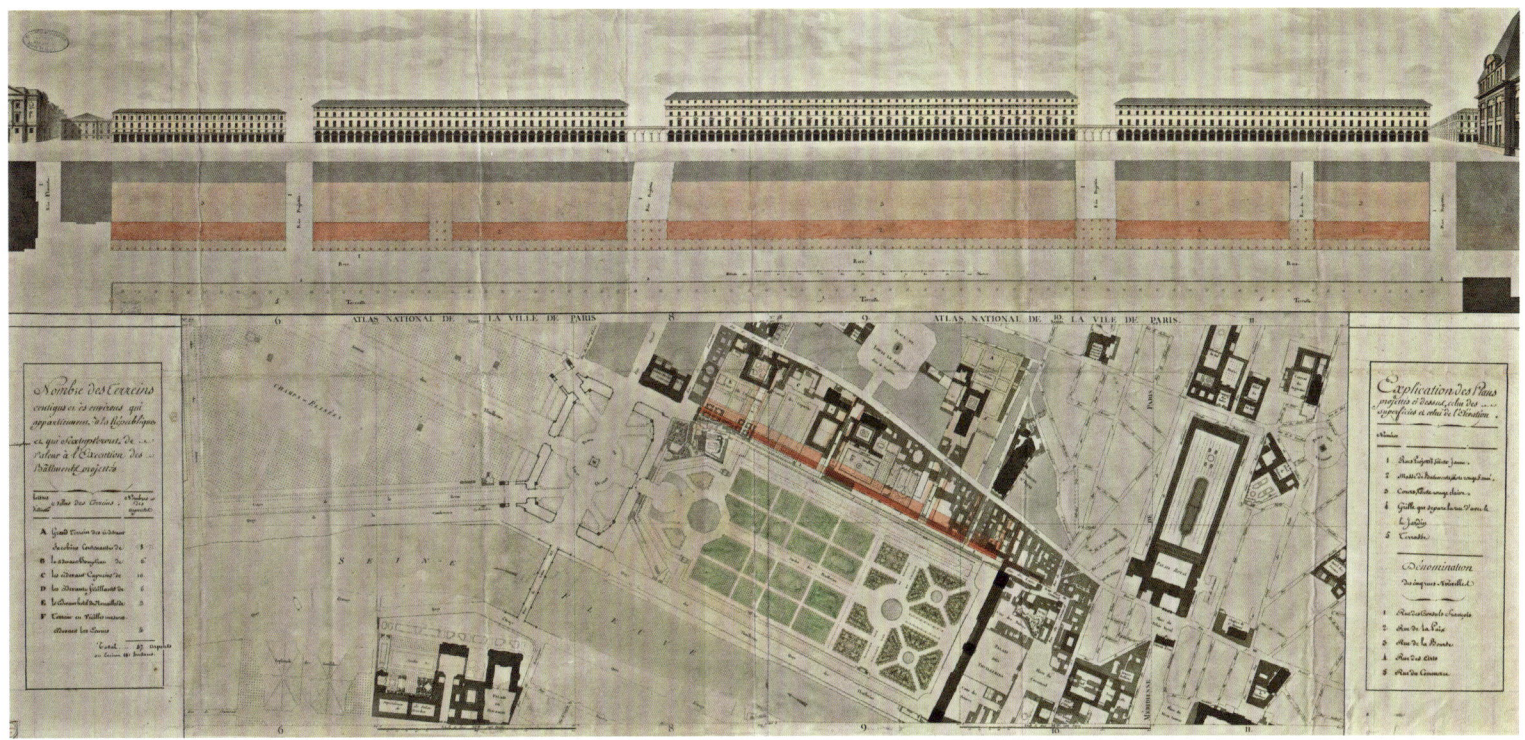

proposal, which dates from 1799, consists of both a plan and a street elevation [FIG. 12.4]. Its title, *Project costing more than 12 million* [livres] *to be subsequently executed and underwritten by an association for the support of workers of all kinds, presented to the Consuls of the French government,*[6] emphasizes that construction of this large undertaking would create many jobs for the unemployed. The design includes four blocks separated by five newly named streets: rue des Consuls Français, rue de la Paix, rue de la Bourse, rue des Arts, and rue du Commerce. The width of the smallest of these blocks corresponds to that of the polygonal space through which one passed when entering the gardens from either the place Louis XV or near the Orangerie. The three principal blocks, linked by an arcade traversing two of the cross streets, constitute a symmetrical composition facing the main part of the gardens and whose central structure is taller than the others. The architecture of the façades is Italianate and stripped down, employing a baseless Doric for the arcade that brings to mind the rue des Colonnes, which was

◂ **FIG 12.3.** Map of Paris 1734–39, pl. 15 of the *Plan Turgot*, showing the Louvre and the Tuileries.

▵ **FIG 12.4.** Anonymous. *Project costing more than 12 million* [livres]…, December 1799. Design for the future rue de Rivoli. Drawing over an engraved plan combined with a drawing of the elevation and plan of the rue de Rivoli, ink and watercolor. Service historique de l'armée de terre, collection du ministre, Fort de Vincennes, Vincennes. Cat. 111.

inaugurated 26 vendémiaire year VI (October 17, 1797) and whose design, as Werner Szambien has shown, influenced that of the rue de Rivoli.[7]

The 1802 project too was intended more to embellish the Tuileries gardens than to ameliorate circulation. Like its precedent, the plan included, in addition to the principal street, perpendicular ones providing access to the quarter beyond, as well as a small square at the corner of the Tuileries palace corresponding to the present place des Pyramides. Its architecture, again in the Italian taste, is similarly austere in character but much more accomplished. The curved profile of its roofs, inspired by the basilicas in Vicenza and Padua, is a brilliant variation on the Parisian broken-eave or hipped model.

The arcades were built first, each property owner being obliged to duplicate the approved façade design [FIG. 12.5]. But construction got off to a slow start, as investors preferred to build in other areas of Paris, and so distance themselves from the center of political power [FIG. 12.6]. It was not until the 1820s and, much later, Haussmann's decision to continue the arcades as far as the rue du Louvre that it assumed its present extent.

In his *Description de Paris*, Jacques Guillaume Legrand insisted on the importance of the urban environment of the Louvre and the Tuileries: "Since great buildings call for great complementary elements, it is no small advantage for the palace of a sovereign, situated in a capital city, to occupy a site that allows for its accessory structures, its avenues and surrounding embellishments, to be proportionate to it."[8] The primary concern here was not functional urban planning but the creation of a monumental architectural setting.

In the aerial view published by Clarac, all of the façades facing the palace complex are represented as uniform, notably the hemispherical composition

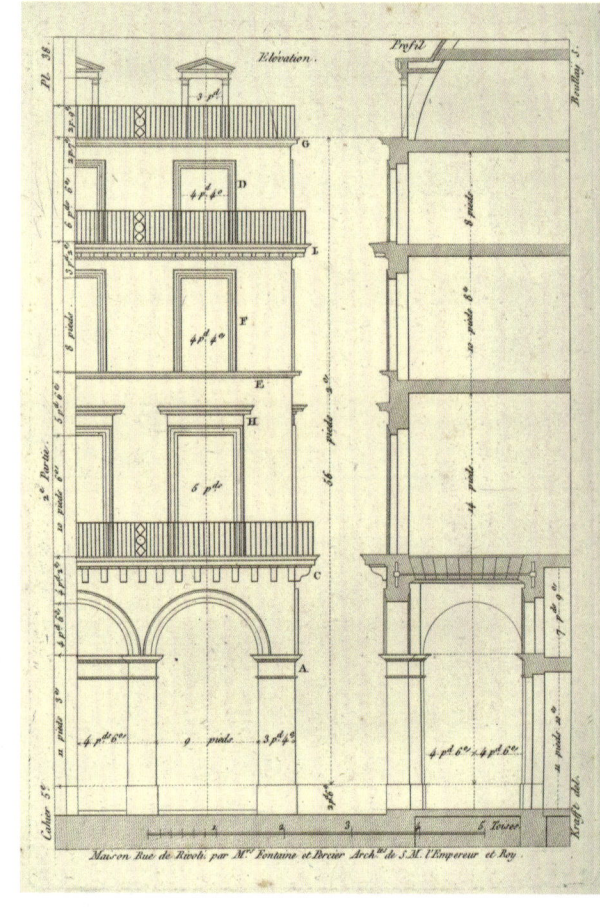

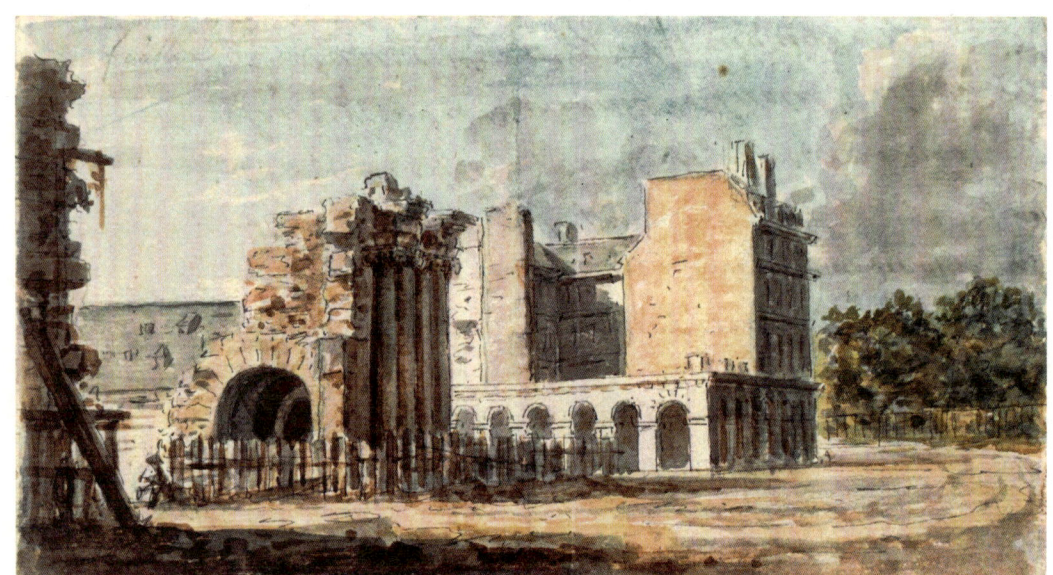

▲ **FIG 12.5.** Charles Percier and Pierre Fontaine. Elevation and cross section of the façades on the rue de Rivoli. From Jean Charles Krafft, *Recueil des plus jolies maisons de Paris* (Paris: Author, 1809), pl. 38. Cat. 114.

◂ **FIG 12.6.** Gautier-Dagoty. *Demolition of Les Feuillants Convent*, View of the rue de Rivoli under construction with the remnants of Les Feuillants in the foreground, 1806. Pen, India ink, and watercolor on paper. Bibliothèque nationale de France, Département des Estampes et de la Photographie, Paris.

fronting a new square opposite the Louvre Colonnade. The creation of this public square would have entailed the demolition of the church of Saint-Germain-l'Auxerrois. It was not realized.

CREATING THE RESIDENCE OF A GREAT SOVEREIGN

The project to connect the two palaces occasioned many proposals, to such an extent that in 1812 Claude Jacques Toussaint published a comparative engraving that shows, in addition to the current state of the complex and the projects of Bernini (1665) and Perrault (1667), no less than twenty others proposed between 1787 and 1810 [FIG. 12.7].[9] Scholars have often evoked the differences between Napoleon, who wanted to link the two palaces as simply as possible with an immense courtyard, and his architects, who lobbied for a more complex solution incorporating two main courtyards. This opposition was cultural, for the emperor failed to see the interest in such a sophisticated articulation of space. But Napoleon's prevarications, which are minutely recorded in Fontaine's diary, doubtless also had a fiscal basis. In any event, despite the acquisition of many buildings between the two palaces preliminary to their demolition and the rapid progress of the rue de Rivoli wing, the projected connection was not realized.

Even so, much was built, but little of this construction survives: essentially, a portion of the structure along the rue de Rivoli, which was completed and widened for some of its length on the courtyard side during the Second Empire, and the arc du Carrousel. The remodeled Tuileries interiors disappeared in 1871 along with the palace itself, notably the salle des Maréchaux—then considered the most beautiful room in Paris—and its casts of the caryatids by Jean Goujon dissimu-

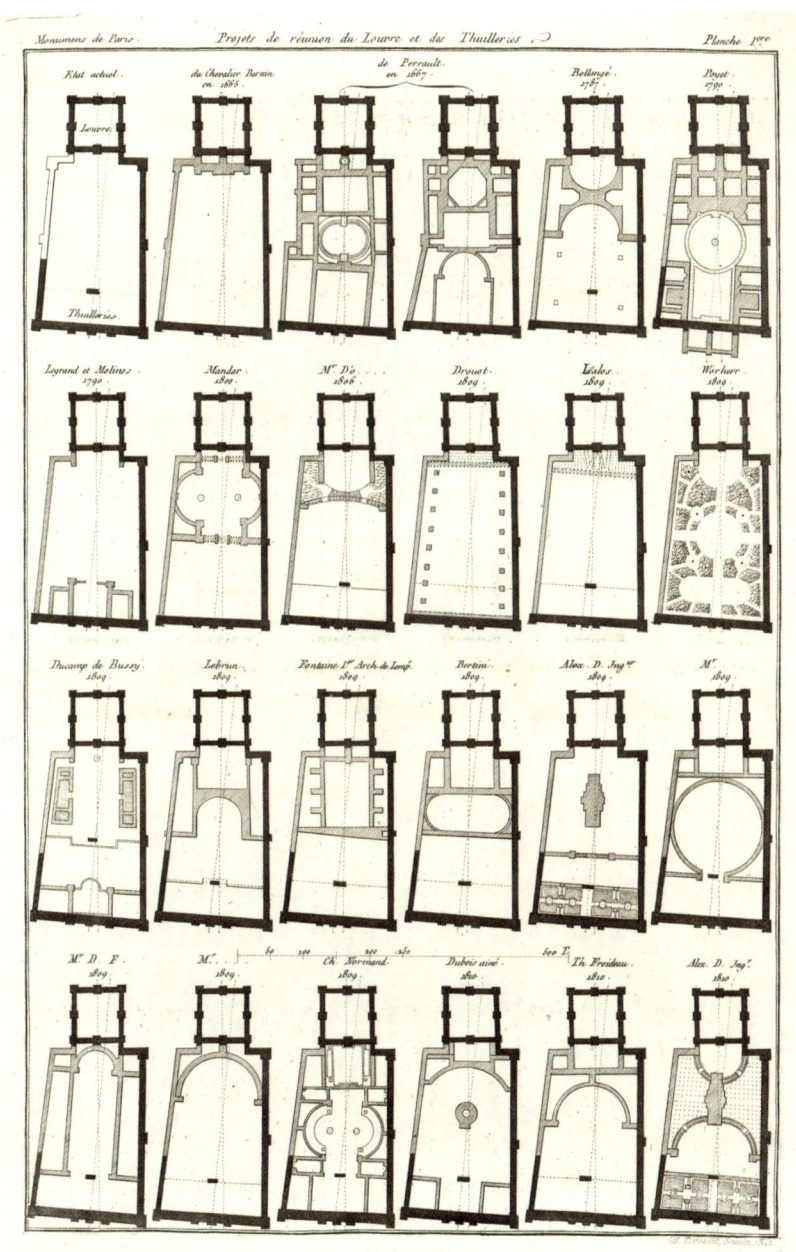

▽ FIG 12.7. Claude Jacques Toussaint. Comparison of projects for the linking of the Louvre and the Tuileries. From Toussaint, *Traité de Géométrie et d'architecture*. Partie théorique (Paris: Author, 1812). The first four plans show the current state, Bernini's design (1665), and two designs by Claude Perrault (1667). The next four show the proposals submitted between 1787 and 1800 from François Joseph Bélanger, Bernard Poyet, Jacques Guillaume Legrand and Jacque Molinos, and Charles François Mandar. The next fourteen were designed between 1806 and 1810.

lating large heaters. Percier and Fontaine included a view of this room in their *Recueil de décorations intérieures* (plate 49), and the young Viollet-le-Duc made a beautiful drawing of it [FIG. 12.8].

The triumphal arch is one of very few built works by Percier and Fontaine to survive, and it is the unique extant example from their ensemble for the Tuileries. Commissioned on March 1, 1806, in honor of the Austrian campaign and the Grande armée, which paid for it, it was also intended to glorify the entrance to the palace. In this capacity, it replaced a less ambitious but more original project for two lanterns—large metal torches surmounting pre-existing masonry guardhouses—designed by Percier and Fontaine the previous year [FIG. 12.9].

The surviving structure is a sophisticated variation on the Arch of Septimius Severus in Rome, here enriched with lateral entries. Awarded the "prix décennal" in 1810 as the finest architectural work of the preceding decade, it ev-

▽ **FIG 12.8.** Eugène Emmanuel Viollet-Le-Duc. *The salle des maréchaux with a view of the Tuileries Gardens*, ca. 1835. Watercolor on paper. Musée d'Orsay, Paris, 33285. Cat. 117.

▷ **FIG 12.9.** Charles Percier and Pierre Fontaine. Design of a lantern to mark the entrance of the Tuileries, elevation and cross section, 1805. Graphite, pen, wash, and watercolor on paper. Private collection, Paris. Cat. 118.

◁ **FIG 12.10.** Arc du Carrousel, south side view, 1806–15. Watercolor and pen on paper. Bibliothèque nationale de France, Département des estampes et de la photographie, Paris, RESERVE FOL-VE-53 (C). Cat. 120.

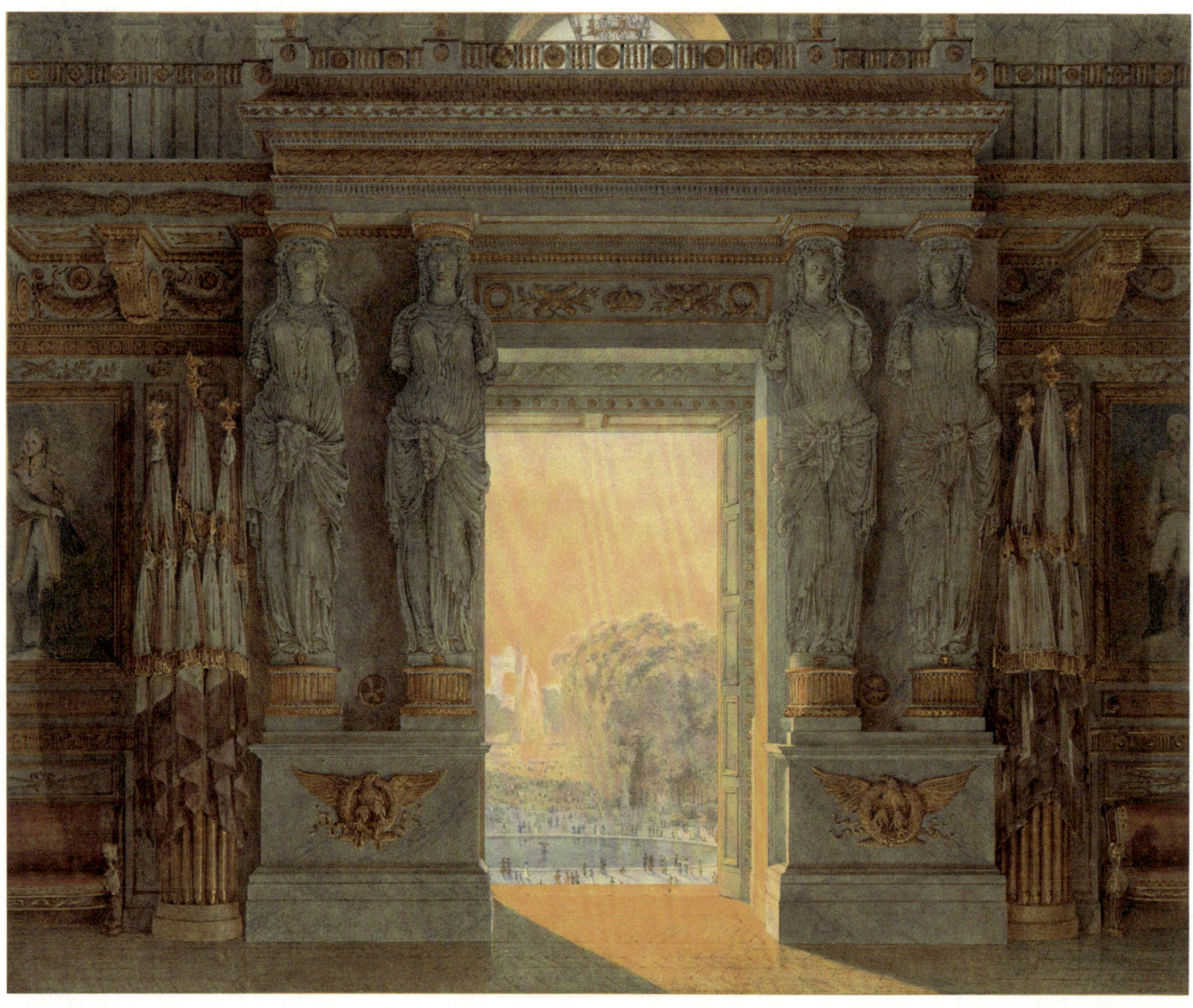

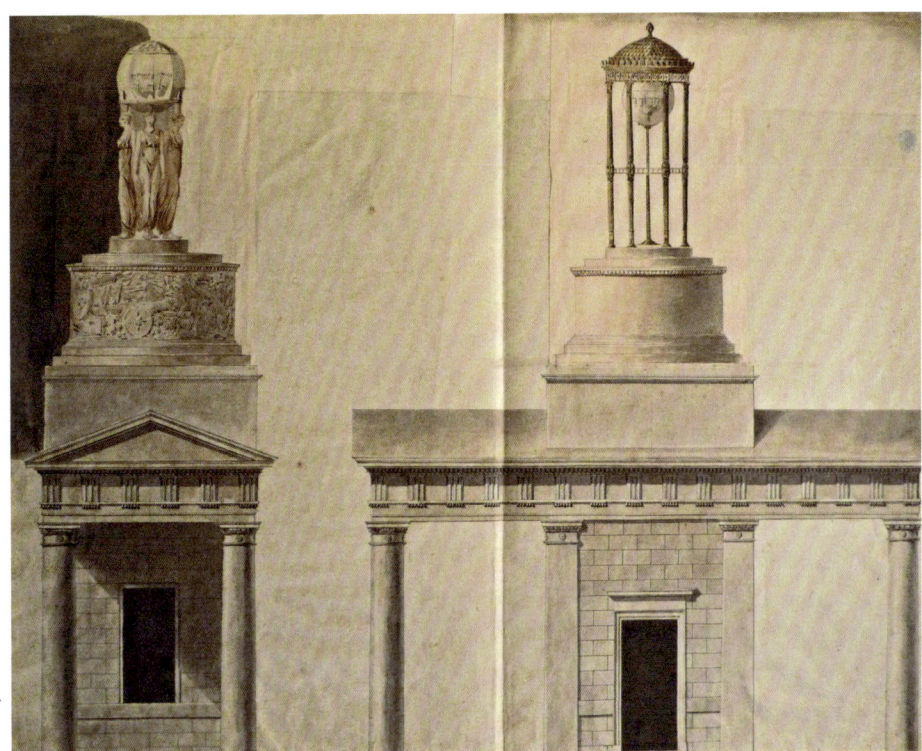

idences considerable archaeological culture and an unsurpassed mastery of detail. Moreover, it was doubtless this project that Percier had in mind when, in the course of a conversation that took place in 1814 and was then reported by Courier W. Stewart, he acknowledged "that the works he himself had superintended were liable to some objections on the score of superfluous ornaments."[10]

Destined to serve as a monumental base for one of the principal artistic appropriations of Napoleon's military campaigns—the bronze horses of Venice, here harnessed to form a quadriga—it was, with its red marble columns and bronze capitals and bases, the first work of nineteenth-century French architecture to break with the classical tradition of monochrome masonry [FIG. 12.10].

OUTFITTING THE WORLD'S LARGEST MUSEUM

By contrast with the Tuileries, several of Percier and Fontaine's interventions at the Louvre palace survive. Around 1800, the still unfinished building was occupied by ateliers and lodgings for scientists, artists, and other variously privileged individuals, notably Percier himself. The considerable sums allotted to it each year—the budget for the Louvre alone was a million francs per annum,

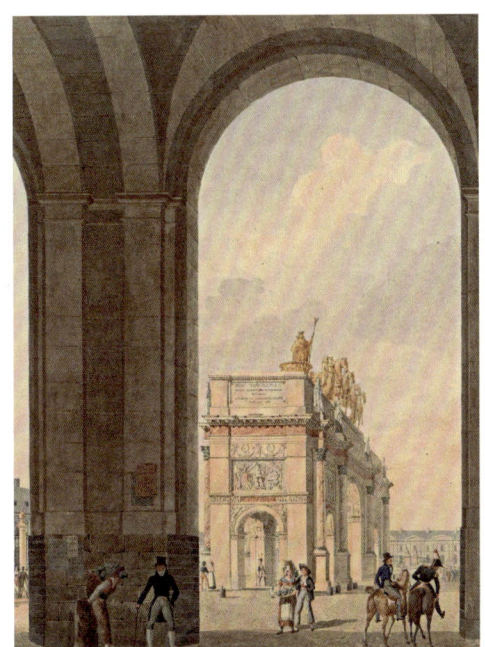

which is what it cost to build the arc du Carrousel—made it possible to complete long-suspended construction work and to restore and sometimes rebuild liberated spaces and structures in relatively poor condition. In his diary, Fontaine was insistent about the importance of completing the Cour Carrée and their decision to disobey Napoleon in order to assure the coherence of the whole. But work on the interiors was just as extensive. In addition to the remodeling of the Grande Galerie and the introduction of skylights there, it is worth mentioning the rooms for the display of sculpture, especially the Salle des Cariatides, an emblematic space, thanks to the importance of Jean Goujon's caryatids to French Renaissance art.

As Clarac emphasized: "The old Louvre projects had nothing to offer in the way of planning and ornament, which were only vaguely indicated and without specific purpose in Perrault's plan. We are wholly indebted for this sequence of rooms to Messrs. Percier and Fontaine."[11] Farther along, he specifies: "It is worth stating here—something not generally known—that the only sculptures then completed were the caryatids, a very small portion of the tribune that they supported, some footings of the entablature in this part of the room, and two capitals; the rest, as well as the transverse arches, existed only in the form of blocked stone, and the columns were not yet fluted....[I]t was only by emulating the style of other works by Jean Goujon and Paul Ponce scattered throughout the Louvre and elsewhere, in accordance with their own ideas, that Messrs. Percier and Fontaine managed to execute the immense and magnificent architectural and ornamental details of this room"[12] As these designs suggest, both architects were familiar with works of the French Renaissance, which inflected their own culture and influenced the evolution of Percier's taste. But more than taste was in play here. The renovations in the salle de Vénus and the Salle des Cariatides, portions of which are reproduced in the last part of the *Recueil de décorations intérieures*, evince changes in their approach to scale and the use of materials [FIGS. 12.11, 12.12]. Most of the designs published in the *Recueil*—stucco and painted decors conceived after antique or mannerist models—consist of new facework and furniture (wood paneling, hangings, paintings, moldings, bronze fittings), but the interventions in the Louvre are more monumental and made of carved stone. This shift, from the detachable and superficial to the permanent, echoes

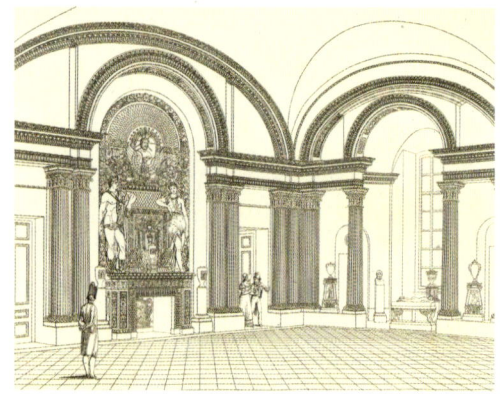 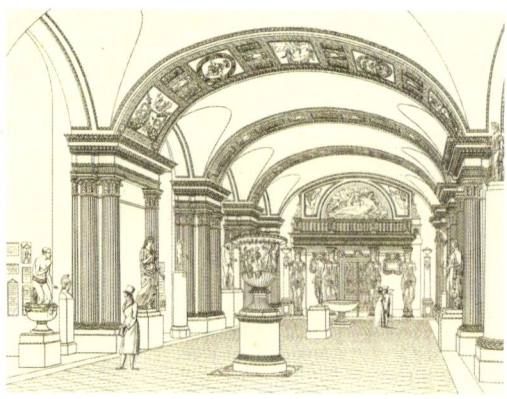

◢ **FIG 12.11–12.** Charles Percier and Pierre Fontaine. Views of the Salle des Cariatides, musée du Louvre, remodeled by Percier and Fontaine. Engravings after drawings by Civeton. From Charles Othon Frédéric Jean-Baptiste de Clarac, *Musée de sculpture antique et moderne* (Paris: Texier, 1826–55), pls. 41, 43.

◣ **FIG 12.13.** Jean-Baptiste Isabey. *The Grand Staircase of the Musée Napoleon*, ca. 1804–14. Destroyed by the construction of the Daru staircase. Watercolor on cardboard. Musée du Louvre, Paris, 27236-recto.

▷ **FIG 12.14.** Charles Percier and Pierre Fontaine. South staircase of the colonnade. Engraving after a drawing by Christophe Civeton. From Charles Othon Frédéric Jean-Baptiste de Clarac, *Musée de sculpture antique et moderne*, (Paris: Texier, 1826-55), atlas vol. 1, pl. 97. Cat. 128.

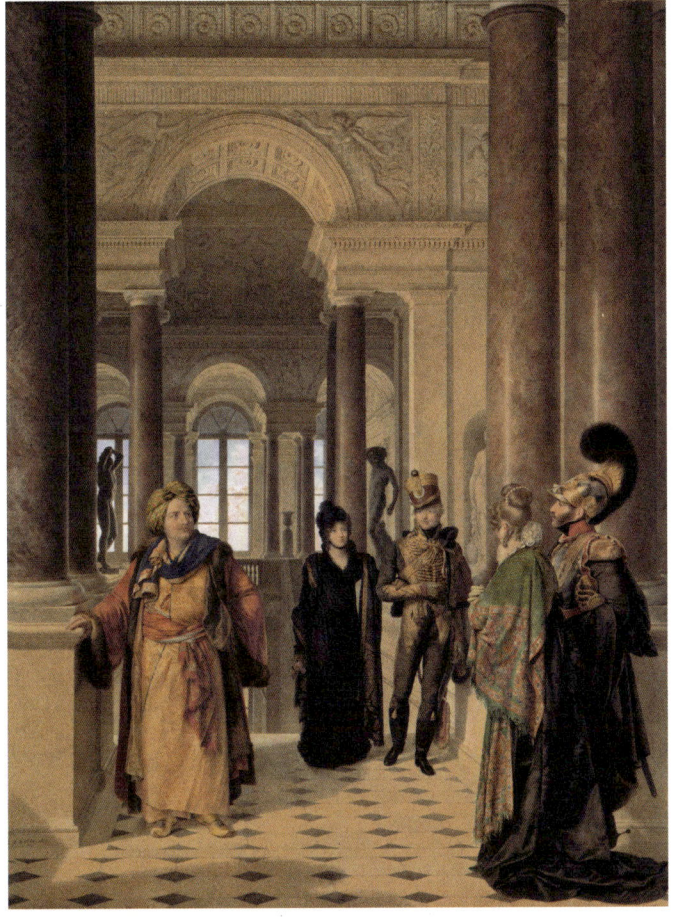

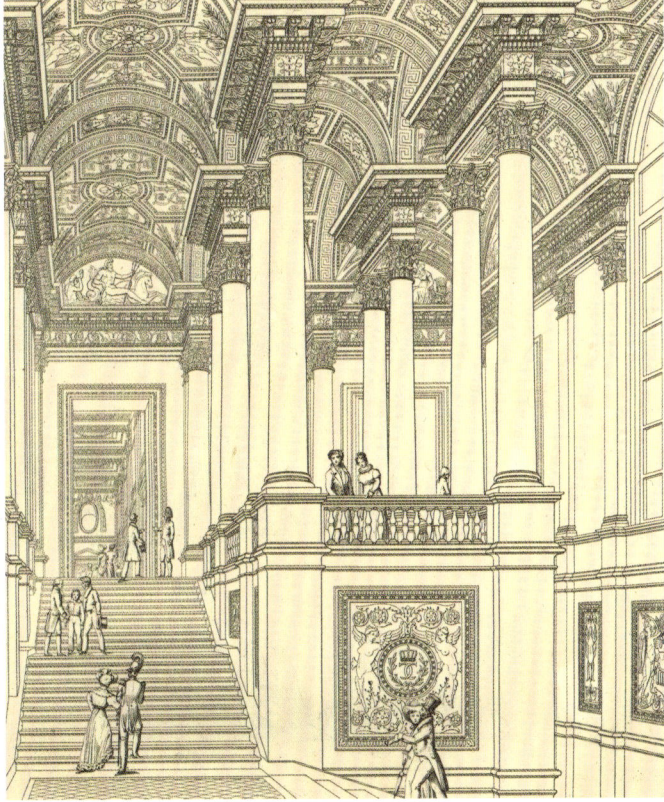

statements in the preliminary discourse, where the authors assert the existence of an organic connection between architecture and interior decoration and call fashion into question. It also grounds their project in the profoundly French material reality of dressed stone, the use of which Fontaine would later perfect in his design for the Chapelle expiatoire.

The most important and spectacular interior spaces built by Percier and Fontaine, however, were their monumental staircases in the Louvre: the grand stairway of the museum, demolished during the Second Empire because it was deemed too narrow, and the staircases in the Colonnade block, of which only the one toward the Seine survives [FIGS. 12.13, 12.14]. All of them featured isolated columns with smooth shafts supporting richly decorated vaults—the sculpture envisioned for the Colonnade staircase was never executed—and a way of organizing their linked spaces into spectacular sequences, in the one case along a linear axis, in the other turning around a central core. These designs are reminiscent of certain Italian mannerist interiors that had especially impressed them during their Italian sojourn, notably the Palazzo Te in Mantua and the palazzi of Strada Nuova in Genoa. As in their volume on the palaces of Rome, there is a penchant here for Italian models in which austere, even primitive façade elevations are combined with principal interior spaces that are dynamic and richly decorated. This marriage of a refined classical vocabulary consistent with the lessons of the early Renaissance—as exemplified by Giacomo Vignola, Baldassare Peruzzi, and Andrea Palladio—with the theatrical splendor of palaces for the Genoese patriciate dating from the second half of the Cinquecento anticipates the main thrust of architectural pedagogy at the École des beaux-arts.

The interventions commissioned by Napoleon and directed by his architects, in view of realizing a long-projected transformation of the heart of Paris by completing the Louvre and connecting it to the Tuileries, illustrate the contradictions characteristic of their built work more generally. Much more was spent on completion and restoration work than on striking new structures, which in any case were largely destroyed in subsequent decades. Nonetheless, it remains true that these several initiatives, whether in the realms of urban planning, architecture, preservation, or decoration, facilitated the transition from the aims and aspirations of the century of Enlightenment to the large-scale projects of the nineteenth century. ●

1 Charles Othon Frédéric Jean-Baptiste de Clarac, *Musée de sculpture antique et moderne* (Paris: Texier, 1826), atlas, 1:1, pls. 110, 110bis, 110ter.
2 This despite the existence of a more developed project dated 1831, and which called for a transformation of the Tuileries palace. See Charles Percier and Pierre Fontaine, *Résidences de souverains. Parallèle entre plusieurs résidences de souverains de France, d'Allemagne, de Suède, de Russie, d'Espagne et d'Italie, à Paris chez les auteurs* (Paris: Authors, 1833), pl. 7.
3 "The project to connect the Louvre with the Tuileries along the rue Honoré with a building similar to the one that overlooks the river was conceived at the same time as the immense gallery that is now part of the museum….Completion of this project has often been contemplated. The plans of Knight Bernini, Perrault, and others are proof of this." ("Le projet de réunion du Louvre avec les Tuileries du côté de la rue Honoré, par un bâtiment semblable à celui qui donne sur la rivière, a été conçu lorsqu'on a projeté cette immense galerie qui sert aujourd'hui au Muséum….On a souvent pensé à effectuer ce projet. Les plans connus du chevalier Bernin, de Perrault et autres, en sont les preuves."). Antoine François Peyre, "Mémoire sur l'achèvement du Louvre, sur l'agrandissement du Muséum national de peinture et de sculpture, et sur la nécessité de former promptement une école spéciale des arts, lu le 23 Messidor an 4," in *Mémoires de l'Institut national des sciences et des arts, pour l'an IV de la République. Littérature et beaux-arts* (Paris: Institut national, 1798), 1:667–68.
4 Ibid., 668.
5 The rue de Rivoli has been much studied. The synthetic discussion that follows is especially indebted to two sources: Werner Szambien, *De la rue des Colonnes à la rue de Rivoli,* exh. cat. (Paris: Délégation à l'Action Artistique de la Ville de Paris, 1992), and Charlotte Duvette, "La rue de Rivoli et le secteur des Tuileries: projets, percements et constructions, depuis la Révolution française à la fin du Premier Empire," Master's thesis, Université Paris 1 Panthéon-Sorbonne, 2014.
6 "Projet de plus de 12 millions à exécuter de suite aux frais d'une compagnie pour le secours des ouvriers de tout genre présenté aux Consuls du gouvernement françois."
7 Werner Szambien, *De la rue des Colonnes à la rue de Rivoli,* exh. cat. (Paris: Délégation à l'Action Artistique de la Ville de Paris, 1992).
8 "Comme les grands édifices veulent de grands accompagnements, ce n'est pas un médiocre avantage pour un palais de souverain, placé dans une capitale, que d'occuper une situation qui permette de lui proportionner ses accessoires, ses avenues et tous embellisements environnants." Jacques Guillaume Legrand, "Les palais réunis des Thuileries et du Louvre," in Charles Paul Landon, *Description de Paris et de ses édifices* (Paris, 1806–9), 2:5.
9 Claude Jacques Toussaint, *Traité de géométrie et d'architecture. Partie Théorique* (Paris: Author, 1812).
10 Courier W. Stewart, *Diary of an Excursion to France in the Months August and September 1814* (Edinburgh: Peter Hill, Manners and Miller, 1814), 153–54.
11 "Les anciens projets du Louvre n'offraient rien pour leur distribution et leurs ornemens; elles n'étaient que vaguement projetées et sans destination dans le plan de Perrault. C'est entièrement à MM. Percier et Fontaine que l'on doit cette suite de pièces." Charles Othon Frédéric Jean-Baptiste de Clarac, *Musée de sculpture antique et modern* (Paris: Texier, 1826), 1:398.
12 "Il est bon de constater ici, ce que l'on ignore généralement, qu'il n'y avait alors de terminé en sculpture que les caryatides, une très petite partie de la tribune qu'elles soutiennent, quelques pieds de l'entablement dans cette partie de la salle, et deux chapiteaux; les autres, ainsi que les arcs doubleaux étaient encore en pierre d'attente, et les cannelures des colonnes n'existaient pas…ce ne fut qu'en se réglant sur le style d'autres ouvrages de Jean Goujon et de Paul Ponce épars dans le Louvre et ailleurs, et d'après leurs propres idées, que MM. Percier et Fontaine firent exécuter les immenses et magnifiques détails de l'architecture et des ornements de cette salle." Ibid., 456.

THE ARCADES ON THE RUE DE RIVOLI

CHARLOTTE DUVETTE

One of the architectural characteristics of the rue de Rivoli, the emblematic thoroughfare on Paris' right bank, is the long enfilade of arcades that enliven the lower part of its façades.[1] These arcaded porticos are an essential element of the architecture of these streets. Once construction began, the arcades were erected first, at government expense; the restrained and uniform façades above them rose later, in a second phase of construction.[2]

Why did the architects, Percier and Fontaine opt for these arcades with piers? Also, why did they exclude almost all ornament, a decision seemingly at odds with their career as decorators? These questions, which have persisted since the nineteenth century, have received much attention; responses have been many and various.

The use of street arcades in Paris has already been the focus of a publication.[3] One of the many propositions advanced there is that our two architects were influenced by the monumental covered galleries of the two large buildings erected to designs by Ange Jacques Gabriel on the place de la Concorde, originally place Louis XV, which prompted them to include a similar feature out of a concern for uniformity. There is no need to detail all previous hypotheses, but it is worth noting that open arcades surmounted by buildings were not unusual in the city's earlier royal squares. A case in point is the place des Vosges, originally place Royale.[4] The rue des Colonnes (opened 1797) is also frequently cited as an important Parisian precedent for the rue de Rivoli.

In addition to these elements of the cityscape familiar to our two architects, there were other likely influences on the monumentality and aesthetic restraint of their arcade design. The abiding taste for ancient models was certainly a factor, and Bonaparte's interest in classical antiquity is well known; consider his declaration, reported by his aide Armand Caulaincourt, that "it is necessary to temper young heads a bit in the Greeks and Romans."[5] Similarly, it is worth remembering the Italian names—Rivoli, Castiglione—that Napoleon himself conferred upon some of the district's new Parisian streets in 1804 to memorialize the Italian campaign (1796–97).[6] Do these names reflect the patron's desire for architectural forms redolent of Italy? Should we construe the stripped-down monumentality of these arcades as an allusion to military rigor? The two possibilities are not mutually exclusive.

Percier and Fontaine shared Napoleon's taste for architecture in the Italian mode, which moreover was consistent with aesthetic views of the period. Their Roman sojourn (1786–91) and their book *Palais, maisons et autres édifices modernes dessinés à Rome*[7] (1798–1801), with its many engravings of domestic interior courtyards with open porticos, sometimes with pillars and arcades, attest to this predilection. Among Percier's many Italian sketches, one representing a small house near the Coliseum in Rome is notable for its depiction of a two-bay arcade very similar to the rue de Rivoli design.[8]

Doubtless our two architects were familiar with the many earlier projects, beginning in the early eighteenth century, that envisioned the construction of a street along the full length of the northern façades of the Louvre and the Tuileries.[9] Some of these included street arcades, although rather differently conceived.[10] A recently discovered anonymous project of December 1799 (SEE FIG. 12.4) is intriguing, since Bonaparte's official directive to work on this district was issued only in 1801.[11] Here the unknown architect imagined an ensemble of buildings, separated by streets, whose façades are basically uniform, but with variations in arcade elevation and increases in building height introduced symmetrically, at every cross street, toward the central, highest block. The Italian influence here is even more pronounced, from the three-bay deep arcades over the start of the perpendicular streets—as in Italian Renaissance squares, such as the piazza del Duomo in Bologna—to the handling of the moldings and cornices, which

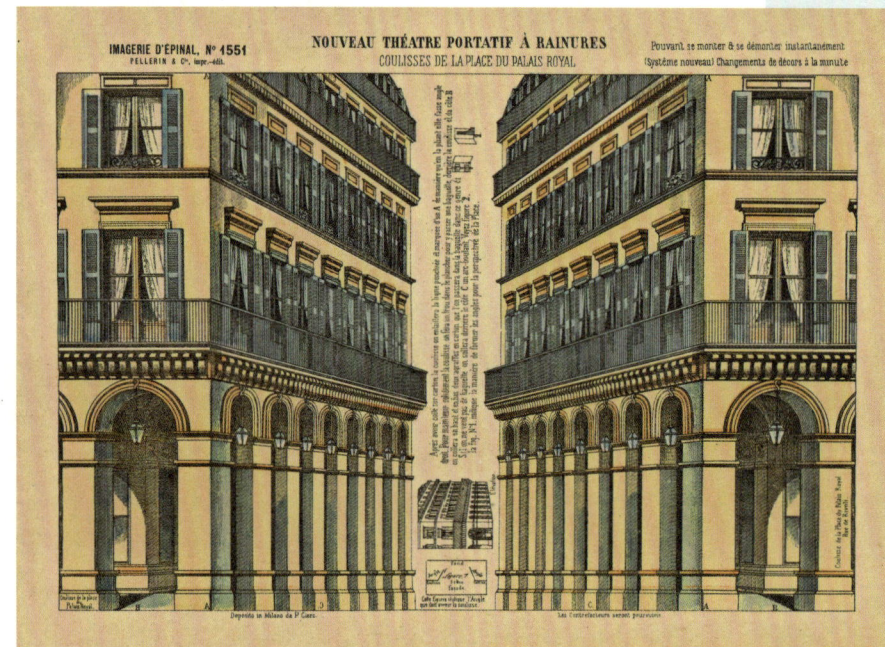

brings to mind that of celebrated Italian palazzi of the sixteenth century. This project remained unrealized, but it may have revived the government's interest in embellishing the district, perhaps prompting the first consul to ask his architects to break ground there. The final scheme, more uniform and restrained, called for shops fronting the covered arcades [FIGS. 12A.1, 12A.2], the simplicity of the design having been deemed consistent with luxury boutiques. Similar commercial arcades could be seen in Turin and Bologna, cities that Percier had visited.

What did contemporary theorists have to say about such arcades? In his *Précis des leçons d'architecture* (1809), Jean Nicolas Louis Durand recommended their use but stipulated that the residential structures accessed through them should vary in a accordance with the wealth and social station of their occupants, while Quatremère de Quincy, in the entry "rue" (street) in his *Encyclopédie méthodique (Architecture*, vol. 3, 1825), acknowledged the utility of such arcades but regretted the attendant

▷ **FIG 12A.1.** Arcades of the Place du Palais Royal, rue de Rivoli. Paper cut-out toy of a portable theater, ca. 1860. Private collection, Paris.

◁ **FIG 12A.2.** Arcades on the rue de Rivoli, toy construction set for the Orléans princes, ca. 1820. Painted and assembled wood blocks. Musée Carnavalet, Paris, PM 109.

▷ **FIG 12A.3.** Charles Percier and Pierre Fontaine, "Design of Monsieur Fontaine for linking the Louvre to the Tuileries," 1812. Graphite, pen, wash, and watercolor on paper. Private collection. Cat. 113.

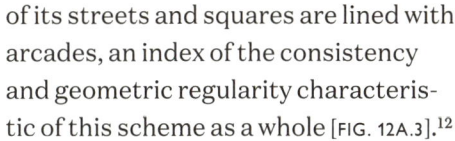

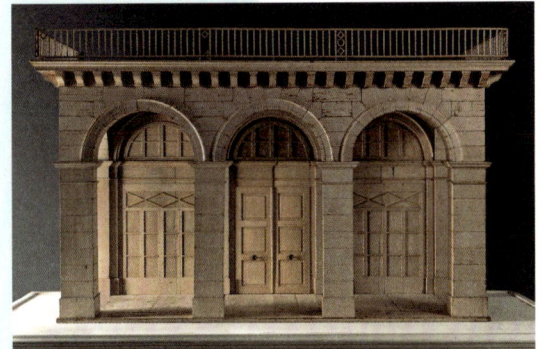

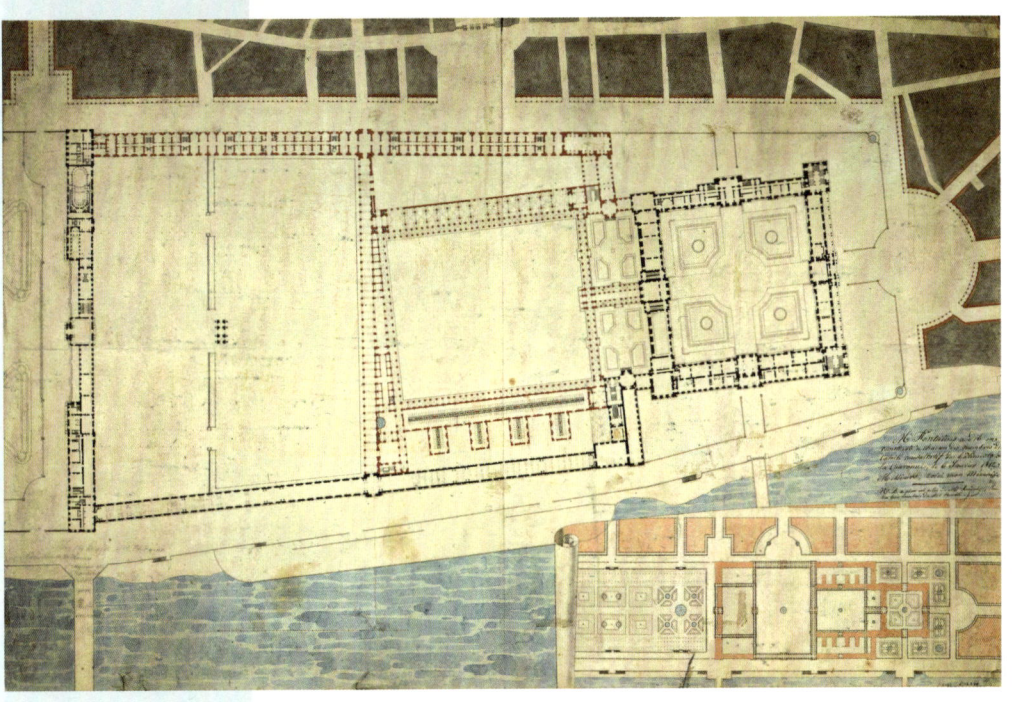

loss of space for habitation.

Despite their different emphases, both of these sources suggest that arcaded porticos were part of the early nineteenth-century idea of what a street could be. Some years later, in 1812, Percier and Fontaine, as part of yet another project to link the Louvre and the Tuileries, proposed a design for recasting the Tuileries district. All of its streets and squares are lined with arcades, an index of the consistency and geometric regularity characteristic of this scheme as a whole [FIG. 12A.3].[12]

There was, then, nothing eccentric about the use of street arcades along the rue de Rivoli, but the severity of the design occasioned criticism. In 1852, when an extension of the street was under consideration, one "J-B" warned against duplicating its architecture on too large a scale: "Let us excuse the architects of the rue de Rivoli, who might have written a great many things on this never-ending page but did not do so, because plainness, the absence of all trappings and ornament, were then the norm for monuments, as they were for men."[13]

Through the elegant sobriety of these buildings, the architects succeeded in adapting their art and aesthetic preferences to the taste of their patron as well as to the design program, which called for the creation of an apt setting for the palaces of the Louvre and the Tuileries, whose elevations were already richly decorated. ●

1 At the same time, arcades were also built along the rue de Castiglione and on the place des Pyramides.
2 An 1806 drawing of the rue de Castiglione by Gautier-Dagoty (Paris, Bibliothèque national de France) shows the interim result of this piecemeal construction.
3 Werner Szambien, *De la rue des Colonnes à la rue de Rivoli*, exh. cat. (Paris: Délégation à l'action artistique de la ville de Paris, 1992); see texts by Béatrice de Andia and Werner Szambien.
4 Ibid., 16.
5 "il faut tremper un peu les jeunes têtes dans les Grecs et les Romains." Armand Augustin Louis de Caulaincourt, *Mémoires du général de Caulaincourt, duc de Vicence, grand écuyer de l'Empereur*, 3 vols. (Paris: Plon et Nourrit, 1933), as cited by Louis Hautecœur, *Histoire de l'Architecture classique en France*, vol. 5: *Révolution et Empire, 1792–1815* (Paris: Picard, 1957), 150.
6 "The Emperor himself designated the names of the new streets" ("L'Empereur a lui-même désigné le nom des nouvelles rues.") Pierre Fontaine, *Journal 1799–1853*. (Paris: ENSBA / Institute français d'architecture / Société de l'histoire de l'art français, 1987), 1:85, entry dated 5 fructidor year XII (August 23, 1804).
7 See the recent edition: Charles Percier and Pierre Fontaine, *Palais de Rome: Palais, maisons, et autres édifices modernes dessinés à Rome*, ed. Jean-Philippe Garric (Wavre, Mardaga/Institut national d'histoire de l'art, 2008).

8 In an album of Italian drawings by Percier in the library of the Institut de France: ms. 1006, fol. 76, drawing 136 (*Vue d'une petite maison près du Colisée à Rome*). For a reproduction, see Sabine Frommel, Jean-Philippe Garric, and Elisabeth Kieven, eds., *Charles Percier e Pierre Fontaine dal soggiorno romano alla trasformazione di Parigi* (Milan: Silvana Editoriale, 2014), 127.
9 Some of these projects are discussed in Jean-Claude Daufresne, *Louvre & Tuileries: architectures de papier* (Paris: Mardaga, 1987).
10 See Alain Manesson-Mallet, *La Géométrie pratique...* (Paris: Anisson, 1702), 3:9, pl. iv ("Veüe générale du Louvre étant achevé").
11 Fontaine, *Journal*, 1:20, entry dated 25 pluviôse year IX (February 14, 1801).
12 The drawings for this scheme, now in the musée Carnavalet, are signed only by Fontaine, but it is generally assumed that Percier continued to collaborate with him during this period.
13 "Excusons les architectes de la rue de Rivoli qui auraient pu écrire tant de choses sur cette page qui n'en finit pas, et qui ne l'ont pas fait, parce que le nu et l'absence de tout vêtement, de tout ornament étaient alors chose courante pour les monuments comme pour les hommes." J-B, *Arcades de la rue de Rivoli, à MM. les membres de la commission municipal de Paris* (Paris: Garnier, 1852).

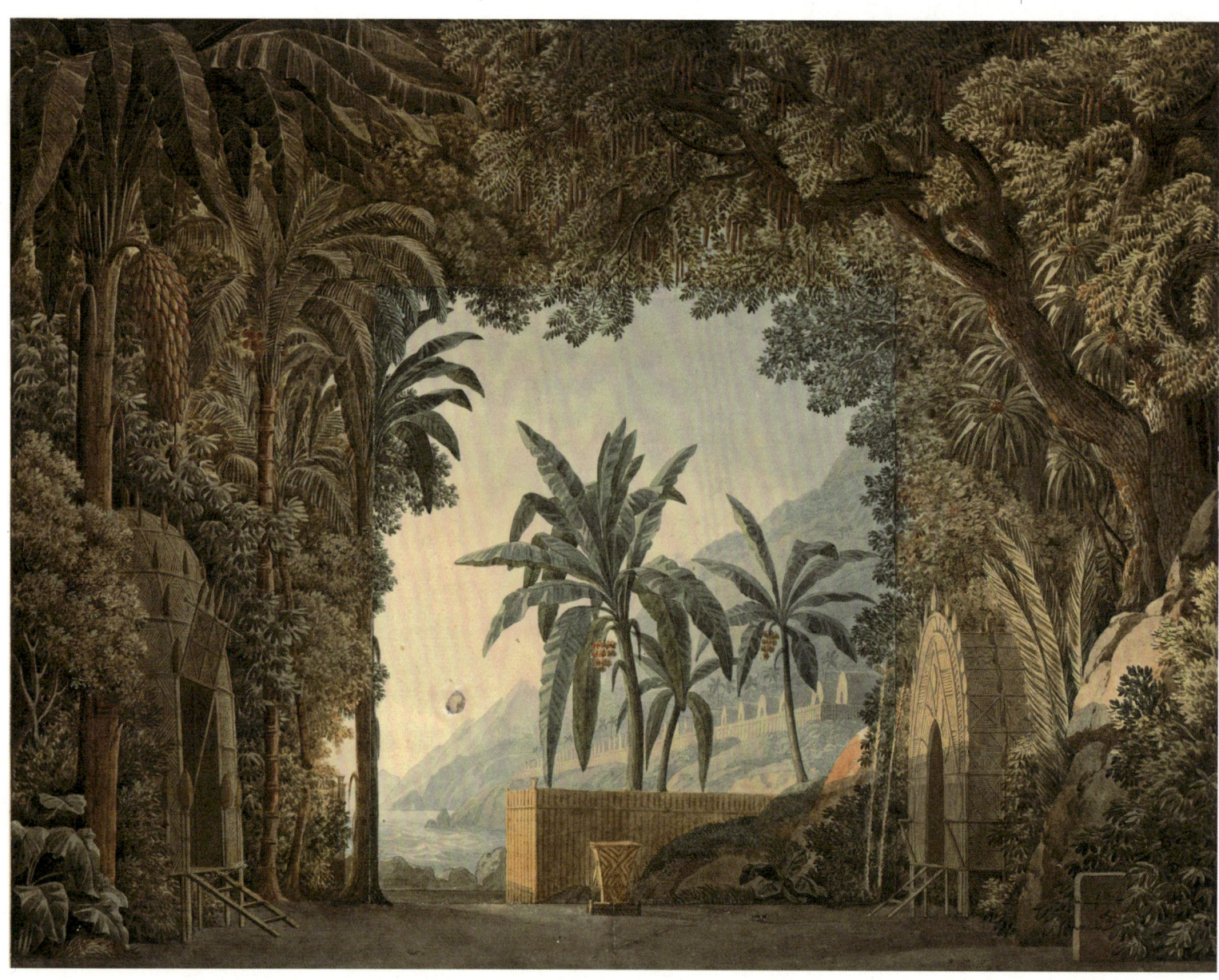

▲ FIG 13.1. Charles Percier, Jean Thomas Thibault, and Pierre Fontaine. Set design for *Elisca ou l'amour maternel*, Act I, 1799. Pen and watercolor on paper. Bibliothèque nationale de France, Bibliothèque-musée de l'opéra, Paris, BMO ESQ 19-30. Cat. 133.

CHAPTER 13

A RHETORIC OF UNBUILT ARCHITECTURE

JEAN-PHILIPPE GARRIC

THE MEAGER CATALOGUE OF PERCIER AND FONTAINE'S BUILT production was typical of their generation, for the period in which they worked was too troubled to allow architectural careers to flourish in real space. Despite being borne up by the extravagant ambition of their principal patron, they managed to build only a small number of important projects, and their contributions to the staging of Napoleonic power, notably the emperor's coronation and his marriage to Marie-Louise, represent a significant portion of their realized work. Understandably, they were bitter about this outcome, as they eventually said in print.[1] Nonetheless, the fact that Percier and Fontaine produced more ephemeral projects and—especially—designs for unrealized buildings reveals more than a series of frustrated opportunities. The resulting corpus of works on paper, in addition to revealing the fecundity and diversity of their imaginations, develops an independent capacity for demonstration: a rhetoric less grandiloquent than that of the "revolutionary" generation of Boullée and Ledoux, but one whose drawn speculations did nothing less than lay the foundations for something like a graphic theory of their art.

In both Fontaine's journals and the accounts of his contemporaries, Percier is depicted as a man more comfortable at the drawing board than on the construction site, an architect more preoccupied with the perfection of his drawings than with their realization.[2] But in assessing this predilection, it is difficult to separate the more personal factors from others determined by the circumstances of his career. Already well known and published while a student,[3] Percier agreed to take on the job—together with Fontaine, whose collaboration he solicited—of supervising set designs for the Paris Opera late in 1792, when such opportunities to draw a regular salary for substantive creative work were rare. In addition to the high degree of visibility this activity brought the two architects, it sharpened their sensitivity to theatrical effects, strengthening their awareness of the visual impact that could be produced by architectural compositions.[4] It also fostered their engagement with a variety of social and historical contexts and broadened their range of cultural references.

Their sets for *Les Mystères d'Isis* (1801)[5]—more inventive than archaeologically accurate—refer to contemporary Egyptomania, and anticipate works of the same kind realized more than twenty years later by Karl Friedrich Schinkel, notably for *The Magic Flute*.[6] For the premiere of *Elisca ou l'amour maternel* (Elisca, or maternal love) by André Grétry in 1799, they conceived huts all but engulfed by tropical jungle on the island of Madagascar, which related to romantic exoticism and a new ethnographic attention to the reality of primitive structures, qualities they share with the first plates of an almost contemporaneous treatise on carpentry by Jean Henri Hassenfratz [FIGS. 13.1, 13.2].[7] The set design for the first act, signed by both Fontaine and Jean Thomas Thibault, translates into vegetal form the dense profusion of

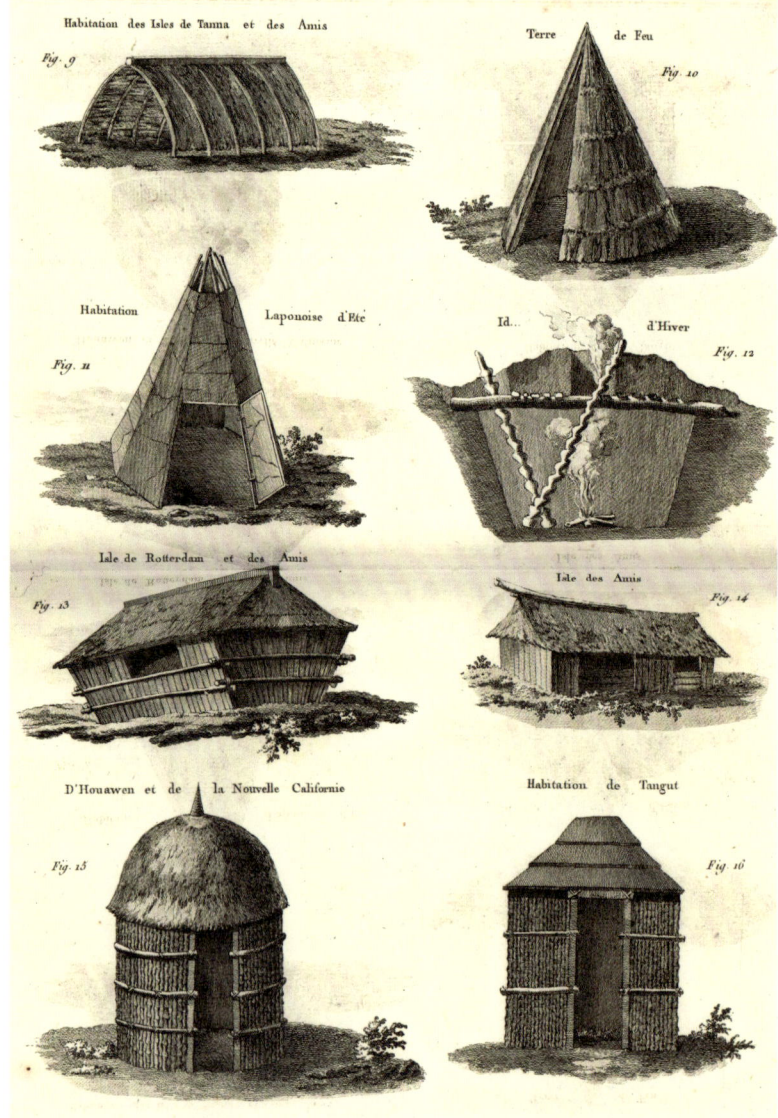

▽ **FIG 13.2.** Jean Henri Hassenfratz. *Housing Structures from the Tonga Islands, Lapland, Tierra del Fuego, New Caledonia, and Tibet.* From Hassenfratz, *Traité de l'art du charpentier* (Paris: Firmin Didot, 1804), pl. 2.

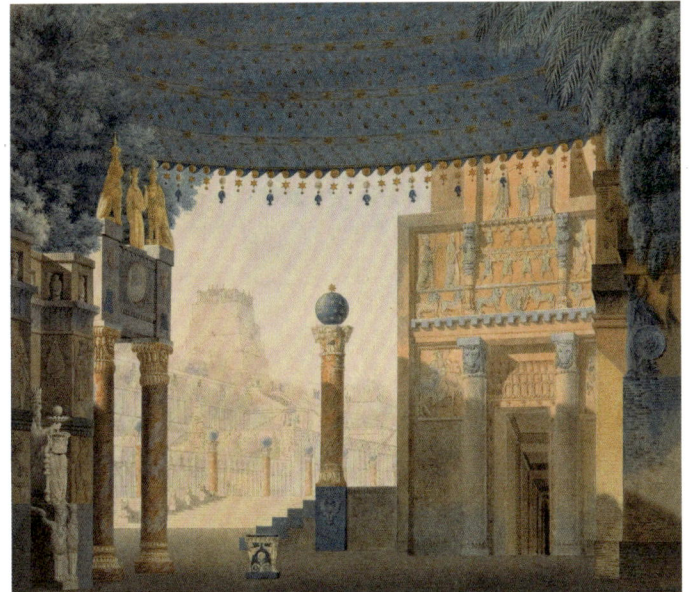

▲ **FIG 13.3.** Charles Percier. Set design for Act III of *Sémiramis* by Charles Simon Catel, 1802. Black chalk and watercolor on beige paper. Musée du Louvre, Paris, RF 54686 recto.

▼ **FIG 13.4.** Charles Percier. Headpiece for Book 8 illustrating the poem "The Two Friends," from Jean de La Fontaine, *Fables* (Paris: Pierre Didot l'aîné, 1802), 2:68. Cat. 44.

Percier's compositions of ancient decorative fragments, from which it took the principle of a perspectival recession opening onto a distant view obstructed by a frontally disposed central motif, here a group of banana trees. The Babylonian sets for Charles Simon Catel's *Sémiramis* (1802) add orientalism to the range of these architectural inventions, an element also present in another work by Percier from the same year, his engraved headpiece for "The Two Friends" in the Didot edition of the fables of La Fontaine, to which—despite the tale's being set in the southern African Kingdom of Mutapa—he gave a distinct Ottoman inflection [FIGS. 13.3, 13.4].[8]

However, the theater, with its demand for cultural and formal diversity, was not, in the last years of the eighteenth century, the only domain in which Percier and Fontaine devised architectural conceptions without any prospect of their realization. The Revolutionary Competitions of the year II (late 1793) spurred artists to seek glory—prosperity being effectively foreclosed at the time—by submitting works that would contribute to the political struggle in which the entire nation was then engaged.[9] Here the rhetorical character of their productions was intended not to serve a dramatic text, however informed by new ideas, but to reinforce official Revolutionary propaganda.

Three designs for these competitions by Percier and Fontaine are known.[10] The first is an urban development project that called for surrounding the

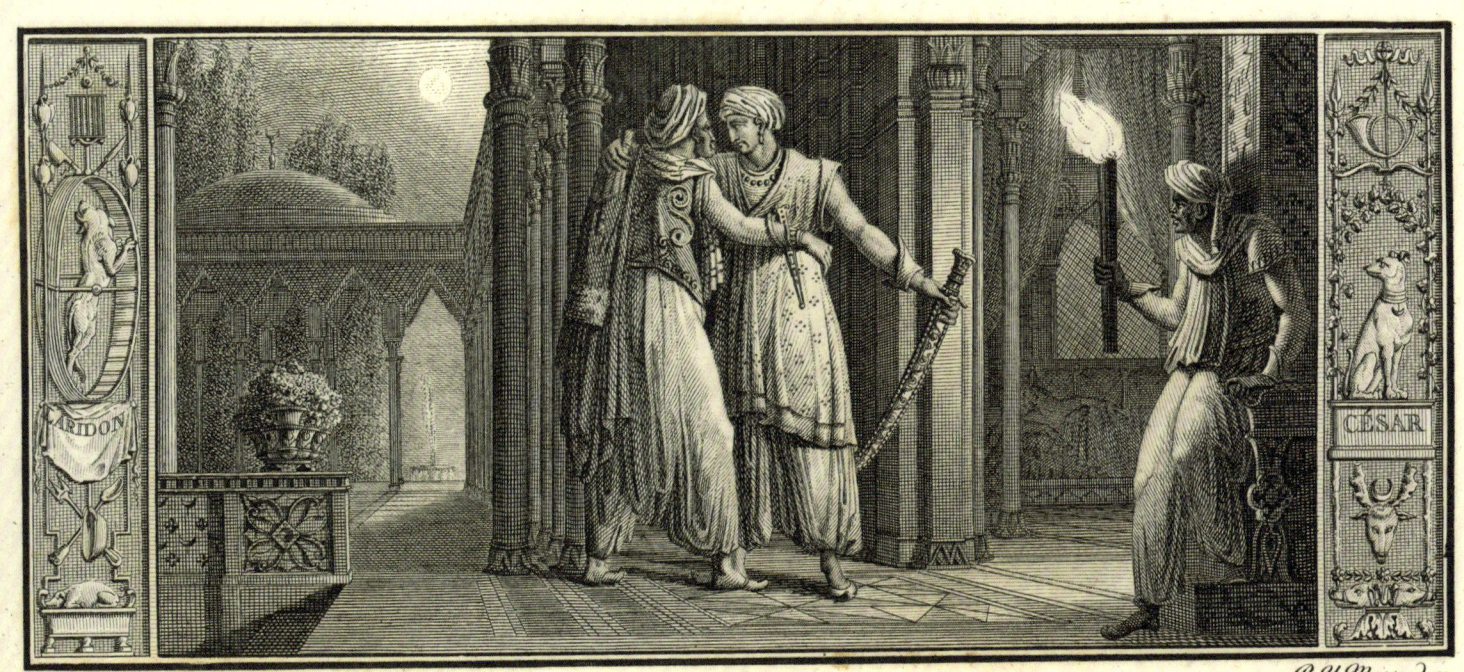

Panthéon with a public space delimited by a portico. The second, also devoted to a commemorative public space, was entitled "Theater for celebrating the triumphs of the Republic with civic songs," wording that insists on the intended purpose: to accommodate government spectacles glorifying the armies of the Republic. This design called for a long façade fronting the Seine and punctuated by three temples dedicated to Good Faith, Concord, and Liberty, as well as an impressive sequence of stepped terraces descending toward the river. These terraces were intended to accommodate huge crowds gathered to watch flotillas of small craft representing victorious French fleets as they passed by. The third design, which Werner Szambien dates a bit later, to 1796, is more modest in scale; a small structure resembling a stepped pyramid and crowned by an open temple surmounted by a figure of Victory was to be a "Monument to Defenders of the Nation"[11] whose exterior surfaces were to be engraved with the names of heroes fallen in battle [FIG. 13.5].

The conception is original and its mode of expression remarkable, insofar as the composition, while consistent with the didactic thrust of Revolutionary

▼ **FIG 13.5.** Charles Percier and Pierre Fontaine. *Design for a Monument to the Defenders of the Homeland in the year II*, elevation (detail), 1796. Pen, wash, and watercolor on paper. Musée Carnavalet, Paris, CARO3681. Cat. 130.

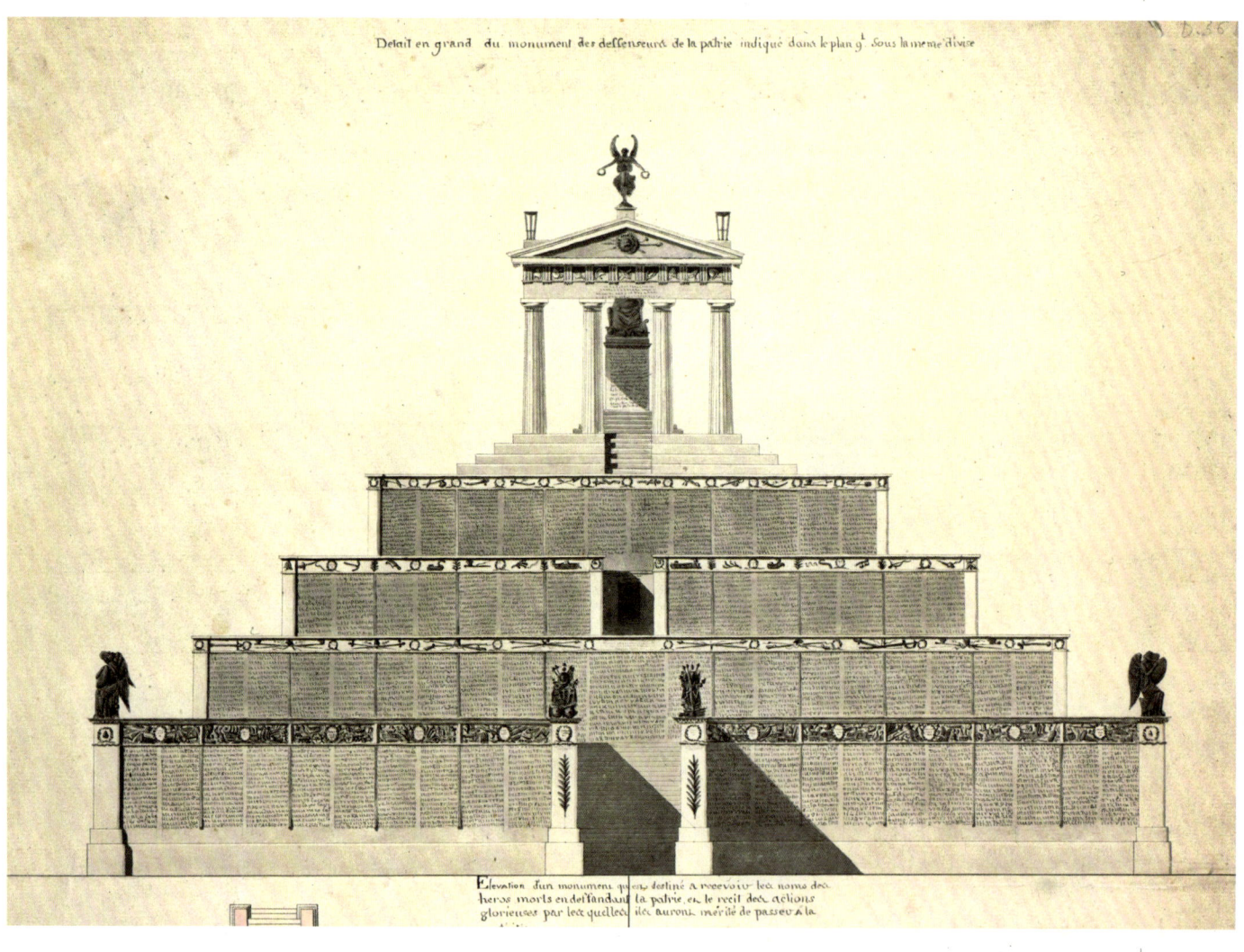

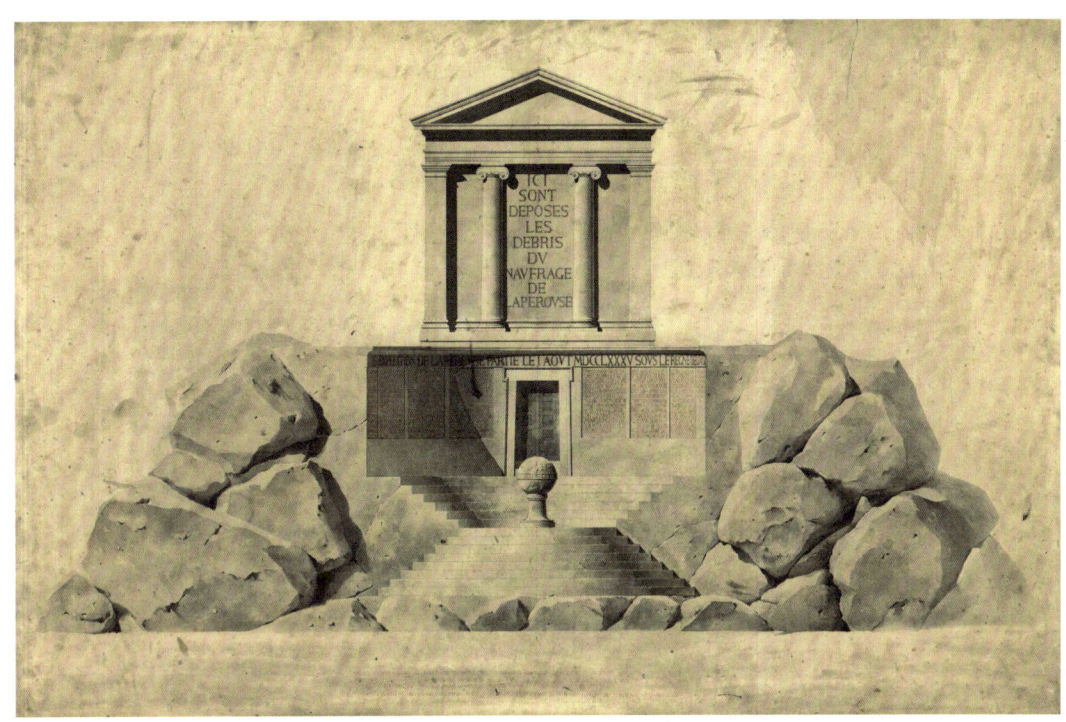

FIG 13.6. Henri Labrouste. *Design for a Cenotaph Commemorating La Pérouse*, principal elevation, 1829. Pencil, pen, wash, and watercolor on paper. Académie d'architecture, Paris, 282.1. Cat. 131.

FIG 13.7. Jean-Baptiste Isabey. *The Distribution of the Eagle Standards on the Champ de Mars* (December 5, 1804), showing the ephemeral tribune designed for the occasion by Percier and Fontaine. Château de Fontainebleau, GM Bibl.3502.

architecture, avoids the latter's characteristic bombast, over-dramatization, and radical formal vocabulary. The proportions of the temple's baseless Doric order are rather slender and the sides of the column shafts are straight. Contrasting with the emphatic power and severity typical of the architecture of the early years of the Revolution, the design creates an impression of balance and restraint. It already belongs entirely to the following century, and Henri Labrouste remembered it when he designed his cenotaph memorializing La Pérouse (1829)[12]; it was also one of his sources for the façade of the Bibliothèque Sainte-Geneviève [FIG. 13.6].

Exercises in either the spectacle of power or spectacle per se, these early efforts were succeeded after 1800 by others that were now centered on the figure of Napoleon: architectural set pieces that, although ephemeral, were brought to realization and recorded in drawings and prints. The most famous of them is perhaps the tribune designed for the distribution of the eagle standards to the heads of the French army on December 5, 1804 [FIG. 13.7; SEE ALSO FIG. 11.2]. In response to the neoclassical conception of the ceremony itself, which was modeled after a practice of the Roman emperor and his legions, Percier and Fontaine came

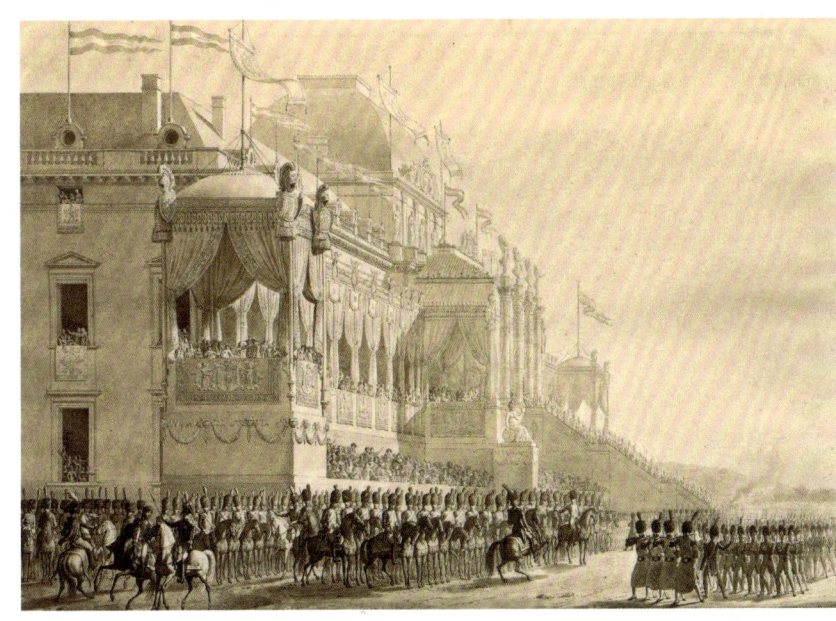

up with a design of emphatic theatricality, full of classical and military allusions exalting the personality of the hero. Despite disastrous weather conditions (the tent proved ineffective in a driving, icy rain), the event would echo down the years. Depicted by Jacques Louis David in an immense canvas conceived as a pendant to his painting of the coronation, the ceremony would be imitated by Napoleon III (May 10, 1852), and Andreas Beyer has demonstrated that it inspired the cornice of the Altes Museum in Berlin designed by Karl Friedrich Schinkel, who was in Paris at the time.[13]

During the same festival days (the distribution of the "Eagles" occurred three days after the coronation), the temporary alterations of the cathedral of Notre Dame for the religious ceremony provided Percier with an occasion to express himself in a very different mode. Far from ancient Rome, this time he could mobilize the intimate knowledge of medieval French art he had acquired during an extended campaign of drawing the collections of the Musée des monuments français by the side of Alexandre Lenoir, especially his familiarity with Parisian work of the early medieval period, which Raoul-Rochette emphasized in his obituary.[14] The perspective view from the porch of the ephemeral portico attached to the façade, engraved and published in the volume commemorating these events, reveals a mastery of, even a delight in, a colorful, highly decorative neo-Gothic idiom [FIG. 13.8].[15] In this context, the large sculpted figures—personifications of French cities on the lower register, a figure of Renown and angels carrying the scepter and crown on the upper register—embody a synthetic architectural and decorative program as contradictory as Napoleon's own views of religion at the time.

However, service as architects to the emperor also entailed the design of many buildings that were meant to endure. Few of these were realized, but the associated design process occasioned much dialogue with the patron, conversations that in the last book Percier and Fontaine published together, *Résidences de souverains*,[16] are revealed to have often been quite personal. Critical discussion of the principal palaces of modern Europe was one way for the emperor to imagine his own place in the gallery of great men; the latter were represented by their resi-

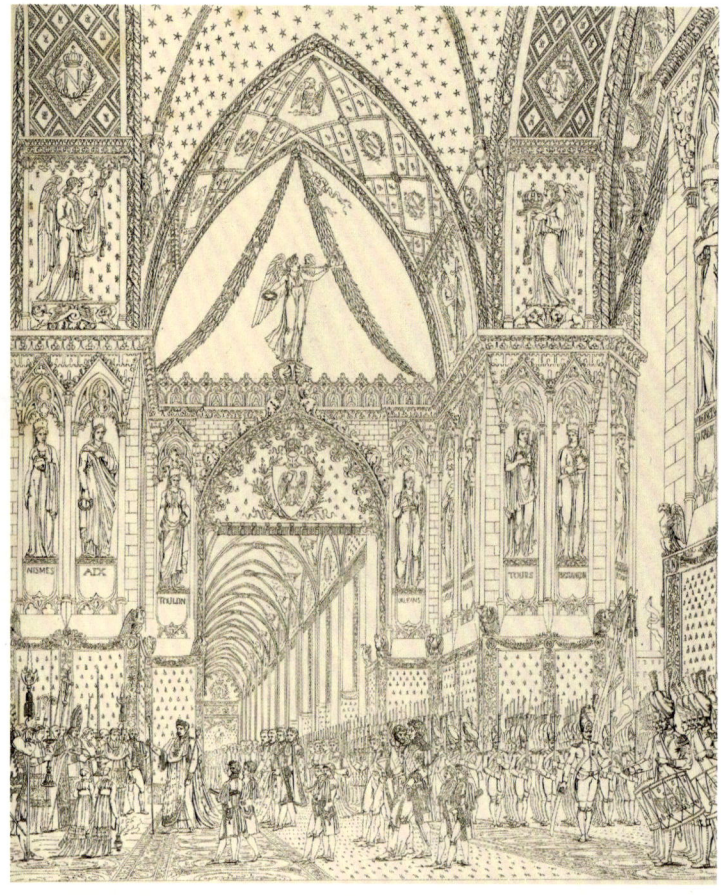

▲ **FIG 13.8.** Charles Percier and Pierre Fontaine. View of the Gallery and the Grand Portico erected at the entrance of the cathedral of Notre Dame. Line engraving. From Percier and Fontaine, *Description des cérémonies et des fêtes* (Paris: Leblanc, 1807), pl. 4.

▷ **FIG 13.9.** Charles Percier and Pierre Fontaine. Sketch of the plan for the version of the palace of the King of Rome that was retained for publication, ca. 1812. Pencil, pen, and ink on paper. Private collection, Paris.

dences, and it was his intention, with his architects' help, to fashion an analogous monumental self-portrait. This goal—to build a palace for himself that would be superior to those of previous kings and emperors, just as he intended to surpass their other achievements—dates from 1806, with the plan to build a palace in Lyon. But another phase, characterized by more focused reflection and more intimate exchanges between the patron and his architects, commenced in June of 1810, less than three years after Napoleon's marriage to Marie Louise, with the project to build a palace for the king of Rome. To quote the architects: "Napoleon himself almost always designated the residences whose plans seemed fitting, and which he wanted to compare with the one he intended to build."[17] This undertaking, which entailed the comparison of a set of examples with a series of proposals, will always retain an element of mystery, but, in addition to the designs in *Résidences de souverains*, it occasioned a large corpus of drawings, some of which were published and some of which survive in the form of spectacular, carefully finished presentation drawings. The most original aspect of the project is to be found not in the compositions themselves but rather in this principle of variation.

Accordingly, we are confronted here not with a project that evolved and matured in successive stages but rather with a corpus of possible alternative designs. The version published by the two architects is a rectangular palace situated at the top of the Chaillot Hill and separated from the Seine by vast stepped terraces [FIG. 13.9]. But drawings exist for several other designs, some of

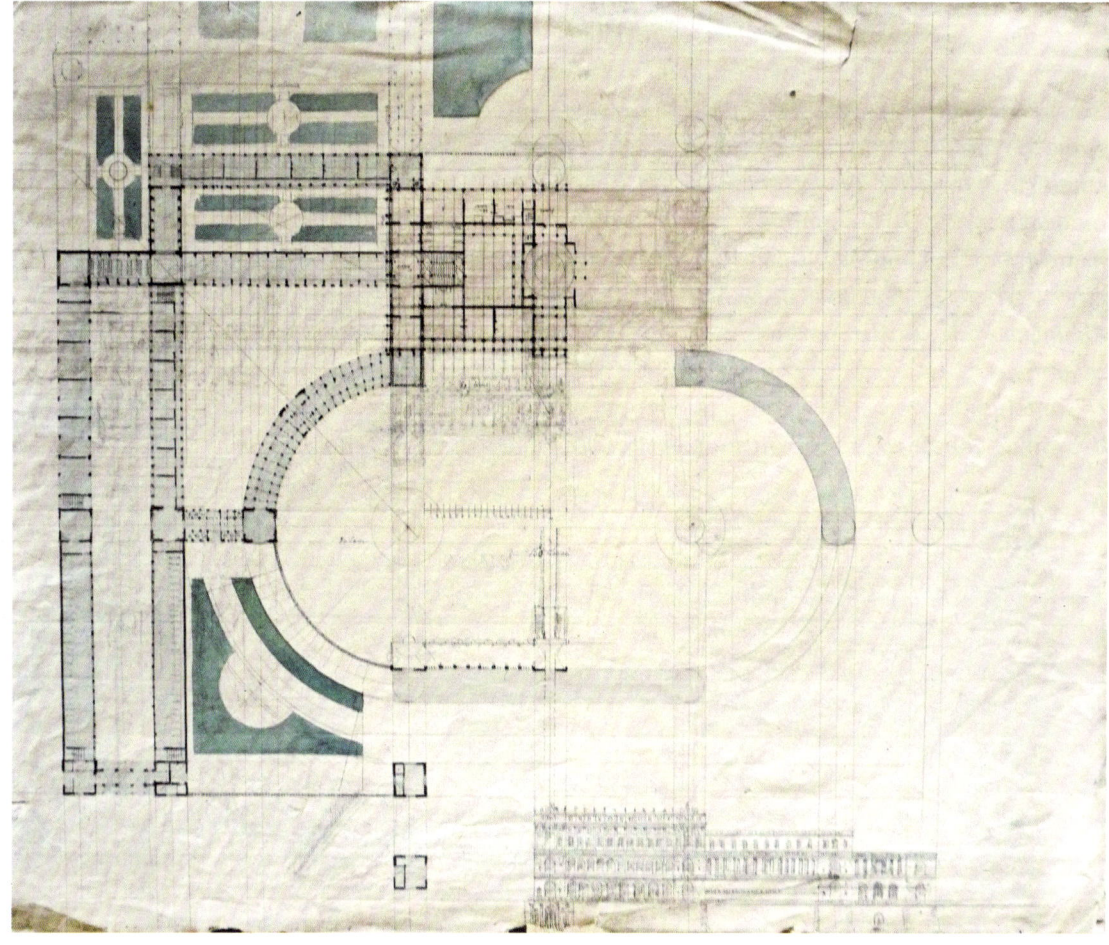

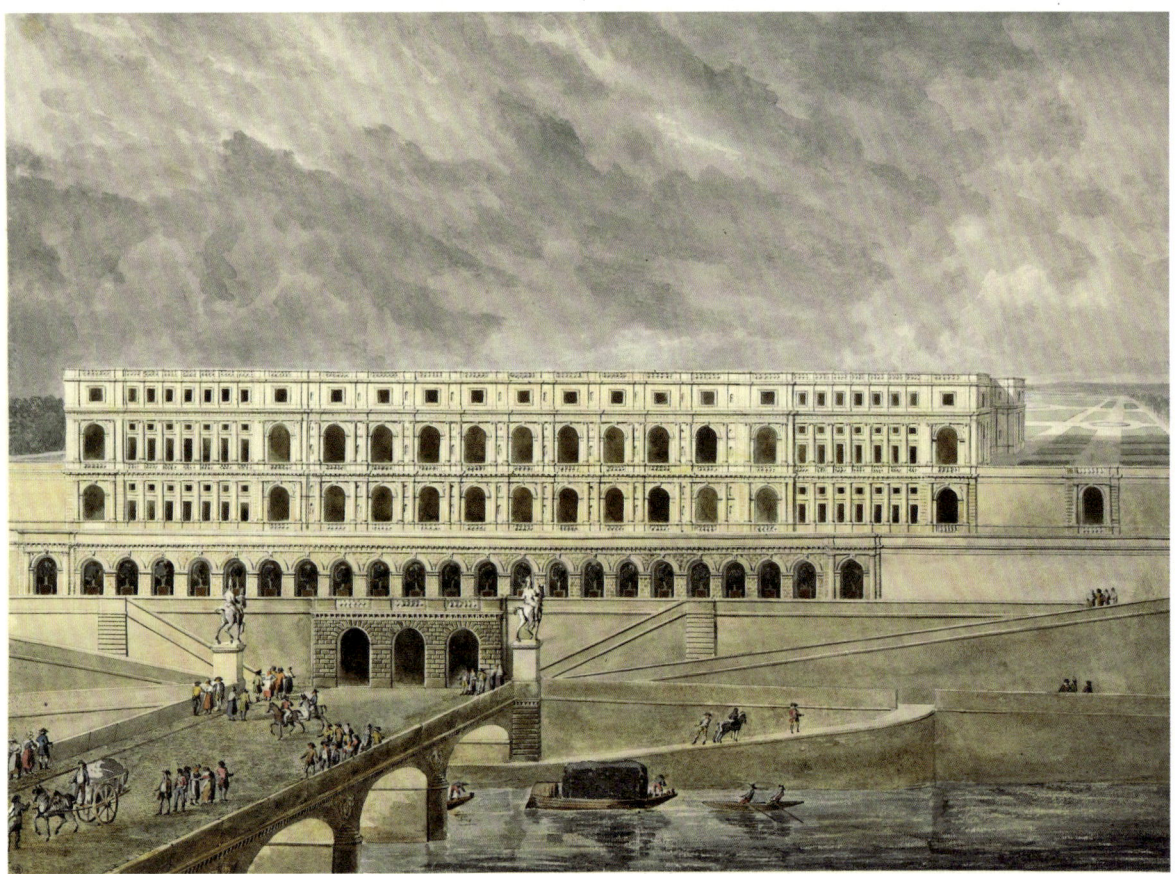

which are variant proposals for the organization of the central block, whereas others offer completely different solutions. The possibility of a structure rising directly from the river is explored in a proposal with a façade in the Italian manner consisting of two basement levels surmounted by three floors with as many superimposed orders. Formal interest is generated by a contrast between ranges of seven narrow windowed bays on either side and, in the center, a range of eleven monumental bays pierced with large arcade openings, with identical single bays terminating the composition at either end [FIG. 13.10]. A much more modest variant corresponds, as we now know, to a specific request made by Napoleon in the context of calls for his abdication. An album in the École des beaux-arts, Paris, includes drawings for a final version in which it is reduced to an unassuming garden pavilion: a "palace" for the king of Rome with no palace at all. The structure consisted entirely of landscaped features that would have recycled completed work on the foundations, which (given the date of the latest drawing it contains) points to a date for the album later than 1815 [FIGS. 13.11, 13.12].

▷ **FIG 13.10.** Charles Percier and Pierre Fontaine. Perspective view of the main façade of a version of the project for the palace of the king of Rome in which it rises directly from a quay on the Seine, ca. 1812. Watercolor and wash on paper. École nationale supérieure des beaux-arts, Paris, PC 65 936–46.

◁ **FIG 13.11.** Charles Percier and Pierre Fontaine. Perspective view of the most modest project for the palace of the king of Rome, which nonetheless retains the composition of riverside ramps and terraces as well as a vast park, 1814. Watercolor and wash on paper. École nationale supérieure des beaux-arts, Paris, PC 65 936-48.

▷ **FIG 13.12.** Charles Percier and Pierre Fontaine, View of a proposed transformation of the Chaillot Hill into a garden, showing a modest pavilion overlooking the pont d'Iena and the Champ de Mars, after 1815. Watercolor and wash on paper. École nationale supérieure des beaux-arts, Paris, PC 65 936-48b.

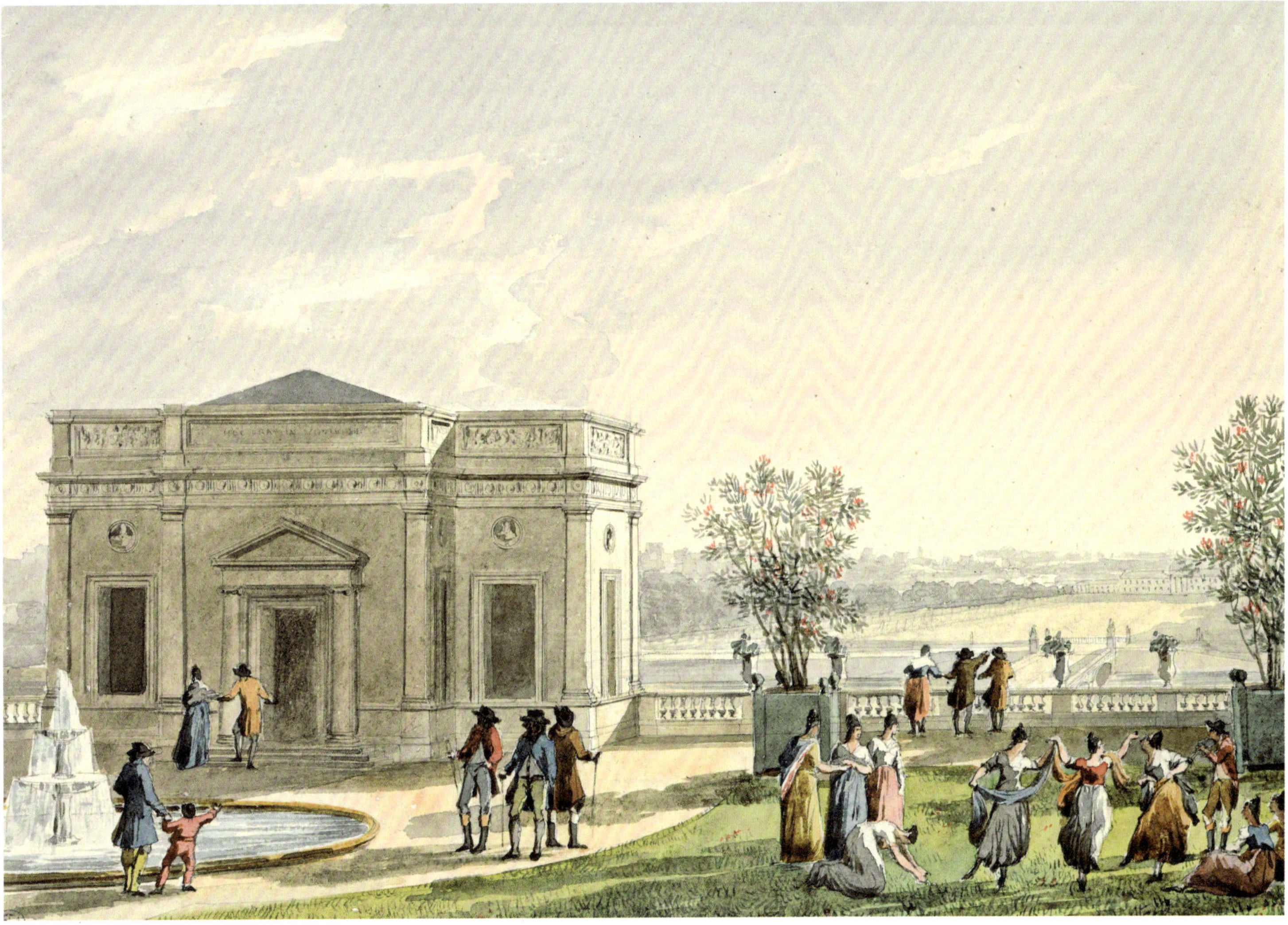

13 UNBUILT ARCHITECTURE

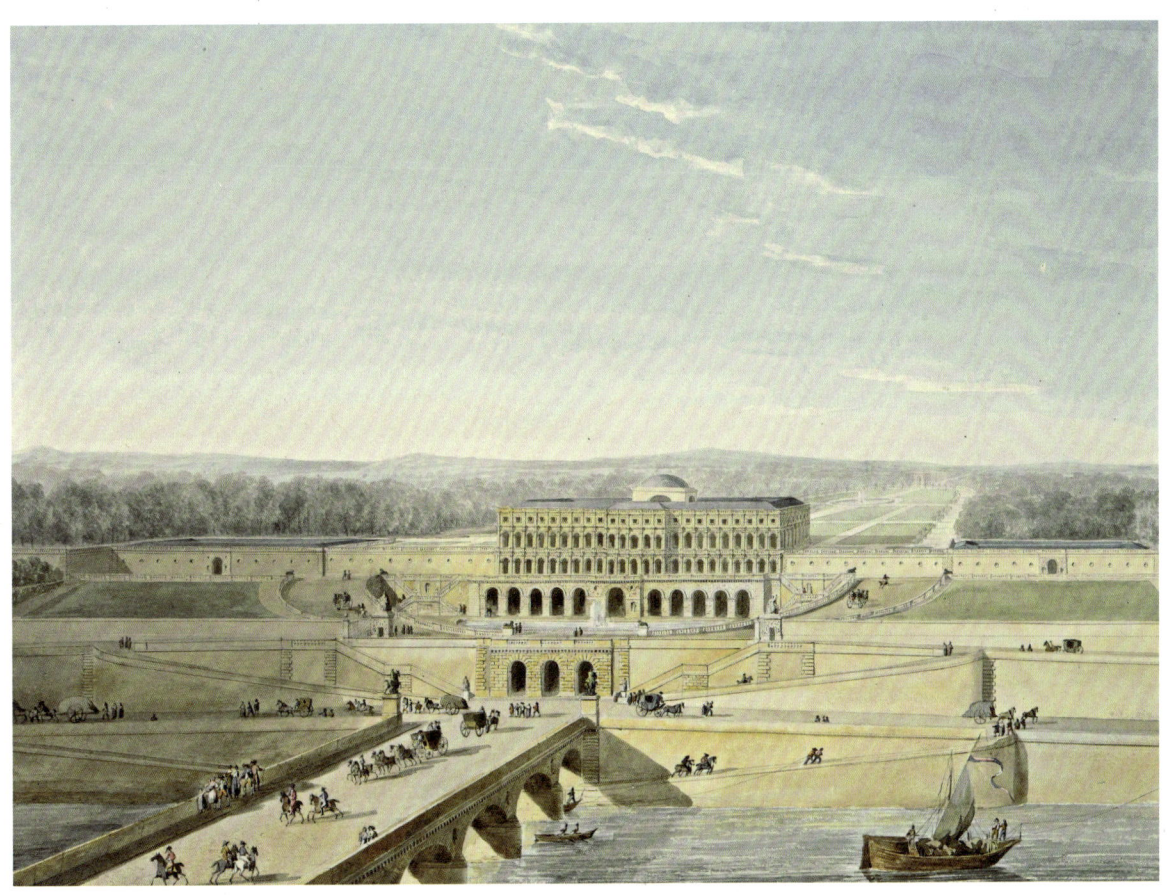

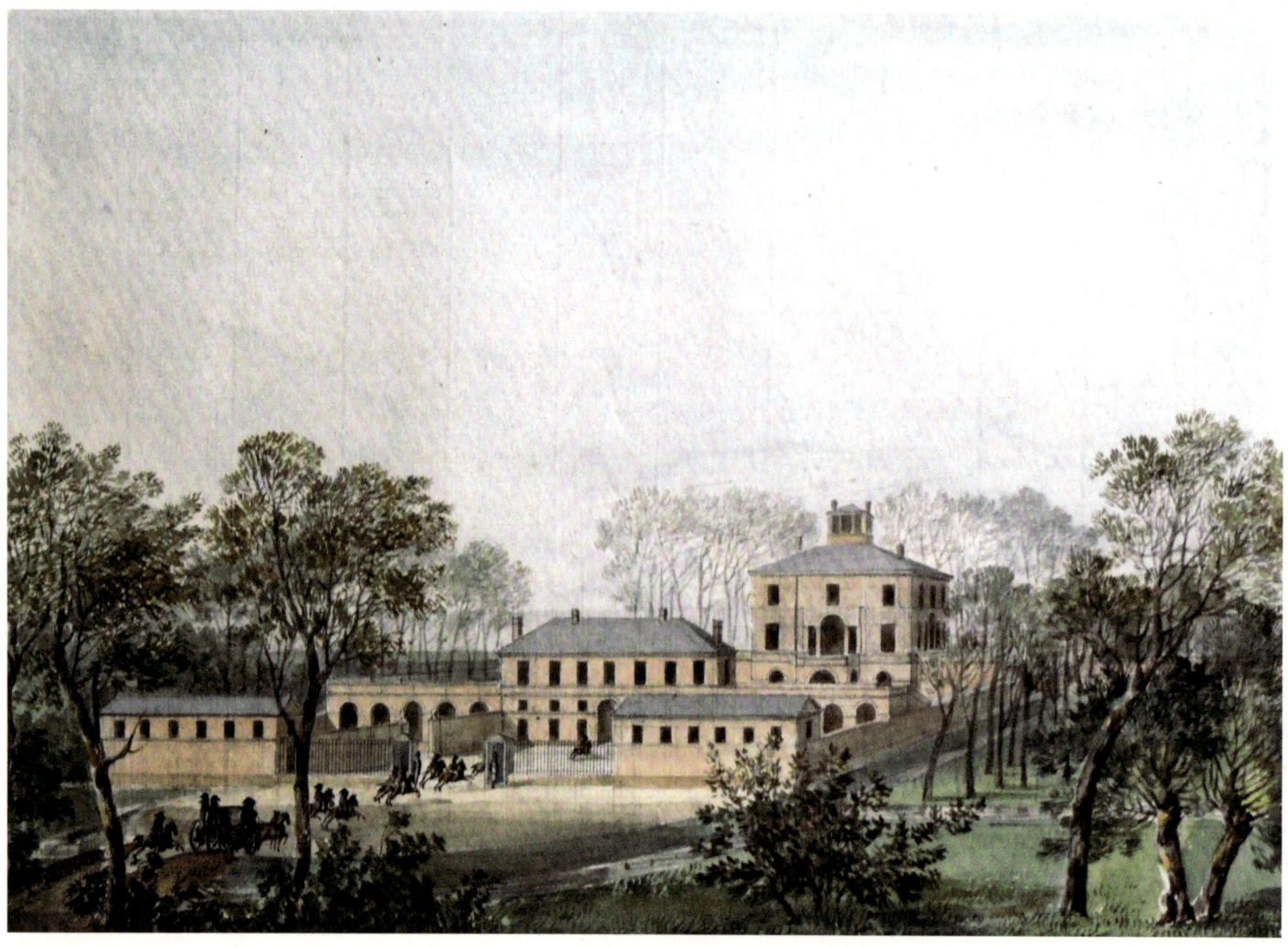

Significantly, we find this same approach—the development of several variations on a single conception—in the response to another, otherwise modest proposal, a house intended to facilitate Napoleon's oversight of the construction of a large port in the bay of Terneuzen, just opposite London on the Dutch coast. In a journal entry dated December 25, 1811, Fontaine briefly refers to this project, which he apparently did not dare present to the emperor because of its high cost, as all three of the resulting proposals greatly exceeded the patron's needs. Clearly, the design process occasioned an effort that, in rhetorical and demonstrative terms, was disproportionate and, in the end, counterproductive. It is difficult to say whether this was because the architects' reflections were somewhat detached from reality, or because they hoped to interest the emperor by initiating another comparative architectural discussion with him, along the lines of their previous exchanges about the design of the palace of the king of Rome.

▷ **FIG 13.14.** Charles Percier and Pierre Fontaine. Project for a house for the emperor overlooking the bay of Terneuzen, sheet with various sketches (plans, elevation, section) of version B, in which the complex is organized around a central observation tower, ca. 1811. Pencil, pen, wash, and watercolor on paper. The Art Institute of Chicago, Percier and Fontaine Collection, Ryerson and Burnham Libraries, 2000.2.

▷▷ **FIG 13.15.** Charles Percier and Pierre Fontaine. Project for a house for the emperor overlooking the bay of Terneuzen, version B, elevation with the observation tower, 1811. Pencil and watercolor on paper. Private collection, Paris.

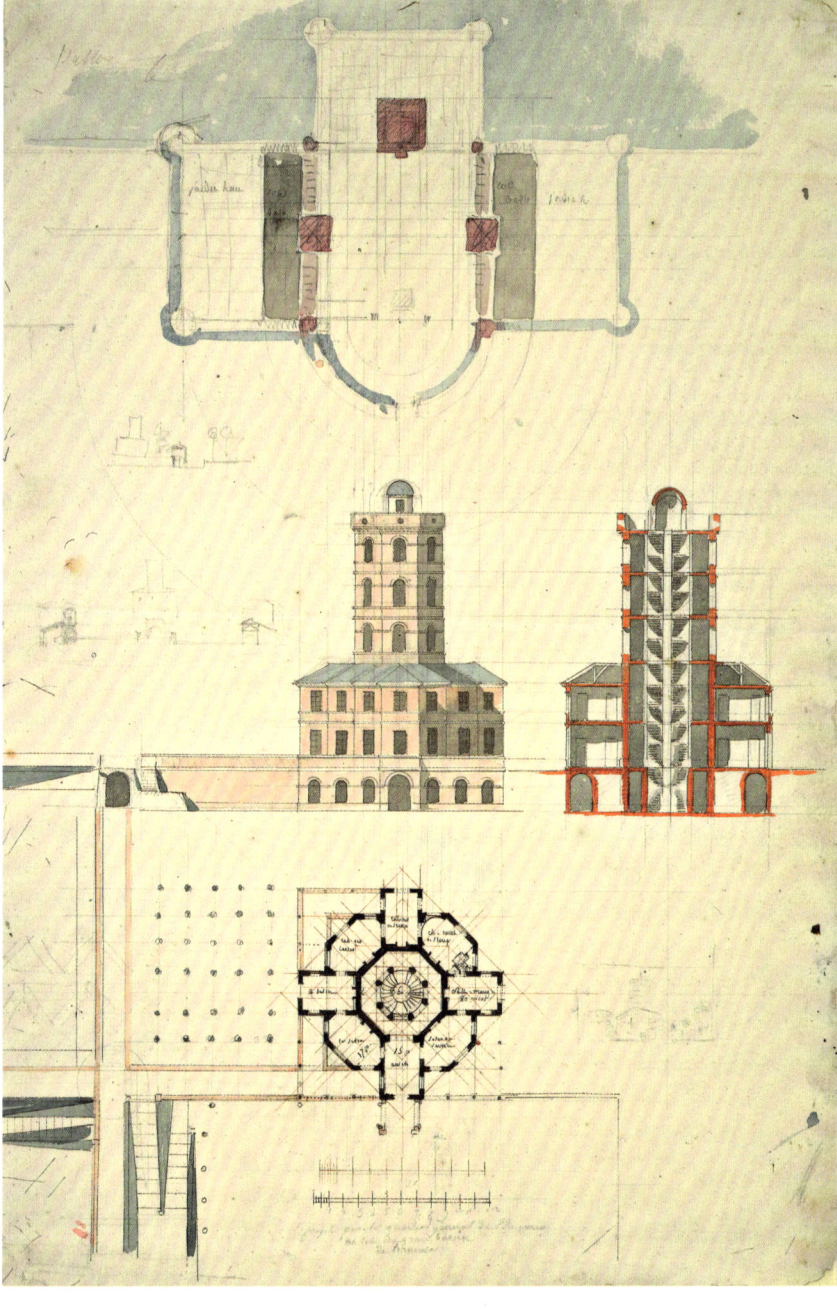

◀ **FIG 13.13.** Charles Percier and Pierre Fontaine. Project for a house for the emperor overlooking the bay of Terneuzen, perspective view of version C, in which the residence is an Italian-style villa in the manner of Serlio, 1811. Pencil and watercolor on paper. Private collection, Paris.

All three of the proposals feature a courtyard providing access to the main building and include a central staircase. One of the designs resembles a small Italian villa culminating in a simple belvedere, whereas the other two are dominated by a powerful central observation tower. In plan, there are similarities with some of Ledoux's *barrières* (toll gates), but here the exterior expression of the brick façades, stripped of all ornament, telegraphs a military austerity and simplicity appropriate to the building's intended function. Above all, the designs reference the Italian Renaissance and Perrault's Observatory in ways that are quite literal, even historicist. The façade pierced by a large Palladian window could have come straight from the pages of a contemporary model book, but the corresponding plan recycles that of the Medici villa at Poggio a Caiano.

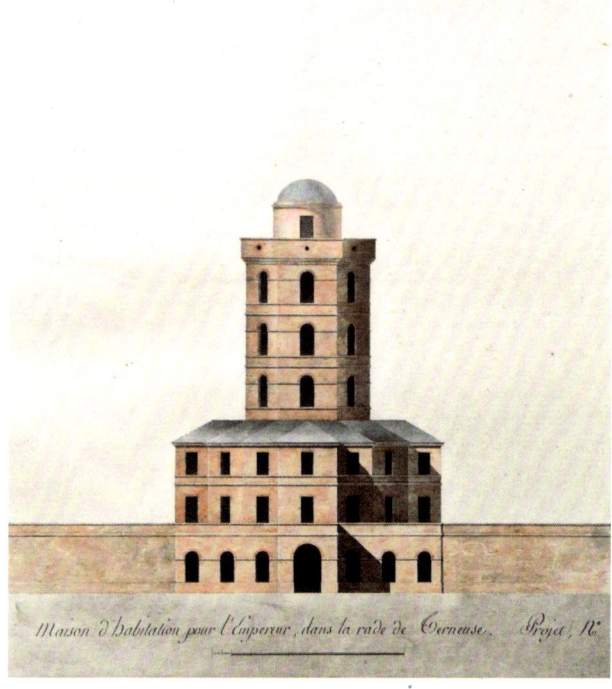

One of the two other circularly disposed plans bears a striking resemblance to one by Brunelleschi for the rotunda at Santa Maria degli Angeli in Florence [FIGS. 13.13–13.15].

Professors at the École des beaux-arts often told students who were hesitant to settle on a single proposal: "several designs: no design," a phrase meant to convey how important it is for an architect to take a position and defend it with conviction. For this project—effectively a reversion to the paper architecture of their youth and early career, at a time when the likelihood of their realizing their dreams as Napoleon's builders was growing ever more remote—Percier and Fontaine returned to architectural speculation and rhetoric, spheres to which Percier would largely devote his energies after 1815. ●

1 Charles Percier and Pierre Fontaine, *Résidences de souverains. Parallèle entre plusieurs résidences de souverains de France, d'Allemagne, de Suède, de Russie, d'Espagne et d'Italie, à Paris chez les auteurs* (Paris: Authors, 1833), 339.

2 Courier W. Stewart, *Diary of an Excursion to France in the Months August and September 1814* (Edinburgh: Peter Hill, Manners and Miller, 1814), 153ff.

3 See especially the designs published in the first collection of engraved designs by students of the Académie royale d'architecture. Armand Parfait Prieur and Pierre Louis Van Cléemputte, *Collection des prix que la ci-devant Académie d'Architecture proposait et couronnait tous les ans, gravée au trait, imprimée sur papier propre à être lavé*, vol. 1 (Paris: Authors, [1787–96]).

4 David Van Zanten, "Architectural composition at the École des Beaux-Arts, from Charles Percier to Charles Garnier," in *The Architecture of the École des Beaux-Arts*, ed. Arthur Drexler (New York: Museum of Modern Art, 1977), 111–324.

5 A radical reworking of Mozart's *The Magic Flute* by Ludwig Wenzel Lachnith (1746–1820), which premiered at the Paris Opera in 1801.

6 Marie Ursula Riemann-Reyher in *Karl Friedrich Schinkel: A Universal Man*, ed. Michael Snodin (New Haven and London: Yale University Press, 1991), 107–11.

7 Jean Henri Hassenfratz, *Traité de l'art du charpentier* (Paris: Firmin Didot, 1804), pls. 1–4.

8 La Fontaine, *Fables de La Fontaine* (Paris: Pierre Didot l'aîné, 1802), 2:68–69.

9 See Werner Szambien, *Les projets de l'an II, concours d'architecture de la période révolutionnaire* (Paris: EnsBa, 1986).

10 Ibid.

11 Ibid., 82.

12 Jean-Philippe Garric, "Alexandre Lenoir et Charles Percier, un compagnonnage oublié," in *Alexandre Lenoir et le Musée des monuments français*, ed. Geneviève Bresc and Béatrice de Chancel Bardelot (Paris: Musée du Louvre / INHA, 2016), 241–50.

13 Andreas Beyer. "Karl Friedrich Schinkel in Paris," in *Interferenzen/Interférences. Deutschland Frankreich Architektur 1800–2000*, ed. Jean-Louis Cohen and Harmut Frank 104–11. Exh. cat. Tübingen: Deutsches Architektur Museum Frankfurt am Main, 2013.

14 Desiré Raoul-Rochette, "Percier, Sa vie et ses ouvrages," *Revue des deux mondes* 4, no. 24 (October 15, 1840): 246–68; the passage regarding Percier's knowledge of Gothic art is on p. 263. See also Garric, "Alexandre Lenoir et Charles Percier."

15 Charles Percier, Pierre Fontaine, and Jean-Baptiste Isabey, *Description des cérémonies et des fêtes qui ont eu lieu pour le couronnement de LL MM Napoléon, empereur des français et roi d'Italie, et Joséphine son auguste épouse* (Paris: Leblanc, 1807).

16 Charles Percier and Pierre Fontaine, *Résidences de souverains. Parallèle entre plusieurs résidences de souverains de France, d'Allemagne, de Suède, de Russie, d'Espagne et d'Italie, à Paris chez les auteurs* (Paris: Authors, 1833).

17 "Napoléon a presque toujours désigné lui-même, les résidences dont les dispositions lui semblaient convenables, et qu'il voulait comparer à celle qu'il avait l'intention de bâtir." Percier and Fontaine, *Résidences de souverains*, 231–32.

CONCLUSION

CHAPTER 14

PERCIER'S LEGACY

JEAN-PHILIPPE GARRIC

CHARLES PERCIER'S LEGACY IS AT ONCE VAST AND VARIOUS. AS IS well known, and as stated at the beginning of this volume, he was active in a dizzying number of fields, from architecture to urban planning, from furniture design to graphic design. Without pretending to be exhaustive, this book and the accompanying exhibition have made it possible to examine his career anew, to reassess its historical impact and to reconsider our understanding of it. The results have confirmed our original hypothesis: reducing Percier to his partnership with Fontaine, and then Percier-and-Fontaine to the Empire style alone, tends to obscure an artistic personality that was open-minded, prolific, and in no way limited to the codification of a single style. But revealing the extent to which Percier's individual activity exceeded his service to the imperial regime has led us to an inescapable ambiguity: he was by no means a struggling, marginal figure, an *artiste maudit*, but neither did he fit comfortably into the uniform of the official artist.

Fontaine's role as a protective buffer allowed Percier to keep a certain distance—to favor interaction with the small but enthusiastic circle of his students

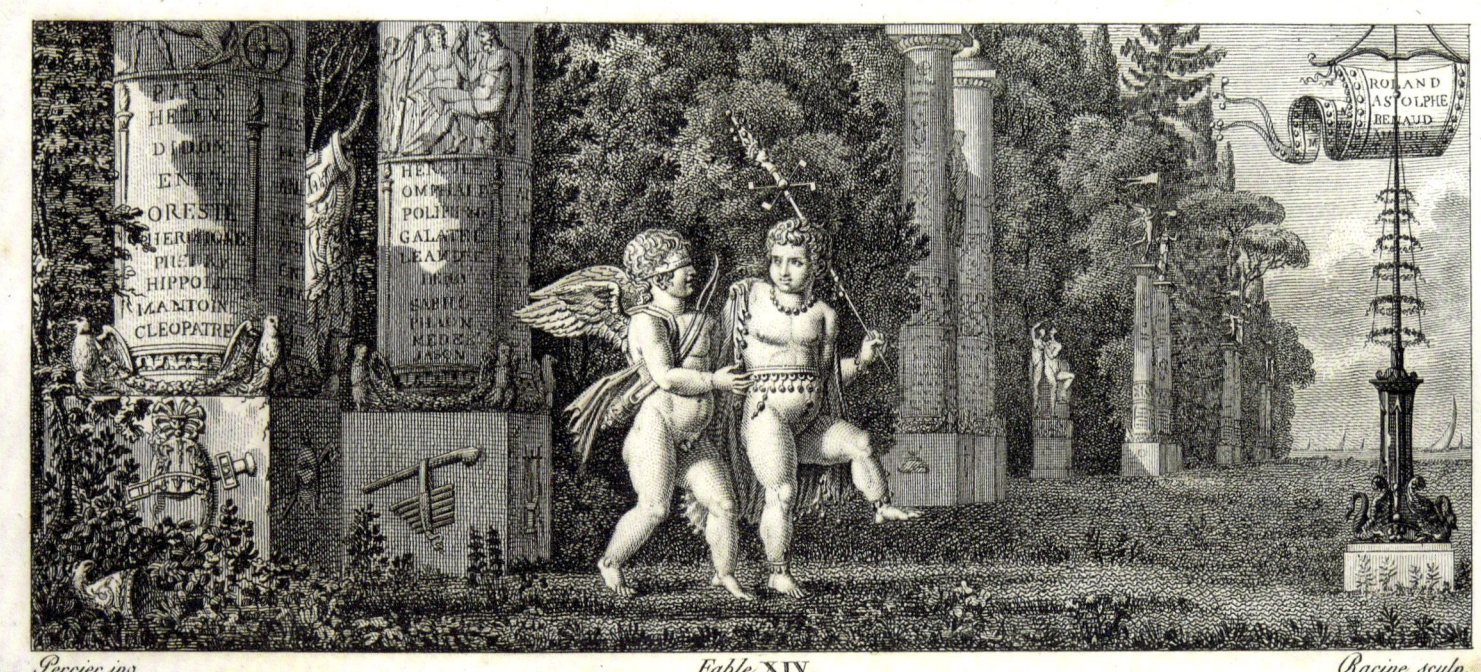

▲ **FIG 14.1.** Charles Percier. *Folly Serving as Love's Guide*. Headpiece for Book 12 illustrating the fable "Love and Folly," from Jean de La Fontaine, *Fables* (Paris: Pierre Didot l'aîné, 1802). Cat. 44.

and the seclusion of his drawing cabinet over socializing with the powerful. He was thus able to occasionally indulge in secondary pursuits—his illustrations for the fables of La Fontaine [FIG. 14.1], the design of frontispieces and ornamental framing devices—and even to wander down a side path such as his collaboration with Alexandre Lenoir on the study and installation of the collection in the Musée des monuments français. This situation made it possible for work of the most spectacular and prestigious kind to coexist with highly speculative and solitary endeavors. It allowed—and indeed explains—Percier's gradual disengagement, the two pivotal moments of which were the coronation of 1804, when he agreed to collaborate in Fontaine's shadow despite his no longer holding an official post in the emperor's household, and Waterloo in 1815, after which he opted not to join his friend in service to the new sovereign, Louis XVIII.

This gradual withdrawal, at a time of life when important architects are usually consolidating their position, was by no means a premature retirement. The architecture schools, from the Académie royale, dominated by the figure of Étienne Louis Boullée, to the École des beaux-arts, officially established in 1819, were laboratories for the gestation of future monuments as much as they were educational institutions. When the future of French and European architecture was being played out on paper to the same extent, if not an even greater one, as it was on the ground, a choice in favor of education and research through drawing was not so much a renunciation as it was an alternative ambition. Moreover, this strategy was crowned with success, at least in quantitative terms, for his students repeatedly won academic success and went on to assume important official positions, to such an extent that seven of them became members of the Institute de France,[1] while others played prominent roles abroad.[2] Percier's role in the birth of the École des beaux-arts in Paris and its architecture department was so important that as late as 1900 he was still revered as that institution's tutelary figure.

His prestigious role as a professor of architecture was decidedly in phase with his status as a winner of the Prix de Rome and a member of the Institut de France, and the institutional framework for his teaching reverberated with his high-profile friendships with painters, from Drouais to Gérard by way of David. In any case, he shifted his orientation, distancing himself from furniture design, interior decoration, and independent draftsmanship, just as he moved away from the world of high-end artisanal fabrication and publishing, where his connections were stronger and more numerous than they were in construction circles. It is easy to imagine that in a different institutional context, one that included a school of the decorative arts, the array of skills commanded by this man—who began his studies at the École gratuite de dessin—might well have led him down another professional path, and that the future of architecture and design in France would, as a consequence, have unfolded differently.

THE PRODIGIOUS INFLUENCE OF PERCIER THE TEACHER

Despite the lack of documents directly related to the content of Percier's teaching, there is reason to believe that his own publications and corpus of drawings served as its foundation, and that there was a marked continuity between his own work and that of his students. The degree to which they imitated him is eloquent; clearly they regarded their teacher as a model. Grandjean de Montigny, as previously noted, is a notable and early example.[3] We may also mention Achille Leclère, who won the Prix de Rome in 1808 and directed an atelier after his return to France in 1812. Leclère published an anthology of architectural models, again closely inspired by the one on Roman palaces by Percier and Fontaine, and was entrusted with Percier's ring upon the latter's death in 1838, whereupon he established the mechanism for its subsequent transmission.[4]

Without going into detail, we can nonetheless emphasize the degree to which several of Percier's favorite interests and themes were taken up by his disciples. The anthologies of Italian architecture, which he cosigned with Fontaine, inspired a series of analogous publications, culminating in *Les édifices de Rome moderne* by Paul Letarouilly.[5] Percier's interest in the use of color in architecture, which he had observed in Italy as well as in the Abbey of Saint-Denis, and which he applied in the arc de Carrousel, preceded by twenty years the "invention" of polychromy by his student Jakob Ignaz Hittorff. Percier's attentiveness to French architectural styles, when he designed and restored the imperial palaces, heralded similar preoccupations in the restoration and transformation of historical monuments—projects of varying quality, to be sure—by François Debret (Saint-Denis), Alphonse Gisors (Luxembourg palace), and Auguste Caristie (triumphal arch in Orange).

In the face of such abundance and diversity, it seems appropriate to assess the coherence of Percier's legacy. Doubtless there is reason to speak of a precocious eclecticism, but only if we specify what is meant by the term. Between, on the one hand, the frivolous variety of garden pavilions and the fantastic exoticism of theater sets characteristic of the late eighteenth century, and on the other hand the rhetorical affirmation of an array of historical styles adapted to different architectural programs for public buildings in the mid-nineteenth century, Percier occupied an intermediary position, one consistent with his role as a transitional figure between the ancien régime and the modern era. His early eclecticism should be distinguished from the one espoused at the same time in the *Recueil et parallèle des édifices en tout genre, anciens et modernes* by Jean Nicolas Louis Durand, a book in which the professor of architecture at the École polytechnique brought together buildings from all periods and all the great civilizations.[6] While Durand, working from a strong foundation of universalist ambitions, built an implacable synthesis at the price of a radical reduction of graphic means, Percier proceeded without global aspirations. He was content merely to establish a hierarchy among the many references that he tried to understand through the many productions that issued from his insatiable drive to draw, honoring their aesthetic and ornamental differences in all their richness and nuance.

But this hierarchy, for all its seeming clarity, is not without ambiguity. Antiquity headed the list, of course, followed closely by Italy; these were the sources from which he drew the models for his official projects, as well as for his furniture designs. The French medieval and Renaissance periods came after: links to great buildings of the past, in which capacity they served in the decorations for Notre Dame de Paris for Napoleon's coronation and in the projects to unite the Louvre and the Tuileries. More exotic allusions were relegated to the realm of theater sets and illustrations. However, this scale of valuations is at odds with something that was even more deeply rooted in Percier—his penchant for accumulation and his Piranesian tendency for ornamental overload, which was seconded by a curiosity about forms that led him to expand his palette to encompass, notably, the Middle Ages.

A SON OF THE ÉCOLE GRATUITE DE DESSIN

Rising from a modest background, Charles Percier made his way to the highest point on his chosen career path, and what we know about his teaching heralded future developments in architectural education and the role of ateliers within the École des beaux-arts. Neither doctrinaire nor a pedagogue (in the conventional sense), he cultivated proximity to his principal students, whether through work and friendship, as with Achille Leclère and Hippolyte Lebas, or through less well-documented collaborations such as the one with André Chatillon that seems to have produced the scrapbook in the Metropolitan Museum. One sens-

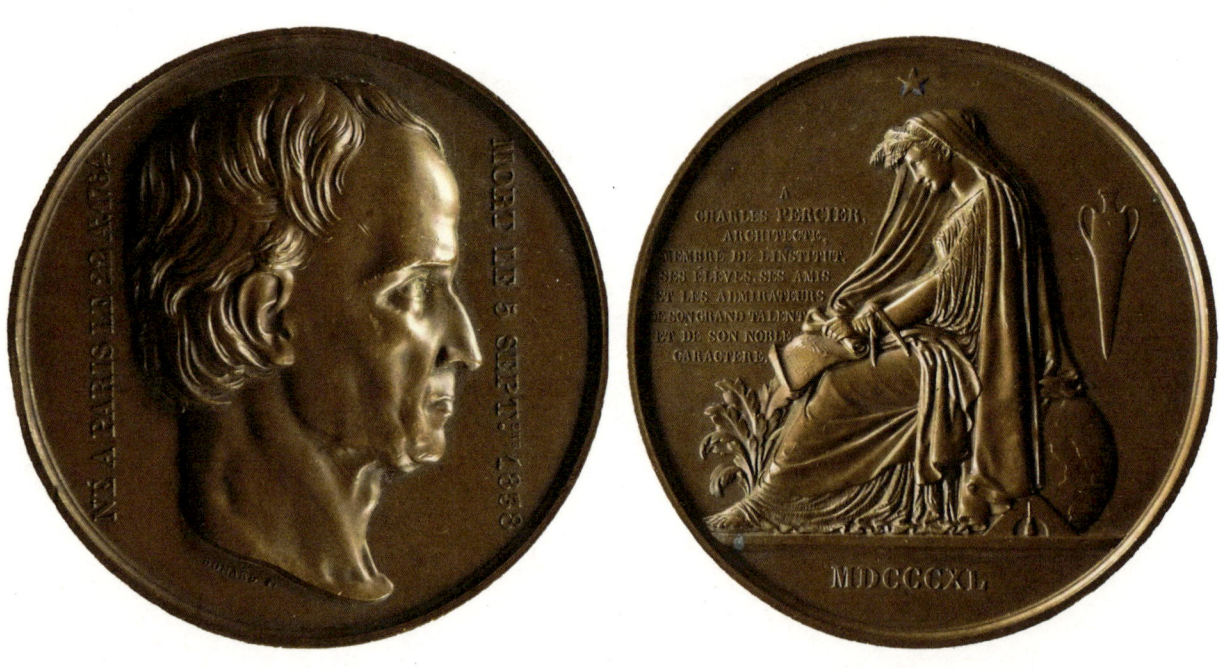

es that Percier's approach was largely intuitive, favoring—to cite a phrase later employed by Charles Garnier—"feeling over theory."[7] Percier was a remarkable draftsman who operated at the heart of an institution that valued drawing above all else. He could not help but reinforce this priority by emphasizing perspective, which was taught by Fontaine during his school's early years and figures prominently in their three principal publications,[8] or by composing architectural fragments, a genre whose mastery remained in his wake a touchstone of Beaux-Arts culture and a way for architecture students to manifest their sensibilities.[9]

However, despite Percier's successes and his central role at this prestigious institution, it was for the benefit of the École gratuite de dessin that he established an annuity one month before his death. In this connection, the historian Jules Michelet, in his book *Le Peuple*, repeats a statement that Percier made toward the end of his life to the painter Hillaire Belloc, then director of the school that had given him his start. As spoken by the aged architect, who was recalling his modest origins, it sounds like a profession of faith: "The most decent men I have known came from this class. They know, when they leave in the morning, that they might not return that evening, and they are always ready to appear before God" [FIG. 14.2].[10]

FIG 14.2. Joseph-François Domard. Medal dedicated to Percier's memory by "his students, his friends, and the admirers of his considerable gifts and his noble character," 1840. Bronze. Recto: Profile portrait of Percier; verso: allegory of Architecture in mourning. Private collection, Paris. Cat. 30.

1 François Debret (1777–1850), Hippolyte Le Bas (1782–1867), Augustin Caristie (1783–1862), Jean Jacques Marie Huvé (1783–1852), Achille Leclere (1785–1853), Martin Pierre Gauthier (1790–1855), and Louis Visconti (1791–1853).

2 Notably Augustin Grandjean de Montigny (1776–1850) in Rio de Janeiro, Brazil; Auguste Ricard de Montferrand (1786–1858) in St. Petersburg, Russia; Tilman François Suÿs (1783–1861) in Belgium; and Frédéric Gaertner (1791–1847) in Germany.

3 Auguste Famin and Augustin Grandjean de Montigny, *Architecture toscane* (Paris: Authors, 1806–15).

4 Achille Leclère, *Recueil d'architecture, lithographié en l'année 1826 par…élèves de Monsieur Achille Leclère* (Paris: Author, 1826). See Garric, *Recueils d'Italie*, 207.

5 Paul Letarouilly, *Édifices de Rome moderne* (Paris: Bance, 1840–57).

6 Jean Nicolas Louis Durand, *Recueil et parallèle des édifices en tout genre, anciens et modernes, remarquables par leur beauté, par leur grandeur ou par leur singularité et dessinés sur une même échelle* (Paris: Author, [1799]–1801).

7 "la préference au sentiment sur la théorie." Charles Garnier, *Le Nouvel opéra de Paris* (Paris: Librairie générale de l'architecture et des travaux publics Duch-er, 1878–81), as quoted in Jacques Lucan, *Composition, non-composition: Architecture et théories, XIXe–XXe siècles* (Lausanne: Presses polytechniques universitaires romandes, 2009).

8 Charles Percier and Pierre Fontaine, *Palais, maisons et autres édifices modernes dessinés à Rome; publiés à Paris, l'an VI de la République française (1798, v. st.)* (Paris, Authors, 1798); Charles Percier and Pierre Fontaine, *Recueil de décorations intérieures* (Paris: Authors and Pierre Didot l'aîné, 1801–12); Charles Percier, Pierre Fontaine, and Jean Charles Bonnard, *Choix des plus célèbres maisons de plaisance de Rome et de ses environs* (Paris: Pierre Didot l'aîne, 1809–13). In Chapter 6 in this volume, Iris Moon explores the role of perspective in the *Recueil de décorations intérieures*.

9 Jean-Philippe Garric, "Des frontispices aux 'éléments analytiques,' les compositions graphiques d'architecture à l'Ecole des Beaux-Arts," in *Livraisons d'histoire de l'architecture*, no. 30 (second semester 2015): 59–68.

10 "Les hommes les plus honnêtes que j'aie connus étaient de cette classe. Ils savent, en partant le matin, qu'ils peuvent ne pas revenir le soir, et ils sont toujours prêts à paraître devant Dieu." Jules Michelet, *Le Peuple* (Paris: Comptoir des imprimeurs réunis, Hachette, Paulin, 1846).

CHECKLIST

SECTION 1

CHARLES PERCIER AND HIS CIRCLES

1

Gathering of Artists, n.d.
Engraved by Alexandre Clément after Louis Léopold Boilly's painting *Gathering of Artists in the Atelier of Isabey* (see cat. 4), exhibited at the 1798 Salon
21 ¼ × 16 ¾ in. (54 × 42.5 cm)
Private collection, Paris

2

Portrait of Charles Percier, 1807
Robert Lefèvre
Oil on canvas
33 ⅛ × 21 ¼ in. (86 × 54 cm)
Châteaux de Versailles et de Trianon, Versailles, MV6313
SEE FIG. I.1.

3

* **Preparatory sketches for the painting *Gathering of Artists in the Atelier of Isabey***, ca. 1798
Louis Léopold Boilly
Oil on paper mounted on canvas

3A Portrait of Percier
11 ¼ × 8 ⅛ in. (28.5 × 20.8 cm)

3B Portrait of Fontaine
7 ¼ × 6 in. (18.4 × 15.3 cm)

3C Portrait of François Gérard
18 ⅛ × 15 in. (46 × 38 cm)

3D Portraits of Jean-Baptiste Isabey and Nicolas Antoine Taunay
12 ¼ × 11 ⅜ in. (31 × 29 cm)
Palais des Beaux-Arts, Lille, P 376; P 381; P 385; P 375
SEE FIG. 2B.2.

4

* **Gathering of Artists in the Atelier of Isabey**, 1798
Louis Léopold Boilly
Oil on canvas
28 × 43 ¾ in. (71 × 111 cm)
Musée du Louvre, Paris, RF1290bis
SEE FIG. 2B.1.

5

* **Portrait of Josephine de Beauharnais**, ca. 1796
Andrea Appiani
Oil on canvas
38 ⅝ × 29 in. (98 × 73.5 cm)
Private collection, Italy

This portrait of the future Empress Josephine was painted by Andrea Appiani, probably in 1796, when Josephine was living in Milan to be near General Bonaparte, who was then engaged in combat with Austrian forces around Mantua. It was conceived as the pendant to the portrait of Bonaparte painted by Appiani earlier in 1796, now in the collection of Lord Rosebery at Dalmeny House.

The portrait of Bonaparte shows the military man, saber in hand, dictating a list of his victories to a winged genius, with the battle of Lodi visible in the distance, but Appiani represents Josephine in the garb of a *merveilleuse* surrounded by many references to the cult of Venus, including statues of Cupid and Venus. The two reliefs on the low wall that separates the foreground from the marine landscape beyond depict episodes from the loves of Jupiter: at left, Leda and the swan; in the center, the rape of Europa. In the background, the retinue of Amphitrite, accompanied by maritime divinities, hastens toward a meeting with Neptune. This too is an allusion to the cult of Venus, as is the myrtle at the right from which Josephine is about to hang a crown of laurel, oak, roses, and jasmine for the victorious hero whose companion she was and whose glory she shared.

Appiani's full-length portraits of Bonaparte and his wife were celebrated in Milan by an ode penned by the poet Angelo Petracchi. The Italian artist twice reprised this portrait of Josephine—in 1801 and 1807, the later version representing her as the queen of Italy (Musée national des châteaux de Malmaison et Bois-Préau).

During Josephine's sojourn in Milan and shortly after, Appiani also painted several members of her entourage. These works include a seductive portrait of Madame Hamelin (Musée Carnavalet), the wife of a wealthy army provisioner, and another of the beautiful Laure de Bonneuil, comtesse Regnaud de Saint-Jean d'Angély (Musée national des châteaux de Versailles et Trianon), spirited portrayals of women who figured prominently in the small court that surrounded General Bonaparte and his wife during the Italian campaign.

—VINCENT DROGUET

6

Percier's *carte de visite*, n.d.
Engraving heightened with bistre wash on heavy paper
3 ½ × 4 ⅜ in. (8.7 × 11 cm)
Private collection, Paris

7

Attendance token, architecture class, ca. 1770
École gratuite de dessin
Copper
Diam. 1 ⅜ in. (3.4 cm)
Private collection, Paris
SEE FIG. 2.2.

8

* **Portrait of Antoine François Peyre**, ca. 1820
Julien Léopold Boilly
Lithograph
24 × 20 in. (62 × 52 cm)
École nationale supérieure des Beaux-Arts, Paris, Est 6479

9

Design of a Menagerie Set within the Park of a Royal Château, arena plan. Second place, Prix de Rome competition (1783)
Charles Percier
From Armand Parfait Prieur and Pierre Louis Van Cléemputte, *Collection des prix que la ci-devant Académie d'Architecture proposait et couronnait tous les ans*
Paris: Authors, 1787–97
Watercolor over engraving
15 ½ × 10 ¼ in. (39.5 × 26 cm)
Private collection, Paris

10

‡ **Edifice to House the Academies, cross section, elevation, and plan. First place, Prix de Rome competition**, 1786
Charles Percier
Pencil, pen and black ink, gray and rose wash on paper
19 ½ × 13 ⅛ in. (49.5 × 33.4 cm)
École nationale supérieure des Beaux-Arts, Paris, PRAE
SEE FIG. 2.8.

11

* **Edifice to House the Academies, cross section and elevation. First place, Prix de Rome competition**, 1786
Charles Percier
From Armand Parfait Prieur and Pierre Louis Van Cléemputte, *Collection des prix que la ci-devant Académie d'Architecture proposait et couronnait tous les ans*, plate VI
Paris: Authors, 1787–97
Line engraving heightened with gray wash and watercolor
20 × 13 ⅜ in. (51 × 34 cm)
Bibliothèque de l'Institut national d'histoire de l'art, Paris, Fol EST 441

12

‡ **Design for a museum, elevation**, 1783
Étienne Louis Boullée
Black ink and wash on paper
20 ¾ × 66 ⅛ in. (53 × 168 cm)
Bibliothèque nationale de France, Paris, HA-56-Ft 7
SEE FIG. 2.9.

* FONTAINEBLEAU ONLY   ‡ BGC GALLERY ONLY

CHECKLIST

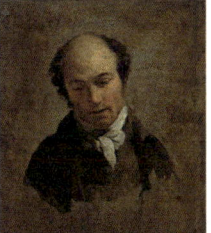
3B

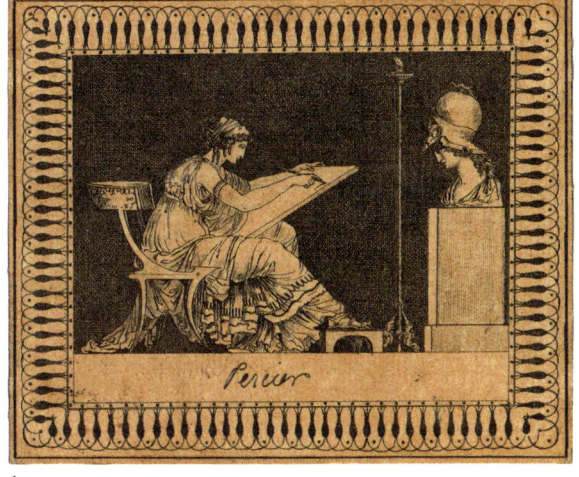
6

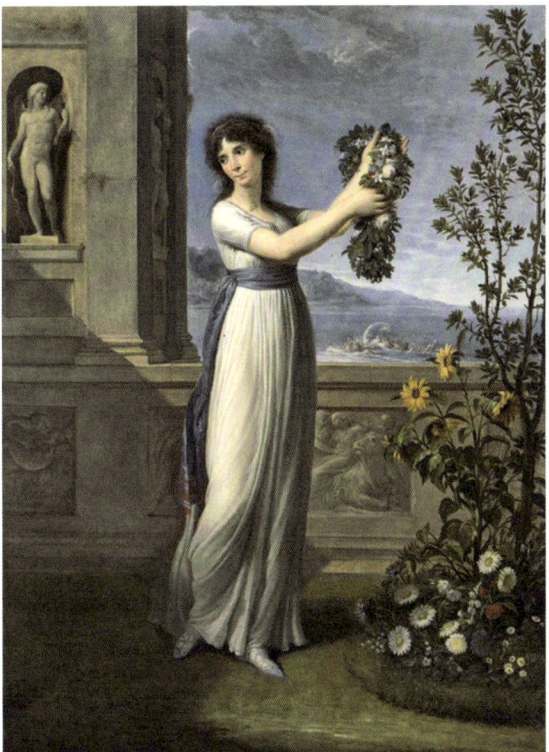
5

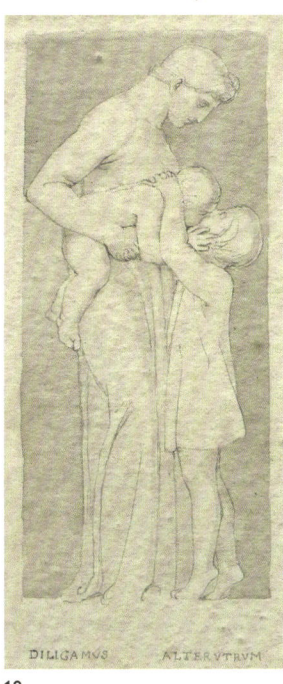
19

13

Trajan's Column, 1788
Charles Percier
India ink and wash on paper mounted on canvas

***13A** Elevation and cross section
38³⁄₈ × 25⅝ in. (97.5 × 65 cm)
SEE FIG. 3.2.

***13B** Reconstruction of the lateral left side of the base
38¼ × 46½ in. (97 × 118 cm)
SEE FIG. 3.3.

‡ **13C** Reconstruction of the entry at the base
38¼ × 46½ in. (97 × 118 cm)
SEE FIG. 2.10.

‡ **13D** Detail of the capital
37⅞ × 26¼ in. (96.5 × 66.5 cm)

École nationale supérieure des Beaux-Arts, Paris, Env. 1-02, Env 1-06, Env. 1-03, Env. 1-08

14

‡ **Trajan's Column, elevation, plan, and cross section**
Charles Percier
From Georges Seure and Hector d'Espouy, *Monuments antiques: relevés et restaurés par les architectes pensionnaires de l'Académie de France à Rome*
Paris: Massin, 1910–12
Heliogravure
17½ × 12⅜ in. (44.5 × 31.5 cm)
Private collection, Paris

15

* **Base of Trajan's Column, lateral left side**, ca. 1860
Attributed to Tomaso Cuccioni
Albumen print from glass-plate negative
8⅝ in × 6½ in. (22 × 16.6 cm)
Private collection, Paris

16

‡ **Base of Trajan's Column, entrance**, ca. 1855
Attributed to Carlo Baldassare Simelli
Albumen print from paper negative
8 × 10½ in. (20.5 × 26 cm)
Private collection, Paris
SEE FIG. 2.11.

17

Duodi Album, album amicorum, with portraits of the friends of Guillaume Guillon Lethière, director of the French Academy in Rome
Album with frontispiece and twelve engraved portraits
Engraved by Angelo Testa after drawings by Charles Percier and Louis Léopold Boilly
14¼ × 9⅞ in. (36.2 × 25 cm)
Bibliothèque musée de l'opéra, Bibliothèque nationale de France, Paris, B-90

18

* ***The Lodge of the Great Sphinx***, 1805
Manuscript sheet
24⅜ × 17¾ in. (62 × 45 cm)
Bibliothèque nationale de France, Paris, Mss Fm2/81

19

Diligamus Alterutrum, 1802
Drawing given by Flaxman to Percier and Fontaine
John Flaxman
Pen and wash on paper mounted on board (drawing) 7¼ × 4⅛ in. (18.5 × 10.5 cm); (mounted) 9½ × 6¼ in. (24 × 16 cm)
Inscriptions: [Verso, in pen] "Mr Flaxman sculpteur anglais An 10–1802"; [in pencil] "Diligamus alterutrum / Aimons-nous l'un l'autre"
Private collection, Paris

20

Percier's ring
Rome, Imperial period, late 1st century BCE–early 2nd century CE
Carnelian intaglio set into a gold ring
Private collection, Paris
SEE FIG. 2A.1.

21

Letter establishing the terms of transmission of Percier's ring and designating his successor, September 15, 1838
Achille Leclère
Pen on paper, wax seal of the ring
8⅛ × 6⅛ in. (20.6 × 15.5 cm)
Private collection, Paris
SEE FIG. 2A.2.

22

* **Bust of Louis Pierre Baltard**, n.d.
Eugène Guillaume
Bronze
25⅝ × 13¾ in. (65 × 35 cm)
École nationale supérieure des Beaux-Arts, Paris, MU 8562

23

* **Allegorical composition for the marriage of Napoleon and Marie-Louise of Austria**, ca. 1810
Attributed to Louis Pierre Baltard
Pencil, pen and black and blue ink, blue-ink wash heightened with white on paper
8¼ × 6⅛ in. (20.5 × 15.6 cm)
Château de Fontainebleau, F-2006.9

24

‡ **Advertisement for Baltard's work as an engraver, mounted in a scrapbook**, ca. 1800
Louis Pierre Baltard
Engraving
12⅝ × 9⅝ × ⅝ in (32 × 24.5 × 1.5 cm)

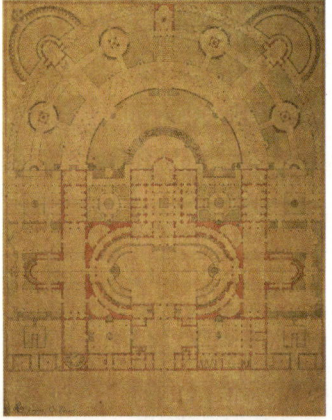

31A

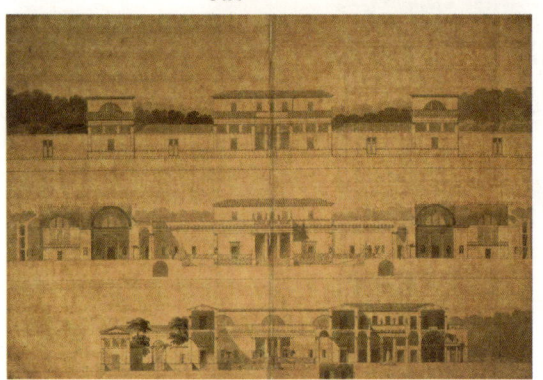

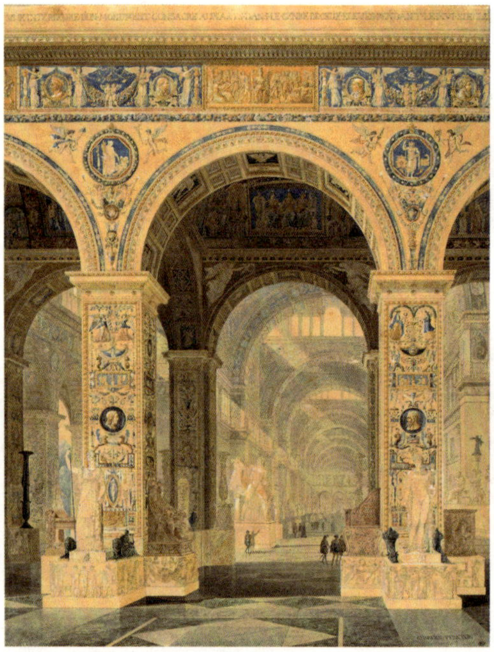

31B

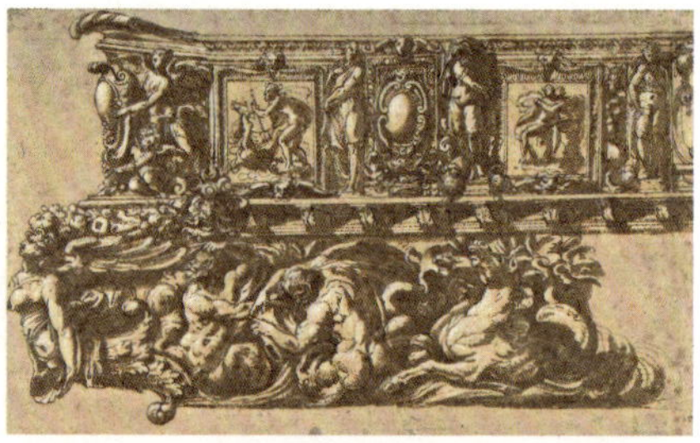

The Metropolitan Museum of Art, New York, The Elisha Whittelsey Collection, The Elisha Whittelsey Fund, 1961, 61.515

25

‡ *Triple Portrait of Percier, Fontaine and Claude Louis Bernier*, before 1807
Louis Léopold Boilly
Black and white chalk on buff paper
5¾ × 13⅛ in. (14.8 × 33.2 cm)
The Clark Institute, Willamstown, Massachusetts, Gift of David Jenness in honor of Arthur F. Jenness (Professor at Williams College, 1946–63), 2005.10.3

26

‡ *The Architects Achille Leclère and Jean Louis Provost, 1812*, ca. 1824–50
Louise Girard; engraving after Jean Auguste Dominique Ingres
Stipple engraving on heavy wove paper (restrike)
12¼ × 9½ in. (31.1 × 24.1 cm)
Smith College Museum of Art, Northampton, Massachusetts, Gift of Priscilla Paine Van der Poel, class of 1928, SC 1977: 32-134

27

‡ *Portrait of Louis Hippolyte Lebas, Architect*, 1811

Merry Joseph Blondel
Oil on canvas
(painting) 28⅛ × 22⅞ in. (71.4 × 58.1 cm); (framed) 36⅜ × 31⅛ × 3 in. (92.4 × 79 × 7.6 cm)
Mount Holyoke College Art Museum, South Hadley, Massachusetts, Purchased with the Friends of Art Fund, MH 1989.2

28

Élysée, or Public Cemetery, project for the Prix de Rome, 1799
Augustin Grandjean de Montigny

28A Elevation of the central chapel
Engraving, heightened with wash and watercolor
13 × 19 ½ in. (33 × 49.5 cm)

28B Cross section of the central chapel
Engraving, heightened with wash and watercolor
13 × 19 in. (33 × 48.5 cm)
Private collection, Paris

29

Architecture Toscane, ou Palais, maisons et autres édifices de la Toscane
Augustin Grandjean de Montigny and Auguste Famin

Paris: Pierre Didot l'aîné, 1806–1815
One volume bound in half-red straight-grain morocco, ornamented with fillets, with paper sides imitating red straight-grain morocco. Plates printed on Holland paper. Pages vii–50, frontispiece, and 109 engraved plates.
18½ × 11¾ × 1⅝ in. (47 × 30 × 4 cm)
Private collection, Paris
SEE FIG. 2.14.

30

Medal dedicated to the memory of Charles Percier and struck at the request of his students, 1840
Joseph François Domard
Bronze
Diam. 2⅞ in. (7.3 cm)
Private collection, Paris
SEE FIG. 14.2.

31

House for a Painter, ca. 1820
Jean François Joseph Lecointe, after Charles Percier
Pen, wash, and watercolor on oiled paper mounted on heavy paper

31A. Plan
17⅜ × 13¾ in. (45 × 35 cm)

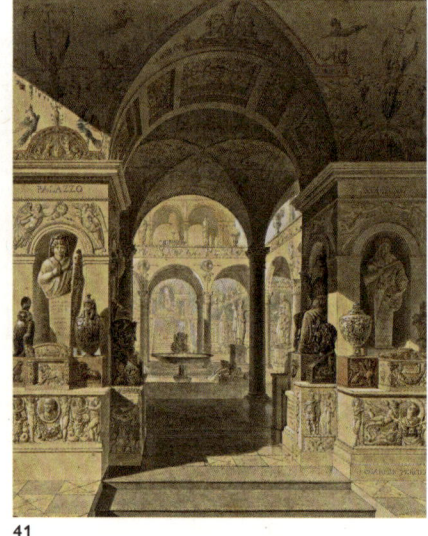

38

41

31B. Elevation and cross section
17⅜ × 25⅝ in. (45 × 65 cm)
Private collection, Paris

In one of the very few publications produced by a workshop of the École des beaux-arts at the beginning of the 19th century, the last plate in the collection lithographed by the students of Achille Leclère shows a ground plan entitled "Plan of the House of a Painter by Mr Percier." The original drawings for the project have been lost, and the volume from the Leclère workshop is so obscure that no scholar has ever discussed it. However, while researching this exhibition, we discovered two drawings on oiled paper in a private collection in Paris that represent this "House of a Painter." These drawings, one of the same ground plan, the other with sections and elevations, are signed by the architect Jean François Joseph Lecointe, with a handwritten inscription: "after C. Percier." These two copies allow us to analyze this project in the absence of the originals.

The plan is organized around a main oblong courtyard preceded by an entrance courtyard giving access to the house itself, which is arranged around another central courtyard with twelve columns, a dodeca-style cavaedium. The lateral concave sides of the main courtyard feature semicircular galleries supported with massive masonry, a clear reference to the central part of Percier's project for the Prix de Rome in 1786 (see fig. 2.8). The elevations, however, demonstrate a more recent date in their very simple and archaeological formal expression. It probably was designed about 1820, and the fact that it was copied at least twice—once by Leclère's students and once by Lecointe—shows that it was available to a certain academic public. Such an academic design produced by a master, probably done as a demonstration piece, is not unique, but we don't have many examples of this kind of composition in the context of the École des beaux-arts, and it points to the strength of Percier's dedication to the school. The choice of the program, a house for a painter, illustrates the proximity of architects with painters, and more broadly the recognition of the figure of the architect-artist.

—JEAN-PHILIPPE GARRIC

SECTION 2
BETWEEN ITALY AND FRANCE

32
‡ *The Colosseum, Rome*, n.d.
Abraham Louis Rodolphe Ducros
Pen and brown ink, watercolor, heightened with white on paper
17½ × 26 in. (44.4 × 66 cm)
The Metropolitan Museum of Art, New York, Purchase, Mrs. Carl L. Selden Gift, in memory of Carl L. Selden, 1987.173

33
Choix des plus célèbres maisons de plaisance de Rome et de ses environs
Charles Percier, Pierre Fontaine, and Charles Bonnard
Paris: Pierre Didot l'aîné, 1809–13

33A Plan of Villa Bologneti
Preparatory drawing for plate 50
Charles Percier
Chalk, pen, and watercolor on paper
14⅛ × 6½ in. (36 × 16.5 cm)
Private collection, Paris

33B *View of the Entrance to one of the Allées of the Garden of the Villa Pamphili*
Plate 18, showing Percier himself drawing
Charles Percier
Engraving
7¾ × 10⅝ in. (19.7 × 27 cm)
Private collection, Paris

* **33C** Villa Mondragone, view of the terrace and fountain
Preparatory sketch for plate 54
Charles Percier
Pen, wash, and gouache on paper
5⅝ × 8½ in. (14.4 × 21.4 cm)
Musée Vivenel, Compiègne, 1980.27

34
View of the courtyard of Villa Barberini, n.d.
Study for an unpublished plate of the *Choix des plus célèbres maisons de plaisance de Rome*
Attributed to Charles Percier
Pencil on paper
4 × 6½ in. (10.1 × 16.5 cm)
Private collection, Paris

35
* **View of Rome from the Tiber River near the Cloaca Maxima**, ca. 1784–88
Jean Germain Drouais
Pencil and gray wash on paper
7¾ × 11 in. (19.7 × 27.9 cm)
Musée des beaux-arts, Rennes, 1974.73.326

36
* **Musée des Monuments Français: View of the 16th–17th-centuries gallery**, 1809
Charles Percier
Pencil and watercolor on paper
10⅛ × 15 in. (25.8 × 38 cm)
Bibliothèque nationale de France, Paris, EST RESERVE VE-53 (C) 948
SEE FIG. 4B.1.

37
Project for an addition of three courtyards representing the 14th, 15th, and 16th centuries to the Musée des monuments français
From Alexandre Lenoir, *Description historique et chronologique des monumens de sculpture réunis au musée des monumens français*, vol. 4
Charles Percier
Paris: Author, 1805
25⅝ × 18⅞ in (65 × 48 cm)

37A View of the entryway leading from the street to the first courtyard, plate 160
SEE FIG. 4B.3.

37B View of a façade from the château de Gaillon to be remounted in the second courtyard, plate 163
SEE FIG. 4B.4.

37C View of a façade from the château de Gaillon to be remounted in the second courtyard, plate 164
Private collection, Paris

SECTION 3
A GRAPHIC ARTIST

38
‡ **Design for a festival float or barge**, ca. 1530–40
Circle of Perino del Vaga, possibly Prospero Fontana
Pen and brown ink, brush and brown wash, highlighted with white, over black chalk, on faded blue paper
10¼ × 16⅞ in. (26.1 × 42.8 cm)
The Metropolitan Museum of Art, New York, Rogers Fund, 1971, 1971.85

39
‡ *Various Modern and Antique Fragments Drawn from Nature in Different Cities in Italy and France*, 1791
Charles Percier
Pen and brown ink, gray and red chalk wash on paper
26⅛ × 40⅛ in. (66.3 × 102 cm)
Musée du Louvre, Paris, RF TGF 52751
SEE FIG. 5.1.

40
* **Interior view of a museum dedicated to the arts in the style of the 16th century**, n.d.
Charles Percier
Watercolor, pen and black and gray ink, gray wash, black chalk, heightened with gouache on paper
24 × 18½ in. (61 × 47 cm)
Musée du Louvre, Paris, 32296, recto

41
‡ *Interior of a Roman Palace*, ca. 1797
Charles Percier
Pen and black ink, grey wash, watercolor over pencil on paper
9¾ × 2⅝ in. (24.7 × 20.3 cm)
Musée du Louvre, Paris, 31900-recto

42
* **Preparatory drawing of the headpiece for Horace's *First Book of Epistles* published by Pierre Didot l'aîné**, ca. 1798
Charles Percier
Pen, black ink, and brown wash on paper
2⅜ × 5¾ in. (6 × 14.7 cm)
Musée des beaux-arts, Angers, Inventaire legs Turpin de Crissé, MTC 120 ; n°1, p. 26
SEE FIG. 5.6.

43
Horace, *Works of Horace*
Illustrated by Charles Percier
Paris: Pierre Didot l'aîné, 1799

* **43A** Horace, *Works of Horace*
Bound in full red morocco with the arms of Napoleon on the lower board
20½ × 15 × 2⅛ in. (52 × 38 × 5.5 cm)
Bibliothèque Paul Marmottan, Paris, 4616

‡ **43B** Horace, *Works of Horace*
Printed book with engraved headpiece illustrations
20½ × 15 × 2⅛ in. (52 × 38 × 5.5 cm)
The Metropolitan Museum of Art, New York, Anonymous Gift, 32.28
SEE FIG. 5.7.

44
Six engraved headpieces illustrating *The Fables of La Fontaine*
Headpieces from Books 4, 5, 7, 8, 9, and 12
Charles Percier
Paris: Pierre Didot l'aîné, 1802
2½ × 6½ in. (6.4 × 16.5 cm); 2½ × 6⅜ in. (6.4 × 16.1 cm); 2⅝ × 6½ in. (6.7 × 16.3 cm); 2⅞ × 6¾ in. (7.2 × 17 cm); 2¾ × 5¾ in. (6.9 × 14.7 cm); 2¾ × 6⅝ in. (7 × 16.8 cm)
Private collection, Paris
SEE FIGS. 13.4, 14.1.

45
‡ *Vignette with two portrait medallions*, n.d.
Charles Percier
Pen and gray ink with brush and gray wash on paper
3⅜ × 5⅜ in. (8.5 × 13.6 cm)
The Metropolitan Museum of Art, New York, Gift of Lincoln Kirstein, 1965, 65.717.3

46
Fan representing Bonaparte crowned by Peace and Victory, 1797
Gift from the City of Paris to Josephine. Designed by Antoine Denis Chaudet, Charles Percier, and Pierre Fontaine; engraved by Adrien Pierre François Godefroy

46A Unmounted fan
Engraving, first state
12 × 20 ½ in. (30.5 × 52 cm)
Bibliothèque nationale de France, Paris, RESERVE QB-370 (50)-FT 4.

‡ 46B Unmounted fan
Engraving printed on silk
10⅜ × 18½ in. (26.4 × 47 cm)
Cooper-Hewitt, Smithsonian Design Museum, New York, Bequest of Richard Cranch Greenleaf in memory of his mother, Adeline Emma Greenleaf, 1962-58-4.

‡ 46C Fan, 1797–99
Paper, wood, bone
9¼ × 17¼ in (23.5 × 43.8 cm)
The Metropolitan Museum of Art, New York, Gift of Mrs. Thomas Hunt, 1933, 33.82.1

47
Eight plates from *Palais, maisons et autres édifices modernes dessinés à Rome*, 1798
Charles Percier and Pierre Fontaine
One engraving on regular paper; seven engravings in sepia ink on Holland paper, of which five are heightened with wash and watercolor
(single sheet) 17¾ × 11⅜ in. (45 × 29 cm); (other sheets) 16½ × 12⅝ in. (42 × 32 cm)
Private collection, Paris
SEE FIGS. 2.15, 5.3, 5.4, 5A.2, 5A.3.

48
‡ *Italian villa at the seaside*, 1797
Charles Percier
Pencil, pen, black and brown ink, black chalk, watercolor on paper
12½ × 10¼ in. (31.5 × 26.1 cm)
Musée du Louvre, Paris, RF3994-recto

49
Drawings for the *Livre du Sacre*, 1811
Jean-Baptiste Isabey, Charles Percier, and Auguste Garneray

49A *The Pope*
Drawing for plate XIII
Pen and brown wash on paper
22 × 15¾ in. (56 × 40 cm)
Château de Fontainebleau, SNAG 92
SEE FIG. 7.6.

49B *The Empress in Lesser Ceremonial Dress* Drawing for plate XII
Pen and brown wash on paper
22 × 15¾ in. (56 × 40 cm)
Château de Fontainebleau, SNAG 92
SEE FIG. 7.4.

50
Description des cérémonies et des fêtes qui ont eu lieu pour le mariage de S.M. l'Empereur Napoléon avec S.A.I. Madame l'archiduchesse Marie Louise d'Autriche
Frontispiece and plate 8
Charles Percier and Pierre Fontaine
Paris: Authors, 1810
Engravings
(image) 15 × 10⅞ in. (38 × 27.5 cm); (sheet) 23¼ × 16½ in. (59 × 42 cm)
Private collection, Paris

51
Frontispiece for Alexandre de Laborde, *Voyage pittoresque et historique de l'Espagne*
Designed by Charles Percier; etching by Georges Malbeste; engraving by Marie Alexandre Duparc
Paris: Pierre Didot l'aine, 1806–20
Engraving mounted on blue paper
(engraving) 10.6 × 11⅜ in. (25.8 × 29 cm); (mounted) 11½ × 15 in. (29.5 × 38 cm)
Private collection, Paris
SEE FIG. 2.4.

52
Seventeen ornamental motifs
Charles Percier
Pen and ink on paper
10 ¼ × 8 ¼ in. (26 × 21 cm)
Les Art Décoratifs, Paris, 6378.1–17

53
Henri IV, roi de France
Frontispiece for Voltaire, *La Henriade*
Designed by Charles Percier and François Gérard; engraved by Henri Charles Müller
Paris: Firmin Didot, 1819 [–23]

* 53A *Henri IV, roi de France*
Engraved plate in volume bound in mottled calf, filetted border aux petits fers on the sides, with the crowned arms of France and the collars of the Orders of the Holy Spirit and Saint Michel. Lower board with gold tooling and monogram of Charles X, part title in green leather, 350 pages.
17¾ × 13⅝ in. (45.1 × 34.6 cm)
Château de Fontainebleau, Library, H 136
SEE FIG. 1.3.

‡ 53B *Henri IV, roi de France*
Engraved plate
17¾ × 13⅝ in. (45.1 × 34.6 cm)
Special Collections and University Archives, Stanford University Libraries, Stanford, California

SECTION 4
THE *RECUEIL DE DÉCORATIONS INTÉRIEURES*

54
Recueil de décorations intérieures comprenant tout ce qui a rapport à l'ameublement comme vases, trépieds, candélabres, cassolettes, lustres, girandoles, lampes, chandeliers, cheminées, feux, poêles, pendules, tables, secrétaires, lits canapés, fauteuils, chaises, tabourets, miroirs, écrans, &, &, &. Composés par C. Percier et P. F. L. Fontaine. Exécutés sur leurs dessins
Charles Percier and Pierre Fontaine
Paris: Authors and Pierre Didot l'aîné, 1801–12

54A One volume, half-bound in calf with marbled paper sides. Half-title, title page, 43 pages, and 72 engraved plates (closed) 18⅝ × 12¼ × 1 in. (47.3 × 31.2 × 2.6 cm)
Château de Fontainebleau, cote 4.8 PERCIER 1812.

54B First title page of the *Recueil de décorations intérieures*, 1801
Line engraving with text and illustration
(design) 9 × 10⅝ in. (22.8 × 27 cm); (sheet) 11½ × 18 in. (29.5 × 45.5 cm)
Private collection, Paris

54C Plate 1, Perspectival view of the interior of Isabey's atelier
Line engraving
(sheet) 11½ × 18 in. (29.5 × 45.5 cm)
Private collection, Paris
SEE FIG. 6.8.

54D Plate 62, Entablature, capital, and details from the Cabinet du Roi d'Espagne
(sheet) 11½ × 18 in. (29.5 × 45.5 cm)
Private collection, Paris
SEE FIG. 10.5.

54E Plate 61, View of the Cabinet du Roi d'Espagne
(sheet) 11½ × 18 in. (29.5 × 45.5 cm)
Private collection, Paris

55
Recueil de décorations intérieures comprenant tout ce qui a rapport à l'ameublement comme vases, trépieds, candélabres, cassolettes, lustres, girandoles, lampes, chandeliers, cheminées, feux, poêles, pendules, tables, secrétaires, lits canapés, fauteuils, chaises, tabourets, miroirs, écrans, &, &, &. Composés par C. Percier et P. F. L. Fontaine. Exécutés sur leurs dessins
Charles Percier and Pierre Fontaine
Paris: Egon Hessling, ca. 1910
New edition in facsimile of the first three hand-colored installments with their wrappers. 3 wrappers, 4 pages of text: pp. [21]–24, 18 plates. Lithography on vellum (text), and on blue paper (wrapper), chromolithography on Holland paper (plates).
16½ × 12½ in. (42 × 32 cm)

55A *Lateral wall of the Painting of the Atelier of C[itizen] I**** [Isabey]*, plate 2
Chromolithography on Holland paper
Private collection, Paris

‡ 55B *Various elements of furniture executed for the bedroom of Citizen V*, plate 15
Chromolithography on Holland paper
Private collection, Paris

56
Recueil de décorations intérieures, ca. 1825
Charles Percier and Pierre Fontaine; hand colored by Benjamin Gotthold, comte de Schlick
Watercolor over engraving
19⅝ × 15 × 2 in. (50 × 38 × 5 cm)
Les Arts Décoratifs, Paris, 33761.42
SEE FIGS. 11.4, 11.5.

57
Design for the ceiling of the library at Malmaison and for an unidentified ceiling, ca. 1799
Charles Percier
India ink and watercolor on paper
9⅝ × 8¼ in. (24.5 × 20.5 cm)
Châteaux de Malmaison et Bois-Préau, Rueil-Malmaison, M.M.71.3.1

CHECKLIST

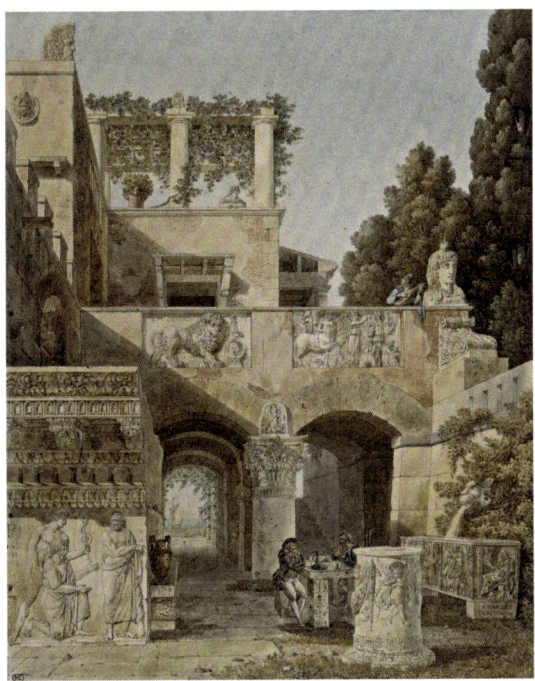

48

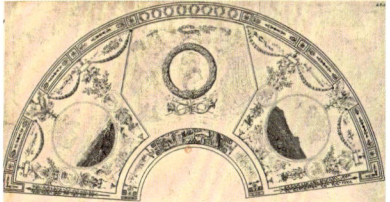

46A

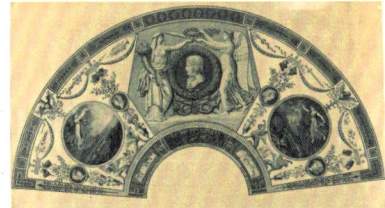

46B

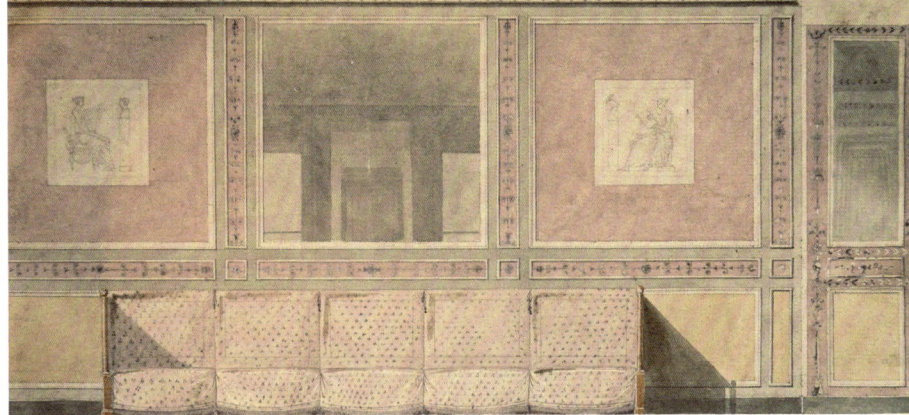

64

58

Bedroom of Mme M. executed in Paris, 1801–12
From Charles Percier and Pierre Fontaine, *Recueil de décorations intérieures*, plate 60
Watercolor over engraving
17¾ × 12¾ in. (45 × 32.5 cm)
Musée Vivenel, Compiègne, L. 162
SEE FIG. 6.7.

59

Scrapbook containing drawings and several prints of architecture, interiors, furniture, and other objects, ca. 1804–14
Workshop of Percier
One volume bound in reused parchment, 128 sheets with drawings of various sizes and media mounted
15⅝ × 10 in. (39.8 × 25.4 cm)
The Metropolitan Museum of Art, New York, The Elisha Whittelsey Collection, The Elisha Whittelsey Fund, 1963, 63.535.1–.128
SEE FIGS. 6.6, 8.18, 8B.1–7, 11A.1–2.

60

‡ *Minerva (Study after a Sculpture)*, ca. 1798
Louis Léopold Boilly
Conté crayon, stumping, heightened with white chalk on faded blue paper
11½ × 8½ in. (29.2 × 21.5 cm)
The Metropolitan Museum of Art, New York, Gift of Louis de Bayser, 2009, 2009.477
SEE FIG. 6.9.

61

Study of a capital for the Platinum Room, Casa Real del Labrador, Aranjuez, 1800
Charles Percier
Graphite and red chalk on paper
18 × 11⅝ in. (45.7 × 29.6 cm)
Private collection, Paris
SEE FIG. 10.4.

62

Entablature, capital, and details from the Platinum Room, Casa Real del Labrador, Aranjuez, 1801–12
Preparatory drawing for the *Recueil de décorations intérieures*, plate 62
Charles Percier
Graphite on paper
15½ × 9⅞ in. (39 × 25 cm)
Private collection, Paris
Provenance: Collection Jacob-Lefuel

63

Design for a bedroom for Josephine, ca. 1802
Charles Percier
Graphite, ink, wash, and watercolor on paper
10½ × 10⅞ in. (26.6 × 27.7 cm)
Private collection, Paris
SEE FIG. 1.4.

This presentation drawing, executed with great care, shows the decor of a bedchamber with an exceptionally high ceiling, at its center some 20 feet high. The monogram JB, doubtless for Josephine Bonaparte, appears in the central myrtle wreath on the blue bed hanging. Within the arch is a mirror in which the draftsman playfully imagined the reflection of an amorous scene, using a form of poetic license similar to that found in plate 60 of the *Recueil de décorations intéreures*, where, contrary to the laws of optics, the mirror above the banquette reflects a statue and some plants in the garden below (see fig. 6.7). The two lovers are Paris and Helen, and the composition here is virtually identical to the one on the central roundel on a tabletop produced by the Sèvres porcelain manufactory for presentation to Josephine, a design engraved about 1802 on plate 35 of the *Recueil*. The inclusion of this motif, the fine draftsmanship, and the presence of certain details, notably the cupids and profile medallions on the door panels, support an attribution to Charles Percier.

The room's dimensions, which imply a building of monumental size, may be a design for the decor of Josephine's bedchamber in the Tuileries, which until 1808 was situated on the ground floor, the fourth room—proceeding from the pavillon de Flore—in an enfilade overlooking the garden, a space subsequently transformed into a billiards room. The bedchamber's dimensions (about 38 feet wide) seem to match those of the room shown here, and, according to Jean-Pierre Samoyault, featured an alcove flanked by columns with bases and capitals. A Miss Berry, who visited the apartment in 1802, mentions a bedchamber whose color scheme is consistent with the one in this design. She wrote: "the next room was the bedchamber, the one in which they slept together in the same bed. The furniture was of blue silk with white and gold fringe. The bed, covered with a simple sheet, is made of mahogany, with rich and even heavy-handed ornament of gilt-bronze."

—JEAN-PHILIPPE GARRIC

64

Design for a boudoir, ca. 1800–2
Charles Percier
Pencil, pen, and watercolor on paper
8¼ × 15⅞ in. (21.1 × 40.2 cm)
Private collection, Paris

This elevation of a boudoir wall—a ravishing example of the refined interiors of the Directory and Consulate—features three molded woodwork panels, the central one occupied by a mirror, above a couch designed to accommodate five. The room, clearly an entresol or mezzanine, features an alcove at right decorated with mirrors that reflect light emanating from the two windows visible in the central mirror flanking what appears to be a fireplace.

Although the dimensions of this drawing exceed those of other interior-decor designs by Percier, notably those for the townhouse of Madame Récamier, this boudoir nonetheless has all the characteristics of his work. The care lavished on the smallest details (such as the knots securing the slipcovers on the couch) betrays Percier's hand, as do the delicately rendered ornament running the full length of slender panels and the repeated reflections in the mirror on the alcove wall, which implies a mirror directly opposite. Moreover, the allegorical figures of Music and Drawing set into the small panels above the couch are very similar to the figures of the Arts incorporated in the atelier of Isabey in 1798.

There are no indications of the residence for which this design was intended. The color scheme on the walls resembles those used for Madame Récamier and General Moreau, but those projects favor draped wall hangings over compartments surrounded by moldings like the ones seen here. The sofa, whose seat and back disappear under slipcovers decorated with scattered florets and trimmed with fringe, is of a kind often found in rooms intended for rest and relaxation. In 1801 François Gérard painted Josephine sitting on a banquette of the same type (Châteaux de Malmaison et Bois-Préau).

—VINCENT COCHET

65

Two fragments of the carpet for the Throne Room in the Tuileries Palace, 1804
Design by Charles Percier and Pierre Fontaine; made by Aubusson Manufactory
Wool
48 3/8 × 46 1/2 in.; 46 1/2 in. × 45 5/8 in. (123 × 118 cm; 118 × 116 cm)
Château de Fontainebleau, F 54 and F 3643

66

Designs for the Townhouse of General Moreau, ca. 1801–2
Charles Percier

66A Two elevations of a salon
Inscription on each of drawings: "salon du général Moreau rue d'Anjou"
Graphite, ink, and watercolor on paper
Upper drawing (fireplace wall): 2 3/8 × 4 3/8 in. (6 × 11 cm); lower drawing (window wall): 2 5/8 × 4 7/8 in. (6.7 × 12.4 cm)

66B Design for a ceiling
Inscription: "salon du général Moreau rue d'Anjou"
Graphite, ink, and watercolor on paper
4 1/2 × 5 in. (11.5 × 12.6 cm)

66C Decorative frieze
Inscription: "atelier de peinture de Me Moreau"
Pen and watercolor on paper
2 3/4 × 9 1/4 in. (7 × 23.5 cm)

Château de Fontainebleau, F-1991.3

67

*****Bed**, 1801–2
Jacob frères
Marks: [stamp] JACOB FRERES / RUE MESLEE; [mark] château de Fontainebleau and inventory numbers.
Mahogany, chiseled, gilt, and enameled bronze
43 × 98 × 59 in. (109 × 250 × 150 cm)
Château de Fontainebleau, F 3706
SEE FIG. 8.23.

68

*****Work table**, 1801–2
Jacob frères
Marks: [stamp] JACOB FRERES / RUE MESLEE; [handwritten label] Jacob Frères / rue Meslée n°77; [mark] palais de Saint-Cloud and inventory numbers.
Mahogany, gilt bronze, sea-green marble
35 7/8 × 15 1/2 in. (91 × 39.5 cm)
Château de Fontainebleau, F 5 C

69

*****Washstand**, 1801–2
Attributed to Jacob frères
Yew wood, gilt bronze, enameled copper
34 5/8 × 19 5/8 in. (88 × 50 cm)
Marks: inventory numbers
Château de Fontainebleau, F 23 C

70

Bed with Endboard Panels, 1806
Pierre Benoît Marcion
Mahogany, gilt and patinated bronze
Marks: [label with inscription] Gard. Imp. Ser.v de / fontainebleau / pour les

66–69

TOWNHOUSE OF GENERAL MOREAU

In March 1801, Jean Victor Marie Moreau, commander in chief of the army of the Rhine and comrade-in-arms of Bonaparte, acquired a townhouse in Paris, on rue d'Anjou, for himself and his young wife, who one month later entrusted its decoration to Percier and Fontaine. The commission was among the most important yet received by the two architects, who at the time were also working at the château de Saint-Cloud for Bonaparte and Josephine.

Moreau's victories had made him a respected figure. Although he took part in the coup d'état of 18 brumaire, he later became an enemy of Bonaparte. Soon after the commutation of Moreau's initial sentence—imprisonment—to exile in North America, the first consul acquired his real estate and his furniture, which was sent to Fontainebleau in November 1804.

The plan of the Moreau townhouse, demolished in 1854, is not known, but a description of its mirrors and furniture attached to the 1804 deed of sale lists the various rooms that might have been redecorated for the couple: in addition to a bedroom, a library, a dining room, a small salon, and a "turkish" boudoir, all for the general, the residence contained an antechamber, another dining room, a large reception salon, and a music room. Madame Moreau had a bedroom of her own as well as an adjacent boudoir.

Several watercolors by Percier represent proposed designs for the rooms, notably the large salon, square in plan, with its pairs of attached columns emphasizing the axis of each wall, and its ceiling, which featured a central roundel and decorated corners (cats. 66a, b). The alternative options for the ceiling corners and the doors suggest that these drawings are from a relatively advanced stage of the design process. The frieze for "the painting atelier of Madame Moreau" repeats, in simpler form, the one from Isabey's atelier with its portrait medallions of great painters, but it is unlikely that the decor for this room was realized (cat. 66c). On the other hand, two plates in the *Recueil de décorations intérieures* are devoted to the bedchamber and boudoir of the general's wife (pls. 19, 60 [see fig. 6.7]), and several pieces of furniture described as "for Madame M. in Paris" appear on plate 23, such as the night table decorated with a reclining dog, included there as a guardian of sleep (see fig. 11a.6, cat. 84). These prints, together with the 1804 inventory and the furniture sent to Versailles, convey something of the elegance of the rue d'Anjou townhouse. The mistress of the place enjoyed a bed in a new form, the prototype of the *lit bateau* (boat bed) (see p. 5 and fig. 8.23): a cross between a day bed (*méridienne*) and a regular bed, it has scrolled endboard panels of equal height, linked by side rails supported by turned baluster legs. Percier and Fontaine explain that their priority here was "comfort" and that they used "shapes without corners; all of the contours are rounded." The front of the mahogany frame is decorated with gilt bronze medallions—featuring motifs set against sky-blue enamel grounds—linked by palmettes from which spring poppy flowers, symbols of

* FONTAINEBLEAU ONLY   ‡ BGC GALLERY ONLY

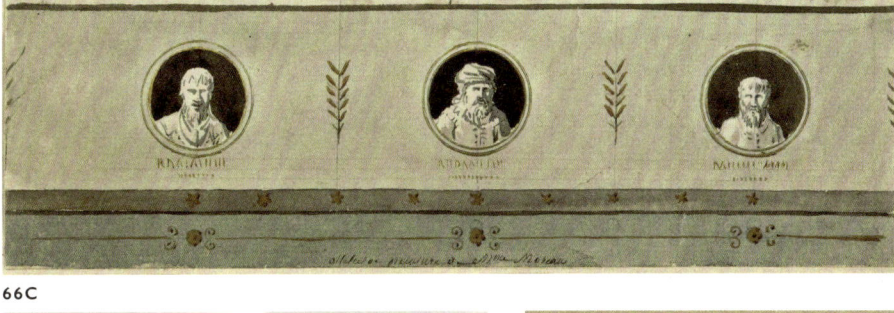
66C

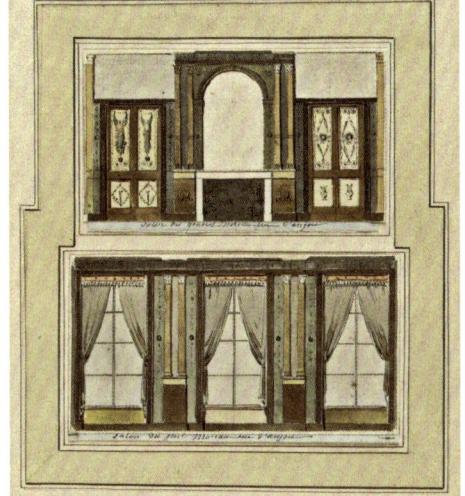
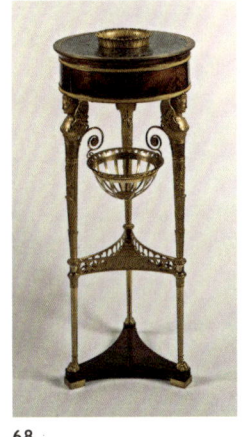
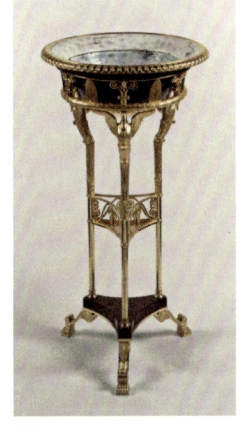
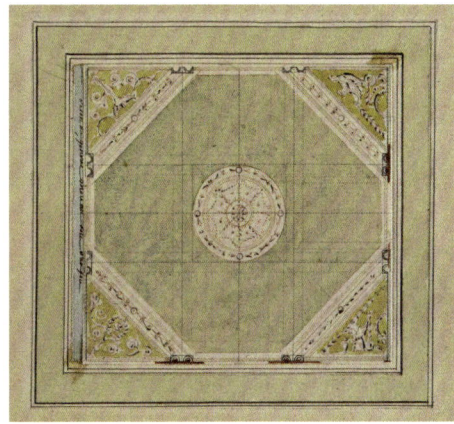

66A 68 69 66B

sleep. In the *Recueil*, the lightness of the silhouette is emphasized by the elegant bed crown suspended above, surmounted by doves linked by swags of strings of pearls, and from which hangs a muslin canopy embroidered with gold. Placed in the empress's bedchamber at Fontainebleau in 1804, this bed was apparently soon deemed unsuitable, for it was replaced in 1805. Another bed now at the château de Fontainebleau (F 2646) is of the same model. Its bronze fittings are virtually identical, though they are not enameled, and its legs are not turned but in the form of pilasters. The details of its design correspond more closely to those seen in plates 14 and 15 (see fig. 8.6) of the *Recueil* ("bed of Citizen V").

The banquette in the boudoir of the Moreau townhouse is a variation on the design of the bed. If plate 60 of the *Recueil* was merely a project (see fig. 6.7), as suggested by the presence of different decorative options on the front, the divan's transfer to Fontainebleau makes it possible for us to know which option was finally realized. An archival document describes the piece in question as "a mahogany day bed, claw feet [my emphasis], curved backs, sculpted bronze ornament, horsehair cushion, pillow with tassel, feather bolster, 15/16 lilacs, trim and decoration [in] buff and white" (Fontainebleau, archives de la régie, 1817, vol. 10, fol. 67, no. 20326).

The refinement of the Moreau townhouse is even more apparent from the small pieces of furniture, notably the washstand included in plate 19 of the *Recueil*, presumably to indicate that it was intended for Madame Moreau. Two realizations of this design have been in the collections at Fontainebleau since the time of Louis-Philippe. One of them was in Josephine's bedchamber at Saint-Cloud in 1804—its harmonious relation to the commode made by the Jacob brothers after a design by Percier and Fontaine (see fig. 8a.1, cat. 86) is undeniable—while the other is documented as being in Napoleon's bedroom in 1805 (cat. 69). Inspired by ancient tripods, these pieces are descendants of the *athéniennes* that began to appear in interiors in the late 18th century. Each of their enameled bowls, lined by copper basins, rest on two circular rings, the upper one decorated with gadrooning and the lower one with a laurel torus, between which alternate vertical palmettes and water leaves. This openwork cradle rests in turn on the wings and necks of three swans, which emerge from slender bronze colonnette legs; these last are reinforced, farther down, by a shelf intended to support a ewer. This frame is set on a base of yew wood, supported in turn by three console legs with claw feet. The allusion to ancient tripods, notably those with sphinxes excavated at Herculaneum, is clear, but Percier's design translates the function of this piece into a luxurious idiom, using the aquatic motif of swans and, above all, making gilt bronze elements dominate the wooden frame, characteristics also found in the washstand made by Biennais for the emperor's bedchamber in the Tuileries (see cat. 88). The model created for Madame Moreau was reprised several times in bronze editions, but its similarity to the sewing table for the same patron secures its attribution to the Jacob brothers.

This small ladies' work table (cat. 68) adheres to the same compositional template. Its three tapering colonnette legs, decorated with foliage, culminate in winged female term figures, whose heads—crowned by small crescents—support a circular mahogany frieze and, above, a marble tabletop. The latter has a central cavity surrounded by a bronze corolla of water leaves to form an incense-burner, originally outfitted with an openwork bronze cover. A mahogany shelf with a low openwork gilt-bronze screen along its edges is situated between the two segments of the legs. Above this, an openwork basket of gilt copper is suspended by small chains from three volutes behind the busts. This basket, intended "for the placement of needlework and other [sewing] tools," was lined with "a network of gold thread": one that, if we can judge from the example formerly in the collection of comte Clary (1837–77), constituted a silk receptacle. In any case, the absence of gilt-bronze mounts on the frieze and of engraved moldings on the base makes this example less rich than the one published in the Recueil (pl. 23, see fig. 8.4). Its presence at Saint-Cloud before the acquisition of Moreau's furniture indicates the degree to which Percier's designs were successful, suggesting that Josephine commissioned a version of Madame Moreau's sewing table—then the epitome of fashion—for her own residence.

—VINCENT COCHET

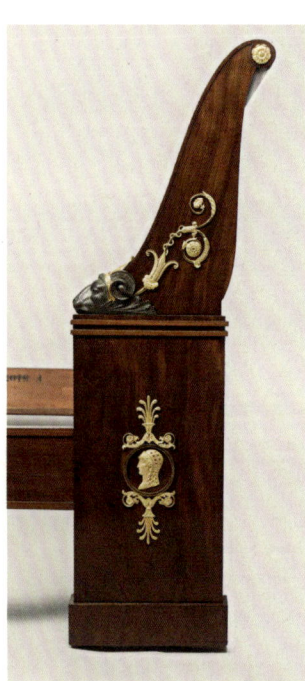

70

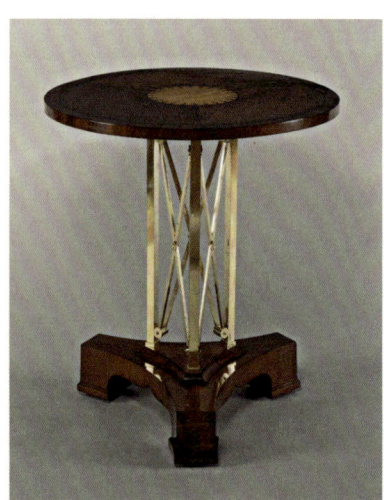

73

princesses / 3 lits à flasques en acajou de / 4 p^d orné / n°; [mark] château de Fontainebleau and inventory numbers.
45¼ × 79⅞ × 54⅞ in. (115 × 203 × 137 cm)
Château de Fontainebleau, F 4244

Although Jacob-Desmalter was the preeminent furniture-maker working for the Mobilier de la Couronne, Marcion executed important pieces for Compiègne, Trianon, and Fontainebleau. Three similar beds and accompanying night tables, intended for princesses of the imperial family, are described in one of Marcion's invoices, the beds as follows: "endboard side panels; ram heads; richly decorated with matte-finished engraved gilt-bronze mounts; the whole carefully made; 1,000 francs each; price based on the model." Were these beds, which remain at Fontainebleau, based on a design published in the Recueil? Its plate 15 (see fig. 8.6) shows an endboard side panel decorated with ram's heads and scrolling rinceaux winding around symbols of sleep, notably the profile of a figure of Night crowned with poppies, and a butterfly. The relationship to the design in the print is unmistakable. The ram's heads, which ease the transition from the side rail to the curving endboard panels (which are of equal height), and from whose horns issue the rinceaux, derive from the antique decorative lexicon. Their use here brings to mind the many eagles, swans, and felines, not to mention hybrid creatures like chimeras and griffins, incorporated into furniture of this period, but ram's heads were used much less frequently. Only a few Empire chairs have arms that incorporate them as terminal elements.

Marcion clearly appropriated one of Percier's inventions but simplified it, leaving more space around the bronze mounts. He evoked the nocturnal realm with profiles resembling those set against enamel grounds on the bed of Madame Moreau, notably the female heads wearing star-strewn Phrygian bonnets that decorate the frame just above the front legs.

—VINCENT COCHET

71

* **Guéridon**, ca. 1798
Attributed to Jacob frères
Mahogany, lemon tree wood, gilt bronze, blue turquin marble
30⅜ × 31⅞ in. (77 × 81 cm)
Château de Versailles, 1982, V. 5211, on deposit at Châteaux de Malmaison et Bois-Préau, Rueil-Malmaison, MMD. 30.3
SEE FIG. 8.14.

Percier and Fontaine published the design of this piece in the Receuil de décorations intérieures (plate 39), where it is described as a "Tea table supported by a bronze column and by delicate rinceaux scrolls" and said to be a "Table executed in Paris for Mme B" (Madame Bonaparte). It comes from Napoleon and Josephine's first residence, situated on rue de la Victoire in Paris, which was redecorated after their marriage (March 9, 1796) and for which the Jacob brothers executed several pieces that were delivered in 1797. The Jacob brothers' close collaboration with Percier and Fontaine is the basis for the attribution of this piece to them.

The antique, or rather pseudo-antique, inspiration of this design, like its prominent use of bronze, make it a perfect example of the archaeological style developed by the two architects in collaboration with the Jacob brothers. The central pedestal, however, was realized not in bronze but in mahogany. Transported from the rue de la Victoire to the Tuileries palace in 1806, the table was moved again during the reign of Louis-Philippe to the palace of Versailles, where it was placed in the queen's private rooms. It was at this time that the table lost its elevated tea tray, a common feature in 18th-century tea tables.

—AMAURY LEFÉBURE

72

* **Design for a guéridon**, ca. 1804
Attributed to Percier
Ink, watercolor on paper
6½ × 9 in. (16.5 × 23.1 cm)
Inscription: [in chalk] en acajou avec marbre bleu / Turquin creuse de 370 cutk. juste
Château de Fontainebleau, F-2001.11

73

* **Guéridon**, ca. 1805
François Honoré Georges Jacob-Desmalter
Mahogany, maple and ebony inlay, gilt bronze
29⅛ × 28 in. (74 × 71 cm)
Marks: [stamp] JACOB D. / R. MESLEE ; [mark]château de Fontainebleau and inventory numbers
Château de Fontainebleau, F 685 C

When the redecoration of the empress's private rooms at Fontainebleau was nearing completion, the Garde-Meuble prepared an invoice for the furniture, notably "a guéridon table, top of blue turquin marble," the realization of which had been entrusted to Jacob-Desmalter. A drawing corresponding to this commission, found in the archives of Jeanselme, Jacob's successor, reveals the table's small dimensions and style, thus supporting an attribution to Percier. The architect departed here from the guéridon design template incorporating a central pedestal support, already widely used by the Jacob brothers, in order to integrate an antique reference. From a triangular footed mahogany base, a leg and crossbar system made of gilt bronze rises to support the tabletop. The result is a deft adaptation of the support system in the athénienne seen on plate 4 of the *Recueil*, whose archaeological character Jacob-Desmalter honored by simulating the hinged bronze elements that made it possible to fold ancient tripods. This detail evokes the moldings on the feet of certain mahogany chairs from the early 19th century that reproduce the folding elements of ancient metal furniture.

This table was in the empress's bedroom in 1810. Although commissioned in 1809, the guéridon sold by Jacob-Desmalter had in fact been executed earlier, as revealed by the tabletop, which was envisioned as marble but finally executed in mahogany, with inlay decoration consisting of a disk circled by a frieze of florets (maple) and three radiating vegetal designs of great delicacy. The guéridon design dates from the early years of the 19th century and was used by Jacob-Desmalter. Reminiscent of the plinth design for the night table decorated with a dog (cat. 84), the en accolade profile on the sides of the mahogany base recurs on the guéridon delivered in 1809 for the emperor's interior cabinet at Fontainebleau (F 2432).

—VINCENT COCHET

74

Sketch of five armchairs for the Jacob firm, ca. 1795
Attributed to Charles Percier
Pen on oiled paper, mounted with three other drawings on a large sheet
(drawing) 9¼ × 12¼ in. (23.5 × 31 cm); (mounted) 19¼ × 24 in. (46.5 × 61 cm)
Private collection, Paris

The sketch on the upper right is very similar to the Kinsky armchair (cat. 76) and the sketch at lower right represents a chair very similar to the so-called Corvisart chair (cat. 77).

75

‡ **Study for two armchairs**, ca. 1800–5
Charles Percier
Graphite on paper
4⅝ × 7⅞ in. (11.8 × 20 cm)
The Metropolitan Museum of Art, New York, The Elisha Whittelsey Collection, The Elisha Whittelsey Fund, 1955, 53.521.11

76

Armchair, ca. 1793
Attributed to Georges Jacob
Mahogany and molded mahogany veneer
37⅜ × 22⅞ × 18½ in. (95 × 48 × 47 cm)
Marks: [stamp on the apron] G. JACOB; [typed label on the rear apron]: Fauteuil en acajou fait par Georges Jacob pour le Pavillon chinois de la Princesse Kinsky. Ancien mobilier du château des Granges
Private collection, Paris

The armrests take the form of sinuous grooved cornucopias. The slightly bowed front apron rests on tapered tubular front legs circled by evenly spaced moldings, while the back legs are of the sabre or klismos type. This armchair was probably made for the Chinese pavilion at the townhouse of Princess Kinsky on rue Saint-Dominique in Paris, the furniture for which also included a set of armless chairs.

CHAIRS

Soon after they completed their work for the assembly hall of the Convention, Percier and Fontaine were entrusted with other furniture commissions. The influence of English fashion and archaeological discoveries, within a political context that encouraged regeneration, led to a purge of design templates associated with the last years of Louis XVI's reign and to the adoption of more Spartan forms. Curule chairs and curved backs were hugely successful during the revolutionary years, as were "etruscan" saber legs and scrolled crest rails (see fig. 8.22). This radical trend petered out a few years later, but the design reforms of the 1790s generated some influential models. Among these, the armchairs designed by Percier for the salon of Madame Récamier, with their curved backs, their combination of saber legs (back) and baluster legs (front), and their incorporation of erect winged sphinxes made of stained wood as armrest supports sparked multiple variations. Chimeras were used as supports in the mahogany armchairs with ebony and pewter inlay from the Tuileries (Fontainebleau, F 83 C) and in those of blond wood, with removable seats, probably delivered in 1799 for Josephine to the Luxembourg palace before being transferred to her rooms in the Tuileries, whence they were moved to her bedchamber at Fontainebleau. These last are notable for having baluster front legs that, like those in the design for Madame Moreau's bed, are exceptionally large. Percier and Fontaine designed chairs of the same kind, but much more richly detailed, for a Russian client (*Recueil*, pl. 29). In 1804, the ceremonial armchairs executed by Jacob-Desmalter after a design by Percier and Fontaine for the throne room in the Tuileries incorporated not sphinxes but winged lions whose tails form volutes under the armrests.

Some chairs lack sculptural elements of this kind but retain the same lines, with front legs in the form of flattened double balusters decorated with palmettes. The ten armchairs made by the Jacob brothers for the first consul's Council Room at Malmaison are the earliest examples. One of them, which Joseph Bonaparte took with him to New Jersey, retains its original upholstery (cat. 78). The use of bronzed wood with gilt ornament, cylindrical armrests, and red wool upholstery fabric reinforces the martial character of these pieces. The fluting on the front surfaces of the curved uprights of the backs lightens the silhouette, while the rinceaux on their side panels—which stand out against the darkened wood—recall the inlay decoration on the mahogany armchairs from the Tuileries (Fontainebleau, F 83 C). There were chairs of this type, made of blond wood, in Josephine's music room at Saint-Cloud, where they remained until 1810. For a time, this model became the prime archetype for chairs, as evidenced by the armchairs in the empress's third salon at Compiègne, upholstered in a lovely green-ground brocaded lampas decorated with flower garlands and cornucopias forming Josephine's initial, woven by Grand frères of Lyon in 1809 (cat. 81).

In a parallel development, simpler models, executed in mahogany, painted wood, or gilt wood, were elaborated by the Jacob brothers in collaboration with Percier and Fontaine. The curved back was retained but given a rectangular form by the addition of a lower rail. The armrest supports became extensions of the front legs to form plinths with claw feet and culminating in Egyptian figures, as in the sofas, bergères, and armchairs delivered for the first consul's salon at Saint-Cloud around 1800, upholstered in brocaded and embroidered gros de Tours made in Lyon in 1786–87 for Marie-Antoinette's bedchamber at Versailles (cat. 79). Napoleon's mother received furniture of this kind for her salon at Saint-Cloud in 1802 (now at Malmaison), as did Cardinal Fesch and Third Consul Charles François Lebrun, for the hôtel de Noailles. Percier devised a version of this armchair—described by him as extraordinarily rich—for the Platinum Room in the Casa del Labrador at Aranjuez, a design in which the Egyptian figures are replaced by helmeted heads with large wings stretching out behind to support the armrests (*Recueil*, pl. 63, see fig. 10.6).

—VINCENT COCHET

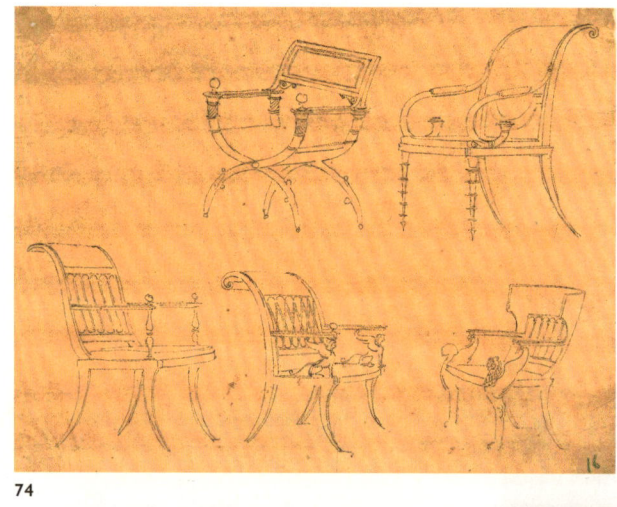
74

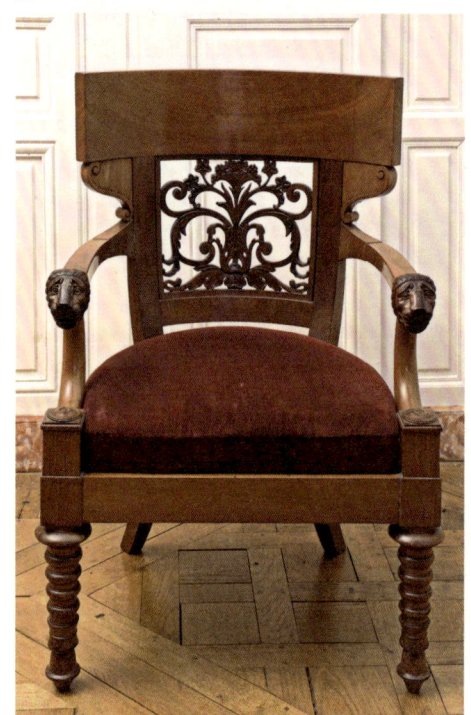
80

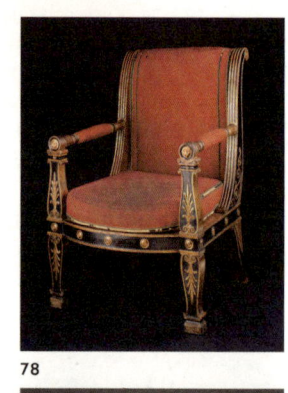
78

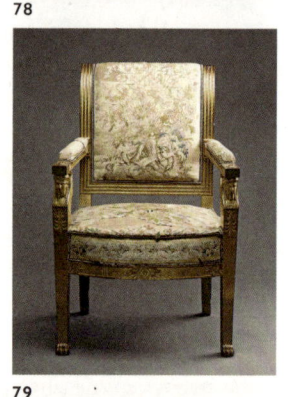
79

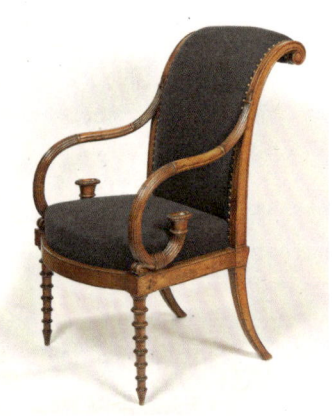
76

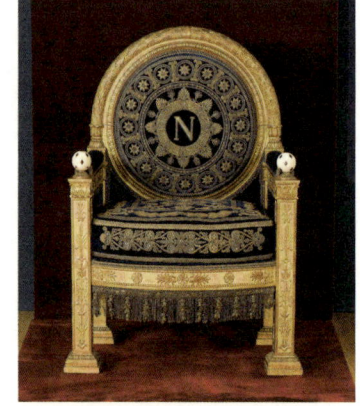
83

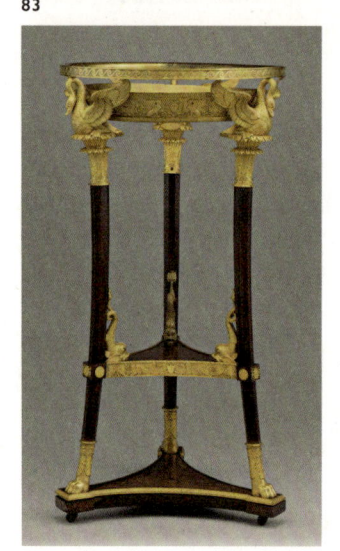
85

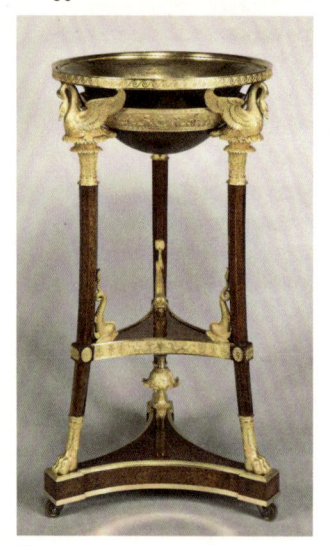
87

88

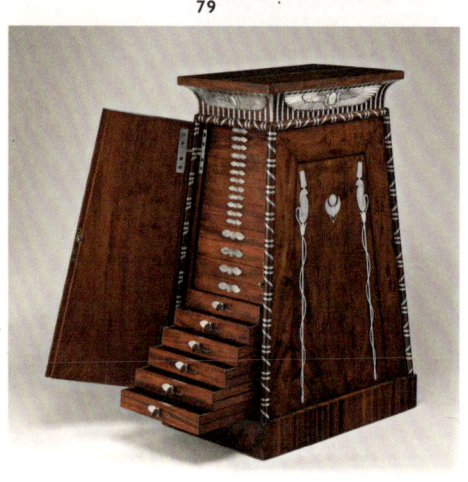
90

* FONTAINEBLEAU ONLY   ‡ BGC GALLERY ONLY

77

"Corvisart" desk chair, ca. 1795
Attributed to Georges Jacob
Mahogany, copper, leather
37¾ × 29⅛ × 18⅞ in. (96 × 74 × 48 cm)
Châteaux de Malmaison et Bois-Préau, Rueil-Malmaison, Don baron Rabusson-Corvisart, 1950, M. M. 50.6.1.
SEE FIG. 8.22.

Although it bears no maker's stamp, this imposing armchair has much in common with the work of Georges Jacob, one of the promoters of the antique revival at the end of the 18th century. It is consistent in many respects with a drawing, now in a private collection, that was probably prepared by Percier and Fontaine for the Jacob firm, and which Hans Ottomeyer has dated to 1797. The decorative vocabulary, notably the lion's-paw feet on the front legs, derives from archaeological remains studied by the two architects in Rome. The back legs, of a saber type used by G. Jacob during the reign of Louis XVI, provide stability, but their curve, which continues into the profile of the concave back, mitigates the sobriety of this exceptionally majestic and enveloping chair. The general austerity of the design is reinforced by the preponderance of wood over textiles.

Thanks to Elisabeth Caude's recent research on the furniture in the Bonaparte townhouse on rue de la Victoire, we know that the Jacob brothers delivered to them an armchair of similar type on December 5, 1797, and that this must have been followed by two more, for three such pieces were removed from the house in 1806. Other examples now at the Mobilier national and the Grand Trianon may correspond to these. The one now at Malmaison came from the descendants of Jean Nicolas Corvisart, Napoleon's official doctor beginning in 1801.

—ISABELLE TAMISIER-VÉTOIS

78

‡ **Armchair from the Council Room at Malmaison**, ca. 1800
Jacob frères
Painted and gilt beech, gilt bronze, wool and metallic braid
38 × 26¾ × 28 in (96.5 × 67.9 × 71.1 cm)
New-York Historical Society, Gift of Louis Borg, 1867, 1867-438

79

Armchair, ca. 1800
Jacob frères
Carved gilt wood, silk, taffeta, Gros de Tours brocaded and embroidered with silk thread, braid
37⅜ × 25¼ × 25¼ in. (95 × 64 × 64 cm)
Marks: [stamp] JACOB FRERES / RUE MESLEE; [handwritten label] Grand salon / des consuls / 1ᵉʳ étage; [marks] châteaux de Saint-Cloud and Fontainebleau and inventory numbers
Château de Fontainebleau, F 3437

80

Armchair from Napoleon's office in the Imperial Palace of Bordeaux, ca. 1804
Attributed to Jacob frères
Mahogany, velvet
38¼ × 26⅜ × 21⅝ in. (97 × 67 × 55 cm)
Inscriptions: [former inventory numbers] B 151, GT 3273, GT 347
Châteaux de Versailles et de Trianon, T 291.1

In 1808, when Napoleon and his army descended on Spain, this armchair was in the imperial palace in Bordeaux. In 1809 it was in the emperor's office there, which under the Restoration became that of the duc d'Angoulême. Upholstered in green morocco by the tapissier Laflèche in 1837 for the Grand Trianon, it was installed in 1839 in the bedchamber of Louis-Philippe, Baron Camille Fain. It remained there until 1893. Doubtless it was designed by Charles Percier in collaboration with Georges Jacob. Armrests like those seen here—with incurving supports and terminating in lion heads—are found on other desk chairs, such as one delivered in 1805 for the topographical cabinet in Fontainebleau and made by Benoît François Boulard (château de Fontainebleau, F 3356). But in the present case, the curve of the back, which has an openwork panel, is continuous with that of the armrests. There are no abrupt transitions here, and the whole has the soft lines of a gondola chair. Similarly, the back legs en jarret recall those of three other armchairs: one that came to the Grand Trianon in 1837 (T 453), another that once belonged to Dr. Corvisart (GMT 3661), and a third that was made available to General de Gaulle in 1966 at Trianon-sous-Bois (GMT 3661), with claw feet and armrest supports in the form of winged chimeras. The last two examples, which recall ancient models, date from the Directory. In terms of style, the present armchair seems to occupy a place somewhere between those two pieces and the chair at Fontainebleau. On the other hand, its front legs, circled by multiple rings in imitation of antique models, are more unusual. They are virtually identical to those found on another armchair recently on the market.

In 1808, Napoleon seems to have abandoned this design for another, simpler one—doubtless also designed by Percier—whose seat and back are covered in silk or morocco. The first example of this later design was delivered to Compiègne; others followed, notably one for Trianon in 1810.

—JÉRÉMIE BENOÎT

81

* **Armchair from the Salon des Dames d'Honneur at Compiègne**, 1809
François Honoré Georges Jacob-Desmalter
Carved gilt wood, silk and metallic thread, taffeta, brocaded Gros de Tours damask, braid
38½ × 29⅛ × 22 in. (98 × 74 × 56 cm)
Marks: [stamp] JACOB D. / R. MESLEE; [mark] château de Compiègne and inventory number
Palais de Compiègne, C 287 C

82

Gondola chair from the Salon d'Argent of the Élysée palace, ca. 1805
François Honoré Georges Jacob-Desmalter
Carved and silver gilt wood
30¼ × 26 × 20 in. (77 × 66 × 51 cm)
Palais de l'Élysée, Paris, Mobilier national, GME 18590
SEE FIG. 11A.5.

83

* **Throne of Napoleon I at the Tuileries palace**, 1804
François Honoré Georges Jacob-Desmalter; after Percier and Fontaine; trimming by Gobert; embroidery by Picot
Gilt wood, velvet
47¼ × 34⅝ × 34⅝ in. (120 × 88 × 88 cm)
Musée du Louvre, Paris, GTMC2

84

* **Night table from Josephine's *petits appartements* at Fontainebleau**, 1804
François Honoré Georges Jacob-Desmalter
Mahogany, gilt bronze, green marble
29¼ × 17 × 14½ in. (75 × 43 × 37 cm)
Château de Fontainebleau, F.4070; GME6879
SEE FIG. 11A.6.

85

* **Night table from the emperor's rooms**, 1802–4
Jacob frères
Mahogany, gilt bronze, turquin blue marble, white marble, enamel
33½ × 18 × 13¾ in. (85 × 45 × 35 cm)
Château de Fontainebleau, F.3728

86

Commode from the bedroom of Josephine's apartments, château de Saint-Cloud, 1802–3
Jacob frères
Mahogany, gilt bronze, white marble, enamel
51 × 23⅝ × 43¼ in. (130 × 60 × 110 cm)
Château de Fontainebleau, F3927
SEE FIG. 8A.1.

87

‡ **Washstand (*athénienne*)**, ca. 1802
Martin Guillaume Biennais, after Charles Percier
Legs, base and shelf of yew wood; gilt-bronze mounts; iron plate beneath shelf
36⅜ × 19½ in. (92.4 × 49.5 cm)
The Metropolitan Museum of Art, New York, Bequest of James Alexander Scrymser, 1918, 26.256.1

88

* **Washstand (*athénienne*)**, ca. 1810
Martin Guillaume Biennais, after Charles Percier
Yew wood, gilt bronze
35⅞ × 19¼ in. (91 × 49 cm)
Château de Fontainebleau, F 24 C

89

‡ **Washstand for the first consul at the Tuileries palace**, 1802
Drawing for Biennais's workshop
Charles Percier
Pen and watercolor on paper (framed) 41¾ × 24⅝ in. (106 × 62.5 cm)
Musée des Arts décoratifs, Paris, 10424

90
Medal cabinet, ca. 1809
Charles Percier, made by François Honoré Georges Jacob-Desmalter; mounts by Martin Guillaume Biennais, after drawings by Dominique Vivant Denon
Mahogany, applied and inlaid silver
35⅜ × 19¾ × 14¾ in. (90 × 50 × 37.5 cm)
The Metropolitan Museum of Art, New York, Bequest of Collis P. Huntington, 1900, 26.168.77

91
‡ **Design for a medal cabinet**, ca. 1809
Attributed to Charles Percier
Graphite, pen, and watercolor on paper
8⅜ × 6¾ in. (21.4 × 17 cm)
Les Arts Décoratifs, Paris, Cabinet es arts graphiques, CD 3240

92
* **Model of the emperor's library in the palais de Compiègne**, ca. 1808
Louis Martin Berthault, Jacob-Desmalter et Cie
Gouache and watercolor on cardboard and paper
18⅛ × 37⅜ in. (46 × 95 cm)
Palais impérial de Compiègne, c.2008.008/3

In 1806, at Josephine's request, Napoleon engaged the architect Louis Martin Berthault to undertake various projects at the palace of Compiègne. Having been instructed to make the building habitable, Berthault presented his proposals on October 22, 1807, but his plans displeased the emperor. Percier and Fontaine were then engaged to reorganize the apartments in a way consistent with main axes determined by Napoleon himself. On November 10, 1807, thanks to Fontaine's involvement, Berthault presented a new design, which was accepted. A library would be created in what was formerly the king's interior cabinet.

The Jacob-Desmalter firm executed the mahogany armoires— as is attested by the copy of a request for a down payment for the library dated May 31, 1808 (Palais impérial de Compiègne archives)— undoubtedly after designs by Berthault.

Although we do not know exactly what part Percier and Fontaine took in reshaping the initial proposal by Berthault, the model relates to one of the emblematic First Empire rooms at Compiègne at a time when they were in charge of supervising the interior arrangement of the palace. The furniture shown in the project differs slightly from what was actually made. Each vertical divider of the executed armoires is decorated with three lion heads, as opposed to the roundels shown in the maquette; likewise, all of the foliage decorating the framing elements in the maquette is similar, while the executed pieces feature, on the upper frieze, branches of laurel flanking a central star. This is a rare surviving example of the type of maquette that architects regularly submitted to their sovereigns for review, as opposed to the two-dimensional renderings previously submitted.

—MARC DESTI

93
* **Design of a tureen for Josephine**, n.d.
Attributed to Charles Percier
Graphite, pen, and gray wash on paper
22¼ × 24⅜ in. (56.5 × 62 cm)
Les Arts Décoratifs, Paris, CD 3172

94
‡ **Design for a tureen**, n.d.
Attributed to Charles Percier
Graphite, pen and gray wash on paper
3⅞ × 5⅞ in. (10 × 15 cm)
Les Arts Décoratifs, Paris, CD 6858

95
‡ **Tureen**, 1794–1814
Charles Percier; made by Martin Guillaume Biennais
Silver gilt
18¼ × 14⅛ in. (46.4 × 35.9) cm
The Metropolitan Museum of Art, New York, Joseph Pulitzer Bequest, 1934, 34.17.1a–c
SEE FIG. 9A.5.

96
Tureen, n.d.
Charles Percier; made by Martin Guillaume Biennais
Silver
20⅞ × 17¾ × 14⅛ in. (53 × 45 × 36 cm)
Banque de France, Paris, 15667
SEE FIG. 9A.4.

This tureen was displayed at the Exposition Universelle of 1900, when it was in the collection of Baron de Bethmann.

97
‡ **Design for a ewer**, n.d.
Attributed to Charles Percier
Graphite, watercolor on paper
17 × 8¼ in. (43.1 × 21 cm)
Les Arts Décoratifs, Paris, CD 3197

98
‡ **Ciborium for the coronation of Napoleon I**, 1804
Charles Percier
Graphite, pen and brown ink, gray and reddish-brown wash on paper
10½ × 7⅜ in. (26.7 × 18.7 cm)
The Metropolitan Museum of Art, New York, Van Day Truex Fund, 2013, 2013.544.1.

99
‡ **Chalice for the coronation of Napoleon I**, 1804
Charles Percier
Graphite, pen and brown ink, gray and reddish-brown wash
10½ × 7⅜ in. (26.7 × 18.6 cm)
The Metropolitan Museum of Art, New York, Van Day Truex Fund, 2013, 2013.544.2

100
‡ **Pair of candelabra with winged victories**, ca. 1810–15
Pierre Philippe Thomire
Gilt bronze
50¼ in. (127.6 cm)
The Metropolitan Museum of Art, New York, Bequest of James Alexander Scrymser, 1918, 26.256.2, .3

101
* **Design of a tea urn for Napoleon**
From the archives of the Biennais workshop, ca. 1810
Attributed to Charels Percier and Louis Hippolyte Lebas
Graphite, pen, and watercolor on paper
33¼ × 22½ in. (87 × 54 cm)
Les Arts Décoratifs, Paris, CD 3184

102
Desk lamp (one of a pair), 1809
Charles Percier, Martin Guillaume Biennais and Jean Charles Cahier
Gilt silver
35 × 17⅜ in. (89 × 44 cm)
Château de Fontainebleau, F 1112 C.2

103
Design of a lamp for the Council Room, 1809
From the archives of the Biennais workshop
Attributed to Charles Percier
Pen and black ink, watercolor, graphite
26¾ × 18¾ in. (67.8 × 47.5 cm)
Les Arts Décoratifs, Paris, CD 3251

104
Clock in the shape of an antique altar dedicated to the sun, 1813
The Four Seasons are represented on the pedestal.
Charles Percier; made by Sèvres Porcelain Manufactory
Bisque porcelain, gold highlights
22¼ × 12¾ × 7⅝ in. (56.5 × 32.3 × 19.4 cm)
Cité de la Céramique, Sèvres, MNC 13022
SEE FIG. 9.4.

105
Clock for the Grand Cabinet of the emperor at the Tuileries Palace, 1809
Pierre Philippe Thomire, after Charles Percier
Griotte marble, chased and gilt bronze
29⅛ × 15¾ × 7½ in. (74 × 40 × 19 cm)
Mobilier national, Paris, GML 2891
SEE FIG. 9.11.

106
* **Bacchus's armchair**, *surtout de table from the Tuileries palace*, 1810
Sèvres Porcelain Manufactory
Bisque porcelain, gilt bronze base
18⅞ × 13¼ × 12⅜ in. (48 × 33.5 × 31.5 cm)
Château de Fontainebleau, Fontainebleau, F-2007.6

107
Designs for the Royal Museums table, 1817
Charles Percier
Graphite, ink, and gouache on paper

‡ **107A** Table pedestal
6⅜ × 9½ in. (16.2 × 24 cm)
Cité de la Céramique, Sèvres, 2012.1.363

‡ **107B** Table top
10¾ × 11¼ in. (27.3 × 28.5 cm)
Cité de la Céramique, Sèvres, 2012.1.227
SEE FIG. 9.6.

* **107C** Cartel for the table top
8⅝ × 12⅝ in. (22 × 32 cm)
Cité de la Céramique, Sèvres, 2012.1.226

CHECKLIST

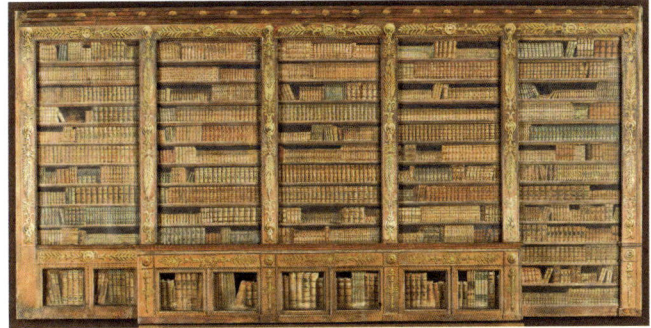
92

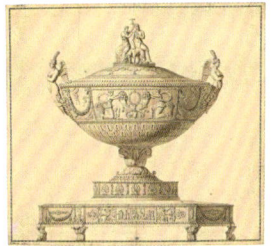
93

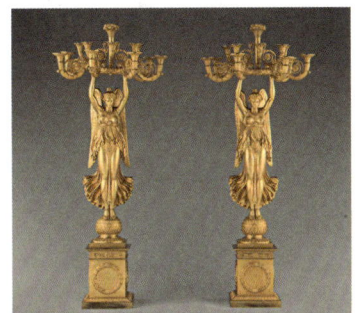
100

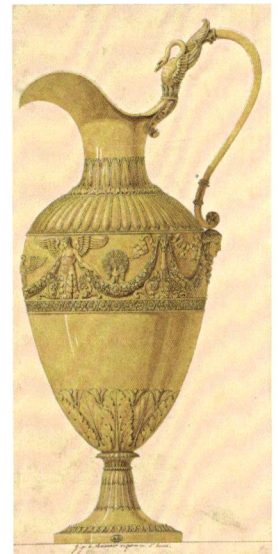
97

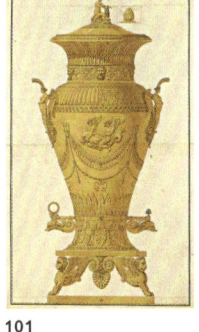
101

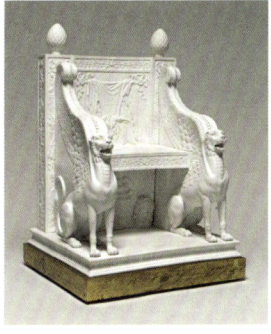
106

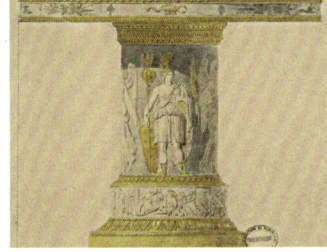
107A

* **107D** Cartel for the table top
8⅝ × 12⅝ in. (22 × 32 cm)
Cité de la Céramique, Sèvres, 2012.1.228
SEE FIG. 9.7.

108

Percier vase (one of a pair), 1805–6
Sèvres Porcelain Manufactory
Porcelain, chased and gilt bronze
22½ × 10⅝ in. (57 × 27 cm)
Château de Fontainebleau, F 3958.1

109

‡ **Vase (one of a pair)**, 19th century
Sèvres Porcelain Manufactory
Porcelain
29½ in. (75 cm); base: 8 9/16 × 8 9/16 in. (21.75 × 21.75 cm)
Wadsworth Atheneum Museum of Art, Hartford, CT, Gift of Mrs. Henry B. Learned, 1948.109

110

Textile panel, 1804/15 or 1852/70
After designs by Charles Percier and Pierre Fontaine
Linen, plain weave; cut and drawn thread work with cotton in interlocking lace, ladder hem, overcast, twisted buttonhole, and wave stitches; buttonhole rings and wheels, padded overcast, satin, and stem stitches
20¾ × 26¾ in. (52.7 × 68.1 cm)
Art Institute of Chicago, Grace R. Smith Textile Endowment, 1993.132
Not in exhibition

SECTION 5

THE LOUVRE, THE TUILERIES, AND THE RUE DE RIVOLI

111

* ***Project costing more than 12 million [livres] to be subsequently executed and underwritten by an association for the support of workers of all kinds, presented to the Consuls of the French government in the month of Brumaire, year VIII***, December 1799
Anonymous
Drawing over an engraved plan combined with a drawing of the elevation and plan of the rue de Rivoli, ink and watercolor
38½ × 75 in. (98 × 190 cm)
Fort de Vincennes, Service historique de l'armée de terre, collection du ministre
SEE FIG. 12.4.

112

Design for the rue de Rivoli, 1802
Charles Percier and Pierre Fontaine
Graphite, pen, wash, and watercolor on paper
25½ × 82⅝ in. (65 × 210 cm)
Private collection, Paris

113

Design of Monsieur Fontaine for linking the Louvre to the Tuileries, 1812
Charles Percier and Pierre Fontaine
Graphite, pen, wash, and watercolor on paper
23¼ × 35 in. (58.9 × 89.2 cm)
Private collection, Paris
SEE FIG. 12A.3.

114

Elevation and cross section of the façades on the rue de Rivoli
Charles Percier and Pierre Fontaine
From Jean Charles Krafft, *Recueil des plus jolies maisons de Paris*, plate 38
Paris: Author, 1809
Engraved plate
13¾ × 10½ in. (35 × 26.6 cm)
Private collection, Paris
SEE FIG. 12.5.

115

Bird's-eye view of the projected linking of the Louvre and Tuileries in 1828
Charles Percier and Pierre Fontaine
From Charles Othon Frédéric Jean-Baptiste de Clarac, *Musée de sculpture antique et moderne*, plate 110bis
Paris: Texier, 1826–55
Engraved plate
8⅛ × 10½ in. (20.7 × 26.6 cm)
Private collection, Paris
SEE FIG. 12.2.

116

Plate from the service de l'Empereur *with a view of the rue de Rivoli and the Palais des Tuileries*, 1807–11
Sèvres Porcelain Manufactory
Hard-paste porcelain
Diam. 9¼ in. (23.4 cm)
Châteaux de Malmaison et Bois-Préau, MM 64.1.215, on deposit at château de Fontainebleau

117

‡ **The Salle des Maréchaux with a view of the Tuileries Gardens**, ca. 1835
Eugène Emmanuel Viollet-Le-Duc
Watercolor on paper
18⅞ × 23⅝ in. (48 × 60 cm)
Musée d'Orsay, Paris, 33285
SEE FIG. 12.8.

118

Design of a lantern to mark the entrance of the Tuileries, 1805
Charles Percier and Pierre Fontaine
Graphite, pen, wash, and watercolor on paper

117A. Elevation
42 × 15 in. (107 × 38 cm)

117B. Cross section
43 × 19¼ in. (109 × 49 cm)
Private collection, Paris
SEE FIG. 12.9.

281

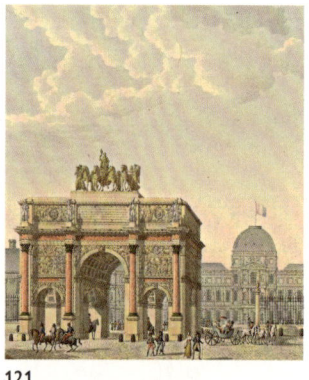
121

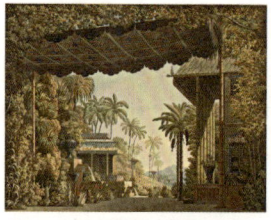
132

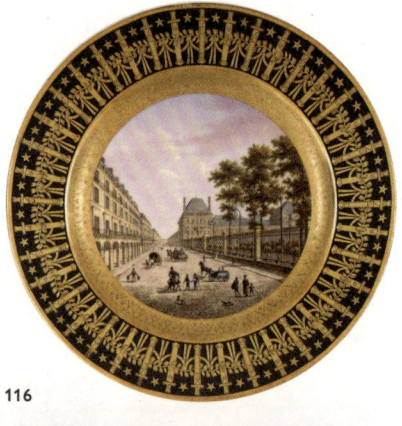
116

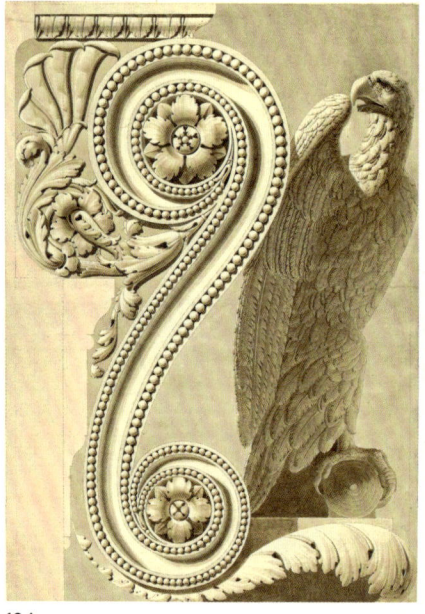
124

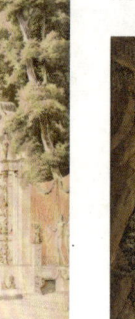
134

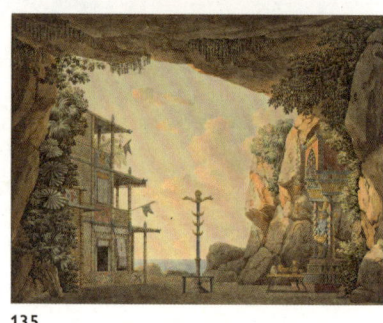
135

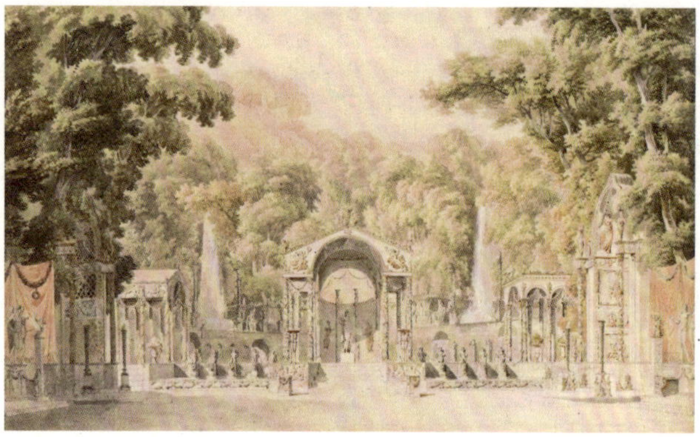

119
Reconstruction of the Arch of Septimius Severus in Rome, ca. 1788
Attributed to Charles Percier and Pierre Fontaine
Pen, ink, and wash on paper
(drawing) 15¾ × 17⅜ in. (40 × 44 cm); (framed) 24 × 26¾ in. (61 × 68 cm)
Private collection, Paris

120
‡ **Arc du Carrousel, south side view**, 1806–15
Charles Percier and Pierre Fontaine
Pen and watercolor on paper
11 × 9¾ in. (28.8 × 24.8 cm)
Bibliothèque nationale de France, départment estampes et photographie, Paris, vol. 1, 28
SEE FIG. 12.10.

121
‡ **Arc du Carrousel, view of east side**, 1806–15
Charles Percier and Pierre Fontaine
Pen and watercolor on paper
12¼ × 9⅛ in. (31.2 × 23.3 cm)
Bibliothèque nationale de France, Paris, EST RESERVE VE-53 (C). Destailleur Paris, t. 1, 29

122
‡ **Arc du Carrousel, view from the Tuileries palace**, 1806
Charles Percier and Pierre Fontaine
Pen and India ink on paper
10½ × 14⅛ in. (26.5 × 35.8 cm)
Bibliothèque nationale de France, départment estampes et photographie, Paris, EST RESERVE VE-53 (C). Destailleur Paris, t. 1, 30

123
* **Arc du Carrousel, view from the Tuileries palace**, 1806
Charles Percier and Pierre Fontaine
Pen and India ink on paper
10½ × 14⅛ in. (26.5 × 35.8 cm)
Bibliothèque nationale de France, , départment estampes et photographie, Paris, RESERVE QB-201 (151)-FOL

124
Side view of the console decorating the central arch of the arc du Carrousel, 1806–10
Charles Percier and Pierre Fontaine
Pen, wash, and watercolor on paper
32 × 22⅞ in. (83.5 × 58 cm)
Musée Carnavalet, Paris, CARD06679

125
Front view of the console decorating the central arch of the arc du Carrousel, 1806–10
Charles Percier and Pierre Fontaine
Pen and ink wash on paper
22⅞ × 32 in. (58 × 83.5 cm)
Musée Carnavalet, Paris, CARD06681

126
* **Study of Victory crowning a trophy for the arc du Carrousel**, ca. 1806
Charles Percier
Pencil, pen, and ink wash on paper
6⅜ × 6 in. (16.3 × 15.3 cm)
Bibliothèque nationale de France, , départment estampes et photographie, Paris, EST RESERVE VE-53 (C), Destailleur Paris, t.1, 31

127
* **Entrance to the musée du Louvre from the rue de Rivoli**, ca. 1806
Charles Percier and Pierre Fontaine
Pen and wash on paper
(Two drawings mounted on one sheet)
15¾ × 24⅞ in. (40 × 63 cm); 11½ × 23¼ in. (29.3 × 59 cm)
Bibliothèque nationale de France, , départment estampes et photographie, Paris, EST RESERVE VE-53 (C). Destailleur Paris, vol. 5, 797

128
South staircase of the colonnade, Louvre
From Charles Othon Frédéric Jean-Baptiste de Clarac, *Musée de sculpture antique et moderne*, atlas, volume 1, plate 97
Designed by Percier and Fontaine; engraving after drawing by Christophe Civeton
Paris: Texier, 1826–27
Engraved plate
9 × 7½ in. (23 × 19 cm)
Private collection, Paris
SEE FIG. 12.14.

SECTION 6

PAPER ARCHITECTURE, EPHEMERAL ARCHITECTURE

129
* **Design for arenas to celebrate the Triumphs of the Republic, façade, plan, and partial cross sections**, 1794
Charles Percier and Pierre Fontaine
Graphite, pen, and wash on paper
(Two drawings mounted on one sheet):
8¼ × 39½ in. (21 × 100 cm); 15¾ × 39½ in. (40 × 100 cm)
Musée Carnavalet, Paris, D 8219 (réserve)

130
* **Monument to the Defenders of the Nation**, ca. 1796
Charles Percier and Pierre Fontaine

Graphite, pen, wash, and watercolor on paper
Musée Carnavalet, Paris, D 3025 (réserve)
SEE FIG. 13.5.

131

* **Project for a cenotaph commemorating La Pérouse** [Jean François de Galaup, 1741–88?], 1829
Henri Labrouste
Graphite, pen, wash, and watercolor on paper
25¼ × 38 2/3 in. (64 × 98.4 cm)
Académie d'architecture, Paris, 282.1
SEE FIG. 13.6.

132

* **Set design for *Elisca ou l'amour maternel*, Act II**, 1799
Charles Percier, Pierre Fontaine, and Jean Thomas Thibault
Pen and watercolor on paper
15¼ × 19⅜ in. (38.8 × 49.3 cm)
Bibliothèque-musée de l'opéra, Bibliothèque nationale de France, Paris, BMO ESQ 19-29

133

‡ **Set design for *Elisca ou l'amour maternel*, Act I**, 1799
Charles Percier, Pierre Fontaine, and Jean Thomas Thibault
Pen and watercolor on paper
15¼ × 15½ in. (38.8 × 39.3 cm)
Bibliothèque-musée de l'opéra, Bibliothèque nationale de France, Paris, BMO ESQ 19-30
SEE FIG. 13.1.

134

‡ **Set design for an opera: a wooded garden with the Temple of Venus**, 1792
Charles Percier
Watercolor, pen, and black ink on paper
15 × 24⅝ in. (38.1 × 62.9 cm)
Philip Hewat-Jaboor

At the end of 1792, one year after his return from Rome, Percier was appointed director of set design at the Paris Opera. He asked Pierre Fontaine, who at the time was in London where he had emigrated, to come back to Paris and assume the role of co-director. Their collaboration began during the first half of December.

This drawing showing a design for a stage set has on its verso an inscription from Jacques Cellerier, the director of the Opera: "Approuvé pour [être] exécuté / Tel qu'il est du côté droit / Paris 13 xbre [December] 1792" (approved to be executed as it is on the right side). Assuming this approval may have taken a few days, we cannot be sure if this composition should be considered a production of Percier alone or whether it was the result of the partnership between Percier and Fontaine, for it corresponds to the very beginning of their association. In any case, the identification with Grétry's opera *Anacreon* that has been accepted until now must be firmly rejected because that opera was not composed until 1797, when Cellerier was no longer the director of the Opera. With its abundant use of ornament and objects like candelabras, torches, and tripods in front of the entrance to the central temple, this drawing represents an interesting link between Percier's studies in Rome and his work in the field of ornament and interior decoration.

—JEAN-PHILIPPE GARRIC

135

‡ **Set design for *Elisca ou l'amour maternel*, Act II**, 1799
Charles Percier, Pierre Fontaine, and Jean Thomas Thibault
Pen and watercolor on paper
13¾ × 18 in. (35 × 45.9 cm)
The Cleveland Museum of Art, Delia E. Holden Fund, 1978.80

136

Sketch for the tribune built for the distribution of the eagle standards on the occasion of Napoleon's coronation, 1804
Charles Percier and Pierre Fontaine
Graphite, pen, and watercolor on paper
31⅛ × 33⅛ in. (79 × 84 cm)
Private collection, Paris
SEE FIG. 11.2.

Erected in front of the façade of the École militaire that faces the Champs-de-Mars, the tribune for the distribution of the eagle standards is known to us through contemporary prints and Jacques Louis David's depiction of the ceremony in a monumental canvas—conceived as a pendant to his painting of Napoleon's coronation—now in the château de Versailles. This large drawing, executed on several conjoined sheets of paper, was a design tool. It is not highly finished throughout, like a presentation drawing, but many of its details are rendered with extreme precision, in a way that made it possible to better envision the final effect of the realized structure. The color scheme is of particular interest. The actual tribune had scarlet curtains, but mauve dominates in the drawing, and the turquoise blue of the carpets that decorate the sub-basement platforms beside the stairs is especially striking.

—JEAN-PHILIPPE GARRIC

137

View of a celebration in honor of the marriage of Napoleon and Marie-Louise, 1810
Louis Pierre Baltard
From an album of 17 drawings; pen and watercolor on paper
30 × 22 in. (76 × 56 cm)
Château de Fontainebleau, F-1996.3

138

Album of designs for the palace of the King of Rome, 1810–after 1815
Charles Percier and Pierre Fontaine
Album of bound drawings. Half shagreen red straight-grain morocco binding, with red paper sides imitating straight-grain morocco. Drawings of various media including pen, wash, chalk, and watercolor.
26 × 20⅞ in. (66 × 51 cm)

‡ **138A** View of the palace
École nationale supérieure des Beaux-Arts, Paris, Pc 65936 - pj 39

* **138B** Ground plan of the palace
École nationale supérieure des Beaux-Arts, Paris, Pc 65936 - pj 31

139

Album of designs for the palace of the King of Rome, 1810–15
Charles Percier and Pierre Fontaine
Album of drawings bound ca. 1820. Half shagreen red straight-grain morocco binding, with red paper sides imitating straight-grain morocco. Title page, 42 sheets of drawings of which 30 are full spreads.
26⅛ × 20⅞ in. (66.5 × 53 cm)
Private collection, Paris

The first thirty-nine drawings in this album are designs for the palace of the king of Rome, and the last three are designs for "cafés in the Tuileries gardens." Eighteen different proposals for the palace are included, all with ground floor plans and most with elevations and cross-sections. Beginning with the eleventh drawing, marginal annotations in pencil specify the buildings that inspired the various projects: the palace of Laecken in Belgium, the château de Meudon, the imperial palace at Bordeaux, the château de Compiègne, the Grand Trianon, the Petit Trianon, the palais de Rohan in Strasbourg, the château de Saint-Cloud, the château de Fontainebleau, and the château de Versailles. Clearly, these "in the manner of" variations grew out of the two architects' presentation to Napoleon of the plans of the principal French and European palaces, which they mention in their book on royal residences.

—JEAN-PHILIPPE GARRIC

140

* **Design for the palace of the King of Rome, elevation**, ca. 1811
Charles Percier and Pierre Fontaine
Pen and wash on paper
6¼ × 30 in. (16 × 77.5 cm)
Châteaux de Malmaison et Bois-Préau; MM 40-47.2406; on deposit at château de Fontainebleau

141

Album of Various Projects, 1805–15
Charles Percier and Pierre Fontaine
Album of drawings bound ca. 1820. Half shagreen red straight-grain morocco binding decorated with compartments; red paper sides imitating straight-grain morocco. Title in gold on spine and front cover: "*Recueil de projets*." One blank sheet and fifty-one sheets of drawings, three of which are full spreads.
25½ × 20½ in. (65 × 52 cm)
Private collection, Paris

The first thirteen drawings relate to work at the parc Monceau, notably the construction of a house and a menagerie there. Drawings 14–28 relate to the project for a house for the emperor overlooking the bay at Terneuzen (Terneuse), three different proposals for which are included. Drawings 29–31 concern the project for a pavilion in the Tuileries gardens; drawings 32–40, three projects for a cemetery; drawings 40–46, four projects for fountains; drawings 47–50, the project for a large townhouse for "the minister of foreign affairs in the kingdom of Italy;" drawing 51 is a project for a panorama.

—JEAN-PHILIPPE GARRIC

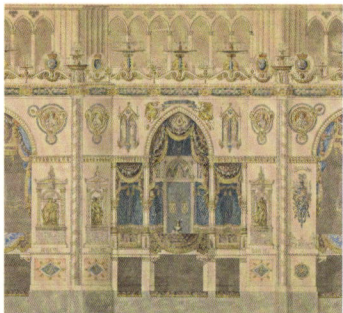

142C

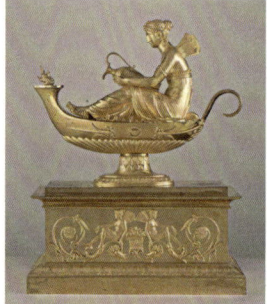

147

146

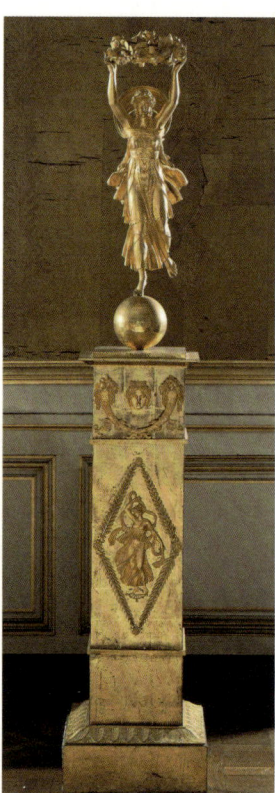

148

143

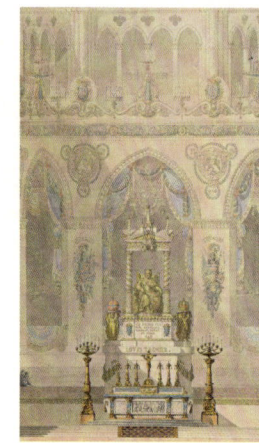

142A

145–48
THE YELLOW SALON AT FONTAINEBLEAU

First envisioned in 1805, the creation of private rooms for the empress at Fontainebleau was delayed until 1807, when Fontaine, during the couple's sojourn there, was asked by the emperor to make design proposals. The architect Antoine Leroy, named Dufour's successor by Fontaine, oversaw the related work there in 1808–9. Josephine was accorded all the rooms situated below the ceremonial apartments and facing the garden of Diana. The etiquette of the imperial palaces, elaborated in 1805, stipulated a very clear division between the ceremonial rooms and the ruling couple's living quarters. The latter should include an "appartement d'honneur," consisting of rooms for sociability, and "appartements intérieurs," or private quarters. At Fontainebleau, apart from service areas and corridors, these last two suites consisted of nine rooms (see fig. 11.8). A large assembly salon was preceded by an antechamber, an intermediary room, and a first salon, known as the *salon de billard* (billiards room). Beyond these were a room for the ladies in waiting, a bathing room, a bedchamber, a boudoir, and a dining room.

Prepared in 1807 by the Percier and Fontaine office, the plan delivered to Leroy included painted decors for the walls of each room except the second, large salon, for which only a carpet design was prepared. This scheme, dominated by grand decorative compositions in antique revival style, incorporating figures and friezes and a great deal of faux marble, occupies a place between the gracious designs from the consular period for Malmaison (1800–1802) and the grand decorative program for the imperial palace of Compiègne (1808–9). In the end it was not executed, since interior designs featuring mirrors and silks set within frames were deemed preferable. Josephine insisted on using the tapissier Michel Jacques Boulard, who provided all of the textile confections, notably the yellow gros de Naples taffeta with red embroidery. The invoice submitted to the administration of the Garde-Meuble on December 4, 1808, includes charges for wall fabric, curtains, and "joined" furniture, which is to say almost forty chairs whose frames had been made by Jacob-Desmalter. It is not known who designed and manufactured the wall fabric, which featured two alternating decorative compositions reminiscent of ancient grotesque designs and separated by pilasters, scrolls, rosettes, and mandorlas. The first composition consists of a lyre set within a laurel wreath from which emerge, both above and below, volutes from which issue palm fronds framing a vegetal vignette that is prolonged first by a mandorla, then by foliage from which spring palmettes. The second composition (cat. 145) features, at the top, two crossed horns surrounded by a laurel wreath; below this, the field is occupied by a sequence of vertically linked motifs: at the bottom, a vegetal vignette incorporating palm leaves gives rise to a symmetrical pair of rinceau scrolls and a large central palmette; above that, another rinceau vignette effects a transition to the bottom of a swag of linked palmettes and a half-velum motif, both suspended from a slender horizontal bar; this last supports, atop

142
Designs for the decoration of Reims Cathedral for the coronation of Louis XVIII, 1815
Charles Percier and Pierre Fontaine

✱ **142A** Raising of the altar with the statue of Louis I
Pen and black ink, watercolor, over graphite on paper
30¼ × 18¾ in. (76.9 × 47.7 cm)
The Metropolitan Museum of Art, New York, Gift of Lincoln Kirstein, 1956, 56.559.2

‡ **142B** Cross section of Reims Cathedral
Pen and black ink, brush and gray, blue, yellow, violet, and rose wash
9⅝ × 27¾ in. (24.6 × 70.5 cm)
The Metropolitan Museum of Art, New York, Gift of Lincoln Kirstein, 1956, 56.559.1

‡ **142C** Elevation of the Royal Box
Pen and black ink with colored wash
30⅛ × 34⅛ in. (76.6 × 86.6 cm)
The Metropolitan Museum of Art, New York, Gift of Lincoln Kirstein, 1956, 56.559.6

143
Design for the Gallery of Diana at Fontainebleau, central elevation, 1810
Charles Percier
Watercolor on paper
9¼ × 13 in. (23.4 × 33.2 cm)
Château de Fontainebleau, F-1992-5

144
Design of the decoration of Gallery of Diana at Fontainebleau, 1810
Maximilien Joseph Hurtault
Watercolor on paper
15¾ × 45⅝ in. (40 × 116 cm)
Château de Fontainebleau, F 3228 C

145
Design for Josephine's *petits appartements* at Fontainebleau, 1807
Charles Percier
Ink and graphite with watercolor highlights on paper
14½ × 28½ in. (36.7 × 72.4 cm)
Château de Fontainebleau, Archives du service d'architecture, carton 11
SEE FIG. 11.8.

146
Textile panel from the Yellow Salon at Fontainebleau, 1809
Michel Jacques Boulard
Embroidered Gros de Naples silk
110¼ × 28 in. (280 × 140 cm)
Château de Fontainebleau, F 2598.2.1

147
Andiron with Psyche, 1809
Pierre Philippe Thomire, after a design by Charles Percier
Chased and gilt bronze
19¾ × 16⅛ × 6¾ in. (50 × 41 × 17 cm)
Château de Fontainebleau, F 943 C

148
Candelabra
Pierre Philippe Thomire
Chased and gilt bronze, gilt wood
80⁵⁄₁₆ × 15¾ × 15¾ in. (204 × 40 × 40 cm)
Inscriptions: [carved in the bronze] THOMIRE and inventory number
Château de Fontainebleau, F 216 C

149
✱ **Album of drawings of the château de Fontainebleau**, 1791–1838
Charles Percier
Thirty-nine drawings, various techniques on paper. Loose sheets and sketchbook sheets of various formats mounted on album pages.
Bibliothèque de l'Institut, Paris, Ms 1014
SEE FIGS. 4.8–11, 4.15.

another pair of delicate scrolling rinceaux, a basket of flowers.

This ornamental lexicon includes motifs that were repeated ad nauseam in the decorative arts during the first quarter of the 19th century, notably the basket of flowers and the lyre set within a wreath, several variations on which figure in Percier and Fontaine's *Recueil*. Boulard here repeated the decoration used on the deep red silk velvet embroidered with gold for the grand bedchamber of the empress in the Tuileries, realized after a design by Charles Percier in 1808, which served to frame the presentation of the new-born king of Rome to Empress Marie-Louise by Napoleon, a scene represented in watercolor by Isabey in 1811.

The harmony of the yellow and amaranth color scheme in the salon was increased by the richness of the gilt-wood furniture, notably the console tables with gilt-bronze fixtures, the result of a collaboration between Jacob-Desmalter and the bronzier Pierre Philippe Thomire. The latter also provided the gilt-bronze wall sconces, torchères, and andirons. His invoice of October 18, 1809, includes a pair of andirons consisting of "decorated antique lamps with seated so-called Psyche figures holding a buire (cat. 146)," or ancient vessel with belly, spout, and handle ("de lampes antiques à ornements sur lesquelles sont des figures de femme assise dites Psiché tenant une buyre;" AN, O² 515, dossier 12, pièce 72). This composition was inspired by the one in biscuit porcelain (dubbed *à l'étude*) modeled by Louis Simon Boizot for the Sèvres manufactory in 1776, but it is also reminiscent of the antique lamp that decorated the bedroom of Juliette Récamier. Nonetheless, Thomire's design is more closely related to the design for a Psyche lamp by Charles Percier (Bibliothèque Marmottan, Paris), one that also figures in the *Recueil* (pl. 18). The inclusion of the Psyche figures here—heads of Psyche had previously been depicted in some of the medallions on the bed of Madame Moreau—added an elegant feminine touch to the salon.

Thomire also delivered two large candelabra on pedestals made of gilt wood with gilt-bronze appliqués (cat. 147). The pedestals are in the same line as Percier's designs for the château of Saint-Cloud in 1802 (see fig. 11a.1), which Thomire had reprised in 1807 (Paris, Mobilier national). But the bronze ornament on these bases is richer, including an eagle on the lower register (removed in 1816), a draped figure set within a lozenge of laurel leaves in the center, and two cornucopias flanking a head toward the top. The pedestal supports a freestanding female figure—likewise gilded—that alights on a globe with one foot and lifts high a crown of roses and lilacs whose flowers serve as candle holders. This lovely conceit brings to mind the sylphs that Louis Lafitte painted on the walls of the dining room at Malmaison as well as the Victories with spread wings that Percier used in his interiors, notably the atelier of Isabey, and in various designs for objects, notably the candelabra for Josephine at Saint-Cloud, later reprised for the large salon in Moreau's townhouse (Fontainebleau, F 671 C). In any case, Thomire here abandoned wings in favor of a backswept veil and restricted the Hellenistic drapery to waist level and below, adding a surplice above the sheer tunic.

—VINCENT COCHET

BIBLIOGRAPHY

ARCHIVES

Percier Manuscripts at the Institut de France

THE TRIP TO ITALY (1786–91)

Mss 1006–1007: Drawings and sketches made of Roman interiors
Ms 1008: Outdoor sketches of Rome
Ms 1009: Outdoor sketches of Rome and along the road to and from Naples
Ms 1010: Sketches and drawings made on the trip from Rome to Paris (1791)
Ms 1011: Sketches of the Vatican

DRAWINGS OF SCULPTURE AND FRENCH BUILDINGS

Ms 1012: Sketches made of the Musée des monuments français
Ms 1013: Sketches made in Paris, Rouen, Cannes, Chartres, Houdan, Jouy-en-Josas, Lagny, Nantes, Josselin, Gouennoux, Plougastel, Quimper, etc.
Mss 1014–1016: Palace of Fontainebleau, Ballroom, different sketches. Gallery of Diane
Ms 1017: Door of the apartment at the old Louvre, during the time of Henri II

DRAWINGS OF ITALY PREPARED FOR PUBLICATION

Ms. 1018: Decorations drawn from several rooms in the Palazzo Tè in Mantua
Ms. 1019: Basilicas of Padua, Vicenza, and Brescia. Souvenirs, by Charles Percier

MANUSCRIPT FOR *PALAIS, MAISONS ET AUTRES ÉDIFICES MODERNES DESSINÉS À ROME* (1798)

Ms. 5380: Original drawings of the palace, houses, and other modern buildings drawn in Rome and published in Paris in year VI by Charles Percier, Pierre Fontaine, and Claude Bernier. The manuscript is stamped by Pierre Fontaine.

PRIMARY SOURCES

Works Published by Percier and Fontaine

Percier, Charles, and Pierre Fontaine [Claude Bernier et Léon Dufourny]. *Palais, maisons et autres édifices modernes dessinés à Rome; publiés à Paris, l'an VI de la République française (1798, v. st.)*, Paris: Authors, 1798. Revised ed., *Palais de Rome. Palais, maisons et autres édifices modernes de Percier et Fontaine*, ed. Jean-Philippe Garric. Wavre, Belgium: Mardaga/Institut national d'histoire de l'art, 2008.

Percier, Charles, and Pierre Fontaine. *Recueil de décorations intérieures, comprenant tout ce qui a rapport à l'ameublement comme vases, trépieds, candélabres, cassolettes, lustres, girandoles, lampes, chandeliers, cheminées, feux, poêles, pendules, tables, secrétaires, lits canapés, fauteuils, chaises, tabourets, miroirs, écrans, &, &, &. Composés par C. Percier et P. F. L. Fontaine. Exécutés sur leurs dessins.* Paris: Authors and Pierre Didot l'aîné, 1801–12.

Percier, Charles, and Pierre Fontaine [Jean Baptiste Isabey]. *Description des cérémonies et des fêtes qui ont eu lieu pour le couronnement de LL MM Napoléon, empereur des français et roi d'Italie, et Joséphine son auguste épouse.* Paris: Leblanc, 1807.

Percier, Charles, and Pierre Fontaine [Jean Charles Bonnard]. *Choix des plus célèbres maisons de plaisance de Rome et de ses environs.* Paris: Pierre Didot, 1809–13. Revised ed., *Villas de Rome de Percier et Fontaine*, ed. Jean-Philippe Garric. Wavre, Belgium: Mardaga, 2007.

Percier, Charles, and Pierre Fontaine. *Description des cérémonies et des fêtes qui ont eu lieu pour le mariage de S.M. l'Empereur Napoléon avec S.A.I. Madame l'archiduchesse Marie-Louise d'Autriche par Charles Percier et P. F. L. Fontaine,* Paris: Pierre Didot l'aîné, 1810.

Percier, Charles, and Pierre Fontaine. *Plans de plusieurs châteaux, palais et résidences de souverains, de France, d'Italie, d'Espagne et de Russie. Dessinés à la même échelle pour être comparés A.P.P.P.L.P.D.R.D.R (au plan projeté pour le palais du roi de Rome).* Paris: Authors [1818].

Percier, Charles, and Pierre Fontaine. *Résidences de souverains. Parallèle entre plusieurs résidences de souverains de France, d'Allemagne, de Suède, de Russie, d'Espagne et d'Italie, à Paris chez les auteurs,* Paris: Authors, 1833.

Works with Engravings after Percier or Reproductions of his Drawings (before 1914)

Baltard, Louis Pierre, Charles Percier, and Pierre Fontaine. *Arc de triomphe du Carrousel édifié par Percier et Fontaine, architectes, gravé d'après leurs dessins par Louis Pierre Baltard.* Paris: Jules Claye, 1875.

Duhamel du Monceau, Henri Louis. *Traité des arbres et des artistes que l'on cultive en France.* Paris: Étienne Michel et Artus Bertrand, [1800]–1819. Frontispiece, with Jean Thomas Thibault.

Horace. *Quintus Horatius Flaccus.* Paris: Pierre Didot l'aîné, 1799. Twelve decorative vignettes.

Laborde, Alexandre de. *Voyage pittoresque et historique de l'Espagne.* Paris: Pierre Didot l'aîné, 1812. Frontispiece.

La Fontaine. *Fables de La Fontaine.* Paris: Pierre Didot l'aîné, 1802. Twelve decorative vignettes. Second edition, Paris: Pierre Didot l'aîné, 1813.

Lenoir, Alexandre. *Musée des monumens français, ou Description historique et chronologique des statues en marbre et en bronze, bas-reliefs et tombeaux des hommes et des femmes célèbres, pour servir à l'histoire de France et à celle de l'art; ornée de gravures et augmentée d'une dissertation sur les costumes de chaque siècle.* 8 vols. Paris: Author, 1800–1821.

Percier, Charles, and Thomas Vaudoyer. *Restaurations des Monuments Antiques par les architectes pensionnaires de l'Académie de France à Rome… Colonne Trajane par Percier… Mémoire historique rédigé en 1839 par Thomas Vaudoyer.* Paris: Firmin Didot, 1877.

Prieur, Armand Parfait, and Pierre Louis Van Cléemputte. *Collection des prix que la ci-devant Académie d'Architecture proposait et couronnait tous les ans, gravée au trait, imprimée sur papier propre à être lave,* vol. 1 (Paris: Authors, [1787–96]).

Taylor, Charles, and Justin Taylor. *Voyages pittoresques et romantiques dans l'ancienne France, Franche Comté.* Paris, 1825. Vignette on title page.

Voltaire. *La Henriade.* Paris: Firmin Didot, 1819. Frontispiece, with François Gérard.

Other Primary Sources

Archives du musée des Monuments français. Inventaire général des richesses d'art de la France. 5 vols. Paris: E. Plon, 1883–97.

Baltard, Louis Pierre. *Paris et ses monumens, mesurés, dessinés et gravés par Baltard, architecte, avec des Descriptions historiques par le cit[oyen] Amaury-Duval.* Paris: Author, 1803[–5].

Baltard, Louis Pierre. *Lettres ou voyage pittoresque dans les Alpes,* Paris: Author, 1806.

Bausset, Louis François Joseph de. *Mémoires anecdotiques sur l'intérieur du palais.* Second edition, Paris: Baudouin frères, 1827.

Beauharnais, Hortense de. *Mémoires.* Paris: Plon, 1927. Revised ed., *Mémoires de la reine Hortense,* Christophe Pincemaille, ed. Paris: Mercure de France, 2006.

Berry, Miss. *Extracts from the Journals and Correspondance of Miss Berry, from the Year 1783 to 1852.* Edited by Lady Theresa Lewis, vol. 3. London: Longmans Green, 1866.

Biet, Joseph Etienne, and Jean Pierre Brès. *Souvenirs du musée des monuments français. Collection de 40 dessins perspectifs gravés au trait… dessinés par M. J.-E. Biet et gravés par MM. Normand père et fils; avec un texte explicatif par M. J.-P. Brès.* Paris: Author, 1821.

Blondel, Jacques François. [Pierre Patte]. *Cours d'architecture ou Traité de la décoration, distribution et construction des bâtiments.* Paris: Desaint, 1771–77.

Castellan, Antoine Laurent. *Fontainebleau: Etudes pittoresques et historiques sur ce château.* Paris and Fontainebleau: Gaillot, 1840.

Clarac, Charles Othon Frédéric Jean-Baptiste de. *Musée de sculpture antique et moderne.* Paris: Texier, 1826.

Coupin, Pierre Alexandre. *Oeuvres postumes de Girodet-Trioson… précédé d'une notice historique.* 2 vols. Paris: Renouard, 1829.

Debret, François, and Louis Hippolyte Lebas. *Oeuvres complète de Vignole.* Paris: Firmin Didot, [1815].

Delécluze, Etienne Jean. *Louis David, son école et son temps: Souvenirs par E.J. Delécluze.* Paris: Didier, 1855.

d'Espouy, Hector. *Fragments d'architecture.* Paris, 1905.

Durand, Jean Nicolas Louis. *Recueil et parallèle des édifices en tout genre, anciens et modernes, remarquables par leur beauté, par leur grandeur ou par leur singularité et dessinés sur une même échelle.* Paris: Author, [1799]–1801.

Fontaine, Pierre. *Mia Vita. Mémoires privés de Pierre François Léonard Fontaine (1762–1853). Architecte des princes à l'âge des révolutions.* Paris: Editions des Cendres, forthcoming March 2017; copy of the original manuscript preserved by Mme Marine Blatin.

Fontaine, Pierre François Léonard. *Journal (1799–1853)*, ed. Marguerite David-Roy. 2 vols. Paris: Ecole nationale supérieure des beaux-arts / Institut français d'architecture / Société de l'histoire de l'art français, 1987.

Fréart de Chambray, Roland. *Parallèle de l'architecture antique avec la moderne.* Paris: Edme Martin, 1650.

Garnier, Charles. *Le Nouvel opéra de Paris.* Paris: Librairie générale de l'architecture et des travaux publics Ducher, 1878–81.

Genlis, Félicité de. *Mémoires inédits sur le dix-huitième siècle et la Révolution française, depuis 1756 jusqu'à nos jours.* Paris: Ladvocat, 1825.

Grandjean de Montigny, Augustin, and Auguste Famin. *Architecture toscane.* Paris: Authors, 1806–15.

Hassenfratz, Jean Henri. *Traité de l'art du charpentier.* Paris: Firmin Didot, 1804.

Hittorff, Jacques Ignace. *Architecture antique de la Sicile.* Paris, 1827.

Hope, Thomas. *Household Furniture and Interior Decoration executed by Thomas Hope.* London: Longman, Hurst, Rees, and Orme, 1807.

Instructions to the art jury of 30 pluviôse an VII (January 28, 1799).

Isabelle, Charles Edouard. *Les Edifices circulaires et les dômes, classés par ordre chronologique et considérés sous le rapport de leur disposition, de leur construction et de leur décoration.* Paris: Firmin Didot, 1835.

Isabelle, Charles Edouard. *Parallèle des salles rondes de l'Italie.* Paris: Firmin Didot, 1831.

J.-B. *Arcades de la rue de Rivoli, à MM. les membres de la commission municipale de Paris.* Paris: Garnier, 1852.

La Mésangère, Pierre. *Collection de meubles et objets de goût*, 8 vols. Paris: Author, 1802–15.

Lafond, Paul. *Une famille d'ébénistes français. Les Jacob. Le mobilier de Louis XV à Louis-Philippe.* Paris, 1894.

Lance, Adolphe. *Notice sur la vie et les travaux de M. Achille Leclère, architecte, membre de l'Institut.* Paris, 1854.

Landon, Charles. *Annales du musée et de l'école moderne des beaux-arts*, vol. 1. Paris: C. P. Landon, 1800.

Landon, Charles. *Nouvelles des arts, peinture, sculpture, architecture et gravure.* Paris: Author, 1801.

Leclère, Achille. *Recueil d'architecture, lithographié en l'année 1826 par… élèves de Monsieur Achille Leclère.* Paris: Author, 1826.

Le Corbusier. *Vers une architecture.* Paris: Crès, 1923.

Legrand, Jacques Guillaume. "Les palais réunis des Thuileries et du Louvre." In Charles Paul Landon, *Description de Paris et de ses édifices*, part 2. Paris, 1806–9.

Lenormant, Amélie. *Souvenirs et correspondances tirés des papiers de Madame Récamier.* Vol. 1. Paris, 1859.

Letarouilly, Paul. *Édifices de Rome moderne.* Paris: Bance, 1840–57.

Manesson-Mallet, Alain. *La Géométrie pratique divisée en quatre livres: le premier enseigne les éléments de la géométrie pratique… le second explique la trigonométrie… le troisième montre la planimétrie,… le quatrième regarde la stéréométrie.* Vol. 3. Paris: Anisson, 1702.

Michelet, Jules. *Le Peuple.* Paris: Comptoir des imprimeurs réunis, Hachette, Paulin, 1846.

Moreau, Charles. *Fragmens et ornemens d'architecture dessinés à Rome, d'après l'antique.* Paris: Vilquin, 1800.

Nietzsche, Friedrich. *The Will to Power*, ed. Walter Kaufmann. New York: Vintage Books, 1968.

Nietzsche, Friedrich. *Nietzsche: Writings from the Late Notebooks*, trans. Kate Sturge, ed. Rüdiger Bittner. Cambridge: Cambridge University Press, 2003.

Palladio, Andrea. *Traicté des cinq ordres d'architecture dont se sont servi les Anciens.* Paris: Langlois, 1645.

Panseron, Pierre. *Éléments d'architecture dédiés à Monsieur de Sartine.* 3 vols. Paris: Author and Desnos, 1772–76.

Peyre, Antoine François. "Mémoire sur l'achèvement du Louvre, sur l'agrandissement du Muséum national de peinture et de sculpture, et sur la nécessité de former promptement une école spéciale des arts, lu le 23 Messidor an 4…." In *Mémoires de l'Institut national des sciences et des arts, pour l'an IV de la République. Littérature et beaux-arts*, vol. 1, 667–74. Paris: Institut national, 1798.

Quatremère de Quincy, Antoine Chrysostôme. *Encyclopédie méthodique. Architecture.* Paris: Panckoucke, 1789–1825.

Quatremère de Quincy, Antoine Chrysostôme. *Essai sur la nature, le but et les moyens de l'imitation dans les beaux-arts.* Paris: Treutel and Würtz, 1823.

Raoul-Rochette, Desiré. "Percier, Sa vie et ses ouvrages." In *Revue des deux mondes* 4, no. 24 (October 15, 1840): 246–68.

Reichardt, Johann Friedrich. *Un hiver à Paris sous le Consulat (1802–1803).* Paris: Tallandier, 2003.

Selvatico, Pietro. *Sull'architettura e sulla scultura in Venezia. Dal Medio Evo sino ai giorni nostri*, Venice: Paolo Ripamondi Carpano, 1847.

Séroux d'Agincourt, Jean Baptiste Louis Georges. *Histoire de l'Art par les Monumens, depuis sa décadence au IVe siècle jusqu'à son renouvellement au XVIe.* 6 vols. Paris: Treutel and Würtz, 1823.

Séroux d'Agincourt, Jean Baptiste Louis Georges. *Storia dell'arte dimostrata coi monumenti dalla sua decadenza nel IV secolo fino al suo risorgimento nel XVI*, vol. 2. Prato: Fratelli Giachetti, 1826.

Stewart, Courier W. *Diary of an Excursion to France in the Months August and September 1814.* Edinburgh: Peter Hill, Manners and Miller, 1814.

Toussaint, Claude Jacques. *Traité de géométrie et d'architecture. Partie Théorique.* Paris: Author, 1812.

Vauchelet, Théophile. "Memoires de Théophile Vauchelet (1802–1873)," manuscript.

Viollet-le-Duc, Eugène. *Dictionnaire raisonné de l'architecture française du XIe au XVIe siècle.* Paris: Bance, Morel, 1854–68.

Viollet-le-Duc, Eugène. *Lettres d'Italie 1836–37.* Paris: Léonce Laget, 1971.

BOOKS AND OTHER SECONDARY SOURCES

Agosti, Giovanni, and Vincenzo Farinella. "Il fregio della Colonna Traina e i Francesi." In *La Colonna Traiana e gli artisti francesi da Luigi XIV a Napoleone I*, ed. Giovanni Agosti, Vincenzo Farinella, and Giorgio Simoncini, 21–40. Rome: Carta Segrete, 1988.

Arizzoli-Clémentel, Pierre. "The Percier and Biennais Album in the Musée des Arts décoratifs, Paris." *Burlington Magazine* (March 1998): 195–201.

Arrizoli-Clémentel, Pierre, Philippe Bordes, and Régis Michel, eds. *Aux armes et aux arts ! Les arts de la Révolution française.* Paris: Éditions Adam Biro, 1988.

Arizzoli-Clémentel, Pierre, and Jean-Pierre Samoyault. *Le Mobilier de Versailles. Chefs-d'œuvre du XIXe siècle.* Dijon: Faton, 2009.

Arts Council of Great Britain. *The Age of Neoclassicism.* Exh. cat. London: Victoria & Albert Museum, 1972.

Austin-Montenay, Florence. *Saint-Cloud, une vie de château.* Geneva: Vogèle Editions, 2005.

Barbanera, Marcello, ed. *Relitti riletti. Metamorfosi delle rovine e identità culturale.* Turin: Bollati Boringhieri, 2009.

Bassi, Elena. "L'architetto Francesco Lazzari." *Rivista di Venezia* 13 (1934): 239–50.

Bédard, Jean-François. "Political Renewal and Architectural Revival during the French Regency: Oppenord's Palais-Royal." *Journal of the Society of Architectural Historians* 68, no. 1 (March 2009): 30–51.

Bellenger, Sylvain, ed. *Girodet 1767–1824*. Paris: Gallimard–Musée du Louvre Editions, 2005.

Bergeron, Louis. *Banquiers, négociants et manufacturiers parisiens du Directoire à l'Empire*. Paris: Editions de l'Ecole des Hautes Etudes en Sciences Sociales, 1978.

Bételu, Claire. "*Réunion d'artistes dans l'atelier d'Isabey*: processus créatifs de Louis-Léopold Boilly." PhD diss. Université Paris 1 – Panthéon-Sorbonne, 2015.

Beyer, Andreas. "Karl Friedrich Schinkel in Paris." In *Interferenzen/Interférences. Deutschland Frankreich Architektur 1800–2000*, ed. Jean-Louis Cohen and Harmut Frank, 104–11. Exh. cat. Tübingen: Deutsches Architektur Museum Frankfurt am Main, 2013.

Bonnet, Jean-Claude, ed. *L'Empire des muses: Napoléon, les arts et les lettres*. Paris: Belin, 2004.

Bouilhet, Henri. *L'orfèvrerie française aux XVIIIe et XIXe siècles*. Paris: Laurens, 1908–12.

Boyer, Ferdinand. "L'installation du premier Consul aux Tuileries et la disgrâce de l'architecte Lecomte (1800–1801)." *Bulletin de la Société de l'Histoire de l'art* (1941–44): 142–84.

Branda, Pierre. *Napoléon et ses hommes: la Maison de l'Empereur 1804–1815*. Paris: Fayard, 2011.

Bresc-Bautier, Geneviève, and Béatrice de Chancel-Bardelot, eds. *Un musée révolutionnaire. Le musée des Monuments français d'Alexandre Lenoir*. Paris: Hazan, 2016.

Brunet, Marcelle. "Eine Dokumentation zu einer Uhr aus Sèvres-Biskuitporzellan nach dem Entwurf von Charles Percier." *Weltkunst* 3 (1979): 162–64.

Caracciolo, Maria-Teresa. "Juliette Récamier et Charles Percier: nouveaux dessins pour l'hôtel de la rue du Mont-Blanc." *Les Cahiers d'histoire de l'art*, no. 12 (2014): 61–70.

Carbonnières, Philippe de. "Les arts florissants." In *La Révolution française: une histoire toujours vivante*, ed. Michel Biard, 377–90. Paris: Tallandier, 2010.

Carlier, Yves. *La galerie de meubles du château de Fontainebleau*. Paris: Somogy, 2009.

Caude, Elisabeth, and Christophe Pincemaille, eds. Exh. cat. *Joséphine et Napoléon: L'hôtel de la rue des Victoires*. Paris: Réunion des musées nationaux, 2013.

Caulaincourt, Armand Louis Augustin de. *Souvenirs du duc de Vicence. Mémoires sur Napoléon et l'Empire*. Series collected and published by Charlotte de Sor. Paris: Barra, 1841.

Château de Fontainebleau. *Enfance impériale. Le roi de Rome, fils de Napoléon*. Exh. cat. Dijon: Editions Faton, 2011.

Château de Fontainebleau. *Pie VII face à Napoléon: La tiare dans les serres de l'Aigle*. Exh. cat. Paris: Réunion des musées nationaux, 2015.

Chevallier, Bernard. *Les Sèvres de Fontainebleau, Porcelaines, terres vernissées, émaux, vitraux (pièces entrées de 1804 à 1904)*. Paris: Réunion des musées nationaux, 1996.

Chevallier, Bernard. *Musée national des châteaux de Malmaison et Bois-préau*. Paris: Réunion des musées nationaux, 2006.

Cochet, Vincent. "Le salon jaune de Joséphine. La sauvegarde d'un décor déraciné." *Revue du Louvre et des musées de France*, no. 5 (2014): 66–77.

Cochet, Vincent. "Les petits appartements de l'empereur et de l'impératrice." In *Fontainebleau: "La vraie demeure des rois*,*"* 268–345. Paris: Swan, 2015.

Cochet, Vincent, and Sylvain Levaissière. *Boilly, 1761–1845. Un grand peintre français de la Révolution à la Restauration*. Lille: Musée des Beaux-Arts, 1988.

Compiègne. *Napoléon Ier ou la légende des arts*. Paris: Réunion des musées nationaux, 2015.

Courajod, Louis. *Alexandre Lenoir, son journal et le Musée des monuments français*. Paris: Honoré Champion, 1878–87.

Crosnier-Leconte, Marie-Laure. *Dictionnaire des élèves architectes de l'Ecole des Beaux-Arts (1800–1968)*; http://agorha.inha.fr/inhaprod/servlet/LoginServlet.

Crosnier-Leconte, Marie-Laure. "Dessins d'école, bibliothèques d'ateliers: une affaire de copies." In *Bibliothèques d'atelier. Édition et enseignement de l'architecture, Paris 1785–1871*, ed. Jean-Philippe Garric. Paris: Institut national d'histoire de l'art, April 2011; http://inha.revues.org/3187.

D'Amia, Giovanna. "Memoria e rappresentazione della storia nel Museo dei Monumenti Francesi di Alexandre Lenoir." In *Memoria, identità, luogo. Il progetto della memoria*, ed. Davide Borsa, 523–48. Milan: Maggs, 2012.

Daufresne, Jean-Claude. *Louvre & Tuileries, architectures de papier*. Paris: Mardaga, 1987.

De Feo, Renato. "Renato De Feo, Une commande de Dominique-Vivant Denon à Giuseppe Borsato: les fêtes vénitiennes pour Napoléon I." *Revue du Louvre* 3 (2002): 66–75.

Dell'Orefici, Anna. "Ernesto Lefebvre." In *Dizionario Biografico degli Italiani*, vol. 64. Rome: Treccani, 2005.

Desti, Marc. "La bibliothèque de Napoléon Ier au palais de Compiègne." *Revue du Louvre et des Musées de France*, no. 5 (2012): 74–77.

Dion-Tenenbaum, Anne. *L'orfèvre de Napoléon, Martin-Guillaume Biennais*. Exh. cat. Paris: Réunion des musées nationaux, 2003.

Dion-Tenenbaum, Anne. "Published Sources of Ornaments." In Odile Nouvel, *Symbols of Power: Napoleon and the Art of the Empire Style 1800–1815*, 62–69. New York: Harry N. Abrams, for the American Federation of the Arts and Musée des Arts décoratifs, 2007.

Dion-Tenenbaum, Anne. "Le mobilier Récamier." In Stéphane Paccoud and Léna Widerkher, *Juliette Récamier: muse et mécène*. Paris: Hazan, 2009.

Droguet, Vincent. "Rosso Fiorentino à Fontainebleau. 'Personne n'a eu plus de génie et plus de feu que lui.'" In *Le Roi et l'Artiste. François Ier et Rosso Fiorentino*, 90–97. Exh. cat. Paris: Réunion des musées nationaux-Grand Palais, 2013.

Dumonthier, Ernest. *Recueil de dessins de tapis et de tapisseries d'ameublement du mobilier de la Couronne*. Paris: Massin, [1900].

Dumonthier, Ernest. *Etoffes d'ameublement de l'époque napoléonienne*. Paris: Ch. Massin, 1909.

Dumonthier, Ernest. *Les bronzes du Mobilier national. Bronzes d'éclairage et de chauffage*. Paris: Ch. Massin, [1911].

Duportal, Jeanne. "Charles Percier 1764–1838." In *Charles Percier. Reproduction de dessins conservés à la Bibliothèque de l'Institut*. Paris: Maurice Rousseau, 1931.

Duportal, Jeanne. *Inventaire des manuscrits [conservés à la bibliothèque de l'Institut] 1 à 3800. Complément. Dessins et estampes*. Paris: Bibliothèque de l'Institut, 1939.

Dupuy, Marie. *Dominique-Vivant Denon l'œil de Napoléon*. Exh. cat. Paris: Réunion des musées nationaux, 1999.

Dupuy-Baylet, Marie-France. *Pendules du Mobilier national 1800–1870*. Paris: Éditions Faton, 2006.

Duvette, Charlotte. "La rue de Rivoli et le secteur des Tuileries: projets, percements et constructions, depuis la Révolution française à la fin du Premier Empire." MA thesis, Université Paris I Panthéon-Sorbonne, 2014.

Epron, Jean-Pierre. *Comprendre l'éclectisme*. Paris: Norma, 1997.

Etlin, Richard. *The Architecture of Death: The Transformation of the Cemetery in Eighteenth-Century Paris*. Cambridge, MA: MIT Press, 1984.

Foray-Carlier, Anne. *Le mobilier du Musée Carnavalet*. Paris: Editions Faton, 2000.

Foucaud, Edouard. *Les artisans illustres*. Paris: Béthune et Plon, 1841.

Fouché, Maurice. *Percier et Fontaine*. Paris: Laurens, 1904.

Frommel, Sabine, Jean-Philippe Garric, and Elisabeth Kieven, eds. *Charles Percier e Pierre Fontaine, dal soggiorno romano alla trasformazione di Parigi*. Rome: Silvana editoriale / Bibliotheca Hertziana, 2014.

Fuhring, Peter. *Juste-Aurèle Meissonnier: un génie du rococo 1695–1750*. 2 vols. Turin: Umberto Allemandi & C., 1999.

Garric, Jean-Philippe. *Recueils d'Italie. Les modèles italiens dans les livres d'architecture français*. Liège: Mardaga, 2004.

Garric, Jean-Philippe. "L'Académie royale d'architecture aux origines de l'art de la composition (1779–1799)." in *L'atelier et l'amphithéâtre: les écoles de l'architecture, entre théorie et pratique*, ed. Guy Lambert and Estelle Thibault, 23–50. Wavre: Mardaga, 2011.

Garric, Jean-Philippe. *Percier et Fontaine, les architectes de Napoléon*. Paris: Belin, 2012.

Garric, Jean-Philippe. "L'architecture Beaux-Arts. Objet d'expositions." In *Les Cahiers du Musée national d'art moderne* 129 (Autumn 2014): 38–49.

Garric, Jean-Philippe. "Le *Recueil de décorations* de Charles Percier et Pierre Fontaine." In *Ornements XVᵉ–XIXᵉ siècles. Chefs-d'œuvre de la bibliothèque de l'INHA*, ed. Lucie Fréjou and Michaël Decrossas, 302–11. Paris: Institut national d'histoire de l'art / Mare et Martin, 2014.

Garric, Jean-Philippe. "Des frontispices aux 'éléments analytiques,' les compositions graphiques d'architecture à l'Ecole des beaux-arts." In *Livraisons d'histoire de l'architecture*, no. 30 (second semester 2015): 59–68.

Garric, Jean-Philippe. "Alexandre Lenoir et Charles Percier, un compagnonnage oublié." In *Un musée révolutionnaire. Le musée des Monuments français d'Alexandre Lenoir*, ed. Geneviève Bresc and Béatrice de Chancel Bardelot, 241–50. Paris: Hazan, 2016.

Garric, Jean-Philippe. "Le monument à La Pérouse: documenter la démarche d'Henri Labrouste." In *Le dessin d'architecture dans tous ses états II. Le dessin d'architecture, document ou monument ?*, ed. Claude Mignot, 97–106. Paris: Salon du dessin, 2016.

Gastinel-Coural, Chantal. "Le cabinet de platine de la Casa del Labrador à Aranjuez. Documents inédits." *Bulletin de la société de l'histoire de l'art français* (1994): 181–205.

Gastinel-Coural, Chantal. *La manufacture des Gobelins au XIXᵉ siècle, tapisseries, cartons, maquettes*. Paris: Mobilier national, 1996.

Gastinel-Coural, Chantal. "Tapis à histoires. Des Savonneries qui n'en sont pas. Quelques identifications de tapis impériaux et royaux." *Bulletin de la Société de l'Histoire de l'Art français*, 2006 (2007): 261–313.

Georgel, Chantal, ed. *La jeunesse des musées: les musées de France au XIXᵉ siècle*. Exh. cat. Paris: Réunion des musées nationaux, 1994.

Giedion, Sigfried. *Mechanization Takes Command*. New York: Oxford University Press, 1948.

Granger, Catherine. *L'Empereur et les Arts: la liste civile de Napoléon III*. Paris: École nationale des chartes, 2005.

Guillaume, J., ed. *Procès-verbaux du Comité d'instruction publique de la convention nationale*, vol. 5. Paris: Imprimerie nationale, 1904.

Hautecœur, Louis. *Histoire de l'Architecture classique en France*. Vol. 5: *Révolution et Empire, 1792–1815*. Paris: Picard, 1953.

Hautecœur, Louis. *Histoire de l'Architecture classique en France*. Vol. 6: *La Restauration et le gouvernement de juillet*. Paris: Picard, 1955.

Heim, Jean-François, Claude Béraud, and Philippe Heim. *Les salons de peinture de la Révolution française 1789-1799*. Paris: C.A.C. sarl Edition, 1989.

Heng, Michèle. "Un fonds inédit d'œuvres, archives et collections provenant de l'architecte Pierre-François-Léonard Fontaine (1762–1853)." *Bulletin de la société de l'histoire de l'art français* (2011): 63–94.

Herbet, Félix. "Fontainebleau révolutionnaire. Liste des personnes mises en arrestation au ci-devant château (1793–1794)." *Annales de la Société historique et archéologique du Gâtinais* 25 (1907): 1–47.

Huard, Georges. "Percier et l'abbaye de Saint-Denis." *Les Monuments Historiques de la France* (1936): 5:134–44; 6: 173–82.

Husserl, Edmund. *L'origine de la géométrie*. Paris: Presses universitaires de France, 1962.

Jacques, Annie. "I viaggi in Italia di Debret et Lebas (1804–1811)." In *Grand Tour: viaggi narrati e dipinti*, ed. Cesare De Seta, 60–73. Naples: Electa, 2001.

Jacques, Annie, and Jean-Pierre Mouilleseaux. *Les architectes de la Liberté*. Paris: Gallimard, Collection découvertes, 1988.

James, André. *Les Didot: Trois siècles de typographie et de bibliophilie 1698–1998*. Paris: Agence culturelle de Paris, 1998.

Jardin, André, and André-Jean Tudesq. *La France des notables. Nouvelle histoire de la France contemporaine*, vols. 6 and 7. Paris: Seuil, 1973.

Jordan, Marc-Henri. "L'étude de l'ornement et l'art du décor." In *Le cabinet de Pierre-Adrien Pâris, architecte, dessinateur des Menus-Plaisirs*, 40–57. Besançon: Musée des Beaux-Arts et d'Archéologie de Besançon, 2008.

Jordán de Urríes y de la Colina, Javier. "Les décors d'Aranjuez: Les *Saisons* du cabinet de platine de la Real Casa del Labrador à Aranjuez." In Bellenger, ed., *Girodet*, 261–65.

Jordán de Urríes y de la Colina, Javier. *La Real Casa del Labrador de Aranjuez*. Madrid: Patrimonio Nacional, 2009.

Jordán de Urríes y de la Colina, Javier, and José Luis Sancho. "Sitel, Percier y el Gabinete de Platino." *Reales Sitios* 50, no. 195 (2013): 28–49.

Jordán de Urríes y de la Colina, Javier, and José Luis Sancho. "El cabinete de platino de la Real Casa del Labrador en Aranjuez." In *Charles Percier e Pierre Fontaine*, eds. Frommel, Garric, and Kieven, 133–43. Milan: Silvana Editoriale, 2014.

Kleinert, Annemarie. *Le "Journal des Dames et des Modes" ou la conquête de l'Europe féminine (1797–1839)*. Stuttgart: Jan Thorbecke, 2001.

Lafont, Anne. "A la recherche d'une iconographie Incroyable et Merveilleuse: les panneaux décoratifs sous le Directoire." *Annales historiques de la Révolution française* 2 (2005): 5.

La Gorce, Jérôme de. "Quand les Menus Plaisirs et les Bâtiments du roi s'associent pour servir la monarchie." In *Les Menus Plaisirs du roi (XVIIᵉ–XVIIIᵉ siècles)*, ed. Pierre Jugie and Jérôme de La Gorce, 101–15. Paris: Presses de l'Université Paris–Sorbonne, 2013.

La Gorce, Jérôme de, and Pierre Jugie. *Dans l'atelier des Menus Plaisirs du roi: spectacles, fêtes et cérémonies aux XVIIᵉ et XVIIIᵉ siècle*. Versailles: Éditions Artlys, 2010.

Laveissière, Sylvain, ed. *Napoléon et le Louvre*. Paris: Fayard / Musée du Louvre, 2004.

Lazaj, Jehanne, ed. *Le bivouac de Napoléon, luxe et ingéniosité en campagne*. Milan: Silvana Editoriale, 2014.

Leben, Ulrich. *Object Design in the Age of Enlightenment: The History of the Royal Free Drawing School in Paris*. Los Angeles: J. Paul Getty Museum, 2004.

Ledoux-Lebard, Guy. "Un Apogée du style consulaire. La décoration et l'ameublement de l'hôtel de Madame Récamier." *L'Estampille l'objet d'art* 278 (March 1994): 64–89.

Ledoux-Lebard, René, and Guy and Christian Ledoux-Lebard. "La décoration et l'ameublement du grand cabinet de Napoléon Ier aux Tuileries." *Bulletin de la Société de l'histoire de l'art français* (1941–44): 185–258.

Lefuel, Hector. *Georges Jacob. Ebéniste du XVIIIᵉ siècle*. Paris: Morancé, 1923.

Lefuel, Hector. *François-Honoré-Georges Jacob-Desmalter, ébéniste de Napoléon 1ᵉʳ et de Louis XVIII*. Paris: Morancé, 1925.

Lelièvre, Pierre. *Vivant Denon, homme des Lumières, ministre des arts de Napoléon*. Paris: Picard, 1993.

Lemoine, Thierry, ed. *Au temps des merveilleuses: la société parisienne sous le Directoire et le Consulat*. Exh. cat. Paris: Paris Musées, 2005.

Loyer, François. *Histoire de l'architecture française de la Révolution à nos jours*. Paris: Mengès-éditions du Patrimoine, 1999.

Lucan, Jacques. *Composition, non-composition. Architecture et théories, XIXᵉ–XXᵉ siècles*. Lausanne: Presses polytechniques universitaires romandes, 2009.

Mairie du Vᵉ arrondissement. *Les Tuileries au XVIIIᵉ siècle*. Paris: Délégation à l'action artistique de la Ville de Paris, 1990.

Mantz, Paul. "Recherches sur l'histoire de l'orfèvrerie française. IV La Révolution et l'Empire." *Gazette des Beaux-Arts* 14 (1863): 238–54.

Marmottan, Paul. "Percier à son collègue Pâris 1804." *Bulletin de la société de l'histoire de l'art français* (1922): 329.

Michel, Régis, and Marie-Catherine Sahut. *David, l'art et le politique*. Paris: Gallimard, "Découvertes" collection, 1988.

Montaiglon, Anatole de. "Artistes français en 1800." *Nouvelles archives de l'Art français*. Vol. 1. Paris, 1872.

Montclos, Jean-Marie Pérouse de. "Les Prix de Rome." *Concours de l'Académie royale d'architecture au XVIIIᵉ siècle*. Paris: Berger-Levrault / École nationale supérieure des Beaux-Arts, 1984.

Montclos, Jean-Marie Pérouse de. *Etienne-Louis Boullée (1728–1799)*. Paris: Flammarion, 1994.

Moon, Iris. "Ornament after the Orders: Percier, Fontaine and the Rise of the Architectural Interior in Post-Revolutionary France." PhD diss., Massachusetts Institute of Technology, 2013.

Morel, Philippe, ed. *La Colonna Traiana e gli artisti francesi da Luigi XIV a Napoleone I*. Rome: Carte Segrete, 1988.

Morel d'Arleux, M.-L. "Les voyages en Italie de Fontaine, Percier et Bernier, d'après leurs carnets de notes." *Bulletin de la Société de l'histoire de l'art français* 1 (1934): 88–103.

Moulier, Igor. "Le ministère de l'Intérieur sous le Consulat et l'Empire (1799–1814). Gouverner la France après le 18 brumaire." PhD diss., Université de Lille III, 2004.

Musée des Arts décoratifs. *Chefs-d'œuvre des grands ébénistes 1790–1850, de G. Jacob à Giroux.* Exh. cat. Paris: Musée des Arts décoratifs, 1951.

Musée du Louvre. *D'après l'antique.* Exh. cat. Paris: Réunion des musées nationaux, 2000.

Musée du Luxembourg. *Joséphine.* Exh. cat. Paris: Réunion des musées nationaux, 2014.

Musée municipal de Saint-Cloud. *Napoléon Bonaparte à Saint-Cloud.* Exh. cat. Saint-Cloud: Association des amis de Saint-Cloud, 1999.

Musée national du château de Malmaison. *Soies tissées, soies brodées chez l'impératrice Joséphine.* Exh. cat. Paris: Réunion des musées nationaux, 2002.

Musée national des châteaux de Malmaison et Bois-Préau. *Jean-Baptiste Isabey (1767–1855), portraitiste de l'Europe.* Exh. cat. Paris: Réunion des musées nationaux, 2005.

Musée national des châteaux de Malmaison et Bois-Préau. *Joséphine, la passion des fleurs et des oiseaux.* Exh. cat. Paris: Artlys, 2014.

Naffah-Bayle, Christiane, and Jehanne Lazaj, eds. *L'esprit et la main.* Paris: Gourcuff-Gradenigo, 2015.

Nègre, Valérie. "Les commencements de l'art industriel. Conception et usages des ornements d'architecture moulés au début de la période contemporaine." In *Le néoclassicisme dans les colonies européennes,* ed. Thierry Nicolas Tchakaloff, 212–33. Saint-Denis de la Réunion: Musée des arts décoratifs de l'Océan indien, 2013.

Niclausse, Juliette. *Thomire fondeur-ciseleur (1751–1843). Thomire, sa vie son œuvre.* Paris: Gründ, 1947.

Nouvel-Kammerer, Odile, ed. *L'aigle et le papillon. Symboles des pouvoirs sous Napoléon.* Exh. cat. Paris: Musée des Arts décoratifs, 2008.

Nouvel-Kammerer, Odile. "La place du *Receuil de décorations intérieures* de Percier Fontaine dans la question de l'ornement." In *Ornament between art and design. Interpretations, paths and mutations in the nineteenth century,* ed. A. Valera Braga, 32–43. Basel: Schwabe, 2013

Nouvel-Kammerer, Odile. "Le vase étrusque à rouleaux représentant 'l'entrée dans Paris des principaux monuments qui composent le musée Napoléon.'" In *Les vases de Sèvres XVIIIe–XXIe siècles. Éloge de la virtuosité,* ed. Antoinette Faÿ-Hallé, 128–39. Dijon: Éditions Faton, 2014.

O'Brien, David. *Antoine-Jean Gros: Peintre de Napoléon.* Paris: Éditions Gallimard, 2006.

Olson, Roberta J. M. "A Selection of European Paintings and Objects." *The Magazine Antiques,* no. 167 (January 2005): 182–87.

Olson, Roberta J. M., and Margaret K. Hofer. *Seat of Empire.* New York: New-York Historical Society, 2002.

Ottomeyer, Hans. *Das frühe Oeuvre Charles Percier (1782–1800). Zu den Anfängen des Historismus in Frankreich.* Munich: Ludwig-Maximilens-Universität, 1981.

Ottomeyer, Hans. "Napoléon Bonaparte erste Möbel." *Kunst und Antiquitäten* (1990): 1–2.

Ottomeyer, Hans, and Peter Pröschel. *Vergoldete Bronzen die Bronzearbeiten des Spätbarock und Klassizismus.* Munich: Klinkhardt & Bermann, 1986–87.

Palais des Beaux-Arts, Lille. *Boilly (1761–1845).* Exh. cat. Paris: Nicolas Chaudun, 2011.

Pavanello, Giuseppe, ed. *La pittura nel Veneto: l'Ottocento.* Milan: Electa, 2003.

Pinon, Pierre. "Les Vaudoyer et les Lebas, dynasties d'architectes." In *Entre le théâtre et l'histoire: la famille Halévy, 1760–1960,* ed. Henri Loyrette, 88–97. Exh. cat. Paris: Réunion des musées nationaux, 1996.

Pinon, Pierre. "Rome antique et moderne vue par Pierre Adrien Pâris." In *Charles Percier e Pierre Fontaine dal soggiorno romano alla trasformazione di Parigi,* ed. Sabine Frommel, Jean-Philippe Garric, and Elisabeth Kieven, 25–39. Milan: Silvana Editoriale, 2014.

Pomarède, Vincent, et al., eds. *Ingres (1780–1867).* Paris: Gallimard–Musée du Louvre Éditions, 2006.

Poulot, Dominique. *Musée, nation, patrimoine, 1789–1815.* Paris: Gallimard, 1997.

Préaud, Tamara, ed. *The Sèvres Porcelain Manufactory: Alexandre Brongniart and the Triumph of Art and Industry, 1800–1847.* Exh. cat. New York: Bard Graduate Center, 1997–98.

Pressouyre, S. "Les fontes de Primatice à Fontainebleau." *Bulletin monumental* 127, no. 3 (1969): 223–39.

René, Guy, and Christian Ledoux-Lebard. "La décoration et l'ameublement du grand cabinet de Napoléon Ier aux Tuileries." *Bulletin de la Société de l'histoire de l'art français* (1941–44): 185–258.

Riemann-Reyher, Marie Ursula. Catalogue entries 27–32 in Michael Snodin (dir.), *Karl Friedrich Schinkel. A universal man,* ed. Michael Snodin, 107–11. London: Yale University Press, 1991.

Robinet, Jacques. *L'art et le goût sous la Restauration.* Paris: Payot, 1927.

Romanelli, Giandomenico. *Venezia Ottocento. L'architettura, l'urbanistica.* Venice: Officina Edizioni, 1988.

Roussel, Jules. *Monographie du palais de Fontainebleau. Décorations intérieures et extérieures.* 8 vols. Paris: Guérinet, [1904].

Rykwert, Joseph. *The First Moderns: The Architects of the Eighteenth Century.* Cambridge, MA: MIT Press, 1980.

Saint-Paul, Evelyne. "Dons des dessins de Charles Percier par ses élèves." In *Charles Percier e Pierre Fontaine,* eds., Frommel, Garric, and Kieven, 159–65.

Samoyault, Jean-Pierre. "Les séjours de Napoléon et de la cour impériale de 1803 à 1810." *Souvenir napoléonien* (September 1974): 9–13.

Samoyault, Jean-Pierre. "Furniture and objects designed by Percier for the Palace of Saint-Cloud." *Burlington Magazine* 868 (July 1975): 457–65.

Samoyault, Jean-Pierre. "Chefs-d'œuvre en tôle vernie de l'époque consulaire et impériale (1801–1806)." *Revue du Louvre et des musées de France,* nos. 5–6 (1977): 322–34.

Samoyault, Jean-Pierre, "L'Ameublement des salles du Trône dans les palais impériaux sous Napoléon 1er." *Bulletin de la Société de l'histoire de l'art français* (1985): 185–206.

Samoyault, Jean-Pierre. *Fontainebleau, musée national du château. Catalogue des collections de mobilier. Pendules et bronzes d'ameublement entrés sous le Premier Empire.* Paris: Réunion des Musées Nationaux, 1989.

Samoyault, Jean-Pierre. *Guide du musée national du château de Fontainebleau.* Paris: Réunion des Musées Nationaux, 1991.

Samoyault, Jean-Pierre. *Le Mobilier du général Moreau, un ameublement à la mode en 1802,* Paris, Réunion des Musées Nationaux, 1992.

Samoyault, Jean-Pierre. "L'Appartement de la générale Bonaparte, puis de l'impératrice Joséphine aux Tuileries (1800–1807)." *Bulletin de la Société de l'Histoire de l'art français* (2000): 215–44.

Samoyault, Jean-Pierre. "L'appartement de Bonaparte aux Tuileries." *Revue du souvenir napoléonien* 449, (November 2003): 7–21.

Samoyault, Jean-Pierre. *Fontainebleau, musée national du château. Catalogue des collections de mobilier. Meubles entrés sous le Premier Empire.* Paris: Réunion des musées nationaux, 2004.

Samoyault, Jean-Pierre. "The Jacob-Lignereux alliance (14 March 1798)." *Furniture History* 43 (2007): 21–28.

Samoyault, Jean-Pierre. "Sur quelques dessins d'art décoratifs provenant de l'architecte Pierre-François-Léonard Fontaine." *Bulletin de la société de l'histoire de l'art français* (2009): 234–55.

Samoyault, Jean-Pierre. *Mobilier français Consulat et Empire.* Paris: Gourcuff-Gradenigo, 2009.

Samoyault, Jean-Pierre, and Pierre Arizzoli-Clémentel. *Le mobilier de Versailles. Chefs d'œuvre du XIXe siècle.* Paris: Faton, 2009.

Samoyault, Jean-Pierre, and Colombe Samoyault-Verlet. eds. *Un ameublement à la mode en 1802: le mobilier du général Moreau.* Paris: Réunion des musées nationaux, 1992.

Sarmant, Thierry. *Le Cabinet des médailles de la Bibliothèque nationale de 1661 à 1848.* Paris: École nationale des chartes, 1994.

Sarmant, Thierry, et al., eds. *Napoléon et Paris: rêves d'une capitale.* Paris: Paris Musées, 2015.

Savage, Nicolas, British Architectural Library, and Royal Institute of British Architects et al. *Early Printed Books: 1478–1840: Catalogue of the British Architectural Library Early Imprints Collection.* London; New Jersey: Bowker-Saur, 1994–2003.

Savorra, Massimiliano. "Francesco Lazzari." In *Dizionario Biografico degli Italiani,* vol. 64. Rome: Treccani, 2005.

Schmidberger, Ekkerhardt and Thomas Richter. *Schatzkunst 800 zu 1800: Kunsthandwerk und Plastik der staatlichen Museen Kassel im hessischen Landesmuseum Kassel.* Exh. cat. Kassel: Éditions Minerva, 2001.

Schnapper, Antoine. *David témoin de son temps.* Fribourg: Office du Livre, 1980.

Sérullaz, Arlette, and Antoine Schnapper. *Jacques-Louis David 1748–1825.* Paris: Réunion des musées nationaux, 1989.

Szambien, Werner. *Les projets de l'an II, concours d'architecture de la période révolutionnaire.* Paris: École nationale supérieure des beaux-arts, 1986.

Szambien, Werner. *De la rue des Colonnes à la rue de Rivoli.* Exh. cat. Paris: Délégation à l'Action Artistique de la Ville de Paris, 1992.

Tentori, Paolo. "Antonelli Giuseppe." In *Dizionario Biografico degli Italiani.* Vol. 3. Rome: Treccani, 1961.

Toews, John E. "Building Historical and Cultural Identities in a Modernist Frame: Karl Friedrich Schinkel's Bauakademie in Context." In *Enlightenment, Passion, Modernity: Historical Essays in European Thought and Culture*, ed. Mark Micale, Robert L. Dietle, and Peter Gay, 167–206. Stanford, CA: Stanford University Press, 2000.

Trombetta, Vincenzo. *L'editoria a Napoli nel decennio francese.* Milan: Franco Angeli, 2011.

Uginet, François-Charles. *Roma Antiqua. Envoi des architectes français (1788–1924) Forum, Colisée, Palatin.* Rome and Paris: École française de Rome, Académie de France à Rome, École nationale supérieure des beaux-arts, 1985.

Van de Sandt, Udolfo. "Le Salon." In *L'Empire des muses*, ed. Jean-Claude Bonnet, 59–78. Paris: Bélin, 2004.

Van Zanten, David. "Architectural composition at the École des Beaux-Arts, from Charles Percier to Charles Garnier." In *The Architecture of the École des Beaux-Arts*, ed. Arthur Drexler, 111–324. New York: Museum of Modern Art, 1977.

Van Zanten, David. "Fontaine in the Burnham Library." *Art Institute of Chicago Museum Studies* 13, no. 2 (1988): 132–45.

Varese, Ranieri. "Giuseppe Borsato Accademico: l'orazione funebre per Antonio Canova." *Arte Documento*, no. 25 (2009): 213–19.

Vincent, Arthur. *Guide illustré dans les petits appartements de Napoléon Ier et de la famille impériale au palais de Fontainebleau.* Versailles: A. Bourdier, [1912].

Warnke, Martin. *The Court Artist: On the Ancestry of the Modern Artist.* Cambridge: Cambridge University Press, 1993.

Zucconi, Guido. *L'invenzione del passato. Camillo Boito e l'architettura neomedievale.* Venice: Marsilio, 1997.

ABOUT THE AUTHORS

Jean-François Bédard is Associate Professor and Chair of the Graduate Programs at Syracuse University's School of Architecture. His research focuses on the architecture and visual culture of court society in early modern France, which he explored in his first book, *Decorative Games: Ornament, Rhetoric, and Noble Culture in the Work of Gilles-Marie Oppenord* (2011). He previously held the position of Assistant Curator, Department of Prints and Drawings, Canadian Centre for Architecture, Montreal.

Jean-François Belhoste has been Director of Studies at the École Pratique des Hautes Études, Paris, since 2004. His teaching and research focuses on the history of industry and technique in Paris, and more specifically in recent years on the decorative arts: costume, jewelry, furniture, and metalwork. He also teaches at the École du Louvre, the Université Paris 1 Panthéon-Sorbonne, the École nationale d'Architecture de Normandie, and the École de Chaillot.

Christophe Beyeler is Chief Curator of Patrimony at the château de Fontainebleau, where he is in charge of the musée Napoléon Ier. He has organized numerous exhibitions including, *Le Pape et l'Empereur. La réception de Pie VII par Napoléon à Fontainebleau* (2004); *Noces impériales. Le mariage de Napoléon et Marie-Louise dessiné par Baltard* (2010); *Enfance impériale. Le Roi de Rome, fils de Napoléon* (2011); and *Pie VII face à Napoléon. La tiare dans les serres de l'aigle. Rome, Paris, Fontainebleau, 1796–1814* (2015).

Vincent Cochet is Chief Curator of Patrimony at the château de Fontainebleau, where he is in charge of the textile collections and other decorative arts. He has helped organize exhibitions on eighteenth- and nineteenth-century French decorative arts, including *Louis XV à Fontainebleau* (2016), and he oversaw the restoration and reopening of several important interiors at Fontainebleau: Napoleon III's study, the Lacquer Salon of Empress Eugénie, and Josephine's Turkish boudoir. He was formerly a curator of historic monuments under France's Ministry of Culture.

Anne Dion-Tenenbaum is Chief Curator of the Department of Decorative Arts at the Musée du Louvre. She has authored numerous catalogues, including *L'orfèvrerie française du XIXe siècle, la collection du musée du Louvre* (2011), and organized several exhibitions on French decorative arts, such as *L'orfèvre de Napoléon: Martin-Guillaume Biennais* (2003), and *Napoléon ou la légende des arts, 1800–1815* (2015), among many others.

Vincent Droguet is Director of Patrimony and Collections at the château de Fontainebleau, where he has served as a curator since 1995. He specializes in French Renaissance painting and decoration and organized the exhibitions, *Le roi et l'artiste. François Ier et Rosso Fiorentino* (2012) and *Henri IV à Fontainebleau. Un temps de splendeur* (2011). He also teaches at the École du Louvre.

Charlotte Duvette is a doctoral candidate at the Université Paris 1 Panthéon-Sorbonne. She was associate curator of the exhibition *Napoléon et Paris. Rêves d'une capitale* at the Musée Carnavalet in Paris in 2015, and co-edited its catalogue. Her research focuses on the history of urbanism and private architecture in Paris during the end of the eighteenth and beginning of the nineteenth century. Her PhD dissertation is entitled "The transformations of Paris from the Revolution to the Restoration, studied through private architecture (1789–1830)."

Jean-Philippe Garric is an architect and a historian; he is Professor of History of Architecture at the Université Paris 1 Panthéon-Sorbonne. He has been a Fellow at the French Academy in Rome and Deputy Director of Research at the Institut national d'histoire de l'art in Paris. Professor Garric has published numerous books, articles, and essays on Charles Percier over the past ten years in both French and Italian, including *Percier et Fontaine, les architectes de Napoléon* (Paris: Belin, 2012). He is currently publishing a critical edition of Pierre Fontaine's memoir, *Mia Vita*, to be released in March 2017.

Iris Moon is Visiting Assistant Professor in the School of Architecture at Pratt Institute. She specializes in eighteenth- and nineteenth-century French art, architecture, and the decorative arts. She earned her PhD from Massachusetts Institute of Technology and has held fellowships at the Metropolitan Museum of Art, the Clark Art Institute, and the Getty Research Institute. Her first book, *Percier, Fontaine, and the Politics of the Empire Style, 1785–1815*, explores the architectural and decorative work of Napoleon's official architects in the cultural context of post-Revolutionary France.

Thierry Sarmant is Deputy Director of the Musée Carnavalet and head of archives at the Service historique de la Défense, Ministry of Defense. He was the lead curator of the exhibition *Napoléon et Paris. Rêves d'une capitale* (Musée Carnavalet, 2015). He received his doctorate from the Université Paris 1 Panthéon-Sorbonne, and his research focuses on the political history of France and the state.

Letizia Tedeschi is Director of the Archivio del Moderno, an archive and research institute of the Accademia di Architettura, Università della Svizzera Italiana, Mendrisio. In partnership with the Centre Ledoux, Université Paris 1 Panthéon-Sorbonne, she has managed a research project on Italian and French architectural culture in the Napoleonic period. She published with Daniel Rabreau the volume *L'architecture et l'Empire entre France et Italie* (2012).

Saskia Wallig is a doctoral candidate at the Université Paris 1 Panthéon-Sorbonne. She was a curatorial assistant at the Academie d'Architecture in 2015. She studies the architect Antoine Laurent Thomas Vaudoyer, and her research more broadly examines the formation of the architect-artist in late eighteenth- and early nineteenth-century France.

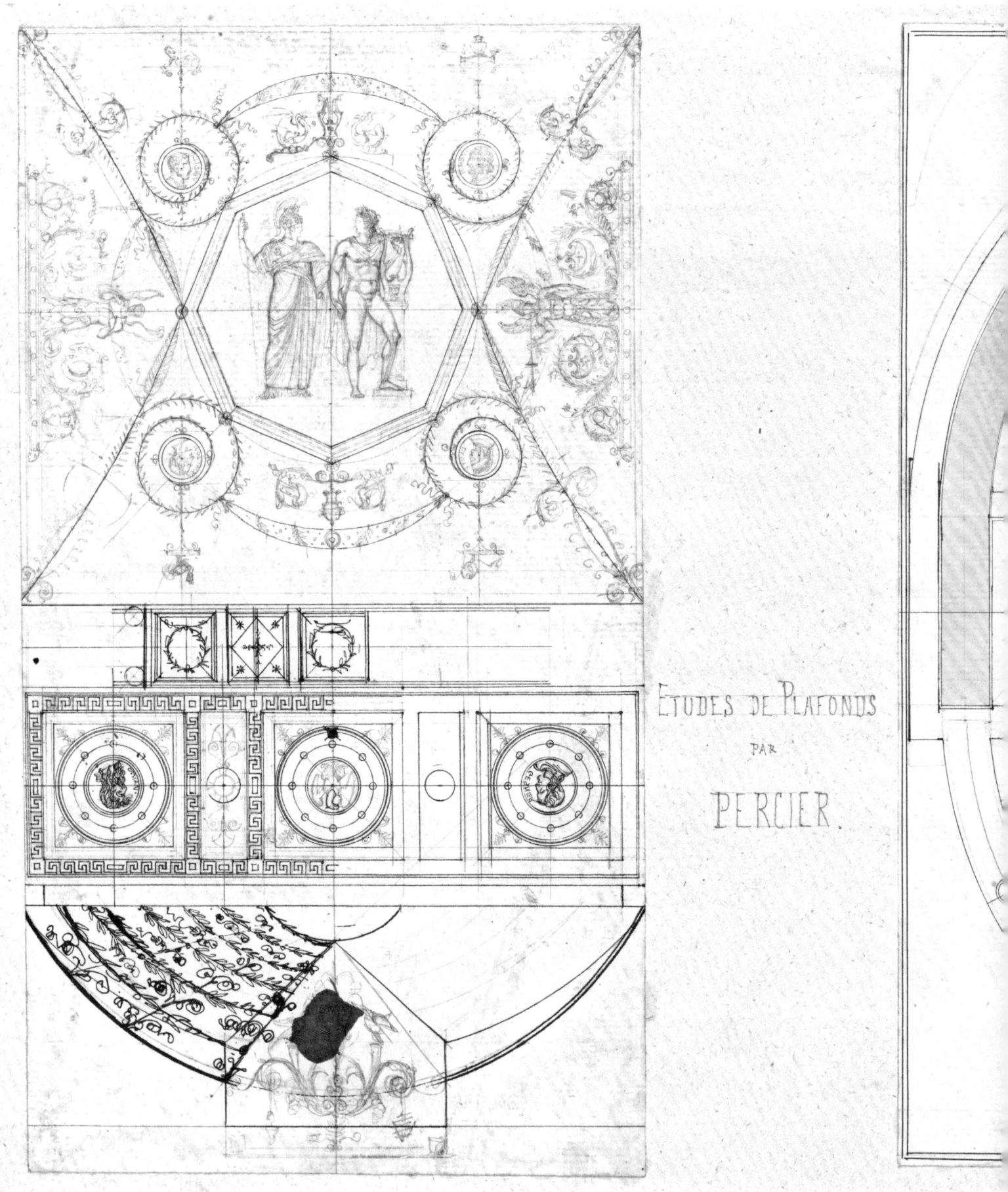

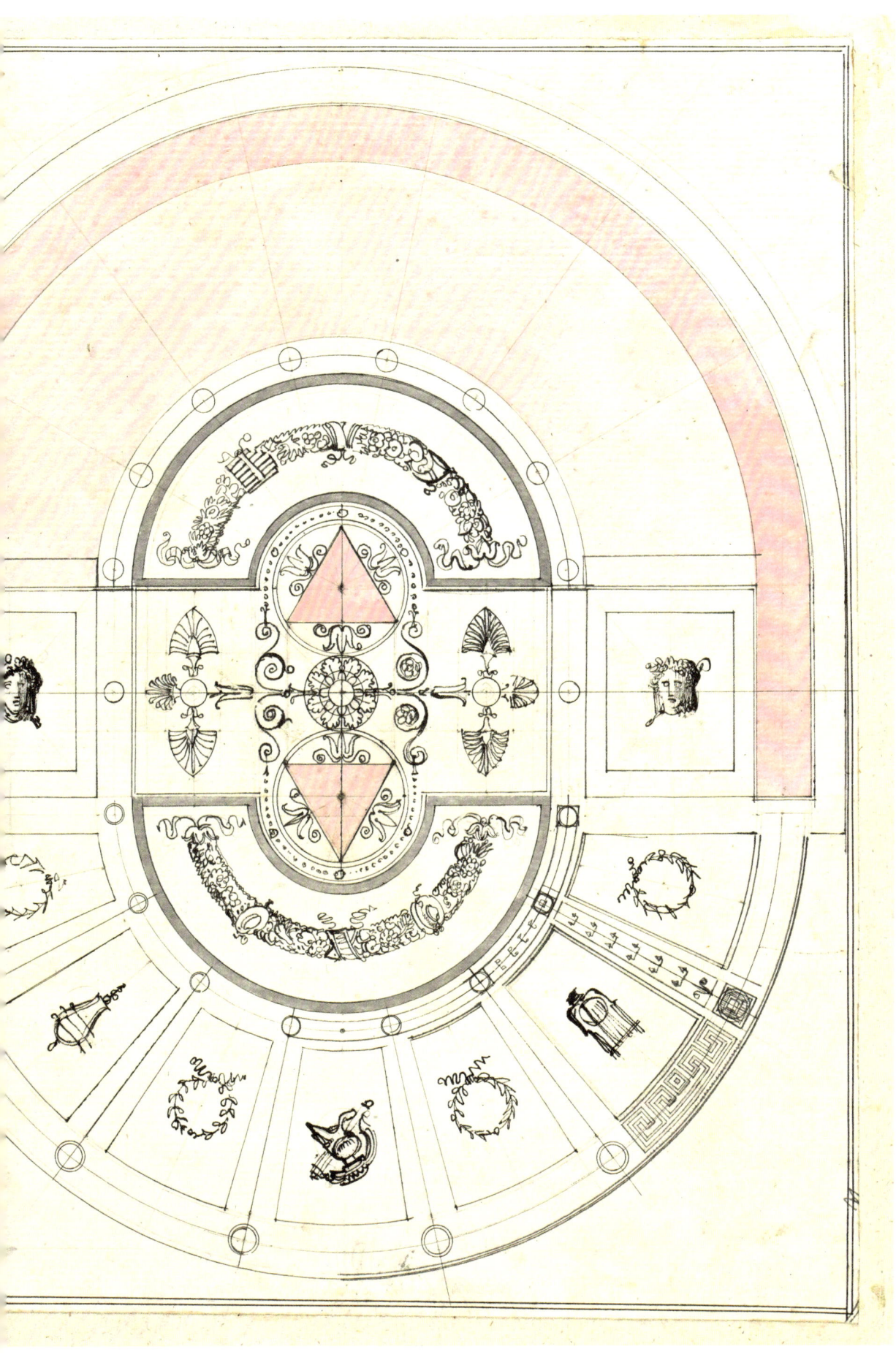

INDEX

Italic page numbers indicate illustrations.

Abbey of Saint-Denis, 99–102, *100–102*, 265
Académie des beaux-arts, 25
Académie royale d'architecture, 48, 50, 63, 83
Accademia delle Belle Arti, Venice, 139n4, 139n6
Accademia di San Luca, 71
Alexander I (czar), 198, 224
Alexander Column, 59
Amsterdam Academy of Fine Arts, 58
antique revival style, 279, 284
Antonelli, Giuseppe, 136, 137, 139n12
Appiani, Andrea (1754–1817): *Portrait of Josephine de Beauharnais*, 268, *269*
Aranjuez. See Casa Real del Labrador.
arc de Triomphe, 26, 30
arc du Carrousel, 11, 14, 18, 26, 30, 52, 132, *186*, 187, 187n11, 192, 224, 225, 239, 240, 242, 265, 282
architectural designs and drawings, 82–106, 206–58; decorative arts and, 206–12; *Edifice to House the Academies*, *55*, 268; *Italian villa at the seaside*, *272*; king of Rome palace, *254*, *256*, 283; Mme Lignereux's country house at Bougival, *157*; *Menagerie Set within the Park of a Royal Château*, *54*, 268; Monceau parc, 283; *Monument to the Defenders of the Homeland*, *252*; Musée du Louvre, *235*, *236*, 239, 242, *247*; Palazzo Te in Mantua, *39*; Reims Cathedral, 285; Roman palace courtyard, *60*; rue de Rivoli, *238*; Saint-Cloud château, 228–32, *229–31*; Salle des Cariatides, musée du Louvre, *242*; Simonetti Staircase Seen from the Gallery of the Candelabra, *72*; Sistine Chapel, *57*, 57; Terneuzen bay, emperor's house overlooking, *258–59*, 283; Trajan's Column, 54, 56, 73, *73–74*, 267; Tuileries, *235*, 240, 281, 283; unbuilt, 249–60, 282–85. *See also Palais, maisons et autres édifices modernes dessinés à Rome; specific buildings.*
Arch of Septimius Severus, Rome, 240

Arnault, Antoine Vincent (1766–1834): *Lucrèce*, 156
Augustin, Jean-Baptiste Jacques, 67
Austerlitz Column, 26, 30

Bachasson, Camille, comte de Montalivet (1801–1880), 34n7
Ballu, Hortense (1815–1896), 156
Ballu, Théodore (1817–1885), 156
Baltard, Louis Pierre (1764–1846), 48, 51–52, 53, 62n3, 97, 269, 284; *Allegorical composition for the marriage of Napoleon and Marie-Louise of Austria*, 269; *Paris et ses monumens, mesurés, dessinés et gravés par Baltard*, 84–85, 97n5
Barbier-Neuville, John Pierre (1754–1822), 34n5
Bard, Jean Auguste: *Inauguration of the Galerie des Batailles, Versailles*, *33*
Barraband, Jacques (1767/8–1809), 171
Barras, Paul (1755–1829), 163, 166
Bâtiments du Roi, 208
Beauharnais, Eugène de, 139n6
Beauharnais, Josephine de (1763–1814), 268, 269. *See also* Bonaparte, Josephine.
Bédard, Jean-François, 38, 44, 206
Bélanger, François Joseph (1744–1818), 224; designs for linking the Louvre and Tuileries, 239
Belhoste, Jean-François, 42, 154, 228
Benneman, Guillaume, 182
Béranger, Charles Antoine, 139n2, 139n3
Bernier, Claude Louis (1755–1830), 45, 52, 57–58, 61, 111, 175n9; tomb of, 18, 46, 47
Bernini, Gian Lorenzo: designs for linking the Louvre and Tuileries, 239
Berthault, Louis Martin (1770–1823), 166, 168, 216, 280
Betou, Alexandre (1607–1693), 92
Beudot, Auguste (1763–1832), 52
Beunat manufactory, 59
Beuth, Peter: *Vorbilder für Fabrikanten und Handwerker*, 123
Beyeler, Christophe, 40, 140
Bibliothèque Sainte-Geneviève, 253
Bidauld, Jean Joseph Xavier (1758–1846), 67, 127, 160, 208

Bielinski, Franciszek, 209
Biennais, Martin Guillaume (1764–1843), 196, 197, 198, 201–3, 275, 279, 280; professional card of, 202, *202*
Biet, Joseph Étienne: *Souvenirs du musée des monuments français*, 104
Blacas, comte de (1771–1839), 34n7
Blanchon, Gilles Barthélémy (1772–1847), 195
Blavette, Victor (1859–1933), 64 –65; *Composition of antique fragments after the Temple of Hercules in Cori*, 117
Blondel, Jacques François (1705–1774), 118
Blondel, Merry Joseph: *Portrait of Louis Hippolyte Lebas, Architect*, 270
Blot, Maurice, 67
Boilly, Julien Léopold (1796–1874), 268; *Charles Percier and Pierre Fontaine*, 37, *38*
Boilly, Louis Léopold (1761–1845), 66–70, 130, 268, 269, 270; *Gathering of Artists in the Atelier of Jean-Baptiste Isabey*, 66–70, *67*, 130, 268, 269; *Jean-Baptiste Isabey and Nicolas Antoine Taunay* (study), 68; *Minerva (Study after a Sculpture)*, 130, 273; *Portrait of Antoine François Peyre*, 53; *Triple Portrait of Percier, Fontaine, and Claude Louis Bernier*, 270
Boiret, Yves (b. 1926), 65
Boizot, Louis Simon, 285
Bonaparte, Caroline, 232
Bonaparte, Jérôme, 59
Bonaparte, Josephine: bedroom interior decoration, 40, 42, 273; commode from bedroom of, 180–81, *181*, 279; Fontainebleau *petits appartements*, 172, 223, *223*, 232, 279, 284–85; furniture designs for, 160, 162, 166, 171; Malmaison renovation and, 17, 123; Percier's commissions from, 213–26; *Portrait of Josephine de Beauharnais* (Appiani), 268, *269*; Saint-Cloud *petits appartements*, 172, 182, 215; tureen designs for, 201. *See also specific residences.*
Bonaparte, Lucien, 159

Bonaparte, Napoleon (1769–1821): Appiani portrait of, 268; coronation of, 69, 283; David and, 29; Denon and, 30; *The Emperor in Grand Ceremonial Dress* (Percier and Isabey), *143*, 145; *Livre du Sacre* and, 140–50; Malmaison and, 17; marriage to Marie-Louise, 269, 283; *Napoleon Distributing the Cross of the Legion of Honor to Artists During His Visit to the Salon on October 22, 1808* (Gros), 30; *Napoleon I on His Imperial Throne* (Ingres), 30, 32; on Paris, 26; Percier's commissions from, 125, 213–26; regime changes and, 11; rue de Rivoli and, 245–47; Terneuzen bay house for, 258–59, 283; Tuileries and, 239–44, 279. *See also specific residences.*
Bonaparte, Pauline, 221
Bonnard, Charles (1765–1818), 20, 271; *Choix des plus célèbres maisons de plaisance de Rome et de ses environs*, 271
Bonneuil, Laure de, 268
Borghese, Camillo, 204
Borsato, Giuseppe (1779–1849), 133, 136, 139n6; *Charles Percier and Pierre Fontaine, Raccolta di decorazione interne che comprende quanto si riferisce all'addobabamento*, 133
Bouchet, Jules Frédéric, 127, *127*, 134n25
Boulard, Benoît François, 279
Boulard, Michel Jacques (1761–1825), 284–85
Boullée, Étienne Louis (1728–1799), 47, 54, 74, 162, 268; design for a museum, elevation, *55*, 264, 268
Bourbon Palais, 32
Bourgeois, Charles Guillaume Alexandre, 66
Brès, Jean Pierre: *Souvenirs du musée des monuments français*, 104
Brongniart, Alexandre (1770–1847), 189–92
Brongniart, Alexandre Théodore (1739–1813), 22, 25, 189
Brosse, Salomon de (1571–1626), 32
Brusa, Eugenio, 203
Bruyère, Louis (1758–1831), 27

Canova, Antonio, 71
Caprarola, Palazzo Farnese, 95
Carlos IV, 170, 179n77, 207, 216
Casa Real del Labrador, Aranjuez: Platinum Room, 38, 52, 160, 170, 171, 207–10, 208, 210, 216, 273, 278; second floor plan, 207, 207
Casino of Pius IV, Vatican, 95
Castellan, Antoine Laurent (1772–1838): *Fontainebleau: Études pittoresques et historiques sur ce château*, 98n14
Catel, Charles Simon: *Sémiramis*, 251, 251
Caude, Elisabeth, 279
Caulaincourt, Armand, 245
Cayla, Madame du, 30
Cellerier, Jacques, 283
Chaillot Hill, 224, 255, 256, 256
Chalgrin, Jean François (1739–1811), 25
Chambray, Roland Fréard de (1606–1676), 118
Chaptal, Jean Antoine (1756–1832), 27, 100, 104
Charles X, 30, 31, 34n7, 132
Chartres, Louis Philippe d'Orléans, duc de (1747–1793), 206
Chatillon, André Marie (1782–1859), 185, 266
Chatillon, Pauline, 46
Chaudet, Antoine Denis (1763–1810), 67, 272, 273
Chaussée d'Antin, 162, 228
Chauvelin, François Bernard, 166, 178n60, 215
Chenard, Simon, 67
Chenu, Pierre: Cabinet of Count Bielinski, 208, 209
Choix des plus célèbres maisons de plaisance de Rome et de ses environs (Percier, Fontaine, and Bonnard), 112, 123, 127, 271
Civeton, Christophe, 242
Civic Buildings Council, 25
Clarac, Charles Othon Frédéric Jean-Baptiste de, 233, 242; *Musée de sculpture antique et moderne*, 235, 242
Claret de Fleurieu, Charles Pierre (1738–1810), 34n7
Cochet, Vincent, 66, 213
Codman, Ogden: sleigh bed for Harold Brown, 133
Colbert, Jean-Baptiste, 29
Column of Trajan. *See* Trajan's Column.
Committee of Public Instruction, 28
Committee of Public Safety, 28
Compiègne, château de, 183, 280
Conservatoire des arts et métiers, 26, 106
Constant-Dufeux, Simon Claude (1801–1870), 51, 60; annex of École gratuite de dessin, 51, 51
Corbet, Charles Louis, 66
Corvisart, Jean Nicolas, 279
Costaz, Baron Louis (1767–1842), 34n6
Coupin, Pierre Alexandre, 163
Crépin-Leblond, Thierry, 98n9
Cuccioni, Tommaso, 269

Dagobert I, 99, 101–102
d'Amia, Giovanna, 103
Dantan, Antoine Laurent (called Dantan L'aîne): *Portrait of François Honoré George Desmalter*, 155
Daru, Pierre (1767–1829), 34n7, 194
Daumier, Honoré (1808–1879), 32
Davent, Léon, 98n19
David, Jacques Louis (1748–1825), 17, 28–29, 45, 59, 69, 156, 189, 215, 254, 283; *The Love of Paris and Helen*, 189, 189; *Self-Portrait*, 26; *The Tennis Court Oath, 20 June 1789* (sketch for), 28, 28
Debret, François (1777–1850), 60, 125, 194, 265
decorative arts: architecture and, 206–12; bedroom of Madame Récamier, 166; designs for manufactories, 188–204; furniture design, 17, 154–87. *See also* furniture design; industrial arts.
de Gaulle, Charles, 279
Delacroix, Eugène (1798–1863): *Liberty Leading the People*, 32
Delafontaine, Pierre Maximilien (1774–1860), 189, 191
Delespine, Pierre Jules (1726–1825), 53
dell'Abate, Niccolo, 92
Demarne, Jean Louis, 66
Denon, Dominique Vivant (1747–1825), 29, 30, 280
Desaix, General, 30
Descartes, René, 138
Description des cérémonies et des fêtes (Percier and Fontaine), 140, 216, 254, 272
Desmaisons, Louis Saint-Ange (1780–1831), 61; View of a Courtyard after Percier and Fontaine, 60, 61
d'Espouy, Hector: *Fragments d'architecture antique*, 117
Diderot, Denis: *Encyclopédie*, 73
Didot l'aîné, Pierre, 40, 47–48, 111, 113, 117, 124, 135
Dion-Tenenbaum, Anne, 42, 188, 201
Direction générale des bâtiments du Roi, 25–26
Domard, Joseph François (1792–1858), 270; medal dedicated to Percier's memory, 267, 270
Dommey, Étienne Théodore (1801–1872), 106
d'Orsay, Palais, 26

Doudeauville, duc de (1765–1841), 34n7
Droguet, Vincent, 82
Drolling, Martin, 66
Drouais, Jean Germain (1763–1788), 48, 57, 264, 271; *Rome from the Tiber River near the Cloaca Maxima*, 271; Sistine Chapel, 57
Duban, Félix (1798–1870), 60
Dubois, Ambroise (1542/43–1614/15), 87, 94
Duc, Joseph Louis (1802–1879), 106
Ducros, Abraham Louis Rodolphe (1748–1810): *The Colosseum, Rome*, 271
Dufour, Alexandre (1760–1835), 86
Duparc, Marie Alexandre (1760?–1829?), 272
Duplessis-Bertaux, Jean, 66, 215
Duportal, Jeanne, 46, 48n2, 103, 116
Dupuis, Sophie, 45
Durand, Jean Nicolas Louis (1760–1834), 27, 138, 265; *Précis des leçons d'architecture*, 246
Duval, Amaury (known as Charles Alexandre Amaury Pineux; 1760–1838), 34n5, 85, 97n5
Duvette, Charlotte, 245
Duvivier, Nicolas Cyprien, 192, 194, 196

École de médicine, 51
École des beaux-arts, 26, 43–44, 48, 50, 60, 63, 64, 117, 129, 156, 243, 256, 260, 264, 266, 270
École gratuite de dessin, 17, 18, 44, 47, 50–51, 51, 52, 53, 60, 111, 121, 125, 264, 266–267
Écouen, château d', 87, 98n9, 99, 116, 117
Elisca ou l'amour maternel (opera), set design, 248, 250, 283
Elysée Palace, 232
Elysian Gardens of Petits-Augustins, 100, 103
Emmanuel, Charles Victoire, General Leclerc (1772–1802), 221
Empire style, 11, 15, 38, 103, 122, 132, 154, 262

Famin, Auguste (1776–1859), 59, 60, 270; *Architecture toscane*, 58
Feuchère, Lucien François, 182
Fiorentino, Rosso (1495–1540), 15, 89
Flaxman, John (1755–1826), 44, 76, 118, 121n3, 269; *Diligamus Alterutrum*, 269, 269
Florence, Palazzo Vecchio, 92, 93
Folie Baujon, 160
Fontaine, Pierre François Léonard (1762–1853): biography, 17; Bonaparte and, 216, 223; caricature of, 37; *Mia Vita*, 39, 42, 45, 134n14, 162; Percier's affiliation with, 11, 14, 36, 37, 38–43, 283; tomb of, 18, 46, 47. *See also Choix des plus célèbres maisons de plaisance de Rome et de ses environs; Recueil de décorations intérieures*; for joint works with Percier, see Percier and Fontaine (joint works).
Fontainebleau, château de, 15, 34n7, 82–98, 223, 284–85; Ballroom, 82, 84, 89, 90, 92, 92, 93, 94; Belle Cheminée Wing, 87, 87; benches, 89; fireplace wall, figures, 93; Fountain Courtyard, 87, 87; furniture design, 182, 183; Gallery of Diana, 61, 82, 89, 94, 94, 96, 285; Gallery of Francis I, 83, 89, 89, 94, 97n8; Grotte des Pins, 82–83; Horseshoe Staircase, 83; Josephine's *petits appartements*, 172, 223, 223, 232, 279, 284–85; mantelpiece design, 192; mural ornamentation and vaults, 89; Oval Courtyard, 82, 83, 97n8; Porte Dorée, 82, 83, 84, 86, 89, 90, 91; Royal Apartments wing, 83, 89; Saint-Saturnin's Chapel, 87, 89; Salle des Fêtes, 61; wood paneling, 89; Yellow Salon, 284–85
Fontana, Prospero (1512–1597), 270, 271
Fourcroy, Antoine (1755–1809), 34n5
Francis I, 83, 85, 86, 89, 204
Frederick William IV, 127
French Academy in Rome, 50, 54, 56, 72, 85, 207
Froidevaux, Yves Marie (1907–1983), 65
furniture design, 154–87; bookcase with a malachite tabletop, 224; chairs, 172–73, 173, 229–31, 231, 277–79, 278; commodes, 180–83, 279; Jacob-Desmalter collaboration with Percier, 154–79; Marshall's table, 191–192, 191; Moreau's townhouse, 173, 274–76, 275; National Convention, 14, 17, 156; Madame Récamier's bed, 168, 172; scrapbook from Percier's workshop, 184–86, 184–87, 231, 273; tea service for the first consul, 196, 197. *See also Recueil de décorations intérieures*.

Gabriel, Ange Jacques (1698–1782), 245
Gaillon, château de, 87, 105–106
Garneray, Auguste Simon (1785–1824), 145, 146–47, 152n16; *Costume of a Grand Officer of the Crown*, 143, 145; *The Empress in Lesser Ceremonial Dress*, 145, 145; *Livre du sacre de S.M. l'empereur Napoléon dans l'Eglise métropolitaine de Paris le XI Frimaire an XIII* (with Isabey et al.),

140–52, 141–44, 147–50, 272; *The Pope*, 145, 147, *148*
Garnier, Charles (1825–1898), 44, 60, 267
Garric, Jean-Philippe, 11–13, 16, 36, 50, 63, 75, 85, 103, 108, 118, 184, 233, 249, 262
Gastinel-Coural, Chantal, 38, 195
Gaudin, Benoît, 162–164, 166, 170, 215
Gaudin, Martin Michel Charles, 162
Gauffier, Louis (1762–1801), 46
Gautier-Dagoty, Jean-Baptiste: *Demolition of Les Feuillants Convent*, *238*
Genlis, Madame de, 226n3
Genoa, palazzi of Strada Nuova, 243
Georget, Jean, 190
Gérard, François (1770–1837), 30, 48, 57, 66, 213, 264; *Flora Caressed by Zephyr*, *164*; Voltaire, *La Henriade* frontispiece (with Percier), *40*, 40, 272
Giedion, Sigfried, 42–43
Ginain, Léon (1825–1898), 63, 64, 65
Ginguené, Pierre Louis (1748–1816), 34n5
Girard, Jean Alexis, 190
Girard, Louise (active 1824–50): *The Architects Achille Leclère and Jean Louis Provost*, *270*
Girodet de Roussy-Trioson, Anne Louis (1767–1824), 52, 66, 127, 160, 208; *Danaë Looking at Herself in a Mirror Held by Cupid*, *162*, 163, *164*, 166
Gisors, Guy de (1762–1835), 214
Gobelins manufactory, 12, 26, 42, 195, 216, 222
Godefroy, Adrien Pierre François (1777–1865), 272
Gonzaga, Federico I, 96
Gothic style, 33, 43, 77, 78, 105, 137, 139n4
Gotthold, Benjamin, comte de Schlick: *Council Room at Malmaison*, *219*; *Library at Malmaison*, *221*
Goujon, Jean, 234, 239, 242
government and the arts, 24–34
Grande Salle, Hôtel de Ville, 92, *93*
Grandjean de Montigny, Augustin (1776–1850), 58, 59, 60, 264, 270; *Architecture Toscane, ou Palais, maisons et autres édifices de la Toscane*, *58*, 270
graphic art and design, 108–52; for *Fables* (La Fontaine), 114, *115*, 118, 251, 263, 271; festival float or barge, 270, *271*; for *First Book of Epistles in Quintus Horatius Flaccus* (Horace), 111, 114, 114–15, 118, 271; *Interior of a Roman Palace*, *271*; for *Livre du Sacre* (with Isabey and Garneray), 147; *Second Book of Epistles in Quintus Horatius Flaccus* (Horace), 114, *115*, 118; *Various Modern and Antique Fragments from Different Cities in Italy and France Drawn from Nature*, 109, 271; for Voltaire, *La Henriade* frontispiece, *40*, 40, 272; for *Voyage pittoresque et historique de l'Espagne* (Laborde), 52, *52*, 118. See also specific books.

Grégoire, Abbé (1750–1831), 29
Grétry, André, 250, 283
Grille, Toussaint (1766–1850), 34n5
Gros, Jean Antoine (1771–1835): *Napoleon Distributing the Cross of the Legion of Honor to Artists During His Visit to the Salon on October 22, 1808*, *30*
Guillaume, Eugène: *Bust of Louis Pierre Baltard*, *269*
Guillon-Lethière, Guillaume (1760–1832), 52, 66

Halls of the Crusades, 33
Hamelin, Madame, 268
Hassenfratz, Jean Henri: *Housing Structures from the Tonga Islands, Lapland, Tierra del Fuego, New Caledonia, and Tibet*, *250*, 250
Haudebourt, Louis Pierre (1788–1849), 58
Hautecoeur, Louis, 39, 43
Hebert, Jean-François, 12, 15
Heim, François Joseph: *Charles X Distributing Prizes after the Salon of 1824 in the Louvre*, *30*
Helman, Isidore Stanislas: *View of the Hall of the National Convention at the Tuileries during the assassination of Deputy Jean-Bertrand Féraud*, *215*
Henri IV, 33, 272
Hindermeyer, Xavier, 170, 208
Hittorff, Jakob Ignaz (1792–1867), 32, 58, 265
Hobsbawm, Eric, 11
Hoffman, François Benoît, 66
Hoffstadt, Friedrich, 137, 139n4
Hope, Thomas, 22, 113
Horace: *First Book of Epistles in Quintus Horatius Flaccus*, 108, 111, 113, 114, 114–15, 118, 190, 271; *Second Book of Epistles in Quintus Horatius Flaccus*, 114, *115*, 118, 271
Hôtel de Ville, Paris, 92, *93*
Hôtel Récamier, 168, *168*, 173
Huard, Georges, 99, 103
Humboldt, Alexander von, 127
Hurtault, Maximilien Joseph (1765–1824), 98n9

Imperial Palace of Bordeaux, 279
industrial arts, 122, 132, 188–204; Londonderry vase, 190, *190*, 281; tureen designs, 201–4, *201–4*, 280, *281*
Ingres, Jean Auguste-Dominique (1780–1867), 30, 64, 270; *The Architects Achille Leclère and Jean-Louis Provost*, 64; *Napoleon I on His Imperial Throne*, 30, *32*; *Vœu de Louis XIII*, 30
Institut de France, 36, 39, 46, 47, 51, 56, 57, 63, 64, 76, 82, 247n8, 264
interior decoration: atelier of Isabey, 21, 66–70, *67–70*, 120, 130, 160, 215, 231, 268, 274, 285; bedroom of Josephine Bonaparte, 40, 273; bedroom of Madame Gaudin, 163, *165*; bedroom of Madame M., 273, 274–275; bedroom of Madame Récamier, 166, 168, *168*, 274; boudoir for château de Saint-Cloud, 186, 228–32, *229–31*; candelabra, 199, 285; carpet for the music room, château de Saint-Cloud, 195, *195*; clock designs, 189, 191, *191*, 196, *196*, 280; commodes, 180–83, 279; dining room of Madame Récamier, 168, *168*; medal cabinet, 199, 280; *petits appartements* of Josephine at Fontainebleau, 172, 223, *223*, 232, 279, 284–85; salon and smoking room of Madame Récamier, *168*; washstands, 280. See also decorative arts; furniture design.
Isabelle, Charles Édouard (1800–1880), 64; *Imaginary Composition of Circular Buildings in a Landscape*, *65*
Isabey, Jean-Baptiste (1767–1855): atelier of, 66–70, *67–70*, 120, 130, 160, 215, 231; *Chief Herald of Arms* (with Percier), 150, *151*; *Costume of a Grand Officer of the Crown* (with Garneray), *143*, 145; *The Distribution of the Eagle Standards on the Champ de Mars*, 253; *The Emperor in Grand Ceremonial Dress* (with Percier), *143*, 145; *The Empress in Lesser Ceremonial Dress* (with Garneray), 145, *145*; *The Grand Staircase of the Musée Napoléon*, *242*; *Livre du sacre de S.M. l'empereur Napoléon dans l'Eglise métropolitaine de Paris le XI Frimaire an XIII* (with Percier et al.), 140–52, *141–44*, *147–50*, 272; Napoleon presenting newborn king of Rome (watercolor), 285; *The Pope* (with Percier and Garneray), 147, *148*; portrait of, 68; *President of the Canton* (with Percier), 150, *151*
Italy: Arch of Septimius Severus, 240, 282; Italian villa at the seaside, 272, 273; Palazzo Ducale, 92, *93*; Palazzo Mancini, 72; Percier's travels to, 17, 56–57, 71–75; Vicenza, basilica in, 40; Villa Albani, 113; Villa Borghese, 113; Villa Madama, 95. See also *Palais, maisons et autres édifices modernes dessinés à Rome*; specific cities and monuments.

Jacob, Georges (1739–1814), 20, 156, 173, 175n8, 179n88, *181*, 188, 214, 277, 279
Jacob, Georges II (1768–1803), 155
Jacob, Georges Alphonse (1799–1870), 156, *157*
Jacob-Desmalter, François Honoré Georges (1770–1841), 154–79, 196, 224, 231, 276, 277, 279, 280, 284–85; bookcase with a malachite tabletop, 224; Gondola chair from the Salon d'Argent of the Elysée Palace, 231; night table from *petits appartements* of the empress at Fontainebleau, 232; portrait, *155*; writing cabinet, *181*
Jacobins, 27
Jordán de Urríes, Javier, 38, 179n74, 179n78, 212n4, 212n7

Krafft, Jean Charles (1764–1833), 30; *Recueil des plus jolies maisons de Paris*, 238

Laborde, Alexandre de: *Voyage pittoresque et historique de l'Espagne*, 52, *52*, 118, 272
La Bouillerie, comte de (1764–1833), 34n7
Labrouste, Henri (1801–1875), 56, 60, 106, 253; *Design for a Cenotaph Commemorating La Pérouse*, 253, *253*
La Fenice theater, 136, 139n6
Lafitte, Louis, 285
La Fontaine, Jean de, 48; *Fables*, 114, *115*, 118, 190, 251, *251*, 263, 271
Lagrenée, Jean Jacques (1739–1821), 194
La Hamayde de Saint-Ange, Jacques Louis de (1780–1860), 194, 195; carpet for the room of the Conseil d'État, 195
La Mésangère, Pierre, 173; *Collection de Meubles et object de goût*, 174, *175*, 182, 232; *Journal des dames et modes*, 182
Landon, Charles, 21, 52, 127, 134n11; *Annales du musée et de l'école moderne des Beaux-Arts*, 52; *Nouvelle des arts*, 124
La Rouchefoucauld, vicomte de (1784–1864), 34n7

Lauriston, marquis de (1768–1828), 34n7

Lazzari, Francesco (1791–1871), 136, 137, 139n4, 139n12; *Compendio delle più interessanti regole di architettura tecnico-pratiche*, 137; *Fabbriche più cospicue di Venezia*, 136; *Principii dello stilo gotico*, 137

Lebas, Louis Hippolyte (1782–1867), 22–23, 25, 60, 61, 64, 97n3, 125, 266, 270, 280

Lebreton, Joachim (1760–1819), 45, 59

Le Brun, Charles (1616–1690), 29

Lebrun, Charles François, 278

Lebrun, Jean-Baptiste Pierre, 159

Leclère, Achille (1785–1853): 22, 65, 265–266; letter from, 64, 64, 269; in Percier's will, 63–64, 176n16; portrait, 64; as student of Percier, 60, 61, 270–71

Leclère, Esther, 64

Lecointe, Jean François Joseph (1783–1858): *House for a Painter*, 270, 270–71

Lecomte, Étienne Chérubin (ca.1760/66–1818), 215

Lefebvre, Charles (1755–1858), 139n3

Lefebvre, Ernest, 135, 139n3

Lefèvre, Robert (1756–1830): *Portrait of Charles Percier*, 16, 268

Legrand, Jacques Guillaume: *Description de Paris*, 238; designs for linking the Louvre and Tuileries, 239

Lemot, François Frédéric, 67

Le Muet, Pierre (1591–1669), 118

Lenoir, Alexandre (1761–1839), 14, 18, 29, 42, 43, 47, 61, 87, 100, 101, 102n14, 103, 104, 105, 106, 108, 116, 254, 263, 271; *Description historique et chronologique des monumens de sculpture réunis au musée des monumens français*, 105–6; *Musée des monumens français*, 117

Lenormant, Amélie (1803–1893), 168, 169, 173

Leopold of Saxe-Coburg, 192

Lepère, Jean-Baptiste (1761–1844), 221

Leroy, Antoine, 223, 284

Le Roy, Julien David (1724–1803), 63, 99

Lignereux, Adélaïde Anne, 156, 157, 157

Ligneruex, Martin Eloy (1751–1809), 156, 173, 230–31, 232n9

Livre du sacre de S.M. l'empereur Napoléon dans l'Eglise métropolitaine de Paris le xi Frimaire an xiii (Isabey et al.), 140–52, 141–44, 148–50, 272

Loménie de Brienne, Cardinal, 45

Louis XIII, 30, 83, 101

Louis XIV, 29

Louis XV, 30, 44, 140, 175n8, 179n88, 237, 245

Louis XVI, 33, 34n7, 45, 54, 140, 182, 277, 279

Louis XVIII, 22–23, 30, 34n7, 263, 285

Louis-Philippe, 26, 32, 33, 34n7, 38, 45, 175n8, 216, 223, 233, 275, 276, 279

Louvet, Albert (1860–1936), 64, 65

Louvre. *See* Musée du Louvre

Luxembourg, palais du, 32, 265, 277

Maison Jacob frères, 127, 154–55, 157–158, 162, 179, 182, 275, 276; bed for Moreau's townhouse, 173, 274; commode from bedroom of Josephine's apartments, 181, 279; tea table from Hôtel Bonaparte, 166

Maisons de plaisance de Rome (Percier and Fontaine), 123, 127, 271

Malbeste, Georges (1754–1843), 52, 145, 151n3, 272

Malmaison, château de, 12, 17, 21, 39, 42, 52, 103, 134n7, 152n11, 160, 166, 166, 170, 171, 173, 209, 224–225, 228, 231, 268, 272, 274, 276, 279, 284, 293; Bonaparte's acquisition of, 215; carpet design, 195; ceiling design, 272; *Council Room at Malmaison* (Gotthold), 219; garden, 123, 221; interior decoration (Percier and Fontaine), 216–22, 219, 221–22; *Library at Malmaison* (Gotthold), 221; *View of Château Malmaison* (Petit), 219

Mandar, Charles François: designs for linking the Louvre and Tuileries, 239

Mantua, Palazzo Te, 15, 18, 39, 40, 61, 78, 95, 96, 243

Marat, Jean Paul, 29

Marcion, Pierre Benoît (1769–1840), 274, 276

Marie-Antoinette (Queen), 17, 44, 278

Marie-Louise (Napoleon Bonaparte's second wife), 61, 157, 171, 249, 269, 283, 285

Massard, Urbain, 151n2, 151n3

Méhul, Etienne Nicolas, 66

Meissonier, Juste-Aurèle, 208, 209

Menus Plaisirs, 54

Metropolitan Museum of Art, New York, 184, 198, 204, 231

Meudon, château de, 85

Meynier, Charles, 67

Michel, Marc Antoine Grégoire, 166, 178n64

Ministry of Culture, 25

Ministry of Foreign Relations, 26

Ministry of the Interior, 25, 29

Moench, Simon Frédéric (1746–1837), 219

Molinos, Jacques: designs for linking the Louvre and Tuileries, 239

Montferrand, Auguste Ricard de (1786–1858), 58, 59

Montmorency, Anne de, 99

Moon, Iris, 122, 180

Moreau, Charles: *Fragmens et ornemens d'architecture*, 184, 185

Moreau, General Jean Victor Marie (1763–1813), 69, 105, 160, 162, 174, 182, 216, 232; townhouse of, 173, 274–76, 275

Moreau, Madame, 129, 131, 172, 274–76, 285

Morel, Jean Marie (1728–1810), 221

Moyroud, Jeanne Sophie, 162

Müller, Henri Charles (1784–1845), 40, 270

Murat, Joachim (1767–1815), 139n2, 215

Musée de Cluny, 102

Musée des monuments français, 14, 18, 29, 103–6, 254; 16th–17th-centuries gallery, 104, 271; addition project incorporating three courtyards, 104, 271; entryway leading from the street to the first courtyard, 105; façade from the château de Gaillon, 104, 105, 106

Musée de Versailles, 33, 34n7. *See also* Versailles

Musée du Louvre: construction and enlargement of, 26, 34n7; David and, 29; designs for linking Tuileries to, 42, 233–44, 235, 239, 281; entrance from rue de Rivoli, 282; name of, 27; renovation by Percier, 14, 281; south staircase of the colonnade, 242, 282; *Views of the Salle des Cariatides*, 242

Musée Napoléon, Salle des Fleuves, 120, 242

Les Mystères d'Isis (play), 250

Napoleon Bonaparte. *See* Bonaparte, Napoleon.

Napoleon III, 26, 254

National Convention (1793), 14, 17, 156

Natoire, Charles Joseph, 73

neoclassical style, 32

neo-Gothic style, 32–33, 137

Neufchâteau, François de (1750–1828), 27, 29, 30

Nicholas I (czar), 59, 224

Nietzsche, Friedrich, 137, 138, 139n15, 139n16

Nodier, Charles: *Voyages romantiques et pittoresques*, 118

Nompère de Champagny, Jean-Baptiste (1756–1834), 34n7

Normand, Charles Pierre Joseph (1765–1840), 51, 62n1, 121, 121n6, 125; fireplace from the Salle des Fleuves, 120; frontispiece for *Annales du musée et de l'école moderne des Beaux-Arts*, 52

Notre-Dame-de-Lorette, 23, 61, 64

Notre-Dame de Paris, 140, 147, 148, 222

opera set designs: for *Elisca ou l'amour maternel*, 248, 250, 283; for *Sémiramis*, 251, 251

Oppenord, Gilles Marie (1672–1742), 206–7

Ottomeyer, Hans, 48n2, 87, 98n9, 133n3, 279

Ouvrard, Augustin (1775–?), 163, 215

Ouvrard, Gabriel Julien (1770–1846), 131, 162, 163, 166, 178n63, 215

Padua, basilica in, 18, 40

Palais, maisons et autres édifices modernes dessinés à Rome (Percier and Fontaine), 10, 17, 74, 74, 110, 112, 118, 119–20, 134n7, 157, 197, 231, 231, 246, 272

Palais Bourbon, 32

Palais d'Écouen, 87, 98n9, 116, 117

Palais d'Orsay, 26

Palais du Luxembourg, 32, 265, 277

Palais-Royal, 23, 30, 233

Palazzo della Strada Nuova, Genoa, 243

Palazzo Ducale, Venice, 92, 93, 139n12

Palazzo Farnese, Caprarola, 95

Palazzo Mancini, Rome, 72

Palazzo Te, Mantua, 15, 18, 23, 39, 40, 61, 78, 95, 96, 243

Palazzo Vecchio, Florence, 92, 93

Palladio, Andrea, 78, 243

Panseron, Pierre (ca. 1736–1787), 118; *Cayer d'attribut de guerre et de fontaine pour orner l'architecture*, 119

Paris: government and the arts in, 26–27; map (1734–39), 236, 237. *See also* Paris Opera; specific locations and museums.

Pâris, Pierre Adrien (1745–1819), 19, 54, 74, 125, 206, 208, 209, 214

Paris Opera, 14, 17, 45, 52, 54, 130, 208–9, 214, 219, 250, 260n5, 283

Percier, Charles: biography, 17–18; caricature of, 37; chronology, 19–23; decorative arts, 154–204; education of, 17, 50–62; family of, 17; Flaxman letter, 76–80, 79; furniture design, 154–87; legacy of, 262–67; political positioning of, 44–45; portrait of, 16; ring of, 63, 63–65, 269; in Rome, 17, 56–57, 71–75; rue de Rivoli and, 245–47; schools of, 50–62; students of, 36, 50–51; tomb of, 18, 46, 47

Percier, Charles (works) *(For joint works with Fontaine, see separate* entry Percier and Fontaine.) Archaeological composition: "8th year of the united and indivisible Republic", 110, 111; architectural designs and drawings, 82–106, 206–58, 285; bed of Madame Récamier, study sketches, 168; bedroom for Josephine Bonaparte, 40, 273; bedroom of Madame Gaudin, 165; boudoir design, 273, 273–74; candelabra, 199; cartel for Royal Museum's table, 192, 192; *Chief Herald of Arms* (with Isabey), 150, 151; clocks, 189, 191, 191, 196, 196; country house of Mme Lignereux at Bougival, 156, 157; designs for manufactories, 188–204; desk chair of Corvisart, 173, 173; dining room of Madame Récamier, 168, 168; *Edifice to House the Academies*, 55, 268; *The Emperor in Grand Ceremonial Dress* (with Isabey), 143, 145; fireplace in marble and bronze, 192, 192; *Folly Serving as Love's Guide*, 263, 263; Fontainebleau, 61, 82, 89, 94, 94, 96, 285; frontispiece for Laborde, *Voyage pittoresque et historique de l'Espagne*, 52, 52, 118; frontispiece for Voltaire, *La Henriade* (with Gérard), 40, 40, 272; graphic art and design, 108–52; headpiece for Horace, *First Book of Epistles in Quintus Horatius Flaccus*, 111, 114, 114–15, 118; headpiece for Horace, *Second Book of Epistles in Quintus Horatius Flaccus*, 114, 115, 118; headpiece for La Fontaine, *Fables*, 114, 115, 118, 251, 263; Isabey's atelier, interior decoration, 120, 130, 160, 215, 231; Italian villa at the seaside, 272, 273; *Livre du sacre de S.M. l'empereur Napoléon dans l'Eglise métropolitaine de Paris le XI Frimaire an XIII* (with Isabey et al.), 140–52, 141–44, 147–50, 272; Loggia of Palazzo Te in Mantua, 39, 40; Londonderry vase, 190, 190; Malmaison ceiling design, 272; Marshall's table, 191, 191–92; medal cabinet, 199, 280; *Menagerie set within the Park of a Royal Château*, 55, 268; Moreau's townhouse, 173, 274–76, 275; Musée des monuments français, 16th–17th-centuries gallery, 104, 271; oeuvre of, 43–44; opera set designs, 251, 251, 283; ornamental motifs, 272; Palais d'Écouen, 87, 98n9, 116, 117; Palazzo Te in Mantua, 39, 40; *petits appartements* of Josephine at Fontainebleau, 172, 223, 223, 232, 279, 284–85; *The Pope* (with Isabey and Garneray), 147, 148; *President of the Canton* (with Isabey), 150, 151; Psyche lamp, 285; Roman Palace, interior, 270, 271; Saint-Cloud château, carpet for music room, 195, 195; salon and smoking room of Madame Récamier, 168, 168; scrapbook from workshop, 184–86, 184–87, 231, 273; Simonetti Staircase Seen from the Gallery of the Candelabra, 72, 72; Sistine Chapel, view of, 57, 57; tea service for the first consul, 196, 197; Trajan's Column, 54, 56, 73, 73–74, 269; Tuileries, 196, 196; tureen designs, 201–4, 201–4, 280, 281; vignette with two portrait medallions, 271; Villa Barberini, view of courtyard, 270, 271. *See also specific books and buildings.*

Percier and Fontaine (joint works): arc du Carrousel, 11, 14, 18, 26, 30, 187, 187n11, 225, 240, 282; bedroom of Mme. M., 273; bedrooms of Mr. and Mme G, 164; bookcase with a malachite tabletop, 224; candelabra made by Mr. D, 159, 159; Casa Real del Labrador, Platinum Room, 38, 52, 160, 170, 171, 207–10, 208, 210, 216, 273, 278; Chaillot Hill, proposed transformation, 256, 256; *Choix des plus célèbres maisons de plaisance de Rome et de ses environ* (with Bonnard), 112, 271; courtyard of a Roman palace, 60, 60; cylinder secrétaire made in Paris for Mr. H, 159, 159; *Description des cérémonies et des fêtes*, 254, 272; designs for linking Tuileries to the Louvres, 42, 233–44, 235, 239, 281; Gallery of Diana, 61, 82, 89, 94, 94, 96, 285; Isabey's atelier, 130, 160; king of Rome palace, 254, 256, 283; lantern to mark entrance of the Tuileries, 240, 281; *Maisons de plaisance de Rome*, 123, 127; Malmaison, 216–22, 219, 221–22; *Monument to the Defenders of the Homeland*, 252, 282–83; Musée du Louvre, 235, 242, 282; opera set design for *Elisca ou l'amour maternel*, 248, 250, 283; *Palais, maisons et autres édifices modernes dessinés à Rome*, 10, 17, 74, 74, 110, 112, 118, 119–20, 134n7, 157, 197, 231, 231, 246, 272; Reims Cathedral, decoration for coronation of Louis XVIII, 284, 285; *Résidences de souverains*, 254; rue de Rivoli, 11, 14, 18, 30, 236, 238, 244n5, 245–48, 246, 281; Salle des Cariatides, Musée du Louvre, 242, 242; tea table for Mr. G, 165, 276; Terneuzen bay, house for the emperor overlooking, 258–59, 283; textile panel, 281; Tuileries, 223, 235, 240, 274, 277, 279; tureen, tea urn, and vases made in Paris for Mr. B, 201; X-frame stool, 231, 231. *See also Recueil de décorations intérieures.*

Père Lachaise Cemetery (Paris), 18, 46, 47, 61
Perino del Vaga (Pietro di Giovanni Buonaccorsi) (1501–1547), 270, 271
Perrault, Claude, 239, 239, 242, 244n3, 259
Peruzzi, Baldassare, 243
Petit, Pierre Joseph: *View of Château Malmaison*, 219
Petits-Augustins, Elysian Gardens of, 100
Petracchi, Angelo, 268
Peyre, Antoine François (1739–1823), 15, 17, 53, 53, 85–86, 96, 206, 214, 234, 236, 268
Peyre, Marie Joseph (1770–1843), 103
Philippon, Charles (1800–1861), 32
Piat Lefebvre manufactory, 195, 195, 196
Piazza del Duomo, Bologna, 246
Picquigny, château de, 102
Pinon, Pierre, 74
Pio Clementino Museum, Vatican, 72
Piranesi, Giovanni Battista, 73, 75n6
Piroli, Tommaso (1752–1824), 20, 118, 121n3
Pius IV (pope), 95
Pius VII (pope), 21, 147–48, 148, 223
place de la Concorde, 236, 245
place des Pyramides, 238, 247n1
place des Vosges, 245
Platinum Room. *See* Casa Real del Labrador.
Plato, 138
Poyet, Bernard: designs for linking the Louvre and Tuileries, 21, 239
Pradel, comte de (1779–1857), 34n7
Primaticcio, Francesco (1504–1570), 15, 82, 87, 89, 90, 92, 98n19
Prix de Rome, 14, 17, 18, 20, 21, 23, 22, 36, 42, 47, 50, 54, 58, 60, 63, 72, 105, 156, 185, 265, 264, 268, 271, 270,
Provost, Jean Louis (1781–1850), 64, 64, 270
Prud'hon, Pierre Paul, 66; *Baron Vivant Denon*, 29
Public Instruction Committee, 28
Public Safety Committee, 28

Quatremère de Quincy, Antoine Chrysostome (1755–1849), 25, 134n32, 246

Raoul-Rochette, Desiré, 188, 254
Raphael, 77, 209, 212n12, 220
Rapilly, A., 198
Récamier, Jacques Rose (1751–1830), 216
Récamier, Juliette, 168, 172, 182, 277, 285
Recueil de décorations intérieures (Percier and Fontaine), 122–39, 125, 129–30, 160, 181, 272–81; architectural design in, 47, 118; bedrooms for Mr. and Mme G, 164; candelabra made by Mr. D, 159; Casa Real del Labrador Platinum Room, 38–39, 171, 208, 210; *Council Room at Malmaison*, 219; cylinder secrétaire made in Paris for Mr. H, 159; Fontainebleau château, 285; furniture design in, 155; influence of, 18, 180, 197; Isabey's atelier, 66, 68, 69, 70, 120; Italian edition, 72, 133, 135–36, 135–39; Malmaison, 219; Musée du Louvre, 242, 242; shared authorship of, 11, 42; tea table executed in Paris for Mr. G, 165, 276; throne at the Palais des Tuileries, 223; title plate, 123; tureen designs, 201–4, 201–4, 280, 281; X-frame stool, 174, 231, 231
Redouté, Pierre Joseph, 67
Regnier, Alexandre (1751–1802), 159
Résidences de souverains (Percier and Fontaine), 254
Restout, Jean Bernard (1732–1797), 28
Ribault, Jean François, 151n3
Romano, Giulio, 95, 96
Rome: Arch of Septimius Severus, 240, 282; French Academy in, 50, 54, 56, 72, 85, 207, 269; *Maisons de plaisance de Rome* (Percier and Fontaine), 112, 123, 127, 271; Palazzo Mancini, 72; Percier's travels to, 17, 56–57, 71–75; Prix de Rome, 14, 17, 36, 47, 54, 105; Villa Barberini, 270, 271; Villa Madama, 95. *See also Palais, maisons et autres édifices modernes dessinés à Rome* (Percier and Fontaine); *specific monuments and structures.*
Rondelet, Jean (1743–1829), 25
Royal Museum, 192, 192, 280
Royer-Collard, Pierre Paul (1754–1822), 34n5
rue de Castiglione, 245, 247n1
rue de Rivoli, 11, 14, 18, 30, 105, 224, 237, 236, 238, 244n5, 245–48, 246, 281
rue des Colonnes, 245
Ruskin, John: *The Stones of Venice*, 139n10
Rykwert, Joseph, 139

Saint-Cloud, château de: boudoir, 173–74, 186, 228–32, 229–31, 274, 275; carpet for music room, 195, 195; furniture design, 183, 279, 285; *petits appartements* of Josephine, 172, 182, 215; renovation of, 170, 221–22; Salon des Consuls, 195, 278
Saint-Denis Abbey. *See* Abbey of Saint-Denis.
Saint-Fargeau, Le Peletier, 29
Saint-Fermin chapel, *101*, 102
Saint-Germain, château de, 85
Saint Isaac's Cathedral, 59
Saint-Ouen, château de, 30
Saint-Saturnin's Chapel, 87, *89*
Sala dei Collegio, Palazzo Ducale, 92, 93
Sala Reggia, Vatican, 92, 93
Salle des Fleuves, Musée Napoléon, 120
Salon du Roi (1833), 32
Salone del Cinquecento, Palazzo Vecchio, 92, 93
Samoyault, Jean-Pierre, 44, 129, 182, 273
Santa Maria degli Angeli, Florence, 260
Sarmant, Thierry, 24, 34n8
Savonnerie manufactory, 192, 195, 195
Schinkel, Karl Friedrich, 23, 250, 254; *Vorbilder für Fabrikanten und Handwerker*, 123
Ségur, Louis Philippe, comte de (1753–1830), 141, 142, 145, 146, 216
Selva, Giannantonio, 136, 137, 139n4
Selvatico, Pietro: *Sull'architettura e sulla scultura in Venezia. Dal Medio Evo sino ai giorni nostri*, 136
Sémiramis (opera), set design, 251, *251*
Serangeli, Gioacchino, 67
Séroux d'Agincourt, Jean-Baptiste Louis Georges, 136
Sèvres Porcelain manufactory, 26, 42, 189, *190*, 191, 199n9, 199n17, 228, 273, 281, 285
Simelli, Carlo Baldassare, 269; Trajan's Column, Entry at the Base of, 56, 269
Sistine Chapel, 57, *57*
Sitel, Michel Léonard, 170, 207, 212n7
Soane Museum, London, 134n7
Société centrale des architectes français, 65, 65n11
Sorel, Alexandre, 102n3
Stewart, Courier W., 241
Suys, Tilman François (1783–1864), 58
Swebach, Jacques François, 66
Szambien, Werner, 238, 252

Talma, François Joseph, 67
Tauney, Nicolas-Antoine, 66, *68*
Taylor, Justin: *Voyages romantiques et pittoresques*, 118

Tedeschi, Letizia, 71, 135
Temple of Diana, 131
Temple of Glory, 26
Terneuzen, house for the emperor overlooking the bay of, 258–59, 283
Testa, Angelo (177?–18??), 269
Thibault, Jean Thomas (1757–1826), 48, 67, 160, 185, 208, 250, 284
Thiers, Adolphe (1797–1877), 32
Thomire, Pierre Philippe (1751–1843), 182, 183, 196, 280, 285
Tipografia del Fibreno, 135, 139n2
Tournon, Paul (1881–1964), 65
Toussaint, Claude Jacques: *Traité de Géométrie et d'architecture*, 239, *239*
Trajan's Column, 54, 56, 73, *73–74*, 269
Tuileries: chairs, 277; clock design, 280; construction of, 26; designs for garden cafés and pavilion, 283; designs for linking the Louvre to, 42, 233–44, 235, 239, 281; gardens, 281; Josephine's bedchamber, 42; lantern to mark entrance of, 240, 281; Louis XVIII at, 30; rue de Rivoli and, 247; throne room, 223, 274, 277, 279

Udine, Giovanni di, 209

Van Daël, Jean François, 67
Vanlerberghe, Ignace Joseph (1758–1819), 160
Van Zanten, David, 43–44
Varcolier, Louis (1864–1948), 65
Vauchelet, Théophile (1802–1873), 213
Vaudoyer, Antoine Laurent Thomas (1756–1846), 25, 53, 54, 60, 74
Vaudoyer, Léon (1803–1872), 106
Vautier, Corneille, 164, 166
Vendôme Column, 26, 30
Venice: Accademia delle Belle Arti, 139n4, 139n6; Palazzo Ducale, 92, 93
Vernet, Carle, 66
Vernet, Horace (1789–1863), 32
Versailles, 27, 33, *33*, 223, 234, 274, 276, 278
Vicenza, basilica in, 40
Vignola, Giacomo, 243
Villa Albani, 113
Villa Barberini, 270, *271*
Villa Borghese, 113
Villain, François Alexandre (1798–1884), 51, 99
Villa Madama, Rome, 95
Viollet-Le-Duc, Eugène Emmanuel, 60, 99, 102; *Dictionnaire raisonné*, 99; *The Salle des Marechaux with a view of the Tuileries Gardens*, 240, *240*, 281
Visconti, Louis (1791–1853), 32, 176n16
Voltaire: *La Henriade*, 40, *40*, 272

Wallig, Saskia, 19
Weber, Susan, 13
Winckelmann, Johann, 132

Zanotto, Francesco, 136
Zucconi, Guido, 136

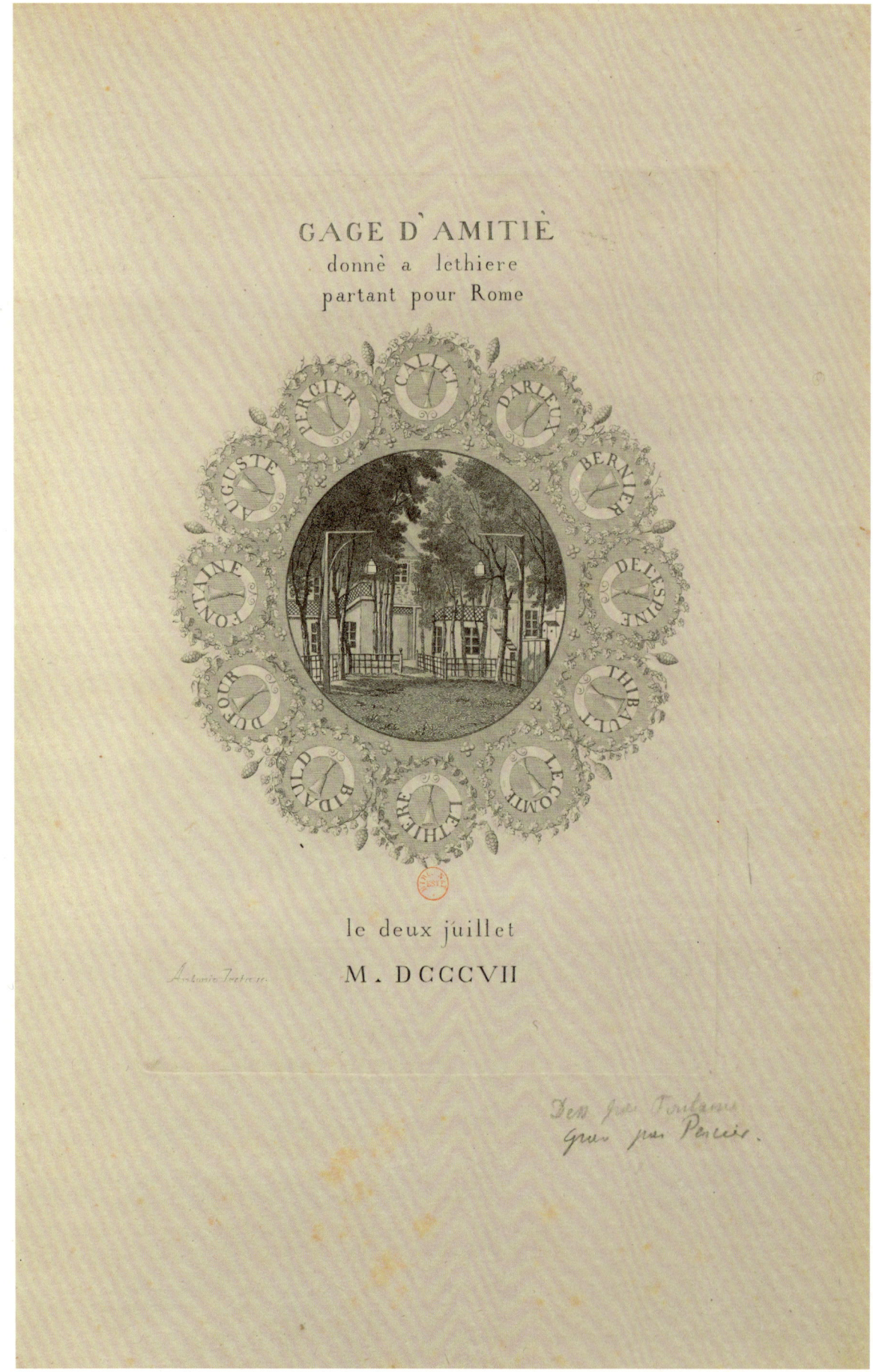

PHOTOGRAPHIC CREDITS

Photographs were taken or supplied by the lending institutions, organizations, or individuals credited in the picture captions and are protected by copyright; many names are not repeated here. Individual photographers are credited below. Permission has been sought for use of all copyrighted illustrations in this volume. In several instances, despite extensive research, it has not been possible to locate the original copyright holder. Copyright owners of these works should contact the Bard Graduate Center, 18 West 86th Street, New York, NY, 10024.

Daniel Arnaudet © RMN–Grand Palais / Art Resource, NY: Fig. 11.4.

Collection Banque de France–tous droits réservés–Cliché P. Assaily: Fig. 9A.4.

© Beaux-Arts de Paris, Dist. RMN–Grand Palais / Art Resource, NY: Figs. 2.10. 3.2–3.4, 5.2, 13.10–13.12.

Martine Beck-Coppola © RMN–Grand Palais / Art Resource, NY: Fig. 9.4.

Michèle Bellot © Musée du Louvre, Dist. RMN–Grand Palais / Art Resource, NY: Cats. 41, 48, 66A, 143.

Jean-Gilles Berizzi © Musée du Louvre, Dist. RMN–Grand Palais / Art Resource, NY: Cats. 40, 83.

Bibliothèque Paul-Marmottan, Ville de Boulogne-Billancourt, Académie des Beaux-Arts, France / Bridgeman Images: Fig. 10.2.

Isabell Bideau © Collection du Mobilier national: Figs. 9.9, 9.11, 11A.5.

Gérard Blot © RMN–Grand Palais / Art Resource, NY: Figs. i.1, iii.1–iii.4, iii.7, 1.1, 2.5, 4.1–4.14, 8.14, 8.22, 9.1, 11.8, 11A.6, 12.8, 12.13; Cats. 57, 66B, 66C, 68, 69, 88, 106, 148.

Harry Brejat © Musée du Louvre, Dist. RMN–Grand Palais / Art Resource, NY: Fig. 13.3.

Adrien Didierjean © RMN–Grand Palais / Art Resource, NY: Fig. 8A.1; Cats. 79, 85, 146.

Matt Flynn / Cooper Hewitt, Smithsonian Design Museum / Art Resource, NY: Cat. 46B.

Philippe Fuzeau © RMN–Grand Palais / Art Resource, NY: Fig. iii.5.

© INHA, Dist. RMN–Grand Palais / Art Resource, NY: Fig. 3.5.

Jean-Pierre Lagiewski © RMN–Grand Palais / Art Resource, NY: Cat. 147.

Thierry Le Mage © RMN–Grand Palais / Art Resource, NY: Figs. 2.13, 5.1; Cat. 92.

Erich Lessing / Art Resource, NY: Fig. 8.9.

Erich Lessing © RMN–Grand Palais / Art Resource, NY: Fig. 8.15.

Jean-Mac Manai © RMN–Grand Palais / Art Resource, NY: Cat. 80.

Steaphane Marechalle © RMN–Grand Palais / Art Resource, NY: Fig. 2B.2; Cat. 3B.

© The Metropolitan Museum of Art. Image source: Art Resource, NY: Figs. 6.6, 6.8–6.10, 6.12, 8.18, 8B.1–8B.7, 9A.5, 11A.1, 11A.2; Cats. 38, 87, 90, 100, 142C.

© Musée Carnavalet / Roger-Viollet: Figs. 8.1, 8.8, 12A.2, 13.5.

© RMN–Grand Palais / Art Resource, NY: Figs. 2B.1, 7.1–7.8, 8.23, 11.7, 13.7.

Jean-Manuel Salingue © RMN–Grand Palais / Art Resource, NY: Fig. 9.2.

Christian Schryve/musée Antoine Vivenel, Compiègne: Figs. 4A.1–4A. 5.

Pascal Segrette © RMN–Grand Palais / Art Resource, NY: Fig. iii.6.

Le Studio Numerique © RMN–Grand Palais / Art Resource, NY: Figs. 9.5–9.8; Cat. 107A.

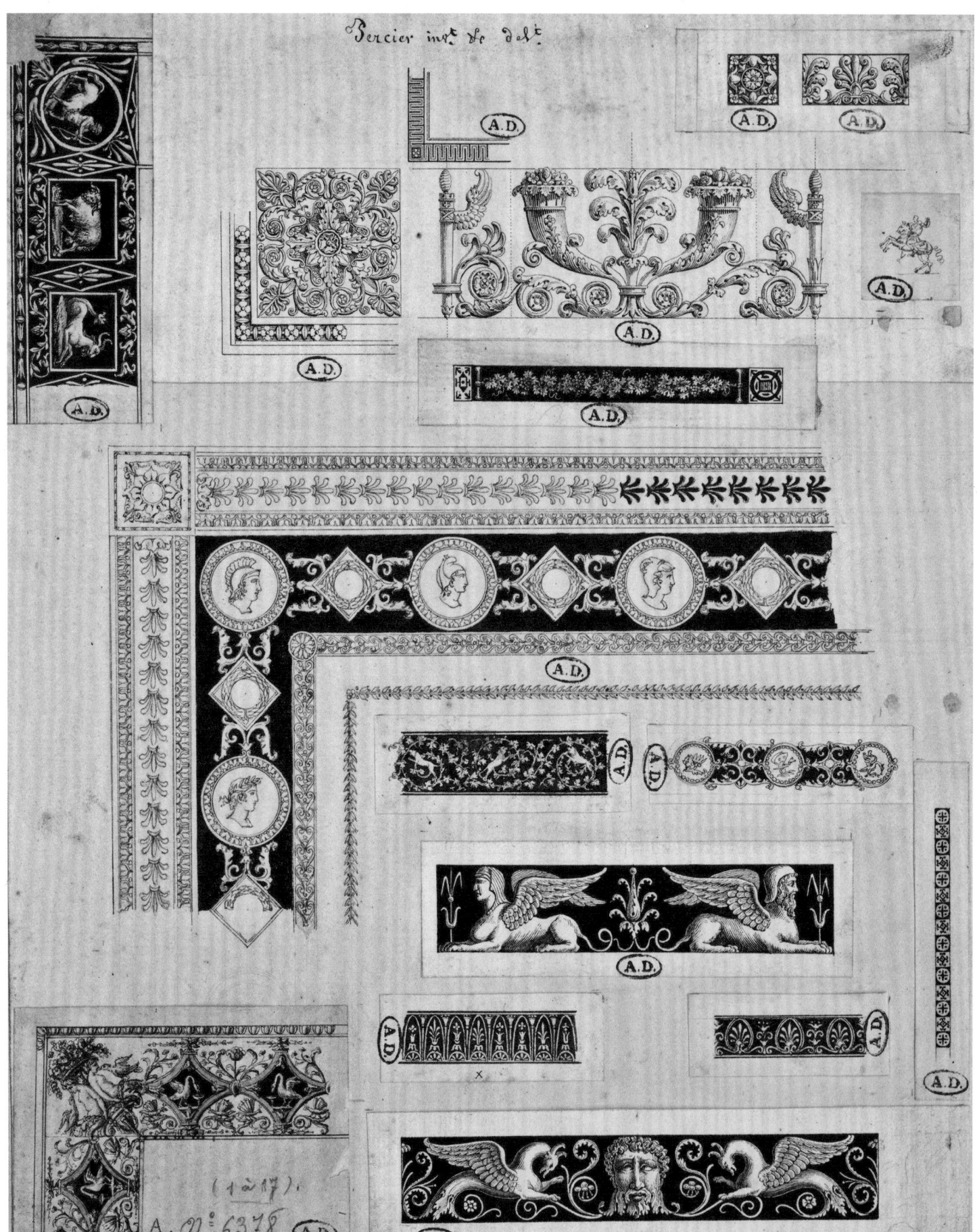

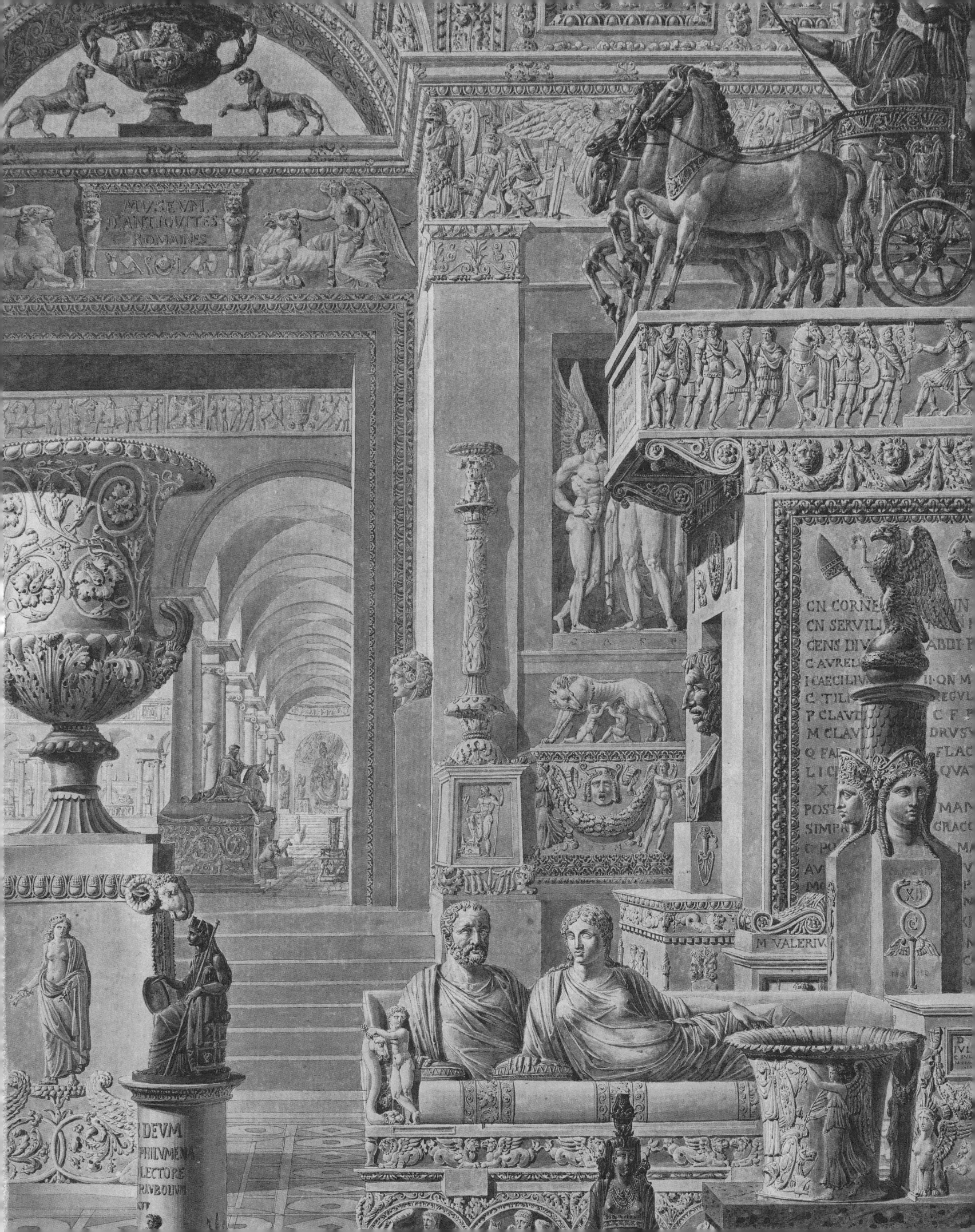

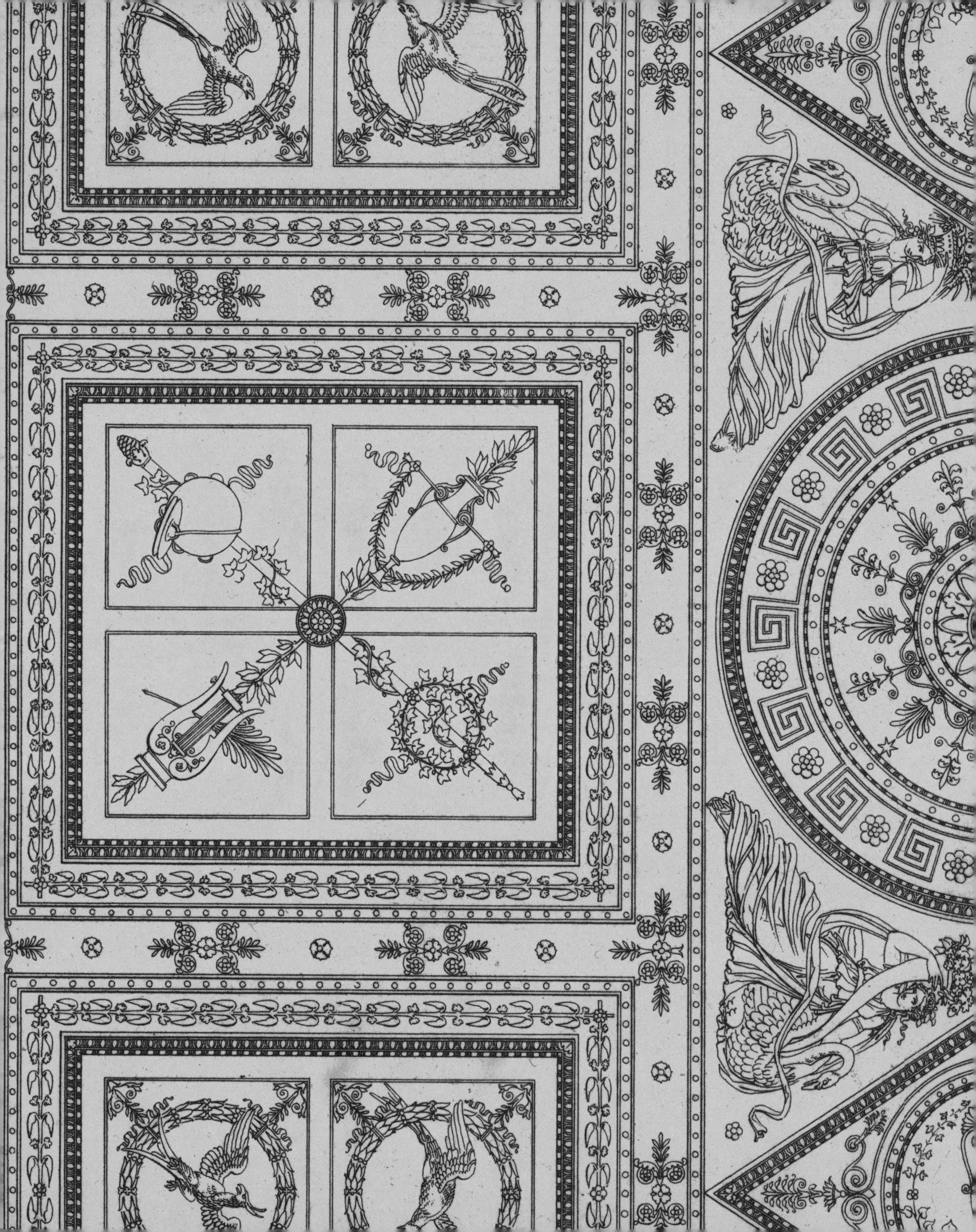